ETHNIC
CULTURES
OF THE WORLD

ETHNIC
CULTURES
OF THE WORLD

A Statistical Reference

Philip M. Parker

CROSS-CULTURAL STATISTICAL
ENCYCLOPEDIA OF THE WORLD
VOLUME 3

GREENWOOD PRESS
Westport, Connecticut • London

Library of Congress Cataloging-in-Publication Data

Parker, Philip, 1960–
    Ethnic cultures of the world : a statistical reference / Philip M.
    Parker.
        p.   cm.—(Cross-cultural statistical encyclopedia of the
    world ; v. 3)
    Includes bibliographical references and indexes.
    ISBN 0–313–29767–3 (alk. paper)
    1. Ethnic groups—Statistics. 2. Demographic surveys. I. Title.
    II. Series: Parker, Philip, 1960–   Cross-cultural statistical
    encyclopedia of the world ; v. 3.
    GN495.4.P37   1997
    305.8—dc20   96–43832

British Library Cataloguing in Publication Data is available.

Library of Congress Catalog Card Number: 96–43832
ISBN: 0–313–29767–3 (vol. 3)
ISBN: 0–313–29768–1 (vol. 1)
ISBN: 0–313–29769–X (vol. 2)
ISBN: 0–313–29770–3 (vol. 4)

First published in 1997

Greenwood Press, 88 Post Road West, Westport, CT 06881
An imprint of Greenwood Publishing Group, Inc.

Printed in the United States of America

The paper used in this book complies with the
Permanent Paper Standard issued by the National
Information Standards Organization (Z39.48–1984).

10 9 8 7 6 5 4 3 2 1

CONTENTS

PREFACE

Work on this book began in early 1993 when, after conversations with international managers, I began work on empirical cross-cultural consumer studies. This work has involved collecting a large quantity of statistics across the world's cultural groups (religious, linguistic, ethnic and national). While there is substantial *soft* or textual information on the world's cultural groups published in anthropological and encyclopedic works, there is no complete source of *hard* or quantitative information which might be used on a global basis for the vast majority of these *trans-national* cultural groups. This book was developed to allow quantitative comparisons across non-national cultures and is one volume of four devoted to this subject (Greenwood Press, 1997):

- Religious Cultures of the World: A Statistical Reference
- Linguistic Cultures of the World: A Statistical Reference
- Ethnic Cultures of the World: A Statistical Reference
- National Cultures of the World: A Statistical Reference

This volume presents various comparative tables across some 300 variables for over 400 ethnic groups (defined in Chapter 1). Approximately 120,000 statistics are given covering: climatic resources, marine resources, land resources, mineral resources, cultural resources, demography and sociology, and economics. These were selected from a much larger data base of over 4000 variables covering a broader range of topics than those given here. The statistics reported were chosen from amongst the larger set for their high potential interest to economists, social scientists, or persons interested in cross-cultural studies. Economic development or strategic planners, for example, might use the variables to estimate market potential sizes, distribution efficiencies or labor force productivity levels across cultural groups. Social planners might use the variables to evaluate the impact of economic development, religion, language or political institutions on cross-cultural behavior. Across all of the areas covered in this book, the statistics provided should be seen as an initial attempt to describe cultural groups along comparable and quantifiable dimensions. Should readers wish more precise or qualitative information on a given culture, in-depth reviews of secondary research and primary research studies, cited in Chapter 1, are recommended.

Given the sheer volume of statistics provided and since this is a first attempt to broadly quantify ethnic groups (as defined in Chapter 1), errors may be present in the figures reported and substantial room for improvement remains (despite great efforts to make the information as accurate as possible, as discussed in Chapter 1). Naturally, the reader held responsible for any errors in or subsequent use of the information provided here. Finally, the book ends with a select bibliography covering physioeconomic effects on religious cultures which motivates the statistical information provided and the discussion in Chapter 2.   Should the reader find important omissions/errors or have comments/questions, please feel free to contact me via the Internet   (e-mail address = parker@insead.fr), or at INSEAD, Bd. de Constance, 77305 Fontainebleau, France (fax: 33-1-60-72-4242).   Information on changes to the data reported can also be requested using these e-mail or postal addresses.

ACKNOWLEDGMENTS

Thanks are owed to a number of persons at the European Institute of Business Administration (INSEAD) including Marie-Louise Berry, William Fisk, and Eva Szekarez for helping me input, proof and format the information given in this book. Thanks are also owed to the Research and Development Committee at INSEAD which provided financial support for this work and to Régine, Paul and Claire who let me invest their time in this effort. Finally, thanks are given to Miklos Sarvary who acted as a sounding board for many of the ideas given in Chapter 1.

ETHNIC
CULTURES
OF THE WORLD

1

ETHNIC CULTURES

AN INTRODUCTION

Both academic and popular presses have recently stressed the importance of "borderless" markets, where national boundaries no longer become the relevant criteria in making international marketing, economic planning and business decisions. Understanding non-political borders is especially important for products and industries which are "culture bound," or those which require local adaptation. Culture is often cited as a critical factor affecting economic development, demographic behavior, and general business policies (e.g. strategies found effective with Norwegians may prove ineffective in Swahili populations). While there is substantial *soft* or textual information on the world's ethnic groups published in various works, there is no complete source of *hard* or quantitative information which might be used on a global basis. This book was developed to allow quantitative comparisons across ethnic groups which are present in multiple countries located in multiple continents. The *hard* information presented in this book allows researchers to begin to answer certain basic questions which have been relatively easy to answer at the national level, but which are illusive for ethnic groups that are trans-national: What is the rank order of ethnic groups by income per capita?; What percent of Japanese speak English?; Which ethnic groups have highest consumption levels of food, or entertainment goods?; What factors best explain differences across ethnic groups in terms of demographic, consumption and production behaviors (e.g. natural resources, political systems, or language differences)?

The book is organized into eleven chapters. This chapter briefly introduces the book's organization, and potential uses across fields (business, economics, sociology, ethnography, demography, etc.). More importantly, this chapter gives a summary of the methodologies used to generate each reported variable; caveats and limitations of the various estimation procedures used are presented. Chapter 2 provides suggestions to applied academic, business or policy researchers on how one might use the data to explain variations in behaviors across cultures (a *physioeconomic* framework). Chapters 3 to 9 present statistical profiles for each of over 400 ethnic groups. Broadly defined, three types of estimates are given for each ethnic group: absolute levels, average levels (e.g. per capita measures), and percentage or penetration measures. Absolute levels include such measures as population sizes. Average levels are a weighted estimate across countries where the ethnic group is present (e.g. average life expectancy or literacy levels). Percent penetration figures indicate, for example, the percentage of an ethnic group's population that lives under a communist regime (or military dictatorship, etc.). In some cases the estimates are unique to the ethnic group in question, while others are shared by multiple ethnic groups simultaneously residing in one or more countries. To the extent that the latter is true, the estimates provided reflect the *prevailing* conditions under which an ethnic group exists (e.g. the weighted estimate of, say, literacy for a ethnic group who's population is located in numerous countries). Estimates of prevailing conditions are most useful in studies of how certain factors affect behaviors within a given ethnic group. Three broad classes of variables of interest to international managers or cross-cultural researchers are given: (1) business, (2) social system, and (3) physioeconomic variables.

Chapter 3 provides a number of economic and business variables. These can be used to estimate, for example, market potential sizes, distribution efficiencies or labor force productivity levels across ethnic groups. These variables include: demographic dimensions (e.g. population sizes, population growth rates, population density, urbanization levels, labor force size, and migration levels), per capita consumption dimensions (e.g. energy, calories, protein, passenger cars, telephones, televisions, radios), production measures across industries (e.g. fish, milk, meat, electricity, coal, petroleum, automobiles), and macroeconomic and infrastructure dimensions (e.g. GNP per capita, GNP growth, highways, ports, aircraft runways, radio stations, television stations, satellite earth stations). Tables 1 to 4 illustrate the variance across some of these statistical measures across ethnic groups. Table 1 reports the 40 most populous ethnic groups. Table 2 reports the top and bottom 20 ethnic groups in terms of GNP/capita; Table 3 does the same in terms of caloric consumption per capita per day. Table 4 reports the top and bottom 20 ethnic groups in terms of literacy.

Chapters 4 and 5 provide social variables that can be used to evaluate the impact of social development, language or political institutions on behavior across ethnic groups. There are several dimensions covered: education (e.g. number of diseases, infant mortality, female life expectancy, male life expectancy, fertility, birth rate, death rate, population/hospital ratio, literacy); political characteristics and systems (e.g. number of parties, number of administrative branches in government, number of governmental changes since 1960, percent of population living under military government, percent of population living under communist government, voting age, percent of population using the metric system, visa requirements, number of border disputes, number of civil wars, number of international wars); frequency of world languages spoken (e.g. number of languages spoken, maximum percent of any one language; percent of population speaking English, French, Spanish, Arabic, Chinese, and Portuguese); and frequency of world religions existing within the same population (e.g. number of major religious groups, maximum percent representation across religious groups; percent Catholic, Protestant or other).

Business and economics literature has long recognized the importance of physical environment on economic behavior (*physioeconomics*). Ethnic groups who's populations are land-locked, and who live in hot climates or high altitudes will have substantially different behavior than, say, a ethnic group living in a temperate climate with an abundance of marine and mineral resources. Two sub-classes of physioeconomic dimensions are covered: (1) natural resources available (e.g. mineral reserves, natural gas reserves, crude petroleum reserves, total land area, arable land area, coastline length), and (2) climate (e.g. absolute latitude, elevation, average temperature, minimum temperature, maximum temperature, humidity, rainfall). Chapters 6 to 9 cover these areas across ethnic groups.

Across all of the areas covered in this book, the statistics provided should be seen as an attempt to describe ethnic groups along comparable and quantifiable dimensions. Should readers wish more precise information on a given ethnic group, in-depth reviews of secondary research and primary research studies are strongly recommended.

Table 1. Population Size Across Ethnic Groups

Top 40

Ethnic Groups	Population 1994
Han Chinese	1,130,000
Indo-Aryan	646,000
White	271,000
Dravidian	224,000
Russian	147,000
Mestizo	146,000
Arab Total	143,000
Japanese	126,000
Bengali	119,000
Arab	102,000
German	87,700
Punjabi	84,600
Jávanese	76,700
Italian	76,400
Black	71,300
Korean	70,700
Vietnamese	62,600
Malay Christian	60,900
French	60,100
Egyptian	55,500
Turkish	54,200
Mulatto	49,100
English	46,800
Ukrainian	45,800
Spanish	45,700
European	40,700
Polish	39,700
Amerind	37,000
Portuguese	34,100
Mongoloid	32,000
Burman	30,800
Siamese	29,900
Sundanese	29,800
Persian	29,000
Hausa	27,500
Chinese	26,100
Malay Coastal	23,400
Yoruba	23,400
Fulani	20,900
Romanian	20,700

Table 2. Economic Affluence Across Ethnic Groups

Top 20

Ethnic Groups	GNP/ Capita
Norwegian	44,000
Romansch	33,200
Swiss	31,000
Liechtensteiner	31,000
Luxemburger	28,700
Japanese	26,600
Finnish	25,900
Swedish	25,200
Danish	24,500
Icelander	23,600
Yugoslav	21,600
German	21,500
French	20,700
Breton	20,400
Austrian	20,200
Dutch	20,200
Sanmarinese	20,000
Arab Emirian	19,900
Belgian	19,500
Fleming	19,200

Bottom 20

Assamese	200
Bihari	188
Abadkis	179
Magars	179
Newar	179
Tamang	179
Tharu	179
Nepalese	179
Somali	175
Sidamo	130
Ometo	130
Gurage	130
Oromo	130
Amhara	130
Tigrinya	127
Tigre	124
Tsonga	121
Saho	120
Makua	116
Malawi	115

Table 3. Caloric Consumption Across Ethnic Groups

Top 20

Ethnic Groups	Calories/Capita/Day
Fleming	3,850
Wallon	3,850
Belgian	3,850
Luxemburger	3,710
Arab Emirian	3,710
Macedonian	3,650
Greek	3,650
Bulgarian	3,630
Arab Berber	3,610
Irish	3,550
Croatian	3,540
Slovene	3,540
Scandinavian	3,510
Hungarian	3,510
Dutch	3,510
Danish	3,510
Russian	3,500
Gypsy	3,470
Yugoslav	3,460
Slovak	3,460

Bottom 20

Ewe	1,730
Ga-Adangme	1,730
Afar	1,660
Amhara	1,660
Gurage	1,660
Ometo	1,660
Oromo	1,660
Sidamo	1,660
Tigre	1,660
Tigrinya	1,660
Bagirmi Sara	1,660
Kotoko	1,660
Masa	1,660
Masalit Maba	1,660
Mubi	1,660
Tama	1,660
Teda	1,660
Tsonga	1,610
Makua	1,610
Malawi	1,610

Table 4. Literacy Across Ethnic Groups

Top 20

Ethnic Groups	Literacy 1994
Abkhaz	100
Andorran	100
Belgian	100
Danish	100
Fleming	100
Greenlandic	100
Icelander	100
Liechtensteiner	100
Luxemburger	100
Ossete	100
Scandinavian	100
Swiss	100
Wallon	100
Tongan	100
Finnish	100
Japanese	100
Belorussian	100
Irish	100
Georgian	99
Dutch	99

Bottom 20

Abadkis	26
Magars	26
Newar	26
Tamang	26
Susu	24
Kissi	23
Bariba	23
Fon	23
Somba	23
Bobo	22
Bullom	21
Kono	21
Koranko	21
Limba	21
Mende	21
Temne	21
Yalunka	21
Saho	20
Grosi	18
Mande	18

QUANTIFYING ETHNIC CULTURES: THE METHODOLOGY

In order to correctly understand the meaning behind the various statistics provided in Chapters 3-9, the reader is advised to carefully review the methodology described in this chapter. Not all of the statistics are direct estimates of the variables reported and reflect, as discussed below, only rough environmental indicators for the ethnic groups covered. In other words, many of the data estimate the environmental conditions under which an ethnic culture lives (e.g. a given ethnic group resides in relatively rich countries), and not the actual level of the ethnic culture itself (e.g. the income per capita of the ethnic group). Special care is needed, therefore, in both interpreting and analyzing these data in applied research settings.

ESTIMATION PROCEDURE

All of the statistics reported in Chapters 3 to 9 are estimates. The procedure used to generate these estimates involved the following steps:

Country Census: First, an exhaustive list of nations, dependencies, and territories was created in order to include all populated areas of the world; these will be referred to as countries, as listed in Appendix B. Total population estimates were obtained for each of these countries. When population estimates across published sources were not consistent (e.g. for the year 1994) or were unavailable, best estimates were obtained via extrapolation from previous years, or from non-published sources (e.g. governmental authorities). Population estimates across countries, in 1994, are given in Appendix B.

Ethnic Group Identification: Second, for each of the 235 countries listed in Appendix B, detailed population statistics broken down by ethnic group were collected from various national and international sources. Inconsistencies which exist across sources include estimates of a given ethnic group's population (usually reported as a percent of the total population), the number of ethnic groups present, the identity of ethnic groups present, or the time period when such estimates are generated. Such inconsistencies were dealt with by (1) setting a target date of mid-1994 for population estimation, and (2) combining estimates across sources while giving more weight to more recent and complete sources. In virtually all cases, this procedure results in original estimates of ethnic group representation within each of the countries present, and, to my knowledge, the most complete enumeration of ethnic representation for the world's population. Not all ethnic groups are, however, represented in official statistics as these may represent too small a percentage (e.g. the Navaho), or are simply unknown with any measure of accuracy. In these cases, a group called "other" has been created for each country. This percent, by country, is reported in Appendix A of this chapter. Given the existence of this "other" category, the reader should understand that the statistics reported for a given ethnic group represent estimates where that group represents enough of a population to be considered a substantial member of the country's social fabric. Appendix A lists the ethnic groups covered in this book, and their populations across countries, as estimated for mid-year 1994. Appendix A provides, therefore, the specific working definition of a particular ethnic group used in this book. It is important to note that the groups are actually ethno-linguistic groups and not racial groups. Appendix C lists a number of references used to identify and quantify ethnic groups across countries. It should be noted that the working definition of an ethnic or ethno-linguistic group has limitations for certain types of research. A number of scholarly works in ethnology note that ethnic groups are often difficult to separate into clean groupings. In this book, a rather pragmatic approach was used to overcome this problem: the groupings reported by national and international sources are used. This causes, for example, certain ethnic groups to be considered separately from others, though some ethnologists would consider these to be identical at a certain level. As the estimates reported are at a certain level of detail using the procedure described above, the reader may be best served by combining estimates across certain groups reported here.

Variable Estimates Across Countries: Third, for each of the variables reported in Chapters 3 to 9, data were collected at the national level for as many countries as possible. For most of the variables reported in Chapters 5 to 9, which describe a ethnic groups' exogenous resources, relatively precise measures were available for all countries of the world (e.g. land areas). For many variables in Chapters 3 and 4 which cover more endogenous social and economic dimensions, as complete an enumeration as possible was conducted by combining various sources, listed in the bibliography. Each chapter reports the number of countries included within the estimation; the higher the number, the more complete the estimate. For many variables, estimates are incomplete by either not existing at all for a given ethnic group or for only a limited number of countries having the group present. As such, for those variables having least cross-country representation, the appropriate caveat should be emphasized. The national estimates are provided in Parker, *National Cultures: A Statistical Reference*, Greenwood Press.

Estimates Across Ethnic Groups: Fourth, given the preceding steps, estimates of variables for a given ethnic group are obtained using an appropriate weighting scheme. This involves first calculating the total population of a given ethnic group, then calculating the percent of that ethnic group residing in every country of the world (in most cases this is equal to zero as most ethnic groups exist to a substantial degree in only a few countries). A given variable is calculated, for a given ethnic group, as a weighted average across countries using these percentages as weights. All figures are reported to the third significant digit. Given this methodology, researchers must recognize certain limitations which, though many can be mitigated, merit great attention.

Finally, it should also be understood that errors are bound to have occurred during the estimation procedure (though great pains were taken to proof-read and cross-validate the input and output statistics). Given the original nature of all of the statistics reported, they should be seen, therefore, as "first generation" estimates which may require external validation (especially if the user is focusing on one particular ethnic group).

INTERPRETING ESTIMATES AND THEIR LIMITATIONS

Given the above outlined methodology with its caveats, the reader is free to interpret the statistics given that due caution is exercised. The most important problem in interpreting the estimates is the fact they are calculated based on country-level statistics, many of which are (1) themselves estimates, and (2) of unknown or possibly skewed distribution within each country. The first issue is a general problem of all cross-cultural research, including those using national definitions of culture. One can better grasp the distribution issue by distinguishing between two types of estimates: (1) *exact estimates*, and (2) *environmental estimates*. The former estimates are not affected by the distribution issue, while the later acknowledge this issue, and are most valid under certain conditions (mostly relating to how the estimates are interpreted or used in subsequent analyses). *Exact estimates* are those which, at the country level, have a uniform distribution across all members of each country where the ethnic group resides. An example of such a variable is "does a country live under a dictatorship (1=yes)." In this case, the distribution across individuals is generally uniform and the estimate provided across ethnic groups reflects the exact estimate for that group (given the steps outlined above and their additional caveats). *Environmental estimates*, on the other hand, measure the conditions under which a given group resides. The estimate for income per capita, for example, is not the exact measure of income per capita for persons in that group. Rather, the estimate indicates that persons in a ethnic group live in societies with the estimated income level. This is true since income may not be uniformly distributed across ethnic groups within a given country. Some ethnic groups may be poorer than the average, while others will be more wealthy than the average. Environmental estimates are most useful when researchers are interested in understanding how the social environment affects the behavior of a given ethnic culture (e.g. as these are exposed to societies having an average level of income, and other forces associated with such a level). Seen in this light, all exact estimates are environmental estimates, yet not all environmental estimates are exact estimates. Most of the variables given in Chapters 5 to 9 are exact estimates as these measure the existence of (and not the consumption or ownership of) natural or cultural resources (and are exogenous variables), while most of those given in Chapters 3 and 4 are environmental (and are endogenous variables).

When and how can environmental estimates be used as proxies for exact estimates? In many cross-cultural studies, researchers are content to use national-level averages (e.g. income per capita) as these represent reasonable proxies for average behavior (even though distributions within each may be skewed). This becomes less of an issue as the number of countries studied increases. So too might researchers use the environmental estimates reported in this book as exact estimates, though the rationale behind this is slightly different. In our case, environmental variables might be reasonable proxies if the research seeks to explain variances across a large number of groups (e.g. 300 ethnic groups) by assuming that biases which tend to over- or under-estimate a behavior will be randomly distributed across groups and, in the aggregate, be offsetting if a large number of groups are investigated simultaneously. A similar argument might be made for those groups which are located in a large number of countries (reported in Appendix A). If biases can be assumed inversely related to the number of countries where an ethnic group is represented, then environmental variables may be reasonable proxies for exact estimates if the study is limited to those groups existing across numerous countries. Additionally, one can attempt to control for biases if these are hypothesized to be based on the extent, say, to which a group is, on average, represented within countries as a minority or a majority (a statistic reported in Chapter 4); other relevant covariates might also be considered. Finally, environmental estimates might be used as proxies for exact estimates if the researcher has prior knowledge of underlying distributions, the ethnic groups themselves, and the variable in question that would suggest that biases are minimal. For example, environmental variables may be deemed to be reasonable exact estimates (i.e. good enough "ball parks") in cases when their distributions overlap, in their absolute levels, to a minimal degree across groups. Consider, for example, the following comparison of ethnic groups and their estimated levels of income per capita:

Ethnic Group	Income per Capita	Countries Covered
Somali	$175	Yemen, Ethiopia, Somalia
Assamese	$200	Bhutan
Japanese	$26649	Northern Mariana Islands, Guam, Canada, United States, Brazil, Japan
Norwegians	$43998	Faroe Islands, Norway

Clearly, the orders-of-magnitude differences observed across ethnic groups in income per capita, for example, allow us to make reasonable conclusions about the relative incomes of these groups and/or analyze these estimates as a dependent variable, despite there being room to improve the estimates by relying on thorough within-country surveys (which are generally not available or incomplete in most countries of the world). As such, even for the environmental variables in Chapters 3 and 9, many of the statistics reported often reflect the "best available" exact estimates to date. Finally, it should be noted that only those ethnic groups and populations which are substantially represented within each country are used (thus eliminating small ethnic groups). As such, the groups ultimately reported in this book are likely to have behaviors reasonably close to average behaviors within the countries where the estimates are derived. Their aggregation, as described above, would tend to reflect this characteristic (i.e. many environmental estimates are reasonable proxies for exact estimates).

ESTIMATION TIMING

The statistics reported in Chapters 3 to 9 are based on the best estimates available during the calendar year 1994. However, in many respects, this timing should not be over emphasized. Rather, the estimates should be seen as covering the ethnic groups during the period of the "early 1990s," or, especially in cases for variables reported in Chapters 3 and 4, the "later part of the 20th century." This perspective is motivated by the fact that data are often inconsistent across sources, or irregular in their availability for 1994 and were extrapolated. By combining various sources and extrapolating, the integrity of the variables was not compromised, though their exact timing (i.e. as required in time series analysis) is not exact. In cases when the variables do not reflect 1994 estimates, these are noted.

Appendix A
Ethnic Groups Across Countries

This appendix lists the ethno-linguistic groups covered in Chapters 3 to 9 in their order of appearance in the comparative tables. Total populations included in the estimation procedures are reported in thousands and are rounded. Due to space limitations, the titles in the comparative tables are abbreviations for the ethnic groups listed here. Countries are given in an order increasing in their absolute population of the ethnic group concerned (e.g. most members of the Afar group live in Djibouti). Many groups represent "ex-patriot" communities with particular national-ethnic identities.

Abadkis, Nepal. Total population covered= 359.

Abkhaz, Georgia. Total population covered= 99.

Acholi, Uganda. Total population covered= 886.

Afar, Eritrea, Djibouti, Ethiopia. Total population covered= 1281.

Afro-European, Jamaica. Total population covered= 379.

Akan, Ghana. Total population covered= 8631.

Albanian, Greece, Macedonia, Serbia & Montenegro, Albania. Total population covered= 5167.

Ambo, Angola. Total population covered= 206.

Amerind, Dominica, St. Vincent & the Grenadines, French Guiana, Suriname, Guyana, Paraguay, Canada, Nicaragua, Ecuador, Panama, Chile, El Salvador, Honduras, Colombia, Peru, Venezuela, United States, Guatemala, Mexico. Total population covered= 37038.

Amerind-Mestizo, Argentina. Total population covered= 5023.

Amhara, Ethiopia. Total population covered= 19953.

Ana-Ife, Togo. Total population covered= 117.

Andorran, Andorra. Total population covered= 15.

Angolares, Sao Tome E Principe, Portugal. Total population covered= 29.

Anouis, Ivory Coast. Total population covered= 1434.

Antandroy, Madagascar. Total population covered= 702.

Arab, other, Gibraltar, Trinidad & Tobago, Djibouti, Canada, Maldives, Bahrain, United Kingdom, Kenya, Senegal, Somalia, Mali, Saudi Arabia, Gaza Strip, Kuwait, Israel, Turkey, United Arab Emirates, France, Iran, Jordan, Tunisia, Syrian Arab Republic, Yemen, Iraq, Morocco, Algeria. Total population covered= 102019.

Arab Berber, Western Sahara, Libya. Total population covered= 4710.

Arab Emirian, United Arab Emirates. Total population covered= 560.

Arab Lebanese, Lebanon. Total population covered= 2381.

Arab Omani, Oman. Total population covered= 1243.

Arab Palestinian, Lebanon, West Bank. Total population covered= 1524.

Arab Qatar, Qatar. Total population covered= 98.

Arab Saudi, Saudi Arabia. Total population covered= 13503.

Arab Sudanic, Chad, Sudan. Total population covered= 15036.

Arab Total, Gibraltar, Trinidad & Tobago, Djibouti, Canada, Maldives, Bahrain, United Kingdom, Kenya, Senegal, Somalia, Mali, Western Sahara, Qatar, Gaza Strip, Kuwait, Israel, Turkey, France, West Bank, Oman, Iran, Chad, United Arab Emirates, Lebanon, Jordan, Libya, Tunisia, Syrian Arab Republic, Yemen, Sudan, Iraq, Saudi Arabia, Morocco, Algeria. Total population covered= 142776.

Araucanian, Chile. Total population covered= 939.

Armenian, Jordan, Canada, Bulgaria, Turkmenistan, Lebanon, Iran, Azerbaijan, Georgia, Armenia. Total population covered= 4785.

Assamese, Bhutan. Total population covered= 217.

Assyrian, Iraq. Total population covered= 159.

Austrian, Liechtenstein, Austria. Total population covered= 7389.

Avar, Azerbaijan. Total population covered= 59.

Aymara, Peru, Bolivia. Total population covered= 2564.

Azande, Central African Republic, Sudan, Zaire. Total population covered= 3574.

Azerbaijani, Armenia, Georgia, Azerbaijan, Iran. Total population covered= 16958.

Bagirmi Sara, Chad. Total population covered= 1827.

Bahraini, Bahrain. Total population covered= 345.

Bai, China. Total population covered= 1695.

Bakhtiari, Iran. Total population covered= 1075.

Bakongo, Angola. Total population covered= 1337.

Balante, Guinea-Bissau. Total population covered= 279.

Baluchi, United Arab Emirates, Afghanistan, Iran, Pakistan. Total population covered= 4864.

Bambara, Mali. Total population covered= 3232.

Bamileke-Bamum, Cameroon. Total population covered= 2322.

Banda, Zaire, Central African Republic. Total population covered= 1348.

Bangi-Ngale, Zaire. Total population covered= 2389.

Bantu, Somalia, Zimbabwe. Total population covered= 1238.

Baoule, Ivory Coast. Total population covered= 1594.

Bari, Sudan. Total population covered= 549.

Bariba, Benin. Total population covered= 492.

Barotze, Zambia. Total population covered= 727.

Baskhir, Russia. Total population covered= 1342.

Basque, St. Pierre & Miquelon, Spain. Total population covered= 904.

Bassa, Liberia. Total population covered= 396.

Batswana, Botswana. Total population covered= 1016.

Bayad, Mongolia. Total population covered= 44.

Beja, Sudan. Total population covered= 1756.

Belgian, Monaco, Luxembourg, Belgium. Total population covered= 310.

Belorussian, Estonia, Lithuania, Latvia, Kazakhstan, Ukraine, Russia, Belarus. Total population covered= 10019.

Bemba, Zambia. Total population covered= 3121.

Bengali, Oman, Bangladesh. Total population covered= 119481.

Berber, Tunisia, Algeria, Morocco. Total population covered= 12796.

Bete, Ivory Coast. Total population covered= 2639.

Betsileo, Madagascar. Total population covered= 1550.

Betsimi-Saraka, Madagascar. Total population covered= 1974.

Bhutia, Bhutan. Total population covered= 1028.

Bihari, Bangladesh, Nepal. Total population covered= 5535.

Black Non-Native (other), Anguilla, British Virgin Islands, Turks and Caicos Islands, Montserrat, Cayman Islands, Maldives, Bermuda, St. Kitts and Nevis, Guadeloupe, Costa Rica, Antigua & Barbuda, Dominica, Grenada, Virgin Islands US, St. Vincent & the Grenadines, Cape Verde, St. Lucia, Guatemala, Honduras, Bahamas, Barbados, Guyana, Nicaragua, Panama, Mexico, Trinidad & Tobago, Puerto Rico, Dominican Republic, Cuba, Colombia, Venezuela, Jamaica, South Africa, Haiti, Brazil, United States. Total population covered= 71283.

Black Amerind, Colombia. Total population covered= 1019.

Boa, Zaire. Total population covered= 947.

Bobo, Mali, Burkina Faso. Total population covered= 909.

Bounty Mutineers, Norfolk Island, Pitcairn Islands, Total population covered= <1.

Brazilian, French Guiana, Portugal. Total population covered= 16.

Breton, St. Pierre & Miquelon, France. Total population covered= 577.

Bubi, Equatorial Guinea. Total population covered= 58.

Bulgarian, Moldova, Ukraine, Bulgaria. Total population covered= 7957.

Bullom, Sierra Leone. Total population covered= 167.

Bura, Nigeria. Total population covered= 1811.

Burman, Burma. Total population covered= 30799.

Bush Negro, French Guiana, Suriname. Total population covered= 43.

Bushman, Botswana. Total population covered= 46.

Capverdien, Portugal. Total population covered= 20.

Carolinians, Northern Mariana I. Total population covered= 19.

Catalan, Spain. Total population covered= 6383.

Chahar Aimak, Afghanistan. Total population covered= 558.

Chamba, Cameroon. Total population covered= 301.

Chamorro, Northern Mariana Islands, Guam. Total population covered= 82.

Chiga, Uganda. Total population covered= 1310.

Chin, Burma. Total population covered= 893.

Chinese, other, Nauru, Seychelles, Solomon Islands, Christmas Island, Northern Mariana Islands, Mauritius, French Polynesia, Suriname, Trinidad & Tobago, Reunion, North Korea, Brunei, Costa Rica, United Kingdom, Canada, Macau,

Cambodia, Philippines, Vietnam, United States, Singapore, Hong Kong, Malaysia, Thailand. Total population covered= 26092.

Chinese Mainland, Taiwan. Total population covered= 2912.

Chokwe, Angola, Zaire. Total population covered= 1173.

Chuang, China. Total population covered= 12110.

Chuvash, Russia. Total population covered= 1789.

Circassian, Jordan, Turkey. Total population covered= 201.

Coloured, South Africa. Total population covered= 3957.

Comorian, Madagascar, Comoros. Total population covered= 636.

Creole, Mayotte, Seychelles, Belize, Suriname, Netherlands Antilles, Mauritius. Total population covered= 1038.

Croatian, Hungary, Slovenia, Bosnia & Hercgovenia, Croatia. Total population covered= 4586.

Czech, Croatia, Slovakia, Canada, Czech Republic. Total population covered= 10094.

Dagestani, Azerbaijan, Russia. Total population covered= 1726.

Dai, China. Total population covered= 1090.

Damara, Namibia. Total population covered= 125.

Dan, Liberia, Ivory Coast. Total population covered= 922.

Danish, Faroe Islands, Iceland, Norway, Denmark. Total population covered= 5028.

Dinka, Sudan. Total population covered= 3155.

Dogon, Mali. Total population covered= 405.

Dong, China. Total population covered= 2664.

Dravidian, Maldives, India. Total population covered= 224225.

Duala, Equatorial Guinea. Total population covered= 11.

Duala- Landa-Basa, Cameroon. Total population covered= 1845.

Dujia, China. Total population covered= 6055.

Dutch Non-Native (other), Suriname, Belgium, Canada. Total population covered= 442.

Dyola, Gambia, Mali. Total population covered= 389.

Edo, Nigeria. Total population covered= 3622.

Egyptian, Egypt. Total population covered= 55482.

English, Monaco, Seychelles, Macau, Guernsey, Jersey, United Kingdom. Total population covered= 46762.

Estonian, Estonia. Total population covered= 976.

Euronesian, Western Samoa. Total population covered= 22.

European Non-Native (other), Kiribati, Tuvalu, Cook Island, Faroe Islands, Montserrat, Niue, Christmas Island, Cocos (Keeling) Islands, Nauru, Sao Tome E Principe, Solomon Islands, Vanuatu, Western Samoa, Bahrain, Fiji, French Polynesia, Togo, Djibouti, Mauritius, Yemen, New Caledonia, Kenya, Angola, Zimbabwe, Costa Rica, New Zealand, Canada, Argentina. Total population covered= 40735.

Ewa-Adja, Togo. Total population covered= 1773.

Ewe, Ghana. Total population covered= 1960.

Fang, Equatorial Guinea, Gabon, Cameroon. Total population covered= 3216.

Fijian, Fiji. Total population covered= 330.

Finnish, Estonia, Canada, Sweden, Finland. Total population covered= 5010.

Fleming, Belgium. Total population covered= 5506.

Fon, Benin. Total population covered= 3324.

Forros, Sao Tome E Principe. Total population covered= 33.

French, Mayotte, Comoros, Andorra, Martinique, Portugal, Reunion, French Guiana, Luxembourg, Monaco, Tunisia, Cameroon, Algeria, Madagascar, Belgium, Switzerland, Canada, France. Total population covered= 60073.

Fulani, Mauritania, Sierra Leone, Gambia, Benin, Guinea-Bissau, Burkina Faso, Niger, Cameroon, Mali, Senegal, Guinea, Nigeria. Total population covered= 20883.

Fur, Sudan. Total population covered= 549.

Ga-Adangme, Ghana. Total population covered= 1285.

Gagauz, Turkey, Moldova. Total population covered= 272.

Galician, Spain. Total population covered= 3211.

Ganda, Uganda. Total population covered= 3429.

Garifuna, Belize. Total population covered= 14.

Gbaya, Central African Republic. Total population covered= 802.

Georgian, Turkey, Georgia. Total population covered= 3965.

German, Andorra, Iceland, Liechtenstein, Guam, Slovakia, Luxembourg, Denmark, Netherlands, Austria, Czech Republic, Paraguay, Romania, Kyrgyzstan, Hungary, Canada, Kazakhstan, France, Switzerland, Brazil, Germany,. Total population covered= 87748.

Gibraltarian, Gibraltar. Total population covered= 21.

Gilaki, Iran. Total population covered= 3352.

Gilbertese, Kiribati. Total population covered= 72.

Gio, Liberia. Total population covered= 224.

Gisu, Uganda. Total population covered= 1387.

Gola, Liberia. Total population covered= 144.

Grebo, Liberia. Total population covered= 258.

Greek, Monaco, Albania, Georgia, Canada, Germany, Cyprus, Greece. Total population covered= 10888.

Greenlandic, Greenland. Total population covered= 47.

Grosi, Burkina Faso. Total population covered= 499.

Guiana Chinese, French Guiana. Total population covered= 17.

Guianese Creole, French Guiana. Total population covered= 52.

Gurage, Ethiopia. Total population covered= 1747.

Gurma, Burkina Faso, Ghana, Togo. Total population covered= 1638.

Gurung, Bhutan. Total population covered= 276.

Gypsy, Albania, Hungary, Czech Republic, Slovakia, Moldova, Bulgaria, Romania. Total population covered= 1017.

Han Chinese, China. Total population covered= 1128903.

Hani, China. Total population covered= 1332.

Hausa, Chad, Cameroon, Niger, Nigeria. Total population covered= 27465.

Haya, Tanzania. Total population covered= 1698.

Hazara-Dari, Afghanistan. Total population covered= 1673.

Hehet-Bena, Tanzania. Total population covered= 1986.

Herero, Namibia. Total population covered= 125.

Hottentot, Botswana. Total population covered= 34.

Hui-Vighur, China. Total population covered= 16349.

Humbe-Nyaneka, Angola. Total population covered= 555.

Hungarian, Slovenia, Czech Republic, Croatia, Canada, Ukraine, Serbia & Montenegro, Slovakia, Romania, Hungary. Total population covered= 13234.

Hutu, Burundi, Rwanda. Total population covered= 11979.

Ibibio, Equatorial Guinea, Nigeria. Total population covered= 5971.

Icelander, Iceland. Total population covered= 273.

Igbo, Nigeria. Total population covered= 19603.

Ijaw, Nigeria. Total population covered= 1918.

Indian Non-Native (other), Gibraltar, Montserrat, St. Kitts and Nevis, St. Vincent & the Grenadines, Grenada, Seychelles, St. Lucia, Belize, Martinique, Swaziland, Madagascar, Brunei, United Arab Emirates, Jamaica, Qatar, Suriname, Panama, Reunion, Singapore, Yemen, Oman, Fiji, United States, Guyana, Mauritius, Trinidad & Tobago, United Kingdom, Malaysia. Total population covered= 5868.

Indo-Aryan, India. Total population covered= 645569.

Indonesian, New Caledonia. Total population covered= 6.

Iranian, Bahrain, Qatar, Pakistan. Total population covered= 10990.

Irish, Isle of Man, United Kingdom, Ireland. Total population covered= 4674.

Issa, Djibouti. Total population covered= 234.

Italian, Vatican City, Slovenia, San Marino, Monaco, Tunisia, Croatia, Luxembourg, Uruguay, France, Belgium, Germany, Canada, Switzerland, Brazil, Italy. Total population covered= 76402.

Japanese, Northern Mariana Islands, Guam, Canada, United States, Brazil, Japan. Total population covered= 126009.

Javanese, Suriname, Indonesia. Total population covered= 76746.

Jewish, Gibraltar, Monaco, Isle of Man, Gaza Strip, Lithuania, Georgia, Canada, Uruguay, Tajikistan, Moldova, West Bank, Belarus, Ukraine, Israel. Total population covered= 5801.

Jola, Senegal. Total population covered= 635.

Kalenjin, Kenya. Total population covered= 2817.

Kamba, Kenya. Total population covered= 2948.

Kanuri, Chad, Niger, Nigeria. Total population covered= 5383.

Karakalpak, Uzbekistan. Total population covered= 455.

Kare, Central African Republic. Total population covered= 79.

Karen, Burma. Total population covered= 2767.

Kavango, Namibia. Total population covered= 141.

Kazakh, Kyrgyzstan, Turkmenistan, Mongolia, Uzbekistan, China, Kazakhstan. Total population covered= 9548.

Kebu-Akposo, Togo. Total population covered= 156.

Khmer, Vietnam, Thailand, Cambodia. Total population covered= 10314.

Kikuyu, Kenya. Total population covered= 5452.

Kimbundu, Angola. Total population covered= 2345.

Kisii, Kenya. Total population covered= 1565.

Kissi, Sierra Leone, Guinea. Total population covered= 513.

Klao, Liberia. Total population covered= 201.

Kongo, Congo, Zaire. Total population covered= 7979.

Kono, Sierra Leone. Total population covered= 234.

Konzo, Zaire. Total population covered= 412.

Koranko, Sierra Leone. Total population covered= 158.

Korean, Northern Mariana Islands, Guam, Canada, Kazakhstan, Uzbekistan, United States, China, North Korea, South Korea. Total population covered= 70715.

Kotoko, Chad. Total population covered= 126.

Kpelle, Guinea, Liberia. Total population covered= 859.

Kru, Liberia. Total population covered= 210.

Kurd, Jordan, Georgia, Armenia, Syrian Arab Republic, Iraq, Iran, Turkey. Total population covered= 16824.

Kuwaiti, Kuwait. Total population covered= 795.

Kyrgyz, Tajikistan, Uzbekistan, Kyrgyzstan. Total population covered= 2667.

Ladino, Guatemala. Total population covered= 4205.

Lango, Uganda. Total population covered= 1156.

Lao, Laos, Thailand. Total population covered= 18320.

Latvian, Latvia. Total population covered= 1388.

Lezgin, Azerbaijan. Total population covered= 220.

Li, China. Total population covered= 1090.

Liechtensteiner, Liechtenstein. Total population covered= 18.

Limba, Sierra Leone. Total population covered= 167.

Lithuanian, Latvia, Lithuania. Total population covered= 3065.

Lobi, Burkina Faso, Ivory Coast. Total population covered= 1399.

Loma, Liberia. Total population covered= 201.

Lomwe, Malawi. Total population covered= 1970.

Lotuko, Sudan. Total population covered= 274.

Luba, Zaire. Total population covered= 7414.

Luchasi, Angola. Total population covered= 247.

Luena, Angola. Total population covered= 350.

Lugbara, Zaire. Total population covered= 824.

Luhya, Kenya. Total population covered= 3600.

Lumbe, Angola. Total population covered= 555.

Lunda, Angola. Total population covered= 123.

Luo, Kenya. Total population covered= 3339.

Luri, Iran. Total population covered= 2719.

Luxemburger, Luxembourg. Total population covered= 276.

Macedonian, Albania, Greece, Bulgaria, Macedonia. Total population covered= 1766.

Madurese, Indonesia. Total population covered= 9342.

Magars, Nepal. Total population covered= 464.

Maka, Equatorial Guinea, Congo, Cameroon. Total population covered= 663.

Makonde, Tanzania. Total population covered= 1669.

Makua, Mayotte, Comoros, Mozambique. Total population covered= 7561.

Malagasy, Mayotte, Seychelles, Madagascar. Total population covered= 3580.

Malawi, Mozambique. Total population covered= 1915.

Malay, Christmas Island, Cocos (Keeling) Islands, Brunei, Singapore, Thailand, Malaysia. Total population covered= 14463.

Malay Christian, Philippines. Total population covered= 60892.

Malay Coastal, Indonesia. Total population covered= 23355.

Malay Muslim, Philippines. Total population covered= 2662.

Malinke, Guinea-Bissau, Gambia, Mali, Ivory Coast, Guinea. Total population covered= 3665.

Maltese, Malta. Total population covered= 345.

Mambwe, Zambia. Total population covered= 408.

Manchu-Tibetian, China. Total population covered= 12716.

Mandara, Cameroon. Total population covered= 715.

Mande, Burkina Faso. Total population covered= 861.

Mandingo, Senegal. Total population covered= 555.

Mandyako, Guinea-Bissau. Total population covered= 109.

Mano, Liberia. Total population covered= 204.

Manx (Norse-Celtic), Isle of Man. Total population covered= 1.

Manzan-Darani, Iran. Total population covered= 2277.

Maori, New Zealand. Total population covered= 312.

Maravi, Zambia, Malawi. Total population covered= 7801.

Masa, Chad. Total population covered= 138.

Masalit Maba, Chad. Total population covered= 377.

Maya, Belize. Total population covered= 20.

Mbaka, Central African Republic. Total population covered= 141.

Mbete, Congo, Gabon. Total population covered= 290.

Mbochi, Congo. Total population covered= 283.

Mbum, Central African Republic, Cameroon, Chad. Total population covered= 699.

Mbunda, Angola. Total population covered= 103.

Melanesian, Vanuatu, Pacific Island Trust, New Caledonia, Solomon Islands, Papua New Guinea. Total population covered= 1016.

Mende, Sierra Leone. Total population covered= 1551.

Merina, Madagascar. Total population covered= 3525.

Meru, Kenya. Total population covered= 1565.

Mestizo, Vanuatu, Sao Tome E Principe, Guadeloupe, Belize, Uruguay, Costa Rica, Panama, Bolivia, Nicaragua, Paraguay, Ecuador, El Salvador, Honduras, Peru, Chile, Venezuela, Brazil, Colombia, Mexico. Total population covered= 146017.

Miao Man, Laos. Total population covered= 235.

Micronesian, Vanuatu, Solomon Islands, Guam, Marshall Islands, Micronesia Federation. Total population covered= 181.

Mixed, St. Kitts and Nevis, Tuvalu, Cook Island, Kiribati, Dominica, Cayman Islands, St. Lucia, Grenada, Barbados, Bahamas, Aruba, Trinidad & Tobago, Cape Verde, Reunion. Total population covered= 1047.

Moldovan, Ukraine, Russia, Moldova. Total population covered= 4105.

Mon, Burma. Total population covered= 893.

Mon-Khmer, Laos. Total population covered= 226.

Monegasque, Monaco. Total population covered= 5.

Mongo, Zaire. Total population covered= 5478.

Mongol-Buryat, Mongolia. Total population covered= 39.

Mongol-Dariganga, Mongolia. Total population covered= 32.

Mongol-Dorbed, Mongolia. Total population covered= 63.

Mongol-Khalka, Mongolia. Total population covered= 1826.

Mongoloid, China, India. Total population covered= 31985.

Montenegroin, Serbia & Montenegro. Total population covered= 633.

Moor, Sri Lanka, Mauritania. Total population covered= 3052.

Moravians, Slovakia. Total population covered= 5.

Mossi, Ghana, Burkina Faso. Total population covered= 7289.

Mpongwe, Gabon. Total population covered= 183.

Mubi, Chad. Total population covered= 252.

Mulatto, Montserrat, Antigua & Barbuda, Turks and Caicos Islands, St. Vincent & the Grenadines, Uruguay, Costa Rica, Guyana, Guadeloupe, Haiti, Martinique, Panama, Cuba, Colombia, Dominican Republic, Brazil. Total population covered= 49060.

Muong, Vietnam. Total population covered= 841.

Nama, Namibia. Total population covered= 78.

Nauruan, Nauru. Total population covered= 6.

Ndebele, Botswana, Zimbabwe. Total population covered= 1741.

Nepalese, Nepal. Total population covered= 12323.

Netherlander, Netherlands. Total population covered= 14573),

Newar, Nepal. Total population covered= 633.

Ngbandi, Central African Republic. Total population covered= 347.

Ngoni, Malawi. Total population covered= 717.

Nkole, Uganda. Total population covered= 1579.

Norman-French Descendants, Guernsey, Jersey. Total population covered= 119.

North-Western (Loz), Zambia. Total population covered= 895.

Norwegian, Faroe Islands, Norway. Total population covered= 4166.

Nuba, Sudan. Total population covered= 2222.

Nuer, Sudan. Total population covered= 1344.

Nung Sukuma, Vietnam. Total population covered= 771.

Nupe, Nigeria. Total population covered= 1278.

Nyamwezi (Galla), Tanzania. Total population covered= 6072.

Nyoros, Uganda. Total population covered= 616.

Ometo, Ethiopia. Total population covered= 1429.

Oromo, Ethiopia. Total population covered= 18683.

Ossete, Georgia. Total population covered= 176.

Ovambo, Namibia. Total population covered= 784.

Ovimbundu, Angola. Total population covered= 3827.

Pacific Islander, Nauru. Total population covered= 3.

Pakistani, Swaziland, Norway, Madagascar, Oman, Suriname, United Arab Emirates, Qatar, United Kingdom. Total population covered= 795.

Palauans, Pacific Island Trust. Total population covered= 6.

Palaung- Wa, Laos. Total population covered= 543.

Papuan New Guinea, Papua New Guinea. Total population covered= 3505.

Pashtun, Afghanistan. Total population covered= 10059.

Pepel, Guinea-Bissau. Total population covered= 103.

Persian, United Arab Emirates, Iraq, Iran. Total population covered= 29027.

Polynesian, Vanuatu, Niue, Tokelau, Pacific Island Trust, Solomon Islands, Cook Island, Micronesia Federation, New Zealand, French Polynesia. Total population covered= 301.

Polynesian- Chinese, French Polynesia. Total population covered= 8.

Polynesian- European, Cook Island, French Polynesia. Total population covered= 22.

Polish, Slovakia, Latvia, Czech Republic, Canada, Ukraine, Lithuania, Germany, Belarus, Poland. Total population covered= 39689.

Portuguese, Swaziland, Andorra, Luxembourg, Macau, Canada, France, Portugal, Brazil. Total population covered= 34117.

Punjabi, Canada, Pakistan. Total population covered= 84616.

Punu, Congo, Gabon. Total population covered= 219.

Puyi, China. Total population covered= 2785.

Pygmy, Congo. Total population covered= 37.

Quechua, Bolivia, Ecuador, Peru. Total population covered= 18453.

Rakhine, Burma. Total population covered= 2009.

Romanian, Hungary, Macedonia, Romania. Total population covered= 20721.

Romansch, Switzerland. Total population covered= 55.

Rundi, Burundi, Zaire. Total population covered= 1673.

Russian, Monaco, Bulgaria, Canada, Armenia, Tajikistan, Lithuania, Georgia, Turkmenistan, Azerbaijan, Estonia, Moldova, Latvia, Kyrgyzstan, Belarus, Uzbekistan, Kazakhstan, Ukraine, Russia. Total population covered= 146614.

Ruthenian, Slovakia. Total population covered= 16.

Rwanda, Uganda, Zaire. Total population covered= 5360.

Saho, Eritrea. Total population covered= 104.

Sakalava, Madagascar. Total population covered= 848.

Samoan, Tokelau, American Samoa, United States, Western Samoa. Total population covered= 293.

Sanga, Congo. Total population covered= 66.

Sanmarinese, San Marino. Total population covered= 18.

Sara, Central African Republic. Total population covered= 229.

Scandinavian, Denmark, Faroe Islands. Total population covered= 72.

Senufo, Burkina Faso, Mali, Ivory Coast. Total population covered= 3704.

Serbian, Slovenia, Macedonia, Canada, Croatia, Bosnia & Hercgovenia, Serbia & Montenegro. Total population covered= 8754.

Serer, Senegal. Total population covered= 1349.

Servicais Tongas, Sao Tome E Principe. Total population covered= 76.

Shan, Burma. Total population covered= 3794.

Shilluk, Sudan. Total population covered= 549.

Shona, Botswana, Mozambique, Zimbabwe. Total population covered= 9693.

Siamese, Thailand. Total population covered= 29899.

Sidamo, Ethiopia. Total population covered= 1270.

Sindhi, Pakistan. Total population covered= 16655.

Sinhalese, Maldives, Sri Lanka. Total population covered= 13347.

Slavic Muslims, Croatia, Bosnia and Hercgovenia. Total population covered= 1777.

Slovak, Hungary, Canada, Czech Republic, Slovakia. Total population covered= 4904.

Slovene, Croatia, Hungary, Slovenia. Total population covered= 1830.

Soga, Uganda. Total population covered= 1579.

Somali, Yemen, Ethiopia, Somalia. Total population covered= 10390.

Somba, Benin. Total population covered= 274.

Songhai, Niger, Mali. Total population covered= 1414.

Soninke, Mauritania, Gambia, Senegal, Mali. Total population covered= 1188.

Sotho, Lesotho, South Africa. Total population covered= 4629.

Sotho North, South Africa. Total population covered= 3957.

Spanish, Monaco, Gibraltar, Virgin Islands US, Portugal, Andorra, Canada, Switzerland, Germany, France, Ecuador, Brazil, Spain. Total population covered= 45699.

Sundanese, Indonesia. Total population covered= 29778.

Suriname, Netherlands Antilles. Total population covered= 5.

Susu, Guinea. Total population covered= 693.

Swahili, Mayotte, Tanzania. Total population covered= 2620.

Swazi, Swaziland. Total population covered= 690.

Swedish, Faroe Islands, Iceland, Norway, Finland, Sweden. Total population covered= 8155.

Swiss, other, Vatican City, Liechtenstein. Total population covered= 5.

Tahitian, New Caledonia. Total population covered= 7.

Tai, Laos, Vietnam. Total population covered= 1404.

Taiwanese (Dari), Taiwan. Total population covered= 17472.

Tajik, Uzbekistan, Tajikistan, Afghanistan. Total population covered= 8643.

Tama, Chad. Total population covered= 377.

Tamang, Nepal. Total population covered= 739.

Tamil (Tubu), Sri Lanka. Total population covered= 3260.

Tatar, Turkmenistan, Kyrgyzstan, Kazakhstan, Uzbekistan, Russia. Total population covered= 6700.

Teda, Chad. Total population covered= 437.

Teke, Congo, Zaire. Total population covered= 1537.

Tem-Kabre, Togo. Total population covered= 937.

Temne, Sierra Leone. Total population covered= 1411.

Teso, Uganda. Total population covered= 1714.

Thai, Vietnam. Total population covered= 841.

Tharu, Nepal. Total population covered= 760.

Tigre, Ethiopia, Eritrea. Total population covered= 2398.

Tigrinya, Eritrea, Ethiopia. Total population covered= 6292.

Tikar, Cameroon. Total population covered= 929.

Tiv, Nigeria. Total population covered= 2344.

Tonga, Zambia. Total population covered= 1339.

Tongan, American Samoa, Tonga. Total population covered= 95.

Toros, Uganda. Total population covered= 597.

Tribal, Bangladesh. Total population covered= 1223.

Tsimihety, Madagascar. Total population covered= 981.

Tsonga, Swaziland, Mozambique. Total population covered= 3739.

Tswana, South Africa. Total population covered= 2374.

Tuareg, Niger, Burkina Faso, Mali. Total population covered= 1319.

Tukolor, Mauritania, Senegal. Total population covered= 830.

Tumbuka, Zambia. Total population covered= 408.

Turkish, Jordan, Denmark, Switzerland, Greece, Austria, Macedonia, Belgium, Cyprus, Netherlands, Bulgaria, Germany, Turkey. Total population covered= 54249.

Turkmen, Turkey, Iraq, Afghanistan, Iran, Turkmenistan. Total population covered= 4959.

Tutsi, Rwanda, Burundi. Total population covered= 1538.

Tuvaluan, Kiribati, Tuvalu. Total population covered= 10.

Twa, Burundi, Rwanda. Total population covered= 138.

Uighur, Kyrgyzstan, Kazakhstan. Total population covered= 234.

Ukrainian, Slovakia, Lithuania, Turkmenistan, Georgia, Estonia, Romania, Latvia, Kyrgyzstan, Belarus, Canada, Poland, Moldova, Kazakhstan, Russia, Ukraine. Total population covered= 45794.

Urdu, Pakistan. Total population covered= 9737.

Uzbek, Turkmenistan, Kazakhstan, Kyrgyzstan, Tajikistan, Afghanistan, Uzbekistan. Total population covered= 19892.

Vanuatuan, Vanuatu. Total population covered= 156.

Vietnamese, New Caledonia, Norway, Canada, Cambodia, United States, Vietnam. Total population covered= 62635.

Wallon, Belgium. Total population covered= 3303.

White Non-Native (other), Dominica, St. Kitts and Nevis, American Samoa, Anguilla, Antigua & Barbuda, Grenada, St. Lucia, Turks and Caicos Islands, British Virgin Islands, St. Vincent & the Grenadines, Cape Verde, Haiti, St. Helena, Barbados, Belize, Guadeloupe, Netherlands Antilles, Cayman Islands, Trinidad & Tobago, Virgin Islands US, Bermuda, Bahamas, El Salvador, Honduras, Jamaica, Namibia, Guatemala, Panama, Nicaragua, Bolivia, Dominican Republic, Peru, Puerto Rico, Venezuela, Colombia, South Africa, Cuba, Mexico, Australia, Brazil, United States. Total population covered= 270905.

Wolof, Gambia, Mauritania, Senegal. Total population covered= 3140.

Xhosa, South Africa. Total population covered= 3957.

Yalunka, Sierra Leone. Total population covered= 158.

Yao, Mozambique, Malawi, China. Total population covered= 4199.

Yi-Miao, China. Total population covered= 13684.

Yoruba, Ghana, Benin, Nigeria. Total population covered= 23358.

Yugoslav, Denmark, Macedonia, Austria, Germany,. Total population covered= 833.

Zambo, Nicaragua. Total population covered= 207.

Zulu, Swaziland, Niger, South Africa. Total population covered= 1086.

Appendix B
List of Countries

The populations of the following countries and territories are those we used in the estimation methodology described in this chapter. The population in 1994, in thousands, and the percent of that population for which ethnic groups were included in this book are reported (100 less this percent is classified as "other"); all figures are rounded.

Countries in Survey	Pop. in 1994	% of Pop. in Survey	Countries in Survey	Pop. in 1994	% of Pop. in Survey
Afghanistan	19234.00	95.90	Cape Verde	403.50	100.00
Albania	3331.00	98.80	Cayman Islands	31.22	100.00
Algeria	27107.50	99.70	Ctrl African Rep.	3272.00	91.30
American Samoa	53.07	94.00	Chad	5991.50	96.40
Andorra	53.00	95.70	Chile	13813.00	88.40
Angola	10287.00	100.00	China	1211009.00	100.00
Anguilla	7.50	70.00	Christmas Island	1.68	97.00
Antigua & Barb.	65.50	99.20	Cocos (Keel.) Isl.	0.59	100.00
Argentina	33487.50	100.00	Colombia	33972.50	100.00
Armenia	3573.50	100.00	Comoros	615.00	98.90
Aruba	63.56	80.00	Congo	2457.50	94.10
Australia	17845.00	99.30	Cook Island	17.95	99.10
Austria	7817.00	98.30	Costa Rica	3273.50	99.00
Azerbaijan	7345.50	99.20	Croatia	4848.00	92.50
Bahamas	286.00	100.00	Cuba	10900.00	99.90
Bahrain	531.50	99.00	Cyprus	718.50	96.80
Bangladesh	122250.50	100.00	Czech Republic	10382.00	99.00
Barbados	280.00	98.00	Denmark	5190.00	99.60
Belarus	10302.00	100.00	Djibouti	498.00	99.00
Belgium	10010.00	98.00	Dominica	77.00	99.20
Belize	200.00	96.90	Dominican Rep.	7634.50	100.00
Benin	5067.50	93.60	Ecuador	11333.00	100.00
Bermuda	61.84	98.00	Egypt	56042.50	99.00
Bhutan	1644.50	92.50	El Salvador	5520.50	97.30
Bolivia	7844.00	88.00	Equatorial Guinea	394.50	97.70
Bosnia and Herz.	4334.00	88.00	Eritrea	3481.50	97.00
Botswana	1346.00	95.10	Estonia	1587.00	97.90
Brazil	156100.00	98.80	Ethiopia	52926.00	95.40
British Virgin Isl.	15.35	70.00	Falkland Islands	2.10	100.00
Brunei	291.00	98.40	Faroe Islands	47.53	99.50
Bulgaria	8951.50	99.50	Fiji	727.50	97.00
Burkina Faso	9784.50	97.20	Finland	5016.50	99.80
Burma	44636.50	92.20	France	57385.50	97.30
Burundi	5984.00	100.00	French Guiana	122.19	94.80
Cambodia	9011.00	97.30	French Polynesia	213.67	96.80
Cameroon	12552.50	85.50	Gabon	1261.50	75.10
Canada	28173.50	95.15	Gambia	928.50	92.20

Countries in Survey	Pop. in 1994	% of Pop. in Survey	Countries in Survey	Pop. in 1994	% of Pop. in Survey
Gaza Strip	691.42	100.00	Macau	498.92	87.50
Georgia	5486.00	99.10	Macedonia	1991.50	98.40
Germany	80621.00	98.00	Madagascar	13251.00	100.00
Ghana	16472.00	92.50	Malawi	10704.00	96.60
Gibraltar	31.25	91.50	Malaysia	19242.00	99.50
Greece	10216.00	98.00	Maldives	232.00	100.00
Greenland	57.27	82.70	Mali	10132.00	98.20
Grenada	88.00	100.00	Malta	360.00	97.80
Guadeloupe	416.06	99.00	Marshall Islands	50.50	100.00
Guam	144.47	100.00	Martinique	380.83	98.00
Guatemala	10011.00	100.00	Mauritania	2185.00	97.50
Guernsey	63.07	100.00	Mauritius	1110.00	99.50
Guinea	6300.50	87.10	Mayotte	89.98	100.00
Guinea-Bissau	1025.00	82.90	Mexico	90020.00	99.50
Guyana	812.50	99.20	Micronesia Fed.	101.00	100.00
Haiti	6917.50	100.00	Moldova	4377.00	100.00
Honduras	5648.50	100.00	Monaco	29.00	100.00
Hong Kong	5895.00	97.00	Mongolia	2317.00	92.40
Hungary	10489.50	98.80	Montserrat	11.83	99.80
Iceland	283.00	98.60	Morocco	26950.50	100.00
India	896623.50	100.00	Mozambique	15961.50	97.70
Indonesia	194627.50	71.50	Namibia	1567.50	86.00
Iran	63239.00	93.30	Nauru	9.70	100.00
Iraq	19931.00	99.10	Nepal	21101.00	91.10
Ireland	3488.00	94.00	Netherlands	15292.00	98.10
Isle of Man	70.13	99.90	Nether Antilles	180.49	97.90
Israel	5486.00	97.90	New Caledonia	178.03	97.50
Italy	57834.00	98.10	New Zealand	3510.00	97.50
Ivory Coast	13397.50	74.50	Nicaragua	4137.50	99.80
Jamaica	2510.50	97.70	Niger	8556.50	97.20
Japan	124711.00	99.40	Nigeria	106539.50	92.30
Jersey	85.45	100.00	Niue	1.99	100.00
Jordan	4447.50	100.00	Norfolk Island	2.66	100.00
Kazakhstan	17151.50	95.10	North Korea	23045.50	100.00
Kenya	26087.50	82.50	Northern Mar. Isl	47.79	97.00
Kiribati	75.00	99.40	Norway	4316.50	98.00
Kuwait	1896.50	94.90	Oman	1679.50	95.00
Kyrgyzstan	4567.00	95.70	Pacific Isl. Trust	16.04	100.00
Laos	4521.50	97.00	Pakistan	128117.00	97.60
Latvia	2679.00	97.00	Panama	2555.50	98.50
Lebanon	2882.50	97.50	Papua N. Guinea	4173.00	99.00
Lesotho	1864.50	99.70	Paraguay	4633.50	95.50
Liberia	2870.50	89.40	Peru	22940.50	98.20
Libya	5062.50	89.00	Philippines	66549.00	97.00
Liechtenstein	28.50	90.60	Pitcairn Islands	0.05	100.00
Lithuania	3782.50	99.20	Poland	38510.50	100.00
Luxembourg	391.50	93.70	Portugal	9888.50	99.80

Countries in Survey	Pop. in 1994	% of Pop. in Survey	Countries in Survey	Pop. in 1994	% of Pop. in Survey
Puerto Rico	3727.54	100.00	Taiwan	20800.00	100.00
Qatar	489.00	95.00	Tajikistan	5731.00	95.40
Reunion	641.81	96.90	Tanzania	28777.50	48.50
Romania	23367.00	98.60	Thailand	56843.00	98.00
Russia	149088.00	92.90	Togo	3905.00	93.20
Rwanda	7778.50	100.00	Tokelau	1.54	100.00
San Marino	22.50	97.10	Tonga	96.00	98.30
Sao Tome E Prin.	127.00	100.00	Trinidad & Tob.	1296.00	99.60
Saudi Arabia	16467.50	95.00	Tunisia	8578.50	99.70
Senegal	7932.50	98.00	Turkey	59601.00	98.90
Serbia & Mont.	10549.77	87.00	Turkmenistan	3977.00	98.10
Seychelles	70.50	100.00	Turks & Caicos I	13.57	100.00
Sierra Leone	4508.00	91.30	Tuvalu	11.05	99.20
Singapore	2863.00	97.70	Uganda	19261.50	79.80
Slovakia	5327.00	99.90	Ukraine	52104.50	98.70
Slovenia	1960.00	96.20	United Arab Emi.	1823.50	99.40
Solomon Islands	333.00	99.30	United Kingdom	57828.00	100.00
Somalia	9522.50	99.90	United States	257856.50	97.40
South Africa	39574.50	100.00	Uruguay	3133.50	97.40
South Korea	44521.50	100.00	Uzbekistan	21679.00	95.10
Spain	39157.00	99.60	Vanuatu	164.00	100.00
Sri Lanka	17910.50	99.30	Vatican City	0.90	100.00
St. Helena	7.36	100.00	Venezuela	20625.50	100.00
St. Kitts & Nevis	42.50	98.30	Vietnam	70071.00	96.10
St. Lucia	147.00	99.40	Virgin Island US	103.06	94.00
St. Pierre & Miqu	6.33	100.00	Wallis and Futuna	14.09	98.40
St. Vincent & Gr	114.00	100.00	West Bank	1404.11	100.00
Sudan	27437.50	89.70	Western Samoa	220.50	100.00
Suriname	440.00	98.30	Western Sahara	206.63	99.00
Swaziland	818.00	98.50	Yemen	12965.00	99.50
Sweden	8666.00	93.40	Zaire	41188.00	84.40
Switzerland	6855.00	96.20	Zambia	8866.00	95.40
Syrian Arab Rep.	13781.00	95.10	Zimbabwe	10907.50	99.60

Appendix C
References: Ethnic Groups of the World

The following references are provided as sources for more detailed or qualitative discussions of the ethnic groups covered in this book.

Asher, R.E. *The Encyclopædia of Language and Linguistics*. 1st ed. Oxford; New York, NY: Pergamon Press, 1994.

Barreau, Daniel, ed. *Inventaire des etudes linguistiques sur les pays d'Afrique noire d'expression francaise et sur Madagascar*. Paris: CILF, 1978.

Bentley, G. Carter. *Ethnicity and Nationality: a Bibliographic Guide*. Seattle, WA: University of Washington Press, 1981.

Comrie, Bernard. *The Languages of the Soviet Union*. Cambridge: Cambridge University Press, 1981.

Coulmas, Florian. *Language and Economy*. Oxford, UK: Blackwell Publishers, 1992.

Crystal, David. *An Encyclopedic Dictionary of Language and Languages*. Oxford, UK: Blackwell Publishers, 1992.

Culbert, S. *The Principal Languages of the World*. NI-25, University of Washington, Seattle, WA 98195.

Fasold, Ralph. *The Sociolinguistics of Language*. Oxford, UK: Basil Blackwell, 1990.

Foss, Donald J. and David T. Hakes. *Psycholinguistics: An Introduction to the Psychology of Language*. Englewood Cliffs, NJ: Prentice-Hall, 1978.

Friedman, Monroe. *A "Brand" New Language: Commercial Influences in Literature and Culture*. Westport, CT: Greenwood Press, 1991.

Giles, Howard and Bernard Saint-Jacques. *Language and Ethnic Relations*. Oxford; New York, NY: Pergamon Press, 1979.

Gonen, Amiram. *The Encyclopedia of the Peoples of the World*. 1st American ed., New York: H. Holt, 1993.

Grimes, Barbara F., ed. *Ethnologue: Languages of the World*. 11th ed., Dallas, TX: Summer Institute of Linguistics, 1988.

Hirschberg, Stuart. *One World, Many Cultures*. 2nd ed., Old Tappan, NJ: Macmillan Publishing Company.

Katzner, Kenneth. *The Languages of the World*. London, UK: Routledge & Kegan Paul, 1986.

Kipfer, Barbara A. *Encyclopedia of World Language*. New York, NY: Henry Holt & Company Incorporated.

Mann, Michael and David Dalby. *A Thesaurus of African Languages*. München: K.G. Saur Verlag, 1987.

Moss, Joyce. *Peoples of the World. The Middle East and North Africa: The Culture, Geographical Setting, and Historical Background of 30 Peoples of the Middle East and North Africa*. 1st ed., Detroit, MI: Gale Research, 1992.

---. *Peoples of the World. Eastern Europe and the post-Soviet Republics: The Culture, Geographical Setting, and Historical Background of 34 Eastern European Peoples*. 1st ed., Detroit, MI: Gale Research, 1993.

---. *Peoples of the World. Asians and Pacific Islanders: the Culture, Geographical Setting, and Historical Background of 41 Asian and Pacific Island Peoples*. 1st ed., Detroit, MI: Gale Research, 1993.

---. *Peoples of the World. Western Europeans: the Culture, Geographical Setting, and Historical Background of 38 Western European Peoples*. 1st ed., Detroit: Gale Research, 1993.

Price, David H. *Atlas of World Cultures: A Geographical Guide to Ethnographic Literature*. Newbury Park, CA: Sage Publications, 1989.

Ruhlen, Merrit. *A guide to the World's Languages*. Volume 1; Classification, Stanford: Stanford University Press, 1987.

Sowell, Thomas. *Race and Culture: A World View*. New York, NY: Basic Books, 1994.

Voegelin, C.F. and F.M. Voegelin. *"Languages of the World,"* Bloomington, IN: Anthropological Linguistics. Vol.6-8, 1964-66.

Appendix D
References: International Statistics

Many of the following references and sources were used in generating estimates in this book.

Society, General

Bureau of Consular Affairs. *Foreign Entry Requirements*. Washington: U.S. Department of State, 1991.

Central Intelligence Agency. *The World Factbook*. Washington: U.S. Government Printing Office, 1994.

Crystal, David, ed. *The Cambridge Factfinder*. Cambridge: Cambridge University Press, 1994.

Dorling Kindersdey. *World Reference Atlas*. London: Dorling Kindersley Limited, 1994.

Encyclopædia Britannica. *Encyclopædia Britannica World Data Annual*. Chicago; Encyclopædia Britannica, 1994.

Encyclopædia Britannica. *The New Encyclopædia Britannica*. Chicago: Encyclopædia Britannica, 1989.

Encyclopædia Universalis. *Payscope; Le nouveau paysage mondial*. Encyclopædia Universalis France S.A., 1994.

Europa Publications. *The Europa World Year Book*. London, UK: Europa Publications Limited, annual.

Frémy, Dominique, Michèle Frémy. *Quid*. Robert Laffont, S.A., et Sté des Encyclopédies Quid, annual.

International Directory of Non-Official Statistical Sources. London, UK: Euromonitor Plc., 1990.

NBC News. *World Atlas & Review*. 1993, Rand McNally,1993.

Paxton, John, ed. *The Statesman's Year-Book 1989-1990*. New York, NY: St. Martin's Press, 1990.

The World Almanac and Book of Facts. Funk & Wagnalls, 1994.

U.S. Department of Health and Human Services. *Health Information for International Travel 1991*. Washington: U.S. Government Printing Office, 1991.

U.S. Department of State, Bureau of Public Affairs. *Background Notes*. Washington: U.S. Government Printing Office, 1981-1991.

Geography and Climate

Financial Times International Yearbooks. *Mining 1992*. Chicago: St. James Press, 1991.

National Climatic Data Center, Asheville, North Carolina.

Rudolff, Willy. *World Climates; with tables of climatic data and practical suggestions.* Stuttgart: Weissenschaftliche, 1981.

Times Books. *The Times Books World Weather Guide.* New York; The New York Times Book Co., Inc. 1984.

U.S. Department of the Interior, Bureau of Mines. *Minerals Yearbook,* vol. III. Washington: U.S. Government Printing Office, annual.

World Meteorological Organization, Geneva, Switzerland.

Culture

Barreau, Daniel, ed. *Inventaire des etudes linguistiques sur les pays d'Afrique noire d'expression francaise et sur Madagascar.* Paris: CILF, 1978.

Comrie, Bernard. *The Languages of the Soviet Union.* Cambridge: Cambridge University Press, 1981.

Katzner, Kenneth. *The languages of the World.* London, UK: Routledge & Kegan Paul, 1986.

Mann, Michael and David Dalby. *A Thesaurus of African Languages.* München: K.G. Saur Verlag, 1987.

O'Brien, Joanne, Martin Palmer. *Atlas des religions dans le Monde.* Paris: Editions Autrement, 1994.

Ruhlen, Merrit. *A guide to the World's Languages.* Volume 1; Classification, Stanford, CA: Stanford University Press, 1987.

Economics

International Monetary Fund. *International Financial Statistics Yearbook.* Washington: International Monetary Fund, various issues.

The World Bank. *The World Bank Atlas 1990.* Washington: Oxford University Press.

The World Bank. *Stars.* version 2.0, World Bank Data on Diskettes, Washington: The International Bank for Reconstruction and Development/ The World Bank, annual, various years.

Business

Consumer International. London: Euromonitor Plc.,1994.

European Marketing Data and Statistics. London: Euromonitor Plc., 1994.

International Marketing Data and Statistics. London: Euromonitor Plc., 1994.

World Marketing Data and Statistics - on CD-ROM, London: Euromonitor Plc., 1994.

World Tourism Organization. *Yearbook of Tourism Statistics.* Madrid: World Tourism Organization, 1994.

2

COMPARING ETHNIC CULTURES

No person who examines and reflects, can avoid seeing that there is but one race of people on the earth, who differ from each other only according to the soil and the climate in which they live. **J. G. Stedman** (1744–1797)[1]

This book considers the use of ethno-linguistic-based social systems as a basis for cross-cultural comparisons (for the remainder of our discussion, we use the terms "ethnic" and "ethno-linguistic" interchangeably). As the reader will quickly surmise from the comparative statistics provided in this book, there are wide variances in estimated economic and social behaviors across the world's ethno-linguistic cultures (cultures aggregated by ethno-linguistic groups, as if they were countries); see Table on page 34 which characterizes a sample of groups along various dimensions: income, literacy, urbanization, population growth rates, and absolute latitude from the equator. For example, Somalis have, in general, lower standards of living than other ethnic groups (e.g. the Finnish). Are these observed differences the result of the cultural groups themselves (e.g. ethnicity drives divergence in behaviors), by economic policies, cultural institutions, other more fundamental mechanisms, or a combination of these? This chapter proposes a framework which can be used to answer this question irrespective of how *culture* is defined (e.g. based on linguistic, national, religious, or ethno-linguistic groups). The framework explicitly integrates both *economic* and *non-economic* dimensions into comparative studies and is an extension of earlier works which considered sources of cross-national or cross-cultural variances in economic and social behavior as originating, in part, from natural resources -- especially *soil* and *climate*. The statistical tables reported later are organized following the logic presented in the framework. Before elaborating on that logic, I will first briefly highlight a number of basic problems frequently observed in cross-cultural or cross-national studies in economics and the social sciences in general. These problems will likely arise in the study of cultures when these are defined as ethnic groups. After that discussion, the *physioeconomic* framework is presented which can overcome many of the problems highlighted.

---

[1] *Narrative of a Five Years' Expedition Against the Revolted Negroes of Surinam*, ch. 15 (1796; repr. 1971).

PROBLEMS WITH CROSS-CULTURAL STUDIES

Several problems arise in cross-cultural or cross-national studies: (1) insufficient variances in either dependent or independent variables, or both, (2) a failure to control for sample heterogeneity, (3) unidentified simultaneity, (4) positive spatial autocorrelation, and (5) measurement problems. Combined, these problems result in biased explanations of cross-cultural differences and/or wholly misleading statements of cause, effects, and magnitudes. We will first review each of these before discussing possible remedies. For the sake of illustration, we will mostly use the case of understanding variances in "economic performance," in the form of production, consumption, or income differences across cultures defined using religious, linguistic, ethno-linguistic or national groupings.

Ethno-linguistic cultures: Some comparative data

Ethnic Group	GNP/ Capita ($ 1994)	Adult Literacy	Urban- ization Percent	Population Growth Rate	Absolute Latitude
Tigrinya	127	57	14	2.70	13
Amhara	130	71	12	2.70	12
Somali	175	28	33	2.88	6
Abadkis	179	26	8	2.40	27
Bihari	188	29	11	2.46	26
Assamese	200	38	10	1.60	27
Danish	24454	100	86	0.50	56
Swedish	25155	99	83	0.49	60
Finnish	25884	100	62	0.32	62
Japanese	26649	100	77	1.21	37
Luxemburger	28730	100	81	0.50	49
Liechtensteiner	31000	100	65	0.60	47
Swiss	31000	100	65	0.60	47
Romansch	33221	99	60	0.50	47
Norwegian	43998	99	74	0.60	64

Insufficient Variance

The Problem. The most common type of cross-cultural study consists in comparing two groups (e.g. using Japanese and French samples) and drawing certain inferences. Beyond providing simple descriptions, *comparative studies* fundamentally lack sufficient variances in or observations of behavior to draw explanatory inferences: the Japanese are different from the French because the Japanese are Japanese and the French are French. The explanation of observed differences in behaviors across cultures is often speculative and tailored to a theory of local interest. The fallacy of *comparative studies* is the lack of degrees of freedom to rigorously test alternative explanations of observed variances; with only two observations all hypotheses are rejected, while many are suggested (e.g. the Japanese are successful due to a homogenous culture; Americans are successful due to a Protestant work ethic, etc.).

The Solution. A solution to this problem is to increase statistical power by collecting information across a large number of cultural groups and to measure explanatory covariates across these groups (e.g. degree of cultural homogeneity, percent of Protestants per country, etc.). If we treat the world as a natural experiment, we can learn from the wide differences in behaviors and factors affecting these behaviors only if a sufficiently large number of cultures/countries are included in the study. The increased variance in both dependent and explanatory variables can, however, lead to additional problems.

Sample Heterogeneity, Omitted Variables and Specification Errors

The Problem. As the number of observations (cultures) increases within a cross-cultural study, we can begin to statistically test theories as to why certain behaviors systematically vary from one to another. This is true so long as we are able to control for factors not related to the theory which independently and exogenously affect the behavior of interest. In essence, we hope that the sample studied is homogenous in all respects, with the exception of the covariate of interest. When dealing with cultures residing in very different parts of the globe, sample heterogeneity cannot be ignored. Consider, for example, development economists or planners who are critically interested in understanding the incremental effects of economic and social policies on various aspects of economic development. Cross-country studies which attempt to measure the incremental effects of differing policies must assume that systematic or exogenous variations which might be confounded with economic performance or behavior are controlled for. If the output of industrial minerals were used as a measure of economic performance across countries, the appropriate measure would control for the differing levels of exogenous natural reserves found in each country. Countries having no natural mineral reserves should not be considered to have ineffective economic policies due to low outputs. Likewise, policies in a country rich in reserves with positive outputs can be found less performing than alternative policies which have engendered relatively higher output levels, given a lower natural resource base.

The Solution. In order to avoid this problem, one can limit the analysis to similar cultures using some matching criteria along the confounding exogenous dimension. Consider, for example, the historical study of communism and its effect on income per capita across countries (or cultures). Without controlling for natural endowments, for example, the average income per capita of existing or former communist countries is compared against those of non-communist countries. Clearly, one should give more weight to comparisons such as North Korea to South Korea, North Vietnam to South Vietnam, Yugoslavia to Italy, East Germany to West Germany, Eastern Europe to Western Europe, Benin to Togo, Cuba to Jamaica, Nicaragua to Honduras, or the Soviet Union to the United States. Across these pairs we matched the samples based on various exogenous natural endowments: locality-driven climatic conditions, physical size of country, mineral and marine resources. Proximity in location is not as critical as proximity in environmental "starting position" (e.g. we can reasonably compare the USA to the former Soviet Union which are centered on opposite sides of the northern hemisphere). Using a sample drawn from United Nations members, traditional comparisons indicate that communism had no effect on income per capita, whereas matched measures of income which control for relative starting positions in natural endowments indicate that, on average, countries governed by communist regimes suffered a average reduction in income per capita by over $3600 per year (1985 dollars). Failing to control for such exogenous factors can lead, therefore, to biased explanations of behavior.

An alternative to matching samples on exogenous dimensions is to control for these dimensions within a multivariate analysis. Only when studies include a large number of dissimilar countries or cultures can this approach be considered. In essence, it would be useful to cross-sectionally filter exogenous factors in a similar fashion to economic models which *deseasonalize* time series data (seasonality often being exogenous and independent of theories being tested). Such a filtering is especially critical to social planners interested in measuring the incremental effect of a specific policy on economic development or progress. By proceeding with a filtering procedure, we can compare the effects of economic policies on countries like Chad, which have no mineral resources, no coastlines, no-inland waterways, desert soils, and long periods of drought, versus countries rich in marine and mineral resources with more generous climates, like the United States. In doing so, we can ascertain the extent to which countries like Chad are "poor" due to their exogenous endowment versus their economic policies. Equivalently, we can determine if Chad has higher "real" economic performance, given its endowment, than endowment rich countries having alternative policies. The examination of the filtered data can provide insights not otherwise evident or measurable from unfiltered data (e.g. measures of economic performance or social behavior relative to each country's exogenous endowment). This option, however, generates additional modeling challenges as there can be a multitude of potential exogenous differences in the world's cultures that might affect any given economic or social behavior.

Summarizing, cross-cultural studies which have large samples assume that observations are independent panel members who's behaviors do not systematically vary via omitted exogenous factors (e.g. countries are assumed to have similar climatic, cultural, or other environmental resources). Controlling for sample heterogeneity presents the challenge of identifying factors which are (1) exogenous to the dependent variable, yet (2) independent to the theory under study. Specification errors in the form of omitted factors can lead to biases in explanation when the exogenous factor is somehow related to both the dependent and explanatory variables of interest.[1]

Simultaneity

The Problem. A problem in designing filters is that it may not be clear which variables are exogenous to the behavior in question. Consider, for example, the study of income per capita or economic wealth across countries or cultures. We might model that changes in wealth depend on and are related to population growth rates. Plausible arguments can be made, however, that population growth rates are driven by changes in wealth. This is a rather general problem within the social sciences with each discipline often treating the others' variables as exogenous to their dependent variables. In the limit, various theories from alternative schools of thought (e.g. sociological versus economic), if added together, may explain more than 100 percent of the variance of certain behaviors. In such cases, both economic and demographic forces are likely to be

---

[1] Of course, including too many exogenous factors simultaneously may lead to multicollinearity and complications in understanding relationships.

simultaneously driven by unidentified exogenous dimensions which have been omitted; as mentioned above this leads to biases in each school's explanation of behavior.

Consider the case of economic growth models which traditionally assume that variables such as land, labor, and capital are exogenous to economic production yet independent from one another. There have been recent calls in the economics literature that research "be directed at explaining why the variables taken to be exogenous in [economic growth] models vary so much from country to country."[1] Should the factors explaining variables held to be exogenous in the economics literature be endogenous to variables which themselves contribute to economic growth and production, then the specification errors and resulting biases may be substantial. Of particular concern is the possibility that the omitted variables may be *non-economic* in nature. In his 250-year review of the literature on economic growth models, Rostow notes[2]:

> The greatest of the unsolved problems in the analysis of economic growth is how to bring to bear in a systematic way the inescapable *non-economic* dimensions of the problem.

Rostow lists a number of non-economic dimensions as including urbanization rates, political systems, literacy rates, crude fertility rates, political strength of the military, and the predominant type of religion.[3] Including these dimensions within a general model becomes problematic in that many of these may be driven by economic processes or be drivers of variables now held to be exogenous within economic models (labor, human capital, investments, etc.). If these non-economic dimensions are included in the model, we are still left with trying to explain the origins of these dimensions. If these origins are themselves retained, then the variables traditionally held as being critical in cross-country economic models (e.g. capital and labor) may therefore have little or no incremental (independent) influence on behaviors studied (e.g. economic wealth or growth).

The Solution. Without a formal statement of "levels of exogeneity" across a given set of variables, debates over cause, effect and explanation are endless. To avoid debates, controlling variables should be broadly seen as exogenous to both dependent and independent variables of interest (e.g. seasonality, generated by the earth's tilt and position to the sun is always seen as exogenous, say, to interest rate fluctuations and can therefore be used as a filter without much controversy). If independent variables are themselves driven by non-economic factors, these too should be filtered or eliminated from the analysis. If multiple filters are used, these should have a strict ordering of exogeneity.

---

[1] Mankiw, Romer and Weil 1992, *Quarterly Journal of Economics*, p.433.
[2] W.W. Rostow, *Theorists of Economic Growth from David Hume to the Present: with a Perspective on the next Century.* Oxford: Oxford University Press, 1990, p. 480.
[3] Rostow, p. 368.

Positive Spatial Autocorrelation

The Problem.   The first problem mentioned above, insufficient variance, might be overcome by collecting data over a large number of countries or cultural groups. While this will   allow researchers to observe variances and increase statistical degrees of freedom, using data collected from a large number of separate geographic locations creates an undesirable side effect not unrelated to sample heterogeneity and specification errors: spatial autocorrelation.   Most comparative studies assume that each country provides as informative and independent an observation as any other. *Statistical degrees of freedom* are assumed to equal *theoretical degrees of freedom.* Yet it is difficult to believe that Belgian and Dutch economic growth would ever significantly diverge, or that substantial productivity gaps would appear within the Benelux or the countries of Central America. Observations from these countries are not independent. Nor would observations be independent from cultural groups having close proximity to each other; see Figure 1 for a graphical representation of spatial correlation. Consider, for example, a study of income per capita across 184 countries (e.g. United Nations members). If France's Departments (states) were to each declare independence and be recognized by the United Nations, we would certainly obtain some 90 new statistical observations, though the theoretical degrees of freedom are far less. In addition to proximity, shared cultural and social values (which can be proximity dependent) would reduce theoretical degrees of freedom. How many of the world's observations are actually independent panel members is difficult to say with precision. Studies which fail to recognize the low levels of theoretical degrees of freedom tend to overstate statistical relationships (i.e. fit statistics of cross-country   or cross-cultural models may be exaggerated as the "theoretical" degrees of freedom in unfiltered data are far less than the number of statistical observations -- countries/cultures -- used in the study).

The lack of independence among spatial observations (leading to spatial autocorrelation) explains, in part, why traditional empirical models of economic growth, for example, often fit well for selected sub-sets of cross-national data (e.g. the OECD countries), yet generally fail to explain under-performance in other groups.   In referring to a cross-national model incorporating initial human capital, Barro finds, for example, that "the results leave unexplained a good deal of the relatively weak performances of countries in sub-Saharan Africa and Latin America. That is, the analysis does not fully capture the characteristics of the typical country on these continents that lead to below average economic growth."[1]

The Solution. Biases resulting from geographic proximity and shared histories are, once again, the result of omitted variables. To eliminate spatial correlation problems, ideally one needs to understand why this correlation exists and quantify the forces behind proximity affecting observation interdependence. If we were able to filter the data of interest for the drivers behind proximity effects, we retain statistical degrees of freedom, but more importantly, we also increase the number of theoretical degrees of freedom and simultaneously eliminate positive spatial autocorrelation. Beyond purely statistical approaches, we need to improve the specification of the model to account for proximity.

---

[1] Barro 1991, *Quarterly Journal of Economics*, p. 437.

Figure 1
Spatial Correlation

Negative

Positive

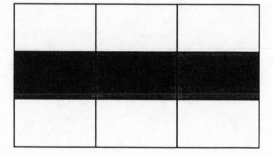

Positive

Measurement Biases

The Problem. Not all cultures perceive the value, or utility, associated with a given behavior equally, yet we often assume so in normative cross-cultural studies (e.g. the utility for films in Hindi varies from one culture to another). Consider cross-country economic studies which use various proxies of economic well-being (e.g. income per capita, caloric intake, ownership of consumer durables, etc.). These studies generally assume that individuals, on average, receive similar levels of utility having consumed similar levels of the proxy (e.g. calories, energy) . This assumption may be strongly violated if one considers a large number of dissimilar cultures or countries. Consider a study of food consumption (e.g. caloric intake) across all countries of the world. As caloric needs are largely dependent on human thermoregulatory needs, utilities derived from consumption will vary across populations having widely different climatic conditions. Equatorial populations obtain similar *basal utilities* to temperate populations while consuming less calories than the later. Measurement biases can exist in both dependent and independent variables, especially those linked to physical/physiological well being (e.g. food consumption, clothing, and housing -- in-door heating, air conditioning, insulation) and psychological well being (e.g. entertainment goods and services, discussed later). Furthermore, any composite index which reflects, even if only partially, differences in basal needs across countries or cultures will suffer from the same biases (e.g. income per capita which reflects consumption potential across goods having physiological and psychological benefits which may generate, at equal amounts, different utilities across cultures); this bias is analogous to composite time series which have one or more components which vary with the seasons. Cultures having lower levels of caloric consumption, housing expenditures, certain forms of entertainment consumption, or even income may therefore have equivalent or higher levels of absolute utility than those with higher levels of consumption. Likewise, the utilities or non-monetary income received from the environment directly (e.g. solar radiation/heat energy) might not be accounted for in economic measures of welfare.

The Solution. Controlling for measurement biases generated from differences in basal needs across countries is challenging. Short of changing proxies, only strong theoretical arguments can be used to give guidance on how to adjust or interpret variances in measured behaviors. For physiological behaviors, theories might come from physiology (e.g. studies of the effects of thermoregulation on the demand for food, clothing and housing).   For psychological and social behaviors, theories might be used from psychology and sociology, respectively.   In general, little work has been done to adjust cross-country estimates of economic performance or social behaviors for differences is basal needs.

PHYSIOECONOMICS

Introduction

The problems discussed above hold irrespective of how one defines a culture, including using ethnic groups as a basis of comparison. The remainder of this chapter proposes a *physioeconomic* framework which can be used to overcome many of these problems. The term *physioeconomics* reflects the wedding of physiological and physical sciences with economics. The key assumption behind this framework is that all humans act within exogenous constraints imposed by nature or environmental endowments. As described later, these constraints result in physical, physiological and psychological mechanisms which affect our utilities for various goods and services, our budget constraints (assets and wealth), as well as the relative prices of alternative choices we face, especially when these are considered on a global basis across national or cultural groups. I will later argue that both dependent and independent variables in many comparative economic and social science studies are endogenous to or are dependent on natural resource endowments (many resulting from soil and climatic conditions). The failure to account for these can lead to biased estimation of tested relationships (e.g. the effect of political economy on income per capita). From this perspective, various economic and social theories can be addressed, including those which would seek to explain variances in behaviors across ethnic groups which transcend national borders. In some cases, physioeconomic models can be used to "partial out" the incremental explained variances across competing schools of thought (e.g. debates concerning the sources of economic and social well being across social systems).

My preliminary use of the framework points to a few interesting conclusions with respect to certain behaviors (e.g. economic growth) across countries/cultures: (1) societies having *absolute* differences in exogenous endowments may have *divergent* long-run *absolute* equilibrium behaviors (i.e. aggregate measures of behavior across countries), (2) societies may be *converging* over time to similar levels of behavior *relative* to their environmental endowments, (3) as time progresses, natural endowments will explain cross-society variances in social and economic behavior to a greater extent (e.g. vis-à-vis public policy, culture, or other variables), and (4) cross-national or cross-cultural studies which fail to control for these physioeconomic constraints can be systematically flawed; this is especially true for studies examining a large number of countries, cultures or social systems.

Physioeconomics: Smith and Montesquieu

It is useful to think of the proposed framework as being consistent with thoughts originating from the 18th century Enlightenment, and, in particular, those of French *philosophes* (e.g. Montesquieu and other *Encyclopedists*)[1] and classical economic thinkers (e.g. David Hume and Adam Smith). Of the philosophes, Montesquieu, a correspondent of Hume, has recently been "...regarded as a precursor of many branches of modern social science"; in particular it was the publication of his *The Spirit of the Laws (De l'esprit des lois)*, which "pioneer[ed] sociology by showing the interrelation of economical, geographical, political, religious, and social forces in history."[2] The *physioeconomic* framework joins his thoughts with that of classical and neo-classical economic theories. The framework is fundamentally based on the assumption that humans are rational utility maximizers seeking individual betterment while simultaneously exploiting, or being constrained by, natural resources. Given this assumption and its importance later in this discussion, it is convenient to contrast the thoughts of Smith and Montesquieu as a point of departure. While both held common views in their criticisms of earlier philosophers' careless evaluation of evidence, the two

---

[1] The encyclopedists include, among others, Montesquieu, Voltaire, Jean Jacques Rousseau, Friedrich Melchior, and Baron von Grimm who participated in the writing of the 18th-century *Dictionnaire Raissoné des Sciences, des Arts et des Métiers*, edited by the French philosopher Denis Diderot.

[2] Citations from Encarata electronic encyclopedia, Microsoft, 1995. Montesquieu is most known, in Anglo-Saxon literature, for his advocacy and influence on American political thought concering the separation and balance of powers within government as the best means of guaranteeing individual freedoms.

generally had independent yet complementary discussions of national characteristics and sources of economic wealth and social behavior. Despite certain divergence, Smith and Montesquieu held a common belief that soil and climate represent powerful forces behind cross-country (in the case of Smith) or cross-cultural (in the case of Montesquieu) variances in both economic and social behavior. The remainder of this chapter will argue that large-scale cross-country/culture studies which systematically ignore these two forces (soil and climate) may be plagued with the problems discussed above.

Smith and Montesquieu on Soil and Climate

Montesquieu's *The Spirit of the Laws* was published in 1748, or 28 years prior to Smith's *An Inquiry into the Nature and Causes of the Wealth of Nations* in 1776. Montesquieu devotes substantial attention, in Books 14 to 19, to the influence of physical terrain (marine biology, mineral resources and topology) and climate on capital formation, labor, technology, and general national socioeconomic conditions. Montesquieu's basis of comparison extended to Africa, South America, Asia and the Pacific Rim. Based on several anecdotal and 18th-century scientific arguments, Montesquieu forecasted prior to the industrial revolution, among other things, that Northern Europe and Northern Asia would industrialize sooner and more so than Southern Europe and Southern Asia, respectively. Countries with similar natural endowments would develop in similar fashions, though quite differently than countries with different environmental endowments. Economic development occurs based on utility maximization constrained by the natural endowments one is forced to or chooses to live with. Montesquieu also conjectured that overall utility levels might be similar across countries or cultures, despite these having taken radically different development paths. Montesquieu suggested that Southern Europeans would have equal or greater overall utilities than Northern Europeans, even though the later would have greater material/industrial wealth. This conclusion is based on the explicit assumption that endowments not only affect one's income generating capacity, but also the utility of consumption itself and the underlying motivation to generate income. Other behaviors and national characteristics attributed to variations in climate and terrain by Montesquieu include culture, work ethic, suicide, alcoholism, aggressivity, religious beliefs (superstition), mortality, fertility, stature, obesity, sexism, combativeness, and industrial development (agriculture, trade, and commerce).

Montesquieu was not unfamiliar to Smith, both having a common correspondent in David Hume. Smith rejoins Montesquieu on the first page of the *Wealth of Nations* when discusses the limit to a social system's wealth as being bounded by its "... soil, climate, or extent of territory..." In passages directly referring to Montesquieu, Smith repeatedly re-emphasizes that a country is affected by "the nature of its soil and climate, and its situation with respect to other countries" and "the nature of its soil, climate, and situation."[1]   While Smith frequently treats social systems in a ceterus paribus setting, holding soil and climate constant, Montesquieu makes these resources his central theme in order to compare behaviors and social institutions across broader cultural dimensions. Beyond this difference in perspective, we will now consider the logic behind their emphasis of soil and climate. These discussions provide avenues to overcome measurement biases, spatial autocorrelation and other problems frequently observed in cross-cultural studies.

---

[1] Smith (pp. 73-74).

Soil: Economics and Sociology

Smith argues that income is generated (caused by) the need to consume, and that, in particular, "After food, clothing and lodging are the two great wants of mankind."[1] Smith's argument that land is an important input into economic models is based on the *physiological* premise that all humans must eat to survive.   Since food demand is inherent, it provides a motivation to generate income and food production becomes the basic source of wealth. Food production inherently depends on the availability of *land*, labor and technology/capital.   Land, therefore, becomes a necessary condition for wealth.   From food demand and its subsequent supply derives profit and the satisfying of demand for other goods and services:

> Human food seems to be the only produce of *land* which always and necessarily affords some rent [profit] to the landlord. Other sorts of produce sometimes may, and sometimes may not, according to circumstances.[2]

> Food is, in this manner, not only the original source of rent [profit], but every other part of the produce of *land* which afterwards affords rent, derives that part of its value from the improvement of the powers of labor in producing food by means of the improvement and the cultivation of the land.[3]

Smith continues,

> The increasing abundance of food, in consequence of increasing improvement and cultivation, must necessarily increase the demand for every part of the produce of *land* which is not food and which can be applied either to use or to ornament[4]

The demand for "ornamental" goods or luxuries, therefore, also becomes dependent on the produce of land:

> Whatever increases the fertility of *land* in producing food, increases not only the value of the lands upon which the improvement is bestowed, but contributes likewise to increase that of many other lands, by creating a demand for their produce. The abundance of food, of which, in consequence of the improvement of land, many people have the disposal beyond what they themselves can consume, is the great cause of the demand both for the precious metals and the precious stones, as well as for every other conveniency and ornament of dress, lodging, household furniture and equipage.[5]

Smith also argues that land becomes a source of population, labor and wages (emphasis added):

---

[1] Smith (p. 128), emphasis added.
[2] Smith (p. 128), emphasis added.
[3] Smith (p. 131), emphasis added.
[4] Smith (p. 140), emphasis added.
[5] Smith (p. 139), emphasis added.

Countries are populous, not in proportion to the number of people whom their produce can clothe and lodge, but in proportion to that of those whom it can *feed*. When food is provided, it is easy to find the necessary clothing and lodging.[1]

The number of workmen increases with the increasing quantity of food, or with the growing improvement and cultivation of *land*.[2]

The high wages of labor encourages population. The cheapness and plenty of *good land* encourage improvement, and enable the proprietor to pay those high wages. In those wages consists almost the whole price of land; and though they are high, considered as the wages of labor, they are low, considered as the price of what is so very valuable. What encourages the progress of population and improvement encourages that of real wealth and greatness.[3]

Smith further emphasizes, for example, the importance of land in characterizing the success of British colonies:

In the plenty of *good land*, the European colonies established in America and the West Indies resemble, and even greatly surpass, those of ancient Greece. ... The progress of all the European colonies in wealth, population, and improvement has accordingly been very great.[4]

Not all countries, however, has equally good land endowments. For example, Smith makes a case that countries having the ability to produce potatoes have the ability to produce a wide variety of produce (emphasis added):

The *land* which is fit for potatoes, is fit for almost every other useful vegetable.[5]

Beyond land as a source of food and the subsequent demand for other goods and services, Smith notes that a country's wealth might also depend on land's ability to produce minerals. The profit and output prices from land, he argues, depend on a mine's fertility:

Whether a coal mine, for example, can afford any rent, depends partly upon its fertility, and partly upon its situation. A mine of any kind may be said to be either fertile or barren, according as the quantity of mineral which can be brought from it by a certain quantity of labor, is greater or less than what can be brought by an equal quantity from the greater part of other mines of the same kind. Some coal-mines advantageously situated, cannot be wrought on account of their barrenness. The produce does not pay the expense. They can afford neither profit, nor rent.

Other coal mines in the same country sufficiently fertile, cannot be wrought on account of their situation. A quantity of mineral sufficient to defray the expense of working, could be brought from the mine by the ordinary, or even less than ordinary, quantity of

---

[1] Smith (p. 130), emphasis added.
[2] Smith (p. 131), emphasis added.
[3] Smith (p. 437), emphasis added.
[4] Smith (p. 438), emphasis added
[5] Smith (p. 128), emphasis added.

labor; but in an inland country, thinly inhabited, and without either good roads or *water-carriage*, this quantity could not be sold.[1]

Smith finds that raw material prices can be affected by a country being endowed with natural reserves: "Coals, in the coal countries, are everywhere much below this highest price."[2] Smith also finds that a country's mineral wealth can affect its economic stature. Countries lacking minerals are not destined to be without minerals, however, so long as they have other land resources which can produce tradable commodities:

> The quantity of the precious metals which is to be found in any country is not limited by anything in its local situation, such as the fertility or barrenness of its own mines. Those metals frequently abound in countries which possess no mines, Their quantity in every particular country seems to depend upon two different circumstances; first, upon its power of purchasing, upon the state of its industry, upon the annual produce of its *land* and labor, in consequence of which it can afford to employ a greater or a smaller quantity of labor and subsistence in bringing or purchasing such superfluities as gold and silver; and, secondly, upon the fertility or barrenness of the mines which may happen at any particular time to supply the commercial world with those metals.[3]

> It was of importance to Columbus that the countries which he had discovered, whatever they were, should be represented to the court of Spain as of very great consequence; and, in what constitutes the real riches of every country, the animal and vegetable productions of the *soil*, there was at that time nothing which could well justify such a representation of them. ... Finding nothing in the animals or vegetables of the newly discovered countries which could justify a very advantageous representation of them, Columbus turned his view towards their minerals; and in the richness of the productions of this third kingdom, he flattered himself, he had found a full compensation for the insignificance of those of the other two.[4]

Montesquieu, in contrast to Smith, considers land as arable and holding mineral reserves, but also more broadly as "terrain." Montesquieu does not treat land as an abstract homogenous unit, but distinguishes between mountainous regions, maritime regions, plains, forests, and deserts (interactions of topology and climate). He holds that terrain has numerous affects on social and cultural structures: forms of government, natural defenses, work ethics, migration and industriousness. The following passages illustrate his general philosophies:

> Wealth consists in land or in movable effects; the land of each country is usually possessed by its inhabitants. Most states have laws that discourage foreigners from acquiring their lands; only the presence of the master can increase their value; therefore, this kind of wealth belongs to each state particularly. But movable effects, such as silver, notes, letters of exchange, shares in companies, ships, and all commodities, belong to the whole world, which, in this regard comprises but a single

---

[1] Smith (pp. 131-132), emphasis added.   Here Smith notes the importance of rivers as a natural endowment.

[2] Smith (p. 133).

[3] Smith (p. 190), emphasis added.

[4] Smith (pp. 432-433), emphasis added.

state of which all the societies are members; the people that possess the most of such movable effects in the universe are the richest.[1]

The goodness of a country's lands establishes dependence there naturally. The people in the countryside, who are the great part of the people, are not very careful of their liberty; they are too busy and too full of their individual matters of business. A countryside bursting with goods fears pillage, it fears an army.[2]

... government by one alone appears more frequently in fertile countries and government by many in the countries that are not, which is sometimes a compensation for them. The barrenness of the Attic terrain establishes popular government there, and the fertility of the Lacedaemonian terrain, aristocratic government.[3]

The fertile countries have plains where one can dispute nothing with the stronger man: therefore, one submits to him. ... But in mountainous countries, one can preserve what one has, and one has little to preserve. Therefore, it reigns more frequently in mountainous and difficult countries than in those which nature seems to have favored more.[4]

The mountain people preserve a more moderate government because they are not as greatly exposed to conquest. They defend themselves easily, they are attacked with difficulty; ammunition and provisions are brought together and transported against them at great expense, as the country provides neither. Therefore, it is more difficult to wage war against them, more dangerous to undertake it, and there is less occasion for all the law one makes for the people's security.[5]

It is natural for a people to leave a bad country in search of a better and not for them to leave a good country in search of a worse. Therefore, most invasions occur in countries nature had made to be happy, and as nothing is nearer to devastation than invasion, the best countries most often lose their population, whereas the wretched countries of the north continue to be inhabited because they are almost uninhabitable.[6]

The bareness of the land makes men industrious, sober, inured to work, courageous, and fit for war; they must procure for themselves what the terrain refuses them. The fertility of a country gives, along with ease, softness and a certain love for the preservation of life.[7]

Island peoples are more inclined to liberty than continental peoples. Islands are usually small; one part of the people cannot as easily be employed to oppress the other; the sea separates them from great empires, and tyranny cannot reach them;

---

[1] Montesquieu (p. 352).
[2] Montesquieu (p. 285).
[3] Montesquieu (p. 285).
[4] Montesquieu (p. 286).
[5] Montesquieu (p. 286).
[6] Montesquieu (p. 287).
[7] Montesquieu (p. 287).

conquerors are checked by the sea; islanders are not overrun by conquest, and they preserve their laws more easily.[1]

The German and Hungarian mines make cultivating the land worthwhile, and working those of Mexico and Peru destroys that cultivation.[2]

There are so many savage nations in America because the land by itself produces much fruit with which to nourish them. If the women cultivate a bit of earth around their huts, corn grows immediately. Hunting and fishing complete their abundance. Moreover, grazing, like cattle, buffalo, etc., succeed better there than carnivorous beasts. The latter have had dominion in Africa from time immemorial. I believe one would not have all these advantages in Europe if the earth were left uncultivated; there would be scarcely anything but forest oak and of other unproductive trees.[3]

While both Montesquieu and Smith find land and terrain to provide sources of wealth and forms of culture, they also share in their appreciation of climate as playing a critical role.

Climate: Economics and Sociology

The fertility of land affects its economic value (e.g. contrasting barren deserts to fertile plains rich in minerals). Smith argues that "whatever increases the fertility of land in producing food increases not only the value of the land upon which the improvement is bestowed, but contributes likewise to increase that of many other lands, by creating a demand for their produce."[4] For both agriculture and basic living conditions, Smith and Montesquieu recognize climate as being critical inputs to fertility and labor productivity. For example, Smith draws a contrast between climatic conditions required for rice farming, versus grain farming:

A field of rice produces a much greater quantity of food than the most fertile field of corn. ... In Carolina, where the planters, as in other British colonies, are generally both farmers and landlords, and where rent consequently is confounded with profit, the cultivation of rice is found to be more profitable than that of corn, though their fields produce only one crop in the year, and though, from the prevalence of the customs of Europe, rice is not there the common and favorite vegetable food of the people. A good rice field is a bog as all seasons, and at one season a bog covered with water. It is unfit for either corn, or pasture, or vineyard, or, indeed, for any other vegetable produce that is very useful to men; and the lands which are fit for those purposes are not fit for rice.[5]

In addition to noting that climate affects the fertility of land, Montesquieu's philosophy also finds that basic needs (basal utilities) vary across climatic regions of the world and that these needs may require different social institutions to insure high welfare:

---

[1] Montesquieu (p. 288).
[2] Montesquieu (p. 396).
[3] Montesquieu (p. 290).
[4] Smith (p. 139).
[5] Smith (p. 127).

If it is true that the character of the spirit and the passions of the heart are extremely different in the various climates, laws should be relative to the differences in these passions and the differences in these characters.[1]

The differing needs of differing climates have formed differing ways of living, and these differing ways have found the various sorts of laws.[2]

In addition to this general view, Montesquieu, as illustrated in the following passages, relates various human endeavors, inventions, passions, and past-times to climatic variations:

Storms and fire led us to discover that the earth contained metals. When they were once separated from the earth, it was easy to use them.[3]

The more communicative peoples are, the more easily they change their manners, because each man is more a spectacle for another; one sees the singularities of individuals better. The climate that makes a nation like to communicate also makes it like to change, and what makes a nation like to change also makes its taste take form.[4]

What has naturalized servitude among the southern peoples [of Europe] is that, as they can easily do without wealth, they can do even better without liberty. But the northern peoples need liberty, which procures for them more of the means of satisfying all the needs nature has given them. The northern peoples are, therefore, in a forced state unless they are either free or barbarians; almost all of the southern people are, in some fashion, in a violent state unless they are slaves.[5]

In northern climates, the physical aspect of love has scarcely enough strength to make itself felt; in temperate climates, love, accompanied by a thousand accessories, is made pleasant by things that at first seem to be love but are still not love; in hotter climates, one makes love for itself; it is the sole cause of happiness; it is life.[6]

In northern countries, a healthy and well-constituted but heavy machine finds its pleasures in all that can start the spirits in motion again: hunting, travels, war, and wine. You will find in the northern climates peoples who have few vices, enough virtues and much sincerity and frankness. As you move toward the countries of the south, you will believe you have moved away from morality itself: the liveliest passions will increase crime; each will seek to take from others all the advantages that can favor these same passions. In temperate countries, you will see peoples whose manners, and even their vices and virtues are inconstant; the climate is not sufficiently settled to fix them.[7]

---

[1] Montesquieu (p. 231).
[2] Montesquieu (pp. 239-240).
[3] Montesquieu (p. 292).
[4] Montesquieu (p.311).
[5] Montesquieu (p. 355).
[6] Montesquieu (p. 234).
[7] Montesquieu (p. 234).

In Asia the number of dervishes, or monks, seems to increase with the heat of the climate; the Indies, where it is extremely hot, are full of them; one finds the same differences in Europe.[1]

One of the consequences of what we have just said is that it is important to a great prince to choose well the seat of his empire. He who puts it in the south will run the risk of losing the north, and he who puts it in the north will easily preserve the south. I do not speak of particular cases: as mechanics has its friction which often change or check its theoretical effects, politics, too, has its friction.[2]

Montesquieu noted that climate may affect psychological mechanisms which would affect, for example, emotions, the utilities derived from entertainment, and one's propensity to commit suicide:

In cold countries, one will have little sensitivity to pleasures; one will have more of it in temperate climates; in hot countries, sensitivity will be extreme. As one distinguishes climates by degrees of latitude, one can also distinguish them by degrees of sensitivity, so to speak. I have seen operas in England and Italy; they are the same plays with the same actors: but the same music produces such different effects in the people of the two nations that it seems inconceivable, the one so calm and the other so transported.[3]

We see in the histories that the Romans did not inflict death on themselves without cause, but the English resolve to kill themselves when one can imagine no reason for their decisions; they kill themselves in the very midst of happiness. ... It is clear that the civil laws of some countries have had reasons to stigmatize the murder of oneself, but in England one can not more punish it than one can punish the effects of madness.[4]

Smith and Montesquieu have similar thoughts with respect to climate's effect on social behaviors surrounding alcohol demand, supply and consumption. Based on certain physiological arguments, Montesquieu concludes:

The law of Mohammed that prohibits the drinking of wine is, therefore, a law of the climate of Arabia; thus, before Mohammed, water was the ordinary drink of the Arabs. The law that prohibits the Carthaginians from drinking wine was also a law of the climate; in effect, the climate of these two countries is about the same. Such a law would not be good in cold climates, where the climate seems to force a certain drunkenness of the nation quite different from drunkenness of the person. Drunkenness is found established around the world in proportion to the cold and dampness of the climate. As you go from the equator to our pole, you will see drunkenness increase with the degree of latitude. As you go from the same equator to the opposite pole, you will find drunkenness to the south, as on our side to the north. ... A German drinks by custom, a Spaniard by choice.[5]

---

[1] Montesquieu (p. 237).
[2] Montesquieu (p. 284).
[3] Montesquieu (p. 233).
[4] Montesquieu (pp. 241-242).
[5] Montesquieu (p. 239).

Smith similarly notes a relationship between alcohol and climate:

> Though individuals, besides, may sometimes ruin their fortunes by an excessive
> consumption of fermented liquors, there seems to be no risk that a nation should do
> so. Though in every country there are many people who spend upon liquors more
> than they can afford, there are always many more who spend less. It deserves to be
> remarked, too, that, if we consult experience, the cheapness of wine seems to be a
> cause, not of drunkenness, but of sobriety. The inhabitants of the wine countries are in
> general the soberest people in Europe; witness the Spaniards, the Italians, and the
> inhabitants of the southern provinces of France. People are seldom guilty of excess in
> what is their daily fare. On the contrary, in the countries which, either from excessive
> heat or cold, produce no grapes, and where wine consequently is dear and a rarity,
> drunkenness is a common vice, as among the northern nations;[1]

> When a French regiment comes from some of the northern provinces of France, where
> wine is somewhat dear, to be quartered in the southern, where it is very cheap, the
> soldiers, I have frequently heard it observed, are at first debauched by the cheapness
> and novelty of the good wine; but after a few months' residence the greater part of
> them become as sober as the rest of the inhabitants.[2]

Smith's observation that individuals acclimate to local conditions is important in
understanding that effects may be more generated from climate, than individual
disposition, culture, race, or ethnic origin. Montesquieu makes a similar observation:

> Indians are by nature without courage; even the children of Europeans born in the
> Indies lose courage of the European climate. [3]

Of importance to economic models is the affect of climate on labor. Here, Montesquieu
holds that there are stronger disutilities to labor in hotter climates than in colder climates
where there may, in fact, be positive utilities to work:

> There is a kind of balance in Europe between the nations of the South and the North.
> The first have all sorts of the comforts of life and few needs; the second have many
> needs and few of the comforts of life. In the former, nature has given much and they
> ask but little of it; to the others nature gives little, and they ask much of it.
> Equilibrium is maintained by the laziness it has given to the southern nations and by
> the industry and activity it has given to those of the north. The latter are obliged to
> work much; if they did not, they would lack everything and become barbarians.[4]

> ...men are more vigorous in cold climates.[5]

> In the time of the Romans, the peoples of northern Europe lived without arts, without
> education, almost without laws, and still, with only the good sense connected with the

---

[1] Smith (p. 376).
[2] Smith (p. 376).
[3] Montesquieu (p. 235).
[4] Montesquieu (p. 355).
[5] Montesquieu (p. 231).

coarse fibers of these climates, they maintained themselves with remarkable wisdom against the Roman power until they came out of their forests to destroy it. [1]

The heat of the climate can be so excessive that the body there [India] will be absolutely without strength. So, prostration will pass even to the spirit; no curiosity, no noble enterprise, no generous sentiment; inclinations will be passive there; in laziness there will be happiness.[2]

In order to conquer the laziness that comes from the climate, the laws must seek to take away every means of living without labor, but in southern Europe they do the opposite: they give to those who want to be idle, places proper for the speculative life, and attach immense wealth to those places. These people who live in an abundance that is burdensome to them correctly give their excess to the common people: the common people have lost the ownership of goods; the people are repaid for it by the idleness they enjoy and they come to love their very poverty.[3]

With respect to food demand, Smith and Montesquieu differ somewhat on perspectives as Smith does not consider variances in climates across countries. To Smith, the demand for food is constant across individuals and "is limited in every man by the narrow capacity of the human stomach,"[4] and "The rich man consumes no more food that his poor neighbor. In quality it may be very different, and to select and prepare it may require more labor and art; but in quantity it is very nearly the same."[5] Montesquieu, on the other hand, notes an important climatic effect on food consumption (which, using Smith's argument, might engender a difference in the motivation to generate income). Montesquieu notes that the basic needs of populations may vary with climate, including the need for food or caloric intake:

In hot countries, relaxation of the fibers produces a great perspiration of liquids, but solids dissipate less. The fibers, which have only a very weak action and little spring, are scarcely used; little nutritious juice is needed to repair them; thus one eats little there.[6]

After Smith and Montesquieu

Smith and Montesquieu are not unique in understanding various effects of natural endowments on national or cross-cultural behavior. In the economics literature, for example, Ricardo and Maltus focus on the role of soil on production and demography. What of climatic effects? Despite a wealth of studies in agriculture, biology, physiology and psychology supporting many of Smith and Montesquieu's speculations, these effects have received far less emphasis in economics and social sciences in general. In his review of the literature on economic growth, for example, Rostow notes Smith's focus on "soil and climate," yet in the same passage, characterizes Smith's view as consisting of three basic elements: "labor, land and capital"; climate disappears.[7] This omission persists in later works including recent exogenous and endogenous models of

---

[1] Montesquieu (p. 235).
[2] Montesquieu (p. 234).
[3] Montesquieu (p. 237).
[4] Smith (p. 131).
[5] Smith (p. 131).
[6] Montesquieu (p. 239).
[7] Rostow (p. 35).

economic growth. Similar omissions exist in other social science disciplines.[1] Climatic effects, for whatever reason, have dropped out of 19th and 20th century analyses which basically assume that all countries or cultures have identical climates. Such reductionist approaches fly in the face of reason when one considers variances across countries with such diverse endowments in natural resources and climates as France and Chad or Mauritania. Figure 2 illustrates some of the more fundamental climatic effects on factor input prices and the utility for various goods and services as hypothesized by Smith, and, especially, Montesquieu. Failure to account for these can be a source for many of the problems mentioned earlier in this chapter.

Physioeconomics versus Environmental Determinism

Before elaborating on statistical methods to filter exogenous endowments, it is important to state that the basic philosophy of the physioeconomic approach is not deterministic. Philosophies of *determinism* hold that events, actions and decisions are deterministically the consequences of factors which are independent of human initiative or genius.[2] Determinism finds that for a given cause, events necessarily follow irrespective of chance or probability. *Environmental determinism*, in particular, holds that variances in exogenous environmental factors deterministically generate economic, social and psychological behaviors across individuals and/or societies.[3]   While biology has found that six basic factors generally determine whether life can exist within a given environment (temperature, pressure, salinity, acidity, water availability, and oxygen content), the philosophy of environmental determinism considers individuals and societies to be locked into a particular path of economic and social development, irrespective of policy or other human-generated initiatives or policies.   Policies and initiatives, themselves, are deterministically a function of a variety of environmental factors.

The lingering problem in most studies of natural endowments following similar arguments made by Montesquieu and Smith is attribution. During the early 20th century, certain geographers, among others, were labeled as holding a determinist view of, for example, climatic effects; climate not only correlates with cross-cultural differences in behavior, but also determined these. The lack of strong theoretical underpinnings and certain extremes in early writings, especially as directed toward individual behavior including generalizations concerning racial differences, lead to a general discredit of geography-based theories of behavior in geography, sociology and economics.   Though some authors have recently argued that these early criticisms were themselves suspect of certain   extremes   or   lacked   rigor,   the   most   important   problem   in

---

[1] For exceptions to this statement, please see the review in Parker (1995*), Climatic Effects on Individual, Social and Economic Behavior*, Westport, Connecticut; London: Greenwood Press.
[2] *Indeterminism*, in contrast, holds that human enterprise is free and not necessarily or at all predetermined by physiological and psychological laws. *Hereditarianism* sees heredity as the primary force in determining human behavior independent of environmental influences. *Naturalism*, especially in literature, finds that natural forces, especially *environmental*, are determining powers(see, for example, the works of Émile Zola and Guy de Maupassant in France, and Stephen Crane, Theodore Dreiser, and James T. Farrell in America).
[3] See, for examples, the work of E. Huntington (referenced in Chapter 2).

Figure 2
Certain Climatic Effects

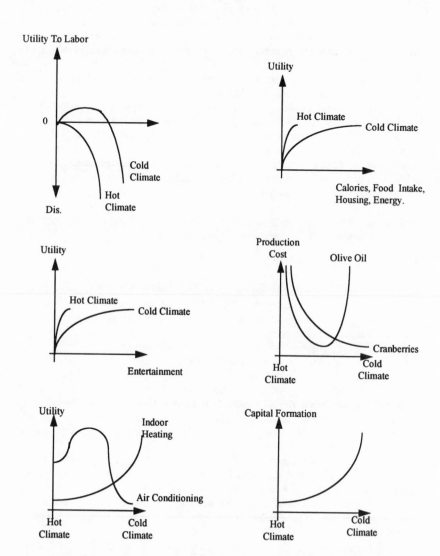

attribution is the identification of physiological and psychological mechanisms. Recent work in these fields, however, fills certain gaps in identifying mechanisms, independent from race, lacking in earlier debates. Together, these would tend to suggest that climate, and other natural resources should be considered as "contributing factors" affecting behavior (rather than factors with determining roles). While some debate has occurred as to whether these effects are direct, or are mediated by social factors, the preponderance of evidence would suggest that both temporal and cross-sectional (cross-cultural) studies of behavior ignoring environmental effects may suffer from substantial specification errors. The physioeconomic framework is presented as to overcome these problems.

In contrast to environmental determinism, the physioeconomic framework blends Smith and Montesquieu by emphasizing that human initiatives can dramatically affect social and economic development, though these cannot ignore local physical environments as constraints or catalysts.[1] Both Smith and Montesquieu stressed that there are no fundamental differences across the world's races: "the difference of natural talents in different men is, in reality, much less than we are aware of."[2] Rather, laws and institutions must maximize welfare in light of natural endowments generating different supply and demand functions across geographic locations. Smith, for example, stresses the importance of individual liberty:

Plenty of good land, and liberty to manage their own affairs their own way, seem to be the two great causes of the prosperity of all new colonies.[3]

Montesquieu has similar philosophies:

Countries are not cultivated in proportion to their fertility, but in proportion to their liberty, and if one divides the earth in thought, one will be astonished to see that most of the time the most fertile parts are deserted and that great peoples are in those where the terrain seems to refuse everything.[4]

Montesquieu sees climate not at a determining force, but one that must be combated against or exploited for the benefit of society: "Countries [Holland and Egypt] have been made inhabitable by the industry of men,"[5] and "Men, by their good nature and their good laws, have made the earth more fit to be their home. We see rivers flowing where there were lakes and marshes; it is a good that nature did not make, but which is maintained by nature." [6] Montesquieu frequently proposes public policies to combat certain climatic effects:

The cultivation of land is the greatest labor of men. The more their climate inclines them to flee this labor, the more their religion and laws should rouse them to it. Thus, the laws of the Indies, which give lands to the princes and take away from individuals the spirit of ownership, increase the bad effects of the climate, that is, natural laziness.[7]

---

[1] Beyond a simple measurement tool, the physioeconomic framework might be seen as blending *liberalism, naturalism* and *indeterminism*.
[2] Smith (p. 12).
[3] Smith (p. 442).
[4] Montesquieu (p. 286).
[5] Montesquieu (p. 288).
[6] Montesquieu (p. 289).
[7] Montesquieu (pp. 236-237).

To Smith and Montesquieu, individual and social responses vary across any two geographic areas having identical environments, even though human behavior in both are affected by physioeconomic constraints. Likewise, racial origins have no independent influences on behavior; these origins are mistakenly confounded with other mechanisms. Finally, environmental determinism would hold that the hula dance of Hawaiians was determined by the existence of ocean waves surrounding the islands; a physioeconomic approach would suggest that one's propensity to be influenced by marine resources is related to one's exposure to these resources and social institutions (culture, public policy, etc.). In all cases, individual differences and initiatives within a society allow for most behaviors to be observed in all locations of the globe. As shown in Figure 3, the frequency of behaviors can be affected by natural endowments across individuals within a population. Similarly, when one wishes to explain cross-country variances in mean behaviors using physioeconomic forces, a high explained variance does not support deterministic philosophies; see Figure 4 which relates solar climate (absolute latitude) to explain behavior and convergence.

A PHYSIOECONOMIC FRAMEWORK

Assumptions

The basic premise of this framework is the assumption that all human behaviors are inherently constrained to time-invariant laws of physiology, among other physical laws, which prevail irrespective of racial, religious, ethnic, cultural, sociological or economic origins and institutions. Two classes of effects encompass most physioeconomic factors: (1) soil (land, terrain, mineral resources), and (2) climate. Of the two, soil-related effects have received the most treatment in the literature. One of the more important distinctions of physioeconomic models compared to alternatives is the explicit measurement of climatic effects on behavior.

Defining Climate

Climate (e.g. tropical, polar, temperate, high-altitude, etc.) is typically defined as average meteorological conditions specific to a geographic region over a period of several years or decades (e.g. 30 years). *Weather* is typically defined as short term fluctuations in meteorology, including changes in temperature, humidity, cloudiness, rainfall, and barometric pressure. General weather patterns are associated with particular climatic conditions (e.g. strong seasonality is highly associated with temperate climates). Climatologists recognize a hierarchy of effects in climate formation. The earth's climates originate from solar radiation which varies in relation to one's absolute latitude from the equator (a power or nonlinear function of latitude provides an approximation of radiation received; the lower the latitude the more the radiation). If the earth had no land masses, the resulting climate would be identical at all points equally distant above and below the equator. Deviations from the solar climate are generated by land areas and topology (including elevation) which result in

Figure 3
Climate and Behavior: Indeterministic Effects

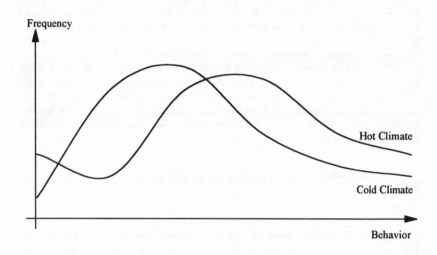

Figure 4
Explained Variance and Convergence

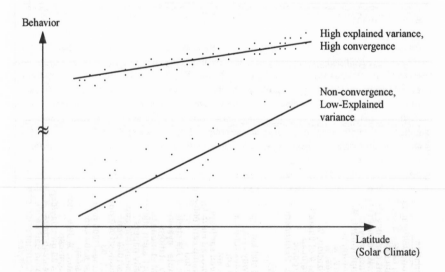

physical climates, ocean currents and wind currents. The interactions amongst these generate prevailing weather patterns and microclimates. No two countries have identical climates. A large portion of countries, however, have similar climates across broad classifications: e.g. mostly desert, or tropical. Many have never experienced a frost over the last 10,000 years; some have almost continual rainfall, while others have virtually no rainfall at all.

Climatic Effects

In addition to direct climatic effects (e.g. rain-based agriculture is less productive in deserts than temperate climates), three climate-induced physiological constraints on human behavior in particular are noteworthy. The first results from humans being homeothermal (or homothermal) mammals (homeotherms). Humans, being warm-blooded, must constantly maintain an internal core body temperature of 37 degrees Celsius, irrespective of where they live or the environments that they face (homoiothermy or homeostatic equilibrium). Heat-exchange behavior balances incoming and outgoing heat by means of physiological processes of thermoregulation in reaction to external factors of radiation, ambient temperature, moisture/humidity, and air movement. This heat transfer relationship can be expressed as:

$$0 = M +- CD +- CV +- R - E$$

where M is the heat generated from metabolism (food consumption, physical labors, exercise), CD is heat gained/lost by conduction, CV the heat gained/lost by convection, R the heat gained/lost by radiation, and E the heat loss due to evaporation.[1] Homeostatic equilibrium, which is controlled by the hypothalamus via nervous and hormonal mechanisms, requires that the human body balance energy absorption and production. In the short-run this process may result in shivering or sweating, or, the long run, adjustments to metabolic functions. In all cases, core or deep body temperature must remain constant irrespective of the environment encountered. Reflecting the need to produce energy via metabolism, physiologists note that some 80 percent of food consumption is required for thermoregulatory needs (the rest being attributed to variety seeking and other behaviors). Failure to maintain energy balance, especially in the extremes, results in various illnesses or death (hypothermia, and heat stroke in the extremes). Bioclimatology and biometeorology attributes a number of consumption behaviors to this constraint: the use of tile floors in hot climates, dressing behaviors, an inverse relationship between caloric intake or digestive energy and ambient temperature (the hotter the climate, the less one eats, especially of foods which require high energies to digest such as meat; the colder the climate, the greater the need to install artificial heating systems and/or wear heavy/layered clothing and the higher our preferences for alcoholic beverages).[2] This climatic effect has further been held to explain differences in physiological utility for physical work or exertion; an equivalent level physical work has greater physiological utility in temperate or polar regions than in equatorial or hot arid regions.

The second mechanism, related to the first, affects physical comfort which is dependent on changes in and long-run levels of ambient temperature and humidity. Acclimatization

---

[1] See Stanier, M.W. et al., *Energy Balance and Temperature Regulation*. Cambridge: Cambridge University Press, 1984.
[2] For a review of the literature, see Chapter 2 and Parker (1995).

(or acclimation) involves an internal physiological adjustment process, also controlled by the hypothalamus. This level is typically expressed as follows:

$$TH = f(Td,Tw,Z)$$

where TH is a temperature humidity index, Td is the dry-bulb temperature, and Tw is the simultaneous wet-bulb temperature; and Z is a vector of constants, which vary by climate. For each climate there exists a temperature-humidity threshold which, if passed, generates physical discomfort or illness for those acclimated to a particular climate; in hotter climates, human physiology acclimates to allow for higher TH levels before discomfort is generated. Persons acclimated to colder climates have lower TH levels (i.e. are able to feel comfortable at lower TH levels). Persons living in the tropics, for example, have less discomfort than tourists visiting the tropics (as Scandinavian's have less discomfort than tourists coming from the tropics to Scandinavia). Thresholds are generated by both mean climatic conditions and seasonal variations. Persons living in climates with marked seasons (very cold winters and very hot summers) have highest levels of discomfort all year round, and will have greatest physiological utility for simultaneously owning both indoor heating and summer air conditioning (non-climatic factors being held constant). Acclimation has also been used to explain variances in labor productivity for a variety of industries including mining where the underground mining environment differs substantially from the surface climate.

Based on these first two physiological mechanisms, certain climatologists and geographers argue that climate is the single most important factor generating variances in numerous human behaviors, including dietary patterns (caloric/protein intake), housing requirements (heating, insulation, architecture), and clothing requirements (light versus heavy). Since these climate-dependent activities alone represent from 30 to 50 percent of total household consumption in developed economies and up to 90 percent in lesser developed economies, climate cannot but have a substantial impact on aggregate measures of behavior which incorporate these items (e.g. cross-cultural measures of aggregate consumption or income per capita).

The third mechanism is the subject of recent studies in medicine and physiology which have demonstrated the role of climate in hormonal secretions, some of which result from thermoregulation, acclimatization and light absorption. Variances in hormone levels in individuals across climates are used to explain, for example, the existence of strong seasonal affective disorders in temperate or polar climates, yet weak affective disorders in equatorial climates; such disorders are commonly treated using light or phototherapy. Evidence of equatorial influences can also be seen in the seasonality of demand for mental health services. Similar tendencies have been observed for suicide and suicide ideation; persons residing closer to the poles are more likely to experience seasonal affective disorders, depression, and suicide ideation. Suicide and mood disorders rise in the winter months in temperate or polar climates and reach their peaks toward the end of winter/early spring when cumulative imbalances are greatest.

Care must be taken not to confuse these mechanisms with direct causes of specific behaviors at the individual level. In the case of suicide, for example, sociologists (including E. Durkheim in the late 19th century) discarded climate as a factor affecting cross-national suicide rates as climate is rarely, if ever, directly linked to a particular act of suicide. It goes without question that individual acts of suicide are frequently brought on by specific tragedy (as opposed to variations in the weather). This observance does not eliminate the possibility that climate affects one's propensity to commit suicide given a specific personal tragedy (i.e. several persons facing similar tragedies may have differing propensities to commit suicide given their respective prevailing climates -- polar versus equatorial). In some cases, climatic effects may be observed through non-meteorological factors (e.g. alcoholism) which themselves are affected by climate (polar countries generally having higher levels of alcoholism than equatorial climates). Likewise, as shown in Figure 3, a climatic effect does not prevent an individual, for example, from owning an air conditioner in a polar region (though on average, utilities are lower there than in temperate climates for this product).

Indirect Effects

To the mechanisms discussed above can be added a variety of physical constraints discussed at length by human and economic geographers. These reflect necessary physical conditions to various behaviors at the individual or societal level. Variances in these necessary conditions, it is argued, affect equilibrium behavior. Certain sports, for example, can only be practiced in geographic areas having appropriate topologies which may interact with climate (e.g. ice fishing, coral photography, alpine skiing). Certain diseases are limited in nature to areas which have not experienced frosts over the last 10,000 years (e.g. tropical diseases, including malaria). Virtually all animal and plant species are geographically bounded by prevailing climatic conditions (e.g. oak forests and their animal inhabitants), the proximity of which affects the economics of human consumption and transformation. Various human activities are also directly bounded by the severity of climate: e.g. the economics of mineral extraction varies by climatic conditions; elevation and/or solar radiation prevents the cultivation of certain crops and directly affects soil fertility. These constraints, including the availability of climate-dependent fresh water, are held to affect the supply and demand of various goods and services, certain cultural traits of populations, economic development patterns, and various vital statistics.

Figure 5 graphically summarizes the various effects discussed by identifying a simply hierarchy; Chapter 10 provides a select bibliography of works discussing various effects mentioned earlier.[1] Using this framework, one can better understand the incremental role of both exogenous climatic factors and endogenous factors which affect behavior. In this case, "exogenous" factors are meant to include all "inherited" or non-human natural resources. Endogenous factors include any of human origin, including population, culture, religion, language, economic policies, and social systems. Within exogenous and endogenous factors, various sub-hierarchies can be considered. Figure 5 notes the existence of human-generated climate (e.g. in-door air conditioning, heating, pollution and human-induced greenhouse effects) as endogenous to natural climates which are mostly time invariant over the last ten centuries (e.g. the absolute latitude of a region, the natural existence of mineral deposits, etc.).

---

1   See also Parker (1995), *Climatic Effects on Individual, Social, and Economic Behavior*. Westport, Connecticut; London: Greenwood Press, for a more detailed summary of climatic effects.

Figure 5
Physioeconomic Framework

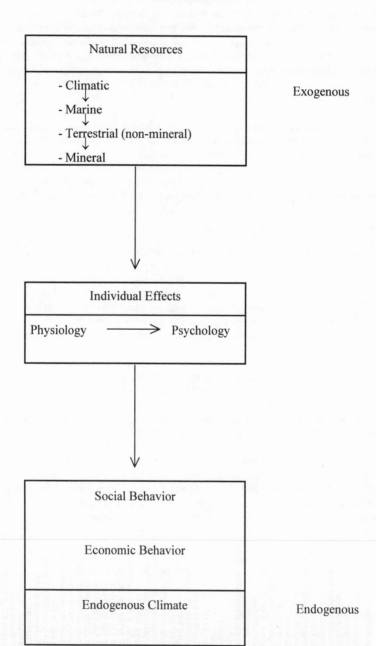

Estimating Physioeconomic Effects

Estimating physioeconomic effects may prove problematic given the complexity of factors affecting behavior. Climate affects water resources and temperature which affects natural vegetation, which in turn affects dietary preferences and consumption patterns. In the case of cross-national comparisons, for example, we might consider the interrelationships between income per capita, political systems, and various demographic variables (e.g. mortality levels). Each of these variables have been shown to be dependent on physioeconomic forces; many of these variables may be mediating factors to others. Short of applying numerous structural variable approaches (LISREL), one can filter each variable for physioeconomic effects in the same vein that we deseasonalize time series data (a form of multivariate "step down" analysis). In this case we are not interested in directly estimating all mediating effects (e.g. the effects of alcoholism, net of climate, on suicide), but rather the net effects of physioeconomic factors on each variable of interest (these in turn can be modeled in some dependence structure).

Figure 6 illustrates a filtering procedure based on the physioeconomic framework. Natural historians have recognized a hierarchy of exogeneity whereby certain natural phenomenon are necessary conditions (and simultaneously historical precedents) to others. Climate, for example, is a necessary condition for marine and animal/human life, which is in turn a necessary condition for culture or economic behavior. Within each level of the hierarchy are sub-hierarchies. The sun, or solar climate is the most exogenous of factors in natural history. Physical climate (continental formation) follows, resulting in land and ocean topology; again, without solar radiation, physical-induced climates would not exist. Following the hierarchy of natural history, climatic forces are generally held responsible for variances in the world's natural marine biology, vegetation and zoological resources. Again, each level in the hierarchy is a necessary condition for the next: terrestrial life depending on prior existence of marine life, which itself depends on climatic formation. Minerals are considered after these (though this might be debated) since many are formed based on the prior existence of topology (physical climate) and animal or plant life; their observance, measurement or extraction also necessarily follows, or is endogenous to, animal life.

Beyond these purely exogenous factors, difficulties arise in establishing hierarchies in human-generated factors. In contrast to the natural endowments, it may be difficult to accept that these factors are necessary conditions by order of exogeneity (e.g. religion may not be a necessary condition to language). For the sake of illustration, Figure 6 follows a hierarchy generally accepted by historians with respect to current social systems. Modern religions, for example, are generally more exogenous than modern languages which are in turn more exogenous than current economic policies, political systems or social institutions.

This framework can be operationalized for any given human behavior via sequential filtering. The dependent variable (e.g. caloric consumption) is first filtered for solar climate. The resulting residuals become the transformed dependent variable which is in turn filtered for physical climate, and so forth through the hierarchy. This process is analogous to that commonly used in time series studies which attempt to measure the short-run affects of policy on economic behavior which varies in a seasonal pattern. An alternative approach is to simultaneously filter the original dependent variable for all exogenous factors (which may have been previously factor analyzed). The primary

Figure 6
Filtering Sequence
(typical incremental explained variance in parentheses)

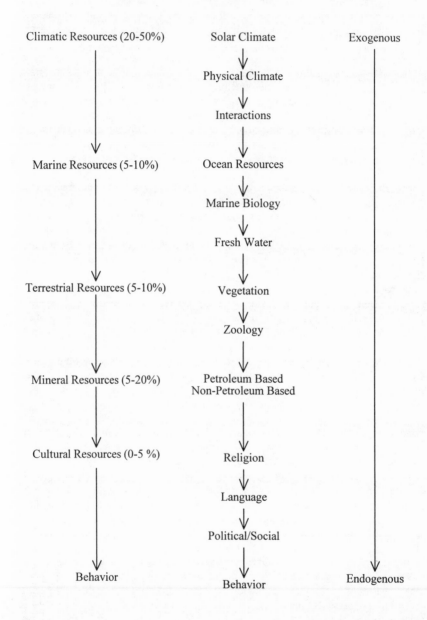

advantage of the sequential filtering process is the insights gained by having a direct measure of the incremental explanatory power of each element along the filtering hierarchy. For example, we can estimate the extent to which Protestantism (or a Protestant work ethic) explains labor productivity beyond variances explained by exogenous elements (i.e. "work ethic" may itself be explained by climate). Similarly, we can test whether religious affiliation (Catholic versus Protestant) affects suicide rates after we control for exogenous geographic effects (given that Catholic countries are more concentrated towards the equator, compared to Protestant countries concentrated towards the poles). Solar climate is measured as absolute latitude squared (to account for the earth's curvature). Measures of physical climate include elevation, and total land area which simultaneously captures other terrestrial resources. Interactions are measured using climatic classifications. Marine life is measured using coastline length. Similar measures are used for land, and mineral resources. Cultural measures include measures of the five largest world religions, numbers of ethnic groups present, and the use of major colonial languages. Political and economic measures include dummy variables for alternative regimes (e.g. communism, dictatorship, democracy). It should be noted that each filter has an equal number of statistical degrees of freedom, yet, as each filter is performed in sequence of exogeneity, theoretical degrees of freedom actual increase (as discussed earlier) despite the data being transformed (re-used) across filters.

For each level of the filtering hierarchy, Figure 6 indicates in parentheses the general range of incremental percent explained variation, adjusted for degrees of freedom, across some thirty cross-national measures frequently used in demography (e.g. mortality, fertility, population, population growth rates), sociology (e.g. crime, suicide) and economics (e.g. manufacturing, mineral extraction, durables consumption, caloric intake, aggregate output, savings). These averages should be seen as typical to many, but not general to all behaviors. These percentages are relatively invariant irrespective of how culture is defined (e.g. as nationalities, linguistic groups, religious groups, or ethno-linguistic groups). Though infrequent, some behaviors are left unexplained by the hierarchy (e.g. short-term inflation rates across countries). Across the various levels in Figure 6, solar climate generally explains the largest variances in behavior; over 70% of the variance observed across the behaviors mentioned are explained by the exogenous factors, including income per capita. Cultural variables explain little variance beyond that already explained by natural endowments (e.g. controlling for climatic effects, religion does not have an impact on labor productivity or "work ethics"). It is interesting to note that solar climate alone (absolute latitude squared) has statistically equal or greater explanatory power than income per capita for a variety of behaviors which are typically thought of as being "development driven" or, if not development driven, "inferior" behaviors (e.g. when the consumption of a good is not positively related to income). Behaviors which are uncorrelated with income per capita but explained by solar climate include (statistically significant Pearson correlation coefficients are given in parentheses): milk consumption per capita (.53), and cereal consumption per capita (.57). Behaviors which are better explained by solar climate than income per capita include: butter consumption per capita (.59), flour consumption per capita (.35), potato consumption per capita (.66), sugar consumption per capita (.46), caloric intake per capita (.74), coffee consumption per capita (.75), cigarette consumption per capita (.33), surface cleaner consumption per capita in Europe (.52), percent of households owning a microwave oven in Europe (.76), percent of households owning a personal stereo (e.g. Sony Walkman) in Europe (.84), percent of households owning a personal computer in Europe (.59), the number of political parties in a country (.34), suicide rates (.62), and homicide rates (-.35). Behaviors which are equally well explained by solar climate and income per capita include: average population growth rates (-.50), number of major diseases present (-.52), literacy rates (.46), the percent of homes with piped water (.66), the percent of homes with flush toilets (.73), daily newspaper circulation per capita (.76), telephones per capita (.65), beef consumption per capita (.36), pork consumption per capita (.64), egg consumption per capita (.54), beer consumption per capita (.56), steel consumption per capita (.65), toilet paper consumption per capita (.72), the percent of homes owning a video camera in Europe (.66), and the percent of homes owning cable television, in Europe (.48). In general, the correlations are higher when the data are limited to European countries, or industrial countries located in very different climatic regions (e.g. desert, polar, temperate, tropical and Mediterranean). When the entire filtering procedure is performed, explained variances are virtually always higher than using income per capita (e.g. when marine, land and mineral resources are included, considering degrees of freedom).[1]

Validation Tests

Approaches used to validate estimated effects when applying the filtering approach include replication using subsets of the data which simultaneously offer sufficient variation in climate and degrees of freedom (i.e. country observations). Clusters can include countries having non-democratic political systems, certain dominating religions, or colonial languages. One can also group the data by exogenous controls including the hemispheres, time zones, form of topology, or wealth in mineral endowments. In both cases, these validity tests must allow for sufficient variation in climate (or climate-dependent variables). Within country tests often do not provide this variation unless these have substantial variances in latitude, elevation, or other environmental factors.

Dynamics

While the percentages reported in Figure 6 are robust to the validity tests discussed above, the results are static (as is common for cross-cultural studies of climate). Two questions arise: (1) are the results robust over time, and (2) in which direction are they likely to change in the future. The first question is best evaluated using data collected over extended time periods using static samples (i.e. the same countries must be represented over time); the variables used in the exogenous filters themselves never change over time. Changes in coefficients and explained variances can address the first question. The second question is best answered by examining the dynamics of the residuals (corrected dependent variables) after the final filter of interest. Strong deviations from the mean (of zero) may foretell future dynamics reflecting a convergence or regression to the mean. In the case of zero mean shifts over time (an empirical question), those countries far below the mean have higher probability of increasing their behaviors toward the mean, whereas those substantially above the mean will eventually fall to the mean. Alternatively (e.g. in cases of positive mean shifts in behavior over time, driven by innovation or other growth mechanisms), those countries/cultures substantially above (or below) the mean may be on a boundary to

---

[1] Data on these behaviors are taken from primary sources or from various Euromonitor publications (European Marketing Data and Statistics; International Marketing Data and Statistics), and from various United Nations statistical reports.

which others converge (e.g. the saturation point on a diffusion curve); of course, this boundary may shift in time.

Some Implications

The implementation of physioeconomic models can be revealing to researchers and policy makers. The filtering of income or consumption per capita, for example, reveals that over 70 percent of variances observed internationally are explained by variances in natural endowments (e.g. countries like Chad are mostly underdeveloped due to their lacking natural resources and having equatorial or desert climates, and less due to economic policy failure). Furthermore, based on cross-sectional data which adjust for purchasing power parity and which are available back to the 1950s, this explained variance has been increasing over time. As information ubiquity and democracy progresses to such an extent that economic planning is conducted to its optimal level within each country, factors which will most explain differences across countries will be exogenous to economic policies (physioeconomic factors). In 1994, solar climate alone explained some 60 percent of the variance of income per capita across countries; also the gradual increases in explained variance has occurred while average consumption levels have substantially increased over time. Furthermore, filtered measures of development are often not correlated with unfiltered measures. When comparing each country's level of "relative development", or its level of economic performance given it exogenous endowments, one finds that resulting income differences are relatively small compared to absolute levels (e.g. within a few thousand dollars, versus tens-of-thousands of dollars). Many "lesser developed" countries (e.g. Costa Rica) have, for example, higher economic performance given their endowments relative to, say, the United States. We can conjecture that if Americans were to inherit Africa, they would do no better in developing Africa with their culture or social system than current Africans with theirs; similarly, if Japan were to have been located on the equator, its social system would have only slightly higher performance to Indonesia (as opposed to several orders of magnitude higher as estimated using absolute measures of development). By focusing on these filtered measures, therefore, one may be able to identify "*relatively* successful" countries; the policies of these countries may prove useful in other countries with relatively low performance or those having similar endowments. Tropical countries, for example, may benefit from studying social and economic policies in Costa Rica or the Cayman Islands which have managed to obtain relatively high economic performance given their natural endowments.

The concept of "relative performance" raises an interesting question concerning cross-national measures of development. There appear to be fundamental cross-country differences in both physiological and psychological utility ("basal utility") for a number of human activities including food consumption, dressing behavior, housing requirements, energy consumption, and the use of in-door entertainment. Cross-country data, including those limited to industrialized countries, seem to indicate that some portion of the observed variances in measures of development can be explained by climatic factors which may affect basal utility. For certain measures of development incorporating these behaviors (e.g. aggregate consumption per capita), holding all countries (or climatic regions) to a unique or absolute standard, regardless of where that standard is established, can be problematic. Considering the case of caloric intake, European data spanning several decades indicate substantially lower caloric consumption in warmer countries, than colder countries (consistent with thermoregulation). These levels have remained relatively constant over time, despite large increases in real income per capita. Similar observations can be made with respect to the consumption of various climate-affected behaviors (e.g. clothing, the use of internal heating, insulation, etc.). If we are interested in measuring development from a general utility perspective, differences in basal utilities should be taken into account (i.e. two divergent levels of absolute consumption may generate similar levels of utility, the difference in consumption being explained by differences in thermoregulatory functions). For example, Belgians consume some 50% more calories per capita than persons living in Bermuda (3850 versus 2545, respectively); it is difficult to imagine that all of this difference is due to economic performance or that Belgians receive that much more absolute utility from their diets.   While adjustments might be made to economic development measures to account for basal utility differences across countries, these adjustments run the risk of overestimating development for those countries having the lowest absolute values on the original scale.   An alternative to adjusting current measures is to place more emphasis on alternative measures not subject to basal utility shifts, or indirect physiological or psychological mechanisms.   The direct or life threatening impacts of climate may also be appropriate (e.g. the prevalence of certain diseases, infant mortality, etc.); these absolute scales should indicate relative levels of development which cannot be confounded with differences in basal utility (a lower level on the scale should always indicate lower performance and, preferably, in a linear manner).

Filtering economic data for physioeconomic factors clearly reveals that countries may develop, in equilibrium, to differing levels of behavior which may reflect, in large part, physiological effects as opposed to endogenous economic policies, culture, ethnic origins, or social institutions.   Estimates of global food supply inadequacies, for example, based on temperate-climate standards are likely therefore to be exaggerated especially given the fact that most persons live closer to the equator, than in temperate climates. While shortages have occurred throughout history, it becomes paramount to objectively estimate basic requirements in order to develop appropriate policies. Otherwise, deviations from "temperate standards" may appear alarming, and result in policies detrimental to welfare. For example, food aid policies including food subsidies based on erroneous needs estimates risk destroying local farming economies.   Filtered measures can also give realistic indications of the likely impact of policies on countries having different endowments (interpreting human experiences as the result of a natural experiment). For example, the application of tight (loose) monetary policy in tropical countries will not necessarily result in levels in consumption per capita as measured in temperate climates with similar policies. The same can be estimated for agricultural policies, educational policies, macroeconomic policies and general economic approaches.   Likewise, the incremental influence of ethnic, religious, language or cultural differences on social behaviors can be measured (or be identified as confounding or irrelevant) using the proposed framework or similar approaches incorporating physioeconomic variables. Again, by focusing on filtered measures we can identify "relatively successful policies" which are more useful than "absolutely successful policies" which can be inappropriate or misleading.

Since climate (and other physioeconomic factors) substantially contribute to human illness (e.g. malaria) and economic poverty (e.g. due to floods or droughts), efforts might be better focused on approaches to directly combat these deleterious effects (as opposed to emphasizing or, worse, blaming confounding factors such as race or culture).

Resources may be better utilized for education, for example, on pre-natal care or nutrition; malnutrition being more critical in many countries than caloric intake which appears low compared to temperate climate standards. Innovation and discovery, in the past, has demonstrated that the parameters of the model can and do change over time. Care must be taken not to interpret strong climatic effects (high explained variances) as indicating that countries will remain underdeveloped. Absolute levels of behavior have shifted over time for all countries despite physioeconomic factors playing a role in affecting variances.

Finally, by explicitly reporting noneconomic dimensions in Chapters 3 to 9 (which are presented in the order of the physioeconomic hierarchy), this book responds to calls to expand the use of non-traditional variables in comparative studies. For example, early neoclassical theories of growth suggest that economic development across countries will ultimately converge since developed economies will grow slower than lesser developed economies due to diminishing returns to reproducible capital. Weak empirical support for neoclassical models has lead to the emergence of endogenous growth models which assume constant returns to broadly defined reproducible capital. Following 18th century economic theories of national wealth, consumption, and growth, these models have historically assumed national production to be a function of capital, technology, land, and labor. More recently, both neoclassical and endogenous growth models have noted the importance of human capital, international trade, and machinery and equipment investment, among other factors, to explain cross-country differences in economic performance and growth. Across all such models, low or inconsistent explained variances across national groupings (OECD versus African countries) has lead to calls for greater inclusion of noneconomic variables. The physioeconomic variables presented later in this book will hopefully foster useful extensions of this research.

3

ECONOMICS ACROSS ETHNIC CULTURES

There are substantial variances in economic measures across the world's ethnic cultures. This chapter provides comparative statistics for a variety of economic variables across ethnic groups. For a full discussion of the methodology used to generate these estimates, please refer to Chapter 1 which gives important caveats. This chapter first gives summary statistics of the variables reported: the number of countries/cultures for which each variable was available, simple averages, and weighted averages (by population); these averages can be used as benchmarks. Then a lengthy comparative table is presented which provides raw statistics across the ethnic groups defined in Chapter 1.

Most of the variables are self explanatory, though some merit commentary. All of the statistics should be considered as estimates which have undergone rounding and certain adjustments. Estimates cover macroeconomics (e.g. gross national product per capita, inflation rates, savings rates, currency convertibility), labor (percent of labor force not employed, and the percent of the population not in the labor force; employment by sector), infrastructure (roads, airports), communications (cable systems, television stations, AM/FM radio, satellite earth stations), ownership and consumption (newspaper circulation, consumer electronics, calories, sugar, energy, and electricity per capita). The estimate of "." signifies a missing value due to a lack of underlying data.

Summary Statistics:
Economic Resources

Characteristics	Number of Countries Covered	Number of Ethnic Groups Covered	Weighted Average by Pop 1994	Simple Average	Simple Standard Deviation
Macroecon: GNP/capita	225	424	4241.62	3600.19	6189.41
: Saving rate	121	330	21.76	13.97	14.08
: Inflation rate	205	399	51.24	155.44	624.29
: Convert currency (1=yes)	192	410	0.73	0.60	0.47
Communist, former (1=yes)	222	420	0.32	0.19	0.39
Labor: Unemployment, %	188	335	10.66	15.21	12.37
: Nonemployment, %	207	415	67.25	66.75	11.81
: Agriculture, %	174	392	46.55	55.18	27.63
: Industry, %	145	314	26.37	24.28	13.59
: Services, %	120	274	28.32	27.72	17.13
: Unionization, %	160	360	27.43	21.00	22.58
Air Trans: # of aircraft	188	394	526.03	90.09	422.31
: # aircraft/cap	188	394	2.94	5.17	23.48
: # of airports	207	404	979.62	227.03	688.55
Runways: Permanent Surf	202	401	349.18	62.43	216.43
: Large	201	400	6.23	1.71	3.87
: Medium	202	401	53.82	12.41	21.96
: Small	200	400	214.81	53.05	127.95
Roads: Total km	194	414	1005662.39	152811.24	394883.53
: Motorways km	215	404	9938.49	882.71	4645.59
: Highways total km	223	425	964050.84	145933.39	383800.04
: Paved km	189	401	269131.29	47448.29	135103.21
: Gravel km	147	348	428949.40	65086.94	189181.32
: Improved earth km	83	243	120377.40	38555.24	98578.68
: Unimproved earth km	106	276	59251.33	27036.18	39895.93
: Ownership car/1000 cap	188	407	73.37	61.79	122.46
Railways km	229	423	41347.06	7874.25	19220.31
Telecom: # AM stations	211	412	414.69	91.63	281.98
: # of cable systems	209	410	2.17	1.23	3.87
: # of TV stations	214	413	715.79	97.02	674.56
: # of FM stations	210	400	365.07	67.50	270.11
: # of SAT earth stations	220	419	6.12	2.17	2.89
: # of daily papers	192	410	872.44	100.74	361.14
: Television/1000 cap	206	417	143.52	106.62	153.55
: Radios/1000 pop	195	402	267.96	214.53	244.60
: Telephones/1000 pop	226	424	126.90	107.72	192.69
: Digital % 1993	96	255	46.19	60.52	31.82
: Main Lines/1000 pop	183	406	113.02	90.56	151.08
: Cellular subs/cap	127	227	10.18	10.18	25.88
: Pagers/cap	39	95	21.89	18.60	23.92
Piped water, % dwellings	113	268	50.34	54.47	30.08
Food: Sugar/cap	143	360	148.39	128.64	113.80
: Protein 1985 grm/day/cap	159	375	69.11	64.05	19.23
: Calories/cap/day	165	384	2656.88	2459.69	521.66
: Meat prod/cap 1988	177	399	0.02	0.02	0.04
Energy: Consumption/cap	186	391	1855.44	1368.12	2627.70
: Electricity/cap	225	423	1994.10	1699.83	2995.32

Characteristics	Abadkis	Abkhaz	Acholi	Afar	Afro-European	Akan	Albanian	Ambo	Amerind	Amerind-Mestizo
Macroecon: GNP/capita	179	4530	300	262	1500	425	1970	950	4620	6800
: Saving rate	9		23	8	6	2	19	28	21	23
: Inflation rate	9			1	61	18	35	92	16	18
: Convert currency (1=yes)	0	0	0	0.1		1	0.7		0.9	1
Communist, former (1=yes)	0	1	0	0	0					0
Labor: Unemployment, %	5	3		40	15	0.5	15	19	5	7
: Nonemployment, %	60		77	66	58	78	57	73	70	67
: Agriculture, %	91	48	90	80	32	55	40	75	30	12
: Industry, %		25			28	20	40	15	29	31
: Services, %		31	3	2	40	25	0.7	10	41	57
: Unionization, %			0.6	21	24	13	15	16	29	56
Air Trans: # of aircraft				0.7			0.1	28	712	2
: # aircraft/cap	0.2		0.3		3	0.5	0.1	3	4	1700
: # of airports	37		35	105	36	10	13	309	2360	137
Runways: Permanent Surf	5			8	13	5	6	30	483	31
: Large	0		1	0.8	2	1	5	2	47	326
: Medium	1		3	11	1		5	15	384	378
: Small			10	33				54		
Roads: Total km	7080	35100	28200	33500	18200	28300	25100	72400	620000	211000
: Motorways km						0	194		8320	378
: Highways total km	7080	33900	26200	33800	18200	32300	24800	73800	603000	208000
: Paved km	2900	29500	1970	2840	12600	6080	22000	8580	53200	47600
: Gravel km	1660	0	5850	7650	3200	26200	7390	29400	26500	39500
: Improved earth km		4400	18400	2670	2400		613	35900	58400	101000
: Unimproved earth km				2470			9090		46700	20300
: Ownership car/1000 cap	0.8	78	1	3	25	4	16	14	97	135
Railways km	52	1570	1270	668	317	953	570	3190	34200	34300
Telecom: # AM stations	88		10	4	10	4	17	17	850	171
: # of cable systems	0		9	0.2	3	4	0.1			
: # of TV stations	1		1	1	8	1	10	6	683	231
: # of FM stations				0.2	17		0.3	13	362	
: # of SAT earth stations	1	149	4	2	2	1	4	2	8	2
: # of daily papers			8	10	124	15	96	6	314	220
: Television/1000 cap	59		22	78	420	185	172	19	164	219
: Radios/1000 pop	2		4	6	83	6	47	5	375	540
: Telephones/1000 pop	25		60	49	100		34		134	134
: Digital % 93	4	96	2	5	83	3	0.2		165	46
: Main Lines/1000 pop	88	11			6	0.2	3		122	143
: Cellular subs/cap	5	97					72		11	
: Pagers/cap									10	2
Piped water, % dwellings	66		29	85	35	41	72	35	50	75
Food: Sugar/cap	14		54	52	398	38	166	70	332	208
: Protein 85 grm/day/cap	52			55	58		84	45	79	106
: Calories/cap/day	2050		2220	1660	2580	1730	2750	1930	3000	3190
: Meat prod/cap 88										0.1
Energy: Consumption/cap	24		25	94	853	115	1310	89	2070	1900
: Electricity/cap	35	2590	31	96	1080	322	1060	215	1970	1700

Characteristics	Amhara	Ana-Ife	Andorran	Angolares	Anouis	Antandroy	Arab, other	Arab Berber	Arab Emirian	Arab Lebanese
Macroecon: GNP/capita	130	421	15400	6310	800	230	2480	5560	19900	2110
: Saving rate	4	14		-3	17	4	21		70	
: Inflation rate	8	3	1	12	1	13	27	8	1	100
: Convert currency (1=yes)	0		0	0.7	1		0	0	1	
: Communist, former (1=yes)	0	0	0	0	0	0	0	0	0	0
Labor: Unemployment, %		2		5	4	63	15	2	2	50
: Nonemployment, %		68	20	63	57	90	79	81	68	77
: Agriculture, %	66	75	80	20	85		36	18	5	11
: Industry, %	80	20	0	35	8	4	29	31	85	79
: Services, %				45	7	8	35	51	10	
: Unionization, %		0.3		55	20	0.6	19	28	0	38
Air Trans: # of aircraft	25	0.8		33	14	148	33	56	5	19
: # aircraft/cap	0.5	9		27		30		11		7
: # of airports	123		220	45	45		96	128	37	9
Runways: Permanent Surf		2	0	25	7		39	51	20	6
: Large	9	2	96	0.7		3		9		0
: Medium	1			0.8	3	34	25	27	5	3
: Small	13	7570	631	6	15	34800	27	44	4360	2
Roads: Total km	38		0	48500	55500	40000	53800	32500	2000	7190
: Motorways km	39500	6460	1	168	155	4690	251	269	1800	0
: Highways total km		1760	0	50900	46600	811	62900	31400	200	7300
: Paved km	44300		0	42600	3600	34500	36600	23000		6200
: Gravel km	3650	4700	0	7960	32000		18900	8500	159	450
: Improved earth km	9650	13	0	2860	11000	2	29500	4750	0	650
: Unimproved earth km	3000	520	0	162	15	960	11000	92	8	175
: Ownership car/1000 cap	28000	2	149	2470	11	17	38	16	4	111
Railways km	1	0	175	40	649		2700	2	12	5
Telecom: # AM stations	835	0	474	4	3	1	17	12	3	13
: # of cable systems	4	3		46	13	0		3	4	3
: # of TV stations	0	0		46	17	3	30	2		2
: # of FM stations	0	2		3	2	0	14		8	40
: # of SAT earth stations	1	1		14	59	5	4	88	109	327
: # of daily papers	0	6		121	129	20	8	210	232	797
: Television/1000 cap	1	214	149	195	11	213	76	52	323	120
: Radios/1000 pop	3	5	175	251	82	3	205		100	
: Telephones/1000 pop	2	98	474	255	0		64	54	343	127
: Digital % 93	80	5		15		3	48		28	2
: Main Lines/1000 pop	39			6			58			
: Cellular subs/cap				58	100	49	2	257	54	287
: Pagers/cap	3	123		293	54	56	49	88	110	82
: Piped water, % dwellings	85	52		78	2550	2410	237	3610	3710	3090
Food: Sugar/cap	25	2220		2900	180	39	2850	4120	20400	0
: Protein 85 grm/day/cap	55	70		0	189	46	1120	3850	7460	1450
: Calories/cap/day	1660	81	2170	1330			952			1630
: Meat prod/cap 88	0			2030						
Energy: Consumption/cap	24									
: Electricity/cap	17									

Characteristics	Arab Omani	Arab Palestin.	Arab Quatar	Arab Saudi	Arab Sudanic	Arab Total	Arauca-nian	Armenian	Assamese	Assyrian
Macroecon: GNP/capita	6670	1370	17000	7050	418	2950	2550	4500	200	2300
: Saving rate	47	28	3	65	0.2	25	8	38		
: Inflation rate	-7	0	1	5	179	43	15	212	9	
: Convert currency (1=yes)	-1	0	0	1	0	0.2	1		0	0
Communist, former (1=yes)	0		0	0	0	0		0.9		0
Labor: Unemployment, %		22			30	15	6	13		5
: Nonemployment, %	74	77	79	70	75	77	66	57	61	78
: Agriculture, %	60	11	10	14	79	37	19	21	93	30
: Industry, %	13	79	70	31	9	28	36	40		22
: Services, %	27	38	20	55	13	35	45	41		48
: Unionization, %	0	19			16	16	13	12	0	10
Air Trans: # of aircraft	19	3	3	104		39	29		0	34
: # aircraft/cap	11	0.6			0.6			0.4		2
: # of airports	134	3	6	211	72	104	390	204	2	113
Runways: Permanent Surf	6	1	4	74	8	38	48	74		73
: Large	1		1	14		4		10		52
: Medium	8			37	5	23	12	13	0	12
: Small	73	2	2	105	30	36	58	57	2	0
Roads: Total km	24700	7190	1500	145000	2210	58000	79200	26000	2280	25500
: Motorways km						202	3460	34		
: Highways total km	26000	7300	1500	74000	21200	56900	79000	27300	1300	34700
: Paved km	6000	6200	1000	35000	1440	31100	9910	18800	418	17500
: Gravel km		450	500	39000	4070	18600	33100	3140	515	
Improved earth km		650			2300	21500	36000	3320	371	5500
Unimproved earth km					1360	11900		2210		11700
Ownership car/1000 cap	104	175	226	145	6	52	50	45	5	34
Railways km	0	111		886	4580	2530	7980	1950		2240
Telecom: # AM stations	0	0.9	2	43	10	18	159	81	0	16
: # of cable systems	0	0.6	2		0.3	3	0	1	0	4
: # of TV stations	7	2	3	80	3	31	131	25	1	13
: # of FM stations	3	0.4	3	13	0.1	11	33		0	
: # of SAT earth stations	3			7	2	4		62		4
: # of daily papers		40	3	10		8			8	8
: Television/1000 cap	762	327	514	277	55	107	201	124	9	68
: Radios/1000 pop	619	797	459	288	220	234	304	374	12	186
: Telephones/1000 pop	99	120	349	152	4	69	112	152	66	56
: Digital % 93	98					50		11	2	
: Main Lines/1000 pop	103	127	270	125	15	62	124	164		43
: Cellular subs/cap	4	2	12	2		8	7	0.4		
: Pagers/cap					3			32		
Piped water, % dwellings				47	65	51	70	53		40
Food: Sugar/cap	287	287		208	125	224	287	199		221
: Protein 85 grm/day/cap	82	82		91	61	78	68	86		81
: Calories/cap/day	3090	3090		3030	2030	2820	2570	3270	2030	2990
: Meat prod/cap 88	0		0							0
Energy: Consumption/cap	3430	1450	22100	6360	59	1810	1210	2080	32	1060
: Electricity/cap	3160	1630	10200	2880	39	1230	1330	2620	973	1470

Characteristics	Austrian	Avar	Aymara	Azande	Azerbai-jani	Bagirmi-Sara	Bahraini	Bai	Bakhtiari	Bakongo
Macroecon: GNP/capita	20200	3830	1140	298	5300	229	7800	417	6150	950
:Saving rate	25		10	15	39	-24	39	28	39	28
:Inflation rate	4	1350	33	2850	498		2	6	23	92
::Convert currency (1=yes)	1			0.1	0.4			1		
:Communist, former (1=yes)	0	1	0	0	33	0	0	1	0	0
Labor: Unemployment, %	5		29	30			9	2	25	19
:Nonemployment, %	56	50	74	67	33	66	74	53	76	73
:Agriculture, %	8	62	43	75	32	85	5	60	33	75
:Industry, %	35	32	18	12	27		85	30	27	15
:Services, %	57	26	39	12	40			10	40	10
:Unionization, %	60		26	9		20				16
Air Trans: # of aircraft	25		50	36	31		27	65	48	28
:# aircraft/cap	3	0		1	0.5	0.3	51	284	0.8	
:# of airports	55	0	678	220	214			330	214	309
Runways: Permanent Surf	20		22	19	81		2	260	81	30
:Large	6			0.7	16	4			16	2
:Medium			15		16	4	2	100		
:Small	4		96	5	71	25		90	71	15
Roads: Total km	107000	30400	55000	60	98700	40000	1	200	139000	54
:Motorways km	1450	0	2460	108000	307		2610	1100000	490	72400
:Highways total km	95400	36700	53900	109000	101000	31300	200	0	140000	73800
:Paved km	21800	31800	4280	2340	38500	32	200	1030000	42700	8580
:Gravel km	60800	0	6700	36500	29400	7300		170000	46900	29400
:Improved earth km	12800		22500	4790	31000			648000	49400	
:Unimproved earth km		4900	48900	72100	2560	24000		211000	1200	35900
:Ownership car/1000 cap	387	33		4	35		182		35	14
Railways km	5820	2070	2910	4580	3720			1	4730	3190
Telecom: # AM stations	6		199	9	77	2	2	54000	77	17
:# of cable systems	0					0		274		
:# of TV stations	47	1	90	13	28	6	6	202	28	0
:# of FM stations	21	151			3		3		3	6
:# of SAT earth stations	3	175		1	2	1	3	6		13
:# of daily papers	33		1		67	1	3	1780	17	
:Television/1000 cap	475		29	14	105	1	402	27	66	2
:Radios/1000 pop	530	98	97	128	178	26	419	69	178	6
:Telephones/1000 pop	469		376		78		282	17	65	19
:Digital % 93	35	101	30	100	11	15	100			
:Main Lines/1000 pop	500	0		2	88	0.9	260	21	80	5
:Cellular subs/cap	12		29		0		40	0.6		
:Pagers/cap								8		
Piped water, % dwellings	99		42	48	49		94	48	49	35
Food: Sugar/cap	298		216	46	139	41		62	139	70
:Protein 85 grm/day/cap	97		57	41	86	53			86	45
:Calories/cap/day	3420		2160	2120	3310	1660		2630	3310	1930
:Meat prod/cap 88	0.1	0					0		0	0
Energy: Consumption/cap	4010		435	65	1650	18	15600	819	1650	89
:Electricity/cap	6400	3040	470	118	1680	14	6880	488	886	215

Characteristics	Balante	Baluchi	Bambara	Bamileke-Bamum	Banda	Bangi-Ngale	Bantu	Baoule	Bari	Bariba
Macroecon: GNP/capita	219	2180	285	1160	378	238	626	800	440	430
: Saving rate	-11	20	-4	-2	-2	21	13	17	3	0.5
: Inflation rate	-50	14	-6		1230	4000	25	1	200	1
: Convert currency (1=yes)	0	0	1	1	0.7	0	1	1	0	1
Communist, former (1=yes)	0	0	0		0	0	0			
Labor: Unemployment, %	17	13		25	30		35	14	30	
: Nonemployment, %	58	77	74	66	72	64	72	57	76	63
: Agriculture, %	90	48	72	74	73	75	74	85	78	60
: Industry, %		18	12	11	13	13	10	8	9	
: Services, %		36	16	15	12	12	16	7	13	38
: Unionization, %		7		45	4	12	16		10	75
Air Trans: # of aircraft	2	41	0		15	45		20	18	0
: # aircraft/cap	2	0.4		0.4	0.8			14	0.7	0
: # of airports	34	139	35	56	133	284	478	45	72	6
Runways: Permanent Surf	4	74	8	10	10	24	22		0	1
: Large	1	5			0.3	1	2	0		0
: Medium		26	5	5	3	6	3	3	5	
: Small	5	50	10	21	38	73	31	15	31	4
Roads: Total km	3500	116000	13300	52200	61300	145000	83300	55000	20000	7420
: Motorways km	0	370	0		0	0	0	155		
: Highways total km	3220	109000	15700	65000	60100	147000	83100	46600	20000	5050
: Paved km	2700	29200	3670	2880	1170	2800	15400	3600	1600	920
: Gravel km		35400		32300	46200	46200	38000	3200	3700	2600
: Improved earth km	520	7060	10400	30000	10500	97500	22700	11000	12400	1530
: Unimproved earth km	4			6	37400		7250			
: Ownership car/1000 cap	0	15	3		11	2	28	15	7	8
Railways km	2	9720	642	1050	1530	5010	2660	649	5110	607
Telecom: # AM stations		36	2	11	4	10	8	3	11	2
: # of cable systems	0	0	0	0	0	0	0	2	3	0
: # of TV stations	1	28	2	1	6	18	8	13	0	2
: # of FM stations	3	6	2	11	2	4	17	17	3	2
: # of SAT earth stations	2	3	2	2	2	4	2	2	0	0
: # of daily papers	0.8	88				4			2	
: Radios/1000 cap	32	31	39	22	71	103	27	59	2	5
: Television/1000 cap	37	108	16	89	4	1	45	129	61	78
: Telephones/1000 pop		30	2	6		1	31	11	243	5
: Digital % 93	7	41	76	6	100		13	82	4	61
: Main Lines/1000 pop		35	2		2				3	4
: Cellular subs/cap		0.3								
: Pagers/cap		0.2						0		
Piped water, % dwellings	32	26	57	30	43	43	80	100	65	25
Food: Sugar/cap	46	138	54	26	13	24	221	54	135	50
: Protein 85 grm/day/cap		67		47	41	34	51			
: Calories/cap/day	2130	2570	2020	2040	2010	2160	2120	2550	2070	2190
: Meat prod/cap 88	0	0	0	0	0	0	0	0	0	
Energy: Consumption/cap	91	738	25	254	53	67	690	180	64	50
: Electricity/cap	17	515	26	225	69	151	907	189	42	39

Characteristics	Barotze	Baskhir	Basque	Bassa	Batswana	Bayad	Beja	Belgian	Belorussian	Bemba
Macroecon: GNP/capita	420	5990	13200	430	2770	1730	440	19500	6010	420
..Saving rate	7		17	6	25		3	14		7
..Inflation rate	155	105	15		15	-1	200	17	898	155
..Convert currency (1=yes)	1	1	1	0	0	1	0	1	0	1
..Communist, former (1=yes)	0							0	1	0
Labor: Unemployment, %		3	18	43	25	1	30	9	1	
..Nonemployment, %	72	47	100	82	70	32	76	59	48	72
..Agriculture, %	58	19	16	82	59	52	78	3	20	58
..Industry, %	11	39	28		23	10	9	28	41	11
..Services, %	31	42	56	2	18		13	68	41	31
..Unionization, %	10	5	209		16	25	18	70	5	10
Air Trans: # of aircraft	12		5	0.3	5	11	0.7	46		12
..# aircraft/cap			105	66	100	81	72	6		
..# of airports	117		60	2		11		41		117
Runways: Permanent Surf	13		4	0	8	4	5	23		13
..Large	1		22	1	1	19	31	14		1
..Medium	4		25	4	27	12		3		4
..Small	22									22
Roads: Total km	37400	854000	158000	5410	13500	3950	20000	124000	329000	37400
..Motorways km	0	0	2280	0	0	0	0	1580	0	0
..Highways total km	36400	879000	150000	10100	11500	46700	20000	100000	199000	36400
..Paved km	6500	653000	62800	603	1600	1000	1600	37000	145000	6500
..Gravel km	7000		85400		1700		3700	57		7000
..Improved earth km		227000			5180		2300	51000		
..Unimproved earth km	22900	0			3040	45700	12400		56100	22900
..Ownership car/1000 cap	9	60	294	1	14	0.8	7	56	51	9
Railways km	1720	871000	15400	485	800	1780	5110	401	16100	1720
Telecom: # AM stations	11	1050	189	3	7	12	1	8140	1000	11
..# of cable systems	1	0	122	0	0			3		1
..# of TV stations	0	310	100	5	0	1	3	5	290	0
..# of FM stations	9	1050	405	4	13	1		31	1000	9
..# of SAT earth stations	5	4		1		1	2	38	3	5
..# of daily papers	2	6	102	2		3		2		2
Television/1000 cap	25	313	390	18	12	56	61	32	174	25
Radios/1000 pop	27		287	185	119	104	243	447	306	27
Telephones/1000 pop	12	166	396	9	37	32	4	470		12
Digital % 93		9	41		100	91		519	184	
Main Lines/1000 pop	10	171	392	2	43	31	3	55	9	10
Cellular subs/cap		0.1	4					475	189	
Pagers/cap								16	0.2	
Piped water, % dwellings	63		91	45	99	0.3	65	23		63
Food: Sugar/cap	101		293	43	268	173	135	100		101
..Protein 85 grm/day/cap	58		97	23	70	93	62	293		58
..Calories/cap/day	2130		3360	2360	2230	2830	2070	105		2130
..Meat prod/cap 88		0.1	0.1	0	0	0.1		3850	0.1	
Energy: Consumption/cap	198		2500	130	425	1870	64	6000		198
..Electricity/cap	909	6810	3860	334	834	1630	42	7210	4120	909

Characteristics	Bengali	Berber	Bete	Betsileo	Betsimi-Saraka	Bhutia	Bihari	Black	Black Amerind	Boa
Macroecon: GNP/capita	212	1500	800	230	230	200	188	11600	1500	238
..Saving rate	5	20	17	4	4	9	9	13	23	21
..Inflation rate	7	15		13	13			0.6	27	4000
..Convert currency (1=yes)	0	0	1	1	1	0	0		1	0
Communist, former (1=yes)	0	0	1	0	0	0	0			0
Labor: Unemployment, %		20	0				12	9	30	64
..Nonemployment, %	30	78	14	63	63	61	63	59	65	75
..Agriculture, %	71	39	57	90	90	93	82	21	30	13
..Industry, %	59	28	85				11	28	24	12
..Services, %	11	32	8				30	51	46	12
..Unionization, %	30	10	7					19	8	45
Air Trans: # of aircraft	3	33	20	4	4		3	3720	83	284
..# aircraft/cap	1.5	1	14	0.6	0.6	0.2	0.2	16	2	24
..# of airports	0.1	98	45	148	148	2	31	7180	1170	1
Runways: Permanent Surf	16	36		30	30	1		2230	70	
..Large	12	2	7				2	28	8	6
..Medium	4	20	3	3	3	2	7	149	191	73
..Small	6	41		34	34			1280		
Roads: Total km	6250	67200	55000	34800	34800	2280	6840	3220000	129000	145000
..Motorways km			155					39100		0
..Highways total km	7250	66400	46600	40000	40000	1300	7130	3160000	75500	147000
..Paved km	3840	39200	3600	4690	4690	418	3170	31100	9350	2800
..Gravel km		27300	32000	811	811	515	1660	778000	66100	46200
..Improved earth km	3400	8600	11000	34500	34500	371	3400	5680		
..Unimproved earth km	0.4		15						33	97500
Railways km	2840	34	649	960	960	5	853	6800	2960	2
..Ownership car/1000 cap	9	2690	15	2	2	1	0.7	269	413	5010
Telecom: # AM stations	11	22	3	17	17		65	127000		0
..# of cable systems	6	25	2	1	1	1	4	2460	33	10
..# of TV stations	59	23	13				2	2	3	
..# of FM stations	4	4	17	3	3			3230		18
..# of SAT earth stations	8	3	2			1	59	2300	33	4
..# of daily papers	19	9	59	20	20		3	28	2	1
..Television/1000 cap	98	74	129	213	213		20	832	32	4
..Radios/1000 pop	3	187	11			9	8	439	108	
..Telephones/1000 pop	0	43	82	4	4	12	88	1070	141	103
..Digital % 93			7	0	0	66	4	392	108	1
..Main Lines/1000 pop	20	39	0	3	3	2		44	100	
..Cellular subs/cap		0.4						314	0.6	
..Pagers/cap								48	5	1
Piped water, % dwellings		58					66	58	54	43
Food: Sugar/cap	20	225	100	49	49		16	78	258	24
..Protein 85 grm/day/cap	41	76	54	56	56		49	269	56	34
..Calories/cap/day	1920	2800	2550	2410	2410	2030	2010	3040	2550	2160
..Meat prod/cap 88	0	0	0	0	0	0	0	0	0	0
Energy: Consumption/cap	70	574	180	39	39	32	37	5080	773	67
..Electricity/cap	67	447	189	46	46	973	44	6100	1200	151

Characteristics	Bobo	Bounty Mutineers	Brazilian	Breton	Bubi	Bulgarian	Bullom	Bura	Burman	Bush Negro
Macroecon: GNP/capita	333		7330	20400	393	3840	330	314	863	3950
..Saving rate	-2		4	18	-0.3	79	-5	23	19	10
..Inflation rate	2		6	12	1		81	45		27
..Convert currency (1=yes)			1	1	0	1				
..Communist, former (1=yes)	0		0	0	0	1	0	0	0	
Labor: Unemployment, %	16		8	11	56	11	70	28	10	16
..Nonemployment, %	68		63	58	50	52	75	60	64	77
..Agriculture, %	79		20	9		33	15	54	65	30
..Industry, %	9		35	45		47		19	25	15
..Services, %	12		45	46		47		27	10	55
..Unionization, %	16		38	20	0	86	35	8	59	42
Air Trans: # of aircraft	1		27	194	1	10		57	17	
..#aircraft/cap	0.1	0.07		3	3		0	0.5	0.4	0.9
..# of airports	45	1	3	469	3	380	12	76	85	2
Runways: Permanent Surf		0		250	2	120	4	33	27	41
..Large	4	0	45	3		20				6
..Medium	3	1	24	36		20	1	15	3	0
..Small	9		0.6	135	1	200	3	22	38	1
Roads: Total km	13200	59	45100	805000	2630	43700	7450	108000	23500	8060
..Motorways km			401	6640		254		115		91
..Highways total km	16300		47200	1540000	2760	44500	7400	108000	27000	7290
..Paved km	1400		39500	799000		40000	1150	30000	3200	501
..Gravel km	3670						490	25400	17000	5400
..Improved earth km	7400		5140	750000		4510	5760		6100	
..Unimproved earth km	8490	27	4100					52600		170
..Ownership car/1000 cap	2		225	421	13		8		2	2400
Railways km	627		3580	34300		4870	84	3510	4250	92
Telecom: # AM stations	2	0	38	41	0	20		35	0	162
..# of cable systems		1	4	24						5
..# of TV stations	2	0	45	841	2	29	0	28	1	
..# of FM stations	1	0	45	796	0	15	1	17	1	0
..# of SAT earth stations	1	0	3	4	1		1		1	6
..# of daily papers	14	0	21	82	0	13		3	2	13
..Television/1000 cap	17		169	401	9	252	10	35	24	136
..Radios/1000 pop		1000	395	858	378	230	208	29		628
..Telephones/1000 pop	2	453	344	692	7	287		79	2	144
..Digital % 93	88			86		37	95	8		23
..Main Lines/1000 pop	2		409	567	4	285	91	0.3	2	162
..Cellular subs/cap			15	17		0.7	4			4
..Pagers/cap								0.5		
Piped water, % dwellings	24		58	100		80	40	17	13	28
Food: Sugar/cap	40		293	293		375	30	23	5	281
..Protein 85 grm/day/cap	61		91	111		106	41	47	70	71
..Calories/cap/day	2040		2990	3270	154	3630	1870	2110	2590	2720
..Meat prod/cap 88	0			0.1		0.1		0		
Energy: Consumption/cap	28		2100	3930	154	5050	76	207	62	1960
..Electricity/cap	19	3780	2810	7280	49	5470	50	111	58	3370

Characteristics	Bushman	Capver-dien	Caroli-nians	Catalan	Chahar Aimak	Chamba	Chamorro	Chiga	Chin	Chinese
Macroecon: GNP/capita	2770	9000	11500	13200	200	1160	13600	300	863	7870
:Saving rate	25	4	7	17	13	20	5	23	19	24
:Inflation rate	15	7		5		-2		0		6
:Convert currency (1=yes)	1	1		1	0	-1				0.9
:Communist, former (1=yes)		0		0	1	0	0		0	0.1
Labor: Unemployment,%	0	5		18		25	3	77	0	
:Nonemployment, %	25	53		100	74	66	68	90	10	53
:Agriculture, %	70	20		16	80	74			64	28
:Industry, %	59	35		28		11			65	39
:Services, %	23	55		56		15		3	25	34
:Unionization, %	18	55		10		45	13	0.3	10	15
Air Trans: # of aircraft	16	43	7	210	0	0.4		0.6	59	644
:# aircraft/cap	5					56	0	35	17	5
:# of airports	100	65	6	105	0	10	5	1	0.4	1070
Runways: Permanent Surf	8	36	3	60	41	1	3	10	85	371
:Large	0		0	4	9	5	0	3	27	
:Medium	1	1	1	22		21	0.5	38	0	30
:Small	27	2	2	25	10					196
Roads: Total km	13500	70200	382	158000	18	52200	597	28200	23500	498000
:Motorways km		243	382	2290	19000		597	26200		5920
:Highways total km	11500	73700		151000	21000	65000		1970	27000	480000
:Paved km	1600	61600		63000	2800	2680		5850	3200	257000
:Gravel km	1700			85400	1650	32300			17000	171000
:Improved earth km	5180	7960		294	16500			18400		62
:Unimproved earth km	3040	4100		15400	2	30000		1	6100	12000
:Ownership car/1000 cap	14	225	0	190	17	6	0		2	95
Railways km	800	3580		100	5	1050	3	1270	4250	22300
Telecom: # AM stations	7	57	2	22		11	0	10	0	421
:# of cable systems	0	6	0	100	1	0	2	0		
:# of TV stations	0	66	1	406	0	1	2	9	1	519
:# of FM stations	13	66	1	5	1	1	2	0	1	393
:# of SAT earth stations		4	2		4	2		1		6
:# of daily papers	1	21		102	3	22		4	1	150
:Television/1000 cap	12	176		389	78	89	672	8	24	222
:Radios/1000 pop	119	171		286	2	6	1210	22	2	412
:Telephones/1000 pop	37	353		396	0		471	4		266
:Main Lines/1000 pop	100	360		41	2	6		60	2	90
:Digital % 93	43	15		392		0	486	2		261
:Cellular subs/cap				10			18			32
:Pagers/cap				4						76
Piped water,% dwellings	99	58		91	25	30		29	13	72
Food: Sugar/cap	268	293		293	26	26		54	5	218
:Protein 85 grm/day/cap	70	91		97	64	47		2220	70	68
:Calories/cap/day	2230	3130		3360	2290	2040	5800		2590	2650
:Meat prod/cap 88	0.1			0.1	0	0	11900	0	0	0
Energy: Consumption/cap	425	1810	732	2490	232	254		25	62	2210
:Electricity/cap	834	2880		3860	69	225		31	58	3110

Characteristics	Chinese Mainland	Chokwe	Chuang	Chuvash	Circassian	Coloured	Comorian	Creole	Croatian	Czech
Macroecon: GNP/capita	10000	500	417	5990	3440	2960	521	3870	6390	7590
: Saving rate	3		28		19	14	4	11	26	24
: Inflation rate	1	2560	6	105	56		3	8	121	
: Convert currency (1=yes)	0	0.4	1	0	0.0			0.9	0.2	1
Communist, former (1=yes)				1	1					0
Labor: Unemployment, %	2	19	2		12	30	16	8	19	48
: Nonemployment, %	62	67	53	47	68	72	69	68	70	12
: Agriculture, %	17	75	60	19	47	25	81	21	14	37
: Industry, %	41	14	30	39	21	39		33	38	51
: Services, %	42	11	10	42	29	36	4	48	33	9
: Unionization, %	35	13	65	45	10	17		40	55	
Air Trans: # of aircraft	0	39	284		49	90	2	6	28	636
: # aircraft/cap	0	2	0.2		1	2		12	3	23
: # of airports	40	293	330		99	901	13	14	8	1360
Runways: Permanent Surf	36	26	260		59	132	6	4	20	455
: Large	3	9	10		3	5	0	0	2	4
: Medium	16	66	90		28	10			7	29
: Small	8		200		24	224	5	7	15	338
Roads: Total km	20000	118000	1100000	854000	53200	181000	2880	2860	26200	73800
: Motorways km	20000			0	735	2040	0	139	251	365
: Highways total km	17100	120000	1030000	879000	45000	188000	3200	2510	30300	74100
: Paved km	2370	4930	170000	653000	24500	54000	490	1130	21200	684000
: Gravel km	575	40000	648000	0	14900	134000	557	2660	8320	8440
: Improved earth km		74800	211000	227000	4000		34500	205	0.9	164000
: Unimproved earth km			1		2200			547	526	251
Railways km	112	4340	54000	87100	7560	20900		52	152	13500
Ownership car/1000 cap	4600	6	274	60	27	95	2	21	2310	863
Telecom: # AM stations	91	13	202	1050	14	14	60	0.3	14	5
: # of cable systems	15	10	6	310	1		3		11	51
: # of TV stations	23	14	1780	1050	318	67		1		28
: # of FM stations	35	7	27	4	84	286			8	5
: # of SAT earth stations	333	3	69		2		0.1	6	8	11
: # of daily papers	269	3	17	313	9	19	0.3	193	204	316
: Television/1000 cap	404	3	21	6	164	101	7	359	540	761
: Radios/1000 pop	71	72	0.6	166	133	282	116	112	206	324
: Telephones/1000 pop	413	3	48	9	193	146	9	87	29	4
: Digital % 93	30		62	171	58	99	3	98	218	227
: Main Lines/1000 pop	80	3		0.1	211	0.5	3	95	5	4
: Cellular subs/cap				0.1	2					32
: Pagers/cap										
Piped water, % dwellings	42	40			92	90		39	84	100
Food: Sugar/cap		41	48		237	232	45	272	406	300
: Protein 85 grm/day/cap		38	62		87	75	41	68	102	96
: Calories/cap/day	2810	2080	2630		3130	2940	2130	2720	3540	3420
: Meat prod/cap 88				0.1			0		0.1	0.1
Energy: Consumption/cap	2390	75	819		1020	2640	46	2100	3700	10900
: Electricity/cap	4310	175	488	6810	975	4140	33	1510	1740	6250

Characteristics	Dagestani	Dai	Damara	Dan	Danish	Dinka	Dogon	Dong	Dravidian	Duala
Macroecon: GNP/capita	5690	417	1300	731	24500	440	285	417	369	393
...Saving rate		28	12	15	14	3	-4	28	22	-0.3
...Inflation rate	275	6	1	1	2	200	-6	6	1	0
...Convert currency (1=yes)	0	1	0	0.8	1		0	1		
Communist, former (1=yes)	1									
Labor: Unemployment, %	2	2	40	19	10	30		2	200	56
...Nonemployment, %	9	53	68	62	50	76	74	53	100	50
...Agriculture, %	49	60		84	6	78	72	60	67	
...Industry, %	21	30		8	27	9	12	30	19	
...Services, %	37	10		7	67	13	16	10	14	
...Unionization, %	42	65	18	17	65			65	5	
Air Trans: # of aircraft		284		12	69			284	93	0
...# aircraft/cap	0	0.2		0.9	13	0.7	0	0.2	0.1	1
...# of airports	0	330	137	49	121	72	35	330	341	3
Runways: Permanent Surf		260	21	6	27	8	8	260	203	3
...Large		10	4	3	9	5	5	10	2	2
...Medium		90	63	13	6	31	10	90	59	0
...Small		200						200	87	1
Roads: Total km	742000	1100000	42800	45700	70900	20000	13300	1100000	2100000	2630
...Motorways km	0			126	649				34000	
...Highways total km	764000	1030000	54500	39800	66500	20000	15700	1030000	1970000	2760
...Paved km	568000	170000	4080	3040	64400	1600	1670	170000	960000	
...Gravel km		648000	2540	32000	2060	3700	3670	648000	1010000	
...Improved earth km	0	211000		11000	10900	2300	10400	211000		
...Unimproved earth km	196000		47900			12400				
...Ownership car/1000 cap	56	1	68	12	313	7	3	1	3	13
...Railways km	75500	54000	2360	618	535	5110	642	54000	61900	
Telecom: # AM stations	1050	274	4	2	19	11	2	274	96	
...# of cable systems		0	0	15	50	3	2	0	2	
...# of TV stations	310	202	3	2	4	2	1	202	274	2
...# of FM stations	1050	6	40	51	7	61		6	4	
...# of SAT earth stations	4		5		49				3	1
...# of daily papers	26									9
...Television/1000 cap	294				528					
...Radios/1000 pop		1780	133	139	392	243	39	1780	2280	378
...Telephones/1000 pop	157	27	36	11	855	4	16	27	27	7
...Digital % 93	9	69	49	82	46	3	76	69	62	
...Main Lines/1000 pop	162	17	78	82	623		2	17	30	4
...Cellular subs/cap	0.1	21	52	0	87		21	21	9	
...Pagers/cap		0.6			14		0.6	0.6	10	
Piped water, % dwellings		8	62	90	97	65	57	8	99	
Food: Sugar/cap		48			284	135		48	54	
...Protein 85 grm/day/cap		62		52	95	62	54	62		
...Calories/cap/day		2630	1840	2510	3510	2070	2020	2630	2200	
...Meat prod/cap 88	0.1		0		0.3					
Energy: Consumption/cap	6290	819	823	171	4420	64	25	819	307	154
...Electricity/cap		488		216	6360	42	26	488	319	49

Characteristics	Duala-Landa-B.	Dujia	Dutch	Dyola	Edo	Egyptian	English	Estonian	Euro-nesian	European
Macroecon: GNP/capita	1160	417	20200	295	314	730	16700	6410	900	8890
..Saving rate	20	28	21	-5	23	17	17			22
..Inflation rate	-2	6	2	-1	45	16	3	3	10	16
..Convert currency (1=yes)		1	1				1	1		1
Communist, former (1=yes)	0	1	0		0	0	0	1	0	0
Labor: Unemployment, %	25			0.8	28	22				8
..Nonemployment, %	66	53	54	70	60	73	55		83	65
..Agriculture, %	74	60	4	73	54	34	2		67	13
..Industry, %	11	30	46	13	19	20	27			35
..Services, %	15	10	50	16	27	46	72			53
..Unionization, %	45	65	40	30	87	50	40			28
Air Trans: # of aircraft	0.4	284	494	1			618	50	0	131
..# aircraft/cap	56	0.2	18		0.5	0.9	11	20	3	5
..# of airports	10	330	1090	27	57	92	498	42	14	1410
Runways: Permanent Surf			351	6	76	66	249		3	163
..Large	5	26	3	4	33	44	37		1	1
..Medium	21	90	26	8	15	24	133		0	26
..Small		200	257		22					279
Roads: Total km	52200	1100000	701000	10600	108000	51900	357000	30200	2090	280000
..Motorways km			1540		115		3090	0	0	361
..Highways total km	65000	1030000	695000	12600	108000	51900	363000	30300	2040	277000
..Paved km	2680	170000	550000	1370	30000	17900	339000	29200	375	136000
..Gravel km	32300	648000	5400	2890	25400	2500	100	0		37000
..Improved earth km		211000	51000			13500		1100		100000
..Unimproved earth km	30000	54000	168000	8340	52600	18000		125		41500
..Ownership car/1000 cap	6		466	4	4	19	367			194
Railways km	1050		149000	484	3510	5110	16600	1030		51300
Telecom: # AM stations	1	274	684	2	35	39	225	1	1	254
..# of cable systems			5				40		1	0.8
..# of TV stations	1	202	48	2	28	5	207	3	0	171
..# of FM stations			31		17	41	525		1	4
..# of SAT earth stations	1		4			6	5		0	2
..# of daily papers	1	6	91		35	17	12		1	172
..Television/1000 cap	2		579	0.8	29	98	479	158	36	278
..Radios/1000 pop	22	1780	692	38	79	174	993	380	437	558
..Telephones/1000 pop	89	27	711	44	8	46	523	238	47	265
..Digital % 93			52			47	100	5		51
..Main Lines/1000 pop	6	69	592	6	3		492	252	100	233
..Cellular subs/cap	6	17	48	81	0.5	0.3	45	9	43	15
..Pagers/cap	0	0.6	30	5			14			8
Piped water, % dwellings	30	21	99	0.4	17	60	99		9	81
Food: Sugar/cap	26	48	298	154	23	233	293		132	249
..Protein 85 grm/day/cap	47	62	98	56	47	81	88		63	101
..Calories/cap/day	2040	2630	3510	2100	2110	3310	3220		2460	3190
..Meat prod/cap 88	0		0.1	0			0	0.1		0.1
Energy: Consumption/cap	254	819	9640	44	207	739	5040		357	3270
..Electricity/cap	225	488	15500	37	111	705	5610	14400	255	4490

Characteristics	Ewa-Adja	Ewe	Fang	Fijian	Finnish	Fleming	Fon	Forros	French	Fulani
Macroecon:: GNP/capita	421	425	1550	1900	25900	19200	430	320	20700	416
::Saving rate	14	18	25	18	24	14	0.5	-20	19	14
::Inflation rate	3	1	-1	6	2	3	1	-25	2	29
::Convert currency (1=yes)	1	0	0	1	1	1	1	0	1	0.9
::Communist, former (1=yes)	0	0	0	0	0	0	0	0	0	0
Labor: Unemployment, %	2	0.5	25	6	9	9	63	83	10	26
::Nonemployment, %	68	78	68	68	49	59	60		57	63
::Agriculture, %	75	55	70	44	9	3	38		8	65
::Industry, %	20	20	14	19	42	28			46	17
::Services, %		25	13	2	80	69	75		46	23
::Unionization, %		13	39	3	50	47	0		21	24
Air Trans:# of aircraft	0.3	3	6	25	173	42	6	10	243	34
::# aircraft/cap	0.8	6	2	20	65	24		79	6	0.6
::# of airports	9	0.5	53	0	22	14	0	2	570	56
Runways: Permanent Surf	2	10	9	1	28	3	6	2	269	22
::Large	0	5	0.8	2			0	0	2	2
::Medium	2	0	4	4	22	42	4	2	35	0.6
::Small		1	19		28	14	7		156	10
Roads: Total km	7570	7	41200	4560	139000	3	7420		795000	18
::Motorways km	0	28300	51000	3300	284	128000	5050	380	6530	72400
::Highways total km	6460	0	2360	1590	108000	1630	920		1440000	88
::Paved km	1760	32300	27500	1290	40800	103000	2600	300	774000	73400
::Gravel km		6080			37000	38000	1530	200	11900	18000
::Improved earth km	4700	26200	26300	420	40600	51000			748000	21000
::Unimproved earth km	13		8	47	387	398	8	100	170000	8390
::Ownership car/1000 cap	520	4	896	620	7560	841	607	22	429	38100
Railways km	0	953	9	7	13	5	2	0	52000	4
Telecom: # AM stations	0	4	9	0	266	32	2	0	139	2340
::# of cable systems	3	0	0	0	118	39	2	2	21	22
::# of TV stations	0	4	1	1	98	33	0	1	734	0.8
::# of FM stations	2	1	9	1	497	447	5	0	697	17
::# of SAT earth stations		3	2	2	979	516	78	250	4	11
::# of daily papers	6	15	23	32	591	54	61	24	85	2
::Television/1000 cap	214	185	117	597	66	471	4		429	21
::Radios/1000 pop	5	6	9	96	582	16		21	835	26
::Telephones/1000 pop	98	3	100		123	23	25		705	66
::Digital % 93	5	0.2	0.1	380	12	100	50		86	77
::Main Lines/1000 pop		41	30	64	95	293	2190	51	577	77
::Cellular subs/cap	0.3	38	41	2900	327	105	50	2390	22	0.4
::Pagers/cap		1730	49		96	3850	39			25
Piped water, % dwellings	123	0	2110	481	3080	0.1		271	100	41
Food: Sugar/cap	52	115	0	598	0.1	5790		126	294	49
::Protein 85 grm/day/cap	2220	322	309		5840	7010			109	2090
::Calories/cap/day	0		290		12800				3290	0
::Meat prod/cap 88	70								0.1	164
Energy: Consumption/cap	81								4710	99
::Electricity/cap									8560	

Characteristics	Fur	Ga-Adangme	Gagauz	Galician	Ganda	Garifuna	Gbaya	Georgian	German	Gibral-tarian
Macroecon: GNP/capita	440	425	3830	13200	300	1970	440	4500	21500	4600
..Saving rate	3	2	21	17	23	7	-9	21	23	4
..Inflation rate	200	18	42	5		2	6	62	6	
..Convert currency (1=yes)	0		0.4	1		0	1		1	
..Communist, former (1=yes)	0		0.6	0				1	0	0
Labor: Unemployment, %	30	0.5	5	18		12	30			
..Nonemployment, %	76	78	58	100	77	74	76	49	55	53
..Agriculture, %	78	55	41	16	90	12	72	26	8	
..Industry, %	9	20	21	28		10		31	40	40
..Services, %	13	25	29	56		44		29	53	
..Unionization, %	0	13	10	10	3	3	1	10	44	1
Air Trans: # of aircraft	18	8	52	210	6			52	230	32
..# aircraft/cap	0.7	0.5	0.9	5	0.3	0	0.6	0.9	4	1
..# of airports	72	10	109	105	35	2	66	109	614	
Runways: Permanent Surf	8	5	65	60	5		4	65	242	1
..Large	0	0	3	4	1				4	0
..Medium	5		30	22			0	30	37	
..Small	31	7	27	25	3		2	27	83	1
Roads: Total km	20000	28300	37700	158000	28200	2000	24400	35800	646000	
..Motorways km	0	0	361	2290				25	8070	50
..Highways total km	20000	32300	33000	151000	26200	2710	22000	34400	512000	50
..Paved km	1600	6080	19600	63000	1970	500	458	29400	173000	50
..Gravel km	3700	26200	7220	85400	5850	1600		496	1090000	
..Improved earth km	2300		1750			300	10500	120	408000	
..Unimproved earth km	12400		4390		18400	310	11000	4330	100000	
..Ownership car/1000 cap	7	4	38	294		85	15	76	354	
Railways km	5110	953	4330	15400	1270	0		1780	39900	1000
Telecom: # AM stations	1	4	15	190	10	6	0	15	143	
..# of cable systems	1	0	1	22		5				
..# of TV stations	0	4	357	100	9	0	1	357	216	0
..# of FM stations	3	1	94	406	0		1	94	434	4
..# of SAT earth stations	0	1	2	5			1		13	6
..# of daily papers	2	3	8	102	4				366	1
..Television/1000 cap	61	15	174	389	8	165	5	145	529	241
..Radios/1000 pop	243	185	119	286	22	506	57	174	408	1170
..Telephones/1000 pop		6	162	396		150	2	119	562	313
..Digital % 93			46	41		100		99	40	
..Main Lines/1000 pop	3	3	172	392	60	157		12	392	
..Cellular subs/cap		0.2		10	2			100	23	
..Pagers/cap				4				2	8	
Food: Piped water, % dwellings	65	41	99	91	29	28	8	99	96	97
..Sugar/cap	135	38	230	293	54	303	44	230	299	501
..Protein 85 grm/day/cap	62		88	97		69		88	99	
..Calories/cap/day	2070	1730	3150	3360	2220	2580	1940	3150	3420	
..Meat prod/cap 88	0	0	0	0.1		0	0	0	0.1	
Energy: Consumption/cap	64	115	1030	2490	25	783	47	1030	5060	600
..Electricity/cap	42	322	1850	3860	31	525	33	2540	6880	6400

Characteristics	Gilaki	Gilber-tese	Gio	Gisu	Gola	Grebo	Greek	Green-landic	Grosi	Guiana Chinese
Macroecon: GNP/capita	6150	732	430	300	430	430	8720	9000	350	4390
Saving rate	39	6	6	23	6	6	19		-2	4
Inflation rate	23	1					15	2	5	
Convert currency (1=yes)	0	0	0	0	0	0	1		1	0
Communist, former (1=yes)	0		0	0	0	0	0			
Labor: Unemployment, %	25	3	0		0	0	8	0	0	14
Nonemployment, %	76	90	43		43	43	63	9	16	81
Agriculture, %	33		82	77	82	82	27		66	
Industry, %	27		82	90	82	82	30		82	
Services, %	40						42			
Unionization, %		32					18		1	7
Air Trans: # of aircraft	48		2	3	2	2	51	35	2	0
# aircraft/cap	0.8		0.3	0.6	0.3	0.3	5		0.2	0
# of airports	214	21	66	35	66	66	102	11	48	0
Runways: Permanent Surf	81	4	2	1	2	2	83	5	2	4
Large	16	0		3			0.2	0	2	
Medium	16	0		10			19	2	8	1
Small	71	5	1		1	1	27	2		1
Roads: Total km	139000	640	5410	28200	5410	5410	65000	80	13100	1100
Motorways km	490	0	0	26200	0	0	347		0	680
Highways total km	140000	640	10100	1970	10100	10100	60500	80	16500	680
Paved km	42700		603	5850	603	603	24600		1300	510
Gravel km	46900			18400			13100		7400	
Improved earth km	49400						5570		7800	
Unimproved earth km	1200						5860			
Ownership car/1000 cap	35	0.8		1			183			170
Railways km	4730		485	1270	485	485	5880		621	
Telecom: # AM stations	77	1	3	10	3	3	40	0	2	5
# of cable systems	0	0	0	0	0	0	8	5	0	0
# of TV stations	28	0	5	9	5	5	332	4	2	9
# of FM stations	3	0	4	9	4	4	30	7	1	7
# of SAT earth stations	3	1	1	1	1	1	2	1	3	1
# of daily papers	17		1	4	1	1	138		5	
Television/1000 cap	66	159	2	8	2	2	235	85	17	158
Radios/1000 pop	178	210	18	22	18	18	420	365	2	789
Telephones/1000 pop	65	22	185	4	185	185	473	327	92	327
Digital % 93			9	60	9	9	56		3	
Main Lines/1000 pop	80			2			479	333	3	494
Cellular subs/cap	0		2		2	2	17			
Pagers/cap							4			
Piped water, % dwellings	49	68		29			82		24	
Food: Sugar/cap	139		45	54	45	45	288		34	93
Protein 85 grm/day/cap	86		43		43	43	113		63	
Calories/cap/day	3310	2940	2360	2220	2360	2360	3650		2050	2750
Meat prod/cap 88	0			25						0
Energy: Consumption/cap	1650	152	130		130	130	3240	3960	29	2610
Electricity/cap	886	104	334	31	334	334	3650	3450	16	2690

Characteristics	Guianese Creole	Gurage	Gurma	Gurung	Gypsy	Han Chinese	Hani	Hausa	Haya	Hazara-Dari
Macroecon: GNP/capita	4390	130	402	200	4000	417	417	318	260	200
:Saving rate	4	4	9	9	26	28	28	21	12	13
:Inflation rate		8	1	0	118	6	6	36	19	
:Convert currency (1=yes)	0	0	0	0	0.4	1	1	0	0	0
Communist, former (1=yes)		0	0				1	0	0	1
Labor: Unemployment, %	14		6	61	7	2	2	31	25	
:Nonemployment, %	81	66	71	93	52	53	53	62	97	74
:Agriculture, %		80	70		25	60	60	60	90	80
:Industry, %	7		20		32	30	30	19		
:Services, %	0	2	25		42	10	10	27	15	
:Unionization, %	0	25	7	0		65	65	47	8	0
Air Trans: # of aircraft	10	0.5	4	2	69	284	284			0
:# aircraft/cap	4	123	0.5	1	5	0.2	0.2	0.5	0.3	0
:# of airports	0	9	21	0	249	330	330	68	104	41
Runways: Permanent Surf					63	260	260	29	12	9
:Large	1		3	0	0.1	0	0	0.8		0
:Medium		13	2	0	17	90	90	13	3	0
:Small	1	38	5	228	17	200	200	21	43	18
Roads: Total km	1100	39500	16000	1300	48200	1100000	1100000	96300	82000	19000
:Motorways km	680	0	0		160	0	0	166	0	0
:Highways total km	680	44300	17900	418	50100	1030000	1030000	96300	81900	21000
:Paved km	510	3650	3080	515	31200	170000	170000	25300	3600	2800
:Gravel km		9650	26200	371	19500	648000	648000	22900	5600	1650
:Improved earth km	170	3000	7400		50	211000	211000		72700	
:Unimproved earth km		28000	6030	5	6620			44300		16500
Ownership car/1000 cap		1	7	0	21	1	1	0.8		
Railways km	5	835	693	1	6830	54000	54000	2900	3780	2
Telecom: # AM stations		4	3	0	16	274	274	31	12	17
:# of cable systems	0	0	0	1	0	0	0		0	5
:# of TV stations	9	1			20	202	202	2	2	0
:# of FM stations	7	0	3		9			15	4	1
:# of SAT earth stations	1	1		0	1	6	6	3	2	0
:# of daily papers			1	0	21	1780	1780		3	1
:Television/1000 cap	158	3	9	0	225	27	27	29	29	4
:Radios/1000 pop	789	80	148	9	189	69	69	34	6	3
:Telephones/1000 pop	327	5	5	12	183	17	17	74	43	78
:Digital % 93		39	95	66	31	21	21	65	3	2
:Main Lines/1000 pop	494	3	4	2	182	0.6	0.6			0
:Cellular subs/cap			0.2		0.6	8	8	0.5		2
:Pagers/cap										
Piped water, % dwellings	93	85	24		81	48	48	17	30	25
Food: Sugar/cap		25	70		273			23		26
:Protein 85 grm/day/cap		55	50		105	62	62	50	55	64
:Calories/cap/day	2750	1660	2010	2030	3470	2630	2630	2150	2210	2290
:Meat prod/cap 88		0	0		0.1	0	0	0	0	0
Energy: Consumption/cap	2610	24	73	32	4660	819	819	182	36	232
:Electricity/cap	2690	17	142	973	4100	488	488	100	36	69

Characteristics	Hehet-Bena	Herero	Hottentot	Hui-Vighur	Humbe-Nyaneka	Hungarian	Hutu	Ibibio	Icelander	Igbo
Macroecon: GNP/capita	260	1300	2770	417	950	5190	276	314	23600	314
Saving rate	12	·	25	28	28	26	7	23	24	23
Inflation rate	19	12	15	6	92	49	8	45	·	45
Convert currency (1=yes)	0	·	·	1	0	0	0	0	1	0
Communist, former (1=yes)	0	0	0	1	1	1	0	0	0	0
Labor: Unemployment, %	25	40	25	2	19	14	·	28	3	28
Nonemployment, %	97	68	70	53	73	50	60	60	53	60
Agriculture, %	90	·	59	60	75	19	92	54	·	54
Industry, %	·	·	23	30	15	45	·	19	·	19
Services, %	·	18	18	10	10	34	·	27	55	27
Unionization, %	15	·	·	·	16	47	·	8	60	8
Air Trans: # of aircraft	·	·	5	65	28	37	·	57	20	57
# aircraft/cap	0.3	·	·	·	·	·	0.2	·	·	·
# of airports	104	137	100	284	309	111	7	76	71	76
Runways: Permanent Surf	12	21	8	330	3	24	2	33	94	33
Large	3	·	·	260	·	2	0	·	4	·
Medium	4	4	1	90	2	2	·	1	·	1
Small	43	63	27	200	15	17	1	15	12	15
Roads: Total km	82000	42800	13500	1100000	72400	44300	10300	108000	11400	108000
Motorways km	81900	·	·	·	·	307	·	115	·	115
Highways total km	3600	54500	11500	1030000	73800	121000	5310	108000	12300	108000
Paved km	5600	4080	1600	170000	8580	35900	435	30000	166	30000
Gravel km	72700	2540	1700	648000	29400	6230	2050	25400	1280	25400
Improved earth km	·	47900	5180	·	·	404	3000	·	·	·
Unimproved earth km	2	·	3040	211000	35900	16700	2700	52600	10900	52600
Ownership car/1000 cap	·	68	800	1	14	159	2	4	464	4
Railways km	3780	2360	·	54000	3190	9590	·	3510	·	3510
Telecom: # AM stations	2	4	7	274	17	35	2	35	19	35
# of cable systems	0	0	0	·	·	0	·	·	2	·
# of TV stations	2	3	0	202	6	36	1	1	13	1
# of FM stations	4	40	13	·	13	13	·	28	30	28
# of SAT earth stations	3	·	·	6	2	·	·	17	·	17
# of daily papers	·	5	1	1780	·	11	·	·	6	·
Television/1000 cap	29	133	12	27	6	368	0.4	3	421	3
Radios/1000 cap	6	36	119	69	19	482	47	35	586	35
Telephones/1000 pop	43	49	37	17	·	172	3	29	542	29
Digital % 93	3	78	100	·	6	26	·	79	66	79
Main Lines/1000 pop	·	52	43	21	5	166	100	8	581	8
Cellular subs/cap	·	·	·	0.6	·	5	0.3	0.3	73	0.3
Pagers/cap	·	·	·	8	·	32	0.1	0.5	25	0.5
Piped water, % dwellings	30	·	99	48	35	84	·	17	100	17
Food: Sugar/cap	55	62	268	·	70	374	15	23	433	23
Protein 85 grm/day/cap	·	·	70	62	45	102	59	47	127	47
Calories/cap/day	2210	1840	2230	2630	1930	3510	2040	2110	3150	2110
Meat prod/cap 88	·	·	0	0.1	·	0.1	·	0	0.1	0
Energy: Consumption/cap	36	823	425	819	89	3870	25	207	5660	207
Electricity/cap	36	·	834	488	215	3790	25	111	16660	111

Characteristics	Ijaw	Indian	Indo-Aryan	Indo-nesian	Iranian	Irish	Issa	Italian	Japanese	Javanese
Macroecon: GNP/capita	314	7070	369	6000	535	13400	1030	15100	26600	683
: Saving rate	23	23	22		12	7		19	32	20
: Inflation rate	45	11		4	11	3	3	0.8		8
: Convert currency (1=yes)	1	0.8	0		0	1			1	1
Communist, former (1=yes)			1		0	0	0		0	0
Labor: Unemployment, %	28	9	20	0	8	13		9	0	3
: Nonemployment, %	60	63	100	16	77	60	40	60	2	66
: Agriculture, %	54	22	67	72	53	11	68	15	8	56
: Industry, %	19	36	19		14	28		31	34	23
: Services, %	27	44	14		34	61		54	58	21
: Unionization, %	8	22	5		10	53		40	29	5
Air Trans: # of aircraft	57	643	93	1	40	200	1	146	407	216
: # aircraft/cap	0.5		0.1		0.5	8	2		3	1
: # of airports	76	1050	341	6	111	173	13	919	283	437
Runways: Permanent Surf	33	362	203	29	74	86	2	169	163	114
: Large	1	5	2	1	31	0.3	2	2	2	1
: Medium	15	30	59	0	43	12	5	32	33	12
: Small	22	194	87	1		44		156	71	64
Roads: Total km	108000	496000	2100000	6340	110000	171000	3070	615000	1140000	214000
: Motorways km	115	6060	34100		337	925		5800	4400	0
: Highways total km	108000	478000	1970000	6340	100000	173000	2900	560000	1150000	119000
: Paved km	30000	55700	1010000	634	39800	162000	2800	214000	747000	500
: Gravel km	25400	2210			22900	4870	2620	345000	368000	5400
: Improved earth km	52600	2450			29000			335000	171000	2400
: Unimproved earth km		3120			9160			8730		
: Ownership car/1000 cap	4	162	3	3	8	266	18	339	282	7
Railways km	3510	20600	61900		12500	6300	99	23500	28900	6830
Telecom: # AM stations	35	363	96	0	19	73	2	383	355	618
: # of cable systems	1	7	2	5	1	13		16	4	
: # of TV stations	28	519	274	0	29	122	1	92	12200	9
: # of FM stations	17	413	4	7	8	187	1	29	89	38
: # of SAT earth stations	3	6	3	3	3	8	2	8	5	5
: # of daily papers	6	132	2280	1	124			144	136	97
: Television/1000 cap	35	273	27	207	20	333	55	378	607	55
: Radios/1000 pop	29	589	62	566	80	616	70	290	718	140
: Telephones/1000 pop	79	238	9	236	17	397	23	441	552	11
: Digital % 93	8	89			43		100	50	28	77
: Main Lines/1000 pop	3	236	30	260	18	382	18	382	511	12
: Cellular subs/cap	0.5	23	39		0.5	28		27	23	0.4
: Pagers/cap		37			0.2	7		4	63	
Piped water, % dwellings	17	75	10	83	15	93		84	98	11
Food: Sugar/cap	23	311	99		144	293	188	312	174	109
: Protein 85 grm/day/cap	47	72	54		59	100		97	88	53
: Calories/cap/day	2110	2880	2200	2980	2240	3550		3300	2860	2510
: Meat prod/cap 88	0	0	0	0	0	0.1	0	0	0	0
Energy: Consumption/cap	207	3400	307	4760	445	4050	445	3210	4000	312
: Electricity/cap	111	2960	319	7230	423	4590	496	3680	6850	230

Characteristics	Jewish	Jola	Kalenjin	Kamba	Kanuri	Kara-kalpak	Kare	Karen	Kavango	Kazakh
Macroecon: GNP/capita	10400	805	376	376	311	2800	440	863	1300	3250
Saving rate	2	-10	14	14	20	600	-9	19		28
Inflation rate	60	2	9	9	36		6		12	128
Convert currency (1=yes)	0.2		1	1	1	0	1	0	1	0.1
Communist, former (1=yes)	0	0	0	0	0	1	0	0	0	1
Labor: Unemployment, %	9		16	16						
Nonemployment, %	70	4	65	65	31	7	30	10	40	53
Agriculture, %	42	68	78	78	62	63	76	64	68	30
Industry, %	50	77	9	9	60	39		65		31
Services, %	78		13	13	19	24	72	25		10
Unionization, %	36		4	4	27		1	10	18	65
Air Trans: # of aircraft	6	3	19	19	48		2	59		258
# aircraft/cap	59	0.4	0.7	0.7	0.5		0.6	17		
# of airports	28	25	249	249	69		66	0.4	137	305
Runways: Permanent Surf		10	21	21	29		4	85	21	235
Large	6		2	2	0.8		0	27		9
Medium	13	15	2	2	0		2	3	4	83
Small			46	46	13		22	38	63	181
Roads: Total km	56600	13900	54600	54600	96600	73100	24400	23500	42800	271000
Motorways km	0	0	0	0	157	0	0	0	0	0
Highways total km	46900	14000	64600	64600	96300	78400	22000	27000	54500	281000
Paved km	177000	3780	7000	7000	25400	67000	458	3200	4080	170000
Gravel km	145		4150	4150	22800			17000	2540	83400
Improved earth km	36000	10200	53400	53400			10500			27400
Unimproved earth km	141				44800	11400	11000	6100	47900	72200
Ownership car/1000 cap	4620	9	5	5	4	37	15		68	36
Railways km	21	1110	2390	2390	2910	3460		4250	2360	18100
Telecom: # AM stations	3	8	16	16	31		1	2		247
# of cable systems	20	3	0	0	0.8		0	0	4	0
# of TV stations	20	1	6	6	26	2	1	1	0	
# of FM stations	3		4	4	15		1	1	3	182
# of SAT earth stations	28	1	2	2	3		1	1	40	
# of daily papers			5	5	29		1	1		2
Television/1000 cap	276	3	9	9	33	279		2	5	257
Radios/1000 pop	281	35	34	34	73	149	57	24	133	227
Telephones/1000 pop	407	70	15	15	7	78	5	2	36	73
Digital % 93	18	9			59		100		49	107
Main Lines/1000 cap	288	74	1.0	1.0	0.5	76	2	2	78	91
Cellular subs/cap	11	2	0.1	0.1		0.2			52	113
Pagers/cap	32	0.1								0.2
Piped water, % dwellings	94	88	32	32	17			13	62	
Food: Sugar/cap	412	92	143	143	23		8	5		0.3
Protein 85 grm/day/cap	98	67	59	59	50		44	70		61
Calories/cap/day	3040	2340	2140	2140	2140		1940	2590	1840	65
Meat prod/cap 88						0			0	2650
Energy: Consumption/cap	3070	176	106	106	181		47	62		926
Electricity/cap	4480	104	129	129	98	2350	33	58	823	3900

Characteristics	Kebu-Akposo	Khmer	Kikuyu	Kimbundu	Kisii	Kissi	Klao	Kongo	Kono	Konzo
Macroecon: GNP/capita	421	524	376	950	376	450	430	370	330	238
: Saving rate	14	75	14	28	14	6		23	-5	21
: Inflation rate	13	0.1	9	92	9	34	6	3360	81	4000
: Convert currency (1=yes)		0.9				0.2		0.2		0
Communist, former (1=yes)	0	0	0		0	0	0		0	0
Labor: Unemployment, %	2	4	16	1	16					64
: Nonemployment, %	68	62	65	19	65	63	43	69	70	75
: Agriculture, %	75	71	78	73	78	81	82	75	75	13
: Industry, %	20	18	9	75	9	10	82	14	15	12
: Services, %		19	13	10	13	9	2	11		12
: Unionization, %		33	4	16	4	87	1	13	35	45
Air Trans: # of aircraft	.3	.7	19	28	19	8	.3	1	0	
: # aircraft/cap	0.8	0.1	0.7	3	0.7	1	66		12	
: # of airports	9	38	249	309	249	14	0.2	246	0	284
Runways: Permanent Surf	2	15	21	30	21	4		21		24
: Large	0	0.1	2	2	2		1	0.8	1	
: Medium	2	0.4	46	15	46	3		5	3	6
: Small		9		54		9	4	64		73
Roads: Total km	7570	28200	54600	72400	54600	25500	5410	123000	7450	145000
: Motorways km	0	0	0	0	0	0		0	0	0
: Highways total km	6460	23800	64600	73800	64600	25500	10100	125000	7400	147000
: Paved km	1760	6950	7000	8580	7000	1150	603	2440	1150	2800
: Gravel km		11100	4150	29400	4150	10400		39000	490	46200
: Improved earth km	4700		53400		53400	5760		5350	5760	
: Unimproved earth km	13	5750		35900		1600		82900		97500
: Ownership car/1000 cap	520	12	5	14	5		1	3	8	2
Railways km		1250	2390	3190	2390	848	485	4340	84	5010
Telecom: # AM stations	0	32	16	17	16	3	3	9		0
: # of cable systems	3	0	0	0	0	0	0	0	0	0
: # of TV stations	0	3	6	6	6	1	5	16	1	18
: # of FM stations	2	15	4	13	4	1	4	4	1	4
: # of SAT earth stations	1	0.5	2	2	2	0.8	1	1		1
: # of daily papers	6	5	5	1	5			4	0	4
: Television/1000 cap	214	26	9	6	9	64	18	2	10	
: Radios/1000 pop	127	127	34	195	34	3	185	96	208	103
: Telephones/1000 pop	98	99	15	5	15	91	9	3	5	1
: Digital % 93	95	77				2	2	2	91	
: Main Lines/1000 pop		8	10	5	10				4	1
: Cellular subs/cap		1	0.1		0.1					
: Pagers/cap		11								
Piped water, % dwellings		34	32	35	32	40		43	40	43
Food: Sugar/cap	123	28	143	70	143	64	45	36	30	24
: Protein 85 grm/day/cap	52	51	59	45	59	40	43	37	41	34
: Calories/cap/day	2220	2180	2140	1930	2140	1800	2360	2230	1870	2160
: Meat prod/cap 88	0	0	0	0	0	0	0	0	0	0
Energy: Consumption/cap	70	126	106	89	106	86	130	116	76	67
: Electricity/cap	81	139	129	215	129	76	334	153	50	151

Characteristics	Koranko	Korean	Kotoko	Kpelle	Kru	Kurd	Kuwaiti	Kyrgyz	Ladino	Lango
Macroecon: GNP/capita	330	4920	229	448	430	4140	16400	3040	1300	300
Saving rate	-5	26	-24	7	6	28	60		10	
Inflation rate	81	14	-2	23		43	8	1400	33	23
Convert currency (1=yes)	1	0.7		0		0.4	1	1	0	0
Communist, former (1=yes)	0	0.4	0		0	0.4	0		0	0
Labor: Unemployment, %		2				14	0		13	
Nonemployment, %	70	60	66	43	43	72	70	3	75	77
Agriculture, %	75	31	85	75	82	39	2	59	60	90
Industry, %	15	27		82	82	24	53	34	26	
Services, %		50				38	45	28	14	
Unionization, %	35	22	20	36		6	9		8	3
Air Trans: # of aircraft	0	167		9	2	45	5		8	
# aircraft/cap	0	2	0.3	0.8	0.3		7		0.8	0.3
# of airports	12	250	0.5	48	66	146	4		448	35
Runways: Permanent Surf	4	108	71			70	4		11	
Large	0	3		3	2	8	4		3	3
Medium	1	27	4	0	1	30	0	32000	19	10
Small	3	54	0	2	4	37	4	34200	13200	28200
Roads: Total km	7450	145000	4	6	5410	77200	4210	26200	26400	26200
Motorways km		2010	25	14100	10100	515	280		2870	1970
Highways total km	7400	150000	40000	17100	603	75900	3900	8020	11400	5850
Paved km	1150	16000	31300	794		29900	3900	3	12100	18400
Gravel km	490	79300	32	13000		28900		624	27	1
Improved earth km	5760	181000	7300	16000	485	19800	226		884	1270
Unimproved earth km		38900	24000		3	4090	3	1	91	
Ownership car/1000 cap	8	41	2	681	0	30	1	153	25	10
Railways km	84	10300	0	3	5	5400	3	16		0
Telecom: # AM stations	1	118	6	0	4	36		82	8	9
# of cable systems	0			4	1	2	281	85	45	1
# of TV stations	1	252	1	3	2	148	306	0.1	45	4
# of FM stations	1	89	1	1	18	37	201		25	8
# of SAT earth stations	1	114	1	2	185		167			22
# of daily papers	0	158	26	13	9	12	48		25	4
Television/1000 cap	10	378	15	130	2	107	58		30	60
Radios/1000 pop	208	257	0.9	7		159	220	0	296	2
Telephones/1000 pop	5	258		2	2	117	92	257	60	
Digital % 93	91	130				55	3080		2300	2220
Main Lines/1000 pop	4	95				125				
Cellular subs/cap	258	100				1			0.5	
Pagers/cap	130									
Piped water, % dwellings	40	95	41	55	45	66	58		30	29
Food: Sugar/cap	30	100	53	42	43	197	220		296	54
Protein 85 grm/day/cap	41	83	1660	2150	2360	85	92		60	2220
Calories/cap/day	1870	2980		115	130	3180	3080	0	2300	
Meat prod/cap 88	0		18	245	334	1250	8830		197	25
Energy: Consumption/cap	76	2450	14			1050	10100	257	240	31
Electricity/cap	50	2670								

Characteristics	Lao	Latvian	Lezgin	Li	Liechten-steiner	Limba	Lithua-nian	Lobi	Loma	Lomwe
Macroecon: GNP/capita	1660	6930	3830	417	31000	330	5980	583	430	200
: Saving rate	20	7		28	5	-5		8	6	13
: Inflation rate	6	1	1350	6		81	174	3		0
: Convert currency (1=yes)	0.2	1		1			1	0	0	
: Communist, former (1=yes)		1	1	1			1		0	
Labor: Unemployment, %		6		2	0.1		0.6	15		
: Nonemployment, %	49		50	53	30			62		96
: Agriculture, %	63	16	62	60	4	70	51	84	43	43
: Industry, %	21	41	32	30	54	75	18	8	82	23
: Services, %	17	47	26	10	41	15	42	7	82	17
: Unionization, %				65		35		11	2	0.5
Air Trans: # of aircraft	34			284		0		8	1	
: # aircraft/cap	0.6			0.2		0		0.6	0.3	0.5
: # of airports	105		0	330		12		46	66	48
Runways: Permanent Surf	43		0	260		4		5	2	6
: Large	0.8			0		0		0	0	0
: Medium	11			90		1		3	1	1
: Small	26			200		3		12	4	9
Roads: Total km	63400	58600	30400	1100000	250	7450	44300	34800	541	12200
: Motorways km	0	0	0	0	0	0	0	80	0	0
: Highways total km	41700	59500	36700	1030000	13100	7400	44400	32100	10100	13100
: Paved km	23700	33000	31800	170000		1150	35500	32490	603	2360
: Gravel km	7450		4900	648000		490		32000		251
: Improved earth km				211000		5760		7400		
: Unimproved earth km	7300	26500		1			8900	9460		10500
: Ownership car/1000 cap	16	101	33	1	603	8	142		1	2
Railways km	3210	2400	2070	54000	19	84	3030	635	485	789
Telecom: # AM stations	169			274		1	13	8	3	10
: # of cable systems				0		0		3	0	0
: # of TV stations	9			202		1	3	1	5	0
: # of FM stations	83			6		1	26	8	4	17
: # of SAT earth stations	2					0	1	9	1	2
: # of daily papers	26			1780				2	2	1
: Television/1000 cap	92		151	27	343	10	339	33	18	2
: Radios/1000 pop	141	419	175	69	654	208		75	185	48
: Telephones/1000 pop	40	311	98	17	846	91	240	87	9	6
: Digital % 93	40			21	99			5	2	52
: Main Lines/1000 pop	5	216	101	0.6		4	344	0		4
: Cellular subs/cap	11	3	0				1	2		
: Pagers/cap				48						
Piped water, % dwellings	42			62		40		24	45	26
Food: Sugar/cap	113			6		30		68		95
: Protein 85 grm/day/cap	51			62		41		58	43	68
: Calories/cap/day	2320			2630		1870		2310	2360	2370
: Meat prod/cap 88	0			0		76		0	0	0
Energy: Consumption/cap	537	0.1	0	819		50	0.1	107	130	35
: Electricity/cap	715	2160	3040	488	5260		6560	105	334	68

Characteristics	Lotuko	Luba	Luchasi	Luena	Lugbara	Luhya	Lumbe	Lunda	Luo	Luri
Macroecon: GNP/capita	440	238	950	950	238	376	950	950	376	6150
: Saving rate	3	21	28	28	21	14	28	28	14	39
: Inflation rate	200	4000	92	92	4000	9	92	92	9	23
: Convert currency (1=yes)	0	0	0	0	0	0	0	0	0	0
Communist, former (1=yes)	0	0	1	1	0	1	1	1	1	0
Labor: Unemployment, %	30		19	19		16	19	19	16	25
: Nonemployment, %	76	64	73	73	64	65	73	73	65	76
: Agriculture, %	78	75	75	75	75	78	75	75	78	33
: Industry, %	9	13	15	15	13	9	15	15	9	27
: Services, %	13	12	10	10	12	13	10	10	13	40
: Unionization, %	0	45	16	16	45	4	16	16	4	0
Air Trans: # of aircraft	18		28	28		19	28	28	19	48
: # aircraft/cap	0.7					0.7			0.7	0.8
: # of airports	72	284	309	309	284	249	309	309	249	214
Runways: Permanent Surf	8	24	30	30	24	21	30	30	21	81
: Large	0	1	2	2	1	2	2	2	2	16
: Medium	5	6	15	15	6	2	15	15	2	16
: Small	31	73	54	54	73	46	54	54	46	71
Roads: Total km	20000	145000	72400	72400	145000	54600	72400	72400	54600	139000
: Motorways km	0	0	0	0	0	0	0	0	0	490
: Highways total km	20000	147000	73800	73800	147000	64600	73800	73800	64600	140000
: Paved km	1600	2800	8580	8580	2800	7000	8580	8580	7000	42700
: Gravel km	3700	46200	29400	29400	46200	4150	29400	29400	4150	46900
: Improved earth km	2300									49400
: Unimproved earth km	12400	97500	35900	35900	97500	53400	35900	35900	53400	1200
: Ownership car/1000 cap	7	2	14	14	2	5	14	14	5	35
Railways km	5110	5010	3190	3190	5010	2390	3190	3190	2390	4730
Telecom: # AM stations	11	10	17	17	10	16	17	17	16	77
: # of cable systems	0	0	0	0	0	0	0	0	0	0
: # of TV stations	3	18	6	6	18	6	6	6	6	28
: # of FM stations	2	4	13	13	4	4	13	13	4	3
: # of SAT earth stations	0	1	2	2	1	2	2	2	2	1
: # of daily papers	2	4	1	1	4	5	1	1	5	17
: Television/1000 cap	61		6	6		9	6	6	9	66
: Radios/1000 pop	243	103	19	19	103	34	19	19	34	178
: Telephones/1000 pop			5	5		15	5	5	15	65
: Digital % 93	4									80
: Main Lines/1000 pop	3	1	5	5	1	10	5	5	10	
: Cellular subs/cap						0.1			0.1	
: Pagers/cap										
Piped water, % dwellings	65	43	35	35	43	32	35	35	32	49
Food: Sugar/cap	135	24	70	70	24	143	70	70	143	139
: Protein 85 grm/day/cap	62	34	45	45	34	59	45	45	59	86
: Calories/cap/day	2070	2160	1930	1930	2160	2140	1930	1930	2140	3310
: Meat prod/cap 88	0	0	0	0	0	0	0	0	0	0
Energy: Consumption/cap	64	67	89	89	67	106	89	89	106	1650
: Electricity/cap	42	151	215	215	151	129	215	215	129	886

Characteristics	Luxem-burger	Macedo-nian	Madurese	Magars	Maka	Makonde	Makua	Malagasy	Malawi	Malay
Macroecon: GNP/capita	28700	3780	680	179	1150	260	116	233	115	3570
: Saving rate	38	19	20	9	21	12	3	4	3	24
: Inflation rate	2	49	8	9	-2	19	39	13	39	3
: Convert currency (1=yes)	1		1	0	1	1	1	1	1	1
Communist, former (1=yes)	0	1								0
Labor: Unemployment,%			3	0	2					
: Nonemployment,%	55	18	66	60	25	25	50	9	50	60
: Agriculture, %	1	70	56	91	68	97	53	63	53	27
: Industry, %	42	12	23		74	90	85	90	85	38
: Services, %	45	38	21		12	9	9	19	9	35
: Unionization, %	56	45	5		14	15	2	32	2	9
Air Trans: # of aircraft	13	11	216		43	8	8	4	8	50
: # aircraft/cap	33	63		0.2	0.5	0.3	0.4	0.6	0.4	
: # of airports	2	7	437	37	55	104	195	148	195	110
Runways: Permanent Surf	1	234	114	5	12	12	27	30	27	34
: Large	0	99								8
: Medium	0	0	12	1	0.9	3	5	3	5	19
: Small	0	19	64	8	5	43	26	34	26	
Roads: Total km	5090	21	214000	7080	21	82000	26100	34	26100	3
: Motorways km	84	19700			49000			34700		43300
: Highways total km	5110	913	120000	7080	61100	81000	26500	40000	26500	3
: Paved km	5000	17200		2900	2540	3600	4590	4690	4590	30100
: Gravel km	57	9980		1660	30200	5600	829	811	829	20400
: Improved earth km	56	3040			25350	72700	21100	34500	21100	720
: Unimproved earth km	479	748	7	0.8	28300		3			
: Ownership car/1000 cap	271	3950	6840	52	6	3780	3200	2	3210	4380
Railways km	2	105	618	88	1030	12	29	959	29	93
Telecom: # AM stations	3	833			10			17		2210
: # of cable systems	3	24	9	1		2	1		1	52
: # of TV stations		49	38	0	0	4	4	1	4	
: # of FM stations		16	2	1	1	3	5	3	5	28
: # of SAT earth stations	4		97	59	10	1	2	5	2	17
: # of daily papers	430	19	55	25	2	29	21	20	21	
: Television/1000 cap	536	201	140		21	6		213		2
: Radios/1000 pop	559	313	11	4	89	43	4		4	39
: Telephones/1000 pop	82	220	77	88			4		4	148
: Digital % 93	613		12	5	6		4	0	4	388
: Main Lines/1000 pop	27	185	0.4		0			3		148
: Cellular subs/cap	18	8				30				90
: Pagers/cap	100	3	11	66	30	55	27	23	27	166
Piped water, % dwellings		80	109	14	31	2210	28	49	28	20
Food: Sugar/cap		335	53	52	47		1610	56	1610	16
: Protein 85 grm/day/cap		110	2510	2050	2080			2410		87
: Calories/cap/day	3710	3650				36	33		33	266
: Meat prod/cap 88		0.1	311	24	262	36	56	40	56	60
Energy: Consumption/cap	12500	4100	311	24	262			40		1490
: Electricity/cap	13400	3490	228	35	220			47		1380

Characteristics	Malay Christian	Malay Coastal	Malay Muslim	Malinke	Maltese	Mambwe	Manchu-Tibetian	Mandara	Mande	Mandingo
Macroecon: GNP/capita	860	680	860	496	7600	420	417	1160	350	805
·· Saving rate	24	20	24	6	26	155	28	20	-2	-10
·· Inflation rate	8	8	8	12	3	0	6	-2	5	-2
·· Convert currency (1=yes)	1	1	1	0.4			1		1	1
Communist, former (1=yes)	0	0	0	0						
Labor: Unemployment, %	10	3	10	14	4	72	2	25	16	4
·· Nonemployment, %	64	66	64	62	65	58	53	66	66	68
·· Agriculture, %	46	56	46	80	2	11	60	74	82	77
·· Industry, %	20	23	20	10	24	31	30	11		
·· Services, %	34	21	34	7	43	10	10	15		
·· Unionization, %	24	5	24	67	40	12	65	45	1	3
Air Trans: # of aircraft	53	216	53	8	47		284	5		
·· # aircraft/cap	0.8		0.8	1			0.2	0.4	0.2	0.4
·· # of airports	278	437	278	25	19	117	330	56	48	25
Runways: Permanent Surf	72	114	72	5	1	13	260	10		10
·· Large							10		2	
·· Medium	9	12	9	0	0	4	90	5		1
·· Small	53	64	53	3	1	22	200	21	8	15
Roads: Total km	162000	214000	162000	29200	1550	3740	1100000	52200	13100	13900
·· Motorways km	0	0	0	0	0	0	0	0	0	0
·· Highways total km	156000	120000	156000	27700	1290	36400	1030000	65000	16500	14000
·· Paved km	29000		29000	1800	1180	6500	170000	2680	1300	3780
·· Gravel km	77000		77000	14600		7000	648000	32300		
·· Improved earth km						22900	211000		7400	
·· Unimproved earth km	50000		50000	11800				30000	7800	10200
·· Ownership car/1000 cap	7	7	7	6	311	9	1	6		
Railways km	592	6840	592	733		1720	54000	1050	621	9
Telecom: # AM stations	267	618	267		8	11	274	11	2	1110
·· # of cable systems	33	9	33						0	8
·· # of TV stations	55	38	55	4	2	9	11	11	2	3
·· # of FM stations	30	2	30	5	4	5	2	2	1	1
·· # of SAT earth stations	41	97	41	1		2	202			0
·· # of daily papers	45	55	45	3	3		6	22	3	3
·· Television/1000 cap	17	140	17	27	741	3	1780	22	5	35
·· Radios/1000 pop	36	17	36	60	398	25	27	89	17	70
·· Telephones/1000 pop	14	77	14	6	510	27	69	6	92	9
·· Digital % 93	0.4	12	0.4	83	100	12	17		3	74
·· Main Lines/1000 pop		0.4		0.1	471		21	6		0.1
·· Cellular subs/cap	3		3		21	10	0.6	0		
·· Pagers/cap		1					8			
·· Piped water, % dwellings	48	11	48	113	90	63	48	30	24	88
Food: Sugar/cap	184	109	184	48	371	101	62	26	34	92
·· Protein 85 grm/day/cap	53	53	53		87	58		47	63	67
·· Calories/cap/day	2350	2510	2350	2080	2880	2130	2630	2040	2050	2340
·· Meat prod/cap 88	0	0	0	0	0	0	0	0	0	0
Energy: Consumption/cap	295	311	295	100	2050	198	819	254	29	176
·· Electricity/cap	402	228	402	94	3060	909	488	225	16	104

Characteristics	Mandyako	Mano	Manx (Norse-C.)	Manzan-Darani	Maori	Maravi	Masa	Masalit Maba	Maya	Mbaka
Macroecon: GNP/capita	219	430	7500	6150	14900	244	229	229	1970	440
Saving rate	-11	6	7	39	21	7	-24	-24	7	-9
Inflation rate	50			23	2	41	2	2		6
Convert currency (1=yes)	0	0	0		1	0	1	1	0	1
Communist, former (1=yes)	0				0		0	0		
Labor: Unemployment, %	17			25	10				12	
Nonemployment, %	58	43		76	54	91	66	66	74	30
Agriculture, %	90	82	1	33	11	46	85	85		76
Industry, %			63	27	41	21				72
Services, %				40	48	20				
Unionization, %					43	10				
Air Trans: # of aircraft	2	2	1	48	40	6	20	20	12	1
# aircraft/cap	.2	0.3	0	0.8	11	0.6	0.5	0.5	2	0.6
# of airports	34	66	1	214	118	62	71	71	10	66
Runways: Permanent Surf	4			81	34	0.2			44	4
Large	0	2		16			4	4	3	0
Medium	1	0		16	2	12				2
Small	5	4		71	43	12	25	25	2	22
Roads: Total km	3500	5410	640	139000	9320	17200	40000	40000	2000	24400
Motorways km	0	0		490	0	0	0	0	0	0
Highways total km	3220	10100	640	140000	92600	17800	31300	31300	2710	22000
Paved km	2700	603		42700	49500	3190	32	32	500	458
Gravel km				46900	43100	1600	7300	7300	1600	
Improved earth km				49400		22900			300	10500
Unimproved earth km	520			1200		10500	24000	24000	310	11000
Ownership car/1000 cap	4	1		35	372	3	2	2	85	15
Railways km	0	485	36	4730	4380	974	0	0	0	0
Telecom: # AM stations	2	3	1	77	64	10	6	6	6	1
# of cable systems	0	0		0		0	0	0	0	0
# of TV stations	1	5		28	14	2	1	1	1	1
# of FM stations	3	4	4	3	2	15	1	1	5	1
# of SAT earth stations	2	1	4		35	2	1	1		1
# of daily papers	0.8	2		17			1	1	1	3
Television/1000 cap	32	18	323	66	372	6	26	26	165	57
Radios/1000 pop		185		178	890	44			506	
Telephones/1000 pop	7	9	323	65	717	52	15	15	150	5
Digital % 93					96				100	100
Main Lines/1000 pop	7	2	385	80	466	5	0.9	0.9	157	2
Cellular subs/cap				0	45				3	
Pagers/cap					17					
Piped water, % dwellings		45		49	99	33			28	8
Food: Sugar/cap	32	43		139	374	96	41	41	303	44
Protein 85 grm/day/cap	46			86		66	53	53	69	
Calories/cap/day	2130	2360		3310	3410	2320	1660	1660	2580	1940
Meat prod/cap 88	0	0		0	0.4	0	0	0	0	
Energy: Consumption/cap	91	130	2710	1650	5050	68	18	18	783	47
Electricity/cap	17	334		886	9140	236	14	14	525	33

Characteristics	Mbete	Mbochi	Mbum	Mbunda	Melanesian	Mende	Merina	Meru	Mestizo	Miao Man
Macroecon: GNP/capita	3100	1070	487	950	1300	330	230	376	2600	270
Saving rate	42	31	-11	28	5	-5	4	14	20	0
Inflation rate	-0.9	-5	2	92	8	81	13	9	31	10
Convert currency (1=yes)	0	0	1	0	0	0	0	1	0	1
Communist, former (1=yes)				1	0		1	1	0	1
Labor: Unemployment, %					0	0	0		0.9	0.9
Nonemployment, %								16	9	
Agriculture, %	93	97	27	19	71	70	63	65	69	19
Industry, %	69	75	68	73	65	75	90	78	29	67
Services, %	26	20	80	75	17	15		9	28	85
Unionization, %	27	5	11	15	12		4	13	43	
Air Trans: # of aircraft	11	20	15	10	9	35		4	112	
# aircraft/cap	8	4	22	16		0	0.6	0.7	2	0
# of airports	60	2	0.5	28	322	12	148	249	1360	57
Runways: Permanent Surf	8	46	67	309	12	4	30	21	152	8
Large	0	0	0.5	30	0.7	0	0	2	19	0
Medium	2	6	0	2	25	3	3	2	214	1
Small	20	0	4	15	13300		34	46		14
Roads: Total km	7810	17	23	54	13000	7450	34800	54600	335000	13900
Motorways km	9320	8310	39900	72400	453	7400	40000	64600	2780	0
Highways total km	560	12000	37400	73800	7420	1150	4690	7000	288000	27500
Paved km	915	560	733	8580		490	811	4150	33200	1860
Gravel km	5350	850	14500	29400	5400	5760	34500	53400	224000	7450
Improved earth km	5660	5350	10500						39800	
Unimproved earth km	13	5200	22900	35900	0	8	2	5	39500	18200
Ownership car/1000 cap	710	11	5	14	21	84	960	2390	44	4
Railways km	5	799	246	3190		1	17	16	12100	0
Telecom: # AM stations	0	4	6	17	0	0	1	6	508	1
# of cable systems	3	0	0	0	2	1	1	4	0.7	0
# of TV stations	4	4	1	6	1	1	3	2	126	1
# of FM stations	2	1	3	13	1	1		5		0
# of SAT earth stations	23	2	1	2	26			9	3	1
# of daily papers	79	5	7	1	114	208	20	34	148	2
Television/1000 cap	20	61	47	6	34	5	213	15	133	114
Radios/1000 pop	100	12	4	19	100	91	4		284	20
Telephones/1000 pop	0.5		36	5	31	4	3	10	87	
Digital % 93		9	20		0.4			0.1	55	2
Main Lines/1000 pop			0						89	0.1
Cellular subs/cap									3	
Pagers/cap										2
Piped water, % dwellings	110	97	30	35	62	40	49	32	49	0.1
Food: Sugar/cap	55	51	31	70	51	30	56	143	307	11
Protein 85 grm/cap/day		2600	50	45	2230	41	2410	59	68	62
Calories/cap/day	2540		1800	1930		1870		2140	2700	2310
Meat prod/cap 88		0	0	0		0	0	0	0	0
Energy: Consumption/cap	580	377	79	89	619	76	39	106	1260	34
Electricity/cap	549	163	67	215	875	50	46	129	1340	219

Characteristics	Microne-sian	Mixed	Moldovan	Mon	Mon-Khmer	Monegas-que	Mongo	Mongol-Buryat	Mongol-Dariganga	Mongol-Dorbed
Macroecon: GNP/capita	4410	4790	4540	863	270	16000	238	1730	1730	1730
: Saving rate	5	8	51	19	10		21			
: Inflation rate	-1	0.1	1		1		4000	-1	-1	-1
: Convert currency (1=yes)			1	0	1	0	0	0	0	0
Communist, former (1=yes)	0	26	1	0	1	0	0			
Labor: Unemployment, %		71	51	0	19		64	2	2	2
: Nonemployment, %		31	29	64	67		75	32	32	32
: Agriculture, %	80	48	27	65	85	1	13	52	52	52
: Industry, %	32	23	42	25	6	1	12	10	10	10
: Services, %	32	8	5	0			12			
: Unionization, %	18	6		59	0		45			
Air Trans: # of aircraft	6	4		17	57		284	25	25	25
: # aircraft/cap		0		0.4	8		24	11	11	11
: # of airports	0	1		85	0	1		81	81	81
Runways: Permanent Surf	10	2		27	14	1	6	11	11	11
: Large	4			38			73	4	4	4
: Medium	0.7							19	19	19
: Small	0.4							12	12	12
Roads: Total km	338	4180	250000	23500	13900	50	145000	3950	3950	3950
: Motorways km	166	1160				0				
: Highways total km	335	4150	258000	27000	27500		147000	46700	46700	46700
: Paved km	39	2600	193000	3200	1860		2800	1000	1000	1000
: Gravel km	18	721		17000	7450		46220			
: Improved earth km	53	269	64500	6100	18200		97500			
: Unimproved earth km	6	2820	52	4250	4	706	2	45700	45700	45700
: Ownership car/1000 cap	0	98	24700	2	0	3	5010	0.8	0.8	0.8
Railways km		0.1	1050				10	1780	1780	1780
Telecom: # AM stations	3	0.2	310	1	0	5	18	12	12	12
: # of cable systems		0.7	1050	1	1	4	4			
: # of TV stations	4	8	4	1	1	0	4	1	1	1
: # of FM stations	2	0.9	6	2	2		4	1	1	1
: # of SAT earth stations	3	2	316	24	5		1	1	1	1
: # of daily papers	0			2	114		103	3	3	3
: Television/1000 cap	267	158	139	2	20	786	1			
: Radios/1000 pop	1090	260	29		0.2	370		56	56	56
: Telephones/1000 pop	178	249	144	2		1660	1	104	104	104
: Digital % 93	100	100	0.1					32	32	32
: Main Lines/1000 pop	194	213						91	91	91
: Cellular subs/cap	21	7						31	31	31
: Pagers/cap										
Piped water, % dwellings		37		13	11	100	43	0.3	0.3	0.3
Food: Sugar/cap	56	314	0.1	5	62		24	173	173	173
: Protein 85 grm/day/cap		76		70	2310		34	93	93	93
: Calories/cap/day	2190	2920		2590	34		2160	2830	2830	2830
: Meat prod/cap 88				62	219		67	0.1	0.1	0.1
Energy: Consumption/cap	5200	1930	3800	62			67	1870	1870	1870
: Electricity/cap	4550	2060		58			151	1630	1630	1630

Characteristics	Mongol-Khalka	Mongoloid	Montene-grin	Moor	Morvians	Mossi	Mpongwe	Mubi	Mulatto	Muong
Macroecon: GNP/capita	1730	377	3000	528	6100	377	4500	229	2420	245
Saving rate	-1	23		10		-0.2	50	-24	17	4
Inflation rate	0	8	0	7	21	9	2	2	14	-0
Convert currency (1=yes)	1			0.4	1	1	1	1	0.1	0
Communist, former (1=yes)	1	0.2	25							1
Labor: Unemployment, %	2	17	5	18	18	10	90	66	10	5
Nonemployment, %	32	93	40	72	53	72	65	85	65	53
Agriculture, %	52	66		47	12	20	30		33	70
Industry, %	10	21		19	33	25	5		27	8
Services, %		13		28		5	32	20	41	22
Unionization, %	25	15		16			15	0.5	23	90
Air Trans: # of aircraft	1	123		5		0.3	12	71	154	
# aircraft/cap	81	0.1		22		34	70	4	2620	100
# of airports	11	339		10		3	10	0	306	50
Runways: Permanent Surf										
Large	4	212		3		8	0	4	17	10
Medium	19	3		12		2	2	25	406	20
Small	12	64							3940	
Roads: Total km	3950	105	46000	3570	17700	18500	7470	40000	1180000	85700
Motorways km	46700	1940000	350	35900	191	22100	7500	31300	1020000	0
Highways total km	1000	28600	46000	12500	17700	3010	560	32	36000	85000
Paved km		1820000	26900	14300		26200	960	7300	995000	9400
Gravel km	45700	834000	10400	14700		7400				48700
Improved earth km		952000		480		7800	5980	24000	1950	
Unimproved earth km	0.8	211000	8700		3670		14		934	26900
Ownership car/1000 cap	1780	3		8		2		2		0.8
Railways km	12	60700	26	1220		740	650	6	22300	2830
Telecom: # AM stations	0	124	0	6		3		0	919	16
# of cable systems	1	2	18	0.8			3	1	2	0
# of TV stations	1	263	9	0.3		3	6	1	87	2
# of FM stations	3	4	1	2		1	3	1	0.3	1
# of SAT earth stations	56	3	2	3	2	3	2	1	3	3
# of daily papers	104	2200	93	7		9	36	26	213	4
Television/1000 cap	32	27		27		77	91	2	179	38
Radios/1000 pop	91	63	65	108	179	4	26	15	328	52
Telephones/1000 pop	31	10		8	192	92	100	0.9	94	4
Main Lines/1000 pop		30		9	1	0.2	28		38	77
Digital % 93	0.3	11		0.3			0.5		97	5
Cellular subs/cap	173	0.6							2	0.1
Pagers/cap	93	0.8								
Piped water, % dwellings		10		18		24	119	41	52	18
Food: Sugar/cap		91		209		36	57	53	356	57
Protein 85 grm/day/cap	93	55		76		54		61	61	
Calories/cap/day	2830	2270		2350	4510	1930	2490	1660	2630	1950
Meat prod/cap 88	0.1	0.1								0
Energy: Consumption/cap	1870	388		425		60	719	18	780	132
Electricity/cap	1630	346	4	112		125	815	14	1430	124

Characteristics	Nama	Nauruan	Ndebele	Nepalese	Netherlander	Newar	Ngbandi	Ngoni	Nkole	Norman-French D.
Macroecon: GNP/capita	1300	18100	661	179	18300	179	440	200	300	
Saving rate	12		13	9	21	9	9	13	23	8
Inflation rate	1	1	25		2	9	6	1	0	0
Convert currency (1=yes)	0	0	1	0	1	0	1	0		
Communist, former (1=yes)		0	0	0	0	0	0	0	0	
Labor: Unemployment, %	40		35		7					
Nonemployment, %	68		72	5	65	5	30	96	77	
Agriculture, %			74	60	5	60	76	43	90	
Industry, %			10	91	26	91	72	23		
Services, %			16		69			17		
Unionization, %	18		17		29					
Air Trans: # of aircraft		3	12	5	98	5				
# aircraft/cap				0.2		0.2	0.6	0.5	0.6	
# of airports	137	1	487	37	28	37	66	48	35	8
Runways: Permanent Surf	21	1	22	5	19	5	4	6	1	
Large		0		0	1	0	0	0		
Medium	4	0	3	1	1	1	2	1	3	
Small	63	1	32	8	6	8	22	9	10	
Roads: Total km	42800	27	84500	7080	118000	7080	24400	12200	28200	
Motorways km	0	0	0	0	2050	0	0	0	0	
Highways total km	54500	27	84500	7080	108000	7080	22000	13100	26200	
Paved km	4080	21	15700	2900	92500	2900	458	2360	1970	
Gravel km	2540		38700	1660	15800	1660		251	5850	
Improved earth km		6	22900				10500			
Unimproved earth km	47900		7210				11000	10500	18400	
Ownership car/1000 cap	68	309	29	0.8	371	0.8	15	2	1	
Railways km	2360	4	2730	52	2930	52		789	1270	
Telecom: # AM stations	4	1	8	88	3	88	0	10	10	
# of cable systems	0	0	0	0	5	0	1	0	0	
# of TV stations	3	0	18	1	8	1	0	0	9	
# of FM stations	40	0	1	0	12	0	1	9	0	
# of SAT earth stations	5	1		1	4	1	1	0	1	
# of daily papers		0	2	59	65	59	1	1		
Television/1000 cap	36	159	27	2	485	2	3	2	4	
Radios/1000 pop	49	750	46	25	793	25	57	48	8	
Telephones/1000 pop	78	213	32	4	625	4	5	6	22	
Digital % 93	52		100	88	93	88	100	52	4	
Main Lines/1000 pop			14	5	530	5	2	4	60	
Cellular subs/cap					20				2	
Pagers/cap					27					
Piped water, % dwellings	62		80	66	100	66	8	26	29	
Food: Sugar/cap			227	14	293	14	44	95	54	
Protein 85 grm/day/cap			51	52	97	52		68		
Calories/cap/day	1840		2120	2050	3260	2050	1940	2370	2220	
Meat prod/cap 88	0				0.1		0	0	0	
Energy: Consumption/cap	823	5900	707	24	6640	24	47	35	25	
Electricity/cap		3320	934	35	5100	35	33	68	31	8320

Characteristics	North-Western	Norwegian	Nuba	Nuer	Nung Sukuma	Nupe	Nyamwezi (Galla)	Nyoros	Ometo	Oromo
Macroecon: GNP/capita	420	44000	440	440	245	314	260	300	130	130
:Saving rate	7	31			4	23	12	23	4	4
:Inflation rate	155	1	200	200	0	45	19		8	8
:Convert currency (1=yes)	0	1	0	0	1			0	0	0
Communist, former (1=yes)		0				0	0			
Labor: Unemployment, %	7	5	30	30	5	28	25	77	66	66
:Nonemployment, %		0	76	76	53	60	97	90	80	80
:Agriculture, %	58	7	78	78	70	54	90			
:Industry, %	11	41	9	9	8	19	15			
:Services, %	31	52	13	13	22	27	8			
:Unionization, %	10	66	18	18	90	8				
Air.Trans:# of aircraft	12	76				57	15		2	2
:# aircraft/cap		.18	0.7	0.7		0.5	0.3	.3	.25	.25
:# of airports	117	103	72	72	100	76	104	6	0.5	0.5
Runways: Permanent Surf	13	64	8		50	33	12	35	123	129
:Large	4	12	5	5	0	15		1	1	1
:Medium	22	16			10	22	3	3	13	13
:Small			31	31	20		43	10	38	38
Roads: Total km	37400	88800	20000	20000	85700	108000	82000	28200	39500	39500
:Motorways km		437	0	0	0	115	0	0		
:Highways total km	36400	79500	20000	20000	85000	108000	81900	26200	44300	44300
:Paved km	6500	38600	1600	1600	9400	30000	3600	1970	3650	3650
:Gravel km	7000	41000	3700	3700	48700	25400	5600	5850	9650	9650
:Improved earth km			2300	2300					3000	3000
:Unimproved earth km	22900		12400	12400	26900	52600	72700	18400	28000	28000
:Ownership car/1000 cap	9	403	7		0.8	0				
Railways km	1720	4220	5110	5110	2830	3510	3780	1270	835	835
Telecom:# AM stations	11	46	11	11	16	35	12	10	4	4
:# of cable systems		4	1	1	0	0	0	0	0	0
:# of TV stations	9	54	0	0	2	28	2	9	1	1
:# of FM stations	5	493	3	3	1	17	4	0	0	0
:# of SAT earth stations	2	3	0	0	3		2	1	1	1
:# of daily papers	3	84	2	2	38	35	3	4	3	3
:Television/1000 cap	25	423	2	2	52	29	29	4	2	2
:Radios/1000 pop	27	411	61	61	4	79	6	22	80	80
:Telephones/1000 pop	12	730	243	243	77	8	43	4	3	3
:Digital % 93		60	4	4	5	0.3		60	39	39
:Main Lines/1000 pop	10	568	3	3	0.1	0.5		2	3	3
:Cellular subs/cap		127								
:Pagers/cap		32								
Piped water,% dwellings	63	98	65	65	18	17	30	29	85	85
Food: Sugar/cap	101		135	135	57	23	55	54	25	25
:Protein 85 grm/day/cap	58	101	62	62		47			55	55
:Calories/cap/day	2130	3220	2070	2070	1950	2110	2210	2220	1660	1660
:Meat prod/cap 88		0	0	0		0				
Energy: Consumption/cap	198	7180	64	64	132	207	36	25	24	24
:Electricity/cap	909	28200	42	42	124	111	36	31	17	17

Characteristics	Ossete	Ovambo	Ovim-bundu	Pacific Islander	Pakistani	Palauans	Palaung-Wa	Papuan New Guin.	Pashtun	Pepel
Macroecon: GNP/capita	4530	1300	950	18100	15000	2260	270	972	200	219
: Saving rate		12	28		27			5	13	-11
: Inflation rate		1	92					5		-50
Convert currency (1=yes)	0	0	0	1	1	0	0	1	0	0
Communist, former (1=yes)	1		1	0	0	20	1	0	1	0
Labor: Unemployment, %	3	40	19		7		1	5		17
: Nonemployment, %	48	68	73		63		19	59	74	58
: Agriculture, %	25		75		11		67	82	80	90
: Industry, %	31		15		36		85	9		
: Services, %			10	3	54		86	9		
: Unionization, %		18	16	309	29	2		1	0	2
Air Trans: # of aircraft	18		28	3	364	2	0	15	0	2
: # aircraft/cap			3			0	0	4		
: # of airports	137	137	309	309	312	0	57	503	41	34
Runways: Permanent Surf	21	21	30	1	149	2	8	18	9	4
: Large				0				0		0
: Medium	4	4	15	0	23	22	14		0	1
: Small	63	63	54		84	22		39	18	5
Roads: Total km	35100	42800	72400		212000		13900	19700	19000	3500
: Motorways km		0	0		1810		0	0	0	0
: Highways total km	33900	54500	73800		216000		27500	19200	21000	3220
: Paved km	29500	4080	8580		199000		1860	640	2800	2700
: Gravel km		2540	29400	6	3060		7450	11000	1650	
: Improved earth km					23500					
: Unimproved earth km	4400	47900	35900	159	2400		18200	7600	16500	520
Ownership car/1000 cap	78	68	14		9750	0	4	4	2	4
Railways km	1570	2360	3190		276	1	0	31	17	0
Telecom: # AM stations	4	4	17	27	133	0	0	0	5	2
: # of cable systems				0	24	2	1	2	0	0
: # of TV stations		0	6	27	124	1	0	2	1	1
: # of FM stations		3	13	21	313		1	1	3	3
: # of SAT earth stations		40	2	6	4			2		
: # of daily papers			1	4	10		2		4	2
: Television/1000 cap		5	6		421	49	5	16	3	
: Radios/1000 pop	149	133	19	750	765	626	114	67	78	
: Telephones/1000 pop	96	36	5	213	403	66	20	16	0	2
: Digital % 93	11	49			68				2	
: Main Lines/1000 pop	97	78	5		376		2	10		0.8
: Cellular subs/cap		52			33		0.1	0.1		37
: Pagers/cap					15					
Piped water,% dwellings		62	35		85		11	62	25	7
Food: Sugar/cap			70		288		62	45	26	32
: Protein 85 grm/day/cap			45		88					46
: Calories/cap/day		1840	1930		3200		2310	2180	2290	2130
: Meat prod/cap 88	0	0	0		0		0			
Energy: Consumption/cap	2590	823	89	5900	7990	638	34	294	232	91
: Electricity/cap			215	3320	6040	1370	219	477	69	17

Characteristics	Persian	Polinisian	Polinesian Chinese	Polinesian European	Polish	Portuguese	Punjabi	Punu	Puyi	Pygmy
Macroecon: GNP/capita	6140	8510	7030	6720	4640	4950	424	3340	417	1070
: Saving rate	39	21	3	3	39	13	12	43	28	31
: Inflation rate	23	3			55	0.3	11	-0.4	6	-5
: Convert currency (1=yes)	0	1	0	0	1		0	0	1	1
Communist, former (1=yes)		0			1					0
Labor: Unemployment, %	0		15	15	13	4	8		2	
: Nonemployment, %	25	13	65	65	55	60	77	93	53	97
: Agriculture, %	76	62			27	27	53	68	60	75
: Industry, %	33	13			50	30	13	27	30	20
: Services, %	27	40			23	43	34	5	10	5
: Unionization, %	40	45			11	32	10	28	65	20
Air Trans: # of aircraft	48	43			52	155	40	11	284	4
: # aircraft/cap	0.1	18					0.3	8	0.2	
: # of airports	213	19	6	6	167	2480	113	62	330	46
Runways: Permanent Surf		62	28	41	88	306	75	9	260	6
: Large	81	23	43	22	35	19	31	0	90	
: Medium	16		23	2	66	385	43	2	200	17
: Small	16	2		11				20		
Roads: Total km	139000	69900	600	574	362000	1190000	112000	7750	1100000	8310
: Motorways km	487	301	600	574	320	3640	340			0
: Highways total km	139000	30800		35	298000	1050000	102000	9000	1030000	12000
: Paved km	42500	33500		35	131000	69300	40600	560	170000	560
: Gravel km	46800	29000		84	2340	1400000	23000	923	648000	5850
: Improved earth km	49200			33	98300	52900	29000	5350	211000	5350
: Unimproved earth km	1250					7150	9270	5720	1	5200
: Ownership car/1000 cap	35	35		84	139	176	6	13	1	11
Railways km	4770	266		33	26900	23400	12700	700	54000	799
Telecom: # AM stations	77	1430			30	861	20	5	274	4
: # of cable systems		24			0.1	4	2	3	202	4
: # of TV stations	28	0.7			41	112	29	4	6	1
: # of FM stations	3	8			31	34	8	2		1
: # of SAT earth stations	3	2			13					2
: # of daily papers	17	2				210	125	26	1780	5
: Television/1000 cap	66	215	156	156	296	202	126		27	5
: Radios/1000 pop	178	626	503	508	250	186	77	81	69	61
: Telephones/1000 pop	66	360	229	218	145	30	15	21	17	12
: Digital % 93	100	99	100	100		190	43	100	21	
: Main Lines/1000 pop	80	293	236	236	146	6	16	21		9
: Cellular subs/cap	0.1	46			0.9	3	0.3	0.5	0.6	
: Pagers/cap		17			32				8	
Piped water, % dwellings	49	94	90	90	57	57	15		48	
Food: Sugar/cap	139	374	75	75	355	350	144	112	62	97
: Protein 85 grm/day/cap	86	88			102	71	59	55		51
: Calories/cap/day	3310	3050	2900	2900	3300	2800	2240	2530	2630	2600
: Meat prod/cap 88	0	0.1	0	0	0.1		0	0		
Energy: Consumption/cap	1670	2580	1440	1380	4560	1210	272	604	819	377
: Electricity/cap	896	3780	1400	1380	4100	2170	355	595	488	163

Characteristics	Quechua	Rakhine	Romanian	Romansch	Rundi	Russian	Ruthenian	Rwanda	Saho	Sakalava
Macroecon: GNP/capita	1270	863	3490	33200	236	5730	6100	251	120	230
: Saving rate	13	19	26	28	20	24	21	21		4
: Inflation rate	53		212	3	3740	129	1	3170	12	13
: Convert currency (1=yes)	0	0	0		0			0	0	1
Communist, former (1=yes)		0	1			1				0
Labor: Unemployment, %	11	10	4	3		3		66		
: Nonemployment, %	73	64	53	52	64	48	18	78		63
: Agriculture, %	38	65	28	6	76	20	53	13		90
: Industry, %	20	25	34	33	13	39	12	12		
: Services, %	42	10	38	61	12	42	33	10		
: Unionization, %	29	59	5	20	12			37		
Air Trans: # of aircraft	39	17	59	89	42	45		0.9		4
: # aircraft/cap	3	0.4	3	13	1	2		232		8
: # of airports	293	85	165	66	266	1050		20		0.6
Runways: Permanent Surf	35	27	25	42	23	337				148
: Large	2				0.9	3		5		30
: Medium	16	3	15	5		27		60		3
: Small	48	38	15	18	6	228				34
Roads: Total km	56900	23500	72600	71100	68	738000	17700	121000		34800
: Motorways km	2460	0	116	1520			191	0	3850	0
: Highways total km	53700	27000	72700	62100	137000	760000	17700	121000	807	40000
: Paved km	5610	3200	35900	62100	2650	569000		2630	840	4690
: Gravel km	14600	17000	27600		43400			37800	402	811
: Improved earth km	16200				3000				1800	34500
: Unimproved earth km	34500		67	430	97500	195000		81000	0.5	
: Ownership car/1000 cap	16	6100	9090	5190	2	59		2	307	2
Railways km	1920				4690	74700	3670	4230		960
Telecom: # AM stations	257	2		7	9	1050		10		17
: # of cable systems	97	4250	11200	0	0	0		0		0
: # of TV stations		0	12	18	17	308		16		1
: # of FM stations	0	1	1	265	4	1050		3		3
: # of SAT earth stations	2	1	5	1	1	4		1		
: # of daily papers	39	1	36	100	4	13	2	2		5
: Television/1000 cap	91	2	194	599	99	308		86	0.5	20
: Radios/1000 pop	267	24	143	367		576	179	2		213
: Telephones/1000 pop	39	2	118	882		163		60	5	4
: Digital % 93	66		26			9		1		
: Main Lines/1000 pop	38	2	121	683	0.1	169	192			3
: Cellular subs/cap	1		0.1	50		0.2	1	43		
: Pagers/cap				13		32		25		
Piped water, % dwellings	46	13	82	100	43	93		38		
Food: Sugar/cap	242	5	195	326	24	326		2170		49
: Protein 85 grm/day/cap	55	70	104	96	37	100		0		56
: Calories/cap/day	2140	2590	3360	3430	2170	3500		58		2410
: Meat prod/cap 88	0	0	0	0.1	0	0.1		126		0
Energy: Consumption/cap	539	62	4490	3660	64	8890	4510			39
: Electricity/cap	596	58	3490	8140	143	6390				46

Characteristics	Samoan	Sanga	Sanmari-nese	Sara	Scandina-vian	Senufo	Serbian	Serer	Servicais Tongas	Shan
Macroecon: GNP/capita	5430	1070	20000	440	17700	568	3530	805	320	863
Saving rate	19	31		-9	14	-0.7	24	-10	-20	19
Inflation rate	8	-5	6	6	2	-0.9	101	2	-25	0
Convert currency (1=yes)	1	1	1	1	1	1	0.2	1	0	0
Communist, former (1=yes)										
Labor: Unemployment, %	9		4		7	14	25	4		10
Nonemployment, %	77	97		30	7	64	73	68	83	64
Agriculture, %	54	75		76	59	80	5	77		65
Industry, %	29	20	81	72	27	10	41			25
Services, %	67	5			67	10	44			10
Unionization, %	3	20		1	65	16	31	3	10	59
Air Trans: # of aircraft	1450	4		2	25	8	636		79	17
# aircraft/cap	15	2		0.6	44	0.6	195	0.4	2	0.4
# of airports	2490	46	74	66	10	42	455	25	2	85
Runways: Permanent Surf	848	6		4		7		10		27
Large	11			0	3		4		0	
Medium	58	0		2	20	4	10	1	2	3
Small	530	17		22	3	12	338	15		38
Roads: Total km	1340000	8310	237	24400	70900	35500	49800	13900	380	23500
Motorways km	14900	0			362	82	295		0	0
Highways total km	1120000	12000	104	22000	24100	32200	50100	14000	300	27000
Paved km	331	560		458	64600	2640	31600	3780	200	3200
Gravel km		850			1930	21200	9820			17000
Improved earth km	200	5350		10500		7400		10200	100	6100
Unimproved earth km		5200		11000	313	10300	8760		22	
Ownership car/1000 cap	128	11	752	15	188	9	80	9		
Railways km	47500	799		0	20	643	10200	1110	1	4250
Telecom: # AM stations	861	4		1		1	36	8	0	2
# of cable systems	1280	0		0	9		0.1	3	0	
# of TV stations	914	4	326	1	20	8	16	0	2	1
# of FM stations	12	1	500	1	3	10	9	3		1
# of SAT earth stations	357	2	680	1	3	2			1	1
# of daily papers	196	5		3	49	3	4			1
Television/1000 cap	864	61		57	528	45	111	35		2
Radios/1000 cap	196	12		5	383	76	761	70	250	24
Telephones/1000 pop	100				658	81	87	74	24	2
Digital % 93		9			46		29	0.1		
Main Lines/1000 pop	160			100	563	5	268		21	2
Cellular subs/cap	93			2	65		12			
Pagers/cap	28				14		32			
Piped water, % dwellings	72	97		8	97	24	100	88		13
Food: Sugar/cap	152	51		44	284	77	300	92	51	5
Protein 85 grm/day/cap					95	55	96	67		70
Calories/cap/day	2710	2600		1940	3510	2310	3420	2340	2390	2590
Meat prod/cap 88				0.3	0.3		0.1	0		0
Energy: Consumption/cap	2540	377		47	5470	108	10900	176	271	62
Electricity/cap	2580	163	0	33	6030	111	601	104	126	58

Characteristics	Shilluk	Shona	Siamese	Sidamo	Sindhi	Sinhalese	Slavic Muslims	Slovak	Slovene	Soga
Macroecon: GNP/capita	440	579	1940	130	410	490	3290	6240	12200	300
: Saving rate	3	11	20	4	12			25	26	
: Inflation rate	200	28	6	8	11	11	123	20	24	23
Convert currency (1=yes)			1						1	0
Communist, former (1=yes)	0	0	0	0	0	0	1	1	1	0
Labor: Unemployment, %	30	38	4		8	14	28	17	13	
: Nonemployment, %	76	68	46	66	77	63	76	53	60	77
: Agriculture, %	78	76	59	80	53	46	45	12	2	90
: Industry, %	13	10	24		34	27		33	46	
: Services, %	13	13	17		10	27		50	33	
: Unionization, %		15	1		40	30		11	55	
Air Trans: # of aircraft	18	11	41	25	40	8	8		28	6
: # aircraft/cap	0.7		0.7	0.5	0.3	0.5		0.3	3	0.3
: # of airports	72	429	115	123	175	14	7		20	35
Runways: Permanent Surf		23	50	9		12			2	5
: Large		3	1	1					2	1
: Medium	5	31	13	13	31	1			9	3
: Small	31		28	38	43	7			15	10
Roads: Total km	20000	73000	73200	39500	111000	74700	21300	24100	15000	28200
: Motorways km					340		7	203	89	0
: Highways total km	20000	73000	44500	44300	101000	75200	21400	24300	16800	26200
: Paved km	1600	13500	28000	3650	40200	27600	11700	235	11000	1970
: Gravel km	3700	31300		9650	23000	32900	8150	2330	4060	5850
: Improved earth km	2300	22700		3000	29000	14700		412	7	
: Unimproved earth km	1240	9750	5130	28000	9160		1560		4	18400
: Ownership car/1000 cap		24	18		6	10	4	259	278	1
Railways km	5110	2800	3850	835	12600	1930	1040	3660	1330	1270
Telecom: # AM stations	11	12	200	4	19	12	14	49	7	10
: # of cable systems			1					25	0	0
: # of TV stations	3	7	100	1	29	5	6	4	8	9
: # of FM stations	15	15	2		8	2	8		5	0
: # of SAT earth stations	2	2	31	1		16	2		0	1
: # of daily papers		2	109	3	125	32		3	3	4
: Television/1000 cap	61	42	146	2	16	117	111	333	268	8
: Radios/1000 pop	243	27	44	80	77	11		691	540	22
: Telephones/1000 pop	4	100	48	39	14	100	81	190	326	4
: Digital % 93			6	3	43	0.3		5	29	60
: Main Lines/1000 pop	3	12	11		16		217	196	282	2
: Cellular subs/cap					0.3		5	1		
: Pagers/cap					0.2					
Piped water, % dwellings	65	80	42	85	15	18		32	84	29
Food: Sugar/cap	135	190	133	25	144	128		95	406	54
: Protein 85 grm/day/cap	62	47	49	55	59	48		334	102	
: Calories/cap/day	2070	2030	2330	1660	2240	2430		3460	3540	2220
: Meat prod/cap 88	0		0	0	0			0.1	0.1	0.1
Energy: Consumption/cap	64	579	637	24	265	115		8630	3700	25
: Electricity/cap	42	770	813	17	343	178	1730	4660	95	31

Characteristics	Somali	Somba	Songhai	Soninke	Sotho	Sotho North	Spanish	Sundanese	Suriname	Susu
Macroecon: GNP/capita	175	430	297	371	1980	2960	9480	680	8700	480
..Saving rate	4	0.5	4	-5	14	14	17	20		8
..Inflation rate	16	1	-7	-3	14	1	17	8	4	23
..Convert currency (1=yes)	0	1		0.9	1	1	0.7			0
..Communist, former (1=yes)	0		0				0		0	0
Labor: Unemployment, %	13		47	8	32	30	13	3		62
..Nonemployment, %	76	63	72	72	69	72	86	66	0	82
..Agriculture, %	82	60	81	72	31	25	21	56	19	9
..Industry, %	22	38	12	13	39	39	28	23	51	9
..Services, %	14		16	19	36	36	51	21		9
..Unionization, %	1	75			10	17	15	5	70	100
Air Trans: # of aircraft	.3	0	0.1	0.8	54	90	202	216	8	10
..# aircraft/cap	0.1	0		0.4	2	2	4		44	2
..# of airports	59	6	32	31	550	901	1290	437	7	15
Runways: Permanent Surf	7	1	8		80	132	185	114	6	4
..Large	2	0	0	0	3	5	3		0	0
..Medium	7	0	4	4	135	10	22	12	2	3
..Small	17	4	11		1220	224	206	64	2	10
Roads: Total km	23100	7420	26200	12400	110000	181000	678000	214000	950	30100
..Motorways km	17700		207		116000	2040	3280		950	0
..Highways total km	2470	5050	27400	14200	32600	188000	600400	120000	300	30100
..Paved km	3470	920	2400	1870	81300	54000	539000		650	1150
..Gravel km	9390	2600	6890	3280	1810	134000	719000			13000
..Improved earth km	25900	1530		10200	2500		18900			16000
..Unimproved earth km			7020	9420		95	190	7		2
..Ownership car/1000 cap	1	8	4	4	58	20900	20600	6840	0	1040
Railways km	72	607	331	666	12500	14	544	618	9	3
Telecom: # AM stations	2	2	8				15		2	0
..# of cable systems	0			0.4	0.6	67	107	9	1	1
..# of TV stations	1	2	10	2	40	286	260	38	4	1
..# of FM stations		2	3	2	172	4	4	3	2	1
..# of SAT earth stations		1	2	2	11	19	167	97		
..# of daily papers	13	5	1	1	62	101	321	55	219	5
..Television/1000 cap	34	78	49	37	180	282	326	140	673	28
..Radios/1000 pop	3	5	32	35	92	146	290	11	168	3
..Telephones/1000 pop	39	61	7	4			37	77		
..Main Lines/1000 pop	0.3	4	72	78	62	99	288	12	9	2
..Digital % 93	0.2		2	0.2	0.5	0.5	7	0.4		
..Cellular subs/cap							3			
..Pagers/cap							77			
Piped water, % dwellings	85		17	88	90	90	320	11	87	72
Food: Sugar/cap	52	25	40	98	232	232	84	109	225	40
..Protein 85 grm/day/cap	65	50	60	58	71	75	3090	53	93	1780
..Calories/cap/day	2050	2190	2180	2100	2680	2940		2510	2930	
..Meat prod/cap 88							1900			88
Energy: Consumption/cap	59	50	42	82	2640	2640	1900	311	9790	88
..Electricity/cap	40	39	33	41	4140	4140	3080	228	3600	82

Characteristics	Swahili	Swazi	Swedish	Swiss	Tahitian	Tai	Taiwanese (Dari)	Tajik	Tama	Tamang
Macroecon: GNP/capita	260	1200	25200	31000	6000	251	10000	1470	229	179
Saving rate	12	-11	18	5	4	.5		13	-24	9
Inflation rate	19	13	1	1		0.3	3	208	2	9
Convert currency (1=yes)	0		0		0	1	1	1	1	0
Communist, former (1=yes)	0	0	0	0.1	0	9	0	1	0	0
Labor: Unemployment,%		76			16	57	2	33		5
Nonemployment,%	25	53	48	30	72	74	62	69	66	60
Agriculture, %	97	9	3	4		7	17	22	85	91
Industry, %		9	29	54	1	22	41		20	5
Services, %	90	10	68	41	6	90	42		3	
Unionization, %	15	4	80		29	89	35	0	0.5	0.2
Air Trans: # of aircraft	8	5	112		1	39	0	0	71	37
# aircraft/cap	0.3	23	13		0	8	0		4	5
# of airports	101	1	250	250	29	18	40	41	4	0
Runways: Permanent Surf	12	1	136		1		36	9	25	1
Large	3	1	0		0		3	10		8
Medium	42		10		2		16	18		
Small			91				8			
Roads: Total km	8200	2740	134000	13000	6340	67700	20000	29500	40000	7080
Motorways km	1		909							0
Highways total km	79200	2850	97600		6340	70600	20000	31600	31300	7080
Paved km	3480	510	51200		634	75000	17100	19700	32	2900
Gravel km	5600	1230	21300		0	38300	2370	745	7300	1660
Improved earth km		1110			5		575			
Unimproved earth km	72700		24800		0	24700		12500	24000	
Ownership car/1000 cap		32	418	603	7	2	112	6	2	0.8
Railways km	3650	334	11400			2120	4600	622		52
Telecom: # AM stations	12	7	5	20	3	14	91	5	0	88
# of cable systems		0	854	23		0	9	0	6	
# of TV stations	2	10	350	0	1		15	0	0	0
# of FM stations	4	6		4		0.7	23		1	1
# of SAT earth stations	2	3		0		3	35		1	
# of daily papers	3		647	2					1	59
Television/1000 cap		16	647	343	207	30	333	67	26	25
Radios/1000 pop	37	154	862	654	566	68	269	84	2	25
Telephones/1000 pop	6	29	926	846	236	8	404	78	15	4
Digital % 93		50	67			77	71	32	0.9	88
Main Lines/1000 pop	43	22	720		260	4	413	0		5
Cellular subs/cap			132			0.1	31	32		
Pagers/cap			26				80	0.1		
Piped water, % dwellings			99	99		18	42	25		66
Food: Sugar/cap	30	48	333		83	46		26	41	14
Protein 85 grm/day/cap	55	60	98			62		64	53	52
Calories/cap/day	2210	2550	3050		2980	2040	2810	2290	1660	2050
Meat prod/cap 88	0		0.1		0	0		0	0	
Energy: Consumption/cap	36	167	5100	5260	4760	107	2390	232	18	24
Electricity/cap	36	189	16800		7230	148	4310	1570	14	35

Characteristics	Tamil (Tubu)	Tatar	Teda	Teke	Tem-Kabre	Temne	Teso	Thai	Tharu	Tigre
Macroecon: GNP/capita	489	5560	229	468	421	330	300	245	179	124
::Saving rate	10		-24	24	14	-5	23	4	9	4
::Inflation rate	11	161	21	2890	3	81		0	0	10
::Convert currency (1=yes)		0	0	0.3	1	1	0	1	0	0
::Communist, former (1=yes)		1								0
Labor: Unemployment, %	1	3			2			5		
::Nonemployment, %	14	49	66	73	68	70	77	53	60	66
::Agriculture, %	63	21	85	75	75	75	90	70	91	80
::Industry, %	46	37		15	20	15	3	8		
::Services, %	27	42		10		35	6	22		
::Unionization, %	27	5	20	14			0.3	90	0.5	2
Air Trans: # of aircraft	30			34	9		35		0.2	.25
::# aircraft/cap	0.8		0.5	0.3	0.3	0	1		37	0.5
::# of airports	0.4		71	218	0.8	12	3	100	5	123
Runways: Permanent Surf	14		4	19	9	4	35	50		9
::Large	12		4	0.7	2	1		0		1
::Medium				58	2	3	1	10	1	13
::Small	7		25				3	20	8	38
Roads: Total km	75300	737000	40000	107000	7570	7450	28200	85700	7080	39500
::Motorways km	0		0					0		0
::Highways total km	75700	760000	31300	109000	6460	7400	26200	85000	7080	20800
::Paved km	27000	567000		2180	1760	1150	1970	9400	2900	9400
::Gravel km	32900		7300	33700		490	5850	48700	1660	4530
::Improved earth km	14700		24000	5350	4700	5760	18400			1490
::Unimproved earth km		197000		72000	13	8	1	26900	0.8	12800
::Ownership car/1000 cap	10	56	2	4	520	84	1270	0.8	52	0.7
Railways km	1950	74700	6	3850	2		10	2830	88	528
Telecom: # AM stations	12	1050	6	8	2	1	10	16		
::# of cable systems			1		0	0	0	2	0	4
::# of TV stations	2	310	1	14	3	1	9	1	1	0
::# of FM stations	5	1050	1	13	0	1	0	3	0	1
::# of SAT earth stations	5	4	1	1	2	0	1	4	1	0
::# of daily papers	2			3	1		4	38		1
::Television/1000 cap	16	30	26	2	6		8	52	59	1
::Radios/1000 pop	32	291	25	91	214	208	22	77	2	80
::Telephones/1000 pop	117	155	15	4	5	5	4		25	4
::Digital % 93	11	9			98	9	60	0.1	4	39
::Main Lines/1000 pop	10	159	0.9	3	5	4	2		88	3
::Cellular subs/cap	0.3	0.1							5	
::Pagers/cap		0.1								
Piped water, % dwellings	18		41	43		40		18	66	85
Food: Sugar/cap	128		53	44	123	30	29	57	14	25
::Protein 85 grm/day/cap	48			39	52	41	54		52	55
::Calories/cap/day	2440		1660	2280	2220	1870	2220	1950	2050	1660
::Meat prod/cap 88	0	0.1	0	0	0	0	0	0	0	0
Energy: Consumption/cap	114	6230	18	153	70	76	25	132	24	24
::Electricity/cap	179		14	154	81	50	31	124	35	17

Characteristics	Tigrinya	Tikar	Tiv	Tonga	Tongan	Toros	Tribal	Tsimihety	Tsonga	Tswana
Macroecon: GNP/capita	127	1160	314	420	1530	300	210	230	121	2960
: Saving rate	4	20	23	7	11		5	4	3	14
: Inflation rate	9	-2	45	155	1	23	7	13	39	1
: Convert currency (1=yes)	0	0	1	1	1	0	0	0	1	0
Communist, former (1=yes)	0		0	0	0	0	0		0	
Labor: Unemployment, %		25	0						50	30
: Nonemployment, %	66	66	28	72	13	77	30	63	53	72
: Agriculture, %	80	74	60	58	75	90	71	90	85	25
: Industry, %		11	54	11	45		59		9	39
: Services, %		15	19	31			11		2	36
: Unionization, %	2		27	10	27		30	4	8	17
Air Trans: # of aircraft	25	45	8	12	1	3		8		90
: # aircraft/cap	0.5	0.4	0.5		0	0.3	0.1	0.6	0.5	2
: # of airports	123	56	76	117	6	35	16	148	194	901
Runways: Permanent Surf	9	10	33	13	1		12	30	27	132
: Large										5
: Medium	13	5	15	4	1	1	4	3	5	10
: Small	38	21	22	22	1	10	6	34	26	224
Roads: Total km	39500	52200	108000	37400	433	28200	6240	34800	26000	181000
: Motorways km	0		115		4					2040
: Highways total km	33100	65000	108000	36400	200	26200	7240	40000	26400	188000
: Paved km	2860	2680	30000	6500	150	1970	3840	4690	4570	54000
: Gravel km	7210	32300	25400	7000	200	5850		811	831	134000
: Improved earth km	2280								1110	
: Unimproved earth km	20800	30000	52600	22900		18400	3400	34500	21100	
: Ownership car/1000 cap	0.9	6	4	9	14		0.4	2	3	95
Railways km	689	1050	3510	1720		1270	2840	960	3190	20900
Telecom: # AM stations	4	11	35	11	1	10	9	17	29	14
: # of cable systems	0		1		0		1	1	1	1
: # of TV stations	1	1		9	1		6	3	4	67
: # of FM stations	0	1	28	5		9	2		5	286
: # of SAT earth stations	1	2	17	2					2	3
: # of daily papers	2		3							19
: Television/1000 cap	2		35			4	59	5	22	101
: Radios/1000 pop	80	89	29	27	795	8		213	5	282
: Telephones/1000 pop	4	6	8	12	39	60	4	4	50	146
: Digital % 93	39			10			8	3	4	99
: Main Lines/1000 pop	3	6		10		2	19			
: Cellular subs/cap		0	0.3			0	2			0.5
: Pagers/cap			0.5				0			
Piped water, % dwellings	85	30	17	63						90
Food: Sugar/cap	25	26	23	101	70	29	20	49	30	232
: Protein 85 grm/day/cap	55	47	47	58		54	41	56	29	75
: Calories/cap/day	1660	2040	2110	2130	2940	2220	1920	2410	1610	2940
: Meat prod/cap 88		0	0							
Energy: Consumption/cap	24	254	207	198	400	25	69	39	34	2640
: Electricity/cap	17	225	111	909	250	31	65	46	57	4140

Characteristics	Tuareg	Tukolor	Tumbuka	Turkish	Turkmen	Tutsi	Tuvaluan	Twa	Uighur	Ukrainian
Macroecon: GNP/capita	306	770	420	4410	3790	261	562	273	3670	5040
: Saving rate	-0.4	-8	7	21	31	7	8	7		24
: Inflation rate	-4	.3	155	60	70	7	1	7	360	91
: Convert currency (1=yes)		0.9	0	1	0	0	0	0	0	0
Communist, former (1=yes)	0	0		0	0.7		3		0.6	1
Labor: Unemployment, %	30	6	72	10	9	62	90	60	53	1
: Nonemployment, %	71	70	58	65	67	92		92	25	51
: Agriculture, %	12	73	11	48	43				31	19
: Industry, %	16	14	31	22	26					40
: Services, %		29	10	30	40					40
: Unionization, %			12	12	37	0.9	1	0.2		5
Air Trans: # of aircraft	0.6	0.3	117	58	0.8	0.1	0	0.4		293
: # aircraft/cap	0.1	0.5	13	123	158	0.7	2	0.7		10
: # of airports	37	25		71	65	2	1	2		683
Air Trans: # of aircraft / airports										233
Runways: Permanent Surf					11					
: Large	0	0	4	30	21	0.9	1	1	138000	31
: Medium	4	2	22	28	49					174
: Small	10	15								
Roads: Total km	18500	12900	37400	76600	52100	9420	31	10200	158000	305000
: Motorways km	83	13100	36400	1070	149	5440	31	5330	156000	2
: Highways total km	20600	3490	6500	62700	52800	427		434		329000
: Paved km	1870	1040	7000	27000	23300	2150	8	2060	66600	273000
: Gravel km	5390	10200	22900	16500	12800	3000		3000	35	246
: Improved earth km	7400	4800		4100	13500	2700		2700	11700	0
: Unimproved earth km	8390			2220	5070		0.8			57400
: Ownership car/1000 cap	3	9	9	39	12	2	0	2		60
Railways km	512	1050	1720	9340	2820		1			29500
Telecom: # AM stations	5	3	11	17	39	2	0	0.4	2	945
: # of cable systems	5	1			50	0.5	0	1	33	0.3
: # of TV stations	2	0	9	344	10	0.2	0	0.4	224	266
: # of FM stations	1	1	5	104	2		0			892
: # of SAT earth stations		3	2	2	44	0.5	0	0.4		3
: # of daily papers	35	33	3	22	27		126	47	119	325
: Television/1000 cap	23	74	25	189	155	45	851	3		451
: Radios/1000 pop	2	8	27	135	66		19	100	126	169
: Telephones/1000 pop	78	76	12	225	18	100		0.1	0.1	12
: Digital % 93	2		10	58	70	0.1				180
: Main Lines/1000 pop		0.1		230	0.2					0.5
: Cellular subs/cap				2						32
: Pagers/cap				17						77
Piped water, % dwellings	21	88	63	99	48	17	68	16		318
Food: Sugar/cap	44	117	101	235	137	62		59		100
: Protein 85 grm/day/cap	59	71	58	88	81	2090	2940	2050		3360
: Calories/cap/day	2090	2330	2130	3170	3060				0.1	0.1
: Meat prod/cap 88	0	0	0	0	0	24	152	25		7190
Energy: Consumption/cap	33	242	198	1260	1250	24	152	25	3820	7190
: Electricity/cap	26	99	909	1270	2670	25	265	25		5050

Characteristics	Urdu	Uzbek	Vanuatuan	Vietnamese	Wallon	White	Wolof	Xhosa	Yalunka	Yao
Macroecon: GNP/capita	410	2590	1180	452	19200	17700	772	2960	330	300
∴ Saving rate	12		4	20	14	20	-9		-5	23
∴ Inflation rate	11	570	0	25	13		0.3	14	81	13
∴ Convert currency (1=yes)	0	1	0		1	0.9	0.9	1	1	0.5
Communist, former (1=yes)				1		0		0		
Labor: Unemployment, %	8	9		5	9	8	4	30	0	13
∴ Nonemployment, %	77	64		53	59	55	68	72	70	67
∴ Agriculture, %	53	42	69	69	3	10	75	25	75	58
∴ Industry, %	13	24			28	30	16	39	15	25
∴ Services, %	34			22	69	60	29	36		11
∴ Unionization, %	10	0		89	70	21	17	17	35	53
Air Trans: # of aircraft	40	0		4400	47	5710	3	90		150
∴ # aircraft/cap	0.3	0	0	18	5	23	0.6	17		0.3
∴ # of airports	112	41	33	216	42	10100	24	901	12	216
Runways: Permanent Surf	75	9	2	89	24	3340	10	132	4	141
∴ Large	1	0	0	0.5	14	43	1	5	0	
∴ Medium	31			13	3	227	14	10	3	5
∴ Small	43	10	1	41		1800		224		48
Roads: Total km	111000	64800	1180	137000	128000	4540000	13100	181000	7450	579000
∴ Motorways km	340	0	0	695	1630	59700		2040		0
∴ Highways total km	101000	69700	1030	137000	103000	4510000	13200	188000	7400	542000
∴ Paved km	40200	58500		9710	38000	77800	3530	54000	1150	89700
∴ Gravel km	23000	139	240	48400		449000	783	134000	490	337000
∴ Improved earth km	29000	0				431000	10200			211000
∴ Unimproved earth km	9160	12600		26800	51000	181000	3540		5760	13700
∴ Ownership car/1000 cap	6	30	26	6	398	429	9	95	8	2
Railways km	12600	3040		5110	8410	190000	1040	20900	84	28800
Telecom: # AM stations	19	5	2	56	3	3490	8	14	4	150
∴ # of cable systems						2		1	1	
∴ # of TV stations	29	1	0	62	32	4990	3	67		105
∴ # of FM stations	8	2		44	39	3540	0.1	286	1	13
∴ # of SAT earth stations	3		0			43		3	1	
∴ # of daily papers	125			18	33	1210		19		922
∴ Television/1000 cap	16	228	9	45	447	624	34	101	10	15
∴ Radios/1000 pop	77	132	242	69	468	1550	74	282	208	55
∴ Telephones/1000 pop	14	78	24	11	516	584	9	146	5	12
∴ Digital % 93	43	71		77	54	48	76	48	91	52
∴ Main Lines/1000 pop	16	0	22	10	471	463	8	99	94	13
∴ Cellular subs/cap	0.3	69	236	0.9	23	76	0.1	0.5		0.6
∴ Pagers/cap	0.2	0.2		91		85				
Piped water, % dwellings	15	25		91	100	76	88	90	40	8
Food: Sugar/cap	144	26	64	19	293	266	116	232	30	26
∴ Protein 85 grm/day/cap	59	64		58	105	97	68	75	41	61
∴ Calories/cap/day	2240	2290	2340	1960	3850	3400	2330	2940	1870	59
Meat prod/cap 88	0	0	0	0	0.1	0.1		0	0	2390
Energy: Consumption/cap	265	232	201	220	5790	7690	195	2640	76	442
∴ Electricity/cap	343	2200	180	232	7010	8990	101	4140	50	284

Characteristics	Yi-Miao	Yoruba	Yugoslav	Zambo	Zulu
Macroecon: GNP/capita	417	317	21600	754	2630
: Saving rate	28	22	24	1	11
: Inflation rate	6	44	4	432	12
: Convert currency (1=yes)	1	1	1	1	1
Communist, former (1=yes)	1	0	1	1	0
Labor: Unemployment, %	2	28	6	74	32
: Nonemployment, %	53	60	55	44	72
: Agriculture, %	60	54	6	13	33
: Industry, %	30	19	40	43	39
: Services, %	10	27	54	35	36
: Unionization, %	65	10	50	9	15
Air Trans: # of aircraft	284	55	194	228	79
: # aircraft/cap	0.2	0.5	3	11	2
: # of airports	330	74	376	2	791
Runways: Permanent Surf	260	32	195	112	116
: Large	10	3			4
: Medium	90	15	33		9
: Small	200	22	44		197
Roads: Total km	1100000	105000	503000	15100	163000
: Motorways km	0	112	7140	384	1830
: Highways total km	1030000	105000	381000	25900	169000
: Paved km	170000	29200	22900	4000	47600
: Gravel km	648000	25000	53200	2170	119000
: Improved earth km	211000	1530	11800	5430	1110
: Unimproved earth km		52600	4100	14300	3470
: Ownership car/1000 cap	1	4	371	12	84
Railways km	54000	3430	33700	347	18300
Telecom: # AM stations	274	34	64	45	14
: # of cable systems		5	5	7	0.9
: # of TV stations	202	27	184	2	61
: # of FM stations		17	374	3	251
: # of SAT earth stations	6	3	12	65	3
: # of daily papers	1780	34	317	278	17
: Television/1000 cap	27	28	530	16	95
: Radios/1000 pop	69	80	427	15	254
: Telephones/1000 pop	17	8	551	0.3	128
: Digital % 93		61	36		66
: Main Lines/1000 pop	21		479		87
: Cellular subs/cap	0.6	0.3	87	15	0.5
: Pagers/cap	8		12	0.3	
Piped water, % dwellings	48	17	98	45	81
Food: Sugar/cap	62	23	294	301	209
: Protein 85 grm/day/cap			100	62	74
: Calories/cap/day	2630	2110	3460	2470	2870
: Meat prod/cap 88	0	0	0.1	0	0
Energy: Consumption/cap	819	203	5100	280	2320
: Electricity/cap	488	112	6880	361	3620

4

DEMOGRAPHY & SOCIOLOGY
ACROSS ETHNIC CULTURES

Ethnic groups are often distinguished by their demographic and social behaviors. This chapter provides comparative statistics for a variety of demographic and sociological variables across ethnic groups. For a full discussion of the methodology used to generate these estimates, please refer to Chapter 1 which gives important caveats. This chapter first gives summary statistics of the variables reported: the number of countries/cultures for which each variable was available, the number of ethnic cultures covered, weighted averages (by population) and simple averages; these averages can be used as benchmarks. Then a lengthy comparative table is presented which provides raw statistics across the ethnic groups defined in Chapter 1.

Most of the variables are self explanatory, though some merit commentary. All of the statistics should be considered as estimates which have undergone rounding and certain adjustments. Estimates in this chapter span a variety of topics. The first three are important as they measure the population covered, the number of countries where the ethnic group is surveyed and the average percent representation each group has within their social systems (i.e. if this number is low, the ethnic group is in the minority within its social systems). After that, various demographic and vital statistics are reported. The variable "Population country" is not the population of the ethnic group, but rather the weighted average population size of the social system where the ethnic group is present in 1994. Various social and political variables are also given covering migration, political systems and censorship, social unrest, and the number and prevalence of certain diseases. The timing of settlements, largest cities, and political independence for each ethnic group (negative numbers signify BC) are also reported. Then various demographic variables are presented. The estimate of "." signifies a missing value due to a lack of underlying data.

Summary Statistics:
Demographic and Sociological Resources

Characteristics	Number of Countries Covered	Number of Ethnic Groups Covered	Weighted Average by Pop 1994	Simple Average	Simple Standard Deviation
Population Covered	234	426	364546.22	12906.37	67446.81
Countries represented, #	234	426	8.12	2.66	4.69
Average representation, %	234	426	49.01	18.35	23.31
Vital Stats: Death rate	225	423	9.22	11.38	4.30
: Birth rate	225	423	26.49	34.55	12.64
: Fertility	221	416	3.36	4.72	1.96
: Female life exp., years	225	423	68.75	63.60	10.49
: Male life exp., years	225	423	65.03	59.63	9.38
: Infant mortality	227	425	69.25	87.37	46.59
: # of major diseases	202	416	3.12	3.30	2.27
Demography: Migration/1000	223	422	0.18	4.94	37.55
: Population of Country	234	426	461500.68	67342.44	213712.75
: Urbanization, %	214	422	43.62	41.30	21.67
: Population growth	204	417	2.11	2.30	0.97
: Females, % of pop	198	402	49.58	49.98	1.95
Male % ages: 0-9 years	176	384	51.15	50.57	1.04
: 10-19 years	176	384	51.27	50.62	1.38
: 20-29 years	176	384	50.82	49.85	3.14
: 30-39 years	176	384	50.63	49.76	3.19
: 40-49 years	176	384	50.86	50.19	2.88
: 50-59 years	176	384	50.83	50.35	3.87
: 60-69 years	176	384	48.68	49.14	3.80
: 70+ years	176	384	44.84	47.11	5.97
Education: Literacy, adult	230	425	72.01	66.61	24.94
Cities: earliest settled, year	182	398	-529.52	910.78	1257.06
: Largest settled, year	182	398	943.61	1368.48	776.99
: Largest, % pop	202	416	5.42	11.72	10.35
Politics: # of parties	228	425	3.97	3.56	2.76
: Largest party, %	206	413	64.42	70.31	26.81
: Top two parties, %	206	413	79.81	84.33	19.29
: Chambers in leg., #	229	426	1.51	1.32	0.44
: # of changes since 1960	202	416	1.82	2.00	1.39
: Independence year	231	425	1922.79	1919.98	134.42
Laws: Censorship (1=high)	192	410	0.56	0.56	0.39
: Metric system (1=yes)	222	420	0.09	0.10	0.29
: Visas needed (3=high)	202	416	2.63	2.62	0.51
: Full soc security (1=yes)	192	410	0.26	0.20	0.38
: Military service (1=yes)	192	410	0.56	0.38	0.47
Crime: Murders/100k pop	82	165	9.60	16.88	31.44
: Thefts/100k pop	51	148	1118.67	1425.78	1997.74
: Suicide/100k pop	64	91	10.89	13.06	10.22
: Prisoners/000 pop	72	172	0.83	0.93	1.24
: Death penalty (1=yes)	191	407	0.70	0.45	0.47
Unrest: Border disputes, #	233	425	4.78	1.75	2.56
: International wars, #	202	416	0.33	0.29	0.70
: # of civil wars	202	416	1.12	1.09	1.18
: # of civil riots	202	416	0.33	0.28	0.47

Characteristics	Abadkis	Abkhaz	Acholi	Afar	Afro-European	Akan	Albanian	Ambo	Amerind	Amerind-Mestizo
Population Covered	359	99	886	1280	379	8630	5170	206	37000	5020
Countries represented, #	1	1	1	3	1	1	4	1	1	1
Average representation %	2	2	5	2	15	52	20	2	7	15
Vital Stats: Death rate	14		14	14	6	13	5	19	6	9
: Birth rate	38	17	51	45	23	45	22	46	29	20
: Fertility	5		7		3	6	3	6	3	3
: Female life exp., years	53	75	55	53	78	58	79	48	75	75
: Male life exp., years	54	72	51	50	72	54	72	45	68	68
: Infant mortality	115	36	112	138	39	105	52	161	56	51
: # of major diseases	5	0	6	4	1	2	5	4	2	2
Demography: Migration/100	0		2	2	-8	-1		0	-0.9	
: Population of Country	21100	5490	19300	39800	2510	16500	5350	10300	84100	33500
: Urbanization, %	8	56	10	23	50	32	40	27	66	86
: Population growth	2	0.8	5	4	1	2	2	3	3	3
: Females, % of pop	49		50	50	51	51	49	48	50	50
Male % ages: 0-9 years	52		50	50	50	49	51	52	51	51
: 10-19 years	52		50	52	50	49	52	52	51	51
: 20-29 years	50		49	47	48	49	52	52	50	51
: 30-39 years	49		49	48	49	49	51	53	49	50
: 40-49 years	51		49	50	49	50	52	53	48	50
: 50-59 years	53		50	53	49	48	50	52	46	46
: 60-69 years	53		50	54	47	50	50	52	46	42
: 70+ years	26		48	56	43	50		42	44	
Education: Literacy, adult		100		62	98	87	87		83	95
Cities: earliest settled, year	723		1890	897	1530	1600	1560	1580	1270	1550
: Largest settled, year	723		1890	1890	1690	1600	1560	1580	1430	1580
: Largest, % pop	5	23	2	13	21	6	7	17	10	9
Politics: # of parties	54	5	0	1	2	4	4	5	5	8
: Largest party %	88	8	100	100	75	95	54	59	58	50
: Top two parties, %		14	100	100	100	95	80	91	79	82
: Chambers in leg., #	2		1	2	1	1	1	2	2	2
: # of changes 60		1	3						0.8	
Independence year	1770	1990	1960	1990	1960	1960	1940	1980	1850	1820
Laws: Censorship (1=high)	0	1	0.5	0.6	0	1	0.3	0.5	0.5	0.5
: Metric system (1=yes)	0	0	0	0	1	0	0	0	0.1	
: Visas needed (3=high)	3	2	3	3	2	3	3	3	0.1	2
: Full soc security (1=yes)	0	0	0	0	0	0	0.3	0	0.1	0
: Military service (1=yes)	0	1	0	1	0	0	1	1	0.9	1
Crime: Murders/100k pop	.		.	0.1	.	.		.	15	2
: Thefts/100k pop	.		.	37	2	.	475	.	4050	153
: Suicide/100k pop	0		0.5	0.3	1	1	0.5		0.5	0.7
: Prisoners/000 pop	0		0		0	0	0.3		0.2	0.8
: Death penalty (1=yes)	0	1	0		1	0	2			.
Unrest: Border disputes, #	0	0	0	0.4	0	3	0	0	0.5	4
: International, #	.	0	2	0.8	0	0	0	1	0.5	1
: # of civil wars	0	1	0	0.2				2	0.5	1
: # of civil riots	1	0	0					0	0.5	0

Characteristics	Amhara	Ana-Ife	Andorran	Angolares	Anouis	Antandroy	Arab, other	Arab Berber	Arab Emirian	Arab Lebanese
Population Covered	20000	117	15	29	1430	702	102000	4710	560	2380
Countries represented, #	1	3	1	1	1	1	26	2	1	1
Average representation %	38	12	28	0.3	1		22	89	31	83
Vital Stats: Death rate	14	48	4	9	12	14	8	7	3	7
..Birth rate	45		11	20	47	46	37	37	29	28
..Fertility		58	1	3	57	57	5	5	5	4
..Female life exp., years	53	54	81	75	53	54	68	70	74	71
..Male life exp., years	50	123	74	69	116	115	65	65	70	67
..Infant mortality	134	5	5	41			82	92	39	64
..# of major diseases	4	2	0	2	3	5	4	5	5	5
Demography: Migration/100	2		1	1	1		0	-0.1	27	-5
..Population of Country	52900	3910	15	6860	13400	13300	204000	4850	1820	2880
..Urbanization, %	12	24	53	34	42	23	52	67	78	82
..Population growth			74	0.9				4		2
Females, % of pop	50	51	47	51	50	51	49	47	29	49
Male % ages: 0-9 years	52	49	51	51	51	49	51	53	51	51
..10-19 years	46	49	53	50	48	49	51	53	63	51
..20-29 years	47	49	56	48	49	49	50	53	81	51
..30-39 years	49	49	56	48	50	49	49	53	82	51
..40-49 years	53	49	54	48	52	49	50	53	78	51
..50-59 years	54	48	51	46	51	50	50	52	74	50
..60-69 years	57	50	54	39	50	50	49	53	59	51
..70+ years	71	43	50	76	46	50	58	62	60	80
Education: Literacy, adult	700	1900	100	-917	54	54	-1140	-585	68	-700
Cities: earliest settled, year	1890	1900		-917	1900	1610	-599	-585	1760	-1500
..Largest settled, year	3	10	34	14	1900	1610	11	21	1800	44
..Largest, % pop	1	5	5	5	14	6	4		11	5
Politics: # of parties	100	44	14	59	4	5	67	100	0	27
..Largest party %	100	87	25	92	93	34	76	100	100	48
..Top two parties, %	1	1	1	1	98	46	1	1	100	1
..Chambers in leg., #	2	2	2	2	1	2	2	2	2	
..# of changes 60	1990	1960	1280	1740	2	1	2	2		
Independence year	0.5	1	0	1990	1960	1960	1950	1950	1970	1940
Laws: Censorship (1=high)	0	0	1	0.2	1	0.5	0.9	1	1	0
..Metric system (1=yes)	3	2	0	0	0	0	0	0	3	0
..Visas needed (3=high)	0	0	0	2	3	3	3	3	1	3
..Full soc security (1=yes)	0	0	0	0.7	0	0	0.2	0		0
..Military service (1=yes)			0	0.7	0	0		0		0
Crime: Murders/100k pop	37			2			-2	3		
..Thefts/100k pop				436			347			
..Suicide/100k pop	0.3			0.8		3	12	211		
..Prisoners/000 pop	0	0	0	0	0	0			1	3
..Death penalty (1=yes)	5	0	0	1	0	1	3	1	4	3
Unrest: Border disputes, #	1	0	0	0.7	0	0	2	2	0	4
..International, #	3	1	0	0	0	1	1	2	0	3
..# of civil wars	3		0		0		0.6	1		4
..# of civil riots	0	1	0	0	1	0		0	0	1

Characteristics	Arab Omani	Arab Palestin.	Arab Quatar	Arab Saudi	Arab Sudanic	Arab Total	Arauca-nian	Armenian	Assamese	Assyrian
Population Covered	1240	1520	98	13500	15000	143000	939	4790	217	159
Countries represented, #	—	2	1	—	2	34	1	9	—	1
Average representation %	74	36	20	82	45	28	7	4	13	0.8
Vital Stats: Death rate	6	6	4	6	14	8	6	7	17	0.9
Birth rate	41	34	21	39	44	38	21	24	40	45
Fertility	—	—	—	7	6	5	3	3	6	7
Female life exp., years	69	71	74	68	53	66	77	74	49	68
Male life exp., years	65	68	69	65	52	64	71	69	50	66
Infant mortality	60	42	45	88	109	84	33	44	147	97
# of major diseases	5	5	4	4	6	4	0	0.5	6	0
Demography: Migration/100	—	0.7	15	0	0	0	0	-5	0	0
Population of Country	1680	1680	489	16500	25200	19200	13800	8120	1640	19900
Urbanization, %	10	82	89	74	26	53	84	65	10	72
Population growth	—	2	6	5	3	3	2	1	2	3
Females, % of pop	47	50	36	47	50	49	51	49	49	48
Male % ages: 0-9 years	53	51	54	53	50	51	51	52	51	52
10-19 years	53	51	71	53	50	51	51	51	51	51
20-29 years	53	51	73	53	50	52	50	51	51	53
30-39 years	52	51	72	53	49	50	49	51	52	52
40-49 years	53	51	73	53	48	50	47	52	51	51
50-59 years	53	51	71	53	47	50	45	51	51	49
60-69 years	53	51	50	53	43	49	41	50	51	52
70+ years	—	—	—	—	27	—	—	48	—	48
Education: Literacy, adult	41	80	76	62	27	55	93	95	38	60
Cities: earliest settled, year	1510	-1670	1870	200	1810	-578	1540	-851	1580	-3000
Largest settled, year	1510	-1820	1870	1700	1830	775	1540	413	1580	762
Largest, % pop	3	44	42	8	3	11	37	31	1	24
Politics: # of parties	—	5	—	—	0.1	3	6	4	—	1
Largest party %	100	86	100	100	100	75	31	46	100	100
Top two parties, %	100	90	100	100	100	82	55	67	100	100
Chambers in leg., #	1	1	1	1	3	2	2	1	1	2
# of changes 60	2	—	—	—	—	—	4	—	—	—
Independence year	1650	1940	1970	1930	1960	1950	1820	1980	1870	1930
Laws: Censorship (1=high)	1	0	1	1	0.9	0.9	0	0	1	—
Metric system (1=yes)	—	0	—	—	—	—	—	—	—	0
Visas needed (3=high)	3	3	2	3	3	—	2	2	3	3
Full soc security (1=yes)	0	0	1	1	0	0.3	1	1	0	1
Military service (1=yes)	1	1	1	—	—	0.8	—	—	0	1
Crime: Murders/100k pop	—	—	—	0.6	—	—	—	—	—	—
Thefts/100k pop	—	—	—	58	—	268	832	2310	—	—
Suicide/100k pop	—	—	—	—	—	12	5	16	—	—
Prisoners/000 pop	—	—	13	—	—	1	0.2	0.2	—	—
Death penalty (1=yes)	1	1	1	1	—	1	—	0.3	—	1
Unrest: Border disputes, #	3	1	1	5	0.9	1	4	0.3	—	5
International, #	2	1	2	1	2	1	0	0.9	0	4
# of civil wars	3	3	0	0	2	3	0	—	0	2
# of civil riots	2	4	0	1	0	2	2	—	0	0

Characteristics	Austrian	Avar	Aymara	Azande	Azerbaijani	Bagirmi Sara	Bahraini	Bai	Bakhtiari	Bakongo
Population Covered	7390	59	2560	3570	17000	1830	345	1700	1080	1340
Countries represented, #	2	1	2	3	4	3	1	1	1	1
Average representation %	94	0.8	8	5	21	31	65	0.1	2	13
Vital Stats: Death rate	11	7	8	13	8	21	4	7	8	19
: Birth rate	12	26	30	45	37	42	27	22	44	46
: Fertility	2	3	4	6	5	5	4	2	7	7
: Female life exp., years	81	74	65	55	70	49	76	73	68	48
: Male life exp., years	74	70	61	52	68	46	71	69	67	45
: Infant mortality	11	47	99	112	72	148	32	52	88	161
: # of major diseases	0	0	3	3	3	4	2	2	5	4
Demography: Migration/100	5	-3	-0.5	0	-1	0	2	0	0	0
: Population of Country	7810	7350	15100	34900	42300	5990	532	1210000	63200	10300
: Urbanization, %	58	54	60	38	55	28	82	29	55	27
: Population growth	0.3	2	3	3	2	2	5	3	3	3
: Females, % of pop	53		50		48	52	40	49	48	48
Male % ages: 0-9 years	51		51	51	52	48	50	52	52	52
: 10-19 years	51		51	51	52	48	51	51	52	52
: 20-29 years	50		50	50	52	48	66	51	52	52
: 30-39 years	50		50	50	52	47	70	52	52	53
: 40-49 years	49		49	49	52	48	64	53	52	53
: 50-59 years	49		49	49	50	48	60	53	52	53
: 60-69 years	39		47	48	48	47	57	49	50	52
: 70+ years	34		44	46	50		54	43	48	42
Education: Literacy, adult	99	98	86	43	70	30	77	73	54	
Cities: earliest settled, year	-400		539	1860	-1100	1900	1510	-2210	-1100	1580
: Largest settled, year	-400		1540	1870	-1200	1900	1510	1100	-1200	1580
: Largest, % pop	20	25	18	0.4	16	10	28	0.6	10	17
Politics: # of parties	4	5	6		1	1	1	1		5
: Largest party %	44	80	47	95	91	100	100	100	100	59
: Top two parties, %	77	80	83	96	91	100	100	100	100	91
: Chambers in leg., #	2		2					3		
: # of changes 60	0	1	4	2	2	4	1	1	2	2
: Independence year	1920	1990	1860	1960	1940	1960	1970	1910	1910	1980
Laws: Censorship (1=high)	0	0	0.7	0	0	0.5	0.5	0	0	0.5
: Metric system (1=yes)	0	1	0	3	3	3	3	3	3	3
: Visas needed (3=high)	2	0	2		0	0		0	0	0
: Full soc security (1=yes)	1	2	0		1		1	1	1	1
: Military service (1=yes)	1	0	1				0.7			
Crime: Murders/100k pop	2	1	7	0.9	0.6		2	177		30
: Thefts/100k pop	2970		351							
: Suicide/100k pop	27		0.5	0.2	0.5			1	5	1
: Prisoners/000 pop	0.7		0.8	0.1	0.6			1	1	1
: Death penalty (1=yes)	0	0	0.5	0.7	0.1		1	2	1	2
Unrest: Border disputes, #	1	400	2			1	1	2		
: International, #	0	0	0			3	1	0	5	0
: # of civil wars	0	0	4			2	0	2	1	2
: # of civil riots	0	1	0			0	0	0	1	0

Characteristics	Balante	Baluchi	Bambara	Bamileke-Bamum	Banda	Bangi-Ngale	Bantu	Baoule	Bari	Bariba
Population Covered	279	4860	3230	2320	1350	2390	1240	1590	549	492
Countries represented, #	1	4	3	1	2	1	2	1	1	1
Average representation %	27	12	32	19	3	6	6	12	13	10
Vital Stats: Death rate	18	4	21	11	16	13	8	12	13	15
: Birth rate	42	43	52	44	44	45	40	47	44	49
: Fertility	6	7	7	6	6	6	5	7	6	7
: Female life exp., years	49	61	48	60	51	56	64	57	54	53
: Male life exp., years	45	61	45	55	48	53	60	53	53	49
: Infant mortality	146	117	132	115	126	112	82	116	105	136
: # of major diseases	5	6	5	6	6	2	3	3	6	5
Demography: Migration/100		-0.6	-5	0	0	0	-3	3	0	0
: Population of Country	1030	104000	10100	12600	14900	41200	10900	13400	27400	5070
: Urbanization, %	26	38	20	41	42	41	28	42	26	31
: Population growth	2	3	2	3	2	3	3	4	3	3
: Females, % of pop	52	48	51	50	51	51	51	50	50	52
Male % ages: 0-9 years	50	51	50	50	50		49	51	51	51
: 10-19 years	51	54	49	50	49		50	48	50	51
: 20-29 years	40	52	49	50	48		49	49	50	38
: 30-39 years	44	51	49	49	48		50	50	49	44
: 40-49 years	46	51	47	49	48		49	52	49	46
: 50-59 years	51	54	48	47	47		49	51	48	49
: 60-69 years	57	56		45	45		48	51	47	49
: 70+ years	59	55	39	54	43		50	46	43	50
Education: Literacy, adult	36	41	32	54	48	72	66	54	43	23
Cities: earliest settled, year	1760	-735	1100	1880	1890	1880	1860	1900	1800	1600
: Largest settled, year	1760	1490	1880	1880	1890	1890	1860	1900	1820	1870
: Largest, % pop	12	6	8	4	16	7	5	14	2	10
Politics: # of parties		4	6	9	3	0				4
: Largest party %	100	61	66	49	58	100	97	93	100	19
: Top two parties, %	100	86	74	87	69	100	99	98	100	33
: Chambers in leg., #	2	2	1	1	2	1	1	1	1	1
: # of changes 60	3	1	3	2		3			3	7
Independence year	1970	1930	1960	1960	1960	1960	1980	1960	1960	1960
Laws: Censorship (1=high)	1	0.7	0	0.5	1	1	0	1	1	1
: Metric system (1=yes)	0	0.3	0	0	0	0	0	0	0	0
: Visas needed (3=high)	3	3	3	3	3	3	2	3	3	3
: Full soc security (1=yes)	0		0	0	0	0	0	0	0	0
: Military service (1=yes)	·	0.3	·	·	·	·	·	·	·	·
Crime: Murders/100k pop	·	78	1	1	0.3	·	18	·	·	1
: Thefts/100k pop	·	18	0	0	·	·	1450	·	·	0
: Suicide/100k pop	·	·	0	0	0.6	·	17	·	·	0
: Prisoners/000 pop	·	0.3	·	·	·	·	2	·	·	·
: Death penalty (1=yes)	0	0.3	2	0	0.2	·	1	0	1	·
Unrest: Border disputes, #	0	4	0	0	0.3	2	0.1	0	2	0
: International, #	0	0.3	0	0		0	1	0	1	0
: # of civil wars	2	1	2	0		1		0	2	0
: # of civil riots	0	0.4	0			1		1	0	5

Characteristics	Barotze	Baskhir	Basque	Bassa	Batswana	Bayad	Beja	Belgian	Belorus-sian	Bemba
Population Covered	727	1340	904	396	1020	44	1760	310	10007	3120
Countries represented, #	1	1	2	1	1	1	1	3	7	1
Average representation %	8	0.9	2	14	76	2	6	10	4	35
Vital Stats: Death rate	11	11	9	13	8	7	13	10	11	11
: Birth rate	48	15	11	44	35	34	44	12	15	48
: Fertility	7	2	1	7	4	5	6			
: Female life exp., years	59	74	82	59	65	68	54	81	76	59
: Male life exp., years	55	70	75	55	59	63	53	74	72	55
: Infant mortality	97	36	11	141	69	75	105		26	97
: # of major diseases					1	3	6	0		2
Demography: Migration/100	-2	0	0	2	0	0	0	1	0.9	-2
: Population of Country	8870	149000	39000	2870	1350	2320	27400	9690	28500	8870
: Urbanization, %	49	71	81	45	26	56	26	96	66	49
: Population growth	3	0.7				3	3	0.3	0.7	3
: Females, % of pop	51		51	49	52	50	50	51	53	51
Male % ages: 0-9 years			52	51	50	50	51	51	51	
: 10-19 years			51	50	50	50	50	51	50	
: 20-29 years			50	48	45	50	50	51	51	
: 30-39 years			50	55	43	50	50	50	51	
: 40-49 years			48	57	46	50	49	49	47	
: 50-59 years			46	61	47	50	48	46	45	
: 60-69 years			46	40	41	50	47	46	36	
: 70+ years			40		74	50	43	37	28	
Education: Literacy, adult	73	99	96		74	90	27	100	100	73
Cities: earliest settled, year	1900		-1200	1820	1900	1650	1800	416		1900
: Largest settled, year	1910		931	1820	1900	1650	1820	610		1910
: Largest, % pop	8	6	1	16	9	24	2	10		
Politics: # of parties	2	8	11		2	3		9	5	2
: Top two parties, %	83	21	46	100	91	92	100	19	78	83
: Largest party %	100	37	86	100	100	97	100	36	88	100
: Chambers in leg., #	2	2	2	1	2	1		2	1	1
: # of changes 60		1	2	3		2	3	1	2	
Independence year	1960	1990	1490	1850	1970	1920	1960	1830	1990	1960
Laws: Censorship (1=high)	0.5	0.5	0.5	1	0	0	0	0.2	0.9	0.5
: Metric system (1=yes)		0	0	1	2	3	3	2	0.0	0.0
: Visas needed (3=high)	3	2	2	3	0	0	0	1	2	3
: Full soc security (1=yes)	0	1	1	0	0	1	0	0	0.1	0
: Military service (1=yes)	0	1	1	0	0		0	1		0
Crime: Murders/100k pop								2		
: Thefts/100k pop			2040					2620		
: Suicide/100k pop			0.7					22		
: Prisoners/000 pop								0.7	0.1	
: Death penalty (1=yes)	0	1	0	1	0	0	1	0		0
Unrest: Border disputes, #	2	1	2	0	4	0	2	0	0	2
: International, #	0	0	0	0	0	0	1	0	0	0
: # of civil wars	0	0	0	0	0	0	2	0	0	0
: # of civil riots	0	0	1	3	0	0	0	0	0	0

Characteristics	Bengali	Berber	Bete	Betsileo	Betsimi-Saraka	Bhutia	Bihari	Black	Black Amerind	Boa
Population Covered	119000	12800	2640	1550	1970	1030	5540	71300	1020	947
Countries represented, #	2	3	1	1	1		4	36	1	1
Average representation %	96	20	20	12	15	63		11	3	2
Vital Stats: Death rate	12	8	12	14	14	17	13	8	5	13
::Birth rate	36	30	47	46	46	40	37	22	24	45
::Fertility	5	4	7	7	7	6	5	3	3	6
::Female life exp., years	54	67	57	57	57	49	53	74	74	56
::Male life exp., years	55	64	53	54	54	50	54	68	69	53
::Infant mortality	129	82	116	118	118	147	119	50	54	112
::# of major diseases	7	4	5	5	5	6	6	2	4	2
Demography: Migration/100	0	-0.6	0	0	0	0	0	0	0	0
::Population of Country	122000	26900	13400	13300	13300	1640	50100	156000	34000	41200
::Urbanization, %	18	47	42	23	23	10	11	68	68	41
::Population growth	3	3	4	3	3	2	2	2	2	3
::Females, % of pop	48	50	50	51	51	49	49	51	50	51
Male % ages: 0-9 years	50	51	51	49	49	51	52	51	51	
::10-19 years	52	51	48	49	49	52	52	51	50	
::20-29 years	51	50	49	49	49	51	51	50	48	
::30-39 years	52	48	50	49	49	52	51	49	49	
::40-49 years	53	46	52	50	49	51	53	49	49	
::50-59 years	55	48	51	50	50	52	53	47	50	
::60-69 years	56	50	50	50	50	52	53	42	49	
::70+ years	35	49	46	50	50	38	29	87	48	72
Education: Literacy, adult		53	54	80	80				87	
Cities: earliest settled, year	800	-1060	1900	1610	1610	1580	745	1560	1530	1880
::Largest settled, year	1610	1310	1900	1610	1610	1580	977	1610	1540	1890
::Largest, % pop	2	9	14	6	6	1	1	6	12	7
Politics: # of parties	5	4	4	5	5		5	4	4	
::Largest party %	46	47	93	34	34	100	52	54	50	0
::Top two parties, %	76	57	98	46	46	100	85	82	77	0
::Chambers in leg., #	4	1	1	2	2	1	2	2	2	1
::# of changes 60			0	1	1					
Independence year	1970	1960	1960	1960	1960	1870	1830	1900	1900	1960
Laws: Censorship (1=high)	0	1	1	0.5	0.5	0	0	0.2	0.5	
::Metric system (1=yes)	0	0	0	0	0	3	3	0.5	0.2	0
::Visas needed (3=high)	2	2	3	3	3		3		2	3
::Full soc security (1=yes)	0	0	0					0.8		
::Military service (1=yes)	0	1	0	3	3			0.3	1	
Crime: Murders/100k pop	2	2		0	0	0	11	19	62	
::Thefts/100k pop	11	204	1	1	1	0		5130	142	
::Suicide/100k pop				0	0	0	0.3	9	4	
::Prisoners/000 pop	0.3	0.8		1	1	0	0.3	0.5		
::Death penalty (1=yes)	1	1		0	0	0	0.3	0.6		
Unrest: Border disputes, #	1	2	0	1	1	0	0.3	3	1	1
::International, #	0		0	0	0	0	0.3	0.9	0	2
::# of civil wars	1	0.4	0	1	1	0	0.7	0.4	2	0
::# of civil riots	0	0.4	1	0	0	0		0.3	0	1

Characteristics	Bobo	Bounty Mutineers	Brazilian	Breton	Bubi	Bulgarian	Bullom	Bura	Burman	Bush Negro
Population Covered	909	0.2	16	577	58	7960	167	1810	30800	43
Countries represented, #	2	2	2	2		2		2	6	2
Average representation %	5	7	0.2	1		12	4		9	8
Vital Stats: Death rate	17		7	9	15	12	20	16	10	6
..Birth rate	50		17	13	42	12	46	46	29	26
..Fertility	7				5	2		7	4	3
..Female life exp., years	52		78	82	53	76	48	54	64	75
..Male life exp., years	50		71	74	49	70	43	51	61	68
..Infant mortality	137		20	10	132	28	163	128	96	47
..# of major diseases	5				6		5	2	8	1
Demography: Migration/100	-3		0	0	0	-5	-28	0	0	-1
..Population of Country	9880	2	63500	57100	395	10300	4510	107000	44600	398
..Urbanization, %	12		50	75	51	67	31	29	24	52
..Population growth	2		1	0.7	2	0.5	2	3	2	-0.2
..Females, % of pop	52		50	51	52	51	50	50	50	51
Male % ages: 0-9 years	49		51	51	48	51	50	51	50	50
..10-19 years	48		51	51	48	51	50	50	50	50
..20-29 years	48		52	50	48	51	50	50	49	48
..30-39 years	48		51	51	48	50	49	50	49	49
..40-49 years	48		50	51	48	50	49	50	49	51
..50-59 years	47		50	49	49	47	49	50	49	50
..60-69 years	46		48	46	48	44	50	51	46	45
..70+ years	22		41	36	50		51	51		
Education: Literacy, adult		94	84	99		96			81	93
Cities: earliest settled, year	1170		-672	-1000	1830	-600	1790	1100	-585	1560
..Largest settled, year	1380		-672	-300	1830	100	1790	1700	-585	1560
..Largest, % pop	6		19	15	16	12	11	1	6	28
Politics: # of parties	6		5	11	4	3	1		1	6
..Largest party %	71	100	59	43	85	45	100	100	100	59
..Top two parties, %	81	100	90	80	93	89		100	100	82
..Chambers in leg., #		1	2	2	4	1	1			
..# of changes 60	4							4	4	2
Independence year	1960	1810	1700	1680	1970	1910	1960	1960	1950	1950
Laws: Censorship (1=high)			0	0	1	0		0.5	1	0.5
..Metric system (1=yes)			0		0	0				
..Visas needed (3=high)	3		2	2	3	2	3	3	3	3
..Full soc security (1=yes)	0		1	1	0	1	0	0	0	
..Military service (1=yes)	0		1	1	0		0	1	1	1
Crime: Murders/100k pop			2	3		3			5	5
..Thefts/100k pop			436	4020		593		1260	56	
..Suicide/100k pop			9	23		17		94		22
..Prisoners/000 pop			0.8	0.8		2				
..Death penalty (1=yes)	1		0	0	1		1		1	
Unrest: Border disputes, #	0	0		7	0	0	0	0	0	0
..International, #	0		2	0	1	0	0	0	0	2
..# of civil wars	0.5		0.6	0	1	0	2	4	3	0
..# of civil riots	0.0		0	1	1	0	0	0	1	0

Characteristics	Bushman	Capver-dien	Caroli-nians	Catalan	Chahar Aimak	Chamba	Chamorro	Chiga	Chin	Chinese
Population Covered	46	20	19	6380	558	301	82	1310	893	26100
Countries represented, #	1	1	1	1	1	1	2	1	1	24
Average representation %	3	0.2	40	16	3	1	43	7	2	6
Vital Stats: Death rate	8	10	45	11	20	11	4	14	10	21
Birth rate	35	12	35	11	44	44	29	51	29	4
Fertility	4	3	3	3	4	6		7	4	75
Female life exp., years	65	78	69	82	44	60	74	55	64	70
Male life exp., years	59	71	66	75	45	55	70	51	61	33
Infant mortality	69	22	38	11	172	115	21	112	96	2
# of major diseases	1	1	0	0	4	6	2	6	8	-0.3
Demography: Migration/100	0	2	0	0	0	0	2	0	0	45500
Population of country	1350	9890		39200	19200	12600	119	19300	44600	54
Urbanization, %	26	33	48	81	18	41	40		24	2
Population growth	4	0.4		1	2	3	3	3	2	50
Females, % of pop	52	52		51	50	50	48	50	50	51
Male % ages: 0-9 years	50	51		51	50	50	52	50	50	51
10-19 years	45	50		52	49	50	53	49	50	51
20-29 years	43	49		51	48	50	52	49	49	51
30-39 years	46	47		50	51	49	52	49	49	51
40-49 years	46	47		48	56	49	53	49	49	50
50-59 years	47	45		46	58	47	54	50	49	47
60-69 years	41	38		40	58	45	50	50	46	42
70+ years		85	97	96	29	54	96	48	81	87
Education: Literacy, adult	74									627
Cities: earliest settled, year	1900	-2000		-1200	-400	1880	1670	1890	-585	1390
Largest settled, year	1900	-2000		931	-400	1880	1670	1890	-585	23
Largest, % pop	9	8		8	9	10	30	2	6	4
Politics: # of parties	2	5	2	11	3	4	2	0	1	65
Largest party %	91	59		46	2	49	2	100	100	78
Top two parties, %	100	90	2	86	4	87	1	100	100	2
Chambers in leg., #	2	1		1		1		1	4	1920
# of changes 60	1	2	1950	1490	1920	1960	1910	1960	1950	0.5
Independence year	1970	1640		0.5		0.5		0.5	1	
Laws: Censorship (1=high)		0		2	0	2			1	0.4
Metric system (1=yes)	2	2		1	2	3	2	3	3	0.4
Visas needed (3=high)	0	1		2	0	0		0	0	6
Full soc security (1=yes)		2		1	2	1		0.5	5	903
Military service (1=yes)	0	436		2040				0	56	10
Crime: Murders/100k pop	4	9		0.7	4	1			1	0.8
Thefts/100k pop	0	0.8		2	1	0	0		0	2
Suicide/100k pop	0	2	0	0	5	0	0	0	0	0.3
Prisoners/000 pop	0	0		1	2	0	0	2	3	0.7
Death penalty (1=yes)		1		0					1	0
Unrest: Border disputes, #										
International, #	4									
# of civil wars	0									
# of civil riots	0									

Characteristics	Chinese Mainland	Chokwe	Chuang	Chuvash	Circassian	Coloured	Comorian	Creole	Croatian	Czech
Population Covered	2910	1170	12100	1790	201	3960	636	1040	4590	10100
Countries represented, #	1	2	1	1	2	1	1	6	4	4
Average representation %	14	15	7	1	0.3	10	5	50	21	21
Vital Stats: Death rate	15	45	22	11	6	8	12	21	10	11
: Birth rate	16	6	2	15	29	34	47	2	12	13
: Fertility	2	53	73	2	4	4	7	75	2	2
: Female life exp., years	78	50	69	74	72	67	59	75	76	77
: Male life exp., years	72	130	52	70	68	62	55	69	70	69
: Infant mortality	5	3	2	36	74	72	107	35	22	19
: # of major diseases	1	0	0	0	0.3	1	4	2	0	0
Demography: Migration/100	0	0	0	0	0.1	0	0	-5	0	0.1
: Population of Country	20800	29800	1210000	149000	53500	39600	1410	761	4740	10700
: Urbanization, %	70	36	29	1	62	59	27	45	46	77
: Population growth	1	50	49	0.7	3	2	3	1	0.6	1
: Females, % of pop	48	52	52	99	49	49	50	50	52	51
Male % ages: 0-9 years	52	52	51		51	50	51	51	51	51
: 10-19 years	52	52	51		51	50	51	51	52	51
: 20-29 years	52	53	52		51	53	46	50	51	50
: 30-39 years	53	53	53		50	53	48	49	51	50
: 40-49 years	52	52	49		51	52	52	50	48	49
: 50-59 years	53	53	43		49	50	51	49	47	46
: 60-69 years	52	52	73		44	47	51	39	43	41
: 70+ years	92	61		99	81	40	50	87	37	
Education: Literacy, adult	1630	1770	-2210		-3100	76	1870	1670	96	99
Cities: earliest settled, year	1710	1770	1100		-377	1650	1870	1670	-100	1580
: Largest settled, year	13	11	0.6		11	1650	4	24	19	1790
: Largest, % pop	2		100	6	42	5	56	52	24	13
Politics: # of parties	79	85	100	8	67	63	97	89	8	6
: Largest party %	97	97		21		84			57	39
: Top two parties, %	2	1	1	37	2	2	5	1	71	57
: Chambers in leg., #	1		3	2	1		1		1	2
: # of changes 60										1
Independence year	1950	1970	1910	1990	1930	1930	1970	1950	1990	1990
Laws: Censorship (1=high)	0.5	0.8	0	0.5	0.2	0.5	0.5	0.1	1	1
: Metric system (1=yes)			3	2				2	0.1	2
: Visas needed (3=high)	3	3	1	1	0.9	3	3	0.3	0.8	0
: Full soc security (1=yes)	0	0.4	2	1	0.9	0	0	0.2		1
: Military service (1=yes)	1		177		68	109	30	0.3	2340	1
Crime: Murders/100k pop										4
: Thefts/100k pop		0.6	1	1	0.9	0.3	1	15	45	5040
: Suicide/100k pop	1	2	12	1	4	1	2	0.3	41	15
: Prisoners/000 pop	2000	1	2	0	2	0	1	0.8	1	0.8
: Death penalty (1=yes)	0	0		0	0.1	0	0	0.2	2	1
Unrest: Border disputes, #	0	0.6		0	0.9	2	0	0.3	1	0
: International, #	0							0	0	0
: # of civil wars										0
: # of civil riots										

Characteristics	Dagestani	Dai	Damara	Dan	Danish	Dinka	Dogon	Dong	Dravidian	Duala
Population Covered	1730	1090	125	922	5030	3160	405	2660	224000	11
Countries represented, #	2			2	4	1	1			1
Average representation %	1	0.1			5			0.2		3
Vital Stats: Death rate	10	7	9	6	11	13	21	7	25	15
: Birth rate	16	22	45	12	12	44	52	22	11	42
: Fertility	2	2	6		2	6	7	2	30	4
: Female life exp., years	74	73	63	57	79	54	48	73	6	53
: Male life exp., years	70	69	58	53	73	53	45	69	61	49
: Infant mortality	38	52	97	120	10	105	132	52	60	132
: # of major diseases		0	4	4	0	6	5	0	103	6
Demography: Migration/100	0.5	0	0			0	-5	0	0	0
: Population of Country	130000	1210000	1570	52	5180	27400	10100	1210000	0	0
: Urbanization, %	69	29	37	11400	86	26	20	29	896000	395
: Population growth	0.8			43	0.5	3	2		27	51
: Females, % of pop		49	51	4	51	50	51	49		2
Male % ages: 0-9 years		52	49	50	51	51	50	52	48	52
: 10-19 years		51	49	51	51	50	49	51	51	48
: 20-29 years		51	49	49	51	50	49	52	52	48
: 30-39 years		52	50	49	51	49	49	53	51	48
: 40-49 years		53	50	49	51	48	47	53	52	48
: 50-59 years		49	48	52	50	47	48	49	53	49
: 60-69 years		43	48	51	47	43	39	43	50	49
: 70+ years			72	49	40	27	32	73	52	48
Education: Literacy, adult	99			51	100		73			50
Cities: earliest settled, year		-2210	1890		1000	1800	1100	-2210	-1500	1830
: Largest settled, year		1100	1890	1880	1040	1820	1880	1100	150	1830
: Largest, % of pop	9	0.6	8	1890	26	2	8	0.6		16
Politics: # of parties	8			15	8				5	4
: Largest party %	29	100	57	3	39	100	66	100	42	85
: Top two parties, %	43	100	86	94	56	100	74	100	64	93
: Chambers in leg., #	2		2	98					2	
: # of changes 60	1	3		0.6	0	3	3	3		4
Independence year	1990	1910	1990	1940	964	1960	1960	1910	1950	1970
Laws: Censorship (1=high)	0.6	1	0.5	1	0	1	0	1	0.5	1
: Metric system (1=yes)	0	0			2		0	0	0	0
: Visas needed (3=high)	2	3	3	0.2		3	3	3	3	3
: Full soc security (1=yes)	0.9	0	0		1	0	0	0	0	0
: Military service (1=yes)	1	1	0	0.3		0	0	0	0	0
Crime: Murders/100k pop				0	5					
: Thefts/100k pop		177			8360			177	49	
: Suicide/100k pop					28				2	
: Prisoners/000 pop				0.2	0.7					
: Death penalty (1=yes)			0	0		1	1			1
Unrest: Border disputes, #	0.9	1	3	0.6	0	2	0	1	1	1
: international, #	10	12	0	0.8	0	1	0	12	3	1
: # of civil wars	0	2	1		0	0	2	2	0	0
: # of civil riots	0.1	0					0	0	1	1

Characteristics	Duala-Landa-B.	Dujia	Dutch	Dyola	Edo	Egyptian	English	Estonian	Euro-nesian	European
Population Covered	1850	6060	442	389	3620	55500	46800	976	22	40700
Countries represented, #	1		3	4	3	1	80	1	1	28
Average representation %	15	0.5		20	16	99	11	62	10	30
Vital Stats: Death rate	11	7	8	51	46	9	11	12	6	8
: Birth rate	44	22	14	7	7	33	14	16	34	20
: Fertility	6		2			4	2			
: Female life exp., years	60	73	81	49	54	65	79	75	70	76
: Male life exp., years	55	69	74	45	51	62	73	71	65	69
: Infant mortality	115	52	9	136	128	89	10	28	66	42
: # of major diseases	6	2		5	2	6				
Demography: Migration/100	0		0	-4	0	0	0	0	-4	0.7
: Population of Country	12600	1210000	23700	7870	107000	56000	57800	1590	221	28000
: Urbanization, %	41	29	81	21	29	45	89	72	21	81
: Population growth	3	2	5	2	3	3	0.2	0.7	0.8	
: Females, % of pop	50	49	51	51	50	49	51		48	50
Male % ages: 0-9 years	50	52	51	50	51	51	52			51
: 10-19 years	50	51	50	48	50	53	51			51
: 20-29 years	50	51	50	49	51	49	51			51
: 30-39 years	49	52	49	50	50	49	50			50
: 40-49 years	49	53	46	49	50	51	50			50
: 50-59 years	47	49	40	49	50	51	49			75
: 60-69 years	45	43	99	42	51	50	47			47
: 70+ years	54	73		31		48	37			42
Education: Literacy, adult						45	99	98	98	95
Cities: earliest settled, year	1880	-2210	1310	1280	1100	-2570	-600		1850	1590
: Largest settled, year	1880	1100	1520	1870	1700	641	43		1850	1640
: Largest, % pop.	10	0.6	5	9	1	20	12	31	17	11
Politics: # of parties	4	1		6	0	2	6	7	2	7
: Largest party, %	49	100	50	62	100	77	52	29	65	52
: Top two parties, %	87	100	68	71	100	78	94	46	98	83
: Chambers in leg., #	1	1	2	1		1	2	1	1	2
: # of changes 60	2	3		3	4	0		0		
: Independence year	1960	1910	1920	1960	1960	1940	1920	1990	1960	1850
Laws: Censorship (1=high)	0.5	0	0.8	0.1	0.5	0.5	1	0.5	0	0.4
: Metric system (1=yes)	0			0.2	0	0		0		0.1
: Visas needed (3=high)	3	3	0.2	0.3	3	3	2	2	2	0.2
: Full soc security (1=yes)	0	0		0	0	0	0	1	0	0.8
: Military service (1=yes)		2	0.8		1	1	3	1		
Crime: Murders/100k pop					94	58				0.3
: Thefts/100k pop	1	177	4480	0.8	1260	0.5	6680	0	0	1230
: Suicide/100k pop	0	1	16	0.2		1	4	1	0	8
: Prisoners/000 pop	0	1	2	0	0	3	0.9	2	2	0.9
: Death penalty (1=yes)	0	2	0	0	0	2	0.0	1	0	
Unrest: Border disputes, #	0	0	0	2	4	0	9	1	0	0.0
: International, #		2	0	0	0	0	0	0	0	0.3
: # of civil wars							0	0	0	0.7
: # of civil riots								0	0	0.0

Characteristics	Ewa-Adja	Ewe	Fang	Fijian	Finnish	Fleming	Fon	Forros	French	Fulani
Population Covered	1770	1960	3220	330	5010	5510	3320	33	60100	20900
Countries represented, #		1	3		4			1	17	12
Average representation %	45	12	23	45	12	55	66	26	34	21
Vital Stats: Death rate	12	13	12	7	10	10	15	8	9	17
: Birth rate	48	45	42	25	12	12	49	38	13	47
: Fertility		6	6	3	2	2	7	5	2	7
: Female life exp., years	58	58	59	74	80	81	53	68	82	53
: Male life exp., years	54	54	54	69	72	74	49	64	74	50
: Infant mortality	123	105	117	39	6	8	136	85	10	131
: # of major diseases	5	2	6	1	6	5	5	5	3	3
Demography: Migration/100	0	-1	0	-10	0.2	0	0	0	2	-5
: Population of Country	3910	16500	9820	728	5360	10000	5070	127	52800	64400
: Urbanization, %	24	32	42	39	62	96	31	38	75	28
: Population growth	3	2	3	2	0.3	0.3	3		0.8	2
: Females, % of pop	51	51	50	50	51	51	52	50	51	50
Male % ages: 0-9 years	49	49	50	51	51	51	51	51	51	50
: 10-19 years	49	49	50	51	51	51	51	51	51	50
: 20-29 years	49	49	50	50	51	50	38	47	51	50
: 30-39 years	49	49	49	49	51	49	44	51	49	49
: 40-49 years	49	50	49	50	49	46	46	49	46	50
: 50-59 years	48	48	48	48	41	37	49	46	37	49
: 60-69 years	48	50	48	48	34		50	41	99	43
: 70+ years	50	60	46	87	100	100	51	57	-739	1300
Education: Literacy, adult	43	1600	55	1880	1190	400	23	1490	-112	1745
Cities: earliest settled, year	1900	1600	1870	1880	1540	600	1600	1490	15	5
: Largest settled, year	1900	6	1870	9	10	10	1870	27	10	2
Politics: # of parties	10	4	14	6	8	5	10	60	45	89
: Largest, % pop		95	4	44	28	18	4	98	79	95
: Largest party %	44	95	53	73	52	35	19		2	1
: Top two parties, %	87	5	85	2	1	2	33		1	3
: Chambers in leg., #		1960	2	1970	0.1	1	1	1980	1720	1960
: # of changes 60	2	0	1	1	1920	1830	7	0.5	0.1	0.5
: Independence year	1960	3	1960	0	0	0	1960	3	0.2	0
Laws: Censorship (1=high)	1	0	0.5	2	2	2	0	0	1	3
: Metric system (1=yes)	0		3	0	1	1	3	0	1	
: Visas needed (3=high)	2	1	0		3340	2620	0	2	3	0.6
: Full soc security (1=yes)	0	0		11	26	22		2	4140	94
: Military service (1=yes)		3	0.9	1	0.6	0.6	1		22	1260
Crime: Murders/100k pop		0	0.2	0	0.1	0	0	0	0.8	0.3
: Thefts/100k pop	0		0.1	0	0	0	0	0	6	0.1
: Suicide/100k pop	0		0.2	0	0.1		5	0	0	0.3
: Prisoners/000 pop	0			0			0	0	0.9	0.1
: Death penalty (1=yes)	1									
Unrest: Border disputes, #	1									
: International, #										
: # of civil wars										
: # of civil riots										

Characteristics	Fur	Ga-Adangme	Gagauz	Galician	Ganda	Garifuna	Gbaya	Georgian	German	Gibral-tarian
Population Covered	549	1280	272	3210	3430	14	802	3960	87700	21
Countries represented, #	1	1	1	1	1	1	2	2	20	1
Average representation %	2	8	0.4	8	18	7	25	6	20	66
Vital Stats: Death rate	13	13	8	9	14	5	18	9	11	8
...Birth rate	44	45	23	11	51	31	43	17	11	18
...Female life exp., years	54	58	73	82	55	73	49	75	79	79
...Male life exp., years	53	54	68	75	51	67	46	72	73	73
...Infant mortality	105	105	56	11	112	53	133	38	15	6
...# of major diseases	6	2	·	0	0	4	5	0	0	3
Demography: Migration/100	0	·	1	0	0	·	·	·	0.3	-9
...Population of Country	27400	16500	28500	39200	19300	200	3270	7110	7910	31
...Urbanization, %	26	32	53	81	10	50	42	56	85	93
...Population growth	3	2	2	·	3	2	2	0.8	0.4	1
...Females, % of pop	50	51	49	51	50	50	52	49	52	·
Male % ages: 0-9 years	51	49	51	51	50	51	50	51	51	·
...10-19 years	50	49	52	52	49	51	49	52	51	·
...20-29 years	50	49	51	51	49	51	48	51	51	·
...30-39 years	49	49	50	50	49	51	48	50	51	·
...40-49 years	48	49	50	50	49	52	47	51	51	·
...50-59 years	47	48	51	48	50	50	45	50	49	·
...60-69 years	43	48	49	46	48	50	43	49	40	·
...70+ years	27	50	43	40	48	47	40	43	34	·
Education: Literacy, adult	27	50	91	96	48	93	38	99	98	94
Cities: earliest settled, year	1800	1600	-3650	-1200	1890	1640	1890	-3650	-509	711
...Largest settled, year	1820	1600	-658	931	1890	1640	1890	-658	1010	711
...Largest, % pop	2	6	13	8	2	21	20	23	4	4
Politics: # of parties	·	4	5	11	·	·	·	9	6	·
...Largest party %	100	95	47	46	100	55	40	16	38	·
...Top two parties, %	100	95	74	86	100	100	55	·	72	·
...Chambers in leg., #	·	·	1	2	·	·	2	1	2	1
...# of changes 60	1	5	1	1	3	2	2	1	1	·
...Independence year	1960	1960	1960	1490	1960	1980	1960	1990	1970	1710
Laws: Censorship (1=high)	·	·	0.7	0.5	0.5	0.5	·	0	0	1
...Metric system (1=yes)	0	0	0	·	0	·	0	1	1	·
...Visas needed (3=high)	3	3	2	2	3	2	3	2	2	·
...Full soc security (1=yes)	0	0	·	1	0	·	0	0	1	·
...Military service (1=yes)	0	0	·	1	0	0	·	1	1	·
Crime: Murders/100k pop	·	·	·	·	·	·	·	·	3	·
...Thefts/100k pop	·	·	68	2040	·	·	·	·	4360	·
...Suicide/100k pop	·	·	0.9	7	·	·	·	68	18	·
...Prisoners/000 pop	·	·	0.4	0.7	·	·	·	0.9	0.7	·
...Death penalty (1=yes)	1	1	0.3	·	0.5	0.4	·	·	1	·
Unrest: Border disputes, #	2	·	0.04	2	·	·	·	0.1	·	·
...International, #	1	0	·	·	0	1	·	0.1	·	·
...# of civil wars	2	0	·	0	0	0	0	·	0	·
...# of civil riots	0	3	0.4	1	2	0	3	0	0.1	0

Characteristics	Gilaki	Gilbertese	Gio	Gisu	Gola	Grebo	Greek	Greenlandic	Grosi	Guiana Chinese
Population Covered	3350	72	224	1390	144	258	10900	47	499	17
Countries represented, #	1	1	1	1	1	1	1	1	1	1
Average representation %	5	96	8	7	5	9	8	83	5	14
Vital Sats: Death rate	8	12	13	14	13	13	9	8	16	5
Birth rate	44	33	44	51	44	44	12	19	49	27
Fertility	7	4	7	7	7	7	2	2	7	4
Female life exp., years	68	58	59	55	59	59	81	69	53	78
Male life exp., years	67	52	55	51	55	55	75	63	52	71
Infant mortality	88	96	141	112	141	141	17	27	139	17
# of major diseases	5	1	2	6	2	2	1	—	5	2
Demography: Migration/100	0	—	265	—	265	265	0.3	0	—	24
Population of Country	63200	75	2870	19300	2870	2870	12000	57	9780	122
Urbanization, %	55	35	45	10	45	45	62	77	9	81
Population growth	3	2	3	3	3	3	0.7	1	2	3
Females, % of pop	48	51	49	50	49	49	51	46	52	47
Male % ages: 0-9 years	52	51	51	50	51	51	52	54	48	51
10-19 years	52	51	50	49	50	50	52	54	48	50
20-29 years	52	47	45	49	45	45	51	54	48	56
30-39 years	52	50	48	49	48	48	50	54	48	54
40-49 years	52	49	55	49	55	55	48	54	48	54
50-59 years	50	47	58	50	58	58	48	54	47	55
60-69 years	48	45	57	48	57	57	46	55	48	51
70+ years	54	40	61	48	61	61	43	56	48	45
Education: Literacy, adult	—	90	40	—	40	40	93	100	18	82
Cities: earliest settled, year	-1100	-1790	1820	1890	1820	1820	-1090	1720	1200	1660
Largest settled, year	-1200	-1790	1820	1890	1820	1820	-1040	1720	1200	1660
Politics: # of parties	10	—	1	2	1	1	10	—	5	—
Largest, % pop	0	30	16	0	16	16	4	21	73	39
Largest party %	100	46	100	100	100	100	55	5	84	5
Top two parties, %	100	87	100	100	100	100	91	—	—	—
Chambers in leg., #	1	1	1	1	1	1	1	2	4	—
# of changes 60	2	3	3	3	3	3	2	—	—	4
Independence year	1910	1980	1850	1960	1850	1850	1920	1380	1960	1820
Laws: Censorship (1=high)	1	0	1	0.5	1	1	0.5	0	1	0
Metric system (1=yes)	0	0	—	0	—	—	0	2	0	—
Visas needed (3=high)	3	3	3	3	3	3	2	—	3	3
Full soc security (1=yes)	0	0	0	0	0	0	1	—	0	0
Military service (1=yes)	1	—	0	0	0	0	1	—	0	0
Crime: Murders/100k pop	—	—	—	—	—	—	—	—	—	—
Thefts/100k pop	1	—	1	—	1	3	659	0	1	2
Suicide/100k pop	—	—	—	—	—	—	0.5	—	—	—
Prisoners/000 pop	—	—	—	—	—	—	0	—	—	—
Death penalty (1=yes)	—	1	—	0.5	—	—	0.4	—	1	1
Unrest: Border disputes, #	1	—	3	2	3	3	2	0	—	—
International, #	5	—	0	0	0	0	0.1	—	—	—
# of civil wars	1	—	—	2	—	—	—	0	0	0
# of civil riots	1	—	—	0	—	—	—	0	0	0

Characteristics	Guianese Creole	Gurage	Gurma	Gurung	Gypsy	Han Chinese	Hani	Hausa	Haya	Hazara-Dari
Population Covered	52	1750	1640	276	1020	1130000	1330	27500	1700	1670
Countries represented, #	1	3	3	1	7	1	1	4	1	1
Average representation %	43	14	5	17	2	93	0.1	21	6	9
Vital Stats: Death rate	5		13	17	11	7	22	17	15	20
Birth rate	27	45	47	40	14	22	22	48	49	44
Fertility	4			6		2	2			6
Female life exp., years	78	53	57	49	75	73	73	54	57	44
Male life exp., years	71	50	53	50	69	69	69	51	53	45
Infant mortality	17	134	122	147	34	52	52	130	123	172
# of major diseases	2	4	4	6	0	2	0	3	5	0
Demography: Migration/100			-0.9		-3	0	0	0	-1	0
Population of Country	122	52900	9760	1640	14000	1210000	1210000	89500	28800	19200
Urbanization, %	81	12	22	10	59	29	29	27	24	18
Population growth	3	3	2	2	0.9			3	3	
Females, % of pop	47	50	51	49	51	49	49	50	51	50
Male % ages: 0-9 years	51	52	49	51	51	52	52	50	50	50
10-19 years	50	46	49	52	51	51	51	50	50	49
20-29 years	56	47	49	51	50	51	51	51	48	48
30-39 years	54	49	49	51	49	52	52	50	46	48
40-49 years	54	53	49	52	49	53	53	51	49	51
50-59 years	55	54	48	51	45	53	53	50	51	56
60-69 years	51	57	48	52	43	49	49	50	48	58
70+ years	45	71	41	51	96	43	43	47	89	29
Education: Literacy, adult	82			38		73	73			
Cities: earliest settled, year	1660	700	1600	1580	-622	-2210	-2210	1190	1600	-400
Largest settled, year	1660	1890	1600	1580	407	1100	1100	1690	1860	-400
Largest, % pop	39	3	7	1	15	0.6	0.6	2	3	9
Politics: # of parties	5	1	5	1	9	1	1		1	3
Largest party %		100	69	100	43	100	100	93	100	
Top two parties, %	2	100	89	100	72	100	100	99	100	2
Chambers in leg., #	1			1	1	1	1		1	4
# of changes 60		2	4		1	3	3	4	1	1
Independence year	1820	1990	1960	1870	1950	1910	1910	1960	1960	1920
Laws: Censorship (1=high)	0	0.5	1	1	0.1	1	1	0.5	0.1	1
Metric system (1=yes)	2	0	0	0	0.02	0	0		0	0
Visas needed (3=high)		3	3	3	0.7	3	3	3	3	2
Full soc security (1=yes)		0	0	0	0.8	0	0	0	0	0
Military service (1=yes)		0	0	0		1	1	0.8	0	0
Crime: Murders/100k pop	1					2	2	94		
Thefts/100k pop		7			387	177	177	1260		4
Suicide/100k pop	0	37			18				1	1
Prisoners/000 pop	0	0.3	0.6	0	1	1	1	0.2	0	
Death penalty (1=yes)	0	0	0	0	0	1	1	0		5
Unrest: Border disputes, #		5	0	0	2	1	1	3	1	2
International, #		1	0	0	0.5	12	12	0	0	
# of civil wars	0	3	1	0	0.5	0	0	3	1	
# of civil riots	0	0	0.4	0	0.5	2	2	0.2	0	2

Characteristics	Hehet-Bena	Herero	Hottentot	Hui-Vighur	Humbe-Nyaneka	Hungarian	Hutu	Ibibio	Icelander	Igbo
Population Covered	1990	125	34	16300	555	13200	12000	5970	273	19600
Countries represented, #	1	1	3	1	5	9	8	6	1	1
Average representation %	7	8	8	7	5	9	7	6	97	8
Vital Stats: Death rate	15	8	8	7	19	12	14	16	7	16
Birth rate	49	45	35	22	46	12	50	46	18	46
Fertility	7	7	4	2	7	2	8		2	
Female life exp., years	57	63	65	73	48	76	55	54	81	54
Male life exp., years	53	58	59	69	45	68	51	51	76	51
Infant mortality	123	97	69	52	161	29	128	128	6	128
# of major diseases	5	4	1		4		7		0	2
Demography: Migration/100	-1	0	0	0	0	-0.4	0	0	-2	0
Population of Country	28800	1570	1350	1210000	10300	12600	7030	106000	283	107000
Urbanization, %	24	37	26	29	27	60	7	29	90	29
Population growth	3	2	4	2	3	0.5	3	3	1	3
Females, % of pop	51	51	52	49	48	52	51	50	50	51
Male % ages: 0-9 years	50	51	52	49	48	51	51	50	51	51
10-19 years	50	49	50	52	52	52	50	51	51	51
20-29 years	48	49	45	51	52	51	50	50	52	50
30-39 years	46	50	43	52	52	51	49	51	50	51
40-49 years	49	49	46	53	53	49	46	50	51	50
50-59 years	51	50	46	53	53	47	45	50	49	50
60-69 years	48	48	47	49	52	43	44	50	43	51
70+ years	48	48	41	43	42	38	46	51	43	51
Education: Literacy, adult	72	72	74	73	42	98	50	51	100	51
Cities: earliest settled, year	1600	1890	1900	-2210	1580	-177	1920	1100	874	1100
Largest settled, year	1860	1890	1900	1100	1580	-124	1920	1700	874	1700
Largest, % pop	3	8	9	0.6	17	19	3		37	1
Politics: # of parties	1	4	2		5	7			5	4
Largest party %	100	57	91	100	59	50	92	100	41	100
Top two parties, %	100	86	100	100	91	55	100	100	62	100
Chambers in leg., #	1	2	2	3	2	1	4	4	1	4
# of changes 60										
Independence year	1960	1990	1970	1910	1980	1930	1960	1960	1940	1960
Laws: Censorship (1=high)	0.1	0.5	0	0	0.5	0.4	0.8	0.5	0	0.5
Metric system (1=yes)	0		0			0			0	
Visas needed (3=high)	3	3	2	3	3	2	3	3	1	3
Full soc security (1=yes)	0	0	0	0	0	3	0	0	0	0
Military service (1=yes)	0	0	0	1	1					
Crime: Murders/100k pop						2		94		94
Thefts/100k pop				177		2030		1260	15	1260
Suicide/100k pop						45			0.3	
Prisoners/000 pop						1				
Death penalty (1=yes)	0	3	4	1	0	0.8	1	0	0	0
Unrest: Border disputes, #		0	0	12	1	0.1	0	0	0	0
International, #	1	1	0	2	2	0.1	1	4	0	4
# of civil wars	0		0	0	0	0.1	0.4	0	0	0
# of civil riots	0									

Characteristics	Ijaw	Indian	Indo-Aryan	Indo-nesian	Iranian	Irish	Issa	Italian	Japanese	Javanese
Population Covered	1920	5870	646000	6	11000	4670	234	76400	126000	76700
Countries represented, #	1	28	7	1	3	3	1	15	6	2
Average representation %	16	2	2	3	9		47	18	22	39
Vital Stats: Death rate		7	11		13	10	16	9	10	8
::Birth rate	46	24	30	23	43	15	43	13		25
::Fertility		3	4	3	6	2	6		2	6
::Female life exp., years	54	74	61	76	59	79	51	79	82	64
::Male life exp., years	51	69	60	70	59	73	47	72	77	59
::Infant mortality	128	35	103	17	127	13	133	29	4	98
::# of major diseases		3	6	1	6	3	5	1		6
Demography: Migration/100	0	-2	0	1	-0.9	-3	0	0.9	0	0
::Population of Country	107000	30800	897000	178	127000	19600	498	79100	126000	194000
::Urbanization, %	29	53	27	58	31	64	80	71	77	31
::Population growth	3	2	2	2	3	0.9	9	0.9	1	2
::Females, % of pop	50	50	48	48	47	52	49	51	51	50
Male % ages: 0-9 years	51	51	51	52	50	51	51	51	51	51
::10-19 years	50	51	52	52	54	51	52	51	51	51
::20-29 years	51	51	51	52	52	51	52	51	50	49
::30-39 years	50	51	51	52	52	51	51	50	50	48
::40-49 years	50	51	52	52	51	50	51	48	49	48
::50-59 years	50	50	52	52	55	48	51	48	43	47
::60-69 years	50	49	50	53	59	40	50	46	40	44
::70+ years	51	44	50	54	58		50	41		
Education: Literacy, adult		84	52	91	35	100	48	93	100	77
Cities: earliest settled, year	1100	918	-1500	1850	-579	315	1890	-489	-664	201
::Largest settled, year	1700	1490	150	1850	1730	601	1890	-394	1210	501
::Largest, % pop		13	5	38	5	22	67	5	8	3
Politics: # of parties	1	62	42	8	5	4	1	9		4
::Largest party %	100	88	64	84	44	44	100	49	43	57
::Top two parties, %	100			97	72	76	100	79	57	69
::Chambers in leg., #		2	2	2	1	1	1	2	2	2
::# of changes 60	1	1	1	0			2	0.7		2
::Independence year	1960	1940	1950	1850	1950	1920	1980	1860	1870	1950
Laws: Censorship (1=high)	0.5	0.3	0.5		1	0.4	1	0	0	0.5
::Metric system (1=yes)		0.3	0.0	2		2		2		
::Visas needed (3=high)	3		3		3	1	3		2	2
::Full soc security (1=yes)		2				0		1		
::Military service (1=yes)	1	0.7	0				1	1		0
Crime: Murders/100k pop		0.4	4					5		0.9
::Thefts/100k pop	94	2770	49		78	6680		2860	1030	41
::Suicide/100k pop	1260	10		0	18	8		8	19	22
::Prisoners/000 pop		0.8		0	0.4	0.7		0.6	0.4	0.2
::Death penalty (1=yes)		2	1	0	3	5		0	3	1
Unrest: Border disputes, #	0	0.5	3		0	0.6	0	2		2
::International, #	0	0.3	0		1	0	0	0	0	0
::# of civil wars	4	0	1			0	0	0.2	0	1
::# of civil riots	0		1	1		0	1	0.7	0	0

Characteristics	Jewish	Jola	Kalenjin	Kamba	Kanuri	Kara-kalpak	Kare	Karen	Kavango	Kazakh
Population Covered	5800	635	2820	2950	5380	455	79	2770	141	9550
Countries representation, #	14	8	1	1	3	2	2	1	1	6
Average representation %	5	13	11	11	17	7	18	10	9	0.8
Vital Stats: Death rate	7									8
Birth rate	20	44	44	44	48	34	43	29	45	24
Fertility	3	6	6	6	7	4	6	8	7	3
Female life exp., years	79	57	64	64	54	74	49	64	63	74
Male life exp., years	75	54	60	60	51	69	46	61	58	70
Infant mortality	19	102	88	88	130	65	133	96	97	47
# of major diseases	0	0	6	6	2	2	0	0	4	0.3
Demography: Migration/100	0	5	0	0	0	−2	0	0	4	−5
Population of Country	11100	7930	26100	26100	89900	21700	3270	44600	1570	169000
Urbanization, %	85	35	24	24	27	41	42	24	37	52
Population growth		3			3	3				4
Females, % of pop	51	51	50	50	50		52	50	51	49
Male % ages: 0-9 years	51	49	51	51	50		50	50	49	52
10-19 years	51	49	50	50	50		49	50	49	51
20-29 years	51	49	48	48	51		48	49	50	51
30-39 years	50	49	48	48	50		48	49	49	52
40-49 years	49	49	48	48	50		48	49	50	53
50-59 years	47	50	48	48	50		47	49	48	49
60-69 years	44	50	45	45	50		45	46	48	44
70+ years	44	38	69	69	47	98	43	81	72	95
Education: Literacy, adult	97						38			
Cities: earliest settled, year	−2870	1860	800	800	1190		1890	−585	1890	−1810
Largest settled, year	−1430	1860	1900	1900	1690		1890	−585	1890	−1160
Largest, % pop	9	17	4	4	2	10	20	6	8	7
Politics: # of parties		8	6	6			4			6
Largest party %	40	70	51	51	94	100	40	100	57	37
Top two parties, %	65	93	66	66	99	100	55	100	86	42
Chambers in leg., #	0.2	1	1	1	4	1	2	4	2	1
# of changes 60			3	3						
Independence year	1950	1960	1960	1960	1960	1990	1960	1950	1990	1980
Laws: Censorship (1=high)	0.9	1	1	1	0.5	1			0.5	
Metric system (1=yes)	1	1	1	1	3	2	3	3	3	0.2
Visas needed (3=high)	0	0	0	0	3	1	0	1	3	
Full soc security (1=yes)	3	3	3	3		1	0	0	0	3
Military service (1=yes)	0.8	0	0	0	0.8		0	1	0	0.1
Crime: Murders/100k pop	1		4	4	94			4		0.1
Thefts/100k pop	2	0	42	42	1260		3	5		177
Suicide/100k pop	2500									
Prisoners/000 pop	7							56		
Death penalty (1=yes)	0.8	0	1	1	0.1	0		1	3	0.1
Unrest: Border disputes, #	4	0	2	2	0.4	0	0	0	0	0.1
International, #	3	0	0	0		0	3	3	3	0.3
# of civil wars	0	0	1	1	0.1	0	0	1	1	0.3
# of civil riots	0	1	0	0		0	0	1	1	0

Characteristics	Kebu-Akposo	Khmer	Kikuyu	Kimbundu	Kisii	Kissi	Klao	Kongo	Kono	Konzo
Population Covered	156	10300	5450	2350	1570	513	201	7980	234	412
Countries represented, #	4	3	2	1		5	1	2	1	1
Average representation %	12	8	1	23	6	2	7	18	5	1
Vital Stats: Death rate		13	21	19	8	21	13	18	20	13
·Birth rate	48	34	44	46	44	46	44	45	46	45
·Fertility	7	6	6	7	6	6	7	6		6
·Female life exp., years	58	56	64	48	64	46	59	56	48	56
·Male life exp., years	54	54	60	45	60	43	55	53	43	53
·Infant mortality	123	123	88	161	88	159	141	112	163	112
·# of major diseases	5	6	6	4	6	5	2	2	5	2
Demography: Migration/100	0	-0.1	0	0	0	-38	265	0	-28	0
·Population of Country	3910	21100	26100	10300	26100	5940	2870	35000	4510	41200
·Urbanization, %	24	13	24	27	24	26	45	42	31	41
·Population growth	3	0.8	4	2		2	3	3	2	3
·Females, % of pop	51	50	50	48	50	51	49	51	50	51
Male % ages: 0-9 years	49	50	51	52	51	49	51	50	50	
·10-19 years	49	50	50	52	50	49	50	49	50	
·20-29 years	49	50	48	52	50	49	45	48	50	
·30-39 years	49	50	48	53	48	49	48	47	49	
·40-49 years	48	49	48	53	48	49	55	49	49	
·50-59 years	50	49	48	52	48	49	58	45	49	
·60-69 years	43	48	45	52	45	50	57	43	49	
·70+ years		48	69	42	69	48	61	47	50	
Education: Literacy, adult			69	42	69	23	40	70	21	72
Cities: earliest settled, year	1900	1140	800	1580	800	1640	1820	1830	1790	1880
·Largest settled, year	1900	1460	1900	1580	1900	1870	1820	1890	1790	1890
·Largest, % pop	10	10	4	17	4	10	16	10	11	7
Politics: # of parties	5	4	6	5	6					0
·Largest party %	44	48	51	59	51	100	100	90	100	100
·Top two parties, %	87	85	66	91	66	100	100	94	100	100
·Chambers in leg., #		1	1	1	1	1	1	1	3	1
·# of changes 60	2	3	3	2	3					
Independence year	1960	1940	1960	1980	1960	1960	1850	1960	1960	1960
Laws: Censorship (1=high)	1	0.2	1	0.5	1	0.6	1	0.9	1	
·Metric system (1=yes)	0	0	0	0	0	0	0	0	0	
·Visas needed (3=high)	2	3	3	3	3	3	3	3	3	3
·Full soc security (1=yes)	0	0	0	0	0	0	0	0	0	0
·Military service (1=yes)	0	1	0	1	0	0	0	0	0	0
Crime: Murders/100k pop		0.1	42		42					
·Thefts/100k pop		10								
·Suicide/100k pop		69								
·Prisoners/000 pop										
·Death penalty (1=yes)	1	1	1	0	1	0	3	2	2	1
Unrest: Border disputes, #		1	2	0	2	0	3	0	0	2
·International, #	0	1	0	2	0	0				0
·# of civil wars	1	2	1		1	4		2	2	1
·# of civil riots	1	0.8	0	0	0	0.4	3	0.8	0	1

Characteristics	Koranko	Korean	Kotoko	Kpelle	Kru	Kurd	Kuwaiti	Kyrgyz	Ladino	Lango
Population Covered	158	70700	126	859	210	16800	795	2670	4200	1160
Countries represented, #	1	9	1	2	1	7	1	3	1	1
Average representation %	20	4	2	9	7	10	42	8	42	6
Vital Stats: Death rate	46	6	21	6	13	7	3	8		14
..Birth rate		19	42	45	44	38	32	31	34	51
..Fertility		7	4	5	5	5	4	4	5	5
..Female life exp., years	48	74	49	54	59	70	76	74	67	55
..Male life exp., years	43	68	46	51	55	67	72	68	62	51
..Infant mortality	163	37	148	147	141	84	26	59	73	112
..# of major diseases	5		0	3	2	2	0			6
Demography: Migration/100	-28	0.7	0	158	265	0	0	-8	-2	0
..Population of Country	4510	73700	5990	4080	2870	49200	1900	5980	10000	19300
..Urbanization, %	31	68	28	38	45	61	95	38	37	10
..Population growth	2	2	2		3	3		2		3
..Females, % of pop	50	50	52	50	49	49	43		50	50
Male % ages: 0-9 years	50	51	48	50	51	52	51		51	50
..10-19 years	50	51	48	50	51	52	51		51	49
..20-29 years	50	51	48	46	45	52	57		50	49
..30-39 years	49	51	48	48	48	51	64		50	49
..40-49 years	49	48	48	53	55	51	67		50	49
..50-59 years	49	45	48	55	58	51	67		50	49
..60-69 years	49	40	47	54	57	50	57		50	50
..70+ years	50		30	56	61	46	43		47	50
Education: Literacy, adult	21	96		34	40	66	74	98		48
Cities: earliest settled, year	1790	-450	1900	1740	1820	-2510	1700		1780	1890
..Largest settled, year	1790	-320	1900	1850	1820	265	1700		1780	1890
..Largest, % pop	11	18	10	13	16	13	7	14	11	2
Politics: # of parties		3		0	0	7				0
..Largest party %	100	68	100	100	100	74	100	100	35	100
..Top two parties, %	100	89	100	100	100	84	100	100	59	100
..Chambers in leg., #	1	1	1	1	1		1	1	1	
..# of changes 60	3	0.7	4	2	3	2	0	1	4	3
Independence year	1960	1950	1960	1890	1850	1920	1960	1990	1840	1960
Laws: Censorship (1=high)	1	0.4	0.5	0.8		1	0.5	0.1	0.5	0.5
..Metric system (1=yes)	0	0	0	0.6		0	0	0.0		
..Visas needed (3=high)	3	2	3	3	3	3	3		3	3
..Full soc security (1=yes)	0	0.6	0	0	0	0.6	1	0.1	0	0
..Military service (1=yes)	0	1	0	0	0	1	0	1	1	0
Crime: Murders/100k pop	·	2	·	·	·	2	0.5		3	·
..Thefts/100k pop		313				66				
..Suicide/100k pop	1	8	3		1		0.5		0.5	0.5
..Prisoners/000 pop		1								
..Death penalty (1=yes)	0	0.3	0	0	0	0.9	0.9	0.9	1	0
Unrest: Border disputes, #	0	0.1	1	0	0	5	0.3	0.9	1	0
..International, #	0	0.6	3	2	3	0.8	3	0	3	0
..# of civil wars	2	0.1	2	2	3	0.8	3	0	3	2
..# of civil riots	0	0.6	0	0	0	0.8	0	0	0	0

Characteristics	Lao	Latvian	Lezgin	Li	Liechten-steiner	Limba	Lithua-nian	Lobi	Loma	Lomwe
Population Covered	18300	1390	220	1090	18	167	3060	1400	201	1970
Countries represented, #	2	1	3					2	1	1
Average representation %	30	52	3	0.1	64	4	47	6	7	8
Vital Stats: Death rate	8	12	7	7	7	20	11	14	13	17
:Birth rate	24	15	26	22	13	46	15	48	44	52
:Fertility	3	2			2		2	7	7	8
:Female life exp., years	68	75	74	73	81	48	77	55	59	51
:Male life exp., years	64	71	70	69	74	43	72	53	55	48
:Infant mortality	62	26	47	52	6	163	21	127	141	153
:# of major diseases	3	4	0	2		5	4	5	2	5
Demography: Migration/100	0	0	-3	0	0	-28	4		2	-17
:Population of Country	48200	2680	7350	1210000	29	4510	3770	11700	2870	10700
:Urbanization, %	20	71	54	29	65	31	68	26	45	13
:Population growth	3	0.6	2		0.6	2	0.8	3	3	3
:Females, % of pop	50			49				51	49	
Male % ages: 0-9 years	51			52	50	50		49	51	52
:10-19 years	51			51	50	50		48	50	50
:20-29 years	50			51	48	50		49	45	49
:30-39 years	50			52	52	50		49	48	47
:40-49 years	49			53	52	49		50	55	42
:50-59 years	46			53	48	49		50	58	47
:60-69 years	43			49	46	49		48	57	50
:70+ years				43	39	50		47	61	54
Education: Literacy, adult	92	98	98	73	100	21	98	37	40	42
Cities: earliest settled, year	807			-2210	1150	1790		1560	1820	1880
:Largest settled, year	1710			1100	1150	1790		1560	1820	1880
:Largest, % pop	35	34	25	0.6	18	11	18	10	16	4
Politics: # of parties	52	8	5		3		6	4		3
:Largest party %	2	36	80	100	51	100	52	83	100	50
:Top two parties, %		51	80	100	92	100	73	91	100	80
:Chambers in leg., #		1	1	3	1	3	1	2	3	1
:# of changes 60										
:Independence year	1890	1990	1990	1910	1720	1960	1990	1960	1850	1960
Laws: Censorship (1=high)	1	0.5	0	0	0	0	0	0	1	1
:Metric system (3=high)	0	0		3	0		0		3	0
:Visas needed (3=high)	2	2	2		2	3	2	3	0	1
:Full soc security (1=yes)	0	1	0	1	1	0	0	0	0	0
:Military service (1=yes)	1	1	1	2	0	0	1	0		0
Crime: Murders/100k pop	0.2	0		177				0.5	1	
:Thefts/100k pop	10		4							1
:Suicide/100k pop	69		0							
:Prisoners/000 pop	1	1	0	12	0		0	0	0	
:Death penalty (1=yes)	1	0	1	0	0	1	1			0
Unrest: Border disputes, #	0	0	4	2	0	0	0	0	3	0
:International, #	0	0			0	0	0			0
:# of civil wars	2	0	0	2	0	2	0	0.5	3	1
:# of civil riots			1		0		0			

Characteristics	Lotuko	Luba	Luchasi	Luena	Lugbara	Luhya	Lumbe	Lunda	Luo	Luri
Population Covered	274	7410	247	350	824	3600	555	123	3340	2720
Countries represented, #	1	1	1	1	1	1	1	1	1	1
Average representation %	1	18	2	3	2	14	5	1	13	4
Vital Stats: Death rate	13	13	19	19	13	8	19	19	8	8
:Birth rate	44	45	46	46	45	44	46	46	44	44
:Fertility	6	6	7	7	6	6	7	7	6	7
:Female life exp., years	54	56	48	48	56	64	48	48	64	68
:Male life exp., years	53	53	45	45	53	60	45	45	60	67
:Infant mortality	105	112	161	161	112	88	161	161	88	88
:# of major diseases	6	4	4	4	2	6	4	4	6	5
Demography: Migration/100	0	0	0	0	0	0	0	0	0	0
:Population of Country	27400	41200	10300	10300	41200	26100	10300	10300	26100	63200
:Urbanization, %	26	41	27	27	41	24	27	27	24	55
:Population growth	3	3	3	3	3	4	3	3	4	3
:Females, % of pop	50	51	48	48	51	50	48	48	50	48
Male % ages: 0-9 years	51		52	52		51	52	52	51	52
:10-19 years	50		52	52		50	52	52	50	52
:20-29 years	50		52	52		50	52	52	48	52
:30-39 years	49		53	53		48	53	53	48	52
:40-49 years	48		53	53		48	53	53	48	52
:50-59 years	47		53	53		48	53	53	48	52
:60-69 years	43		52	52		45	52	52	45	48
:70+ years			42	42		45	42	42	45	54
Education: Literacy, adult	27	72	42	42	72	69	42	42	69	54
Cities: earliest settled, year	1800	1880	1580	1580	1880	800	1580	1580	800	-1100
:Largest settled, year	1820	1890	1580	1580	1890	1900	1580	1580	1900	1200
:Largest, % pop	2		17	17		4	17	17	6	0
Politics: # of parties		0	5	5	0	6	5	5	6	10
:Largest party %	100	100	59	59	100	51	59	59	51	100
:Top two parties, %	100	100	91	91	100	66	91	91	66	100
:Chambers in leg., #	3	1	2	2	1	3	2	2	3	2
:# of changes 60										
:Independence year	1960	1960	1980	1980	1960	1960	1980	1980	1960	1910
Laws: Censorship (1=high)	0	0	0.5	0.5	0	0	0.5	0.5	0	0
:Metric system (1=yes)										
:Visas needed (3=high)	3	3	3	3	3	3	3	3	3	3
:Full soc security (1=yes)	0	0	0	0	0	0	0	0	0	0
:Military service (1=yes)	0	0	1	1	0	0	1	1	0	1
Crime: Murders/100k pop						4			4	
:Thefts/100k pop						42			42	
:Suicide/100k pop										
:Prisoners/000 pop										
:Death penalty (1=yes), #	1	1			1	1			1	1
Unrest: Border disputes, #	2	2	0	0	2	2	0	0	2	5
:International, #	1	0	0	0	0	0	0	0	0	1
:# of civil wars	2	1	2	2	1	1	2	2	1	1
:# of civil riots	0	1	0	0	1	0	0	0	0	1

Characteristics	Luxem-burger	Macedo-nian	Madurese	Magars	Maka	Makonde	Makua	Malagasy	Malawi	Malay
Population Covered	276	1770	9340	464	663	1670	7560	3580	1920	14500
Countries represented, #	1	4	1	1	3	1	1	3	1	6
Average representation %	71	7	5	2	4	6	4	2	1	18
Vital Stats: Death rate	10	8	8	14	11	15	17	14	17	6
:Birth rate	12	15	25	38	44	49	46	46	46	27
:Female life exp., years	80	76	64	53	60	57	50	57	50	73
:Male life exp., years	73	71	59	54	55	53	47	54	47	69
:Infant mortality	10	44	98	115	115	123	151	118	151	35
:# of major diseases	7	5	6	5	6	5	5	5	5	4
Demography: Migration/100	0.7	-0.6			0	-1	0			0.1
:Population of Country	392	3830	195000	21100	11800	28800	15900	13200	16000	24000
:Urbanization, %	81	56	31	8	41	24	26	23	26	38
:Population growth	0.5	0.6	2	2	3	3	3	3	3	3
:Females, % of pop	52	51	50	49	50	51	51	51	51	50
Male % ages: 0-9 years	51	51	51	52	50	50	49	49	49	51
:10-19 years	50	52	51	52	50	50	52	49	52	51
:20-29 years	51	51	50	50	50	48	44	49	44	49
:30-39 years	51	50	49	49	49	46	45	49	49	50
:40-49 years	49	49	48	51	49	49	49	49	49	51
:50-59 years	42	47	48	53	47	51	51	50	51	49
:60-69 years	36	44	47	53	46	48	48	50	50	47
:70+ years		44	44	26	54	89	50	50	50	47
Education: Literacy, adult	100	93	77	26	54	89	33	80	33	81
Cities: earliest settled, year	963	-914	200	723	1860	1600	1540	1610	1540	317
:Largest settled, year	963	-551	500	723	1880	1860	1540	1610	1540	1820
:Largest, % pop	20	5	3		11	3		5	7	8
Politics: # of parties	6	5	5	5	4	1		5		6
:Largest party %	37	36	57	54	48	100	100	34	100	65
:Top two parties, %	67	66	69	88	85	100	100	46	100	77
:Chambers in leg., #	2	1	2	2	1	1	2	2	1	2
:# of changes 60		2	2	2		1		2	1	1
Independence year	1870	1970	1950	1770	1960	1960	1970	1960	1980	1950
Laws: Censorship (1=high)	0	0.1	0.5	0	0.5	0.1	0	0.5	0	0.2
:Metric system (1=yes)	0	0	0	0	0	0	0	0	0	0
:Visas needed (3=high)	1	2	2	3	3	3	3	3	3	2
:Full soc security (1=yes)	1	0	0	0	0	0	0	0	0	0
:Military service (1=yes)	0	1	0	0	0	0	0	0	1	0
Crime: Murders/100k pop	2									
:Thefts/100k pop	20	537	0.9		0.1					314
:Suicide/100k pop	0.9	11	41							12
:Prisoners/000 pop		0.8	0.2							1
:Death penalty (1=yes)	0	0	1	0	0	1	1	3	0	1
Unrest: Border disputes, #	0	1	1	0	0	1	0	0	0	1
:International, #	0	0	2	0	1	1	0	1	0	2
:# of civil wars	0	0.99	1	0	0	1	1	1	1	1
:# of civil riots	0	0	0	1	0	0	0	0	0	0.30

Characteristics	Malay Christian	Malay Coastal	Malay Muslim	Malinke	Maltese	Mambwe	Manchu-Tibetian	Mandara	Mande	Mandingo
Population Covered	60900	23400	2660	3670	345	408	12700	715	861	555
Countries represented, #	1	1	4	1	1	1	1	1	1	1
Average representation %	92	12	7	12	96	5	7	6	9	7
Vital Stats: Death rate		8		18	8	11	7	11	16	13
··Birth rate	28	25	28	47	14	48	22	44	49	44
··Fertility	4	3	4	6	2	7	2	6	7	6
··Female life exp., years	68	64	68	50	79	59	73	60	53	57
··Male life exp., years	63	59	63	46	74	55	69	55	52	54
··Infant mortality	71	98	71	142	17	97	52	115	139	102
··# of major diseases	5	6	5	5	2	2	2	6	6	5
Demography: Migration/100	-1	0	-1	-18		-2		2	-2	0
··Population of Country	66500	195000	66500	7960	360	8870	1210000	12600	9780	7930
··Urbanization, %	42	31	42	28	86	49	29	41	9	35
··Population growth	3	2	3	2		3	2	3	2	3
··Females, % of pop	50	50	50	51	51	51	49	50	52	51
Male % ages: 0-9 years	51	51	51	50	51		52	50	48	49
··10-19 years	51	51	51	49	52		51	50	48	49
··20-29 years	50	50	51	48	51		51	50	48	49
··30-39 years	49	49	50	49	50		52	50	48	49
··40-49 years	49	48	49	50	48		53	49	48	49
··50-59 years	48	48	49	50	47		53	49	47	50
··60-69 years	47	44	48	50	42		49	47	48	50
··70+ years			47	47			43	45		50
Education: Literacy, adult	90	77	90	33	96	73	73	18	18	38
Cities: earliest settled, year	1400	200	1400	1610	1570	1900	-2210	1880	1200	1860
··Largest settled, year	1400	500	1400	1880	1570	1910	1100	1880	1200	1860
··Largest, % pop	3	3	3	11	6	10	0.6	4	5	17
Politics: # of parties				3		2	1			8
··Largest party %	36	57	36	87	52	83	100	49	73	70
··Top two parties, %	53	69	53	91	100	100	100	87	84	93
··Chambers in leg., #	2	2	2	1	1	2	1	1	1	1
··# of changes 60	2	2	2	1		1	3	3	4	0
··Independence year	1950	1950	1950	1960	1960	1960	1910	1960	1960	1960
Laws: Censorship (1=high)	0.5	0.5	0.5	0.5	0	0.5		0.5	0.5	1
··Metric system (1=yes)			0	0.1	0		0			0
··Visas needed (3=high)	2	2	2	3	2	3	3	3	3	3
··Full soc security (1=yes)	0	0	0	0	-1	0	0	0	0	0
··Military service (1=yes)	0	0	0	0		0	1	0	0	
Crime: Murders/100k pop	30	0.9	30		0.9					
··Thefts/100k pop	72	41	72	0.6	0.3					
··Suicide/100k pop	0.5		0.5	0.1	0.6					
··Prisoners/000 pop	0.2	0.2	0.2	0.4	0		177			
··Death penalty (1=yes)	-1	-1	-1	0.2	0	0	1	1	1	1
Unrest: Border disputes, #	2	2	2		0	2	12	0		0
··International, #	0	0	0			0	0	0		1
··# of civil wars	0	1	2			0	2	0		0
··# of civil riots	0	0	0			0	0	0	0	1

Characteristics	Mandyako	Mano	Manx (Norse-C.)	Manzan-Darani	Maori	Maravi	Masa	Masalit Maba	Maya	Mbaka
Population Covered	109	204	0.7	2280	312	7800	138	377	20	141
Countries represented, #	1	1	1	1	1	2	1	1	1	1
Average representation %	1	7	1	4	9	40	2	6	10	4
Vital Stats: Death rate	18	13	14	8	8	16	21	21	5	18
:Birth rate	42	44	11	44	16	51	42	42	31	43
:Fertility					2	57			4	6
:Female life exp., years	49	59	78	68	80	53	49	49	73	49
:Male life exp., years	45	55	73	67	73	49	46	46	67	46
:Infant mortality	146	141	9	88	14	142	148	148	53	133
:# of major diseases	5	2	4	5	0	4	4	4	1	5
Demography: Migration/100	2			-1100	-2	-14	0	0	4	0
:Population of Country	1030	265	70	63200	3510	10300	5990	5990	200	3270
:Urbanization, %	26	2870	57	55	84	20	28	28	50	42
:Population growth	2	45		3	1	3	2	2	2	2
:Females, % of pop	52	3		48	50	51	52	52	50	52
Male % ages: 0-9 years	50	49		52	51	50	48	48	50	50
:10-19 years	51	51		52	51	49	48	48	51	49
:20-29 years	40	50		52	51	47	48	48	51	48
:30-39 years	44	45		52	50	42	47	47	51	48
:40-49 years	46	48		52	50	47	48	48	52	48
:50-59 years	51	55		50	51	50	48	48	51	47
:60-69 years	57	58		48	47	50	47	47	51	45
:70+ years	59	57		54	40	54	30	30	47	43
Education: Literacy, adult	36	61	99	54	99	48	30	30	93	38
Cities: earliest settled, year	1760	40	1250	-1100	1840	1880	1900	1900	1640	1890
:Largest settled, year	1760	1820	1250	-1200	1840	1880	1900	1900	1640	1890
:Largest, % pop	12	1820		10	25	5	10	10	21	20
Politics: # of parties	1	16	0	0	4	3	1	1	2	2
:Largest party %	100	1	100	100	51	57	100	100	55	40
:Top two parties, %	100	100	100	100	96	84	100	100	100	55
:Chambers in leg., #	2	100	1	1	1	1	1	1	2	2
:# of changes 60	3	1		2	0	1	4	4	0	7
:Independence year	1970	3	1770	1910	1950	1960	1960	1960	1980	1960
Laws: Censorship (1=high)		1850	1	1	0	0.9	0.5	0.5	0.5	1
:Metric system (1=yes)	0	1		0	0	0	0	0	1	0
:Visas needed (3=high)	3	1		3	2	1	3	3	2	3
:Full soc security (1=yes)	0	3		0	1	0	0	0	1	0
:Military service (1=yes)	0	0		1	0	0.8	0	0	0	0
Crime: Murders/100k pop		0			2	1		1	0.4	
:Thefts/100k pop		1			4340				1	
:Suicide/100k pop	0		0	5	13	0	0	0	1	0
:Prisoners/000 pop	0	0		1	1	0.8	1	1	0	0
:Death penalty (1=yes)	0	0		1	0		3	3		0
Unrest: Border disputes, #	0	3			0		2	2		0
:International, #	0	0			0		0	0		0
:# of civil wars	2									
:# of civil riots	0	0		1	0	0.8	0	0	0	3

Characteristics	Mbete	Mbochi	Mbum	Mbunda	Melanesian	Mende	Merina	Meru	Mestizo	Miao Man
Population Covered	290	283	699	103	1020	1550	3520	1570	146000	235
Countries represented, #	2	1	3	1	25	1	2	1	19	1
Average representation %	8	12	18	19	21	34	27	6	38	5
Vital Stats: Death rate	14	13			9	20	14	8	6	16
:Birth rate	34	42	43	46	35	46	46	44	28	44
:Fertility	5	6	6	7	5	7	7	6	3	6
:Female life exp., years	56	56	52	48	63	48	57	64	74	53
:Male life exp., years	52	53	48	45	60	43	54	60	68	50
:Infant mortality	117	116	138	161	75	163	118	88	61	131
:# of major diseases	5	5	5	4	4	5	5	6		11
Demography: Migration/100	0	0	0	0	0.1	-28	0	0	-0.5	0
:Population of Country	1750	2460	7000	10300	2690	4510	13300	26100	60400	4520
:Urbanization, %	43	44	34	27	18	31	23	24	70	17
:Population growth	3	3	2	3	3	2	3	4	3	2
:Females, % of pop	51	51	52	48	48	50	51	50	51	50
Male % ages: 0-9 years	49	50	52	52	52	50	49	51	50	50
:10-19 years	49	49	49	52	52	50	49	50	50	50
:20-29 years	48	48	48	52	53	50	49	48	49	50
:30-39 years	48	47	48	53	51	50	49	48	49	50
:40-49 years	49	47	48	53	52	49	49	48	49	51
:50-59 years	48	45	48	53	52	49	50	48	47	51
:60-69 years	47	43	47	52	52	49	50	45	45	51
:70+ years	48	47	46	52	54	50	50	45	45	50
Education: Literacy, adult	59	57	37	42	57	21	80	69	86	84
Cities: earliest settled, year	1750	1600	1890	1580	1890	1790	1610	800	1330	1350
:Largest settled, year	1860	1880	1890	1580	1890	1790	1610	1900	1470	1350
Politics: # of parties	30	26	12	17	8	11	6	4	13	9
:Largest, % pop	5				6		5	6		
:Largest party %	48	38	77	59	33	100	34	51	48	100
:Top two parties, %	67	60	88	91	47	100	46	66	71	100
:Chambers in leg., #	1	2	1	1	1	3	2	1	2	1
:# of changes 60	4	3	4		0.3		1	3		2
Independence year	1960	1960	1960	1980	1970	1960	1960	1960	1850	1950
Laws: Censorship (1=high)	0.2	0.5	0.6	0.5	0.4	1	0.5	1	0.5	1
:Metric system (1=yes)					0.9			0	0	0
:Visas needed (3=high)	2	3	3	3	0.2	3	3	3	0.2	3
:Full soc security (1=yes)	0	0	0	0	0	0	0	0	0.4	0
:Military service (1=yes)	0	0	0	1	0	0	0	0	0.9	1
Crime: Murders/100k pop								4	25	
:Thefts/100k pop			0.2				3	42	382	
:Suicide/100k pop	0.4	1	0.6				0	1	3	
:Prisoners/000 pop	1	1	2				1	2	0.8	1
:Death penalty (1=yes)	0	0	0				1	1	0.1	0
Unrest: Border disputes, #	0.6	0		2		1	3	1	0.8	0
:International, #				0		0	0	0	0.1	0
:# of civil wars						0	1	1	0.8	1
:# of civil riots	0.6	0	2		0.1	2	1	0	0.3	0

Characteristics	Microne-sian	Mixed	Moldovan	Mon	Mon-Khmer	Monegas-que	Mongo	Mongol-Buryat	Mongol-Dariganga	Mongol-Dorbed
Population Covered	181	1050	4100	893	226	5	5480	39	32	63
Countries represented, #	5	14	3	2	1	1	13	1	1	1
Average representation %	23	30	2	2	5	7	13	2	1	3
Vital Stats: Death rate	6	7	10	10	16	7	13			7
:Birth rate	34	30	18	29	44	7	45	34	34	34
:Fertility	5	4	2	4	6		6	5	5	5
:Female life exp., years	74	73	74	64	53	80	56	68	68	68
:Male life exp., years	70	67	69	61	50	72	53	63	63	63
:Infant mortality	46	33	38	96	131	14	112	75	75	75
:# of major diseases	0.4	2	3	8	11		2	3	3	3
Demography: Migration/100	6	-3	0	0	0	0	0	0	0	0
:Population of Country	104	639	44800	44600	4520	29	41200	2320	2320	2320
:Urbanization, %	26	54	55	24	17	100	41	56	56	56
:Population growth	3	1	0.9	2	2	0.9	3	3	3	3
Females, % of pop	48	52	54	50	50	53	51	50	50	50
Male % ages: 0-9 years	52	50	51	50	50	51		50	50	50
:10-19 years	52	49	51	50	50	49		50	50	50
:20-29 years	52	48	50	49	50	48		50	50	50
:30-39 years	53	46	49	49	51	48		50	50	50
:40-49 years	54	46	47	49	51	47		50	50	50
:50-59 years	51	47	45	49	50	44		50	50	50
:60-69 years		47	35	46	50	40		50	50	50
:70+ years		46	27							
Education: Literacy, adult	91	77	98	81	84	99	72	90	90	90
Cities: earliest settled, year	1700	1660		-585	1350	-600	1880	1650	1650	1650
:Largest settled, year	1700	1660		-585	1350	-600	1890	1650	1650	1650
:Largest, % pop	28	16	12	6	9	43	7	24	24	24
Politics: # of parties	1	4	6		1	2	0	3	3	3
:Largest party %	98	65	43	100	100	83	100	92	92	92
:Top two parties, %	98	97	67	100	100	94	100	97	97	97
:Chambers in leg., #	2	2	1	4	2	1	1	2	2	2
:# of changes 60										
Independence year	1960	1820	1990	1950	1950	1860	1960	1920	1920	1920
Laws: Censorship (1=high)		0.1	0.5	1	1	0	1	0	0	0
:Metric system (1=yes)	0.3			1		2				
:Visas needed (3=high)	2	0.2	0.2	3	3	1	3	3	3	3
:Full soc security (1=yes)	0	0.5	0.9	0	0	0	0	0	0	0
:Military service (1=yes)	0	0.7	0.3		1		0	1	1	1
Crime: Murders/100k pop				5						
:Thefts/100k pop	0.3	5	0.3	56			2			
:Suicide/100k pop		0.5								
:Prisoners/000 pop	0.3	0.5								
:Death penalty (1=yes)	0	0	0	1	1	0	0	0	0	0
Unrest: Border disputes, #	0	0	0	0	0	0	1	0	0	0
:International, #	0	0	0	0	0	0	1	0	0	0
:# of civil wars	0			3	1	0	0	0	0	0
:# of civil riots	0			1	0	0	1	0	0	0

Characteristics	Mongol-Khalka	Mongoloid	Montene-grin	Moor	Morvians	Mossi	Mpongwe	Mubi	Mulatto	Muong
Population Covered	1830	32000	633	3050	5	7290	183	252	49100	841
Countries represented, #	1	2	1	2		2	1	1	15	1
Average representation %	79	2	6	15	0.1	28	15	4	22	
Vital Stats: Death rate	7	10		12	9	15	14	21	7	8
: Birth rate	34	29		36	15	48	29	42	25	29
: Fertility	5	5		5	2	7	4	5	3	4
: Female life exp., years	68	63		60	77	55	56	49	70	67
: Male life exp., years	63	61		56	68	53	52	46	65	63
: Infant mortality	75	95	52	81	20	127	118	148	77	69
: # of major diseases	3	5		4	4	4	5	4	4	5
Demography: Migration/100	2			-0.8	0	-2			-0.2	-1
: Population of Country	2320	947000	10500	8740	5330	12200	1260	5990	114000	70100
: Urbanization, %	56	28	47	33	77	17	42	28	72	21
: Population growth	3	2		2		2	4	2	2	2
: Females, % of pop	50	48		50		51	51	52	50	52
Male % ages: 0-9 years	50	51		51		49	49	48	51	
: 10-19 years	50	52		51		49	49	48	50	
: 20-29 years	50	52		48		48	49	48	50	
: 30-39 years	50	51		48		49	49	47	50	
: 40-49 years	50	52		49		49	49	48	50	
: 50-59 years	50	52		50		47	50	48	50	
: 60-69 years	50	52		49		49	49	47	49	
: 70+ years	50	49		46		33		30	47	
Education: Literacy, adult	90	55	89	56	93		61		83	88
Cities: earliest settled, year	1650	-1610		884		1340	1850	1900	1530	-200
: Largest settled, year	1650	301		884		1340	1850	1900	1550	1700
: Largest, % pop	24	0.9		16	7	5	33	1	10	5
Politics: # of parties	3	4	5	4		5	1	1	1	
: Largest party %	92	51	34	73	49	81	55	100	32	100
: Top two parties, %	97	70	59	86	69	88	71	100	53	100
: Chambers in leg., #	1	2	2	2	1	4	2	4	2	1
: # of changes 60	2	1		3					4	3
: Independence year	1920	1940	1990	1960	1990	1960	1960	1960	1840	1980
Laws: Censorship (1=high)	0	0.6	1	1	0	1	0	0.5	0.2	0.5
: Metric system (1=yes)	0	0		0		0	0	0	0	
: Visas needed (3=high)	3	3	1	3	1	3	2	3	3	3
: Full soc security (1=yes)	0	0	1	0	1	0	0	0	1	0
: Military service (1=yes)	1			0		0	0			1
Crime: Murders/100k pop		0.2		0.8				0	0.9	
: Thefts/100k pop		4		0.6					13	
: Suicide/100k pop		69		0.6					142	
: Prisoners/000 pop		1							3	
: Death penalty (1=yes)		1	1	1	0	1	0	0	0.6	-1
Unrest: Border disputes, #	0	4			0	0	1	1	0	6
: International, #	0	0				0	0	3	0.2	3
: # of civil wars	0	1				1	0	2	0.1	2
: # of civil riots	0	0.8	1	1	0	0	1	0	0.8	0

Characteristics	Nama	Nauruan	Ndebele	Nepalese	Nether-lander	Newar	Ngbandi	Ngoni	Nkole	Norman-French D.
Population Covered	78	6	1740	12300	14600	633	347	717	1580	119
Countries represented, #	1	1	1	1	1	1	1	1	1	2
Average representation %	5	58	4	58	95	3	11	7	8	80
Vital Stats: Death rate	9	18	14	14	8	14	18	17	14	10
∴ Birth rate	45	2	40	38	13	38	43	52	51	12
∴ Fertility	7	69	5	5	2	5	6	8	7	1
∴ Female life exp., years	63	64	64	53	81	53	49	51	55	79
∴ Male life exp., years	58	62	60	54	75	54	46	48	51	74
∴ Infant mortality	97	3	80	115	9	115	133	153	112	6
∴ # of major diseases	4		2	5		5			6	
Demography: Migration/100	0	0	3	0	0	0	0	-17	0	0
∴ Population of Country	1570	100	10800	21100	15300	21100	3270	10700	19300	6
∴ Urbanization, %	37	70	27	8	89	8	42	13	10	76
∴ Population growth	2	1	3		0.9	2	2	3	3	
∴ Females, % of pop	51	44	51	49	50	49	52	52	50	
Male % ages: 0-9 years	49	52	50	52	51	52	50	49	50	
∴ 10-19 years	49	52	50	52	51	50	48	47	49	
∴ 20-29 years	49	53	45	50	51	49	48	42	49	
∴ 30-39 years	50	52	43	49	51	51	48	47	49	
∴ 40-49 years	49	53	46	51	50	53	45	50	50	
∴ 50-59 years	48	54	47	53	46	53	43	54	48	
∴ 60-69 years	48	53	41	53	38	36	38	42	48	
∴ 70+ years	72	99	67	26	99	26	1890	1880	1890	0
Education: Literacy, adult										0
Cities: earliest settled, year	1890		1890	723	200	723	1890	1880	1890	100
∴ Largest settled, year	1890		1890	723	900	723	1890	1880	1890	100
∴ Largest, % pop	8	67	6	1	5	5	20	4	2	1
Politics: # of parties	4		5	5	9	5	4	3		
∴ Largest, % pop	57	100	97	54	25	54	40	50	100	1070
∴ Top two parties, %	86	100	99	88	48	88	55	80	100	1
∴ Chambers in leg., #	2	1	1	2	2	2	2	1	3	
∴ # of changes 60	1	0	1	1	0	1	1	1	1	
∴ Independence year	1990	1970	1980	1770	1820	1770	1960	1960	1960	1070
Laws: Censorship (1=high)	0.5	0	0	0	0	0	0	0	0.5	1
∴ Metric system (1=yes)	3	0	0	0	2	0	0	0	3	
∴ Visas needed (3=high)	3	3	2	3	1	3	3	3	0	
∴ Full soc security (1=yes)	0	1	0	0	1	0	0	0	0	
∴ Military service (1=yes)	0	0	0	0	8	0	0	0		
Crime: Murders/100k pop			18		5550					
∴ Thefts/100k pop			1450		11					
∴ Suicide/100k pop			17		0.4					
∴ Prisoners/000 pop	0	0	2	0	0	0	0	0	0.5	0
∴ Death penalty (1=yes)	3	0	1	0	0	0	0	0	0	
Unrest: Border disputes, #	0	0	1	0	0	0	0	1	0	
∴ International, #	1	0	0	0	0	0	0	0	0	
∴ # of civil wars	1	0	0	1	0	1	3	1	2	0
∴ # of civil riots			1							

Characteristics	North-Western	Norwegian	Nuba	Nuer	Nung Sukuma	Nupe	Nyamwezi (Galla)	Nyoros	Ometo	Oromo
Population Covered	895	4170	2220	1340	771	1280	6070	616	1430	18700
Countries represented, #	1	1	1	1	1	1	2	1	1	1
Average representation %	10	95	8	5		16	21	3	3	35
Vital Stats: Death rate	11	10	13	13	8	46	15	14	14	14
: Birth rate	48	14	44	44	29	54	49	51	45	45
: Female life exp., years	57	81	54	54	67	51	57	55	53	53
: Male life exp., years	59	74	53	53	63	128	53	51	53	50
: Infant mortality	55	8	105	105	69		123	112	134	134
: # of major diseases	97	0	6	6	5	2	5	6	4	4
Demography: Migration/100	-2		0	0	-1	0	-1	0	2	2
: Population of Country	8870	4320	27400	27400	70100	107000	28800	19300	52900	52900
: Urbanization, %	49	74	26	26	21	29	24	10	12	12
: Population growth	0.6	0.6	3	3		3	3	3	1	1
: Females, % of pop	51	51	50	50	52	50	51	50	50	50
Male % ages: 0-9 years	51	51	50	51		51	50	50	50	50
: 10-19 years		51	50	51		50	48	49	52	52
: 20-29 years		51	50	50		50	46	49	46	46
: 30-39 years		51	49	49		50	49	49	47	47
: 40-49 years		51	48	48		50	51	49	49	49
: 50-59 years		47	47	47		50	48	50	53	53
: 60-69 years		40	43	43		51	48	50	54	54
: 70+ years			27	27		51	89	48	57	57
Education: Literacy, adult	73	99			88				71	71
Cities: earliest settled, year	1900	900	1800	1800	-200	1100	1600	1890	700	700
: Largest settled, year	1910	1050	1820	1820	1700	1700	1860	1890	1890	1890
Politics: # of parties	10	11	2	2	5	1	3	2	3	3
: Largest, % pop	2	8	0	0	1	0	1	0	1	1
: Largest party %	83	41	100	100	100	100	100	100	100	100
: Top two parties, %	100	60	100	100	100	100	100	100	100	100
: Chambers in leg., #	2	1	1	1		1	1	51	1	1
: # of changes 60		0	3	3	3	4		3	2	2
Independence year	1960	1900	1960	1960	1980	1960	1960	1960	1990	1990
Laws: Censorship (1=high)	0.5	0	1		0.5	0.5	0.1	0.5	0.5	0.5
: Metric system (1=yes)	3	2							3	3
: Visas needed (3=high)	0	1	0	0	3	3	3	3	0	0
: Full soc security (1=yes)		1	3	3	0	0	0	0	3	3
: Military service (1=yes)		2	0	0	1	1		3	7	7
Crime: Murders/100k pop						94				
: Thefts/100k pop		4150			6	1260			37	37
: Suicide/100k pop		16			3				0.3	0.3
: Prisoners/000 pop		0.5			2	0	0	0.5		
: Death penalty (1=yes)		0	1	1	0	0				
Unrest: Border disputes, #	2	2	2	2	6	4	1	2	5	5
: International, #	0	0	1	1	3	0	0	0	1	1
: # of civil wars	0	0	2	2	2	0	0	0	3	3
: # of civil riots	0	0	0	0	0	0	0	0	0	0

Characteristics	Ossete	Ovambo	Ovim-bundu	Pacific Islander	Pakistani	Palauans	Palaung-Wa	Papuan New Guin.	Pashtun	Pepel
Population Covered	176	784	3830	3	795	6	543	3510	10100	103
Countries represented, #	1	1	1	26	1	1	1	1	1	1
Average representation %	3	50	37	5	9	40	12	84	52	10
Vital Stats: Death rate	9	9	19	18	20	7	16	11	20	18
..Birth rate	17	45	46	2	3	23	44	34	44	42
..Fertility	2	7	7	69	76	3	6	5	6	6
..Female life exp., years	75	63	48	64	71	73	53	57	44	49
..Male life exp., years	72	58	45	62	27	69	50	55	45	45
..Infant mortality	36	97	161	3	2	25	131	85	172	146
..# of major diseases	0	4	4		4		11			5
Demography: Migration/100		0	0	0	0	2	0	0	0	0
..Population of Country	5490	1570	10300	100	34300	16	4520	4170	1920	1030
..Urbanization, %	56	37	27	70	76		17	16	18	26
..Population growth	0.8	2	3	1	2		2	2	2	2
Females, % of pop		51	48	44	47	49	50	48		52
Male % ages: 0-9 years		49	52	52	51		50	52	50	50
..10-19 years		49	52	52	53		50	52	50	51
..20-29 years		49	52	52	56		50	54	50	40
..30-39 years		50	52	53	56		51	51	49	44
..40-49 years		49	53	53	55		51	51	48	46
..50-59 years		50	53	54	55		50	51	51	51
..60-69 years		48	52	53	51		50	51	56	57
..70+ years		48	42		43		50	57	58	59
Education: Literacy, adult	100	72	72	99	88	92	84	52	29	36
Cities: earliest settled, year		1890	1580		348	1520	1350	1870	-400	1760
..Largest settled, year		1890	1580		728	1520	1350	1870	-400	1760
..Largest, % pop	23	8	17	67	15		9	7	3	12
Politics: # of parties	5	4	5	0	4	3	1	4		
..Largest party %	8	57	59	100	66		100	20	2	100
..Top two parties, %	14	86	91	100	93		100	34	4	100
..Chambers in leg., #	1					2	2			
..# of changes 60		2	2	0	0.6	1		1	2	3
Independence year	1990	1990	1980	1970	1920		1950	1980	1920	1970
Laws: Censorship (1=high)	1	0.5	0.5	0	0.4	1	1	0.5		
..Metric system (3=high)	0	0	0	3	0.8		0	1	0	0
..Visas needed (3=high)	2	3	3	1	0.9		3	2		
..Full soc security (1=yes)	0	0	1	0	0.4		0	0	0	
..Military service (1=yes)	1	0	0		6630		1	0		
Crime: Murders/100k pop					3				200	300
..Thefts/100k pop					21				0	
..Suicide/100k pop					0.3					
..Prisoners/000 pop					6					
..Death penalty (1=yes)					0.1					
Unrest: Border disputes, #	1	0	0	0	0.4	0	1	0	4	0
..International, #	0	3	1	0	0.0		0	0	1	0
..# of civil wars	0	0	0	0			0	0	5	2
..# of civil riots	1	1	2	0			1	0	2	0

Characteristics	Persian	Polinisian	Polynesian Chinese	Polinesian European	Polish	Portuguese	Punjabi	Punu	Puyi	Pygmy
Population Covered	29000	301	8	22	39700	34100	84600	219	2790	37
Countries represented, #	3	9	1	2	9	8	2	2	1	1
Average representation %	34	7	4	9	17	13	54	14	0.2	2
Vital Stats: Death rate	4	6	5	5	14	8	13	33	2	13
: Birth rate	44	24	28	28	14	21	43	7	22	42
: Fertility	7	3	3	3	7	7	7	7	6	6
: Female life exp., years	68	75	73	73	77	72	59	56	73	56
: Male life exp., years	67	70	68	68	69	66	59	52	69	53
: Infant mortality	88	20	15	16	27	65	128	118	52	116
: # of major diseases	5	0.8	1	1	5	4	6	5	2	5
Demography: Migration/100	0	-0.3	0	-0.6	-0.8	0.6	-1	0	0	0
: Population of Country	62900	1270	214	201	38200	111000	128000	1660	1210000	2460
: Urbanization, %	55	64	62	62	62	63	31	43	29	44
: Population growth	3	2	63	63	0.8		3	3		3
Females, % of pop	48	50	49	49	51	51	48	51	49	51
Male % ages: 0-9 years	52	51	51	51	51	51	50	49	52	50
: 10-19 years	52	51	51	51	51	50	54	49	51	49
: 20-29 years	52	51	51	51	50	49	52	49	52	48
: 30-39 years	52	50	51	51	49	48	51	49	53	47
: 40-49 years	52	51	51	51	47	44	51	48	53	49
: 50-59 years	50	51	51	51	43	48	55	48	49	45
: 60-69 years	48	49	50	50	35	44	59	48	43	43
: 70+ years	54	47	50	50	99	83	58	60	73	47
Education: Literacy, adult		96	98	98	99	472	35			57
Cities: earliest settled, year	-1110	1840	1840	1840	693	472	-598	1770	-2210	1600
: Largest settled, year	-1200	1840	1840	1840	1000	499	1730	1860	1100	1880
Politics: # of parties	10	17	12	12	5	7	6	30	0.6	26
: Largest, % pop	0	5	4	4	38	33	43	49	100	5
: Largest party %	100	59			66	55	79	67	100	38
: Top two parties, %	100	93	2	2	2	3	1	1		60
: Chambers in leg., #		2								2
: # of changes 60	1	0.6	1	1				1	1	3
: Independence year	1910	1900	1850	1850	1950	1770	1950	1960	1910	1960
Laws: Censorship (1=high)	1	0.1	0	0	0	0	1	0.2	1	0.5
: Metric system (1=yes)	0									0
: Visas needed (3=high)	3	0.2	2	2	2	3	3	2	3	3
: Full soc security (1=yes)	0	0.7								0
: Military service (1=yes)	1		0	0	0	1	0	0	1	1
Crime: Murders/100k pop	·						78		2	
: Thefts/100k pop	·	4340			1680	729	22		177	
: Suicide/100k pop	1	13			13	0.5	15	0.3		1
: Prisoners/100k pop	5						0.3		1	1
: Death penalty (1=yes)	1	0.3	0	0	0.1	0	30	0.1	12	0
Unrest: Border disputes, #	1				0	30	1	0	2	0
: International, #	1	0	0	0	0	1	0	0.7	0	0
: # of civil wars	1	0	0	0	1	0				0
: # of civil riots	1									

Characteristics	Quechua	Rakhine	Romanian	Romansch	Rundi	Russian	Ruthenian	Rwanda	Saho	Sakalava
Population Covered	18500	2010	20700	55	1670	147000	16	5360	104	848
Countries representation, #	3	1	3		2	18	1	2	1	1
Average representation %	44	5	58	0.8	4	44	0.3	9	3	6
Vital Stats: Death rate	7	10	10	9	13	11	9	13		14
·Birth rate	28	29	14	12	45	16	15	46		46
·Fertility	3	4	2	2	6	2	2	6		7
·Female life exp., years	68	64	75	83	56	74	77	56		57
·Male life exp., years	64	61	69	76	53	70	68	53		54
·Infant mortality	87	96	40	6	113	36	20	112	175	118
·# of major diseases	4	8	0	3	2	6	0	3		5
Demography: Migration/100	-0.1	0	-3	3	0	0.6		0	0	0
·Population of Country	17800	44600	23300	6860	38900	1290000	5330	36600	3480	13300
·Urbanization, %	63	24	53	60	39	69	77	35	20	23
·Population growth	3	2		0.5	3	0.7		3		
·Females, % of pop	50	50	51	51	51	54		51		51
Male % ages: 0-9 years	51	50	51	51	50	51		50		49
·10-19 years	51	50	51	51	50	51		49		49
·20-29 years	50	49	51	50	49	50		49		49
·30-39 years	50	49	49	50	48	49		49		49
·40-49 years	49	49	49	49	45	47		49		49
·50-59 years	47	49	49	46	44	45		49		50
·60-69 years	44	46	44	38	45	35		50		50
·70+ years	90	81	42	39	50	28	93	50		50
Education: Literacy, adult	952	-585	96	99	71	99		67	20	80
Cities: earliest settled, year	1540	-585	-700	-3000	1880	819		1880		1610
·Largest settled, year	18	6	630	-3000	1890	1200		1890		1610
·Largest, % pop	46		17	5	7	7	7	6		6
Politics: # of parties	80	100	15	6	0.1	8	49		100	5
·Largest party %		100	34	22	99	24	69	100	100	34
·Top two parties, %		1	58	43	100	40	1	100	1	46
·Chambers in leg., #	4		2	2	1	2		1		2
·# of changes 60	1830	1950	1950	1820	1960	1990	1990	1960	1990	1960
Independence year	0.6	1	1		1	0.5	0	0.9	1	0.5
Laws: Censorship (1=high)	0.0					0.0		0.0		
·Metric system (1=yes)	2	3	3	2	3	2	1	3		3
·Visas needed (3=high)		0	0	1	0	0.9		0	0	0
·Full soc security (1=yes)	0.7	1	1	1	0	1	1	0		0
·Military service (1=yes)	0.8	5	1	3		4				
Crime: Murders/100k pop	351	56	141	4590	1	3500		0.5		3
·Thefts/100k pop	2		45	24	2	15		0.8		0
·Suicide/100k pop	0.8	1	2	0.7	0.9	0.8	0	0.2	0	1
·Prisoners/000 pop	0.9	0		0.0	1	0	0	0.1		0
·Death penalty (1=yes)	0.1	3	2	0		0		1		1
Unrest: Border disputes, #	0	1	0	0	0.9	0		0.8		0
·International, #	3		1		1					
·# of civil wars	0		1	0						

Characteristics	Samoan	Sanga	Sanmari-nese	Sara	Scandina-vian	Senufo	Serbian	Serer	Servicais Tongas	Shan
Population Covered	293	66	18	229	72	3700	8750	1350	76	3790
Countries represented, #	4	1	1	1	1	3	6	17	1	1
Average representation %	0.1	3	80	7		11	17	13	60	9
Vital Stats: Death rate	6	13	7	18	9	16	8	13	8	10
...Birth rate	31	42	8	43	16	49	13	44	38	29
...Fertility	4	6	1	6	2	7	2	6	5	4
...Female life exp., years	73	56	79	49	80	53	77	57	68	64
...Male life exp., years	67	53	74	46	74	50	71	54	64	61
...Infant mortality	49	116	21	133	8	124	45	102	85	96
...# of major diseases	0.8	0	0	0	0.4	5	0.3	5	0	8
Demography: Migration/100	-1		5	0	0.4	-0.3	0.3		0	
...Population of Country	45500	2460	23	3270	1900	11800	9320	7930	127	44600
...Urbanization, %	30	44	85	42	47	3	46	35	38	24
...Population growth	1	3	0.6	2	0.5	3	0.7	3	2	2
...Females, % of pop	49	51	52	50	49	51	51	51	50	50
Male % ages: 0-9 years	51	50	52	49	51	50	51	49	51	50
...10-19 years	51	49	50	48	51	49	50	49	49	50
...20-29 years	51	48	50	48	51	49	50	49	47	49
...30-39 years	50	47	51	48	51	49	49	49	51	49
...40-49 years	50	49	50	47	50	51	49	49	49	49
...50-59 years	49	45	48	45	47	49	46	49	49	49
...60-69 years	49	45	42	43	40	44	41	50	41	46
...70+ years	44	47	98	38	100	42	90	38	57	81
Education: Literacy, adult	98	57	98	38	100	42	90	38	57	81
Cities: earliest settled, year	1800	1600		1890	1380	1540	1580	1860	1490	-585
...Largest settled, year	1810	1880		1890	1400	1800	1790	1860	1490	-585
...Largest, % pop	13	26	30	20	26	11	22	17	27	6
Politics: # of parties	2	2	6	4	4	5	5		4	
...Largest party %	64	38	43	40	32	81	36	70	60	100
...Top two parties, %	98	60	66	55	52	88	61	93	98	100
...Chambers in leg., #			1	2	1	1	2		1	
...# of changes 60	1	3	0	0	0	2	0.2	0	0.5	4
...Independence year	1950	1960	301	1960	1230	1960	1990	1960	1980	1950
Laws: Censorship (1=high)		0.5	0	0	0	0.7	0	0	0.5	1
...Metric system (1=yes)	0.3		0	1	0		1	1		1
...Visas needed (3=high)	0.2	3	2	3	2	3	0	3	3	3
...Full soc security (1=yes)	0.2	0	1	0	1	0	1	0	0	0
...Military service (1=yes)	0.0	0	0		1	0	0.8		0	1
Crime: Murders/100k pop	9				5		4			
...Thefts/100k pop	5350				8370		5040			
...Suicide/100k pop	13				28		15			56
...Prisoners/000 pop	0.3				0.7	0.5	0.8			
...Death penalty (1=yes)	0.2				0.4	0.0	0.3	0	0	
Unrest: Border disputes, #	0.7	1	0	0	0	0.7	0.8	0	0	1
...International, #	0.4	-1	0	0	0	0.5	0.1	-1	0	0
...# of civil wars	0	0	0	3	0	0.7	0.8	0	0	3
...# of civil riots	0	0	0	3	0	0.5	1	1	0	1

Characteristics	Shilluk	Shona	Siamese	Sidamo	Sindhi	Sinhalese	Slavic Muslims	Slovak	Slovene	Soga
Population Covered	549	9690	29900	1270	16700	13300	1780	4900	1830	1580
Countries represented, #	1	3	1	1	1	1	2	4	3	1
Average representation %	13	34	53	1	1	74	19	9	3	8
Vital Stats: Death rate	44	10	6	14	13	6	7	10	11	14
:Birth rate	46	41	20	45	43	20	14	14	9	51
:Fertility		6	2				2		15	57
:Female life exp., years	54	61	71	53	59	74	72	77	78	55
:Male life exp., years	53	58	67	50	59	70	72	68	70	51
:Infant mortality	105	93	49	134	128	39	26	20	23	112
:# of major diseases	6		2	4	6	2		0.3	0.6	6
Demography: Migration/100		-0.2			-1	-2				
:Population of Country	27400	11700	56800	52900	128000	17800	4350	5760	2140	19300
:Urbanization, %	26	27	20	12	31	22	36	77	47	10
:Population growth	3	3	3	3	3	22	0.6	1	0.6	3
Females, % of pop	50	51	50	50	48	49		51	52	50
Male % ages: 0-9 years	51	49	51	52	50	51		51	51	50
:10-19 years	50	52	51	46	54	51		51	52	49
:20-29 years	50	44	51	47	52	50		50	51	49
:30-39 years	49	44	50	49	51	51		49	48	49
:40-49 years	48	44	48	53	51	52		45	47	49
:50-59 years	47	51	46	54	55	53		40	43	50
:60-69 years	43	48	42	57	59	54		93	37	50
:70+ years	27	49		71	58	88		1050	99	48
Education: Literacy, adult		61	93		35	-530	93	1230	-100	
Cities: earliest settled, year	1800	1830	700	700	-600	-530		15	19	1890
:Largest settled, year	1820	1830	1780	1890	1730		24	48	15	1890
:Largest, % pop	2	7	10	3	4	4	5	68	25	2
Politics: # of parties	0	4	6		6	6	37		42	
:Largest party %	100	97	22	100	43	56	66		2	100
:Top two parties, %	100	99	43	100	79	86			1	100
:Chambers in leg., #			2	1	2	2		1		1
:# of changes 60	3		3	2						3
Independence year	1960	1980	1880	1990	1950	1950	1990	1990	1990	1960
Laws: Censorship (1=high)	1	0	1	0.5	0	1	1	0.7	0	0.5
:Metric system (1=yes)	0	0			1		0	0.2		
:Visas needed (3=high)	3	2	2	3	3	2	1	0.9	1	0
:Full soc security (1=yes)	0	0			0	0		1	0	3
:Military service (1=yes)		0.2			78			1	1	0
Crime: Murders/100k pop		18	10	37	18	0.2		4	3	0
:Thefts/100k pop		1450	69					4180	2340	
:Suicide/100k pop		17		0.3	0.3	0.8		24	45	0.5
:Prisoners/000 pop		0.8		5	3			0.8	1	0
Death penalty (1=yes)	1	0.9	1	1	0	0	0	0.1	2	0
Unrest: Border disputes, #	2			3	1	0	3	0.6	1	0
:International, #	1	0.2				1		0.3	0	0
:# of civil wars	2		2			1	1		1	2
:# of civil riots	0	0.8					0	0		

Characteristics	Somali	Somba	Songhai	Soninke	Sotho	Sotho North	Spanish	Sundanese	Suriname	Susu
Population Covered	10400	274	1410	1190	4630	3960	45700	29800	5	693
Countries represented, #	3	1	4	4	1	1	12	1	1	1
Average representation %	14	5	6	6	11	10	12	15	3	11
Vital Stats: Death rate	13	15	19	19	11	8	8	8	6	21
: Birth rate	46	49	55	50	34	34	16	25	18	46
: Fertility	7	7	7	7	5	4	2	3	2	6
: Female life exp., years	57	53	50	49	65	67	77	64	79	46
: Male life exp., years	55	49	47	46	61	62	71	59	74	43
: Infant mortality	135	136	136	128	83	72	38	98	11	158
: # of major diseases	5	5	5	5	5	1	2	6	5	5
Demography: Migration/100	-11	.	-3	-4	0	0	0	0	-9	-40
: Population of Country	13300	5070	9370	8840	24400	39600	78600	195000	180	6300
: Urbanization, %	33	31	20	23	43	59	79	31	53	25
: Population growth	3	3	2	2	2	2	2	2	2	2
: Females, % of pop	51	52	51	51	50	49	51	50	52	51
Male % ages: 0-9 years	49	51	50	50	49	50	51	51	51	49
: 10-19 years	50	51	49	49	51	53	51	50	50	48
: 20-29 years	49	38	49	49	51	53	50	49	48	49
: 30-39 years	49	44	49	49	50	52	50	48	47	49
: 40-49 years	49	44	48	50	49	50	49	48	46	49
: 50-59 years	50	49	48	48	48	47	49	48	47	48
: 60-69 years	51	49	48	48	48	47	47	47	47	48
: 70+ years	51	51	43	41	43	40	42	44	37	50
Education: Literacy, adult	28	23	30	33	75	76	91	77	94	24
Cities: earliest settled, year	890	1600	1340	1290	1740	1650	-215	200	1530	1600
: Largest settled, year	994	1870	1750	1880	1740	1650	1140	500	1530	1890
: Largest, % pop	14	10	8	10	5	7	8	3	68	1
Politics: # of parties	0.1	.	.	.	.	.	9	4	.	.
: Largest party %	99	4	63	66	78	63	37	57	.	100
: Top two parties, %	100	19	84	76	90	84	69	69	.	100
: Chambers in leg., #	1	1	1	1	2	2	2	2	1	1
: # of changes 60	3	7	3	3	.	.	2	2	.	.
Independence year	1960	1960	1960	1960	1950	1930	1620	1950	1820	1960
Laws: Censorship (1=high)	0.1	0	0.2	0.2	0.7	0.5	0.3	0.5	.	0.5
: Metric system (1=yes)	0	.	.	0.1	0	0	0	0	.	.
: Visas needed (3=high)	3	3	3	3	3	3	2	2	.	3
: Full soc security (1=yes)	3	0	0	0	0	0	1	0	.	.
: Military service (1=yes)	0	0	0	0	0	0	1	0	.	.
Crime: Murders/100k pop	37	.	.	.	109	109	.	.	.	.
: Thefts/100k pop	.	.	1	0.8	.	.	2090	41	.	.
: Suicide/100k pop	0.3	.	.	0.1	0.3	0.3	0.7	0.9	.	1
: Prisoners/000 pop	0.9	.	0	.	0.4	.	.	0.2	.	.
: Death penalty (1=yes)	5	1	0	0.2	0.6	.	2	1	0	.
Unrest: Border disputes, #	1	.	2	0.2	0.4	1	.	2	2	.
: International, #	2	0	0	0.2	2	0	1	1	.	.
: # of civil wars	0	5	.	.	.	0	0	.	0	0
: # of civil riots	.	0	0.5	.	2	2	.	0	0	0

Characteristics	Swahili	Swazi	Swedish	Swiss	Tahitian	Tai	Taiwanese (Dari)	Tajik	Tama	Tamang
Population Covered	2620	690	8160		7	1400	17500	8640	377	739
Countries represented, #	2	1	5	2	1	2		3	1	1
Average representation %	15	84	44	15	4	10	84	19	6	4
Vital Stats: Death rate		12	11	7	5		5	13	21	14
Birth rate	49	44	13	13	23	33	16	41	42	38
Fertility		6	2	2	3	4	2	6	5	5
Female life exp., years	57	60	81	81	76	63	78	60	49	53
Male life exp., years	53	56	75	74	70	60	72	59	46	54
Infant mortality	122	121	6	6	17	85	5	117	148	115
# of major diseases	5	2	2	0	1	7	1		4	
Demography: Migration/100	-1	-6	-6	0		-0.7	0	-0.7	0	0
Population of Country	27800	818	8520		178	53600	20800	13700	5990	21100
Urbanization, %	24	30	83	65	58	20	70	27	28	8
Population growth	3	3	0.5	0.6		2	1	3	2	2
Females, % of pop	51	53	51	50	48	51	48	50	52	49
Male % ages: 0-9 years	50	50	51	50	52	50	52	50	48	52
10-19 years	50	48	51	50	52	50	52	49	48	52
20-29 years	48	42	51	48	52	50	52	48	48	50
30-39 years	46	44	51	52	52	51	53	51	47	49
40-49 years	49	44	49	48	52	51	52	56	48	51
50-59 years	51	43	48	46	53	50	53	58	48	53
60-69 years	48	33	48	39	54		52	58	47	53
70+ years	48		41					67		53
Education: Literacy, adult	88	68	99	100	91	87	92		30	26
Cities: earliest settled, year	1600	1900	911	1150	1850	189	1630	-400	1900	723
Largest settled, year	1860	1900	1270	1150	1850	1610	1710	-400	1900	723
Largest, % pop	3	5	8	18	38	6	13	13	10	
Politics: # of parties			8	3	8	1	1	4	1	5
Largest party %	100	100	40	51	84	100	79	95	100	54
Top two parties, %	100	100	63	92	97	100	97	95	100	88
Chambers in leg., #		2	1	1	2	3	2	1	4	2
# of changes 60	1		1				1	2		
Independence year	1960	1970	1910	1720	1850	1970	1950	1960	1960	1770
Laws: Censorship (1=high)	0	0	0	0	0	0.6	0.5	1	0.5	0
Metric system (1=yes)			2	2	2		0	0	0	0
Visas needed (3=high)	3	2	1	1	2	3	3	2	3	3
Full soc security (1=yes)	0	1	1	0		0	0		0	0
Military service (1=yes)		1	7	0		1	1			0
Crime: Murders/100k pop	0.1			0				0.1		
Thefts/100k pop			8400	0			2	0.8	0	
Suicide/100k pop			19	0			0	0.2	1	
Prisoners/000 pop	0		0.5	0			0	0.5	3	
Death penalty (1=yes)	1	1	0	0			0	0.9	2	0
Unrest: Border disputes, #	1			0	0	4				0
International, #				0	0	2				0
# of civil wars	1		0	0	0	0				0
# of civil riots	0	0	1	0	1					1

Characteristics	Tamil (Tubu)	Tatar	Teda	Teke	Tem-Kabre	Temne	Teso	Thai	Tharu	Tigre
Population Covered	3260	6700	437	1540	937	1410	1710	841	760	2400
Countries represented, #	1	5	1	2	1	1	1	1	1	2
Average representation %	8	3	7	4	24	3	9	1	4	4
Vital Stats: Death rate	6	10	21	13	12	20	14	8	14	14
..Birth rate	20	17	42	44	48	46	51	29	38	45
..Fertility		2	5	6	6			4	5	7
..Female life exp., years	74	74	49	56	58	48	55	67	53	53
..Male life exp., years	70	70	46	53	54	43	51	63	54	50
..Infant mortality	39	40	148	113	123	163	112	69	115	158
..# of major diseases	2	0	4	3	5	5	6	5	5	4
Demography: Migration/100	-2	0.2	0			-28	0	-1	0	2
..Population of Country	17900	129000	5990	30500	3910	4510	19300	70100	21100	24200
..Urbanization, %	22	67	28	42	24	31	10	21	8	17
..Population growth	2	0.9				2	3	2	2	3
..Females, % of pop	49		52	51	51	50	50	52	49	50
Male % ages: 0-9 years	51		48	50	49	50	50		52	50
..10-19 years	50		48	49	49	50	50		52	52
..20-29 years	51		48	47	49	50	49		50	46
..30-39 years	51		47	49	49	49	49		49	47
..40-49 years	52		48	45	49	49	49		51	49
..50-59 years	52		48	43	48	49	49		53	53
..60-69 years	54		47	47	43	50	50		53	54
..70+ years			30			21	48			57
Education: Literacy, adult	88	99		68				88	26	41
Cities: earliest settled, year	-543		1900	1800	1900	1790	1890	-200	723	700
..Largest settled, year	-543		1900	1890	1900	1790	1890	1705	723	1890
Politics: # of parties	4	7	1			1	2			3
..Largest, % pop	56	29	100	83	44	100	100	100	54	100
..Top two parties, %	86	43	100	89	87	100	100	100	88	100
..Chambers in leg., #	1	2	1	2	2	3	3	1	2	1
..# of changes 60		1	4							2
..Independence year	1950	1990	1960	1960	1960	1960	1960	1980	1770	1990
Laws: Censorship (1=high)	1	0.6	0.5	0.9	1	3	0.3	0.5		0.8
..Metric system (1=yes)	0	0	0	0	0	0	0	0	0	0
..Visas needed (3=high)	2	2	3	3	2	3	3	3	3	0
..Full soc security (1=yes)	0	0	0	0	0	0	0	0	0	0
..Military service (1=yes)	0	0	0	0	0	0	0	1	0	0
Crime: Murders/100k pop		0.9					0.5			7
..Thefts/100k pop										37
..Suicide/100k pop	0.8							6		
..Prisoners/000 pop	0			0.7						0.3
..Death penalty (1=yes)	0	0	0	1	1	1	2	1	0	0
Unrest: Border disputes, #	0	0	1	2		3		3	0	2
..International, #	0	0	3			1		2	0	1
..# of civil wars	1	0	2			2			0	3
..# of civil riots	1	0	0		1	0		0	1	0

Characteristics	Tigrinya	Tikar	Tiv	Tonga	Tongan	Toros	Tribal	Tsimihety	Tsonga	Tswana
Population Covered	6290	929	2340	1340	95	597	1220	981	3740	2370
Countries represented, #	2	1	1	1	2	1	1	1	2	1
Average representation %	11	7	2	15	64	14	12	7	22	6
Vital Stats: Death rate	14	11	16	11				14	17	8
: Birth rate	45	44	46	48	26	51	36	46	46	34
: Fertility		6	7		4		5	7	6	4
: Female life exp., years	53	60	54	59	70	55	54	57	50	67
: Male life exp., years	50	55	51	55	65	51	55	54	47	62
: Infant mortality	145	115	128	97	53	112	129	118	151	72
: # of major diseases	4	6	2	2		6	7	5	5	1
Demography: Migration/100	2	0	0	-2	-11	0	0	0	12	
: Population of Country	39200	12600	107000	8870	96	1930	122000	13300	15900	39600
: Urbanization, %	13	41	29	49	27	10	18	23	26	59
: Population growth		3	3	3	0.9	3	3	1	3	2
: Females, % of pop	50	50	51	51	51	50	48	51	51	49
Male % ages: 0-9 years	52	50	50		51	50	50	49	52	50
: 10-19 years	46	50	50		50	50	52	49	44	50
: 20-29 years	47	50	51		50	49	51	49	45	53
: 30-39 years	49	49	50		51	49	53	49	49	53
: 40-49 years	53	49	50		51	49	53	50	49	52
: 50-59 years	54	47	50		51	50	55	50	51	50
: 60-69 years	57	45	51		50	50	35	50	48	47
: 70+ years	57	54	54		50	48		50	50	40
Education: Literacy, adult			51	73	100				33	76
Cities: earliest settled, year	700	1880	1100	1900	1860	1890	800	1610	1550	1650
: Largest settled, year	1890	1880	1700	1910	1860	1890	1610	1610	1550	1650
: Largest, % pop.	3	10	1	2	28	2	2	5	7	5
Politics: # of parties	1	4	0	0			5	3	0	7
: Largest party %	100	49	100	83	100	100	46	34	100	63
: Top two parties, %	100	87	100	100	100	100	76	46	100	84
: Chambers in leg., #	1	2	1	2	1	1	4	2	2	2
: # of changes 60	2		4	1	1	3				
Independence year	1990	1960	1960	1960	1970	1960	1970	1960	1970	1930
Laws: Censorship (1=high)	0.6	0.5	0.5	0.5	1	0.5	0	0.5	0	0.5
: Metric system (1=yes)		0	0	0		0	0	0	0	0
: Visas needed (3=high)	3	3	3	3	2	3	2	3	3	3
: Full soc security (1=yes)	0	0	0	0	0	0	0	0	0	0
: Military service (1=yes)	0	0	1	0	0	0	0	0	1	0
Crime: Murders/100k pop	37		94				2			109
: Thefts/100k pop			1260				11			
: Suicide/100k pop								3		
: Prisoners/000 pop	0.3				0.6	0.5	0.3			0.3
: Death penalty (1=yes)	0	1	0	0	0	0	1	0	0	0
Unrest: Border disputes, #	4	0	0	2	0	0	1	1	0	1
: International, #	1	0	0	0	0	0	0	0	0	0
: # of civil wars	3	0	4	0	0	2	1	1	1	0
: # of civil riots	0	0	0	0	0	0	0	0	0	2

Characteristics	Tuareg	Tukolor	Tumbuka	Turkish	Turkmen	Tutsi	Tuvaluan	Twa	Uighur	Ukrainian
Population Covered	1320	830	408	54200	4960	1540	10	138	234	45800
Countries represented, #	3	2	1	12	5	2	2	1	2	15
Average representation %	5	8	5	26	3		12			13
Vital Stats: Death rate	20	14	11	6	10	14	12	14	8	12
Birth rate	52	45	48	26	39	49	28	49	25	14
Fertility		56	59	72	70	54	64	55	74	75
Female life exp., years	50	53	55	68	65	50	61	51	70	71
Male life exp., years	47	103	97	73	93	128	54	128	46	28
Infant mortality	135	5	2	0.1	2	7	1	7	0	0
# of major diseases	5	0	-2			0	0	0	-7	0.8
Demography: Migration/100	-3	7130	8870	58900	22400	6800	13	7000	14700	59200
Population of Country	9740	36	49	62	47	7	29	3	54	67
Urbanization, %	17		3		3				1	0.4
Population growth	2	51	51	49	49	51	55	51		54
Females, % of pop	51	50		51	52	50	48	50		51
Male % ages: 0-9 years	49	49		52	51	49	47	49		51
10-19 years	50	49		51	51	46	47	46		50
20-29 years	49	49		50	51	45	47	45		49
30-39 years	49	49		51	52	44	48	44		47
40-49 years	49	50		51	49	46	48	46		45
50-59 years	48	49		48		52	47	52		35
60-69 years	47	47		43				50		28
70+ years	28	37	73	82	79		96		98	98
Education: Literacy, adult	1220	1860	1900	-3470	-1450	1910	1790	1920		941
Cities: earliest settled, year	1660	1860	1910	-577	677	1910	1790	1920		1300
Largest settled, year	6	18	10	9	11	3	33	3		6
Largest, % pop		72	83	39	0.5	89	0.1	0.9	8	12
Politics: # of parties	67	92	100	65	98	100	98	91	6	26
Largest party %	81		2	2	99	5	100	100	33	48
Top two parties, %		0.6			2		0.1	4	38	1
Chambers in leg., #	3	1960	1960	1920	1960	1960	1980	1960	1	1990
# of changes 60	1960	1	0.5	0.9	1	0.7		0.8	1990	0.1
Independence year	0.3			0	0		3		0.8	0
Laws: Censorship (1=high)		3	3	2	2	3	0	3	2	0
Metric system (1=yes)	3	0	0	1	0.1	0	1	0	1	2
Visas needed (3=high)	0				0.9	1	0	1		0.1
Full soc security (1=yes)				248	68		0		0.2	3
Military service (1=yes)	1	0.1	2	18	0.9	0		1		2920
Crime: Murders/100k pop	0	0.1		0.9	1	0.9		0	0	14
Thefts/100k pop	0	0.1	0	0.9	0.6	0.5	0	1	0	1
Suicide/100k pop	1	1	0	4	0.7			0.4	0	0.1
Prisoners/000 pop	0.2			2	0.4					0
Death penalty (1=yes)				0						0
Unrest: Border disputes, #				0.9						0

Characteristics	Urdu	Uzbek	Vanuatuan	Vietnamese	Wallon	White	Wolof	Xhosa	Yalunka	Yao
Population Covered	9740	19900	156	62600	3300	271000	3140	3960	158	4200
Countries represented, #	1	6	1	6	1	41	3	10	1	3
Average representation %	8	27	95	17	33	38	28	8		0.3
Vital Stats: Death rate	13	8		8	10	17	44	34	4	12
·Birth rate	43	35	35	29	12		6	4	20	36
·Fertility		4		4		2			46	5
·Female life exp., years	59	71	72	67	81	78	53	67	48	62
·Male life exp., years	59	67	67	63	74	72	53	62	43	59
·Infant mortality	128	74	61	69		27	105	72	163	100
·# of major diseases	6			5	0	0.8			5	3
Demography: Migration/100	-1	-2	0	-1	0	2	0	0	-28	-4
·Population of Country	128000	19400	164	71200	10000	196000	7360	39600	4510	635000
·Urbanization, %	31	38	23	21	96	74	34	59	31	23
·Population growth	3	0.3		2	0.3	1			2	
·Females, % of pop	48	50	47	51	51	51	51	49	50	50
Male % ages: 0-9 years	50	50		50	51	51	50	50	50	51
·10-19 years	54	49		51	51	51	49	53	50	51
·20-29 years	52	48		50	51	50	49	53	49	49
·30-39 years	51	51		49	51	49	49	52	49	48
·40-49 years	51	56		49	50	48	50	50	49	51
·50-59 years	55	58		48	49	47	49	47	50	52
·60-69 years	59	58		43	46	40	50	40	49	49
·70+ years	58			88	37		37	76	50	49
Education: Literacy, adult	35	92	53	88	100	95	37	76	21	57
Cities: earliest settled, year	-600	-400	1860	-174	400	1520	1860	1650	1790	-290
·Largest settled, year	1730	-400	1860	1700	600	1610	1860	1650	1790	1430
·Largest, % pop	4	10	9	5	10	6	17	5	11	3
Politics: # of parties	6	2	4		5		8	7	0	2
·Largest party %	43	98	41	99	18	57	70	63	100	83
·Top two parties, %	79	98	63	100	35	91	91	84	100	93
·Chambers in leg., #	2	1	1	1	2		2	2	1	
·# of changes 60	1	1		3			0.2		3	-2
·Independence year	1950	1980	1980	1980	1830	1930	1960	1930	1960	1940
Laws: Censorship (1=high)	0	1	1	0.5		0.1		0.5	0	0.9
·Metric system (1=yes)	1	0	1	0.0		0.7	0	3		0.0
·Visas needed (3=high)	3	2	0	3	2	0.9	3	0	3	0
·Full soc security (1=yes)	0	0.8		1	1	0.2	0	0	0	2
·Military service (1=yes)	0	0.9			0	14	0		1	0.7
Crime: Murders/100k pop	78			9		4970		109		
·Thefts/100k pop	18			5310	2620	11				177
·Suicide/100k pop				13	22	0.4				
·Prisoners/000 pop	0.3	0.1	0	0.3	0.6	0.7		0.3		0.9
·Death penalty (1=yes)	0	0.4	0	6	0	3	0	1	1	7
Unrest: Border disputes, #	3	0.1	0	3		0.2	0	0	0	0
·International, #	0	0.4	0	2		0.1	0	2	2	1
·# of civil wars	1	0.2	0	0			1		0	0.3
·# of civil riots	0									

Characteristics	Yi-Miao	Yoruba	Yugoslav	Zambo	Zulu
Population Covered	13700	23400	833	207	10900
Countries represented, #	1	3	4	1	3
Average representation %	7	18	0.9	5	22
Vital Stats: Death rate	7	16	11	5	10
: Birth rate	22	46	11	37	37
: Female life exp., years	73	54	79	68	65
: Male life exp., years	69	51	73	65	60
: Infant mortality	52	128	12	83	81
: # of major diseases	2	2	5	4	1
Demography: Migration/100	0	0	0	-1	-1
: Population of Country	1210000	104000	64000	4140	35600
: Urbanization, %	29	29	81	59	54
: Population growth		3	0.2	3	2
: Females, % of pop	49	50	52	50	49
Male % ages: 0-9 years	52	50	51	54	50
: 10-19 years	51	50	51	47	50
: 20-29 years	51	50	51	48	52
: 30-39 years	52	51	51	49	52
: 40-49 years	53	51	49	48	51
: 50-59 years	53	50	39	46	50
: 60-69 years	49	50	33	45	47
: 70+ years	43	50	33	57	41
Education: Literacy, adult	73	51	99	57	70
Cities: earliest settled, year	-2210	1110	-461	1520	1650
: Largest settled, year	1100	1700	901	1520	1650
: Largest, % pop	0.6	0.1	7	18	5
Politics: # of parties	1		6	6	7
: Largest party %	100	98	41	55	63
: Top two parties, %	100	99	76	98	85
: Chambers in leg., #	1			2	2
: # of changes 60	3	4			
: Independence year	1910	1960	1960	1840	1940
Laws: Censorship (1=high)	1	0.5	0	0	0.5
: Metric system (1=yes)	0	0	0	0	0.3
: Visas needed (3=high)	3	3	2	2	0
: Full soc security (1=yes)	1	1	1	0	0
: Military service (1=yes)		1	2	0	
Crime: Murders/100k pop	2	94	2	.	109
: Thefts/100k pop	177	1260	4130		.
: Suicide/100k pop	1	.	21	0	0.3
: Prisoners/000 pop	1	0	0.7	2	0.1
: Death penalty (1=yes)	1	0	0	1	0.9
Unrest: Border disputes, #	12	4	1	1	0.1
: International, #	2	0	0	1	0.1
: # of civil wars	2	4	0	1	0.1
: # of civil riots	0	0	0	1	2

5

CULTURAL RESOURCES ACROSS ETHNIC CULTURES

A given ethnic culture will rarely exist in isolation and is likely to co-exist with others within a given social or cultural milieu. This chapter provides comparative statistics for a variety of cultural variables across ethnic groups. For a full discussion of the methodology used to generate these estimates, please refer to Chapter 1 which gives important caveats. This chapter first gives summary statistics of the variables reported: the number of countries/cultures for which each variable was available, the number of ethnic cultures covered, weighted averages (by population) and simple averages; these averages can be used as benchmarks. Then a lengthy comparative table is presented which provides raw statistics across the ethnic groups defined in Chapter 1.

Most of the variables are self explanatory, though some merit commentary. All of the statistics should be considered as estimates which have undergone rounding and certain adjustments. Culture is broadly defined as a group's ethnic, religious and linguistic heritage. The variable "Ethnic Groups: # present" measures the average number of ethnic groups co-living within the social systems of the ethnic group. The higher this number, the more the ethnic group is exposed to multiple ethnic groups. The variable "Max ethnic %" estimates the percent of the highest represented ethnic group in the social systems of the ethnic group. The higher this number, the more homogeneous (the less dominated by one) the ethnic group is in terms of its exposure to multiple ethnic groups; similarly for religions and colonial languages. For these latter two, estimates are given covering the percent of the groups residing in social systems having certain religious beliefs (practiced and official) and colonial languages (spoken as mother tongues, being official, or being used, in part, in commercial settings).

Summary Statistics:
Cultural Resources

Characteristics	Number of Countries Covered	Number of Ethnic Groups Covered	Weighted Average by Pop 1994	Simple Average	Simple Standard Deviation
Ethnic Groups: # present	234	426	8.04	7.36	3.33
: Max % present	233	426	74.31	55.12	24.71
Religions: # present	234	426	10.48	8.32	2.73
: Max % present	233	426	67.82	62.88	19.63
Beliefs: Anglican %	233	426	0.79	1.84	6.96
: Buddhist %	233	426	5.89	4.69	16.92
: Christian Total %	233	426	28.15	48.30	35.99
: Hindu %	233	426	13.83	2.63	12.78
: Jewish %	233	426	0.27	0.27	3.20
: Islam %	233	426	21.17	23.23	31.79
: Protestant Total %	233	426	6.05	14.19	20.06
: Roman Catholic %	234	426	15.39	24.10	29.09
: Traditional %	233	426	2.15	10.52	15.17
Official: Anglican	234	426	0.01	0.00	0.06
: Buddhism	234	426	0.01	0.01	0.11
: Christianism	234	426	0.00	0.00	0.02
: Greek Orthodox	234	426	0.00	0.00	0.04
: Hinduism	234	426	0.00	0.02	0.12
: Islam	234	426	0.13	0.10	0.29
: Lutheran-Evangelical	234	426	0.00	0.01	0.12
: Monotheism	234	426	0.03	0.01	0.10
: Orthodox	234	426	0.00	0.01	0.07
Languages: # present	234	426	7.55	5.98	3.26
: Max % present	233	426	64.51	55.95	27.54
: Number official	192	410	1.33	1.39	1.42
: None official (1=yes)	222	420	0.04	0.00	0.04
Mother Tongue: Arabic %	231	425	5.54	4.71	16.59
: Chinese (all) %	231	425	20.95	3.21	15.82
: English %	232	425	5.16	2.33	11.11
: French %	231	425	0.99	0.97	6.73
: German %	231	425	1.71	1.40	10.86
: Spanish %	233	426	5.33	3.08	14.65
Official: Arabic %	234	426	7.00	8.52	27.04
: Chinese %	234	426	22.55	3.57	18.06
: English %	234	426	28.34	28.27	43.41
: French %	234	426	4.51	23.98	41.27
: German %	234	426	1.88	2.40	15.00
: Spanish %	234	426	5.96	3.73	18.24
Commercial: Arabic %	228	423	0.07	0.11	0.30
: Chinese %	228	423	0.23	0.05	0.21
: English %	228	423	0.63	0.58	0.47
: French %	228	423	0.15	0.34	0.45
: German %	228	423	0.04	0.06	0.23
: Italian %	228	423	0.02	0.03	0.17
: Portuguese %	228	423	0.03	0.05	0.21
: Russian %	228	423	0.08	0.08	0.26
: Spanish %	228	423	0.11	0.05	0.21

Characteristics	Abadkis	Abkhaz	Acholi	Afar	Afro-European	Akan	Albanian	Ambo	Amerind	Amerind-Mestizo
Ethnic Groups: # present	7	10	11	8	4	6	4	12	5	2
:Max % present	58	70	18	40	76	52	85	37	57	85
Religions: # present	10	5	8	15	15	8	8	8	10	9
:Max % present	86	75	50	58	87	28	65	69	85	93
Beliefs: Anglican %	0	0	26	0	0	0	0	0	0	0
:Buddhist %	8	0	0	0	0	0	0	0	0	0
:Christian Total %	0.2	83	76	42	58	62	47	90	94	95
:Hindu %	86	0	0	0	0	0	0	0	0.1	0
:Jewish %	0	0	0	0	0	0	0	0	0.2	0.8
:Islam %	80	1	7	46	0	16	48	20	0.2	0
:Protestant Total %	3	1	26	0.1	53	28	0.4	69	9	2
:Roman Catholic %	0	0	50	0.4	5	21	0	100	85	93
:Traditional %	0.6	0	13	8	0	0	1	0	0.1	0.1
Official: Anglican	0	0	0	0	0	0	0	0	0	0
:Buddhism	0	0	0	0	0	0	0	0	0	0
:Christianism	0	0	0	0	0	0	0	0	0	0
:Greek Orthodox	0	0	0	0	0	0	0	0	0	0
:Hinduism	0	0	0	0	0	0	0	0	0	0
:Islam	1	0	0	0	0	0	0	0	0	0
:Luthren Evangelical	0	0	0	0	0	0	0	0	0	0
:Monotheism	0	0	0	0	0	0	0	0	0	0
:Orthodox	0	0	0	0	0	0	0	0	0	0
Languages: # present	10	4	10	9	3	9	2	9	8	3
:Max % present	51	69	16	35	70	44	95	37	82	96
Number official	1	1	1	2	1	1	1	1	1	1
None official (1=yes)	0	0	0	0	0	0	0	0	0	0
Mother Tongue: Arabic %	0	0	0	0	0	0	0	0	0	0
:Chinese (all) %	0	0	0	0	0	0	0	0	0	0
:English %	0	0	0	0	27	0	0	0	0.1	0
:French %	0	0	0	0.6	0	0	0	0	0	0
:German %	0	0	0	0	0	0	0	0	0	0
:Spanish %	0	0	0	0	0	0	0	0	76	96
Official: Arabic %	0	0	0	15	0	0	0	0	0	0
:Chinese %	0	0	0	0	0	0	0	0	0	0
:English %	0	0	100	0	100	100	0	96	0.7	0
:French %	0	0	0	15	0	0	0	0	0	0
:German %	0	0	0	0	0	0	0	0	0	0
:Spanish %	0	0	0	0	0	0	0	0	92	100
Commercial: Arabic %	0	0	0	0	0	0	0	0	0	0
:Chinese %	0	0	0	0	0	0	0	0	0	0
:English %	0	0	1	0	0	0	0	0	0	1
:French %	0	0	0	0	0	0	0	0	0	1
:German %	0	0	0	0	0	0	0	0	0	0
:Italian %	0	0	0	0.7	0	0	0.9	0	0	0
:Portuguese %	0	0	0	0	0	0	0	0	0.8	0
:Russian %	1	1	0	0	0	0	0	0	0	0
:Spanish %	0	0	0	0	0	0	0	0	1	1

Characteristics	Amhara	Ana-Ife	Andorran	Angolares	Anouis	Antandroy	Arab, other	Arab Berber	Arab Emirian	Arab Lebanese
Ethnic Groups: # present	9	6	6	7	7	11	4	1	9	3
::Max % present	38	45	46	87	20	27	83	89	56	83
Religions: # present	9	5	4	8	9	1	7	5	6	12
::Max % present	48	50	99	89	37	47	83	97	79	30
Beliefs: Anglican %	0	0	0	0	0	0	0	0	0	0
::Buddhist %	0	0	0	0	0	0	0	0	0	0
::Christian Total %	53	35	100	95	20	50	3	0	4	15
::Hindu %	0	0	0	0	0	0	0	0	0	0
::Jewish %	0	0	0.4	0.1	0	0	0.8	0	0	0
::Islam %	32	12	0	0.6	20	3	95	97	95	50
::Protestant Total %	0	9	0.5	0	5	23	0.1	0	0	0
::Roman Catholic %	0	26	99	89	15	26	0	0	0	4
::Traditional %	11	50	0	0.5	37	47	0	0	0	0
Official: Anglican	0	0	0	0	0	0	0	0	0	0
::Buddhism	0	0	0	0	0	0	0	0	0	0
::Christianism	0	0	0	0	0	0	0	0	0	0
::Greek Orthodox	0	0	0	0	0	0	0	0	0	0
::Hinduism	0	0	0	0	0	0	0	0	0	0
::Islam	0	0	0	0	0	0	1	1	1	1
::Luthren Evangelical	0	0	0	0	0	0	0	0	0	0
::Monotheism	0	0	0	0	0	0	0	0	0	0
::Orthodox	0	0	0	0	0	0	0	0	0	0
Languages: # present	11	1	3	3	5	9	4	2	9	2
::Max % present	31	1	56	56	41	99	82	95	48	93
::Number official	0	0	1	1	1	2	1	1	1	1
::None official (1=yes)	0	0	0	0	0	0	1	0	0	0
Mother Tongue: Arabic %	0	0	0	0	0	0	79	95	48	93
::Chinese (all) %	0	0	0	0	0	0	0.1	0	0	0
::English %	0	0	0	0	0	0	0.1	0	0	0
::French %	0	0	0	0	0	0	0	0	0	0
::German %	0	0	0	0	0	0	0	0	0	0
::Spanish %	0	0	8	0	0	0	0	0	0	0
Official: Arabic %	0	0	0	0	0	0	96	100	100	100
::Chinese %	0	0	0	0	0	0	0	0	0	0
::English %	0	0	0	0	0	0	0	0	0	0
::French %	0	100	0	0	100	100	0.8	0	0	0
::German %	0	0	0	0	0	0	0	0	0	0
::Spanish %	0	0	56	0	0	0	0	0	0	0
Commercial: Arabic %	0	0	0	0	0	0	0	0	0	0
::Chinese %	0	0	0	0	0	0	0	0	0	0
::English %	1	1	1	0.7	1	1	0.7	1	1	1
::French %	0	0	0	0.7	0	0	0.4	0	0	1
::German %	1	0	0	0	0	0	0.6	1	1	1
::Italian %	0	0	0	0	0	0	0	0	0	0
::Portuguese %	0	0	0	100	0	0	0	0	0	0
::Russian %	0	0	0	0	0	0	0	0	0	0
::Spanish %	0	0	1	0.3	0	0	0.2	0	0	0

Characteristics	Arab Omani	Arab Palestin.	Arab Quatar	Arab Saudi	Arab Sudanic	Arab Total	Arauca-nian	Armenian	Assamese	Assyrian
Ethnic Groups: # present	4	2	5	3	10	4	3	5	3	5
:Max % present	74	87	25	82	47	79	80	87	63	77
Religions: # present	6	5	6	6	8	7	9	4	5	12
:Max % present	72	71	92	99	70	83	81	87	70	60
Beliefs: Anglican %	0	0	0	0	2	0.2	0	0	0	0
:Buddhist %	0	0	0	0.8	0	0	0	0	0	0
:Christian Total %	0	9	6	0	10	4	87	79	0	4
:Hindu %	13	0	1	0	0	0.1	0.1	0.1	70	0
:Jewish %	0	10	0	0	0	0.6	0	0.1	0	0
:Islam %	87	74	92	99	70	92	0.1	19	25	94
:Protestant Total %	0	0	0	0	3	0.4	6	0.2	0	0
:Roman Catholic %	0	0.8	0	0	6	2	81	0.3	0	3
:Traditional %	0	0	0	0	18	2	0.7	0	5	0
Official: Anglican	0	0	0	0	0	0	0	0	0	0
:Buddhism	0	0	0	0	0	0	0	0	0	0
:Christianism	0	0	0	0	0	0	0	0	0	0
:Greek Orthodox	0	0	0	0	0	0	0	0	0	0
:Hinduism	0	0	0	0	0	0	0	0	0	0
:Islam	1	1	1	1	0.9	0.9	0	0	0	1
:Luthren Evangelical	0	0	0	0	0	0	0	0	0	0
:Monotheism	0	0	0	0	0	0	0	0	0	0
:Orthodox	0	0	0	0	0	0	0	0.1	0	0
Languages: # present	6	2	3	1	7	4	2	4	5	5
:Max % present	68	89	56	99	49	81	92	84	30	78
:Number official	1	1	1	1	1	1	1	1	1	1
:None official (1=yes)	0	0	0	0	0	0	0	0	0	0
Mother Tongue: Arabic %	68	89	56	99	49	78	0	3	0	78
:Chinese (all) %	0	0	0	0	0	0	0	0	0	0
:English %	0	0	0	0	0	0.7	0	0.2	0	0
:French %	0	0	0	0	0	0.1	0	0.1	0	0
:German %	0	0	0	0	0	0	0	0	0	0
:Spanish %	0	0	0	0	0	0	92	0	0	0
Official: Arabic %	100	100	100	100	100	97	0	0	0	100
:Chinese %	0	0	0	0	0	0	0	0	0	0
:English %	0	0	0	0	0	1	0	0	0	0
:French %	0	0	0	0	0	2	0	0	0	0
:German %	0	0	0	0	0	0	0	0	0	0
:Spanish %	0	0	0	0	0	0	100	0	0	0
Commercial: Arabic %	1	1	1	1	1	0.8	0	3	0	1
:Chinese %	0	0	0	0	0	0	0	0	0	0
:English %	0	0.8	0	0	0	0.6	0	0.4	1	0
:French %	0	0.2	0	0	0	0.5	0	0.4	0	0
:German %	0	0	0	0	0	0	0	0.1	0	0
:Italian %	0	0	0	0	0	0	0	0.1	0	0
:Portuguese %	0	0	0	0	0	0	0	0	0	0
:Russian %	0	0	0	0	0	0	0	0.9	0	0
:Spanish %	0	0	0	0	0	0.1	1	0	0	0

Characteristics	Austrian	Avar	Aymara	Azande	Azerbai-jani	Bagirmi Sara	Bahraini	Bai	Bakhtiari	Bakongo
Ethnic Groups: # present	4	6	4	12	9	11	5	16	11	12
: Max % present	94	81	39	25	59	31	65	93	46	37
Religions: # present	8	5	8	9	9	8	7	8	12	8
: Max % present	83	60	92	53	80	43	60	59	91	69
Beliefs: Anglican %	0	0	0	0.5	0	0	0	0	0	0
: Buddhist %	0	0	0	0	0	0	0	0.2	0	0
: Christian Total %	88	11	95	74	6	33	7	6	0.7	90
: Hindu %	0	0	0	0	0	0	0	0	0	0
: Jewish %	0.2	0	0	0	0	0	2	0	0	0
: Islam %	2	80	0	17	90	43	90	2	98	0
: Protestant Total %	6	0	3	24	0	9	0	0	0	20
: Roman Catholic %	83	0	92	38	0	8	0	0	0	69
: Traditional %	0	0	0.8	7	0	24	0	0.1	0	10
Official: Anglican	0	0	0	0	0	0	0	0	0	0
: Buddhism	0	0	0	0	0	0	0	0	0	0
: Christianism	0	0	0	0	0	0	0	0	0	0
: Greek Orthodox	0	0	0	0	0	0	0	0	0	0
: Hinduism	0	0	0	0	0	0	0	0	0	0
: Islam	0	0	0	0.2	0	0	1	0	1	0
: Luthren Evangelical	1	0	0	0	0	0	0	0	0	0
: Monotheism	0	0	0	0	0	0	0	0	0	0
: Orthodox	0	0	0	0	0.6	0	0	0	0	0
Languages: # present	1	4	3	5	8	7	3	8	1	9
: Max % present	99	78	52	20	60	30	80	67	100	37
: Number official	1	1	3	1	1	1	1	1	1	1
: None official (1=yes)	0	0	0	0	0	0	0	0	0	0
Mother Tongue: Arabic %	0	0	0	1	0	0	80	0	0	0
: Chinese (all) %	0	0	0	0	0	0	0	93	0	0
: English %	0	0	0	0	0	0	0	0	0	0
: French %	0	0	0	0	0	30	0	0	0	37
: German %	99	0	0	0	0	0	0	0	0	0
: Spanish %	0	0	51	0	0	0	0	0	0	0
Official: Arabic %	0	0	0	0	0	0	100	0	0	0
: Chinese %	0	0	0	0	0	0	0	100	0	0
: English %	0	0	0	21	0	0	0	0	0	0
: French %	0	0	0	79	0	100	0	0	0	0
: German %	99	0	0	0	0	0	0	0	0	0
: Spanish %	0	0	100	0	0	0	0	0	0	0
Commercial: Arabic %	0	0	0	0.2	0	0	1	0	0	0
: Chinese %	0	0	0	0	0	0	0	1	0	0
: English %	0	0	0	0.2	0	0	0	0	0	0
: French %	0	0	0	0.8	0	1	0	0	0	1
: German %	100	0	0	0	0	0	0	0	0	0
: Italian %	0	0	0	0	0	0	0	0	0	0
: Portuguese %	0	0	0	0	0	0	0	0	0	0
: Russian %	0	1	0	0	0.6	0	0	0	1	0
: Spanish %	0	0	1	0	0.4	0	0	0	0	0

Characteristics	Balante	Baluchi	Bambara	Bamileke-Bamum	Banda	Bangi-Ngale	Bantu	Baoule	Bari	Bariba
Ethnic Groups: # present	5	7	11	11	10	13	4	7	10	5
:Max % present	27	59	32	20	25	18	72	20	49	66
Religions: # present	7	12	6	8	7	9	10	9	8	8
:Max % present	58	81	89	34	43	48	42	37	73	63
Beliefs: Anglican %	0	0	0	0	0	0	0	0	0	0
:Buddhist %	0	0	0	0	0	0	0	0	0	0
:Christian Total %	6	1	1	52	77	94	41	20	8	23
:Hindu %	0	1	0	0	0	0	0	0	0	0
:Jewish %	0	0	0	0	0	0	0	0	0	0
:Islam %	34	97	89	22	6	0	3	20	73	13
:Protestant Total %	0	0	0	18	37	29	17	5	2	3
:Roman Catholic %	0	0	9	34	35	48	11	15	6	20
:Traditional %	58	0	0	25	14	3	39	37	17	63
Official: Anglican	0	0	0	0	0	0	0	0	0	0
:Buddhism	0	0	0	0	0	0	0	0	0	0
:Christianism	0	0	0	0	0	0	0	0	0	0
:Greek Orthodox	0	0	0	0	0	0	0	0	0	0
:Hinduism	0	0	0	0	0	0	0	0	0	0
:Islam	0	1	0	0	0	0	0	0	1	0
:Luthren Evangelical	0	0	0	0	0	0	0	0	0	0
:Monotheism	0	0	0	0	0	0	0	0	0	0
:Orthodox	0	0	0	0	0	0	0	0	0	0
Languages: # present	6	9	9	6	4	4	6	5	7	10
:Max % present	30	49	38	9	35	7	56	41	51	26
:Number official	1	1	1	2	1	1	1	1	1	1
:None official (1=yes)	0	0.4	0	0	0	0	0	0	0	0
Mother Tongue: Arabic %	0	0	0	0	0	0	0	0	51	0
:Chinese (all) %	0	0	0	0	0	0	0	0	0	0
:English %	0	0	0	0	0	0	7	0	0	0
:French %	0	0	0	0	0	0	0	0	0	0
:German %	0	0	0	0	0	0	0	0	0	0
:Spanish %	0	0	0	0	0	0	0	0	0	0
Official: Arabic %	0	0.3	0	0	0	0	0	0	100	0
:Chinese %	0	0	0	0	0	0	0	0	0	0
:English %	0	0	0	100	0	0	3	0	0	0
:French %	0	0	100	100	100	100	97	100	0	100
:German %	0	0	0	0	0	0	0	0	0	0
:Spanish %	0	0	0	0	0	0	0	0	0	0
Commercial: Arabic %	0	0	0	0	0	0	0	0	1	0
:Chinese %	0	0	0	0	0	0	0	0	0	0
:English %	0	0	0	0	0	0	0	0	0	0
:French %	0	0	0	0	0	0	0	0	0	0
:German %	0	0	0	0	0	0	0	0	0	0
:Italian %	0	0	0	0	0	0	0	0	0	0
:Portuguese %	0	0	0	0	0	0	0	0	0	0
:Russian %	1	0.3	1	1	1	1	1	1	1	1
:Spanish %	0	0	0	0	0	0	0	0	0	0

Characteristics	Barotze	Baskhir	Basque	Bassa	Batswana	Bayad	Beja	Belgian	Belorus-sian	Bemba
Ethnic Groups: # present	7	8	4	10	5	6	10	8	6	7
Max % present	35	82	73	19	76	79	49	55	77	35
Religions: # present	9	6	7	5	7	6	8	8	3	9
Max % present	34	75	95	67	50	49	73	79	62	34
Beliefs: Anglican %	0	0	0	0	0	0	2	0	0	0
Buddhist %	0	0	0	0	0	2	0	0	0	0
Christian Total %	69	84	96	67	48	0	8	79	70	69
Hindu %	0	0	0.3	0	0	0	0	0.3	0	0
Jewish %	0.3	1	0	0	0	0	0	0	0.1	0.3
Islam %	34	5	0.4	14	0	1	73	0	0.2	34
Protestant Total %	26	5	0	0	27	0	2	0	1	26
Roman Catholic %	27	4	95	19	9	0	6	79	8	27
Traditional %	0	0	0	0	50	0	17	0	0	0
Official: Anglican	0	0	0	0	0	0	0	0	0	0
Buddhism	0	0	0	0	0	0	0	0	0	0
Christianism	0	0	0	0	0	0	0	0	0	0
Greek Orthodox	0	0	0	0	0	0	0	0	0	0
Hinduism	0	0	0	0	0	0	0	0	0	0
Islam	0	0	0	0	0	0	1	0	0	0
Luthren Evangelical	0	0	0	0	0	0	0	0	0	0
Monotheism	0	0	0	0	0	0	0	0	0	0
Orthodox	0	0	0	0	0	0	0	0	0	0
Languages: # present	8	4	4	8	3	4	7	4	4	8
Max % present	25	87	70	23	75	90	51	60	71	25
Number official	3	1	4	1	1	1	1	3	1	3
None official (1=yes)	0	0	0	0	0	0	0	0	0	0
Mother Tongue: Arabic %	0	0	0	0	0	0	51	0	0	0
Chinese (all) %	0	0	0	0	0	0	0	0	0	0
English %	1	0	0	0	0	0	0	0	0	1
French %	0	0	0.3	0	0	0	0	0	0	0
German %	0	0	0	0	0	0	0	0.1	0	0
Spanish %	0	0	70	0	0	0	0	0.6	0	0
Official: Arabic %	0	0	0	0	0	0	100	0	0	0
Chinese %	0	0	0	0	0	0	0	0	0	0
English %	100	0	0	100	100	0	0	0	0	100
French %	0	0	0.3	0	0	0	0	100	0	0
German %	0	0	0	0	0	0	0	100	0	0
Spanish %	0	0	100	0	0	0	0	0	0	0
Commercial: Arabic %	0	0	0	0	0	0	1	0	0	0
Chinese %	0	0	0	0	0	0	0	0	0	0
English %	1	0	0	1	1	0	1	1	0.1	1
French %	0	0	0	0	0	0	0	1	0	0
German %	0	0	0	0	0	0	0	1	0	0
Italian %	0	0	0	0	0	0	0	0	0	0
Portuguese %	0	0	0	0	0	0	0	0	0	0
Russian %	0	1	0	0	0	1	0	0	1	0
Spanish %	0	0	1	0	0	0	0	0	0	0

Characteristics	Bengali	Berber	Bete	Betsileo	Betsimi-Saraka	Bhutia	Bihari	Black	Black Amerind	Boa
Ethnic Groups: # present	3	2	7	11	11	3	6	12	6	13
:Max % present	98	75	20	27	27	63	70	58	58	18
Religions: # present	8	7	9	10	10	5	9	20	9	9
:Max % present	87	99	37	47	47	70	86	46	93	48
Beliefs: Anglican %	0	0	0	0	0	0	0	0.1	0	0
:Buddhist %	0	0	0	0	0	70	6	0	0	0
:Christian Total %	12	0.8	20	50	50	0	0.1	72	93	94
:Hindu %	0	0	0	0	0	25	65	0.4	0	0
:Jewish %	0	0	0	0	0	0	0	1	0	0
:Islam %	87	99	20	3	3	5	27	22	0	1
:Protestant Total %	0.1	0	5	23	23	0	0	43	93	29
:Roman Catholic %	0	0.1	15	26	26	0	0.5	0	0.8	48
:Traditional %	0.1	0	37	47	47	0	0	0	0	3
Official: Anglican	0	0	0	0	0	0	0	0	0	0
:Buddhism	0	0	0	0	0	1	0	0	0	0
:Christianism	0	0	1	0	0	0	0	0	0	0
:Greek Orthodox	0	0	0	0	0	0	0	0	0	0
:Hinduism	0	0	0	0	0	0	0	0	0	0
:Islam	1	1	0	0	0	0	0	0	0	0
:Luthren Evangelical	0	0	0	0	0	0	0	0	0	0
:Monotheism	0	0	0	0	0	0	0	0	0	0
:Orthodox	0	0	0	0	0	0	0	0	0	0
Languages: # present	2	4	5	3	3	3	3	8	1	4
:Max % present	98	72	41	99	99	30	64	88	99	7
:Number official	1	2	1	2	2	1	1	2	1	1
:None official (1=yes)	0	0	0	0	0	0	0	0	0	0
Mother Tongue: Arabic %	0	72	0	0	0	0	0	0.4	0	0
:Chinese (all) %	0	0	0	0	0	0	0	0.2	0	0
:English %	0	0	0	0	0	0	0	41	0	0
:French %	0	0	0	0	0	0	0	0.4	0	0
:German %	0	0	0	0	0	0	0	0.3	0	0
:Spanish %	0	0	0	0	0	0	0	13	99	0
Official: Arabic %	0	100	0	0	0	0	0	0	0	0
:Chinese %	0	0	0	0	0	0	0	0	0	0
:English %	1	0	0	0	0	0	0	57	0	0
:French %	0	0	100	100	100	0	0	10	0	100
:German %	0	0	0	0	0	0	0	0	0	0
:Spanish %	0	0	0	0	0	0	0	11	100	0
Commercial: Arabic %	0	0.6	0	0	0	0	0	0	0	0
:Chinese %	0	0	0	0	0	0	0	0	0	0
:English %	1	1	0	0	0	0	1	0.9	0	0
:French %	0	0	1	1	1	0	0	0.1	0	1
:German %	0	0	0	0	0	0	0	0.2	0	0
:Italian %	0	0	0	0	0	0	0	0	0	0
:Portuguese %	0	0	0	0	0	0	0	0	0	0
:Russian %	0	0	0	0	0	0	0	0	0	0
:Spanish %	0	0.6	0	0	0	0	0	0.6	1	0

Characteristics	Bobo	Bounty Mutineers	Brazilian	Breton	Bubi	Bulgarian	Bullom	Bura	Burman	Bush Negro
Ethnic Groups: # present	10	2	8	7	5	6	9	11	6	8
:Max % present	44	89	78	90	78	84	34	21	69	33
Religions: # present		5	10	10	8	7	7	9	12	11
:Max % present	57	56	88	77	85	77	52	45	89	34
Beliefs: Anglican %	0	28	0	0	0	0	1	0	0	0
:Buddhist %	0	0	0	0	0	0	0	0	89	
:Christian Total %	9	79	90	82	85	79	8	49	5	47
:Hindu %	0	0	0	0	0	0	0	0	0	23
:Jewish %	0	0	0.5	1	0.5	0.1	0	0	0	0.1
:Islam %	55	0	0	3	0	12	39	45	4	17
:Protestant Total %	2	71	2	2	5	0.7	6	26	0	16
:Roman Catholic %	7	8	88	77	85	0.5	2	12	0	30
:Traditional %	35	0	0.3	0	5	0	52	6	1	5
Official: Anglican	0	0	0	0	0	0	0	0	0	0
:Buddhism	0	0	0	0	0	0	0	0	0	0
:Christianism	0	0	0	0	0	0	0	0	0	0
:Greek Orthodox	0	0	0	0	0	0	0	0	0	0
:Hinduism	0	0	0	0	0	0	0	0	0	0
:Islam	0	0	0	0	0	0	0	0	0	0
:Luthren Evangelical	0	0	0	0	0	0	0	0	0	0
:Monotheism	0	0	0	0	0	0	0	0	0	0
:Orthodox	0	0	0	0	0	1	0	0	0	0
Languages: # present	8	3	1	8	4	3	12	12	8	5
:Max % present	45	50	96	83	75	84	31	21	69	41
:Number official	1		1	1	1	1	1	1	1	1
:None official (1=yes)	0	0	0	0	0	0	0	0	0	0
Mother Tongue: Arabic %	0	0	0	0	0	0	0	0	0	0
:Chinese (all) %	0	0	0	0	0	0	0	0	0	0
:English %	0	50	0	3	0	0	0	0	0	0
:French %	0.3	0	0	83	0	0	0	0	0	13
:German %	0	0	0	0	0	0	0	0	0	0
:Spanish %	0	0	0	0	0	0	0	0	0	0
Official: Arabic %	0	0	0	0	0	0	0	0	0	0
:Chinese %	0	0	0	0	0	0	0	0	0	0
:English %	0	100	0	0	0	0	100	100	0	0
:French %	100	0	0	100	0	0	0	0	0	0
:German %	0	0	0	0	0	0	0	0	0	0
:Spanish %	0	0	0	0	100	0	0	0	0	0
Commercial: Arabic %	0	0	0	0	0	0	0	0	0	0
:Chinese %	0	0	0	0	0	0	0	0	0	0
:English %	0	1	36	1	1	0	1	1	1	0.9
:French %	1	0	0	0	1	0	0	0	0	0.1
:German %	0	0	0.6	0	0	0	0	0	0	0
:Italian %	0	0	0	0	0	0	0	0	0	0
:Portuguese %	0	0	0	0	0	0	0	0	0	0
:Russian %	0	0	0	0	0	1	0	0	0	0
:Spanish %	0	0	1	0	1	0	0	0	0	0

Characteristics	Bushman	Capver-dien	Caroli-nians	Catalan	Chahar Aimak	Chamba	Chamorro	Chiga	Chin	Chinese
Ethnic Groups: # present	5	8	6	4	7	11	6	11	6	5
Max % present	76	99	45	73	52	20	43	18	69	72
Religions: # present	7	9	5	5	7	8	4	8	12	12
Max % present	50	92	49	95	74	34	72	50	89	61
Beliefs: Anglican %	0	0	0	0	0	0	0	26	0	0.4
Buddhist %	0	0	0	0	0	0	0	0	89	41
Christian Total %	48	94	95	96	0	52	96	76	5	15
Hindu %	0	0	0	0	0	0	0	0	0	0.2
Jewish %	0	0.1	0	0.3	0	0	0	0	0	2
Islam %	0	0.6	0	0.4	89	22	0	7	4	15
Protestant Total %	27	0	49	0	0	18	25	26	0	4
Roman Catholic %	59	92	46	95	0	34	71	50	0	1
Traditional %	50	0	4	0	0	25	0	13	0	0
Official: Anglican	0	0	0	0	0	0	0	0	0	0
Buddhism	0	0	0	0	0	0	0	0	0	0.3
Christianism	0	0	0	0	0	0	0	0	0	0
Greek Orthodox	0	0	0	0	0	0	0	0	0	0
Hinduism	0	0	0	0	0	0	0	0	0	0.2
Islam	0	0	0	0	1	0	0	0	0	0
Luthren Evangelical	0	0	0	0	0	0	0	0	0	0
Monotheism	0	0	0	0	0	0	0	0	0	0
Orthodox	0	0	0	0	0	0	0	0	0	0
Languages: # present	3	1	3	4	6	6	4	10	8	7
Max % present	75	100	43	70	51	9	48	16	69	63
Number official	1	1	.	4	2	2	.	1	1	2
None official (1=yes)	0	0	0	0	0	0	0	0	0	0
Mother Tongue: Arabic %	0	0	0	0	0	0	0	0	0	0
Chinese (all) %	0	0	0	0	0	0	0	0	0	34
English %	0	0	0	0	0	0	21	0	0	8
French %	0	0	0	0	0	0	0	0	0	0.3
German %	0	0	0	0	0	0	0	0	0	0.1
Spanish %	0	0	0	70	0	0	0	0	0	0.8
Official: Arabic %	0	0	0	0	0	0	0	0	0	0
Chinese %	0	0	0	0	0	0	0	0	0	30
English %	100	0	100	0	0	100	100	100	0	43
French %	0	0	0	0	0	0	0	0	0	1
German %	0	0	0	0	0	0	0	0	0	0
Spanish %	0	0	0	100	0	0	0	0	0	0.4
Commercial: Arabic %	0	0	0	0	0	0	0	0	0	0
Chinese %	0	0	0	0	0	0	0	0	0	0.6
English %	1	1	1	1	1	1	1	1	1	0.1
French %	0	0	0	0	0	0	0	0	0	0
German %	0	0	0	0	0	0	0	0	0	0
Italian %	0	0	0	0	0	0	0	0	0	0
Portuguese %	0	1	0	0	0	0	0	0	0	0
Russian %	0	0	0	0	0	0	0	0	0	0
Spanish %	0	0	0	1	0	0	0	0	0	0.1

Characteristics	Chinese Mainland	Chokwe	Chuang	Chuvash	Circassian	Coloured	Comorian	Creole	Croatian	Czech
Ethnic Groups: # present	3	13	16	8	7	9	4	5	6	7
:Max % present	84	25	93	82	87	24	93	57	72	93
Religions: # present	10	9	8	6	9	17	4	10	6	14
:Max % present	49	56	59	75	98	34	96	56	71	40
Beliefs: Anglican %	0	0	0	0	0	4	0	1	0	0.1
:Buddhist %	43	0	6	0	0	0	0	0.2	0	0.0
:Christian Total %	7	93	0.2	84	0.8	68	4	49	83	49
:Hindu %	0	0	0	0	0	0.6	0	35	0	0.1
:Jewish %	0.5	0	0	1	0	0	0	0.1	0	0.0
:Islam %	0	0.9	2	5	98	1	93	10	8	8
:Protestant Total %	0.1	26	0	5	0	13	1	8	2	39
:Roman Catholic %	0	56	0.1	4	0	8	2	40	67	0
:Traditional %	0.1	6	0	0	0	20	3	1	0	0
Official: Anglican	0	0	0	0	0	0	0	0	0	0
:Buddhism	0	0	0	0	0	0	0	0	0	0
:Christianism	0	0	0	0	0	0	0	0	0	0
:Greek Orthodox	0	0	0	0	0.1	0	0	0	0	0
:Hinduism	0	0	0	0	0	0	0	0	0	0
:Islam	0	0	0	0	0	0	0.9	0	0	0
:Luthren Evangelical	0	0	0	0	0	0	0	0	0	0
:Monotheism	0	0	0	0	0	0	0	0	0	0
:Orthodox	0	0	0	0	0	0	0	0	0	0
Languages: # present	3	8	8	4	2	10	0.9	6	1	6
:Max % present	69	18	67	87	91	25	0	59	96	66
:Number official	1	1	1	1	1	13	1	1	1	1
:None official (1=yes)	0	0	0	0	0	0	0	0	0	0
Mother Tongue: Arabic %	0	0	0	0	1	0	100	0	0	0
:Chinese (all) %	31	0	93	0	0	0	2	0	0	0
:English %	0	0	0	0	0	9	0	1	0	0
:French %	0	63	0	0	0	0	0	3	0	0
:German %	0	0	0	0	0	0	0	2	0	0.5
:Spanish %	0	0	0	0	0	0	0	0	0	0
Official: Arabic %	0	0	0	0	1	0	94	0	0	0
:Chinese %	100	0	100	0	1	0	0	72	0	0
:English %	0	0	0	0	0	9	0	65	0	2
:French %	0	0	0	0	0	0	100	0	0	2
:Spanish %	0	0	0	0	0	100	0	0	0	0
Commercial: Arabic %	0	0	0	0	0.1	0	0.9	0	0	0
:Chinese %	0	0	0	0	0	0	0	0	0	0
:English %	1	0.6	1	1	0	1	0	1	1	1
:French %	0	0	0	0	0.9	0	1	0.7	0	1
:German %	0	0	0	0	0	0	0	0	0	0
:Italian %	0	0.4	0	0	0	0	0	0	0	0
:Portuguese %	0	0	0	0	0	0	0	0	0	0
:Russian %	0	0	0	0	0	0	0	0	1	0
:Spanish %	0	0	0	0	0	0	0	0.1	0	0

Characteristics	Dagestani	Dai	Damara	Dan	Danish	Dinka	Dogon	Dong	Dravidian	Duala
Ethnic Groups: # present	8	16	6	8	7	10	11	16	3	5
.Max % present	81	93	50	20	97	49	32	93	72	78
Religions: # present	6	8	8	8	10	8	6	8	14	8
.Max % present	73	59	51	43	88	73	89	59	80	85
Beliefs: Anglican %	0	0	5	0	0	0	0	0	0	0
.Buddhist %	74	6	82	29	89	8	1	6	0.7	85
.Christian Total %	0.9	0.2	0.1		0.1	0	0	0.2	0.2	0.5
.Hindu %	15	0	0	19	88	73	89	2	80	85
.Jewish %	4	2	62	4	0.5	2	9	0.1	11	
.Islam %	3	0.1	20	12		6			0	
.Protestant Total %			3	34		17			1	
.Roman Catholic %										
.Traditional %										
Official: Anglican										
.Buddhism										
.Christianism						1				
.Greek Orthodox										
.Hinduism					1					
.Islam	4	8	9	6	2	7	9	8	14	4
.Luthren Evangelical	86	67	47	38	97	51	38	67	28	75
.Monotheism	1	1	1	1		0	1	2	2	1
.Orthodox		0	0			0	0	0	0	
Languages: # present		93	3	19		51	1	93		
.Max % present				81						
.Number official (1=yes)										
.None official (1=yes)					1	1	1			
Mother Tongue: Arabic %										
.Chinese (all) %		100	100			100	100	100	100	100
.English %	1				1					
.French %										
.German %										
.Spanish %										
Official: Arabic %										
.Chinese %		1	1			1	1	1	1	1
.English %	0	0	0	0.2		0	0	0	0	1
.French %				0.8		1				
.German %										
.Spanish %										
Commercial: Arabic %										
.Chinese %										
.English %										
.French %										
.German %										
.Italian %										
.Portuguese %										
.Russian %	1									
.Spanish %	0									1

Characteristics	Duala-Landa-B.	Dujia	Dutch	Dyola	Edo	Egyptian	English	Estonian	Euro-nesian	European
Ethnic Groups: # present	11	16	23	10	11	1	11	5	3	6
Max % present	20	93	39	34	21	99	81	62	88	78
Religions: # present	8	8	13	6	9	7	15	3	6	10
Max % present	34	59	53	90	45	88	57	100	47	80
Beliefs: Anglican %	0	0	4	0	0	0	57	0	0	2
Buddhist %	0	6	0	0	0	0	0.2	0	0	0
Christian Total %	52	0.2	85	2	49	11	87	100	93	90
Hindu %	0	0	0.7	0	0	0	0.7	0.2	0	0.1
Jewish %	0	0	0.1	0	0	0	0.5	0	0	0.4
Islam %	22	2	1	90	45	88	1	0	0	0.4
Protestant Total %	18	0	32	0	26	0	72	100	71	11
Roman Catholic %	34	0	52	0	12	0	13	0	22	79
Traditional %	25	0.1	0.1	7	6	0	0	0	0	0.4
Official: Anglican	0	0	0	0	0	0	1	0	0	0
Buddhism	0	0	0	0	0	0	0	0	0	0
Christianism	0	0	0	0	0	0	0	0	0	0
Greek Orthodox	0	0	0	0	0	0	0	0	0	0
Hinduism	0	0	0	0	0	0	0	0	0	0
Islam	0	0	0	0	0	1	0	0	0	0
Luthren Evangelical	0	0	0	0	0	0	0	0	0	0
Monotheism	0	0	0	0	0	0	0	0	0	0
Orthodox	0	0	0	0	0	0	0	0	0	0
Languages: # present	6	8	23	8	12	3	2	3	1	7
Max % present	9	67	60	38	21	99	98	65	99	90
Number official	2	1	2	1	1	1	1	1	2	1
None official (1=yes)	0	0	0	0	0	0	0	0	0	0
Mother Tongue: Arabic %	0	0	0.1	0	0	99	0	0	0	0.2
Chinese (all) %	0	93	0	0	0	0	0	0	0	0.1
English %	0	0	0.7	0	0	1	98	0	0	15
French %	0	0	46	0.8	0	0	0	0	0	0.3
German %	0	0	19	0	0	0	0	0	0	74
Spanish %	0	0	0	0	0	0	0	0	0	0.3
Official: Arabic %	0	0	0	0	0	100	0	0	0	0
Chinese %	0	100	0	0	0	0	0	0	0	0
English %	100	0	76	25	100	0	100	0	100	22
French %	100	0	99	75	0	0	0	0	0	14
German %	0	0	23	0	0	0	0	0	0	77
Spanish %	0	0	0	0	0	0	0	0	0	0
Commercial: Arabic %	0	0	0	0	0	99	0	0	0	0
Chinese %	0	1	0	0	0	0	0	0	0	0
English %	1	0	46	0.8	1	1	100	0	1	0
French %	0	0	1	0.2	0	1	0	0	0	0
German %	0	0	0.2	0	0	0	0	0	0	0
Italian %	0	0	0	0	0	0	0	0	0	1
Portuguese %	0	0	0	0	0	0	0	0	0	0.8
Russian %	0	0	0	0	0	0	0	1	0	0.7
Spanish %	0	0	0	0	0	0	0	0	0	0.8

Characteristics	Ewa-Adja	Ewe	Fang	Fijian	Finnish	Fleming	Fon	Forros	French	Fulani
Ethnic Groups: # present	6	6	9	3	2	8	5	5	9	10
:Max % present	45	52	27	50	93	55	66	60	83	28
Religions: # present	7	8	8	9	8	8	8	5	11	8
:Max % present	50	28	43	52	86	79	63	81	72	57
Beliefs: Anglican %	0	0	0	0	0	0	0	0	0.6	0
:Buddhist %	0	0	0	0	0	0	0	0	0	0
:Christian Total %	35	62	61	52	88	79	23	98	83	32
:Hindu %	0	0	0	38	0	0	0	0	0	0
:Jewish %	0	0	0	0	0	0.3	0	0	0	0
:Islam %	12	16	17	8	0	3	13	0	1	56
:Protestant Total %	9	28	16	0	86	0	3	17	3	16
:Roman Catholic %	26	21	43	0	0.4	79	20	81	72	9
:Traditional %	50	0	20	0	0	0	63	2	0	1
Official: Anglican	0	0	0	0	0	0	0	0	0	0
:Buddhism	0	0	0	0	0	0	0	0	0	0
:Christianism	0	0	0	0	0	0	0	0	0	0
:Greek Orthodox	0	0	0	0	0	0	0	0	0	0
:Hinduism	0	0	0	0	0	0	0	0	0	0
:Islam	0	0	0	0	0	0	0	0	0	0
:Luthren Evangelical	0	0	0	0	1	0	0	0	0	0
:Monotheism	0	0	0	0	0	0	0	0	0	0
:Orthodox	0	0	0	0	0	0	0	0	0	0
Languages: # present	11	9	6	3	0.9	4	10	1	10	10
:Max % present	22	44	18	49	93	59	26	100	80	28
:Number official	3	1	2	1	2	3	1	1	1	1
:None official (1=yes)	0	0	0	0	0	0	0	0	0	0
Mother Tongue: Arabic %	0	0	0	0	0	0	0	0	0	0.2
:Chinese (all) %	0	0	0	0	0	0	0	0	0.1	0
:English %	0	0	0	0	0.4	0	0	0	2	0
:French %	0	0	0.8	0	0.2	0.6	0	0	74	0
:German %	0	0	0	0	0	0	0	0	4	0.2
:Spanish %	0	0	0	0	0	0	0	0	0	0
Official: Arabic %	0	0	0	0	0	0	0	0	0	0
:Chinese %	0	0	0	0	0	0	0	0	0.1	0
:English %	0	100	0	100	0.7	0	0	0	12	0.1
:French %	100	0	77	0	0	100	100	0	100	65
:German %	0	0	90	0	0	100	0	0	2	40
:Spanish %	0	0	1	0	0	0	0	0	0	0
Commercial: Arabic %	0	0	0	0	0	0	0	0	0	0.6
:Chinese %	0	0	0	0	0	0	0	0	0	0.4
:English %	0	1	0	1	0.9	1	0	0	1	0
:French %	1	0	0.1	0	0	1	1	1	0	0
:German %	0	0	0	0	0	1	0	0	0	0
:Italian %	0	0	0	0	0	0	0	0	0	0
:Portuguese %	0	0	0	0	0	0	0	1	0	0
:Russian %	0	0	0	0	0	0	0	0	0	0
:Spanish %	0	0	0	0	0	0	0	0	0	0

Characteristics	Fur	Ga-Adangme	Gagauz	Galician	Ganda	Garifuna	Gbaya	Georgian	German	Gibral-tarian
Ethnic Groups: # present	10	6	7	4	11	6	8	10	7	6
: Max % present	49	52	73	73	18	38	29	71	87	66
Religions: # present	8	8	7	7	8	16	6	5	8	8
: Max % present	73	28	98	95	50	58	40	76	45	74
Beliefs: Anglican %	0	0	0	0	26	12	0	0	0	8
: Buddhist %	0	0	0	0	0	0	0	0	0	0
: Christian Total %	8	62	55	96	76	89	69	81	63	85
: Hindu %	0	0	0	0.3	0	3	0	0	0.1	0
: Jewish %	0	0	0.9	0	0	0	0	1	0.3	1
: Islam %	73	16	43	0.4	7	1	0	14	41	8
: Protestant Total %	2	28	0	0	26	31	40	0	20	11
: Roman Catholic %	6	0	0.6	95	50	58	29	0	0	74
: Traditional %	17	21	0	0	13	4	18	0	0	0
Official: Anglican	0	0	0	0	0	0	0	0	0	0
: Buddhism	0	0	0	0	0	0	0	0	0	0
: Christianism	0	0	0	0	0	0	0	0	0	0
: Greek Orthodox	0	0	0	0	0	0	0	0	0	0
: Hinduism	0	0	0	0	0	0	0	0	0	0
: Islam	1	0	0	0	0	0	0	0	0	0
: Luthren Evangelical	0	0	0	0	0	0	0	0	0	0
: Monotheism	0	0	0	0	0	0	0	0	0	0
: Orthodox	0	0	0	0	0	0	0	0	0	0
Languages: # present	7	9	4	4	10	4	4	4	3	5
: Max % present	51	44	74	70	16	60	47	70	95	86
: Number official	1	1	1	4	1	1	1	1	1	1
: None official (1=yes)	0	0	0	0	0	0	0	0	0	0
Mother Tongue: Arabic %	51	0	0	0	0	0	0	0	0	0
: Chinese (all) %	0	0	0	0	0	0	0	0	0	2
: English %	0	0	0	0	0	0	0	0	0.4	0
: French %	0	0	0	0	0	0	0	0	0.2	0
: German %	0	0	0	0	0	0	0	0	88	0
: Spanish %	0	0	0	70	0	25	0	0	0.1	11
Official: Arabic %	100	0	0	0	0	0	0	0	0	0
: Chinese %	0	0	0	0	0	0	0	0	0	0
: English %	0	100	0	0	100	0	0	0	0.7	100
: French %	0	0	0	0	0	0	100	0	0.7	0
: German %	0	0	0	0	0	0	0	0	91	0
: Spanish %	0	0	0	100	0	100	0	0	0.1	0
Commercial: Arabic %	1	0	0	0	0	0	0	0	1	0
: Chinese %	0	0	0	0	0	0	0	0	0.1	0
: English %	1	1	0	0	1	1	0	0	0.9	1
: French %	0	0	0	0	0	0	1	0	0.1	0
: German %	1	0	0.4	0	0	0	0	0	0.1	0
: Italian %	0	0	0.4	0	0	0	0	0	0.1	0
: Portuguese %	0	0	0	0	0	0	0	0	0.9	0
: Russian %	0	0	0	0	0	0	0	1	0.1	0
: Spanish %	0	0	0.6	1	0	1	0	0	0	1

Characteristics	Gilaki	Gilber-tese	Gio	Gisu	Gola	Grebo	Greek	Green-landic	Grosi	Guiana Chinese
Ethnic Groups: # present	11	4	10	11	10	10	4	1	9	8
:Max % present	46	96	19	18	19	19	93	83	48	43
Religions: # present	12	7	5	8	5	5	9	5	7	11
:Max % present	91	53	67	50	67	67	93	98	45	80
Beliefs: Anglican %	0	0	0	26	0	0	0.1	0	0	0
:Buddhist %	0.7	0	0	0	0	0	0	0	0	0
:Christian Total %	0	95	67	76	67	67	95	98	12	84
:Hindu %	0	0	0	0	0	0	0.1	0	0	0
:Jewish %	0	0	0	0	0	0	0.3	0	0	0
:Islam %	98	0	14	7	14	14	2	0	42	1
:Protestant Total %	0	43	0	26	0	0	1	98	2	4
:Roman Catholic %	0	53	0	50	0	0	0	0	10	80
:Traditional %	0	0	19	13	19	19	0	0	45	0.9
Official: Anglican	0	0	0	0	0	0	0	0	0	0
:Buddhism	0	0	0	0	0	0	0	0	0	0
:Christianism	0	0	0	0	0	0	0	0	0	0
:Greek Orthodox	0	0	0	0	0	0	0.9	0	0	0
:Hinduism	0	0	0	0	0	0	0	0	0	0
:Islam	1	0	0	0	0	0	0	0	0	0
:Luthren Evangelical	0	0	0	0	0	0	0	1	0	0
:Monotheism	0	0	0	0	0	0	0	0	0	0
:Orthodox	0	0	0	0	0	0	0	0	0	0
Languages: # present	1	2	8	10	8	8	4	2	7	2
:Max % present	100	97	23	16	23	23	93	86	48	90
:Number official	1	1	1	1	1	1	1	1	1	1
:None official (1=yes)	0	0	0	0	0	0	0	0	0	0
Mother Tongue: Arabic %	0	0	0	0	0	0	0	0	0	0
:Chinese (all) %	0	0	0	0	0	0	0	0	0	0
:English %	0	3	0	0	0	0	0.7	0	0	0
:French %	0	0	0	0	0	0	0.3	0	0	0
:German %	0	0	0	0	0	0	0	0	0	0
:Spanish %	0	0	0	0	0	0	0	0	0	0
Official: Arabic %	0	0	0	0	0	0	0	0	0	0
:Chinese %	0	0	0	0	0	0	0	0	0	0
:English %	0	0	100	100	100	100	1	0	100	100
:French %	0	0	0	0	0	0	0	0	0	0
:German %	0	0	0	0	0	0	0	0	0	0
:Spanish %	0	0	0	0	0	0	3	0	0	0
Commercial: Arabic %	0	0	0	0	0	0	0	0	0	0
:Chinese %	0	0	0	0	0	0	0	0	0	0
:English %	0	0	0	0	0	0	0.9	0	0	0
:French %	0	0	0	0	0	0	0	0	0	0
:German %	0	0	0	0	0	0	0	0	0	0
:Italian %	1	1	1	1	1	1	1	0	1	1
:Portuguese %	0	0	0	0	0	0	0	0	0	0
:Russian %	0	0	0	0	0	0	0	0	0	0
:Spanish %	0	0	0	0	0	0	0	0	0	0

Characteristics	Guianese Creole	Gurage	Gurma	Gurung	Gypsy	Han Chinese	Hani	Hausa	Haya	Hazara-Dari
Ethnic Groups: # present	8	9	7	3	6	16	16	10	5	7
Max % present	43	38	48	63	84	93	93	26	21	52
Religions: # present	11	9	7	5	8	8	8	8	12	7
Max % present	80	48	41	70	74	59	59	52	33	74
Beliefs: Anglican %	0	0	0	0	0	0	0	0	0	0
Buddhist %	0	0	0	70	0	6	6	0	0	0
Christian Total %	84	53	37	0	85	0.2	0.2	41	34	0
Hindu %	0	0	0	25	0.3	0	0	0	0	0
Jewish %	0	0	0	0	0.4	0	0	0	0	0
Islam %	4	32	22	5	5	2	2	52	33	89
Protestant Total %	80	0	13	0	9	0	0	22	26	0
Roman Catholic %	0.9	11	13	0	0	0	0	10	32	0
Traditional %	0	0	39	0	0	0.1	0.1	0	0	0
Official: Anglican	0	0	0	0	0	0	0	0	0	0
Buddhism	0	0	0	1	0	0	0	0	0	0
Christianism	0	0	0	0	0	0	0	0	0	0
Greek Orthodox	0	0	0	0	0	0	0	0	0	0
Hinduism	0	0	0	0	0	0	0	0	0	0
Islam	0	0	0	0	0	0	0	0	0	1
Luthren Evangelical	0	0	0	0	0	0	0	0	0	0
Monotheism	0	0	0	0	0	0	0	0	0	0
Orthodox	0	0	0	0	0	0	0	0	0	0
Languages: # present	2	11	0	0	0	8	8	11	10	6
Max % present	90	31	37	30	82	67	67	25	13	51
Number official	.	1	2	1	1	1	1	1	2	2
None official (1=yes)	0	0	0	0	0	0	0	0	0	0
Mother Tongue: Arabic %	0	0	0	0	0	0	0	0.2	0	0
Chinese (all) %	0	0	0	0	0	93	93	0	0	0
English %	0	0	0	0	0	0	0	0	0	0
French %	0	0	0	0	0.9	0	0	0	0	0
German %	0	0	0	0	0	0	0	0	0	0
Spanish %	0	0	0	0	0	0	0	0	0	0
Official: Arabic %	0	0	0	0	0	0	0	0.5	0	0
Chinese %	0	0	0	0	0	100	100	0	0	0
English %	100	1	33	0	0	0	0	83	100	0
French %	0	0	67	0	0	0	0	17	0	0
German %	0	0	0	0	0	0	0	0	0	0
Spanish %	0	0	0	0	0	0	0	0	0	0
Commercial: Arabic %	0	0	0	0	0	0	0	0	0	0
Chinese %	0	0	0	0	0	1	1	0	0	0
English %	1	1	0.3	1	0.5	0	0	0.8	1	1
French %	0	0	0.7	0	0	0	0	0.2	0	0
German %	0	0	0	0	0	0	0	0	0	0
Italian %	0	0	0	0	0	0	0	0	0	0
Portuguese %	0	0	0	0	0	0	0	0	0	0
Russian %	0	0	0	0	0	0	0	0	0	0
Spanish %	0	0	0	0	0.5	0	0	0	0	0

Characteristics	Hehet-Bena	Herero	Hottentot	Hui-Vighur	Humbe-Nyaneka	Hungarian	Hutu	Ibibio	Icelander	Igbo
Ethnic Groups: # present	5	6	5	16	12	7	3	11	5	11
Max % present	21	50	76	93	37	93	87	21	97	21
Religions: # present	12	8	7	8	8	10	6	9	8	9
Max % present	33	51	50	59	69	59	67	45	93	45
Beliefs: Anglican %	0	5	0	0	0	0	0	0	0	0
Buddhist %	0	0	0	6	0	0	0	0	0	0
Christian Total %	34	82	48	0.2	90	82	76	49	97	49
Hindu %	0	0.1	0	0	0	0	0	0	0	0
Jewish %	0	0	0	2	0	0.6	0	0	0	0
Islam %	33	0	0	0	20	0.7	6	45	0	45
Protestant Total %	26	62	27	0.1	69	18	9	26	96	26
Roman Catholic %	32	20	50	0	10	48	67	12	1	12
Traditional %	0	3	0	0	0	0	14	6	0	6
Official: Anglican	0	0	0	0	0	0	0	0	0	0
Buddhism	0	0	0	0	0	0	0	0	0	0
Christianism	0	0	0	0	0	0	0	0	0	0
Greek Orthodox	0	0	0	0	0	0	0	0	0	0
Hinduism	0	0	0	0	0	0	0	0	0	0
Islam	0	0	0	0	0	0	0	0	0	0
Luthren Evangelical	0	0	0	0	0	0	0	0	1	0
Monotheism	0	0	0	0	0	0	0	0	0	0
Orthodox	0	0	0	0	0	0	0	0	0	0
Languages: # present	10	9	3	8	9	5	1	12	1	12
Max % present	13	47	75	67	37	96	99	21	100	21
Number official	2	1	1	1	1	1	2	1	1	1
None official (1=yes)	0	0	0	0	0	0	0	0	0	0
Mother Tongue: Arabic %	0	0	0	0	0	0	0	0	0	0
Chinese (all) %	0	0	0	93	0	0	0	0	0	0
English %	0	1	0	0	0	0.4	0	0.1	0	0
French %	0	0	0	0	0	0.2	0	0	0	0
German %	0	3	0	0	0	0.6	0	0	0	0
Spanish %	0	0	0	0	0	0	0	0	0	0
Official: Arabic %	0	0	0	0	0	0	0	0	0	0
Chinese %	0	0	0	100	0	0	0	0	0	0
English %	100	100	100	0	0	0.7	0	100	0	100
French %	0	0	0	0	0	0	100	0	0	0
German %	0	0	0	0	0	0.7	0	0	0	0
Spanish %	0	0	0	0	0	0	0	0	0	0
Commercial: Arabic %	0	0	0	0	0	0	0	0	0	0
Chinese %	0	0	0	1	0	0	0	0	0	0
English %	1	1	1	0	0	0.8	0	1	1	1
French %	0	0	0	0	0	0.2	1	0	0	0
German %	0	0	0	0	0	0.8	0	0	0	0
Italian %	0	0	0	0	0	0	0	0	0	0
Portuguese %	0	0	0	0	1	0	0	0	0	0
Russian %	0	0	0	0	0	0	0	0	0	0
Spanish %	0	1	0	0	0	0.8	0	0	0	0

Characteristics	Ijaw	Indian	Indo-Aryan	Indo-nesian	Iranian	Irish	Issa	Italian	Japanese	Javanese
Ethnic Groups: # present	11	6	3	6	5	4	4	3	1	4
: Max % present	21	61	72	43	66	90	47	80	98	39
Religions: # present	9	12	14	7	12	10	7	8	9	12
: Max % present	45	51	80	72	77	82	94	77	55	81
Beliefs: Anglican %	0	10	0.7	0	0	19	0	0.1	0	0
: Buddhist %	0	5	0	0	0	0.1	0	0.1	54	0.9
: Christian Total %	49	38	0.2	8	2	93	5	81	3	0.9
: Hindu %	0	4	80	0	0	0.2	0	0.1	0	0.2
: Jewish %	0	0.2	0	0	1	0.4	0	0.1	0	0
: Islam %	45	28	1	88	97	0	94	0.1	0	81
: Protestant Total %	26	18	1	3	0	24	0	2	0.3	5
: Roman Catholic %	12	14	0	16	0	69	0	77	0.8	4
: Traditional %	6	0.1	0	72	0	0.3	3	0	0	4
Official: Anglican	0	0	0	0.1	0	0	0	0	0	0
: Buddhism	0	0	0	0	0	0	0	0	0	0
: Christianism	0	0	0	0	0	0	0	0	0	0
: Greek Orthodox	0	0	0	0	0	0	0	0	0	0
: Hinduism	0	0.4	1	0	0	0	0	0	0	0
: Islam	0	0	0	0	1	0	0	0	0	0
: Luthren Evangelical	0	0	0	0	0	0	0	0	0	0
: Monotheism	0	0	0	0	0	0	0	0	0	1
: Orthodox	0	0	0	0	0	0	0	0	0	0
Languages: # present	12	6	14	3	8	2	4	4	1	10
: Max % present	21	65	28	42	48	96	47	94	99	42
: Number official	1	1	2		1	2	2	1	1	1
: None official (1=yes)	0	0	0	0	0	0	0	0	0	0
Mother Tongue: Arabic %	0	0	0	0	0	0	12	0	0	0
: Chinese (all) %	0	0	0	0	0	0	0	0	0.6	2
: English %	0	8	0	0	0.6	96	0	0.5	0	0
: French %	0	0	0	0	0	0	0	0.6	0	0
: German %	0	0	0	0	0	0	0	0.1	0	0
: Spanish %	0	0	0	0	0	0	0	0	0	0
Official: Arabic %	0	0	0	0	0	0	100	0	0	0
: Chinese %	0	0	0	0	0	0	0	0	0.6	0
: English %	100	54	100	35	0	100	0	0.8	0	0
: French %	0	0	0	0	0	0	0	0	0	0
: German %	0	0	0	0	0	0	0	0.2	0	0
: Spanish %	0	0	0	0	0	0	0	0.1	0	0
Commercial: Arabic %	0	0	0	0	0	0	100	0	0	0
: Chinese %	0	0	0	0	0	0	0	0	0.6	0
: English %	1	18	1	1	1	1	1	0.8	0	1
: French %	0	0.7	0	0	0	0	1	0	0	0
: German %	0	0.1	0	0	0.9	0	0	0.8	0	0
: Italian %	0	0.3	0	0	0	0	0	0.2	0	0
: Portuguese %	0	0.9	0	0	0	0	0	0	0	0
: Russian %	0	0.2	0	0	0	0	0	0	0	0
: Spanish %	0	0.2	0	0	0	0	0	0	0	0

Characteristics	Jewish	Jola	Kalenjin	Kamba	Kanuri	Kara-kalpak	Kare	Karen	Kavango	Kazakh
Ethnic Groups: # present	3	8	10	10	10	8	8	6	6	10
Max % present	80	36	21	21	26	71	29	69	50	52
Religions: # present	7	5	13	13	8	3	6	12	8	4
Max % present	82	91	26	26	51	88	40	89	51	53
Beliefs: Anglican %	0	0	0	0	0	0	0	0	5	0
Buddhist %	0	0	0	0	0	0	0	89	0	0.8
Christian Total %	18	5	73	73	42	0	69	5	82	14
Hindu %	0	0	0	0	0	0	0	0	0	0
Jewish %	65	0	0	0	0	0	0	0	0.1	0
Islam %	12	91	6	6	51	88	8	4	0	45
Protestant Total %	0.3	0	29	29	22	0	40	0	62	2
Roman Catholic %	0.3	3	26	26	17	0	29	1	20	0
Traditional %	0	0	19	19	0	0	18	0	3	0
Official: Anglican	0	0	0	0	0	0	0	0	0	0
Buddhism	0	0	0	0	0	0	0	0	0	0
Christianism	0	0	0	0	0	0	0	0	0	0
Greek Orthodox	0	0	0	0	0	0	0	0	0	0
Hinduism	0	0	0	0	0	0	0	0	0	0
Islam	0	0	0	0	0	0	0	0	0	0
Luthren Evangelical	0	0	0	0	0	0	0	0	0	0
Monotheism	0	0	0	0	0	0	0	0	0	0
Orthodox	0	0	0	0	0	0	0	0	0	0
Languages: # present	5	7	8	8	11	5	4	8	9	5
Max % present	69	44	20	20	25	69	47	69	47	55
Number official	1	1	1	1	1	1	1	1	1	1
None official (1=yes)	0	0	0	0	0	1	0	1	0	0
Mother Tongue: Arabic %	17	0	0	0	0	0	0	0	0	0
Chinese (all) %	0	0	0	0	0	0	0	0	0	0
English %	0.4	0	0	0	0.8	0	0	0	0	0
French %	0.1	0	0	0	0	0	0	0	0	0
German %	0.9	0	0	0	0	0	0	0	0	0
Spanish %	0	0	0	0	0	0	0	0	0	0
Official: Arabic %	80	0	0	0	3	0	0	0	0	0
Chinese %	0	0	0	0	0	0	0	0	0	0
English %	4	0	100	100	83	0	0	1	100	12
French %	0.6	100	0	0	0	0	100	0	0	0
German %	0.9	0	0	0	0	0	0	0	0	3
Spanish %	0.8	0	0	0	0	0	0	0	0	0
Commercial: Arabic %	0	0	0	0	0	0	0	0	0	0
Chinese %	0	0	0	0	0	0	0	0	0	0
English %	0.8	0	1	1	0.8	0	0	1	1	13
French %	0	1	0	0	0	0	1	0	0	0
German %	0	0	0	0	0	0	0	0	0	0.1
Italian %	0	0	0	0	0	0	0	0	0	0
Portuguese %	0	0	0	0	0	0	0	0	0	0
Russian %	0.2	0	0	0	0	1	0	0	0	0.9
Spanish %	0	0	0	0	0.2	0	0	0	0	0.0

Characteristics	Kebu-Akposo	Khmer	Kikuyu	Kimbundu	Kisii	Kissi	Klao	Kongo	Kono	Konzo
Ethnic Groups: # present	6	4	10	12	10	6	10	12	9	13
:Max % present	45	83	21	37	21	38	19	23	34	18
Religions: # present	7	9	13	8	13	7	5	9	7	9
:Max % present	50	86	26	69	26	74	67	49	52	48
Beliefs: Anglican %	0	0	7	0	7	0.2	0	0	1	0
:Buddhist %	0	86	0	0	0	0	0	0	0	0
:Christian Total %	35	0.8	73	90	73	3	67	92	8	94
:Hindu %	0	0	0	0	0	0	0	0	0	0
:Jewish %	0	0	0	0	0	0	0	0	0	0
:Islam %	12	2	6	0	6	72	4	1	39	1
:Protestant Total %	9	0	29	20	29	1	14	28	6	29
:Roman Catholic %	26	0.6	26	69	26	0.4	0	49	2	48
:Traditional %	50	0.9	19	10	19	14	19	6	52	3
Official: Anglican	0	0	0	0	0	0	0	0	0	0
:Buddhism	0	0	0	0	0	0	0	0	0	0
:Christianism	0	0	0	0	0	0	0	0	0	0
:Greek Orthodox	0	0	0	0	0	0	0	0	0	0
:Hinduism	0	0	0	0	0	0	0	0	0	0
:Islam	0	0	0	0	0	0	0	0	0	0
:Luthren Evangelical	0	0	0	0	0	0	0	0	0	0
:Monotheism	0	0	0	0	0	0	0	0	0	0
:Orthodox	0	0	0	0	0	0	0	0	0	0
Languages: # present	11	5	8	9	8	7	8	4	12	4
:Max % present	22	75	20	37	20	38	23	13	31	7
:Number official	3	1	1	1	1	1	1	1	1	1
:None official (1=yes)	0	0	0	0	0	0	0	0	0	0
Mother Tongue: Arabic %	0	0	0	0	0	0	0	0	0	0
:Chinese (all) %	0	3	0	0	0	0	0	0	0	0
:English %	0	0	0	0	0	0	0	0	0	0
:French %	0	0	0	0	0	0	0	0	0	0
:German %	0	0	0	0	0	0	0	0	0	0
:Spanish %	0	0	0	0	0	0	0	0	0	0
Official: Arabic %	0	0	0	0	0	0	0	0	0	0
:Chinese %	0	0	0	0	0	0	0	0	0	0
:English %	0	0	100	0	100	20	100	0	100	100
:French %	100	0	0	0	0	80	0	100	0	0
:German %	0	0	0	0	0	0	0	0	0	0
:Spanish %	0	0	0	0	0	0	0	0	0	0
Commercial: Arabic %	0	0	0	0	0	0	0	0	0	0
:Chinese %	0	0.1	0	0	0	0	0	0	0	0
:English %	0	0.2	1	0	1	0.2	1	0	1	1
:French %	1	0.9	0	0	0	0.8	0	1	0	0
:German %	0	0	0	0	0	0	0	0	0	0
:Italian %	0	0	0	0	0	0	0	0	0	0
:Portuguese %	0	0	0	1	0	0	0	0	0	0
:Russian %	0	0	0	0	0	0	0	0	0	0
:Spanish %	0	0	0	0	0	0	0	0	0	0

Characteristics	Koranko	Korean	Kotoko	Kpelle	Kru	Kurd	Kuwaiti	Kyrgyz	Ladino	Lango
Ethnic Groups: # present	9	2	11	8	10	8	3	8	4	11
:Max % present	34	99	31	26	19	70	42	54	55	18
Religions: # present	7	9	8	6	5	11	4	3	9	8
:Max % present	52	36	43	71	67	86	45	72	74	50
Beliefs: Anglican %	1	0	0	0	0	0	0	0	0	26
:Buddhist %	0	15	0	0	0	2	0	0	0	0
:Christian Total %	8	22	33	44	67	0	0	19	98	76
:Hindu %	0	0	0	0	0	0	0	0	0	0
:Jewish %	0	0	0	0	0	0	0	0	0	0
:Islam %	39	0.5	43	37	14	97	85	72	24	7
:Protestant Total %	6	15	9	0	0	0	0	0	74	26
:Roman Catholic %	2	7	8	14	19	0.6	0	0	0	50
:Traditional %	52	5	24	0	0	0	0	0	0	13
Official: Anglican	0	0	0	0	0	0	0	0	0	0
:Buddhism	0	0	0	0	0	0	0	0	0	0
:Christianism	0	0	0	0	0	0	0	0	0	0
:Greek Orthodox	0	0	0	0	0	0	0	0	0	0
:Hinduism	0	0	0	0	0	0	0	0	0	0
:Islam	0	0	0	0	0	0.6	1	0	0	0
:Luthren Evangelical	0	0	0	0	0	0	0	0	0	0
:Monotheism	0	0	0	0	0	0	0	0	0	0
:Orthodox	0	0	0	0	0	0	0	0	0	0
Languages: # present	12	1	7	7	8			5	6	10
:Max % present	31	99	30	29	23	73	85	50	66	16
:Number official	1	1	1	1	1	1	1	1	1	1
:None official (1=yes)	0	0	0	0	0	0	0	0	0	0
Mother Tongue: Arabic %	0	0	0	0	0	22	85	0	0	0
:Chinese (all) %	0	0	0	0	0	0	0	0	0	0
:English %	0	3	0	0	0	0	0	0	0	0
:French %	0	1	0	0	0	0	0	0	0	0
:German %	0	0	0	0	0	0	0	2	0	0
:Spanish %	0	0	0	0	0	0	0	0	66	0
Official: Arabic %	0	0.1	0	0	0	28	100	0	0	0
:Chinese %	0	0	0	0	0	0	0	0	0	0
:English %	100	3	100	65	100	0	0	0	0	100
:French %	0	1	100	35	0	0	0	0	0	0
:German %	0	0	0	0	0	0	0	0	0	0
:Spanish %	0	0	0	0	0	0	0	0	100	0
Commercial: Arabic %	0	0	0	0	0	0.3	1	0	0	0
:Chinese %	0	0	0	0	0	0	0	0	0	0
:English %	1	0.6	1	0.6	1	0	1	0	0	1
:French %	0	0	0	0.4	0	0	0	0	0	0
:German %	0	0	0	0	0	0.8	0	0	0	0
:Italian %	0	0	0	0	0	0	0	0	0	0
:Portuguese %	0	0	0	0	0	0	0	0	0	0
:Russian %	0	0	0	0	0	0.8	0	66	0	0
:Spanish %	0	0	0	0	0	0	0	0	1	0

Characteristics	Lao	Latvian	Lezgin	Li	Liechten- steiner	Limba	Lithua- nian	Lobi	Loma	Lomwe
Ethnic Groups: # present	5	6	6	16	4	9	6	8	10	4
..Max % present	55	52	81	93	64	34	80	33	19	58
Religions: # present	11	5	5	8	6	7	4	8	5	8
..Max % present	87	35	60	59	86	52	79	41	67	34
Beliefs: Anglican %	0	0	0	0	0	1	0	0	0	0
..Buddhist %	87	0	0	6	0	0	0	0	0	0
..Christian Total %	1	65	11	0.2	95	8	95	16	67	64
..Hindu %	0	0	0	0	0	0	0	0	0	0
..Jewish %	0	0	0	0	0.1	0	0.3	0	0	0
..Islam %	3	0	80	2	0	39	0	31	14	16
..Protestant Total %	0	25	0	0	9	6	15	4	0	34
..Roman Catholic %	0	20	0	0	86	2	79	12	0	28
..Traditional %	6	0	0	0.1	0	52	0	41	19	19
Official: Anglican	0	0	0	0	0	0	0	0	0	0
..Buddhism	0.8	0	0	0	0	0	0	0	0	0
..Christianism	0	0	0	0	0	0	0	0	0	0
..Greek Orthodox	0	0	0	0	0	0	0	0	0	0
..Hinduism	0	0	0	0	0	0	0	0	0	0
..Islam	0	0	0	0	0	0	0	0	0	0
..Luthren Evangelical	0	0	0	0	0	0	0	0	0	0
..Monotheism	0	0	0	0	0	0	0	0	0	0
..Orthodox	0	0	0	0	0	0	0	0	0	0
Languages: # present	7	2	4	8	1	12	5	6	8	4
..Max % present	47	54	78	67	100	31	80	44	23	50
..Number official (1=yes)	1	1	1	1	1	1	1	1	1	2
..None official	0	0	0	0	0	0	0	0	0	0
Mother Tongue: Arabic %	0	0	0	0	0	0	0	0	0	0
..Chinese (all) %	2	0	0	93	0	0	0	0	0	0
..English %	0	0	0	0	0	0	0	0	0	0
..French %	0	0	0	0	0	0	0	0	0	0
..German %	0	0	0	0	100	0	0	0	0	0
..Spanish %	0	0	0	0	0	0	0	0	0	0
Official: Arabic %	0	0	0	0	0	0	0	0	0	0
..Chinese %	0	0	0	100	0	0	0	0	0	0
..English %	0	0	0	0	0	0	0	0	0	0
..French %	0	0	0	0	0	0	0	0	0	0
..German %	0	0	0	0	100	0	0	0	0	0
..Spanish %	0	0	0	0	0	0	0	0	0	0
Commercial: Arabic %	0.8	0	0	0	0	0	0	0	0	0
..Chinese %	0.8	0	0	1	0	0	0	0	0	0
..English %	0.2	0	0	0	0	100	0	100	100	0
..French %	0	0	0	0	0	0	0	0	0	0
..German %	0	0	0	0	100	0	0	0	0	0
..Italian %	0	0	0	0	0	0	0	0	0	0
..Portuguese %	0	0	0	0	0	0	0	0	0	100
..Russian %	0	1	1	1	1	0	1	1	1	1
..Spanish %	0	0	0	0	0	0	0	0	0	0

Cultural Resources Across Ethnic Cultures 185

Characteristics	Lotuko	Luba	Luchasi	Luena	Lugbara	Luhya	Lumbe	Lunda	Luo	Luri
Ethnic Groups: # present	10	13	12	12	13	10	12	12	10	11
Max % present	49	18	37	37	18	21	37	37	21	46
Religions: # present	8	8	8	8	9	13	8	8	13	12
Max % present	73	48	69	69	48	26	69	69	26	91
Beliefs: Anglican %	2	0	0	0	0	0	0	0	7	0
Buddhist %	0	0	0	0	0	0	0	0	0	0
Christian Total %	8	94	90	90	94	73	90	90	73	0.7
Hindu %	0	0	0	0	0	0	0	0	0	0
Jewish %	0	0	0	0	0	0	0	0	0	0
Islam %	73	1	0	0	1	0	0	0	6	98
Protestant Total %	2	29	20	20	29	6	20	20	29	0
Roman Catholic %	6	48	69	69	48	29	69	60	26	0
Traditional %	17	3	10	10	3	19	10	10	19	0
Official: Anglican	0	0	0	0	0	0	0	0	0	0
Buddhism	0	0	0	0	0	0	0	0	0	0
Christianism	0	0	0	0	0	0	0	0	0	0
Greek Orthodox	0	0	0	0	0	0	0	0	0	0
Hinduism	0	0	0	0	0	0	0	0	0	0
Islam	1	0	0	0	0	0	0	0	0	1
Luthren Evangelical	0	0	0	0	0	0	0	0	0	0
Monotheism	0	0	0	0	0	0	0	0	0	0
Orthodox	0	0	0	0	0	0	0	0	0	0
Languages: # present	7	4	9	9	4	8	9	9	8	1
Max % present	51	7	37	37	7	20	37	37	20	100
Number official	1	1	1	1	1	1	1	1	1	1
None official (1=yes)	0	0	0	0	0	0	0	0	0	0
Mother Tongue: Arabic %	51	0	0	0	0	0	0	0	0	100
Chinese (all) %	0	0	0	0	0	0	0	0	0	0
English %	0	0	0	0	0	0	0	0	0	0
French %	0	0	0	0	0	0	0	0	0	0
German %	0	0	0	0	0	0	0	0	0	0
Spanish %	0	0	0	0	0	0	0	0	0	0
Official: Arabic %	100	0	0	0	0	0	0	0	0	50
Chinese %	0	0	0	0	0	0	0	0	0	0
English %	0	0	0	0	100	100	0	0	100	0
French %	0	100	0	0	0	0	0	0	0	0
German %	0	0	0	0	0	0	0	0	0	0
Spanish %	0	0	0	0	0	0	0	0	0	0
Commercial: Arabic %	0	0	0	0	0	0	0	0	0	0
Chinese %	0	0	0	0	0	0	0	0	0	0
English %	0	0	0	0	0	0	0	0	0	0
French %	1	1	0	0	1	1	0	0	1	1
German %	0	0	0	0	0	0	0	0	0	1
Italian %	0	0	0	0	0	0	0	0	0	0
Portuguese %	0	0	1	1	0	0	1	1	0	0
Russian %	0	0	0	0	0	0	0	0	0	0
Spanish %	0	0	0	0	0	0	0	0	0	0

Characteristics	Luxem-burger	Macedo-nian	Madurese	Magars	Maka	Makonde	Makua	Malagasy	Malawi	Malay
Ethnic Groups: # present	6	6	4	7	11	5	5	11	5	3
:Max % present	71	73	39	58	22	21	47	27	47	60
Religions: # present	7	6	12	10	8	12	7	10	7	11
:Max % present	92	66	81	86	36	33	48	47	48	59
Beliefs: Anglican %	0	0	0	0	0	0	0	0	0	0
:Buddhist %	0	0	0	8	0	0	0	0	0	28
:Christian Total %	93	70	0.9	0.2	54	34	31	50	31	6
:Hindu %	0	0	2	86	0	0	0	0	0	6
:Jewish %	0.3	0	0	0	0	0	0	0	0	0
:Islam %	0	22	81	3	20	33	13	3	13	45
:Protestant Total %	1	0.9	5	0	18	0	31	23	31	0.1
:Roman Catholic %	92	3	4	0	36	26	48	26	48	0.2
:Traditional %	0	0	4	0.6	24	32	0	47	0	0.1
Official: Anglican	0	0	0	0	0	0	0	0	0	0
:Buddhism	0	0	0	0	0	0	0	0	0	0
:Christianism	0	0.1	0	0	0	0	0	0	0	0
:Greek Orthodox	0	0	0	0	0	0	0	0	0	0
:Hinduism	0	0	0	1	0	0	0	0	0	0
:Islam	0	0	0	0	0	0	0	0	0	0
:Luthren Evangelical	0	0	0	0	0	0	0	0	0	0
:Monotheism	0	0.1	1	0	0	0	0	0	0	0
:Orthodox	0	4	0	0	0	0	0	0	0	0
Languages: # present	1	4	10	10	6	10	9	1	9	9
:Max % present	100	75	42	51	12	13	38	99	38	46
:Number official	1	1	1	1	2	2	1	2	1	1
:None official (1=yes)	0	0	0	0	0	0	0	0	0	0
Mother Tongue: Arabic %	0	0	0	0	0	0	0	0	0	0
:Chinese (all) %	0	0	0	0	0	0	0	0	0	25
:English %	0	0	0	0	0	0	0	0	0	0.3
:French %	0	0	0	0	0	0	0	0	0	0
:German %	0	0	0	0	0	0	0	0	0	0
:Spanish %	0	0	0	0	0	0	0	0	0	0
Official: Arabic %	0	0	0	0	0	0	0	0	0	0
:Chinese %	0	0	0	0	0	0	0	0	0	0
:English %	0	0	0	0	93	100	0.1	0	1	3
:French %	100	0	0	0	99	0	0	0.1	0	3
:German %	100	0	0	0	0.6	0	0	0	0	0
:Spanish %	0	0	0	0	0	0	0	0	0	0
Commercial: Arabic %	0	0	0	0	0	0	0	0	0	0
:Chinese %	0	0	0	0	0	0	0	0	0	0
:English %	1	0	1	1	0.9	1	0.1	1	1	1
:French %	1	0	0	0	0.1	0	0	100	0	0
:German %	0	0.5	0	0	0	0	0	0	0	0
:Italian %	0	0	0	0	0	0	0	0	0	0
:Portuguese %	0	0	0	0	0	0	0	0	0	0
:Russian %	0	0.5	0	0	0	0	0	0	0	0
:Spanish %	0	0	0	0	0	0	0	0	0	0

Characteristics	Malay Christian	Malay Coastal	Malay Muslim	Malinke	Maltese	Mambwe	Manchu-Tibetan	Mandara	Mande	Mandingo
Ethnic Groups: # present	3	4	3	7	2	7	16	11	9	8
: Max % present	92	39	92	33	96	35	93	20	48	36
Religions: # present	11	12	11	7	6	9	8	8	7	5
: Max % present	84	81	84	72	97	34	59	34	45	91
Beliefs: Anglican %	0	0	0	0	0	0	0	0	0	0
: Buddhist %		0.99					6			
: Christian Total %	88	2	88	6	97	69	0.2	52	12	5
: Hindu %	0	0	0	0	0	0	0	0	0	0
: Jewish %										
: Islam %	4	81	4	67	0	0.3	2	22	42	91
: Protestant Total %	4	5		1	0	34		18	2	
: Roman Catholic %	84	4	84	4	97	26		34	19	
: Traditional %	0.6	4	0.6	15		27	0.1	25	45	3
Official: Anglican	0	0	0	0	0	0	0	0	0	0
: Buddhism	0	0	0	0	0	0	0	0	0	0
: Christianism	0	0	0	0	0	0	0	0	0	0
: Greek Orthodox	0	0	0	0	0	0	0	0	0	0
: Hinduism	0	0	0	0	0	0	0	0	0	0
: Islam	0	0	0	0	0	0	0	0	0	0
: Luthren Evangelical	0	0	0	0	0	0	0	0	0	0
: Monotheism	0	0	0	0	0	0	0	0	0	0
: Orthodox	0	1	0	0	0	0	0	0	0	0
Languages: # present	8	10	8	6	3	8	8	6	7	7
: Max % present	29	42	29	40	96	25	67	9	48	44
: Number official (1=yes)	2	1	2	1	2	3	1	2	1	1
: None official (1=yes)	0	0	0	0	0	0	0	0	0	0
Mother Tongue: Arabic %	0	0	0	0	0	0	0	0	0	0
: Chinese (all) %	0	0	0	0	0	0	93	0	0	0
: English (all) %	0	2	0	0	2	0	0	0	0	0
: French %	0	0	0	0.2	0	0	0	0	0	0
: German %	0	0	0	0	0	0	0	0	0	0
: Spanish %	0	0	0	0	0	0	0	0	0	0
Official: Arabic %	0	0	0	0	0	0	0	0	0	0
: Chinese %	0	0	0	0	0	0	100	0	0	0
: English %	100	100	100	100	100	100	0	100	100	100
: French %	0	0	0	86	0	0	0	100	0	0
: German %	0	0	0	0	0	0	0	0	0	0
: Spanish %	0	0	0	0	0	0	0	0	0	0
Commercial: Arabic %	0	0	0	0	0	0	0	0	0	0
: Chinese %	0	0	0	0	0	0	1	0	0	0
: English %	1	1	1	0.1	1	1	0	1	1	1
: French %	0	0	0	0.9	0	0	0	1	0	0
: German %	0	0	0	0	0	0	0	0	0	0
: Italian %	0	0	0	0	1	0	0	0	0	0
: Portuguese %	0	0	0	0	0	0	0	0	0	0
: Russian %	0	0	0	0	0	0	0	0	0	0
: Spanish %	0	0	0	0	0	0	0	0	0	0

Characteristics	Mandyako	Mano	Manx (Norse-C.)	Manzan-Darani	Maori	Maravi	Masa	Masalit Maba	Maya	Mbaka
Ethnic Groups: # present	5	10	4	11	3	5	11	11	6	8
: Max % present	27	19	89	46	86	54	31	31	38	29
Religions: # present	7	5	6	12	14	8	8	8	16	6
: Max % present	58	67	61	91	22	34	43	43	58	40
Beliefs: Anglican %	0	0	61	0	22	0	0	0	12	0
: Buddhist %	0	0	0	0.7	0	0	0	0	0	0
: Christian Total %	6	67	91	0	63	65	33	33	89	69
: Hindu %	0	0	0	0	0.1	0	0	0	3	0
: Jewish %	0	0	0.1	0	0	0	0	0	0	0
: Islam %	34	14	0	98	0	13	43	43	1	8
: Protestant Total %	0	0	80	0	48	34	9	9	31	40
: Roman Catholic %	0	0	11	0	15	27	8	8	58	29
: Traditional %	58	19	0	0	0.2	21	24	24	4	18
Official: Anglican	0	0	0	0	0	0	0	0	0	0
: Buddhism	0	0	0	0	0	0	0	0	0	0
: Christianism	0	0	0	0	0	0	0	0	0	0
: Greek Orthodox	0	0	0	0	0	0	0	0	0	0
: Hinduism	0	0	0	0	0	0	0	0	0	0
: Islam	0	0	0	1	0	0	0	0	0	0
: Luthren Evangelical	0	0	0	0	0	0	0	0	0	0
: Monotheism	0	0	0	0	0	0	0	0	0	0
: Orthodox	0	0	0	0	0	0	0	0	0	0
Languages: # present	6	8	3	1	2	5	7	7	4	4
: Max % present	30	23	89	100	93	45	30	30	60	47
: Number official	1	1	0	1	1	2	1	1	1	1
: None official (1=yes)	0	0	0	0	0	0	0	0	0	0
Mother Tongue: Arabic %	0	0	0	0	0	0	30	30	0	0
: Chinese (all) %	0	0	0	0	0	0	0	0	0	0
: English %	0	0	89	0	93	0.2	0	0	0	0
: French %	0	0	0	0	0	0	0	0	0	0
: German %	0	0	0	0	0	0	0	0	0	0
: Spanish %	0	0	0	0	0	0	0	0	25	0
Official: Arabic %	0	0	0	50	0	0	100	100	0	0
: Chinese %	0	0	0	0	0	0	0	0	0	0
: English %	0	100	100	0	100	100	0	0	0	0
: French %	0	0	0	0	0	0	100	100	0	100
: German %	0	0	0	0	0	0	0	0	0	0
: Spanish %	0	0	0	0	0	0	0	0	100	0
Commercial: Arabic %	0	0	0	1	0	0	1	1	0	0
: Chinese %	0	0	0	0	0	0	0	0	0	0
: English %	0	1	1	0	1	1	0	0	0	0
: French %	0	0	0	0	0	0	1	1	0	1
: German %	0	0	0	0	0	0	0	0	0	0
: Italian %	0	0	0	0	0	0	0	0	0	0
: Portuguese %	1	0	0	0	0	0	0	0	0	0
: Russian %	0	0	0	0	0	0	0	0	0	0
: Spanish %	0	0	0	0	0	0	0	0	1	0

Characteristics	Mbete	Mbochi	Mbum	Mbunda	Melanesian	Mende	Merina	Meru	Mestizo	Miao Man
Ethnic Groups: # present	6	8	10	12	3	9	11	10	5	5
:Max % present	42	52	28	37	84	34	27	21	57	67
Religions: # present	7	8	8	8	12	7	10	13	9	9
:Max % present	61	54	40	69	38	52	47	26	88	58
Beliefs: Anglican %	0	0	0	0	10	1	0	7	0	0
:Buddhist %	0	0	0	0	0	0	0	0	0	58
:Christian Total %	89	78	44	90	91	8	50	73	92	2
:Hindu %	0	0	0	0	0.1	0	0	0	0.1	0
:Jewish %	0	0	0	0	0.2	0	0	0	0	0
:Islam %	0.9	1	31	20		39	3	6	0	1
:Protestant Total %	21	24	17	69	60	6	23	29	3	0
:Roman Catholic %	61	54	23	10	31		26	19	88	0
:Traditional %	9	19			2	52	47		0.4	33
Official: Anglican	0	0	0	0	0	0	0	0	0	0
:Buddhism	0	0	0	0	0	0	0	0	0	0
:Christianism	0	0	0	0	0	0	0	0	0	0
:Greek Orthodox	0	0	0	0	0	0	0	0	0	0
:Hinduism	0	0	0	0	0	0	0	0	0	0
:Islam	0	0	0	0	0	0	0	0	0	0
:Luthren Evangelical	0	0	0	0	0	0	0	0	0	0
:Monotheism	0	0	0	0	0	0	0	0	0	0
:Orthodox	0	0	0	0	0	0	0	0	0	0
Languages: # present		4	6		5	12	1	8	4	4
:Max % present	36	47	28	37	69	31	99	20	90	79
:Number official	1	1	1	1	2	1	2	1	1	1
:None official (1=yes)										
Mother Tongue: Arabic %			17							
:Chinese (all) %										1
:English %					3					
:French %	4									
:German %										
:Spanish %									75	
Official: Arabic %										
:Chinese %										
:English %			57			100		100		
:French %	100	100	100				100			
:German %										
:Spanish %										
Commercial: Arabic %										
:Chinese %									0.1	
:English %									87	
:French %	1	1								
:German %									0.7	
:Italian %										
:Portuguese %				1	0.9				0.1	
:Russian %										
:Spanish %					0.1				0.9	

Characteristics	Micronesian	Mixed	Moldovan	Mon	Mon-Khmer	Monegasque	Mongo	Mongol-Buryat	Mongol-Dariganga	Mongol-Dorbed
Ethnic Groups: # present	2	4	7	6	5	11	13	6	6	6
:Max % present	74	63	68	69	67	52	18	79	79	79
Religions: # present	2	7	6	12	9	4	9	6	6	6
:Max % present	83	75	89	89	58	90	48	49	49	49
Beliefs: Anglican %	2	5	0	0	0	0	0	0	0	0
:Buddhist %	0	0	0	89	58	0	0	2	2	2
:Christian Total %	97	84	93	5	2	90	94	0	0	0
:Hindu %	0	5	0	0	0	0	0	0	0	0
:Jewish %	0	0	1	0	0	2	0	0	0	0
:Islam %	0	2	2	4	0	0	1	1	1	1
:Protestant Total %	56	11	1	0	0	0	29	0	0	0
:Roman Catholic %	45	73	3	1	0	90	48	0	0	0
:Traditional %	0.2	0	0	0	33	0	3	0	0	0
Official: Anglican	0	0	0	0	0	0	0	0	0	0
:Buddhism	0	0	0	0	0	0	0	0	0	0
:Christianism	0	0	0	0	0	0	0	0	0	0
:Greek Orthodox	0	0	0	0	0	0	0	0	0	0
:Hinduism	0	0	0	0	0	0	0	0	0	0
:Islam	0	0	0	0	0	0	0	0	0	0
:Luthren Evangelical	0	0	0	0	0	0	0	0	0	0
:Monotheism	2	2	0	0	0	0	0	0	0	0
:Orthodox	0	0	0	0	0	0	0	0	0	0
Languages: # present	66	76	5	8	4	5	4	4	4	4
:Max % present	1	1	69	69	79	58	7	90	90	90
:Number official	0	0	1	1	1	1	1	1	1	1
:None official (1=yes)	0	0	0	0	0	0	0	0	0	0
Mother Tongue: Arabic %	0	0	0	0	0	0	0	0	0	0
:Chinese (all) %	0	0	0	0	0	0	0	0	0	0
:English %	18	11	0	0	0	5	0	0	0	0
:French %	0.5	4	0	0	0	58	0	0	0	0
:German %	0	0	0	0	0	0	0	0	0	0
:Spanish %	0	0	0	0	0	0	0	0	0	0
Official: Arabic %	0	0	0	0	0	0	0	0	0	0
:Chinese %	0	0	0	0	0	0	0	0	0	0
:English %	100	29	0	0	0	0	0	0	0	0
:French %	0.4	39	0	0	0	100	100	0	0	0
:German %	0	0	0	0	0	0	0	0	0	0
:Spanish %	0	0	0	0	0	0	0	0	0	0
Commercial: Arabic %	0	0	0	0	0	0	0	0	0	0
:Chinese %	0	0	0	0	0	0	0	0	0	0
:English %	1	0.3	0	1	1	1	0	0	0	0
:French %	0	0.6	0	0	0	1	1	0	0	0
:German %	0	0	0	0	0	0	0	0	0	0
:Italian %	0	0	0	0	0	1	0	0	0	0
:Portuguese %	0	0.3	0	0	0	0	0	0	0	0
:Russian %	0	0	1	0	0	0	0	1	1	1
:Spanish %	0	0.2	0	0	0	0	0	0	0	0

Characteristics	Mongol-Khalka	Mongoloid	Montene-grin	Moor	Morvians	Mossi	Mpongwe	Mubi	Mulatto	Muong
Ethnic Groups: # present	6	5	4	4	9	8	4	11	8	7
: Max % present	79	75	63	78	86	50	36	31	35	88
Religions: # present	6	13	5	8	8	7	6	4	12	10
: Max % present	49	77	65	86	60	39	65	43	70	55
Beliefs: Anglican %	0	0	0	0	0	0	0	0	0.1	0.1
: Buddhist %	2	2	0	28	0	0	0	0	0.2	55
: Christian Total %	0	2	70	3	80	30	96	33	80	0
: Hindu %	0	0	0	0	0	0	0	0	0.1	0
: Jewish %	1	67	19	61	16	33	0.8	30	0.1	0
: Islam %	0	0	1	0	60	11	19	0	0.1	0
: Protestant Total %	1	0	4	0	0	6	65	43	5	7
: Roman Catholic %	0	1	0	0	0	36	3	9	68	3
: Traditional %	0	0	0	0	0	0	0	8 24	0.1	0
Official: Anglican	0	0	0	0	0	0	0	0	0	0
: Buddhism	0	0	0	0	0	0	0	0	0	0
: Christianism	0	0	0	0	0	0	0	0	0	0
: Greek Orthodox	0	0	0	0	0	0	0	0	0	0
: Hinduism	0	0	0	0	0	0	0	0	0	0
: Islam	0	0	0	0	0	0	0	0	0	0
: Luthren Evangelical	0	0	0	0	0	0	0	0	0	0
: Monotheism	0	0	0	0	0	0	0	0	0	6
: Orthodox	0	0	0	0.6	0	0	0	0	2	0
Languages: # present	4	13	2	4	85	8	5	7	97	90
: Max % present	90	34	95	74	1	47	29	30	1	1
: Number official	1	2	1	1		1	1	1		
: None official (1=yes)	0	0		0		0	0	0	0	0
Mother Tongue: Arabic %	1	15		47			6	30		
: Chinese (all) %									27	
: English %										
: French %										
: German %		16								
: Spanish %										
Official: Arabic %	1	84		58		36	100	100	0.3	1
: Chinese %						64				
: English %									0.2	
: French %									28	
: German %										
: Spanish %	0	0.2		0.6		0.4		100		
Commercial: Arabic %	1	0.8		0.4		0.6	1	1	0.9	1
: Chinese %		0		0.6						
: English %	0	0		0		0	0	0		0
: French %										
: German %										
: Italian %									0.7	
: Portuguese %	1									
: Russian %	0								0.3	
: Spanish %	0	0		0		0	0	0		0

Characteristics	Nama	Nauruan	Ndebele	Nepalese	Nether-lander	Newar	Ngbandi	Ngoni	Nkole	Norman-French D.
Ethnic Groups: # present	6	4	4	7	4	7	8	4	11	2
: Max % present	50	58	71	58	95	58	29	58	18	80
Religions: # present	8	8	10	10	10	10	6	8	8	7
: Max % present	51	54	40	86	36	86	40	34	50	63
Beliefs: Anglican %	5	3	0	0	0	0	0	0	26	63
: Buddhist %	0	2	0	8	0	8	0	0	0	0
: Christian Total %	82	81	43	0.2	62	0.2	69	64	76	95
: Hindu %	0	0	0	86	0	86	0	0	0	0
: Jewish %	0.1	0	0	0	0.2	0	0	0	0	0
: Islam %	0	0	0	3	0.3	3	8	16	7	0
: Protestant Total %	62	57	18	0	26	0	40	34	26	77
: Roman Catholic %	20	24	12	0	36	0	29	28	50	18
: Traditional %	3	0	40	0.6	0	0.6	18	19	13	0
Official: Anglican	0	0	0	0	0	0	0	0	0	0
: Buddhism	0	0	0	0	0	0	0	0	0	0
: Christianism	0	0	0	0	0	0	0	0	0	0
: Greek Orthodox	0	0	0	0	0	0	0	0	0	0
: Hinduism	0	0	0	1	0	1	0	0	0	0
: Islam	0	0	0	0	0	0	0	0	0	0
: Luthren Evangelical	0	0	0	0	0	0	0	0	0	0
: Monotheism	0	0	0	0	0	0	0	0	0	0
: Orthodox	0	0	0	0	0	0	0	0	0	0
Languages: # present	9	6	6	10	2	10	4	4	10	
: Max % present	47	58	55	51	93	51	47	50	61	
: Number official	1	1	1	1	1	1	1	2	1	
: None official (1=yes)	0	0	0	0	0	0	0	0	0	
Mother Tongue: Arabic %	0	0	0	0	0	0	0	0	0	
: Chinese (all) %	0	0	0	0	0	0	0	0	0	
: English %	1	9	7	0	0	0	0	0	16	42
: French %	0	0	0	0	0	0	0	0	0	58
: German %	3	0	0	0	0	0	0	0	0	0
: Spanish %	0	0	0	0	0	0	0	0	0	0
Official: Arabic %	0	0	0	0	0	0	0	0	0	0
: Chinese %	0	0	0	0	0	0	0	0	0	0
: English %	100	100	100	0	0	0	0	100	100	0
: French %	0	0	0	0	0	0	100	0	0	0
: German %	0	0	0	0	0	0	0	0	0	0
: Spanish %	0	0	0	0	0	0	0	0	0	0
Commercial: Arabic %	0	0	0	0	0	0	0	0	0	0
: Chinese %	0	0	0	0	0	0	0	0	0	0
: English %	1	1	1	1	1	1	0	1	1	1
: French %	0	0	0	0	0	0	1	0	0	1
: German %	1	0	0	0	0	0	0	0	0	0
: Italian %	0	0	0	0	0	0	0	0	0	0
: Portuguese %	0	0	0	0	0	0	0	0	0	0
: Russian %	0	0	0	0	0	0	0	0	0	0
: Spanish %	0	0	0	0	0	0	0	0	0	0

Characteristics	North-Western	Norwegian	Nuba	Nuer	Nung Sukuma	Nupe	Nyamwezi (Galla)	Nyoros	Ometo	Oromo
Ethnic Groups: # present	7	7	10	10	7	11	5	11	9	9
:Max % present	35	97	49	49	88	21	21	18	38	38
Religions: # present	9	7	8	8	10	9	12	8	9	9
:Max % present	34	88	73	73	55	45	33	50	48	48
Beliefs: Anglican %	0	0	0	0	0	0	0	26	0	0
:Buddhist %	0	0	0	0	0	0	0	0	0	0
:Christian Total %	69	92	8	8	55	49	34	76	53	53
:Hindu %	0	0	0	0	0	0	0	0	0	0
:Jewish %	0.3	0	0	0	0	0	0	0	0	0
:Islam %	34	0	73	73	7	45	33	0	32	32
:Protestant Total %	26	88	2	2	0	26	26	26	0	0
:Roman Catholic %	0	0	7	7	7	12	26	50	0	0
:Traditional %	27	0	17	17	3	6	32	13	11	11
Official: Anglican	0	0	0	0	0	0	0	0	0	0
:Buddhism	0	0	0	0	0	0	0	0	0	0
:Christianism	0	0	0	0	0	0	0	0	0	0
:Greek Orthodox	0	0	0	0	0	0	0	0	0	0
:Hinduism	0	0	0	0	0	0	0	0	0	0
:Islam	0	0	1	1	0	0	0	0	0	0
:Luthren Evangelical	1	1	0	0	0	0	0	0	0	0
:Monotheism	0	0	0	0	0	0	0	0	0	0
:Orthodox	0	0	0	0	0	0	0	0	0	0
Languages: # present	8	2	7	7	6	12	10	10	11	11
:Max % present	25	99	51	51	90	21	13	16	31	31
:Number official	3	1	1	1	1	1	2	1	1	1
:None official (1=yes)	0	0	0	0	0	0	0	0	0	0
Mother Tongue: Arabic %	1	0	51	51	1	0	0	0	0	0
:Chinese (all) %	0	0	0	0	0	0	0	0	0	0
:English %	0	0	0	0	0	0	0	0	0	0
:French %	0	0	0	0	0	0	0	0	0	0
:German %	0	0	0	0	0	0	0	0	0	0
:Spanish %	0	0	0	0	0	0	0	0	0	0
Official: Arabic %	0	0	100	100	0	0	0	0	0	0
:Chinese %	0	0	0	0	0	0	0	0	0	0
:English %	100	0	0	0	0	100	100	100	0	0
:French %	0	0	0	0	0	0	0	0	0	0
:German %	0	0	0	0	0	0	0	0	0	0
:Spanish %	0	0	0	0	0	0	0	0	0	0
Commercial: Arabic %	0	0	1	1	0	0	0	0	0	0
:Chinese %	0	0	0	0	0	0	0	0	0	0
:English %	1	0	1	1	1	1	1	1	1	1
:French %	0	0	0	0	0	0	0	0	0	0
:German %	0	0	0	0	0	0	0	0	0	0
:Italian %	0	0	0	0	0	0	0	0	1	1
:Portuguese %	0	0	0	0	0	0	0	0	0	0
:Russian %	0	0	0	0	0	0	0	0	0	0
:Spanish %	0	0	0	0	0	0	0	0	0	0

Characteristics	Ossete	Ovambo	Ovim-bundu	Pacific Islander	Pakistani	Palauans	Palaung-Wa	Papuan New Guin.	Pashtun	Pepel
Ethnic Groups: # present	10	6	12	4	9	4	5	2	7	5
:Max % present	70	50	37	58	66	40	67	84	52	27
Religions: # present	5	8	8	8	12	4	9	13	7	7
:Max % present	75	51	69	54	61	97	58	35	74	58
Beliefs: Anglican %	0	5	0	3	33	0	0	0	0	0
:Buddhist %	0	0	0	2	0.1	0	58	0	0	0
:Christian Total %	83	82	90	81	58	0	2	91	0	6
:Hindu %	0	0	0	0	4	0	0	0	0	0
:Jewish %	1	0.1	0	0	0.3	0	0	0.2	0	0
:Islam %	11	0	0	0	29	0	1	0	89	34
:Protestant Total %	0	62	20	57	45	0	0	58	0	0
:Roman Catholic %	0	20	69	24	10	0	0	33	0	0
:Traditional %	0	3	10	0	0.6	0.9	33	3	0	58
Official: Anglican	0	0	0	0	0	0	0	0	0	0
:Buddhism	0	0	0	0	0	0	0	0	0	0
:Christianism	0	0	0	0	0	0	0	0	0	0
:Greek Orthodox	0	0	0	0	0	0	0	0	0	0
:Hinduism	0	0	0	0	0.3	0	0	0	0	0
:Islam	0	0	0	0	0	0	0	0	1	0
:Luthren Evangelical	0	0	0	0	0	0	0	0	0	0
:Monotheism	0	0	0	0	0	0	0	0	0	0
:Orthodox	0	0	0	0	0	0	0	0	0	0
Languages: # present	4	9	9	6	3	3	4	4	6	6
:Max % present	69	47	37	58	80	45	79	73	51	30
:Number official	1	1	1	1	1	0	1	2	2	1
:None official (1=yes)	0	0	0	0	0	0	0	0	0	0
Mother Tongue: Arabic %	0	0	0	0	0	0	0	0	0	0
:Chinese (all) %	0	0	0	9	0	0	0	0	0	0
:English %	0	1	0	7	16	15	0	0	0	0
:French %	0	0	0	0	0	0	0	0	0	0
:German %	0	3	0	0	0	0	0	0	0	0
:Spanish %	0	0	0	0	0	0	0	0	0	0
Official: Arabic %	0	0	0	0	0	0	0	0	0	0
:Chinese %	0	0	0	0	0	0	0	0	0	0
:English %	0	100	0	0	57	100	0	100	0	0
:French %	0	0	0	0	0	0	0	0	0	0
:German %	0	0	0	0	0	0	0	0	0	0
:Spanish %	0	0	0	0	0	0	0	0	0	0
Commercial: Arabic %	0	0	0	0	0.3	0	0	0	0	0
:Chinese %	0	0	0	0	0	0	0	0	0	0
:English %	0	1	0	1	29	1	1	1	1	1
:French %	0	0	0	0	0	0	0	0	0	0
:German %	0	1	0	0	0	0	0	0	0	0
:Italian %	0	0	0	0	0	0	0	0	0	0
:Portuguese %	0	0	1	0	0	0	0	0	0	1
:Russian %	1	0	0	0	0.9	0	1	1	1	0
:Spanish %	0	0	0	0	0	0	0	0	0	0

Characteristics	Persian	Polinisian	Polinesian Chinese	Polinesian European	Polish	Portu-guese	Punjabi	Punu	Puyi	Pygmy
Ethnic Groups: # present	11	4	5	5	2	9	5	5	16	8
::Max % present	46	76	68	69	98	46	66	41	93	52
Religions: # present	12	9	8	8	6	12	12	7	8	8
::Max % present	90	42	47	50	87	72	77	61	59	54
Beliefs: Anglican %	0	0	0	0	0	0.2	0	0	0	0
::Buddhist %	0	0	0	0	0	83	0	0	6	0
::Christian Total %	0.7	83	97	97	89	0.1	2	90	0.2	78
::Hindu %	0	0	0	0	0	0.1	1	0	0	0
::Jewish %	0	0	0	0	0.1	0.5	0	0.9	0	1
::Islam %	98	0	0	0	0.7	72	97	20	2	24
::Protestant Total %	0	47	50	47	86	0	0	61	0	54
::Roman Catholic %	0	28	39	37	0	0	0	8	0.1	19
::Traditional %	0	0.2	0	0	0	0	0	0	0	0
Official: Anglican	0	0	0	0	0	0	0	0	0	0
::Buddhism	0	0	0	0	0	0	0	0	0	0
::Christianism	0	0	0	0	0	0	0	0	0	0
::Greek Orthodox	0	0	0	0	0	0	0	0	0	0
::Hinduism	0	0	0	0	0	0	0	0	0	0
::Islam	1	0	0	0	0	0	0	0	0	0
::Luthren Evangelical	0	0	0	0	0	0	0	0	0	0
::Monotheism	0	0	0	0	0	0	0	0	0	0
::Orthodox	0	0	0	0	0	0	0	0	0	4
Languages: # present	10	3	5	5	2	2	8	35	8	47
::Max % present	50	79	69	71	97	97	48	1	67	1
::Number official (1=yes)	1	1	0	0	1	1	1	0	1	0
::None official	0	0	0	0	0	0	0	0	0	0
Mother Tongue: Arabic %	1	0	0	0	0	0.2	0	0	0	0
::Chinese (all) %	0	0	0	6	0.2	0.3	0	4	93	0
::English %	0	37	9	8	0.1	0.1	0	0	0	0
::French %	0	5	0	0	0.8	0	0	0	0	0
::German %	0	0	0	0	0	0	0	0	0	0
::Spanish %	0	0	0	0	0	0	0	0	0	0
Official: Arabic %	0	0	0	0	0	0.5	0	0	0	0
::Chinese %	0	52	100	6	0.4	0.1	0	100	100	100
::English %	0.7	48	0	94	0.4	0	0.1	0	0	0
::French %	0	0	0	0	0.8	0	0.1	0	0	0
::German %	0	0	0	0	0	0	0	0	0	0
::Spanish %	0	0	0	0	0	0	0	0	0	0
Commercial: Arabic %	0	0	0	0	0	1	0	0	0	1
::Chinese %	0	0.5	1	0.1	1	0.3	1	1	1	0
::English %	1	0.5	0	0.9	0	0	0	0	0	0
::French %	1	0	0	0.9	0	0	0	0	0	0
::German %	0	0	0	0	0	0.7	0	0	0	0
::Italian %	0	0	0	0	0	0	0	0	0	0
::Portuguese %	0	0	0	0	0	0.7	0	0	0	0
::Russian %	0	0	0	0	0	0	0	0	0	0
::Spanish %	0	0	0	0	0	0	0	0	0	0

Characteristics	Quechua	Rakhine	Romanian	Romansch	Rundi	Russian	Ruthenian	Rwanda	Saho	Sakalava
Ethnic Groups: # present	5	6	5	6	12	8	9	13	4	11
..Max % present	46	69	88	65	22	78	86	18	50	27
Religions: # present	9	12	9	8	9	6	8	9	2	10
..Max % present	92	89	70	48	50	74	60	49	80	47
Beliefs: Anglican %	0	0	0	0	0	0	0	5	0	0
..Buddhist %	0	89	0	0	0	0	0	0	0	0
..Christian Total %	95	5	90	92	93	80	80	91	20	50
..Hindu %	0	0	0	0.3	0	0	0	0	0	0
..Jewish %	0	0	0.1	2	0	0.8	0	0	0	0
..Islam %	0	4	0.3	44	1	9	0	2	80	3
..Protestant Total %	3	0	7	48	28	5	16	28	0	23
..Roman Catholic %	92	0	5	48	50	5	60	49	0	26
..Traditional %	0.7	1	0	0	4	0	0	5	0	47
Official: Anglican	0	0	0	0	0	0	0	0	0	0
..Buddhism	0	0	0	0	0	0	0	0	0	0
..Christianism	0	0	0	0	0	0	0	0	0	0
..Greek Orthodox	0	0	0	0	0	0	0	0	0	0
..Hinduism	0	0	0	0	0	0	0	0	0	0
..Islam	0	0	0	0	0	0	0	0	0	0
..Luthren Evangelical	0	0	0	0	0	0	0	0	0	0
..Monotheism	0	0	0	0	0	0	0	0	0	0
..Orthodox	0	0	0	0	0	0	0	0	0	0
Languages: # present	3	8	4	6	4	4	2	5	4	1
..Max % present	72	69	87	65	13	83	85	9	50	99
..Number official	2	1	1	3	1	1	1	1	2	2
..None official (1=yes)	0	0	0	0	0	0	0	0	0	0
Mother Tongue: Arabic %	0	0	0	0	0	0	0	0	3	0
..Chinese (all) %	0	0	0	0	0	0	0	0	0	0
..English %	0	0	0	0	0	0	0	0	0	0
..French %	0	0	0	0	0	0	0	21	0	0
..German %	0	0	0	18	0	0	0	0	0	0
..Spanish %	72	0	0	0	0	0	0	0	0	0
Official: Arabic %	0	0	0	0	0	0	0	0	0	0
..Chinese %	0	0	0	0	0	0	0	0	0	0
..English %	0	0	0	0	0	0	0	0	0	0
..French %	0	0	0	0	100	0	0	79	0	100
..German %	0	0	2	65	0	0.2	0	0	0	0
..Spanish %	100	0	0	0	0	0	0	0	0	0
Commercial: Arabic %	0	0	0	0	0	0	0	0	1	0
..Chinese %	0	0	0	0	0	0	0	0	0	0
..English %	0	1	1	100	0	0	0	0	0	0
..French %	0	0	0	100	1	0	0	0.2	0	1
..German %	0	0	0	1	0	0	0	0.8	0	0
..Italian %	0	0	0	1	0	0	0	0	0	0
..Portuguese %	0	0	0	1	0	0	0	0	0	0
..Russian %	0	0	0	0	0	1	0	0	0	0
..Spanish %	1	0	0	0	0	0	0	0	0	0

Characteristics	Samoan	Sanga	Sanmari-nese	Sara	Scandina-vian	Senufo	Serbian	Serer	Servicais Tongas	Shan
Ethnic Groups: # present	6	8	2	8	6	9	4	8	5	6
Max % present	85	52	80	29	97	28	60	36	60	69
Religions: # present	10	8	4	6	6	8	5	5	5	12
Max % present	43	54	95	40	94	55	62	91	81	89
Beliefs: Anglican %	0	0	0	0	0	0	0.1	0	0	0
Buddhist %	0	0	0	0	0	0	0	0	0	89
Christian Total %	89	78	95	69	94	13	69	5	98	5
Hindu %	0	0	0	0	0	0	0	0	0	0
Jewish %	0.4	0	0	0	0.5	0	0	0	0	0
Islam %	0.4	1	0	8	0	46	21	91	17	4
Protestant Total %	66	24	0	40	94	3	2	0	81	0
Roman Catholic %	22	54	95	29	0.2	9	12	3	2	1
Traditional %	0	19	0	18	0	29	0	3	0	0
Official: Anglican	0	0	0	0	0	0	0	0	0	0
Buddhism	0	0	0	0	0	0	0	0	0	89
Christianism	0	0	0	0	0	0	0	0	0	0
Greek Orthodox	0	0	0	0	0	0	0	0	0	0
Hinduism	0	0	0	0	0	0	0	0	0	0
Islam	0	0	0	0	0	0	0	0	0	0
Luthren Evangelical	0	0	0	0	0.4	0	0	0	0	0
Monotheism	0	0	0	0	0	0	0	0	0	0
Orthodox	0	0	0	0	0	0	2	0	0	0
Languages: # present	3	4	1	4	2	7	2	7	1	1
Max % present	96	47	100	47	97	41	95	44	100	69
Number official	2	1	1	1	1	1	1	1	1	1
None official (1=yes)	0	0	0	0	0	0.3	0	0	0	0
Mother Tongue: Arabic %	0	0	0	0	0	0	0	0	0	0
Chinese (all) %	0.1	0	0	0	0	0	0	0	0	0
English %	16	0	0	0	0	0	0.7	0	0	0
French %	0.1	0	0	0	0	0	0	0	0	0
German %	0.1	0	0	0	0	0	0.3	0	0	0
Spanish %	0	0	0	0	0	0	0	0	0	0
Official: Arabic %	0	0	0	0	0	0	0	0	0	0
Chinese %	0	0	0	0	0	0	0	0	0	0
English %	100	0	0	0	0	0	1	0	0	0
French %	0	100	0	100	0	100	1	100	0	0
German %	0	0	0	0	0	0	0	0	0	0
Spanish %	0	0	0	0	0	0	0	0	0	0
Commercial: Arabic %	0	0	0	0	0	0	0	0	0	0
Chinese %	0	0	0	0	0	0	0	0	0	0
English %	1	0	0	0	0.4	0	0.1	0	0	1
French %	0	0	0	0	0	0	0	0	0	0
German %	0	0	0	0	0	0	0.9	0	0	0
Italian %	0	0	1	0	0	0	0	0	0	0
Portuguese %	0	0	0	0	0	0	0	0	1	0
Russian %	0	0	0	0	0	0	0.9	0	0	0
Spanish %	0.2	0	0	0	0	0	0	0	0	0

Characteristics	Shilluk	Shona	Siamese	Sidamo	Sindhi	Sinhalese	Slavic Muslims	Slovak	Slovene	Soga
Ethnic Groups: # present	10	4	5	9	5	3	3	9	5	11
Max % present	49	67	53	38	66	74	41	86	90	18
Religions: # present	8	9	11	9	12	12	6	8	4	8
Max % present	73	42	92	48	77	67	44	59	93	50
Beliefs: Anglican %	2	2	0	0	0	0	0	0	0	26
Buddhist %	0	0	92	0	0	67	0	0	0	0
Christian Total %	8	41	1	53	2	7	53	78	96	76
Hindu %	0	0	0	0	2	15	0	0	0	0
Jewish %	0	0	0	0	0	0	0	0	0	0
Islam %	73	0	4	32	97	8	42	0	0.4	7
Protestant Total %	2	14	0	0	0	0	4	15	0	0
Roman Catholic %	6	15	0	0	0	0	18	59	93	26
Traditional %	17	42	0.5	11	0	0	0	0	0	50
Official: Anglican	0	0	0	0	0	0	0	0	0	0
Buddhism	0	0	1	0	0	1	0	0	0	0
Christianism	0	0	0	0	0	0	0	0	0	0
Greek Orthodox	0	0	0	0	0	0	0	0	0	0
Hinduism	0	0	0	0	0	0	0	0	0	0
Islam	1	0	0	0	1	0	1	0	0	0
Luthren Evangelical	0	0	0	0	0	0	0	0	0	0
Monotheism	0	0	0	0	0	0	0	0	0	0
Orthodox	0	0	0	0	0	0	0	0	0	0
Languages: # present	7	7	7	11	8	2	1	2	2	10
Max % present	51	52	41	31	48	66	99	84	91	16
Number official	1	1	1	1	1	1	1	1	1	1
None official (1=yes)	0	0	0	0	0	0	0	0	0	0
Mother Tongue: Arabic %	51	0	0	0	0	0	0	0	0	0
Chinese (all) %	0	0	2	0	0	0	0	0	0	0
English %	0	6	0	0	0	0	0	0.3	0	0
French %	0	0	0	0	0	0	0	0.1	0	0
German %	0	0	0	0	0	0	0	0.1	0	0
Spanish %	0	0	0	0	0	0	0	0	0	0
Official: Arabic %	100	0	0	0	0	0	0	0	0	0
Chinese %	0	0	0	0	0	0	0	0	0	0
English %	0	81	0	0	0	0	0	0.5	0	100
French %	0	0	0	0	0	0	0	0	0	0
German %	0	0	0	0	0	0	0	0.5	0	0
Spanish %	0	0	0	0	0	0	0	0	0	0
Commercial: Arabic %	1	0	0	0	0	0	0	0	0	0
Chinese %	0	0	0	0	0	0	0	0	0	0
English %	1	1	1	1	1	1	1	0.1	1	1
French %	0	0	0	0	0	0	0	0	0	0
German %	0	0	0	0	0	0	0	0.3	0	0
Italian %	0	0	0	0	0	0	0	0	0	0
Portuguese %	0	0.2	0	0	0	0	0	0	0	0
Russian %	0	0	0	0	0	0	0	0.3	0	0
Spanish %	0	0	0	0	0	0	0	0	0	0

Characteristics	Somali	Somba	Songhai	Soninke	Sotho	Sotho North	Spanish	Sundanese	Suriname	Susu
Ethnic Groups: # present	4	5	9	10	6	9	6	4	4	5
...Max % present	93	66	42	36	54	24	55	39	84	39
Religions: # present	6	8	5	9	14	17	17	12	9	7
...Max % present	95	63	89	90	38	34	84	81	85	80
Beliefs: Anglican %	0	0	0	0	7	4	0.1	0	0	0
...Buddhist %	0	0	0	0	0	0	0	0.9	0	0
...Christian Total %	5	23	0.5	2	78	68	89	9	97	2
...Hindu %	0	0	0	0	0	0	0	2	0	0
...Jewish %	0	0	0	0	0.3	0.6	0.2	0	0.4	0
...Islam %	94	13	89	90	0.6	1	3	81	12	80
...Protestant Total %	0	20	0	0	24	13	0	5	85	0
...Roman Catholic %	0	63	9	7	22	8	84	4	0	5
...Traditional %	1	0	9	0	14	20	0	4	0	0
Official: Anglican	0	0	0	0	0	0	0	0	0	0
...Buddhism	0	0	0	0	0	0	0	0	0	0
...Christianity	0	0	0	0	0.4	0	0.4	0	0	0
...Greek Orthodox	0	0	0	0	0	0	0	0	0	0
...Hinduism	0	0	0	0	0	0	0	0	0	0
...Islam	0.9	0	0.7	0.1	0	0	0	1	0	0
...Luthren Evangelical	0	0	0	0	0	0	0	0	0	0
...Monotheism	0	0	0	0	0	0	0	0	0	0
...Orthodox	0	0	0	0	0	0	0	0	0	0
Languages: # present	4	10	7	8	7	10	3	10	2	6
...Max % present	91	26	42	41	49	25	80	42	86	40
...Number official	2	1	1	1	9	13	3	1	1	1
...None official (1=yes)	0	0	0.5	0	0	0	3	0	0	0
Mother Tongue: Arabic %	0	0	0	0	0	0	0	0	0	0
...Chinese (all) %	0	0	0	0	0	0	0	0	0	0
...English %	0	0	0	0	0	0	0.1	0	8	0
...French %	0	0	0.5	5	0	0	0.5	0	0	0
...German %	0	0	0	0	0	0	0	0	0	0
...Spanish %	0	0	0	0	0	0	46	0	0	0
Official: Arabic %	0	0	0	0	0	0	0.2	0	0	0
...Chinese %	0	0	0	0	0	0	0.9	0	0	0
...English %	0	0	0	6	100	100	0.6	0	0	0
...French %	0	100	100	88	0	0	0	0	0	100
...German %	0	0	0	0	0	0	0	0	0	0
...Spanish %	0	0	0	0	0	0	64	0	0	0
Commercial: Arabic %	1	0	0	0.1	0	0	0	0	0	0
...Chinese %	0	0	0	0.1	0	0	0.4	0	0	0
...English %	1	0	0	0.9	1	1	0	1	1	0
...French %	0	1	1	0	0	0	0	0	0	1
...German %	0	0	0	0	0	0	0	0	0	0
...Italian %	0.9	0	0	0	0	0	0	0	0	0
...Portuguese %	0	0	0	0	0	0	0.3	0	0	0
...Russian %	0	0	0	0	0	0	0	0	0	0
...Spanish %	0	0	0	0	0	0	0.6	0	0	0

Characteristics	Swahili	Swazi	Swedish	Swiss	Tahitian	Tai	Taiwanese (Dari)	Tajik	Tama	Tamang
Ethnic Groups: # present	5	6	2	4	6	6	3	6	11	7
Max % present	24	84	91	64	43	83	84	60	31	58
Religions: # present	12	6	7	6	7	10	10	5	8	10
Max % present	35	37	78	86	72	56	49	78	43	86
Beliefs: Anglican %	0	0	0	0	0	0	0	0	0	0
Buddhist %	0	0	0	0	3	56	43	0	0	8
Christian Total %	33	77	81	95	88	0.3	7	0	33	0.2
Hindu %	0	0	0	0	0	0	0	0	0	86
Jewish %	0	0	0.2	0.1	0	0	0	0	0	0
Islam %	35	0	0	0	0	6	0.5	87	43	3
Protestant Total %	0	37	79	9	72	0	0	0	9	0
Roman Catholic %	25	11	1	86	16	11	0.1	0	8	0
Traditional %	31	21	0	0	0.1	0	0	0	24	0.6
Official: Anglican	0	0	0	0	0	0	0	0	0	0
Buddhism	0	0	0	0	0	1	0	0	0	0
Christianism	0	0	0	0	0	0	0	0	0	0
Greek Orthodox	0	0	0	0	0	0	0	0	0	0
Hinduism	0	0	0	0	0	0	0	0	0	1
Islam	0	0	0	0	0	0	0	1	1	0
Luthren Evangelical	0	0	1	0	0	0	0	0	0	0
Monotheism	0	0	0	0	0	0	0	0	0	0
Orthodox	0	0	0	0	0	0	0	0	0	0
Languages: # present	10	2	2	0	3	5	0	0	7	0
Max % present	15	91	93	0	42	87	69	57	30	51
Number official	2	2	1	0	1	1	1	1	1	1
None official (1=yes)	0	0	0	0	0	0	0	0	0	0
Mother Tongue: Arabic %	0	0	0	0	0	0	0	0	30	0
Chinese (all) %	0	0	0	0	0	0	39	0	0	0
English %	0	0	0	0	0	0	0	0	0	0
French %	0	0	0	0	35	0	0	0	0	0
German %	0	0	0	0	0	0	0	0	0	0
Spanish %	0	0	0	0	0	0	0	0	0	0
Official: Arabic %	0	0	0	0	0	0	0	0	100	0
Chinese %	0	0	0	0	0	0	100	0	0	0
English %	97	100	0	0	0	0	0	0	0	0
French %	3	0	0	100	100	0	0	0	0	0
German %	0	0	0	100	0	0	0	0	0	0
Spanish %	0	0	0	0	0	0	0	0	0	0
Commercial: Arabic %	0	0	0	0	0	0	0	0	100	0
Chinese %	0	0	0	0	0	0	0	0	0	0
English %	1	1	1	1	1	1	1	0.5	1	1
French %	0	0	0	0	0	0	0	0	0	0
German %	0	0	0	100	0	0	0	0	0	0
Italian %	0	0	0	0	0	0	0	0	0	0
Portuguese %	0	0	0	0	0	0	0	0	0	0
Russian %	0	0	0	0	0	0	0	0.5	0	0
Spanish %	0	0	0	0	0	0	0	0	0	0

Characteristics	Tamil (Tubu)	Tatar	Teda	Teke	Tem-Kabre	Temne	Teso	Thai	Tharu	Tigre
Ethnic Groups: # present	3	8	11	12	6	9	11	7	7	6
Max % present	74	78	31	27	45	34	18	88	58	45
Religions: # present	12	6	8	9	7	7	8	10	10	5
Max % present	67	75	43	50	50	52	50	55	86	67
Beliefs: Anglican %	0	0	0	0	0	1	26	0	0	0
Buddhist %	67	0	0	0	0	0	0	55	0.2	0
Christian Total %	8	73	33	90	35	8	76	7	0	34
Hindu %	16	0	0	0	0	0	0	0	86	0
Jewish %	0	0.8	0	0	0	0	0	0	0	0
Islam %	8	15	43	1	12	39	7	7	3	60
Protestant Total %	0	4	9	28	9	2	26	0	0	0
Roman Catholic %	0	3	8	50	26	6	50	3	0.6	0
Traditional %	0	0	24	8	50	52	13	0	0	5
Official: Anglican	0	0	0	0	0	0	0	0	0	0
Buddhism	0	0	0	0	0	0	0	0	0	0
Christianism	0	0	0	0	0	0	0	0	0	0
Greek Orthodox	0	0	0	0	0	0	0	0	0	0
Hinduism	0	0	0	0	0	0	0	0	1	0
Islam	0	0	0	0	0	0	0	0	0	0
Luthren Evangelical	0	0	0	0	0	0	0	0	0	0
Monotheism	0	0	0	0	0	0	0	0	0	0
Orthodox	0	0	0	0	0	0	0	0	0	0
Languages: # present	2	4	7	4	11	12	10	6	10	7
Max % present	66	83	30	18	22	31	16	90	51	42
Number official	1	1	1	1	3	1	1	1	1	2
None official (1=yes)	0	0	0	0	0	0	0	0	0	0
Mother Tongue: Arabic %	0	0	30	0	0	0	0	0	0	2
Chinese (all) %	0	0	0	0	0	0	0	0	0	0
English %	0	0	0	0	0	0	0	0	0	0
French %	0	0	0	0	0	0	0	0	0	0
German %	0	0.2	0	0	0	0	0	0	0	0
Spanish %	0	0	0	0	0	0	0	0	0	0
Official: Arabic %	0	0	100	0	0	0	0	0	0	0
Chinese %	0	0	0	0	0	0	0	0	0	0
English %	0	0	0	0	0	100	100	0	0	0
French %	0	0	100	100	100	0	0	0	0	0
German %	0	0	0	0	0	0	0	0	0	0
Spanish %	0	0	0	0	0	0	0	0	0	0
Commercial: Arabic %	0	0	1	0	0	0	0	0	0	0
Chinese %	0	0	0	0	0	0	0	0	0	0
English %	1	0	0	0	0	1	1	1	1	0
French %	0	0	1	1	1	0	0	0	0	0
German %	0	0	0	0	0	0	0	0	0	0
Italian %	0	0	0	0	0	0	0	0	0	0.4
Portuguese %	0	0	0	0	0	0	0	0	0	0
Russian %	0	1	0	0	0	0	0	0	0	0
Spanish %	0	0	0	0	0	0	0	0	0	0

Characteristics	Tigrinya	Tikar	Tiv	Tonga	Tongan	Toros	Tribal	Tsimihety	Tsonga	Tswana
Ethnic Groups: # present	8	11	11	7	1	11	3	11	5	9
:Max % present	41	20	21	35	98	18	98	27	48	24
Religions: # present	5	8	9	9	7	8	8	10	7	17
:Max % present	7	34	45	34	43	50	87	47	48	34
Beliefs: Anglican %	0	0	0	0	0	26	0	0	0	4
:Buddhist %	0	0	0	0	0	0	0	0	0	0
:Christian Total %	44	52	49	69	93	76	12	50	32	68
:Hindu %	0	0	0	0	0	0	0	0	0	2
:Jewish %	0	0	0	0	0	0	0	0	0	0.6
:Islam %	45	22	45	0.3	0	7	0	3	13	1
:Protestant Total %	0	18	26	34	54	26	0	23	0.2	13
:Roman Catholic %	0	34	12	26	16	50	0.1	26	31	8
:Traditional %	8	25	6	27	0	13	87	47	48	20
Official: Anglican	0	0	0	0	0	0	0	0	0	0
:Buddhism	0	0	0	0	0	0	0	0	0	0
:Christianism	0	0	0	0	0	0	1	0	0	0
:Greek Orthodox	0	0	0	0	0	0	0	0	0	0
:Hinduism	0	0	0	0	0	0	0	0	0	0
:Islam	0	0	0	0	0	0	0	0	0	0
:Luthren Evangelical	0	0	0	0	0	0	0	0	0	0
:Monotheism	0	0	0	0	0	0	0	0	0	0
:Orthodox	0	0	0	0	0	0	0	0	0	0
Languages: # present	9	6	12	8	1	10	2	1	9	10
:Max % present	36	9	21	25	98	16	98	99	38	25
Number official	1	2	1	3	1	1	1	2	1	1
None official (1=yes)	0	0	0	0	0	0	0	0	0	3
Mother Tongue: Arabic %	0.8	0	0	0	0	0	0	0	0	0
:Chinese (all) %	0	0	0	0	0	0	0	0	0	0
:English %	0	0	0	1	0	0	0	0	0	9
:French %	0	0	0	0	0	0	0	0	0	0
:German %	0	0	0	0	0	0	0	0	0	0
:Spanish %	0	0	0	0	0	0	0	0	0	0
Official: Arabic %	1	0	0	0	0	0	0	0	0	0
:Chinese %	0	0	0	0	0	0	0	0	0	0
:English %	0	100	100	100	100	100	0	0	0.5	100
:French %	0	100	0	0	0	0	0	100	0	0
:German %	0	0	0	0	0	0	0	0	0	0
:Spanish %	0	0	0	0	0	0	0	0	0	0
Commercial: Arabic %	0.7	0	0	0	0	0	0	0	0	0
:Chinese %	0	0	0	0	0	0	0	0	0	0
:English %	0	1	1	1	1	1	1	0	1	1
:French %	0	1	0	0	0	0	0	1	0	0
:German %	0	0	0	0	0	0	0	0	0	0
:Italian %	0	0	0	0	0	0	0	0	0	0
:Portuguese %	0	0	0	0	0	0	0	0	0	0
:Russian %	0	0	0	0	0	0	0	0	0	0
:Spanish %	0	0	0	0	0	0	0	0	0	0

Characteristics	Tuareg	Tukolor	Tumbuka	Turkish	Turkmen	Tutsi	Tuvaluan	Twa	Uighur	Ukrainian
Ethnic Groups: # present	10	8	7	7	8	4	3	3	9	8
:Max % present	40	42	35	86	66	86	91	87	44	73
Religions: # present	6	5	9	9	6	7	5	6	4	4
:Max % present	78	92	34	96	86	68	91	67	51	75
Beliefs: Anglican %	0	0	0	0	0	0	0	0	0	0
:Buddhist %									18	0
:Christian Total %	4	4	69	4	7	77	94	76		87
:Hindu %	0	0	0	0	0	0	0	0	0	0.1
:Jewish %	0	0	0.3	0	0	0	0	0	0	0.9
:Islam %	78	92		94	91	5		6	51	1
:Protestant Total %	0.6	0	34	0.2	0.1	9	92	9	2	1
:Roman Catholic %		3	26	0.9		68	2	67		13
:Traditional %	18		27			13		14		
Official: Anglican	0	0	0	0	0	0	0	0	0	0
:Buddhism	0	0	0	0	0	0	0	0	0	0
:Christianism	0	0	0	0	0	0	0	0	0	0
:Greek Orthodox	0	0	0	0	0	0	0	0	0	0
:Hinduism	0	0	0	0	0	0	0	0	0	0
:Islam	0	0	0	0	0	0	0	0	0	0
:Luthren Evangelical	0	0	0	0	0	0	0	0	0	0
:Monotheism	0	0	0	0	0	0	0	0	0	0
:Orthodox	0	0	0	0	0	0	0	0	0	0
Languages: # present	8	7	8	2	6	1	2	1	4	2
:Max % present	42	49	25	90	64	98	97	99	50	68
:Number official	1	1	3	1	1	2		2	1	1
:None official (1=yes)	0	0	0	0	0	0	0	0	0	0
Mother Tongue: Arabic %	0.6									
:Chinese (all) %										
:English %										
:French %		11								
:German %										
:Spanish %										
Official: Arabic %										
:Chinese %									4	
:English %			100				96			
:French %	100	86				100		100		
:German %										
:Spanish %										
Commercial: Arabic %										
:Chinese %									1	
:English %			1	0.9			1			
:French %	1	14				1		1		
:German %				0.3						
:Italian %										
:Portuguese %		0.1								
:Russian %					0.6					0.7
:Spanish %		1								

Characteristics	Urdu	Uzbek	Vanuatuan	Vietna-mese	Wallon	White	Wolof	Xhosa	Yalunka	Yao
Ethnic Groups: # present	5	8	7	7	8	14	8	9	9	10
:Max % present	66	68	95	88	55	66	38	24	34	75
Religions: # present	12	3	10	10	8	24	5	17	7	8
:Max % present	77	85	37	55	79	36	92	34	52	49
Beliefs: Anglican %	0	0	14	0	0	2	0	4	1	0
::Buddhist %	0	0	0	55	0	0	0	0	0	3
::Christian Total %	2	8	76	8	79	68	5	68	8	0
::Hindu %	2	0	0	0	0	0.1	0	0.2	0	0
::Jewish %	0	0.7	0	0	0.3	0.2	0	0.6	0	0
::Islam %	97	87	0	0.3	0.3	2	92	1	39	26
::Protestant Total %	0	0	61	8	0	28	0	13	6	9
::Roman Catholic %	0	0	15	3	79	35	0	8	2	11
::Traditional %	0	0	0	0	0	0.6	3	20	52	14
Official: Anglican	0	0	0	0	0	0	0	0	0	0
::Buddhism	0	0	0	0	0	0	0	0	0	0
::Christianism	0	0	0	0	0	0	0	0	0	0
::Greek Orthodox	0	0	0	0	0	0	0	0	0	0
::Hinduism	0	0	0	0	0	0	0	0	0	0
::Islam	1	0.1	0	0	0	1	0	0	0	0
::Luthren Evangelical	0	0	0	0	0	0	0	0	0	0
::Monotheism	0	0	0	0	0	0	0	0	0	0
::Orthodox	0	0	0	0	0	0	0	0	0	0
Languages: # present	8	5	7	7	4	11	7	10	12	7
::Max % present	48	66	94	90	59	88	46	25	31	57
::Number official	1	1	2	1	3	1	1	13	1	1
::None official (1=yes)	0	0	0	0	0	0.7	0	0	0	0
Mother Tongue: Arabic %	0	0	0	0	0	0.1	0	0	0	0
::Chinese (all) %	0	0	0	0.8	0	0.3	0	0	0	0
::English %	0	0	0	0.1	0	66	0	9	0	48
::French %	0	0.1	0	0	0.6	0.5	0	0	0	0
::German %	0	0	0	0	0	0.4	0	0	0	0
::Spanish %	0	0	0	0	0	18	0	0	0	0
Official: Arabic %	0	0	0	0	0	0	0	0	0	0
::Chinese %	0	0	0	0.9	0	0	0	0	0	0
::English %	0	0	100	0.1	0	78	5	100	100	52
::French %	0	0	100	0	100	0	4	0	0	34
::German %	0	0	0	0	100	0	91	0	0	0
::Spanish %	0	0	0	0	0	15	0	0	0	0
Commercial: Arabic %	0	0	0	0	0	0	0	0	0	0
::Chinese %	0	0	0	0	0	0	0	0	0	0
::English %	1	0.1	1	1	1	1	1	1	1	0.5
::French %	0	0	0	1	1	0	0	0	0	0.5
::German %	0	0	0	0	0	0	0	0	0	0
::Italian %	0	0	0	0	0	0	0	0	0	0
::Portuguese %	0	0	0	0	0	0.1	0	0	0	0.1
::Russian %	0	0.9	0	0	0	0.1	0	0	0	0
::Spanish %	0	0	0	0	0	0.8	0	0	0	0

Characteristics	Yi-Miao	Yoruba	Yugoslav	Zambo	Zulu
Ethnic Groups: # present	16	11	6	5	9
Max % present	93	22	93	69	28
Religions: # present	8	9	8	11	15
Max % present	59	45	52	87	41
Beliefs: Anglican %	0	0	0	0	3
Buddhist %	6	0	0	92	0
Christian Total %		49	67		60
Hindu %	0.2	0	0.1	0	0.2
Jewish %	0	0	0.3	0	0
Islam %	0	44	36	5	12
Protestant Total %	2	26	28	87	11
Roman Catholic %	0	12			7
Traditional %	0.1	7			19
Official: Anglican	0	0	0	0	0
Buddhism	0	0	0	0	0
Christianism	0	0	0	0	0
Greek Orthodox	0	0	0	0	0
Hinduism	0	0	0	0	0
Islam	0	0	0	0	0
Luthren Evangelical	0	0	0	0	0
Monotheism	0	0	0	0	0
Orthodox	0	0	0	0	0
Languages: # present	8	12	2	3	9
Max % present	67	21	98	95	28
Number official	1	1	1	1	2
None official (1=yes)	0	0	0	0	0
Mother Tongue: Arabic %	0	0	0	0	0
Chinese (all) %	93	0	0	0	0
English %	0	0	0	0	8
French %	0	0	0	0	0
German %	0	0	0	0	0
Spanish %	0	0	95	95	0
Official: Arabic %	0	0	0	0	0
Chinese %	100	0	0	0	0
English %	0	98	97	0	88
French %	0	2	0	0	12
German %	0	0	0	0	0
Spanish %	0	0	0	100	0
Commercial: Arabic %	0	0	0	0	0
Chinese %	0	0	0	0	0
English %	1	1	0.8	1	0.9
French %	0	0	0	0	0.1
German %	0	0	1	0	0
Italian %	0	0	0	0	0
Portuguese %	0	0	0.8	0	0
Russian %	0	0	0	0	0
Spanish %	0	0		1	0

6

MINERAL RESOURCES ACROSS ETHNIC CULTURES

This chapter provides comparative statistics for a variety of variables covering each ethnic group's mineral resources. For a full discussion of the methodology used to generate these estimates, please refer to Chapter 1 which gives important caveats. This chapter first gives summary statistics of the variables reported: the number of countries/cultures for which each variable was available, simple averages, and weighted averages (by population); these averages can be used as benchmarks. Then a lengthy comparative table is presented which provides raw statistics across the ethnic groups defined in Chapter 1.

Most of the variables are self explanatory, though some merit commentary. All of the statistics should be considered as estimates which have undergone rounding and certain adjustments. First, across 44 minerals, each ethnic group is characterized as living in areas holding a given percent of the world's known reserves. A value of "0" should be interpreted as a negligible level or a very small percentage of known world reserves. These reserves may not be economically viable, so the measure reflects an exogenous presence, rather than a mining activity. For example, Araucanians reside in areas which contain 27 percent of the world's known reserves of copper. The sum of these percentages is then reported as "Total minerals: % sum." The number of minerals which are heavily mined are then given: "Number of Minerals." Finally, per capita oil reserves are estimated. Some ethnic groups do not reside in areas with these mineral resources.

Summary Statistics:
Mineral Resources

Characteristics	Number of Countries Covered	Number of Ethnic Groups Covered	Weighted Average by Pop 1994	Simple Average	Simple Standard Deviation
World Reserves %: Bauxite	234	426	1.46	0.43	2.02
: Antimony	234	426	11.75	1.73	8.70
: Barytes	234	426	9.21	1.00	4.33
: Beryllium	234	426	4.14	0.60	2.55
: Bismuth	234	426	4.94	0.69	3.23
: Boron	234	426	3.57	0.58	2.88
: Cadmium	234	426	1.98	0.45	1.36
: Chromium	234	426	1.25	1.04	7.72
: Cobalt	234	426	0.46	1.28	6.21
: Copper	234	426	0.97	0.47	1.96
: Fluorspar	234	426	2.83	0.85	3.21
: Gold	234	426	0.86	0.67	5.10
: Indium	234	426	2.88	0.46	1.97
: Ind. diamond	234	426	0.33	0.52	2.50
: Iron ore	234	426	2.38	0.32	1.14
: Kaolin	234	426	2.83	0.33	1.73
: Lead	234	426	3.22	0.47	1.69
: Lithium	234	426	0.87	0.24	2.89
: Magnesium	234	426	7.01	1.00	5.03
: Manganese	234	426	1.13	0.71	4.96
: Mercury	234	426	2.42	0.79	5.41
: Molybdenum	234	426	4.10	0.55	2.69
: Nickel	234	426	0.73	0.31	1.23
: Niobium	234	426	2.24	0.52	4.16
: Phosphate	234	426	1.09	0.40	2.37
: Platinium group	234	426	0.64	1.16	9.66
: Potash	234	426	1.02	0.26	1.86
: Rare minerals	234	426	12.38	1.62	8.61
: Rhenium	234	426	0.76	0.20	2.66
: Selenium	234	426	1.03	0.49	2.03
: Silver	234	426	0.76	0.13	0.95
: Sulphur	234	426	2.32	0.41	1.54
: Talc	234	426	1.75	0.16	1.47
: Tantalum	234	426	0.73	0.68	2.76
: Tellurium	234	426	0.88	0.52	2.11
: Tin	234	426	6.63	1.14	4.55
: Titanium A	234	426	6.11	0.90	3.42
: Titanium B	234	426	6.33	1.03	4.80
: Tungsten	234	426	10.30	1.48	7.49
: Uranium	234	426	0.82	0.18	0.60
: Vanadium	234	426	3.40	0.70	3.21
: Vermiculite	234	426	2.49	0.74	4.87
: Zinc	234	426	2.82	0.44	1.29
: Zirconium	234	426	1.59	0.50	3.13
Total minerals: % sum	234	426	137.43	29.15	83.01
Number of Minerals	234	426	13.72	3.23	6.32
Oil reserves (/cap bbl)	187	405	209233.49	287513.98	2850597.39

Characteristics	Abadkis	Abkhaz	Acholi	Afar	Afro-European	Akan	Albanian	Ambo	Amerind	Amerind-Mestizo
World Reserves %: Bauxite	0	0	0	0	9	0	0	0	0	0
Antimony	0	0	0	0	0	0	0	0	0.3	0
Barytes	0	0	0	0	0	0	0	0	0.4	0
Beryllium	0	0	4	0	0	0	0.3	0	7	7
Bismuth	0	0	0	0	0	0	0	0	3	0
Boron	0	0	0	0	0	0	0	0	6	1
Cadmium	0	0	0	0	0	0	0	0	0	0
Chromium	0	0	0	0	0	0	0	0	4	0
Cobalt	0	0	0	0	0	0	0	0	6	0
Copper	0	0	0	0	0	0	0	0	0.8	0
Fluorspar	0	0	0	0	0	0	0	0	0.3	0
Gold	0	0	0	0	0	0.1	0	0	0.3	0
Indium	0	0	0	0	0	0	0	0	0.5	0
Ind. diamond	0	0	0	0	0	0	0	0	0	0
Iron ore	2	0	0	0	0	0	0	0	3	0
Kaolin	0	0	0	0	0	0	0	0	4	0
Lead	0	0	0	0	0	0	0	0	2	0
Lithium	0	0	0	0	0	0	0	0	0	0
Magnesium	0	0	0	0	0	0	0.3	0	0.4	0
Manganese	0	0	0	0	0	0	0	0	3	0
Mercury	0	0	0	0	0	0	0	0	5	0
Molybdenum	0	0	0	0	0	0	0	0	0.1	0
Nickel	0	0	0	0	0	0	0	0	0	0
Niobium	0	0	0	0	0	0	0	0	0.7	0
Phosphate	0	0	0	0	0	0	0	0	0.2	0
Platinium group	0	0	0	0	0	0	0	0	0	0
Potash	0	0	0	0	0	0	0	0	1	0
Rare minerals	0	0	0	0	0	0	0	0	0	0
Rhenium	0	0	0	0	0	0	0	0	5	0
Selenium	0	0	0	0	0	0	0	0	10	0
Silver	0	0	0	0	0	0	0	0	5	0
Sulphur	0	0	0	0	0	0	0	0	2	0
Talc	0	0	0	0	0	0	0	0	0	0
Tantalum	0	0	0	0	0	0	0	0	1	0
Tellurium	0	0	0	0	0	0	0	0	0	0
Tin	0	0	0	0	0	0	0	0	0.3	0.4
Titanium A	0	0	0	0	0	0	0	0	0.7	0
Titanium B	0	0	0	0	0	0	0	0	0.2	0
Tungsten	0	0	0	0	0	0	0	0	3	0
Uranium	0	0	0	0	0	0	0	0	0	0
Vanadium	0	0	0	0	0	0	0	0	0.5	0
Vermiculite	0	0	0	0	0	0	0	0	0	0
Zinc	2	0	4	0	9	0.1	0.6	0	4	0
Zirconium	0	0	0	0	0	0	0	0	0.5	0
Total minerals: % sum	2	0	4	0	9	0.1	0.6	0	90	3
Number of Minerals	1	0	1	0	1	1	1	0	15	8
Oil reserves (/cap bbl)	0	0	0	0	0	30	30900	146000	444000	46900

Characteristics	Amhara	Ana-Ife	Andorran	Angolares	Anouis	Antandroy	Arab, other	Arab Berber	Arab Emirian	Arab Lebanese
World Reserves %: Bauxite							0.3			
Antimony				0.2			1			
Barytes										
Beryllium										
Bismuth										
Boron							0.3			
Cadmium										
Chromium				0.6						
Cobalt										
Copper							0.1			
Fluorspar							0.1			
Gold						0.5				
Ind. diamond										
Iron ore										
Kaolin										
Lead							0.2			
Lithium							0.5			
Magnesium										
Manganese										
Mercury							0.4			
Molybdenum										
Nickel										
Niobium										
Phosphate							4			
Platinium group								1		
Potash										
Rare minerals										
Rhenium										
Selenium										
Silver							1			
Sulphur										
Talc										
Tantalum										
Tellurium										
Tin				0.8						
Titanium A										
Titanium B										
Tungsten				0.8						
Uranium										
Vanadium										
Vermiculite										
Zinc										
Zirconium						0.3				
Total minerals: % sum				2		0.8	9	1		
Number of Minerals				3		2	2			
Oil reserves (/cap bbl)	0	0	0	0	7460	0	1530000	4500000	53800000	0

Characteristics	Arab Omani	Arab Palestin.	Arab Quatar	Arab Saudi	Arab Sudanic	Arab Total	Arauca-nian	Armenian	Assamese	Assyrian
World Reserves %: Bauxite	0	0	0	0	0	0.2	0	0	0	0
Antimony	0	0	0	0	0	1	0	0	0	0
Barytes	0	0	0	0	0	0	1	0	0	0
Beryllium	0	0	0	0	0	0	0	0.1	0	0
Bismuth	0	0	0	0	0	0.2	0	0	0	0
Boron	0	0	0	0	0	0	3	0	0	0
Cadmium	0	0	0	0	0	0	0	0	0	0
Chromium	0	0	0	0	0	0	0	0	0	0
Cobalt	0	0	0	0	0	0	0	0	0	0
Copper	0	0	0	0	0	0	27	0.1	0	0
Fluorspar	0	0	0	0	0	0	0	0	0	0
Gold	0	0	0	0	0	0	0	0.1	0	0
Indium	0	0	0	0	0	0.1	0	0	0	1
Ind. diamond	0	0	0	0	0	0	0	0	0	0
Iron ore	0	0	0	0	0	0.1	0	0	0	0
Kaolin	0	0	0	0	0	0.4	0	0.1	0	0
Lead	0	0	0	0	0	0	0	0.1	0	0
Lithium	0	0	0	0	0	0	58	0	0	0
Magnesium	0	0	0	0	0	0	0	0	0	0
Manganese	0	0	0	0	0	0	0	0	0	0
Mercury	0	0	0	0	0	0.3	0	0.1	0	0
Molybdenum	0	0	0	0	0	0	21	0.2	0	0
Nickel	0	0	0	0	0	0	0	0	0	0
Niobium	0	0	0	0	0	0	0	0	0	0
Phosphate	0	0	0	7	0	3	0	0	0	0
Platinium group	0	0	0	0	0	0	0	0	0	0
Potash	0	0	0	0	0	3	0.1	0	0	9
Rare minerals	0	0	0	0	0	0	53	0.2	0	0
Rhenium	0	0	0	0	0	0	23	0	0	0
Selenium	0	0	0	0	0	0	0	0	0	0
Silver	0	0	0	0	0	2	0	0.1	0	0
Sulphur	0	0	0	0	0	0	25	0	0	0
Talc	0	0	0	0	0	0	0	0	0	0
Tantalum	0	0	0	0	0	0	0	0	0	0
Tellurium	0	0	0	0	0	0	0	0	0	0
Tin	0	0	0	0	0	0	0	0	0	0
Titanium A	0	0	0	0	0	0	0	0	0	0
Titanium B	0	0	0	0	0	0	0	0	0	0
Tungsten	0	0	0	0	0	0	0	0	0	0
Uranium	0	0	0	0	0	0	0	0	0	0
Vanadium	0	0	0	0	0	0	0	0	0	0
Vermiculite	0	0	0	0	0	0	0	0	0	0
Zinc	0	0	0	0	0	0	0	0.1	0	0
Zirconium	0	0	0	0	0	0	0	0.1	0	0
Total minerals: % sum	0	0	0	7	0	7	210	0.3	0	1
Number of Minerals	0	0	0	1	0	2	9	1	0	2
Oil reserves (/cap bbl)	2670000	0	7630000	15700000	9800	3180000	21700	16000	0	5020000

Characteristics	Austrian	Avar	Aymara	Azande	Azerbai-jani	Bagirmi Sara	Bahraini	Bai	Bakhtiari	Bakongo
World Reserves %: Bauxite	0	0	0	0	0	0	0	0.7	0	0
Antimony	0	0	0.5	0	0	0	0	52	0	0
Barytes	0	0	0	0	0	0	0	24	0	0
Beryllium	0	0	7	1	0	0	0	0	0	0
Bismuth	0	0	1	0	0	0	0	19	0	0
Boron	0	0	2	0	0	0	0	8	0	0
Cadmium	0	0	0	3	0	0	0	3	0	0
Chromium	0	0	0	29	0	0	0	0	0	0
Cobalt	0	0	1	6	0	0	0	0	0	0
Copper	0	0	0	0	0	0	0	11	0	0
Fluorspar	0	0	0	0	0	0	0	0	0	0
Gold	0	0	3	1	0	0	0	9	0	0
Indium	0	0	0	1	0	0	0	1	0	0
Ind. diamond	0	0	0	0	0	0	0	5	0	0
Iron ore	0	0	0	0	0	0	0	1	0	0
Kaolin	0	0	0	0	0	0	0	9	0	0
Lead	0	0	1	0	0	0	0	0	0	0
Lithium	0	0	0	0	0	0	0	30	0	0
Magnesium	0.6	0	0	0	0	0	0	2	0	0
Manganese	0	0	0	0	0	0	0	8	0	0
Mercury	0	0	0	0.6	0.6	0	0	9	0.9	0
Molybdenum	0	0	1	0	0	0	0	2	0	0
Nickel	0	0	0	0	0	0	0	0	0	0
Niobium	0	0	0	0	0	0	0	2	0	0
Phosphate	0	0	0	0	0	0	0	0	0	0
Platinium group	0	0	0	0	0	0	0	3	0	0
Potash	0	0	0	7	0	0	0	51	0	0
Rare minerals	0	0	0	0	0	0	0	0	0	0
Rhenium	0	0	0	0	0	0	0	7	0	0
Selenium	0	0	0	0	0	0	0	0	0	0
Silver	0	0	0.9	5	0	0	0	0	0	0
Sulphur	0	0	0	0.2	0	0	0	7	0	0
Talc	0.4	0	0	0	0	0	0	0	0	0
Tantalum	0	0	4	0	0	0	0	0	0	0
Tellurium	0	0	0	0.1	0	0	0	0	0	0
Tin	0	0	1	0	0	0	0	25	0	0
Titanium A	0	0	1	0	0	0	0	15	0	0
Titanium B	0	0	0	0	0	0	0	15	0	0
Tungsten	0	0	0	0	0	0	0	45	0	0
Uranium	0	0	1	0	0	0	0	4	0	0
Vanadium	0	0	0	2	0	0	0	14	0	0
Vermiculite	0	0	0	0	0	0	0	0	0	0
Zinc	0	0	2	0	0.8	0	0	3	0	0
Zirconium	0	0	0	0	0	0	0	1	0	0
Total minerals: % sum	1	0	35	70	1	0	0	375	1	0
Number of Minerals	2	0	10	9	2	0	0	29	2	0
Oil reserves (/cap bbl)	11900	177000	15400	5460	63000	0	131000	19800	1470	146000

Characteristics	Balante	Baluchi	Bambara	Bamileke-Bamum	Banda	Bangi-Ngale	Bantu	Baoule	Bari	Bariba
World Reserves %: Bauxite	o	o	o	3	o	o	o	o	o	o
Antimony	o	o	o	o	o	o	o	o	o	o
Barytes	o	o	o	o	o	o	o	o	o	o
Beryllium	o	o	o	o	o	o	o	o	o	o
Bismuth	o	o	o	o	o	o	o	o	o	o
Boron	o	o	o	o	o	o	o	o	o	o
Cadmium	o	o	o	o	0.6	2	0.3	o	o	o
Chromium	o	o	o	o	o	o	o	o	o	o
Cobalt	o	o	o	o	o	4	o	o	o	o
Copper	o	o	o	o	1	41	1.0	o	o	o
Fluorspar	o	o	o	o	2	8	0.1	o	o	o
Gold	o	o	o	o	o	o	o	o	o	o
Indium	o	o	o	o	o	o	o	o	o	o
Ind. diamond	o	o	o	o	5	5	1	o	o	o
Iron ore	o	o	o	o	o	15	o	o	o	o
Kaolin	o	0.3	o	o	o	o	o	o	o	o
Lead	o	o	o	o	o	o	o	o	o	o
Lithium	o	o	o	o	o	o	o	o	o	o
Magnesium	o	o	o	o	o	o	o	o	o	o
Manganese	o	o	o	o	o	o	o	o	o	o
Mercury	o	o	o	o	0.2	0.8	0.2	o	o	o
Molybdenum	o	o	o	o	o	o	o	o	o	o
Nickel	o	o	o	o	o	o	o	o	o	o
Niobium	o	o	o	o	o	1	o	o	o	o
Phosphate	o	0.1	o	o	3	o	o	o	o	o
Platinum group	o	o	o	o	o	o	o	o	o	o
Potash	o	o	o	o	2	7	0.3	o	o	o
Rare minerals	o	o	o	o	0.1	8	o	o	o	o
Rhenium	o	o	o	o	o	0.3	0.2	o	o	o
Selenium	o	0.4	o	o	0.4	o	o	o	o	o
Silver	o	0.7	o	o	o	0.1	o	o	o	o
Sulphur	o	0.6	o	o	1	0.1	12	o	o	o
Talc	o	o	o	3	31	3	7	o	o	o
Tellurium	o	o	o	1	4	99	0	o	o	o
Total minerals: % sum	0	164000	0	31900	1390	12		7460	10900	3930
Number of Minerals						4540				
Oil reserves (/cap bbl)										

Characteristics	Barotze	Baskhir	Basque	Bassa	Batswana	Bayad	Beja	Belgian	Belorussian	Bemba
World Reserves %: Bauxite	0	0	0	0	0	0	0	0	0	0
Antimony	0	0	0	0	0	0	0	0	0	0
Barytes	0	0	0	0	0	0	0	0	0	0
Beryllium	0	0	0	0	0	0	0	0	0	0
Bismuth	0	0	0	0	0	0	0	0	0	0
Boron	0	0	0	0	0	0	0	0	0	0
Cadmium	0	0	4	0	0	0	0	0	0	0
Chromium	0	0	0	0	0	0	0	0	0	0
Cobalt	11	0	0	0	0	0	0	0	0	11
Copper	4	0	2	0	0.2	0.9	0	0	0	4
Fluorspar	0	0	0.8	0	0	21	0	0	0	0
Gold	0	0	0.3	0	0	0	0	0	0	0
Indium	0	0	0	0	0	0	0	0	0	0
Ind. diamond	0	0	0	0	13	0	0	0	0	0
Iron ore	0	0	0	0.8	0	0	0	0	0	0
Kaolin	0	0	0	0	0	0	0	0	0	0
Lead	0	0	0.4	0	0	0	0	0	0	0
Lithium	0	0	0	0	0	0	0	0	0	0
Magnesium	0	0	0	0	0	0	0	0	0	0
Manganese	0	0	0	0	0	0	0	0	0	0
Mercury	0	0	59	0	0	0	0	0	0	0
Molybdenum	0	0	0	0	0	0	0	0	0	0
Nickel	0	0	0	0	1	0	0	0	0	0
Niobium	0	0	0	0	0	0	0	0	0	0
Phosphate	0	0	0	0	0	0	0	0	0	0
Platinium group	0	0	0	0	0	0	0	0	0	0
Potash	0	0	0.3	0	0	0	0	0	0	0
Rare minerals	0	0	0	0	0	0	0	0	0	0
Rhenium	0	0	0	0	0	0	0	0	0	0
Selenium	4	0	0	0	0	0	0	0	0	4
Silver	9	0	0	0	0	0	0	0	0	9
Sulphur	0	0	4	0	0	0	0	0	0	0
Talc	0	0	0	0	0	0	0	0	0	0
Tantalum	0	0	0	0	0	0	0	0	0	0
Tellurium	0	0	0	0	0	0	0	0	0	0
Tin	0	0	0	0	0	0	0	0	0	0
Titanium A	0	0	0	0	0	0	0	0	0	0
Titanium B	0	0	0	0	0	0	0	0	0	0
Tungsten	0	0	0	0	0	0	0	0	0	0
Uranium	0	0	0	0	0	0	0	0	0	0
Vanadium	0	0	0	0	0	0	0	0	0	0
Vermiculite	0	0	0	0	0	0	0	0	0	0
Zinc	0	0	3	0	0	0	0	0	0	0
Zirconium	0	0	0	0	0	0	0	0	0	0
Total minerals: % sum	27	0	76	0.8	14	22	0	0	0	27
Number of Minerals	4	0	9	1	3	2	0	0	0	4
Oil reserves (/cap bbl)	0	.	575	0	0	0	10900	0	0	0

Characteristics	Bengali	Berber	Bete	Betsileo	Betsimi-Saraka	Bhutia	Bihari	Black	Black Amerind	Boa
World Reserves %: Bauxite	0	0	0	0	0	0	0	4	0	0
Antimony	0	0.9	0	0	0	0	0	1	0	0
Barytes	0	0.4	0	0	0	0	0	8	0	0
Beryllium	0	0	0	0	0	0	0	12	0	0
Bismuth	0	0	0	0	0	0	0	4	0	2
Boron	0	0	0	0	0	0	0	17	0	0
Cadmium	0	0	0	0	0	0	0	6	0	0
Chromium	0	0	0	0	0	0	0	5	0	4
Cobalt	0	0	0	0	0	0	0	0.7	0	0
Copper	0	0	0	0	0	0	0	8	0	41
Fluorspar	0	0	0	0	0	0	0	1	0	0
Gold	0	0	0	0.5	0.5	0	0	8	0	8
Indium	0	0	0	0	0	0	0	0.1	0	0
Ind. diamond	0	0	0	0	0	0	0	3	0	0
Iron ore	0	0	0	0	0	0	0	18	0	0
Kaolin	0	0	0	0	0	0	0	7	0	15
Lead	0	2	0	0	0	0	0	0.6	0	0
Lithium	0	0	0	0	0	0	0	4	0	0
Magnesium	0	0.1	0	0	0	0	0	1	0	0
Manganese	0	0.6	0	0	0	0	0	22	0	0
Mercury	0	0	0	0	0	0	0	1	0	0
Molybdenum	0	0	0	0	0	0	0	9	0	0
Nickel	0	0	0	0	0	0	0	6	0	0
Niobium	0	0	0	0	0	0	1	0.5	1	0
Phosphate	0	15	0	0	0	0	0	7	0	0
Platinum group	0	0	0	0	0	0	0	7	0	0
Potash	0	0	0	0	0	0	0	7	0	0
Rare minerals	0	0	0	0	0	0	0	5	0	0
Rhenium	0	0	0	0	0	0	0	4	0	0
Selenium	0	0	0	0	0	0	0	16	0	0.8
Silver	0	0	0	0	0	0	0	0.8	0	1
Sulphur	0	0	0	0	0	0	0	7	0	0
Talc	0	0	0	0	0	0	0	5	0	0
Tantalum	0	0	0	0	0	0	0	4	0	0
Tellurium	0	0	0	0	0	0	0	16	0	7
Tin	0	0	0	0	0	0	0	0.8	0	8
Titanium A	0	0	0	0	0	0	0	7	0	0.3
Titanium B	0	0	0	0	0	0	0	5	0	0
Tungsten	0	0	0	0	0	0	0	3	0	0
Uranium	0	0	0	0	0	0	0	19	0	0
Vanadium	0	0	0	0	0	0	0	3	0	0.1
Vermiculite	0	0	0	0	0	0	0	1	0	0
Zinc	0	0	0	0	0	0	0	26	0	3
Zirconium	0	0	0	0.3	0.3	0	0	6	0	0
Total minerals: % sum	0	22	0	0.8	0.8	0	0.7	301	1	99
Number of Minerals	0	4	0	2	2	0	1	25	1	12
Oil reserves (/cap bbl)	938	124000	7460	0	0	0	0	135000	57	4540

Characteristics	Bobo	Bounty Mutineers	Brazilian	Breton	Bubi	Bulgarian	Bullom	Bura	Burman	Bush Negro
World Reserves %: Bauxite	0	0	0	0	0	0	0.6	0	0	2
Antimony	0	0	0.2	1	0	0	0	0	0	0
Barytes	0	0	0	0	0	0	0	0	0	0
Beryllium	0	0	0	0	0	0	0	0	0	0
Bismuth	0	0	0	0	0	0	0	0	0	0
Boron	0	0	0	0	0	0	0	0	0	0
Cadmium	0	0	0	0	0	0	0	0	0	0
Chromium	0	0	0	0	0	3	0	0	0	0
Cobalt	0	0	0.6	4	0	4	0	0	0	0
Copper	0	0	0	5	0	0	0	0	0	0
Fluorspar	0	0	0	1	0	0	0	0	0	0
Gold	0	0	0	0	0	0	0	0	0	0
Indium	0	0	0	0	0	0	0	0	0	0
Ind. diamond	0	0	0	0	0	0	0	0	0	0
Iron ore	0	0	0	0	0	0	0	2	0	0
Kaolin	0	0	0	0	0	0	0	0	0	0
Lead	0	0	0	0	0	0	0	0	0	0
Lithium	0	0	0	0	0	0	0	0	0	0
Magnesium	0	0	0	0	0	0	0	0	0	0
Manganese	0	0	0	0.2	0	0	0	0	0	0
Mercury	0	0	0	0	0	0	0	0	0	0
Molybdenum	0	0	0	0	0	0	0	0	0	0
Nickel	0	0	0	0	0	0	0	0	0	0
Niobium	0	0	0	0.7	0	0	0	0	0	0
Phosphate	0	0	0	0	0	0	0	0	0	0
Platinum group	0	0	0	0	0	0	0	0	0	0
Potash	0	0	0	0	0	0	0	0	0	0
Rare minerals	0	0	0	0	0	0	0	0	0	0
Rhenium	0	0	0	0	0	0	0	0	0	0
Selenium	0	0	0	0	0	0	0	0	0	0
Silver	0	0	0	0	0	0.2	0	0	0	0
Sulphur	0	0	0	0	0	0	0	0	0	0
Talc	0	0	0	0	0	0	0	0	0	0
Tantalum	0	0	0	0.8	0	0	0	0	0	0
Tellurium	0	0	0	0	0	0	0	0	0	0
Tin	0	0	0.8	0	0	0	0.5	12	0.3	0
Titanium A	0	0	0.7	0	0	0	0.2	0.3	0.6	0
Titanium B	0	0	0	0	0	0	0	0	0	0
Tungsten	0	0	0	0	0	0	0	0	0	0
Uranium	0	0	0	0	0	0	0	0	0	0
Vanadium	0	0	0	0	0	0	0	0	0	0
Vermiculite	0	0	0	0	0	0	0	0	0	0
Zinc	0	0	2	0	0	0	1	0	0	0.2
Zirconium	0	0	0	0	0	0	0	0	0	0
Total minerals: % sum	0	0	3	14	0	8	5	14	0.9	0.9
Number of Minerals			3	7		3	4	3	2	
Oil reserves (/cap bbl)	0	.	0	3090	9130	33	0	168000	0	0

Characteristics	Bushman	Capver-dien	Caroli-nians	Catalan	Chahar Aimak	Chamba	Chamorro	Chiga	Chin	Chinese
World Reserves %: Bauxite	0	0	0	0	0	3	0	0	0	0
Antimony	0	0	0	0	0	0	0	0	0	2
Barytes	0	0	0	0	0	0	0	0	0	0.4
Beryllium	0	0.3	0	0	0	0	0	4	0	0.6
Bismuth	0	0	0	0	0	0	0	0	0	0.3
Boron	0	0	0	4	0	0	0	0	0	1
Cadmium	0.2	0	0	0	0	0	0	0	0	0
Chromium	0	0	0	0	0	0	0	0	0	0
Cobalt	0	0	0	0	0	0	0	0	0	1
Copper	0	0.9	0	0	0	0	0	0	0	0.8
Fluorspar	0	0	0	3	0	0	0	0	0	1
Gold	0	0	0	0	0	0	0	0	0	0
Indium	0	0	0	0	0	0	0	0	0	0.5
Ind. diamond	13	0	0	0	0	0	0	0	0	0.3
Iron ore	0	0	0	0	0	0	0	0	0	1
Kaolin	0	0	0	0.8	0	0	0	0	0	1
Lead	0	0	0	0	0	0	0	0	0	0
Lithium	0	0	0	0	0	0	0	0	0	0.1
Magnesium	0	0	0	0.4	0	0	0	0	0	0
Manganese	0	0	0	0	0	0	0	0	0	0.2
Mercury	0	0	0	59	0	0	0	0	0	0
Molybdenum	0	0	0	0	0	0	0	0	0	0.3
Nickel	1	0	0	0	0	0	0	0	0	0
Niobium	0	0	0	0	0	0	0	0	0	0.2
Phosphate	0	0	0	0	0	0	0	0	0	0
Platinium group	0	0	0	0.3	0	0	0	0	0	0.1
Potash	0	0	0	0	0	0	0	0	0	0
Rare minerals	0	0	0	0	0	0	0	0	0	0.7
Rhenium	0	0	0	0	0	0	0	0	0	0
Selenium	0	0	0	0	0	0	0	0	0	0.5
Silver	0	0	0	4	0	0	0	0	0	0
Sulphur	0	0	0	0	0	0	0	0	0	1
Talc	0	0	0	0	0	0	0	0	0	1
Tantalum	0	0	0	0	2	0	0	0	0	1
Tellurium	0	1	0	0	0	0	0	0	0	0.9
Tin	0	1	0	2	0	0	0	0	0.3	0
Titanium A	0	0	0	0	0	0	0	0	0	0.8
Titanium B	0	0	0	0	0	0	0	0	0	2
Tungsten	0	0	0	0	0	0	0	0	0.6	8
Uranium	0	0	0	0	0	0	0	0	0	1
Vanadium	0	0	0	0	0	0	0	0	0	0.5
Vermiculite	0	0	0	0	0	0	0	0	0	0
Zinc	0	0	0	3	0	0	0	0	0	0.4
Zirconium	0	0	0	0	0	0	0	0	0	0
Total minerals: % sum	14	3	0	77	2	3	0	4	0.9	52
Number of Minerals	3	4	0	9	1	1	0	1	2	6
Oil reserves (/cap bbl)	0	0	.	575	0	31900	.	0	0	63800

Characteristics	Chinese Mainland	Chokwe	Chuang	Chuvash	Circassian	Coloured	Comorian	Creole	Croatian	Czech
World Reserves %: Bauxite	0	0	0.7	0	0	0	0	0.3	0	0
: Antimony	0	0	52	0	2	6	0	0	0	0
: Barytes	0	0	24	0	2	0	0	0	0	0
: Beryllium	0	1	0	0	0	4	0	0	0	0
: Bismuth	0	0	19	0	0	0	0	0	0	0.1
Boron	0	0	8	0	28	0	0	0	0	0
: Cadmium	0	2	3	0	0	7	0	0	0	0.3
Chromium	0	0	0	0	0	71	0	0	0	0
Cobalt	0	26	0	0	0.5	0.6	0	0	0	0
Copper	0	5	0	0	0	0.6	0	0	0	0.1
Fluorspar	0	0	11	0	0	13	0	0	0	0
Gold	0	0	0	0	0	47	0	0	0	0.1
Indium	0	0	9	0	0	0	0	0	0	0
Ind. diamond	0	10	1	0	0	0	0	0	0	0.6
Iron ore	0	0	5	0	0	4	0	0	0	0
Kaolin	0	0	1	0	0	2	0	0	0	0.2
Lead	0	0	9	0	0	3	0	0	0	0
Lithium	0	0	0	0	0	0	0	0	0	0
Magnesium	0	0	30	0	2	0.2	0	0	0	0.2
Manganese	0	0	2	0	2	45	0	0	0	0.2
Mercury	0	0	8	0	0	0	0	0	0	0
Molybdenum	0	0	9	0	0	0	0	0	0	0
Nickel	0	0	2	0	0.1	5	0	0	0	0
Niobium	0	0.5	0	0	0	0	0	0	0	0.2
Phosphate	0	0	2	0	0.1	20	0	0	0	0
Platinium group	0	0	0	0	0	89	0	0	0	0.3
Potash	0	0	51	0	0	0	0	0	0	0
Rare minerals	0	0	0	0	0	0	0	0	0	0.1
Rhenium	0	0	0	0	0	0	0	0	0	0
Selenium	0	6	7	0	0	0	0	0	0	0
Silver	0	0	0	0	0	0	0	0	0	1
Sulphur	0	0	0	0	0	0	0	0	0	0
Talc	0	4	25	0	0	0	0	0	0	0
Tantalum	0	5	15	0	0	0	0	0	0	0.2
Tellurium	0	0.2	45	0	0	0	0	0	0	0
Tin	0	0	2	0	2	0.5	0	0	0	0.3
Titanium A	0	0	14	0	0	18	0	0	0	0
Titanium B	0	0.1	0	0	0	4	0	0	0	0.3
Tungsten	0	0	3	0	0	0	0	0	0	0
Uranium	0	0	0	0	0	20	0	0	0	0.1
Vanadium	0	0	0	0	0	40	0	0	0	0
Vermiculite	0	2	0	0	0	2	0	0	0	0.3
Zinc	0	0	0	0	0	28	0	0	0	0
Zirconium	0	0	0	0	0	4	0	0	0	0.2
Total minerals: % sum	0	63	375	0	39	428	0.1	0.3	0	5.0
Number of Minerals	0	8	29	0	6	23	0.1	0.1	0	0.7
Oil reserves (/cap bbl)	0	56600	19800	.	7180	0	0	0	183	4160

Characteristics	Dagestani	Dai	Damara	Dan	Danish	Dinka	Dogon	Dong	Dravidian	Duala
World Reserves %: Bauxite	0	0.7	0	0	0	0	0	0.7	4	0
Antimony	0	52	0	0	0	0	0	52	0	0
Barytes	0	24	0	0	0	0	0	24	18	0
Beryllium	0	0	0	0	0	0	0	0	17	0
Bismuth	0	19	0	0	0	0	0	19	0	0
Boron	0	8	0	0	0	0	0	8	0	0
Cadmium	0	3	0	0	0	0	0	3	3	0
Chromium	0	0	0	0	0	0	0	0	4	0
Cobalt	0	0	0	0	0	0	0	0	0.5	0
Copper	0	1	1	0	0	0	0	1	0	0
Fluorspar	0	1	0	0	0	0	0	1	0	0
Gold	0	0	0	0	0	0	0	0	0	0
Indium	0	9	0	0	0	0	0	9	0	0
Ind. diamond	0	1	0	0.1	0	0	0	1	0	0
Iron ore	0	5	0	0	0	0	0	5	5	0
Kaolin	0	1	0	0	0	0	0	1	5	0
Lead	0	9	0	0	0	0	0	9	3	0
Lithium	0	0	0	0	0	0	0	0	0	0
Magnesium	0	30	0	0	0	0	0	30	1	0
Manganese	0	2	0	0	0	0	0	2	2	0
Mercury	0	8	0	0	0	0	0	8	0	0
Molybdenum	0	9	0	0	0	0	0	9	0	0
Nickel	0	2	0	0	0	0	0	2	0	0
Niobium	0	0	0	0	0	0	0	0	0	0
Phosphate	0	2	0	0	0	0	0	2	0	0
Platinium group	0	0	0	0	0	0	0	0	0	0
Potash	0	3	0	0	0	0	0	3	3	0
Rare minerals	0	51	0	0	0	0	0	51	0	0
Rhenium	0	0	0	0	0	0	0	0	0	0
Selenium	0	0	0	0	0	0	0	0	0	0
Silver	0	7	1	0	0	0	0	7	0.8	0
Sulphur	0	0	0	0	0	0	0	0	0	0
Talc	0	0	0	0	0	0	0	0	0	0
Tantalum	0	0	0	0	0.1	0	0	0	1	0
Tellurium	0	0	0	0	0	0	0	0	0	0
Tin	0	25	0	0	0	0	0	25	0	0
Titanium A	0	15	0	0	0	0	0	15	15	0
Titanium B	0	15	0	0	0	0	0	15	5	0
Tungsten	0	45	0	0	0	0	0	45	0	0
Uranium	0	2	4	0	0	0	0	2	2	0
Vanadium	0	14	0	0	0	0	0	14	0	0
Vermiculite	0	0	0	0	0	0	0	0	7	0
Zinc	0	0	0	0	0	0	0	0	4	0
Zirconium	0	3	3	0	0	0	0	3	4	0
Total minerals: % sum	0	375	6	0.2	0.1	0	0	375	101	0
Number of Minerals	0	29	3	3	1	0	0	29	19	0
Oil reserves (/cap bbl)	177000	19800	0	6070	147000	10900	0	19800	6740	9130

Characteristics	Duala-Landa-B.	Dujia	Dutch	Dyola	Edo	Egyptian	English	Estonian	Euro-nesian	European
World Reserves %: Bauxite	3	0.7	0	0	0	0	0	0	0	0.2
:Antimony	0	52	1	0	0	0	0	0	0	0.3
:Barytes	0	24	2	0	0	0	0	0	0	0.5
:Beryllium	0	0	4	0	0	0	0	0	0	0.7
:Bismuth	0	19	0	0	0	0	0	0	0	0.2
:Boron	0	8	1	0	0	0	0	0	0	0.1
:Cadmium	0	3	0	0	0	0	0	0	0	0.2
:Chromium	0	0	1	0	0	0	0	0	0	0.5
:Cobalt	0	0	0	0	0	0	0	0	0	0.1
:Copper	0	0	1	0	0	0	0	0	0	0.6
:Fluorspar	0	1	0.3	0	0	0	0	0	0	0
:Gold	0	1	0	0	0	0	0.8	0	0	40
:Indium	0	0	6	0	0	0	0	0	0	0.1
:Ind. diamond	0	9	21	0	0	0	0	0	0	1
:Iron ore	0	1	0.5	0	0	0	9	0	0	0.2
:Kaolin	0	5	0.6	0	0	0	0	0	0	0
:Lead	0	1	8	0	0	0	0	0	0	1
:Lithium	0	0	6	0	0	0	0	0	0	2.4
:Magnesium	0	9	0.9	0	0	0	0	0	0	0.1
:Manganese	0	0	0	0	0	0	0	0	0	0.6
:Mercury	0	30	0	0	0	0	0	0	0	0.2
:Molybdenum	0	2	6	0	0	0	0	0	0	0.1
:Nickel	0	8	1	0	0	0	0	0	0	2
:Niobium	0	9	0	0	2	0	0	0	0	0.1
:Phosphate	0	2	2	0	0	0	0	0	0	0.5
:Platinium group	0	0	0.3	0	0	0	0	0	0	0.1
:Potash	0	2	35	0	0	0	0	0	0	0.2
:Rare minerals	0	0	0.8	0	0	0	0	0	0	0.3
:Rhenium	0	3	1	0	0	0	0.3	0	0	0
:Selenium	0	51	0	0	0	0	0	0	0	0
:Silver	0	0	8	0	0	0	0	0	0	2
:Sulphur	0	0	0	0	0	0	0	0	0	0.1
:Talc	0	7	9	0	0	0	0	0	0	0
:Tantalum	0	0	0	0	0	0	0	0	0	0
:Tellurium	0	0	5	0	0	0	0	0	0	0
:Tin	0	25	0.3	0	12	0	1	0	0	0
:Titanium A	0	15	0.8	0	0.3	0	0	0	0	0
:Titanium B	0	15	10	0	0	0	0	0	0	0
:Tungsten	0	45	0	0	0	0	3	0	0	0
:Uranium	0	0	8	0	0	0	0	0	0	0.3
:Vanadium	0	14	0	0	0	0	0	0	0	0
:Vermiculite	0	0	0	0	0	0	0	0	0	0
:Zinc	0	3	1	0	0	0	0	0	0	2
:Zirconium	0	1	1	0	0	0	0	0	0	0
Total minerals: % sum	3	375	187	0	14	0	15	0	0	40
Number of Minerals	1	29	23	0	3	0	5	0	0	6
Oil reserves (/cap bbl)	31900	19800	141000	0	168000	111000	71600	0	0	63400

Characteristics	Ewa-Adja	Ewe	Fang	Fijian	Finnish	Fleming	Fon	Forros	French	Fulani
World Reserves %: Bauxite	0	0	2	0	0	0	0	0	0.2	3
:Antimony	0	0	0	0	0	0	0	0	1	0
:Barytes	0	0	0	0	0	0	0	0	0.5	0
:Beryllium	0	0	0	0	0	0	0	0	2	0
:Bismuth	0	0	0	0	0	0	0	0	0.2	0
:Boron	0	0	0	0	0	0	0	0	0.4	0
:Cadmium	0	0	0	0	0.1	0	0	0	0.5	0
:Chromium	0	0	0	0	0.27	0	0	0	8	0
:Cobalt	0	0	0	0	0	0	0	0	2	0
:Copper	0	0	0	0	0.2	0	0	0	1	0
:Fluorspar	0	0	0	0	0	0	0	0	9	0
:Gold	0	0	0.9	0	0.2	0	0	0	0	0
:Indium	0	0	0	0	0.2	0	0	0	9	0
:Ind. diamond	0	0	0	0	0.1	0	0	0	1	0
:Iron ore	0	0	0	0	0	0	0	0	0	0.9
:Kaolin	0	0	0	0	0	0	0	0	6	0
:Lead	0	0	0	0	0.3	0	0	0	1	0
:Lithium	0	0	0	0	0	0	0	0	1	0
:Magnesium	0	0	0	0	0.3	0	0	0	2	0
:Manganese	0	0.1	0	0	0	0	0	0	8	0
:Mercury	0	0	0	0	0.1	0	0	0	4	0
:Molybdenum	0	0	0	0	0.1	0	0	0	0.1	0
:Nickel	0	0	0	0	0.1	0	0	0	2	0
:Niobium	0	0	0	0	0	0	0	0	0	0
:Phosphate	0	0	0	0	0.6	0	0	0	2	7
:Platinium group	0	0	0	0	0	0	0	0	0	0
:Potash	0	0	0	0	0.1	0	0	0	2	0
:Rare minerals	0	0	0	0	0	0	0	0	0	0
:Rhenium	0	0	0	0	0	0	0	0	0.8	0
:Selenium	0	0	0	0	0	0	0	0	0.4	0
:Silver	0	0	0	0	0	0	0	0	0.1	0
:Sulphur	0	0	0	0	0	0	0	0	2	0
:Talc	0	0	0	0	0	0	0	0	0	0
:Tantalum	0	0	0	0	0	0	0	0	2	0
:Tellurium	0	0	0	0	0	0	0	0	0	0
:Tin	0	0	0.1	0	0	0	0	0	2	2
:Titanium A	0	0	0	0	0	0	0	0	0	0
:Titanium B	0	0	0	0	0	0	0	0	2	0
:Tungsten	0	0	0	0	0.1	0	0	0	0	0
:Uranium	0	0	0	0	0.05	0	0	0	0	0
:Vanadium	0	0	0	0	0	0	0	0	2	0
:Vermiculite	0	0	0	0	0	0	0	0	0	0
:Zinc	0	0.1	0	0	0.1	0	0	0	2	2
:Zirconium	0	0	0	0	0	0	0	0	0	0
Total minerals: % sum	0	0.1	3	0	5	0	0	0	40	12
Number of Minerals	0	1	3	0	4	0	0	0	9	2
Oil reserves (/cap bbl)	0	30	106000	0	1360	0	3930	0	24100	97900

Characteristics	Fur	Ga-Adangme	Gagauz	Galician	Ganda	Garifuna	Gbaya	Georgian	German	Gibraltarian
World Reserves %: Bauxite	0	0	0	0	0	0	0	0	0	0
Antimony	0	0	0.9	0	0	0	0	0.1	0.7	0
Barytes	0	0	0.9	0	0	0	0	0.1	0.9	0
Beryllium	0	0	0.04	0	4	0	0	0	0	0
Bismuth	0	0	0	4	0	0	0	0	0.2	0
Boron	0	0	14	0	0	0	0	0.9	0	0
Cadmium	0	0	0.3	0	0	0	0	0	0	0
Chromium	0	0	0	0	0	0	0	0	0.1	0
Cobalt	0	0	0	0	0	0	0	0	0	0
Copper	0	0	0	3	0	0	0	0	0	0
Fluorspar	0	0	0	0	0	0	0	0	0	0
Gold	0	0	0	0	0	0	0	0	0	0
Indium	0	0	0	0	0	0	0	0	0.1	0
Ind. diamond	0	0	0	0	0	0	0	0	0	0
Iron ore	0	0	0	0	0	0	0	0	0.2	0
Kaolin	0	0	1	0.8	0	0	0	0	0.1	0
Lead	0	0	0	0.3	0	0	0	0	0	0
Lithium	0	0	0	0	0	0	0	0	0.4	0
Magnesium	0	0.1	0	0.4	0	0	0	0	0.1	0
Manganese	0	0	1	59	0	0	0	0.1	0.1	0
Mercury	0	0	0	0	0	0	0	0.1	0.1	0
Molybdenum	0	0	0	0	0	0	0	0	0	0
Nickel	0	0	0	0	0	0	0	0	0.1	0
Niobium	0	0	0	0	0	0	0	0	0.2	0
Phosphate	0	0	0	0.3	0	0	0	0	0	0
Platinium group	0	0	0	0	0	0	0	0	0.4	0
Potash	0	0	0	0	0	0	0	0	0	0
Rare minerals	0	0	0	0	0	0	0	0	0	0
Rhenium	0	0	0	0	0	0	0	0	5	0
Selenium	0	0	0	0	0	0	0	0	0	0
Silver	0	0	0	0	0	0	0	0	0.1	0
Sulphur	0	0	0	4	0	0	0	0	0	0
Talc	0	0	0	0	0	0	0	0	0.1	0
Tantalum	0	0	0	0	0	0	0.6	0	0	0
Tellurium	0	0	0	0	0	0	0	0	0.2	0
Tin	0	0	1	0	0	0	0	0.1	0.2	0
Titanium A	0	0	0	0	0	0	0	0	0	0
Titanium B	0	0	0	0	0	0	0	0	0	0
Tungsten	0	0	0	0	0	0	0	0	0.1	0
Uranium	0	0	0	0	0	0	0	0	0.4	0
Vanadium	0	0	0	0	0	0	0	0	0.1	0
Vermiculite	0	0	0	0	0	0	0	0	0.3	0
Zinc	0	0	0	3	0	0	0	0	0.4	0
Zirconium	0	0	0	0	0	0	0	0	0.2	0
Total minerals: % sum	0	0.1	19	77	4	0	0.6	0.2	5	0
Number of Minerals	0	1	3	9	1	0	1	5	25	0
Oil reserves (/cap bbl)	10900	30	3490	575	0	0	0	239	7220	0

Characteristics	Gilaki	Gilber-tese	Gio	Gisu	Gola	Grebo	Greek	Green-landic	Grosi	Guiana Chinese
World Reserves %: Bauxite							20			
Antimony							0.1			
Barytes				4						
Beryllium							0.1			
Bismuth							0.2			
Boron							0.1			
Cadmium							0.0			
Chromium										
Cobalt										
Copper										
Fluorspar										
Gold										
Indium							0.1			
Ind. diamond							0.4			
Iron ore			0.8		0.8	0.8	0.1			
Kaolin							0.1			
Lead							0.1			
Lithium							1			
Magnesium							0.1			
Manganese										
Mercury										
Molybdenum							0.1			
Nickel										
Niobium										
Phosphate										
Platinium group							0.7			
Potash							0.0			
Rare minerals										
Rhenium										
Selenium							0.2			
Silver							0.2			
Sulphur										
Talc							0.1			
Tantalum										
Tellurium										
Tin							0.2			
Titanium A										
Titanium B										
Tungsten										
Uranium										
Vanadium										
Vermiculite										
Zinc	0.9						0.2			
Zirconium										
Total minerals: % sum	1		0.8	4	0.8	0.8	8			
Number of Minerals	2		1	1	1	1	4			
Oil reserves (/cap bbl)	1470	0	0	0	0	0	6320		0	

Characteristics	Guianese Creole	Gurage	Gurma	Gurung	Gypsy	Han Chinese	Hani	Hausa	Haya	Hazara-Dari
World Reserves %: Bauxite	0	0	0	0	0.1	0.7	0.7	0	0	0
Antimony	0	0	0	0	0	52	52	0	0	0
Barytes	0	0	0	0	0	24	24	0	0	0
Beryllium	0	0	0	0	0	0	0	0	0	0
Bismuth	0	0	0	0	0	0	0	0	0	0
Boron	0	0	0	0	0	19	19	0	0	0
Cadmium	0	0	0	0	0	8	8	0	0	0
Chromium	0	0	0	0	0	3	3	0	0	0
Cobalt	0	0	0	0	0	0	0	0	0	0
Copper	0	0	0	0	0	0	0	0	0	0
Fluorspar	0	0	0	0	0	0	0	0	0	0
Gold	0	0	0	0	0	11	11	0	0	0
Indium	0	0	0	0	0	0	0	0	0	0
Ind. diamond	0	0	0	0	1	9	9	0	0	0
Iron ore	0	0	0	0	0	1	1	0	0.5	0
Kaolin	0	0	0	0	0	5	5	0	0	0
Lead	0	0	0	0	0	1	1	0	0	0
Lithium	0	0	0	0	0	0	0	0	0	0
Magnesium	0	0	0	0	0	9	9	0	0	0
Manganese	0	0	0	0	0	0	0	0	0	0
Mercury	0	0	0	0	0	30	30	0	0	0
Molybdenum	0	0	0	0	0	2	2	0	0	0
Nickel	0	0	0	0	0	8	8	0	0	0
Niobium	0	0	0	0	0	9	9	0	0	0
Phosphate	0	0	0	0	0	2	2	0	0	0
Platinum group	0	0	0	0	0	0	0	0	0	0
Potash	0	0	0	0	0	2	2	0	0	0
Rare minerals	0	0	0	0	0	0	0	0	0	0
Rhenium	0	0	0	0	0	2	2	0	0	0
Selenium	0	0	0	0	0	0	0	0	0	0
Silver	0	0	0	0	0	3	3	0	0	2
Sulphur	0	0	0	0	0	51	51	0	0	0
Talc	0	0	0	0	0	0	0	0	0	0
Tantalum	0	0	0	0	0	0	0	10	0	0
Tellurium	0	0	0	0	0	0	0	0	0	0
Tin	0	0	0	0	0	7	7	0.2	0	0
Titanium A	0	0	0	0	0	25	25	0	0	0
Titanium B	0	0	0	0	0	15	15	0	0	0
Tungsten	0	0	0	0	0	15	15	0	0	0
Uranium	0	0	0	0	0.3	45	45	1	0	0
Vanadium	0	0	0	0	0	2	2	0	0	0
Vermiculite	0	0	0	0	0	14	14	0	0	0
Zinc	0	0	0	0	0	3	3	0	0	0
Zirconium	0	0	0	0	0	1	1	0	0	0
Total minerals: % sum	0	0	0.3	0	3	375	375	13	0.5	2
Number of Minerals	0	0	0	0	2	29	29	3	1	1
Oil reserves (/cap bbl)	.	0	10	0	31200	19800	19800	139000	0	0

Characteristics	Hehet-Bena	Herero	Hottentot	Hui-Vighur	Humbe-Nyaneka	Hungarian	Hutu	Ibibio	Icelander	Igbo
World Reserves %: Bauxite	0	0	0	0.7	0	1	0	0	0	0
Antimony	0	0	0	52	0	0	2	0	0	0
Barytes	0	0	0	24	0	0	0	0	0	0
Beryllium	0	0	0	0	0	0	0	0	0	0
Bismuth	0	0	0	19	0	0.1	0	0	0	0
Boron	0	0	0.2	8	0	0	0	0	0	0
Cadmium	0	0	0	3	0	0	0	0	0	0
Chromium	0	0	0	0	0	0	0	0	0	0
Cobalt	0	0	0	0	0	0	0	0	0	0
Copper	0	1	0	1	0	0.2	0	0	0	0
Fluorspar	0	0	0	1	0	0	0	0	0	0
Gold	0.5	0	0	0	0	0.2	0	0	0	0
Indium	0	0	0	9	0	0	0	0	0	0
Ind. diamond	0	0	13	1	0	0	0	0	0	0
Iron ore	0	0	0	5	0	0.1	0	0	0	0
Kaolin	0	0	0	1	0	0	0	0	0	0
Lead	0	0	0	9	0	0.1	0	0	0	0
Lithium	0	0	0	0	0	0.1	0	0	0	0
Magnesium	0	0	0	30	0	0	0	0	0	0
Manganese	0	0	0	2	0	0.1	0	0	0	0
Mercury	0	0	0	8	0	0	0	0	0	0
Molybdenum	0	0	0	9	0	0.1	0	0	0	0
Nickel	0	1	0	2	0	0	0	1	0	2
Niobium	0	0	1	0	0	0	0	0	0	0
Phosphate	0	0	0	2	0	0.1	0	0	0	0
Platinium group	0	0	0	0	0	0	0	0	0	0
Potash	0	0	0	3	0	0.3	0	0	0	0
Rare minerals	0	0	0	51	0	0	0	0	0	0
Rhenium	0	0	0	0	0	0.1	0	0	0	0
Selenium	0	0	0	0	0	0.1	0	0	0	0
Silver	0	0	0	7	0	0	0	0	0	0
Sulphur	0	0	0	0	0	0	0	0	0	0
Talc	0	0	0	0	0	0.1	0	0	0	0
Tantalum	0	4	0	25	0	0	0	0	0	0
Tellurium	0	0	0	15	0	0	0	0	0	0
Tin	0	0	0	15	0	0.1	0	12	0	12
Titanium A	0	0	0	45	0	0.2	0	0.3	0	0.3
Titanium B	0	0	0	2	0	0	0	0	0	0
Tungsten	0	0	0	14	0	0	0	0	0	0
Uranium	0	0	0	0	0	0	0	0	0	0
Vanadium	0	0	0	3	0	0.1	0	0	0	0
Vermiculite	0	0	0	0	0	0	0	0	0	0
Zinc	0	0	0	0	0	0.1	0.6	0	0	0
Zirconium	0	0	0	0	0	0	0	0	0	0
Total minerals: % sum	0.5	6	14	375	0	3	2.6	14	0	14
Number of Minerals	1	3	3	29	0	2	2	3	0	3
Oil reserves (/cap bbl)	0	0	0	19800	146000	22600	0	168000	0	168000

Characteristics	Ijaw	Indian	Indo-Aryan	Indo-nesian	Iranian	Irish	Issa	Italian	Japanese	Javanese
World Reserves %: Bauxite	0	0.4	5	0	0	0	0	0.3	0.1	3
: Antimony	0	0.1	0	0	0	0.7	0	0.8	0.1	0
: Barytes	0	.1	18	0	0	0	0	1	0.4	0
: Beryllium	0	0.3	17	0	0	0	0	8	0.2	0
: Bismuth	0	0.6	0	0	0	0	0	0	0.2	0
: Boron	0	0.3	0	0	0	0	0	0	0	0
: Cadmium	0	0.9	3	0	0	0	0	0.3	0.1	0
Chromium	0	0.0	4	0	0	0	0	0.1	0.1	0
Cobalt	0	0	0.5	7	0	0	0	0.2	0.3	0
Copper	0	0.1	0	0	0	0.2	0	0.5	0	0.7
Fluorspar	0	0.7	0	0	0	0	0	0.2	0	0
Gold	0	0.9	0	0	0	0	0	0.1	0	0
Indium	0	0.4	0	0	0	0	0	0.1	0.3	0
Ind. diamond	0	0.4	0	0	0	0	0	0.1	0.1	0
Iron ore	0	1	0	0	0	3	0	0.4	0	0
Kaolin	0	0	5	0	0	0	0	0.6	0	0
Lead	0	1	5	0	0	0	0	0.4	0	0
Lithium	0	0	3	0	0	0	0	8	0	0
Magnesium	0	0.2	0	0	0	0	0	0	0	0
Manganese	0	0.3	1	0	0	0	0	0	0	0
Mercury	0	0	0	0	0	0	0	0.7	0.3	0
Molybdenum	0	0	2	0	0	0	0	0.1	0.1	0
Nickel	2	0.6	0	1	0	0.1	0	0.1	0.1	7
Niobium	0	0.1	0	0	0	0	0	0.6	0	0
Phosphate	0	1	0	0	0	0	0	0.8	0	0
Platinum group	0	0	0	0	0	0	0	0.8	0	0
Potash	0	0	0	0	0	0	0	0	0	0
Rare minerals	0	0	0	0	0	0	0	0	0	0
Rhenium	0	0	0	0	0	0	0	0	0	0
Selenium	0	0	3	0	0	0	0	0.5	0	0
Silver	0	0.7	0	0	0	0.4	0	0.3	0.2	0
Sulphur	0	0.7	0.8	0	0	0	0	0.8	0.8	0
Talc	0	0.5	0	0	0	0.9	0	0.8	0.1	0
Tantalum	12	1	0	0	0	0	0	0	0.4	0
Tellurium	0.3	0.3	1	0	0	0	0	0	0.3	0
Tin	0	0	0	0	0	0	0	0	0.1	0
Titanium A	0	1	0	0	0	0	0	0.5	0.2	0
Titanium B	0	0.2	0	0	0	0	0	0.3	0.8	0
Tungsten	0	0.3	15	0	0	0	0	17	0.1	0
Uranium	0	0.9	5	0	0	0	0	0.3	0.4	1
Vanadium	0	0.4	0	0	0	0	0	0	0.3	1
Vermiculite	0	0.2	2	0	0	0	0	0.2	0.1	0
Zinc	0	0.3	7	0	0	2	0	0.4	0.3	0
Zirconium	0	0.9	4	0	0	0	0	0.5	0.1	0
Total minerals: % sum	14	39	101	16	0	9	0	67	23	22
Number of Minerals	3	5	19	2	0	4	0	10	6	4
Oil reserves (/cap bbl)	168000	1170000	6750	.	51100	21300	0	15500	1280	29700

Characteristics	Jewish	Jola	Kalenjin	Kamba	Kanuri	Kara-kalpak	Kare	Karen	Kavango	Kazakh
World Reserves %: Bauxite	0	0	0	0	0	0	0	0	0	0.1
Antimony	0	0	0	0	0	0	0	0	0	0.7
Barytes	0	0	0	0	0	0	0	0	0	3
Beryllium	0	0	0	0	0	0	0	0	0	0
Bismuth	0	0	0	0	0	0	0	0	0	2
Boron	0	0	0	0	0	0	0	0	0	0
Cadmium	0.1	0	0	0	0	0	0	0	0	0.4
Chromium	0	0	0	0	0	0	0	0	0	0
Cobalt	0	0	0.8	0.8	0	0	0	0	0	0
Copper	0	0	0	0	0	0	0	0	0	0
Fluorspar	0	0	0	0	0	0	0	0	0	0
Gold	0	0	0	0	0	0	0	0	1	2
Indium	0	0	0	0	0	0	0	0	0	0
Ind. diamond	0.2	0	0	0	0	0	0	0	0	1
Iron ore	0	0	0	0	0	0	0	0	0	0.7
Kaolin	0	0	0	0	0	0	0	0	0	0.0
Lead	0.1	0	0	0	0	0	0	0	0	0.1
Lithium	0	0	0	0	0	0	0	0	0	0
Magnesium	0	0	0	0	0	0	0	0	0	0
Manganese	0	0	0	0	0	0	0	0	0	4
Mercury	0	0	0	0	0	0	0	0	0	0.2
Molybdenum	0	0	0	0	0	0	0	0	0	1
Nickel	0.1	0	0	0	0	0	0	0	0	1
Niobium	0	0	0	0	0	0	0	0	0	0
Phosphate	0	0	0	0	1	0	0	0	0	0
Platinium group	0	0	0	0	0	0	0	0	0	2
Potash	0.7	0	0	0	0.2	0	0	0	1	0.0
Rare minerals	0	0	0	0	0	0	0	0	0	2
Rhenium	0	0	0	0	0	0	0	0	0	0.0
Selenium	0.1	0	0	0	0	0	0	0	0	4
Silver	0.1	0	0	0	0	0	0	0	0	0.47
Sulphur	0	0	0	0	0	0	0	0	0	0
Talc	0	0	0	0	0	0	0	0	0	0
Tantalum	0	0	0	0	0	0	0	0	0	0
Tellurium	0	0	0	0	0	0	0	0	0	9
Tin	0.1	0	0	0	0	0	0.6	0.3	4	0.9
Titanium A	0.1	0	0	0	0	0	0	0	0	0
Titanium B	0	0	0	0	0.9	0	0	0.6	0	0
Tungsten	0	0	0	0	0	0	0	0	0	0
Uranium	0	0	0	0	0	0	0	0	0	0
Vanadium	0.1	0	0	0	0	0	0	0	0	3
Vermiculite	0	0	0	0	0	0	0	0	0	2
Zinc	0.2	0	0	0	0	0	0	0.9	0	6
Zirconium	0	0	0	0	0	0	0	0.2	0	0.2
Total minerals: % sum	0.9	0	0.8	0.8	1.3	0	0.6	0.9	6	48
Number of Minerals		0	1	1	3	0	1		3	4
Oil reserves (/cap bbl)	1260	0	0	0	140000	0	0	0	0	2510

Characteristics	Kebu-Akposo	Khmer	Kikuyu	Kimbundu	Kissi	Kisii	Klao	Kongo	Kono	Konzo
World Reserves %: Bauxite	0	0	0	0	21	0	0	0	0	0
Antimony	0	0.6	0	0	0	0	0	0	0.6	0
Barytes	0	0	0	0	0	0	0	0	0	0
Beryllium	0	0	0	0	0	0	0	0	0	0
Bismuth	0	0	0	0	0	0	0	2	0	2
Boron	0	0	0	0	0	0	0	0	0	0
Cadmium	0	0	0	0	0	0	0	0	0	0
Chromium	0	0	0	0	0	0	0	3	0	4
Cobalt	0	0	0	0	0	0	0	34	0	0
Copper	0	0	0	0	0	0.8	0	7	0	4
Fluorspar	0	0.1	0	0	0	0	0	0	0	1
Gold	0	0	0.8	0	0	0	0.8	0	0	8
Ind. diamond	0	0	0	0	0	0	0	0	0	0
Indium	0	0	0	0	0	0	0	0	0	0
Iron ore	0	0	0	0	0	0	0	13	0	15
Kaolin	0	0	0	0	0	0	0	0	0	0
Lead	0	0	0	0	0	0	0	0	0	0
Lithium	0	0	0	0	0	0	0	0	0	0
Magnesium	0	0	0	0	0	0	0	0	0	0
Manganese	0	0	0	0	0	0	0	0	0	0
Mercury	0	0	0	0	0	0	0	0	0	0
Molybdenum	0	0	0	0	0	0	0	0	0	0
Nickel	0	0	0	0	0	0	0	0	0	0
Niobium	0	0	0	0	0	0	0	0	0	0
Phosphate	0	0	0	0	0	0	0	0.7	0	0.8
Platinium group	0	0	0	0	0	0	0	0	0	0
Potash	0	0	0	0	0	0	0	0	0	0
Rare minerals	0	0	0	0	0	0	0	0	0	0
Rhenium	0	0	0	0	0	0	0	0	0	0
Selenium	0	0	0	0	0	0	0	0	0	0
Silver	0	0	0	0	0	0	0	8	0	1
Sulphur	0	0	0	0	0	0	0	0	0	0
Talc	0	0	0	0	0	0	0	0	0	0
Tantalum	0	0	0	0	0	0	0	0	0	0
Tellurium	0	0	0	0	0	0	0	0	0	0
Tin	0	4	0	0	0.1	0	0	6	0.5	0.7
Titanium A	0	0.7	0	0	0.5	0	0	7	0.2	8
Titanium B	0	0	0	0	0	0	0	0.3	0	0.3
Tungsten	0	0.2	0	0	0	0	0	0	0	0
Uranium	0	0	0	0	0	0	0	0	0	0
Vanadium	0	0	0	0	0	0	0	0.1	0	0.1
Vermiculite	0	0	0	0	0	0	0	0	0	0
Zinc	0	0	0	0	0.2	0	0	0	0.1	0
Zirconium	0	7	0	0	0	0	0	3	0	3
Total minerals: % sum	0	7	0.8	0	22	0.8	0.8	83	1.5	99
Number of Minerals	0	1	1	0	2	1	1	10	4	12
Oil reserves (/cap bbl)	0	1210	0	146000	0	0	0	57400	0	4540

Characteristics	Koranko	Korean	Kotoko	Kpelle	Kru	Kurd	Kuwaiti	Kyrgyz	Ladino	Lango
World Reserves %: Bauxite	0.6	0.2	0	9	0	0	0	0	0	0
Antimony	0	0.9	0	0	0	0.8	0	0	0	0
Barytes	0	0.1	0	0	0	0.8	0	0	0	0
Beryllium	0	0.6	0	0	0	0	0	0	0	4
Bismuth	0	0.2	0	0	0	0.0	0	0	0	0
Boron	0	0.0	0	0	0	12	0	0	0	0
Cadmium	0	0	0	0	0	0.2	0	0	0	0
Chromium	0	0.2	0	0	0	0.2	0	0	0.3	0
Cobalt	0	0.3	0	0	0	0	0	0	0	0
Copper	0	0.1	0	0	0	1	0	0	0	0
Fluorspar	0	0.4	0	0	0	1	0	0	0	0
Gold	0	0	0	0	0	0	0	0	0	0
Indium	0	0.2	0	0	0	0	0	0	0	0
Ind. diamond	0	0.4	0	0	0.8	0	0	0	0	0
Iron ore	0	0.4	0	0.5	0	0.3	0	0	0	0
Kaolin	0	0.7	0	0	0	0	0	0	0	0
Lead	0	0	0	0	0	0	0	0	0	0
Lithium	0	0.3	0	0	0	0	0	0	0	0
Magnesium	0	0.8	0	0	0	0	0	0	0	0
Manganese	0	0.0	0	0	0	0	0	0	0	0
Mercury	0	0	0	0	0	2	0	0	0	0
Molybdenum	0	0.2	0	0	0	0	0	0	0	0
Nickel	0	0.1	0	0	0	0	0	0	0	0
Niobium	0	0.2	0	0	0	0	0	0	0	0
Phosphate	0	0.2	0	0	0	0	0	0	0	0
Platinium group	0	0.1	0	0	0	0	0	0	0	0
Potash	0	0.3	0	0	0	0	0	0	0	0
Rare minerals	0	0	0	0	0	0	0	0	0	0
Rhenium	0	0.3	0	0	0	0	0	0	0	0
Selenium	0	0	0	0	0	0	0	0	0	0
Silver	0	0.2	0	0	0	0	0	0	0	0
Sulphur	0	0.7	0	0	0	0	0	0	0	0
Talc	0	0.5	0	0	0	0	0	0	0	0
Tantalum	0	0.4	0	0	0	0	0	0	0	0
Tellurium	0	0	0	0	0	0	0	0	0	0
Tin	0.5	0.4	0	0	0	1	0	0	0	0
Titanium A	0.2	0.3	0	0	0	0	0	0	0	0
Titanium B	0	0.4	0	0	0	0	0	0	0	0
Tungsten	0	0.5	0	0	0	0	0	0	0	0
Uranium	0	0	0	0	0	0	0	0	0	0
Vanadium	0	0.1	0	0	0	0	0	0	0	0
Vermiculite	0	0	0	0	0	0	0	0	0	0
Zinc	0	0	0	0	0	0.4	0	0	0	0
Zirconium	0	0	0	0	0	0	0	0	0	0
Total minerals: % sum	1	5	0	10	0.8	20	0	0	0.3	4
Number of Minerals	5	30	0	1	1	4	0	0	1	1
Oil reserves (/cap bbl)	0	1670	0	0	0	1140000	0	0	2700	0

Characteristics	Lao	Latvian	Lezgin	Li	Liechten-steiner	Limba	Lithua-nian	Lobi	Loma	Lomwe
World Reserves %: Bauxite	5			0.7		0.6				
Antimony	3			52						
Barytes				24						
Beryllium				1						
Bismuth				9						
Boron				8						
Cadmium				3						
Chromium										
Cobalt										
Copper										
Fluorspar				1						
Gold	0.3			1					0.8	
Indium										
Ind. diamond				9						
Iron ore				1						
Kaolin				5						
Lead				1						
Lithium										
Magnesium				9						
Manganese				30						
Mercury				2						
Molybdenum				8						
Nickel				9						
Niobium				2						
Phosphate				2						
Platinium group										
Potash				3						
Rare minerals										
Rhenium				51						
Selenium										
Silver	23			7						
Sulphur										
Talc										
Tantalum	4									
Tellurium				25						
Tin				15		0.5				
Titanium A	1			15		2				
Titanium B				45						
Tungsten				2						
Uranium				14						
Vanadium										
Vermiculite				3						
Zinc						1				
Zirconium										
Total minerals: % sum	37	0	0	375	0	5	0	0	0.8	0
Number of Minerals	6	0	0	29	0	4	0	0	1	0
Oil reserves (/cap bbl)	3550	0	177000	19800	0	0	0	3860	0	0

Characteristics	Lotuko	Luba	Luchasi	Luena	Lugbara	Luhya	Lumbe	Lunda	Luo	Luri
World Reserves %: Bauxite	0	0	0	0	0	0	0	0	0	0
: Antimony	0	0	0	0	0	0	0	0	0	0
: Barytes	0	2	0	0	2	0	0	0	0	0
: Beryllium	0	0	0	0	0	0	0	0	0	0
: Bismuth	0	0	0	0	0	0	0	0	0	0
: Boron	0	0	0	0	0	0	0	0	0	0
: Cadmium	0	4	0	0	4	0	0	0	0	0
: Chromium	0	0	0	0	0	0	0	0	0	0
: Cobalt	0	41	0	0	41	0.8	0	0	0.8	0
: Copper	0	8	0	0	8	0	0	0	0	0
: Fluorspar	0	0	0	0	0	0	0	0	0	0
: Gold	0	0	0	0	0	0	0	0	0	0.9
: Indium	0	0	0	0	0	0	0	0	0	0
: Ind. diamond	0	15	0	0	15	0	0	0	0	0
: Iron ore	0	0	0	0	0	0	0	0	0	0
: Kaolin	0	0	0	0	0	0	0	0	0	0
: Lead	0	0	0	0	0	0	0	0	0	0
: Lithium	0	0	0	0	0	0	0	0	0	0
: Magnesium	0	0	0	0	0	0	0	0	0	0
: Manganese	0	0	0	0	0	0	0	0	0	0
: Mercury	0	0	0	0	0	0	0	0	0	0
: Molybdenum	0	0.8	0	0	0.8	0	0	0	0	0
: Nickel	0	0	0	0	0	0	0	0	0	0
: Niobium	0	0	0	0	0	0	0	0	0	0
: Phosphate	0	0	0	0	0	0	0	0	0	0
: Platinium group	0	0	0	0	0	0	0	0	0	0
: Potash	0	0	0	0	0	0	0	0	0	0
: Rare minerals	0	0	0	0	0	0	0	0	0	0
: Rhenium	0	0	0	0	0	0	0	0	0	0
: Selenium	0	0	0	0	0	0	0	0	0	0
: Silver	0	1	0	0	1	0	0	0	0	0
: Sulphur	0	0	0	0	0	0	0	0	0	0
: Talc	0	7	0	0	7	0	0	0	0	0
: Tantalum	0	8	0	0	8	0	0	0	0	0
: Tellurium	0	0	0	0	0	0	0	0	0	0
: Tin	0	0.3	0	0	0.3	0	0	0	0	0
: Titanium A	0	0	0	0	0	0	0	0	0	0
: Titanium B	0	0	0	0	0	0	0	0	0	0
: Tungsten	0	0	0	0	0	0	0	0	0	0
: Uranium	0	0.1	0	0	0.1	0	0	0	0	0
: Vanadium	0	0	0	0	0	0	0	0	0	0
: Vermiculite	0	0	0	0	0	0	0	0	0	0
: Zinc	0	3	0	0	3	0	0	0	0	1
: Zirconium	0	0	0	0	0	0	0	0	0	0
Total minerals: % sum	0	99	0	0	99	0.8	0	0	0.8	2
Number of Minerals	0	12	0	0	12	1	0	0	1	2
Oil reserves (/cap bbl)	10900	4540	146000	146000	4540	0	146000	146000	0	1470

Characteristics	Luxem-burger	Macedo-nian	Madurese	Magars	Maka	Makonde	Makua	Malagasy	Malawi	Malay
World Reserves %: Bauxite	0	0.3	4	0	3	0	0	0	0	0.9
Antimony	0	0	0	0	0	0	0	0	0	0.6
Barytes	0	0	0	0	0	0	0	0	0	0
Beryllium	0	0	0	0	0	0	1	0	1	0
Bismuth	0	0	0	0	0	0	0	0	0	0
Boron	0	0	0	0	0	0	0	0	0	0
Cadmium	0	0	0	0	0	0	0	0	0	0
Chromium	0	0	0	0	0	0	0	0.5	0	0
Cobalt	0	0	0.7	0	0	0	0	0	0	1
Copper	0	0	0	0	0	0	0	0	0	0
Fluorspar	0	0	0	0	0	0	0	0	0	0
Gold	0	0	0	0	0	0	0	0	0	0.1
Ind. diamond	0	0	0	0	0	0.5	0	0	0	0
Iron ore	0	0	0	0	0	0	0	0	0	0
Kaolin	0	0	0	0	0	0	0	0	0	0
Lead	0	0.5	0	0	0	0	0	0	0	0
Lithium	0	0.5	0	0	0	0	0	0	0	0
Magnesium	0	0	0	0	0	0	0	0	0	0
Manganese	0	0	0	2	0	0	0	0	0	0
Mercury	0	0.1	0	0	0	0	0	0	0	0
Molybdenum	0	0.1	0	0	0	0	0	0	0	0
Nickel	0	0.1	7	0	0	0	0	0	0	0.1
Niobium	0	0	0	0	0	0	0	0	0	0
Phosphate	0	0	0	0	0	0	1	0	1	0
Platinium group	0	0	0	0	0	0	0	0	0	0
Potash	0	0	0	0	0	0	0	0	0	0
Rare minerals	0	0	0	0	0	0	0	0	0	0
Rhenium	0	0	0	0	0	0	0	0	0	0
Selenium	0	0	0	0	0	0	0	0	0	0
Silver	0	0	0	0	0	0	0	0	0	0
Sulphur	0	0	0	0	0	0	0	0	0	0
Talc	0	0	0	0	0	0	0	0	0	0
Tantalum	0	0	0	0	0	0	0	0	0	0
Tellurium	0	0	0	0	0	0	0	0	0	0
Tin	0	0	12	0	0	0	0	0	0	5
Titanium A	0	0	0	0	0	0	0	0	0	16
Titanium B	0	0	0	0	0	0	0	0	0	0
Tungsten	0	0	0	0	0	0	0	0	0	0
Uranium	0	0	0	0	0	0	0	0	0	0
Vanadium	0	0	0	0	0	0	0	0	0	0
Vermiculite	0	0	0	0	0	0	0	0	0	0
Zinc	0	0	0	0	0	0	0	0.3	0	0.8
Zirconium	0	0	0	0	0	0	0	0	0	0
Total minerals: % sum	0	0.8	22	2	0.3	0.5	2	0.8	2	24
Number of Minerals	0	2	4	1	0.9	1	2	2	2	5
Oil reserves (/cap bbl)	0	562	29700	0	52100	0	0	0	0	218000

Characteristics	Malay Christian	Malay Coastal	Malay Muslim	Malinke	Maltese	Mambwe	Manchu-Tibetian	Mandara	Mande	Mandingo
World Reserves %: Bauxite	0	4	0	11	0	0	0	3	0	0
Antimony	0	0	0	0	0	0	0.7	0	0	0
Barytes	0	0	0	0	0	0	52	0	0	0
Beryllium	0	0	0	0	0	0	24	0	0	0
Bismuth	0	0	0	0	0	0	0	0	0	0
Boron	0	0	0	0	0	0	19	0	0	0
Cadmium	0.6	0.7	0.6	0	0	0	8	0	0	0
Chromium	0	0	0	0	0	0	3	0	0	0
Cobalt	3	0	3	0	0	11	0	0	0	0
Copper	0	0	0	0	0	4	11	0	0	0
Fluorspar	0	0	0	0	0	0	9	0	0	0
Gold	0	0	0	0	0	0	1	0	0	0
Indium	0	0	0	0	0	0	5	0	0	0
Ind. diamond	0	0	0	0	0	0	0	0	0	0
Iron ore	0	0	0	0	0	0	1	0	0	0
Kaolin	0	0	0	0	0	0	0	0	0	0
Lead	0	0	0	0	0	0	9	0	0	0
Lithium	0	0	0	0	0	0	0	0	0	0
Magnesium	0	0	0	0	0	0	30	0	0	0
Manganese	0	0	0	0	0	0	2	0	0	0
Mercury	0	0	0	0	0	0	8	0	0	0
Molybdenum	0	0	0	0	0	0	9	0	0	0
Nickel	0.9	7	0.9	0	0	0	2	0	0	0
Niobium	0	0	0	0	0	0	2	0	0	0
Phosphate	0	0	0	0	0	4	2	0	0	0
Platinium group	0	0	0	0	0	0	3	0	0	0
Potash	0	0	0	0	0	0	0	0	0	0
Rare minerals	0	0	0	0	0	0	51	0	0	0
Rhenium	3	0	3	0	0	0	0	0	0	0
Selenium	0	0	0	0	0	0	0	0	0	0
Silver	0	0	0	0	0	9	7	0	0	0
Sulphur	0	0	0	0	0	0	7	0	0	0
Talc	0	0	0	0	0	0	0	0	0	0
Tantalum	0	0	0	0	0	0	0	0	0	0
Tellurium	0	0	0	0	0	0	0	0	0	0
Tin	3	12	3	0	0	0	25	0	0	0
Titanium A	0	0	0	0	0	0	15	0	0	0
Titanium B	0	0	0	0	0	0	15	0	0	0
Tungsten	0	0	0	0	0	0	45	0	0	0
Uranium	0	0	0	0	0	0	2	0	0	0
Vanadium	0	0	0	0	0	0	14	0	0	0
Vermiculite	0	0	0	0	0	0	0	0	0	0
Zinc	0	0	0	0	0	0	3	0	0	0
Zirconium	0	0	0	0	0	0	0	0	0	0
Total minerals: % sum	10	22	10	11	0	27	375	3	0	0
Number of Minerals	5	4	5	1	0	4	29	1	0	0
Oil reserves (/cap bbl)	2220	29700	2220	1770	0	0	19800	31900	0	0

Characteristics	Mandyako	Mano	Manx (Norse-C.)	Manzan-Darani	Maori	Maravi	Masa	Masalit Maba	Maya	Mbaka
World Reserves %: Bauxite	0	0	0	0	0	0	0	0	0	0
Antimony										
Barytes										
Beryllium										
Bismuth										
Boron										
Cadmium										
Chromium										
Cobalt						0.2				
Copper						0.7				
Fluorspar										
Gold		0.8								
Indium										
Ind. diamond										
Iron ore										
Kaolin										
Lead										
Lithium										
Magnesium										
Manganese										
Mercury				0.9						
Molybdenum										
Nickel										
Niobium										
Phosphate						0.7				
Platinium group										
Potash										
Rare minerals										
Rhenium										
Selenium						0.2				
Silver										0.6
Sulphur										
Talc										
Tantalum										
Tellurium										
Tin										
Titanium A										
Titanium B										
Tungsten										
Uranium										
Vanadium										
Vermiculite										
Zinc					0.3					
Zirconium					0.3					
Total minerals: % sum	0	0.8	0	1 0 2	0.3	0.5 0.8	0	0	0	0.6
Number of Minerals		1		2	1					1
Oil reserves (/cap bbl)	0	0	.	1470	48300	0	0	0	0	0

Characteristics	Mbete	Mbochi	Mbum	Mbunda	Melanesian	Mende	Merina	Meru	Mestizo	Miao Man
World Reserves %: Bauxite	0	0	0.7	0	0	0.6	0	0	0	0
Antimony	0	0	0	0	0	0	0	0	2	0
Barytes	0	0	0	0	0	0	0	0	2	0
Beryllium	0	0	0	0	0	0	0	0	5	0
Bismuth	0	0	0	0	0	0	0	0	4	0
Boron	0	0	0	0	0	0	0	0	0.4	0
Cadmium	0	0	0	0	0	0	0	0	0.3	0
Chromium	0	0	0	0	0	0	0	0	0.1	0
Cobalt	0	0	0	0	0.5	0	0.5	0.8	0.4	0
Copper	0	0	0	0	0.1	0	0	0	3	0
Fluorspar	0	0	0	0	0	0	0	0	0.3	0
Gold	0	0	0	0	0	0	0	0	0.1	0
Indium	0	0	0	0	0	0	0	0	0.2	0
Ind. diamond	0	0	0	0	0	0	0	0	0.8	0
Iron ore	0	0	0	0	0	0	0	0	2	0
Kaolin	0	0	0	0	0	0	0	0	0	0
Lead	0	0	0	0	0	0	0	0	4	0
Lithium	0	0	0	0	0	0	0	0	0.5	0
Magnesium	0	0	0	0	0	0	0	0	1	0
Manganese	0	0	0	0	0	0	0	0	2	0
Mercury	0	0	0	0	0	0	0	0	0.3	0
Molybdenum	4	0	0	0	0	0	0	0	10	0
Nickel	0	0	0	0	0.7	0	0	0	0.1	0
Niobium	0	0	0	0	0	0	0	0	0	0
Phosphate	0	0	0.1	0	0	0	0	0	4	0
Platinium group	0.4	0	0	0	0	0	0	0	4	0
Potash	0	0	0	0	0	0	0	0	5	0
Rare minerals	0	0	0	0	0.5	0	0	0	2	0
Rhenium	0	0	0	0	0	0	0	0	0	0
Selenium	0	0	0	0	0	0.5	0	0	0.5	0
Silver	0	0	0	0	0	0.2	0	0	0.4	0
Sulphur	0	0	0	0	0	0	0	0	2	0
Talc	0	0	0	0	0	0	0	0	3	0
Tantalum	0	0	0	0	1	0	0	0	0.1	0
Tellurium	0	0	0	0	0	0	0	0	10	0
Tin	0	0	0	0	0	0.1	0	0	0.3	0
Titanium A	0	0	0	0	0	0	0.3	0	0.8	0
Titanium B	0	0	0	0	0	0	0.8	0	0.9	0
Tungsten	0	0	0	0	0	0	0	0	0.3	0
Uranium	0	0	0	0	0	0	0	0.8	0.9	0
Vanadium	0	0	0	0	0	0	0	0	0.2	0
Vermiculite	0	0	0	0	0	0	0	0	0	0
Zinc	0.4	0	0	0	0	0	0	0	0.2	0
Zirconium	0	0	0	0	0	0	0	0	0.3	0
Total minerals: % sum	0.4	0	0.9	0	4	5	0.3	0.8	80	0
Number of Minerals	4	0	0.4	0	2	4	0.8	1	11	0
Oil reserves (/cap bbl)	481000	338000	7440	146000	54400	0	2	0	495000	0

Characteristics	Microne-sian	Mixed	Moldovan	Mon	Mon-Khmer	Monegas-que	Mongo	Mongol-Buryat	Mongol-Dariganga	Mongol-Dorbed
World Reserves %: Bauxite	0	0	0	0	0	0	0	0	0	0
: Antimony	0	0	0	0	0	0	0	0	0	0
: Barytes	0	0	0	0	0	0	0	0	0	0
: Beryllium	0	0	0	0	0	0	0	0	0	0
: Bismuth	0	0	0	0	0	0	0	0	0	0
: Boron	0	0	0	0	0	0	2	0	0	0
: Cadmium	0	0	0	0	0	0	0	0	0	0
: Chromium	0	0	0	0	0	0	4	0	0	0
: Cobalt	0	0	0	0	0	0	41	0	0	0
: Copper	0	0	0	0	0	0	8	0	0	0
: Fluorspar	0	0	0	0	0	0	0	0.9	0.9	0.9
: Gold	0	0	0	0	0	0	0	21	21	21
: Indium	0	0	0	0	0	0	0	0	0	0
: Ind. diamond	0	0	0	0	0	0	15	0	0	0
: Iron ore	0	0	0	0	0	0	0	0	0	0
: Kaolin	0	0	0	0	0	0	0	0	0	0
: Lead	0	0	0	0	0	0	0	0	0	0
: Lithium	0	0	0	0	0	0	0	0	0	0
: Magnesium	0	0	0	0	0	0	0	0	0	0
: Manganese	0	0	0	0	0	0	0	0	0	0
: Mercury	0	0	0	0	0	0	0	0	0	0
: Molybdenum	0	0	0	0	0	0	0.8	0	0	0
: Nickel	0	0	0	0	0	0	1	0	0	0
: Niobium	0	0	0	0	0	0	0.3	0	0	0
: Phosphate	0	0	0	0	0	0	0	0	0	0
: Platinium group	0	0	0	0	0	0	0	0	0	0
: Potash	0	0	0	0	0	0	0	0	0	0
: Rare minerals	0	0	0	0	0	0	0	0	0	0
: Rhenium	0	0	0	0	0	0	0	0	0	0
: Selenium	0	0	0	0	0	0	0	0	0	0
: Silver	0	0	0	0	0	0	7	0	0	0
: Sulphur	0	0	0	0	0	0	8	0	0	0
: Talc	0	0	0	0	0	0	0	0	0	0
: Tantalum	0	0	0	0	0	0	0.3	0	0	0
: Tellurium	0	0	0	0	0	0	0	0	0	0
: Tin	0	0	0	0.3	0	0	0	0	0	0
: Titanium A	0	0	0	0	0	0	0	0	0	0
: Titanium B	0	0	0	0	0	0	0	0	0	0
: Tungsten	0	0	0	0.6	0	0	0.1	0	0	0
: Uranium	0	0	0	0	0	0	0	0	0	0
: Vanadium	0	0	0	0	0	0	0	0	0	0
: Vermiculite	0	0	0	0	0	0	0	0	0	0
: Zinc	0	0	0	0	0	0	3	0	0	0
: Zirconium	0	0	0	0	0	0	0	0	0	0
Total minerals: % sum	0	0	0	0.9	0	0	99	22	22	22
Number of Minerals	0	0	0	2	0	0	12	2	2	2
Oil reserves (/cap bbl)	0	159000	0	0	0	0	4540	0	0	0

Characteristics	Mongol-Khalka	Mongoloid	Montene-grin	Moor	Morvians	Mossi	Mpongwe	Mubi	Mulatto	Muong
World Reserves %: Bauxite	0	4	0	0	0	0	0	0	9	0
Antimony	0	8	0	0	0	0	0	0	0.7	0
Barytes	0	19	0	0	0	0	0	0	26	0
Beryllium	0	14	0	0	0	0	0	0	0	0
Bismuth	0	3	0	0	0	0	0	0	0.6	0
Boron	0	1	0	0	0	0	0	0	0.4	0
Cadmium	0	3	0	0	0	0	0	0	2	0
Chromium	0	4	0	0	0	0	0	0	0	0
Cobalt	0.9	0.4	0	0	0	0	0	0	0	0
Copper	21		0	0	0	0	0	0	2	0
Fluorspar	0	2	0	0	0	0	0	0	0	0
Gold	0	0.1	0	0	0	0	0	0	0.4	0
Indium	0		0	0	0	0	0	0	0.1	0
Ind. diamond	0	0.2	0	0	0	0	0	0	5	0
Iron ore	0	5	0	0	0	0	0	0		0
Kaolin	0	4	0	0	0	0	0	0	0.1	0
Lead	0	4	0	0	0	0	0	0	1	0
Lithium	0	0	0	0	0	0	0	0	2	0
Magnesium	0	6	0	0	0	0	0	0	0	0
Manganese	0	2	0	0	0	0	0	0	3	0
Mercury	0	1	0	0	0	0	0	0	55	0
Molybdenum	0	0.1	0	0	0	0	0	0	0.1	0
Nickel	0		0	0	0	0	0	0		0
Niobium	0	0.2	0	0	0	0	7	0	0.4	0
Phosphate	0	0.3	0	0.8	0	0	0	0	0.2	0
Platinium group	0	0.5	0	0.4	0	0	0	0	0	0
Potash	0	10	0	0	0	0	0	0	0	0
Rare minerals	0		0	0	0	0	0	0	0	0
Rhenium	0	0.7	0	0	0	0	0	0	0	0
Selenium	0		0	0	0	0	0	0	3	0
Silver	0	0.1	0	0	0	0	0	0	2	0
Sulphur	0		0	0	0	0	0	0	0	0
Talc	0	0.9	0	0	0	0	0	0	14	0
Tantalum	0	0	0	0	0	0	0	0	0.7	0
Tellurium	0		0	0	0	0	0	0	54	0
Tin	0	4	0	0	0	0	0	0	0.6	0
Titanium A	0	15	0	0	0	0	0	0	0.4	0
Titanium B	0	7	0	0.1	0	0.4	0.6	0		0
Tungsten	0	7	0	0.8	0	0	0	0	0	0
Uranium	0	2	0	0	0	0	0	0	5	0
Vanadium	0	2	0	0	0	0	0	0	0	0
Vermiculite	0	0	0	0	0	0	0	0	0	0
Zinc	0	7	0	0	0	0	0	0	0.9	0
Zirconium	0	4	0	0	0	0	0	0		0
Total minerals: % sum	22	145	0	0.8		0.4	7	0	193	
Number of Minerals	2	21	0			11	2	0	20	
Oil reserves (/cap bbl)	0	8830	0	0			579000	0	14200	7140

Characteristics	Nama	Nauruan	Ndebele	Nepalese	Nether-lander	Newar	Ngbandi	Ngoni	Nkole	Norman-French D.
World Reserves %: Bauxite										
Antimony			0.3							
Barytes										
Beryllium									4	
Bismuth										
Boron										
Cadmium			1							
Chromium			0							
Cobalt	1									
Copper			0.1							
Fluorspar										
Gold			0.1							
Indium										
Ind. diamond			0.1							
Iron ore										
Kaolin			1							
Lead										
Lithium										
Magnesium										
Manganese				2		2				
Mercury			0.2							
Molybdenum										
Nickel										
Niobium										
Phosphate										
Platinium group										
Potash										
Rare minerals										
Rhenium										
Selenium										
Silver	1									
Sulphur										
Talc										
Tantalum										
Tellurium			0.3							
Tin	4		0.2							
Titanium A										
Titanium B										
Tungsten										
Uranium										
Vanadium										
Vermiculite										
Zinc							0.6			
Zirconium										
Total minerals: % sum	6	0	13	2	9460	2	0.6	0	4	0
Number of Minerals	3	0	7	1		1	1	0	1	0
Oil reserves (/cap bbl)	0	0	0	0		0	0	0	0	

Characteristics	North-Western	Norwegian	Nuba	Nuer	Nung Sukuma	Nupe	Nyamwezi (Galla)	Nyoros	Ometo	Oromo
World Reserves %: Bauxite										
Antimony										
Barytes								4		
Beryllium										
Bismuth										
Boron										
Cadmium	11									
Chromium										
Cobalt	4									
Copper										
Fluorspar										
Gold							0.5			
Indium										
Ind. diamond										
Iron ore										
Kaolin										
Lead										
Lithium										
Magnesium										
Manganese										
Mercury										
Molybdenum										
Nickel										
Niobium						2				
Phosphate										
Platinium group										
Potash										
Rare minerals										
Rhenium										
Selenium	4									
Silver										
Sulphur	9									
Talc										
Tantalum						12				
Tellurium						0.3				
Tin		16								
Titanium A										
Titanium B										
Tungsten										
Uranium										
Vanadium										
Vermiculite										
Zinc										
Zirconium										
Total minerals: % sum	27	16	0	0	0	14	0.5	4	0	0
Number of Minerals	4	1	0	0	0	3	1	1	0	0
Oil reserves (/cap bbl)	0	2040000	10900	10900	7140	168000	0	0	0	0

Characteristics	Ossete	Ovambo	Ovim-bundu	Pacific Islander	Pakistani	Palauans	Palaung-Wa	Papuan New Guin.	Pashtun	Pepel
World Reserves %: Bauxite	0	0	0	0	0.2	0	0	0	0	0
: Antimony	0	0	0	0	0	0	0	0	0	0
: Barytes	0	0	0	0	0	0	0	0	0	0
: Beryllium	0	0	0	0	0	0	0	0	0	0
: Bismuth	0	0	0	0	0	0	0	0	0	0
: Boron	0	0	0	0	0	0	0	0	0	0
: Cadmium	0	0	0	0	0	0	0	2	0	0
: Chromium	0	0	0	0	0	0	0	0	0	0
: Cobalt	0	0	0	0	0	0	0	0	0	0
: Copper	0	1	0	0	0	0	0	0	0	0
: Fluorspar	0	0	0	0	0	0	0	0	0	0
: Gold	0	0	0	0	0.5	0	0	0	0	0
: Ind. diamond	0	0	0	0	0	0	0	0	0	0
: Iron ore	0	0	0	0	5	0	0	0	0	0
: Kaolin	0	0	0	0	0	0	0	0	0	0
: Lead	0	0	0	0	0	0	0	0	0	0
: Lithium	0	0	0	0	0	0	0	0	0	0
: Magnesium	0	0	0	0	0	0	0	0	0	0
: Manganese	0	0	0	0	0	0	0	0	0	0
: Mercury	0	0	0	0	0	0	0	0	0	0
: Molybdenum	0	0	0	0	0.2	0	0	0	0	0
: Nickel	0	0	0	0	0	0	0	0	0	0
: Niobium	0	0	0	0	0	0	0	0	0	0
: Phosphate	0	0	0	0	0	0	0	0	0	0
: Platinium group	0	0	0	0	0	0	0	0.8	0	0
: Potash	0	0	0	0	0	0	0	0	0	0
: Rare minerals	0	0	0	0	0	0	0	0	0	0
: Rhenium	0	0	0	0	0	0	0	2	0	0
: Selenium	0	0	0	0	0	0	0	0	0	0
: Silver	0	0	0	0	0.9	0	0	0	0	0
: Sulphur	0	0	0	0	0.2	0	0	0	2	0
: Talc	0	0	0	0	0.2	0	0	0	0	0
: Tantalum	0	0	0	0	0	0	0	0	0	0
: Tellurium	0	0	0	0	2	0	0	0	0	0
: Tin	0	1	0	0	0	0	0	0	0	0
: Titanium A	0	0	0	0	0	0	0	0	0	0
: Titanium B	0	4	0	0	0	0	0	0	0	0
: Tungsten	0	0	0	0	0	0	0	0	0	0
: Uranium	0	0	0	0	0	0	0	0	0	0
: Vanadium	0	0	0	0	0	0	0	0	0	0
: Vermiculite	0	0	0	0	0	0	0	0	0	0
: Zinc	0	0	0	0	0	0	0	0	0	0
: Zirconium	0	0	0	0	0	0	0	0	0	0
Total minerals: % sum	0	6	0	0	9	.	0	5	2	0
Number of Minerals	0	3	0	0	3		0	3	1	0
Oil reserves (/cap bbl)	0	0	146000	0	6660000		0	81500	0	0

Characteristics	Persian	Polinisian	Polinesian Chinese	Polinesian European	Polish	Portu-guese	Punjabi	Punu	Puyi	Pygmy
World Reserves %: Bauxite	0	0	0	0	0	9	0	0		0
Antimony	0	0	0	0	0	0	0	0	0.7	0
Barytes	0	0	0	0	0	0.7	0	0	52	0
Beryllium	0	0	0	0	0	26	0	0	24	0
Bismuth	0	0	0	0	0	0	0	0	0	0
Boron	0	0	0	0	0	0.7	0	0	19	0
Cadmium	0	0	0	0	0	0.4	0	0	8	0
Chromium	0	0	0	0	2	0.4	0	0	3	0
Cobalt	0	0	0	0	0	0.3	0	0	0	0
Copper	0	0	0	0	0	0.1	0	0	0	0
Fluorspar	0	0	0	0	3	0.2	0	0	11	0
Gold	0	0	0	0	0	0	0	0	0	0
Indium	0	0	0	0	0	0.3	0	0	9	0
Ind. diamond	0	0	0	0	0.1	0.3	0	0	1	0
Iron ore	0	0	0	0	0	0.1	0	0	5	0
Kaolin	0	0	0	0	0	5	0	0	1	0
Lead	0	0	0	0	0	0.1	0	0	9	0
Lithium	0.9	0	0	0	0	1	0	0	0	0
Magnesium	0	0	0	0	3	0	0	0	30	0
Manganese	0	0	0	0	0	2	0	0	2	0
Mercury	0	0	0	0	0.4	0	0	0	8	0
Molybdenum	0	0	0	0	0	0	0	0	9	0
Nickel	0	0	0	0	0	1	0	0	2	0
Niobium	0	0	0	0	0	54	0	0	0	0
Phosphate	0	0	0	0	0	0.1	0	0	2	0
Platinium group	0	0	0	0	0	0	0	0	0	0
Potash	0	0	0	0	0	0.6	0	0	3	0
Rare minerals	0	0	0	0	0.2	0.2	0	0	51	0
Rhenium	0	0	0	0	0	0	0	0	0	0
Selenium	0	0	0	0	0	0	0	0	0	0
Silver	0.1	0	0	0	2	0.1	0	0	7	0
Sulphur	0	0	0	0	9	0.1	0	0	0	0
Talc	0	0	0	0	0	0.1	0	0	0	0
Tantalum	0	0	0	0	0	3	0	0	0	0
Tellurium	0	0	0	0	0	0	0	0	0	0
Tin	0	0	0	0	0	2	0	0	25	0
Titanium A	0	0	0	0	0	14	0	0	15	0
Titanium B	0	0	0	0	0	0.8	0	0	15	0
Tungsten	0	0	0	0	0	53	0	0	45	0
Uranium	0	0	0	0	0	0	0	0.4	2	0
Vanadium	1	0	0	0	0	4	0	0	14	0
Vermiculite	0	0.1	0	0	0	0	0	0	0	0
Zinc	0	0	0	0	2	5	0	0	3	0
Zirconium	2	0.1	0	0	0	1	0	0		
Total minerals: % sum	2	0.1			22	189	0.2	0	375	
Number of Minerals		0.3			7	21		1	29	
Oil reserves (/cap bbl)	86500	36100	.		1770	14400	3340	497000	19800	338000

Characteristics	Quechua	Rakhine	Romanian	Romansch	Rundi	Russian	Ruthenian	Rwanda	Saho	Sakalava
World Reserves %: Bauxite	0	0	0.2	0	0	0	0	0	0	0
Antimony	0.6	0	0	0	0	0	0	0	0	0
Barytes	0	0	0	0	0	0	0	0	0	0
Beryllium	7	0	0	0	2	0	0	2	0	0
Bismuth	1	0	0	0	0	0	0	0	0	0
Boron	0	0	0	0	0	0	0	0	0	0.5
Cadmium	3	0	0	0	0	0	0	0	0	0
Chromium	0	0	0	0	3	0	0	3	0	0
Cobalt	0	0	0	0	38	0	0	32	0	0
Copper	1	0	0	0	8	0	0	6	0	0
Fluorspar	0	0	0	0	0	0	0	0	0	0
Gold	0	0	0.6	0	0	0	0	0	0	0
Indium	3	0	0	0	0	0	0	0	0	0
Ind. diamond	0	0	0	0	14	0	0	12	0	0
Iron ore	0	0	0	0	0	0	0	0	0	0
Kaolin	0	0	0	0	0	0	0	0	0	0
Lead	2	0	0	0	0	0	0	0	0	0
Lithium	0	0	0	0	0	0	0	0	0	0
Magnesium	0	0	0	0	0	0	0	0	0	0
Manganese	0	0	0	0	0	0	0	0	0	0
Mercury	0	0	0	0	0	0	0	0	0	0
Molybdenum	1	0	0	0	0	0	0	0	0	0
Nickel	0	0	0	0	0	0	0	0	0	0
Niobium	0	0	0	0	0.7	0	0	0.6	0	0
Phosphate	0	0	0	0	0	0	0	0	0	0
Platinium group	0	0	0	0	0	0	0	0	0	0
Potash	0	0	0	0	0	0	0	0	0	0
Rare minerals	0	0	0	0	0	0	0	0	0	0
Rhenium	1	0	0	0	9	0	0	8	0	0
Selenium	1	0	0	0	0	0	0	0	0	0
Silver	5	0	0	0	7	0	0	6	0	0
Sulphur	0	0	0	0	7	0	0	6	0	0
Talc	0	0	0	0	0.3	0	0	0.2	0	0
Tantalum	0	0	0	0	0	0	0	0	0	0
Tellurium	1	0	0	0	0	0	0	0	0	0
Tin	0.3	0.3	0	0	0.1	0.1	0	0.1	0	0
Titanium A	0	0	0	0	0	0	0	0	0	0
Titanium B	0	0	0	0	0	0	0	0	0	0
Tungsten	0.3	0	0	0	0	0	0	0	0	0
Uranium	0.1	0	0	0	0	0	0	0	0	0
Vanadium	0	0	0	0	0	0	0	0	0	0
Vermiculite	0	0	0	0	0	0	0	0	0	0
Zinc	3	0.6	0	0	3	0	0	3	0	0.3
Zirconium	0	0	0	0	0	0	0	0	0	0
Total minerals: % sum	32	0.9	0.8	0	93	0.1		79	0	0.8
Number of Minerals	9	2	2	0	11	0		10	0	2
Oil reserves (/cap bbl)	11300	0	67800	0	4250	5800	.	3590	0	0

Characteristics	Samoan	Sanga	Sanmarinese	Sara	Scandinavian	Senufo	Serbian	Serer	Servicais Tongas	Shan
World Reserves %: Bauxite	0	0	0	0	0	0	0	0	0	0
Antimony	0.3	0	0	0	0	0	0	0	0	0
Barytes	0.3	0	0	0	0	0	0	0	0	0
Beryllium	0.9	0	0	0	0	0	0	0	0	0
Bismuth	1	0	0	0	0	0	0.1	0	0	0
Boron	7	0	0	0	0	0	0.2	0	0	0
Cadmium	2	0	0	0	0	0	0	0	0	0
Chromium	0	0	0	0	0	0	0	0	0	0
Cobalt	0	0	0	0	0	0	0	0	0	0
Copper	0.3	0	0	0	0	0	0.3	0	0	0
Fluorspar	0.1	0	0	0	0	0	0.1	0	0	0
Gold	2	0	0	0	0	0	0	0	0	0
Indium	0	0	0	0	0	0	0.1	0	0	0
Ind. diamond	1	0	0	0	0	0	0.1	0	0	0
Iron ore	6	0	0	0	0	0	0	0	0	0
Kaolin	3	0	0	0	0	0	0.1	0	0	0
Lead	0.1	0	0	0	0	0	0.1	0	0	0
Lithium	0	0	0	0	0	0	0	0	0	0
Magnesium	0.5	0	0	0	0	0	0.5	0	0	0
Manganese	9	0	0	0	0	0	0	0	0	0
Mercury	0	0	0	0	0	0	0.1	0	0	0
Molybdenum	0	0	0	0	0	0	0.1	0	0	0
Nickel	2	0	0	0	0	0	0	0	0	0
Niobium	0.1	0	0	0	0	0	0.1	0	0	0
Phosphate	0.1	0	0	0	0	0	0.1	0	0	0
Platinium group	3	0	0	0	0	0	0	0	0	0
Potash	3	0	0	0	0	0	0.1	0	0	0
Rare minerals	3	0	0	0	0	0	0.1	0	0	0
Rhenium	2	0	0	0	0	0	0	0	0	0
Selenium	6	0	0	0.6	0	0	0.1	0	0	0
Silver	0.3	0	0	0	0	0	0.1	0	0	0
Sulphur	0.7	0	0	0	0	0	0	0	0	0
Talc	0.1	0	0	0	0	0	0.1	0	0	0
Tantalum	1	0	0	0	0	0	0.1	0	0	0.3
Tellurium	0.6	0	0	0.6	0	0	0	0	0	0
Tin	9	0	0	1	0	0	0	0	0	0.6
Titanium A	2	0	0	0	0	0	0	0	0	0
Titanium B	0	0	0	0	0	0	0	0	0	0
Tungsten	0	0	0	0	0	0	0	0	0	0
Uranium	0	0	0	0	0	0	0.2	0	0	0.9
Vanadium	0	0	0	0	0	0	0	0	0	0.2
Vermiculite	0	0	0	0	0	0	0	0	0	0
Zinc	0	0	0	0	0	0	0	0	0	0
Zirconium	0	0	0	0	0	0	0	0	0	0
Total minerals: % sum	82	0	0	0	0	0	0.3	0	0	0
Number of Minerals	87	0	0	0	0	0	0.3	0	0	0
Oil reserves (/cap bbl)	20100	338000	0	0	141000	3970	2170	0	0	0

Characteristics	Shilluk	Shona	Siamese	Sidamo	Sindhi	Sinhalese	Slavic Muslims	Slovak	Slovene	Soga
World Reserves %: Bauxite	0	0	0	0	0	0	0	0	0	0
::Antimony	0	0	6	0	0	0	0	0	0	0
:Barytes	0	0.5	4	0	0	0	0	0	0	0
:Beryllium	0	0	0	0	0	0	0	0	0	4
:Bismuth	0	0	0	0	0	0	0	0	0	0
::Boron	0	0	0	0	0	0	0	0	0	0
:Cadmium	0	0	0	0	0	0	0	0.1	0	0
:Chromium	0	8	0	0	0	0	0	0	0	0
:Cobalt	0	0.1	0	0	0	0	0	0	0	0
:Copper	0	0	0.4	0	0	0	0	0	0	0
:Fluorspar	0	0	0	0	0	0	0	0.1	0	0
:Gold	0	0.2	0	0	0	0	0	0	0	0
:Indium	0	0	0	0	0	0	0	0	0	0
:Ind. diamond	0	0	0	0	0	0	0	0	0	0
:Iron ore	0	0	0	0	0	0	0	0	0	0
:Kaolin	0	0	0	0	0	0	0	0	0	0
:Lead	0	0	0	0	0	0	0	0.1	0	0
:Lithium	0	0.8	0	0	0	0	0	0	0	0
:Magnesium	0	0	0	0	0	0	0	0	0	0
:Manganese	0	0	0	0	0	0	0	0.2	0	0
:Mercury	0	0	0	0	0	0	0	0	0	0
:Molybdenum	0	0	0	0	0	0	0	0	0	0
:Nickel	0	0.2	0	0	0	0	0	0	0	0
:Niobium	0	0	0	0	0	0	0	0	0	0
:Phosphate	0	0	0	0	0	0	0	0	0	0
:Platinium group	0	0	0	0	0	0	0	0	0	0
:Potash	0	0	0	0	0	0	0	0	0	0
:Rare minerals	0	0	0	0	0	0	0	0	0	0
:Rhenium	0	0	0	0	0	0	0	0	0	0
:Selenium	0	0	0	0	0	0	0	0	0	0
:Silver	0	0.2	0	0	0	0	0	0.1	0	0
:Sulphur	0	0.2	0	0	0	0	0	0.1	0	0
:Talc	0	0	0	0	0	0.9	0	0	0	0
:Tantalum	0	0	0	0	0	0	0	0	0	0
:Tellurium	0	0	0	0	0	0	0	0	0	0
:Tin	0	0.2	28	0	0	0	0	0.1	0	0
:Titanium A	0	0	5	0	0	0	0	0.1	0	0
:Titanium B	0	0	0	0	0	0	0	0	0	0
:Tungsten	0	0	1	0	0	0	0	0	0	0
:Uranium	0	0	0	0	0	0	0	0	0	0
:Vanadium	0	0	0	0	0	0	0	0	0	0
:Vermiculite	0	0	0	0	0	0	0	0	0	0
:Zinc	0	0.2	0	0	0	0	0	0.1	0	0
::Zirconium	0	0	0	0	0	0	0	0	0	0
Total minerals: % sum	0	11	45	0	0	3	0	0.1	0	4
Number of Minerals	0	6	7	0	0	2	0	0.1	0	1
Oil reserves (/cap bbl)	10900	0	4260	0	3220	0	0	12500	244	0

Characteristics	Susu	Suriname	Sundanese	Spanish	Sotho North	Sotho	Soninke	Songhai	Somba	Somali
World Reserves %: Bauxite	26	0	4	4	0	0	0	0	0	0
Antimony	0	0	0	0.4	6	3	0	0	0	0
Barytes	0	0	0	13	0	0	0	0	0	0
Beryllium	0	0	0	0	4	2	0	0	0	0
Bismuth	0	0	0	0	0	0	0	0	0	0
Boron	0	0	0	3	0	0	0	0	0	0
Cadmium	0	0	0	0.2	7	4	0	0	0	0
Chromium	0	0	0	0.2	71	42	0	0	0	0
Cobalt	0	0	0.7	0	0.6	0.4	0	0	0	0
Copper	0	0	0	2	0.6	0.4	0	0	0	0
Fluorspar	0	0	0	0.8	13	8	0	0	0	0
Gold	0	0	0	0.1	47	28	0	0	0	0
Indium	0	0	0	0.2	0	0	0	0	0	0
Ind. diamond	0	0	0	0.3	0	0	0	0	0	0
Iron ore	0	0	0	0	4	2	0	0	0	0
Kaolin	0	0	0	2	2	1	0	0	0	0
Lead	0	0	0	0.9	3	2	0	0	0	0
Lithium	0	0	0	0.9	0	0	0	0	0	0
Magnesium	0	0	0	37	0.2	0.1	0	0	0	0
Manganese	0	0	0	0	45	27	0	0	0	0
Mercury	0	0	0	0.5	0	0	0	0	0	0
Molybdenum	0	0	0	27	0	0	0	0	0	0
Nickel	0	0	0	0.1	5	3	0	0	0	0
Niobium	0	0	0	0.5	0	0	0	0	0	0
Phosphate	0	0	0	0.1	0	0	0	0	0	0
Platinium group	0	0	0	0	20	12	0	0	0	0
Potash	0	0	0	0	89	53	0	0	0	0
Rare minerals	0	0	0	0	0	0	0	0	0	0
Rhenium	0	0	0	2	0	0	0	0	0	0
Selenium	0	0	0	1	0	0	0	0	0	0
Silver	0	0	0	1	0	0	0	0	0	0.2
Sulphur	0	0	0	0.7	0	0	0	0	0	0
Talc	0	0	0	0.4	0	0	0	0	0	0
Tantalum	0	0	0	27	0	0	0	0	0	0
Tellurium	0	0	0	0.3	0	0	0	0	0	0
Tin	0	0	12	0	0.5	0.3	0	3	0	0
Titanium A	0	0	0	2	18	11	0	0	0	0
Titanium B	0	0	0	0.7	4	3	0	0	0	0
Tungsten	0	0	0	0	0	0	0	0	0	0
Uranium	0	0	0	0	0	0	0	0	0	0
Vanadium	0	0	0	0	20	12	0	0	0	0
Vermiculite	0	0	0	0	40	24	0	0	0	0
Zinc	0	0	0	0	2	0	0	0	0	0
Zirconium	0	0	0	0.7	28	17	0	0.3	0	0
Total minerals: % sum	26	0	22	141	428	256	0	0.5	0	0.2
Number of Minerals	1	0	4	15	23	14	0	0	0	0.9
Oil reserves (/cap bbl)	0		29700	7340	0	0	0	0	3930	3850

Characteristics	Swahili	Swazi	Swedish	Swiss	Tahitian	Tai	Taiwanese (Dari)	Tajik	Tama	Tamang
World Reserves %: Bauxite	0	0	0	0	0	0	0	0	0	0
Antimony	0	0	0	0	0	0	0	0	0	0
Barytes	0	0	0	0	0	0	0	0	0	0
Beryllium	0	0	0	0	0	0	0	0	0	0
Bismuth	0	0	0	0	0	0	0	0	0	0
Boron	0	0	0	0	0	0	0	0	0	0
Cadmium	0	0	0	0	0	0	0	0	0	0
Chromium	0	0	0	0	0	0	0	0	0	0
Cobalt	0	0	0	0	7	0	0	0	0	0
Copper	0	0	0.1	0	0	0	0	0	0	0
Fluorspar	0	0	0	0	0	0	0	0	0	0
Gold	0.5	0	0	0	0	0	0	0	0	0
Indium	0	0	0	0	0	0	0	0	0	0
Ind. diamond	0	0	0	0	0	0	0	0	0	0
Iron ore	0	0	2	0	0	0	0	0	0	0
Kaolin	0	0	3	0	0	0	0	0	0	0
Lead	0	0	0	0	0	0	0	0	0	0
Lithium	0	0	0	0	0	0	0	0	0	0
Magnesium	0	0	0	0	0	0	0	0	0	2
Manganese	0	0	0	0	0	0	0	0	0	0
Mercury	0	0	0	0	1	0	0	0	0	0
Molybdenum	0	0	0	0	0	0	0	0	0	0
Nickel	0	0	0	0	0	0	0	0	0	0
Niobium	0	0	0	0	0	0	0	0	0	0
Phosphate	0	0	0	0	0	0	0	0	0	0
Platinium group	0	0	0	0	0	0	0	0	0	0
Potash	0	0	0	0	0	0	0	0	0	0
Rare minerals	0	0	0	0	0	0	0	0	0	0
Rhenium	0	0	0	0	0	0	0	0	0	0
Selenium	0	0	0	0	0	0	0	0	0	0
Silver	0	0	0	0	0	0	0	0	0	0
Sulphur	0	0	0	0	0	0	0	0	0	0
Talc	0	0	0	0	0	0	0	0	0	0
Tantalum	0	0	0	0	0	0	0	0	0	0
Tellurium	0	0	0	0	0	0	0	0	0	0
Tin	0	0	0	0	0	0	0	1	0	0
Titanium A	0	0	0	0	0	0	0	0	0	0
Titanium B	0	0	0	0	0	0	0	0	0	0
Tungsten	0	0	0	0	0	0	0	0	0	0
Uranium	0	0	0	0	0	0	0	0	0	0
Vanadium	0	0	0	0	0	0	0	0	0	0
Vermiculite	0	0	0	0	0	0	0	0	0	0
Zinc	0	0	0	0	0	0	0	0	0	2
Zirconium	0	0	0	0	0	0	0	1	0	1
Total minerals: % sum	0.5	0	5	0	16	0	0	0	0	2
Number of Minerals	1	0	2	0	2	0	0	0	0	1
Oil reserves (/cap bbl)	0	0	2160	0	.	5340	0	0.5	0	0

Characteristics	Tamil (Tubu)	Tatar	Teda	Teke	Tem-Kabre	Temne	Teso	Thai	Tharu	Tigre
World Reserves %: Bauxite	0	0	0	0	0	0.6	0	0	0	0
Antimony	0	0	0	0	0	0	0	0	0	0
Barytes	0	0	0	1	0	0	0	0	0	0
Beryllium	0	0	0	0	0	0	0	0	0	0
Bismuth	0	0	0	0	0	0	4	0	0	0
Boron	0	0	0	0	0	0	0	0	0	0
Cadmium	0	0	0	3	0	0	0	0	0	0
Chromium	0	0	0	0	0	0	0	0	0	0
Cobalt	0	0	0	30	0	0	0	0	0	0
Copper	0	0	0	6	0	0	0	0	0	0
Fluorspar	0	0	0	0	0	0	0	0	0	0
Gold	0	0	0	0	0	0	0	0	0	0
Indium	0	0	0	0	0	0	0	0	0	0
Ind. diamond	0	0	0	11	0	0	0	0	0	0
Iron ore	0	0	0	0	0	0	0	0	0	0
Kaolin	0	0	0	0	0	0	0	0	0	0
Lead	0	0	0	0	0	0	0	0	0	0
Lithium	0	0	0	0	0	0	0	0	0	0
Magnesium	0	0	0	0	0	0	0	0	0	0
Manganese	0	0	0	0	0	0	0	0	2	0
Mercury	0	0	0	0	0	0	0	0	0	0
Molybdenum	0	0	0	0	0	0	0	0	0	0
Nickel	0	0	0	0	0	0	0	0	0	0
Niobium	0	0	0	0.6	0	0	0	0	0	0
Phosphate	0	0	0	0	0	0	0	0	0	0
Platinium group	0	0	0	0	0	0	0	0	0	0
Potash	0	0	0	0	0	0	0	0	0	0
Rare minerals	0	0	0	0	0	0	0	0	0	0
Rhenium	0	0	0	7	0	0	0	0	0	0
Selenium	0	0	0	0	0	0	0	0	0	0
Silver	0	0	0	5	0	0	0	0	0	0
Sulphur	0	0	0	6	0	0	0	0	0	0
Talc	0	0	0	0	0	0	0	0	0	0
Tantalum	0	0	0	0.2	0	0	0	0	0	0
Tellurium	0	0	0	0	0	0	0	0	0	0
Tin	0.2	0	0	0	0	0.5	0	0	0	0
Titanium A	0.9	0	0	0.1	0	0.2	0	0	0	0
Titanium B	0	0	0	0	0	0	0	0	0	0
Tungsten	0	0	0	0	0	0	0	0	0	0
Uranium	0	0	0	0	0	0	0	0	0	0
Vanadium	0	0	0	0	0	0	0	0	0	0
Vermiculite	0	0	0	0	0	0	0	0	0	0
Zinc	0	0	0	2	0	0	0	0	0	0
Zirconium	0	0	0	0	0	1	0	0	0	0
Total minerals: % sum	3	0	0	72	0	5	4	0	2	0
Number of Minerals	2	0	0	9	0	4	1	0	1	0
Oil reserves (/cap bbl)	0	0	0	96700	0	0	0	7140	0	0

Characteristics	Tigrinya	Tikar	Tiv	Tonga	Tongan	Toros	Tribal	Tsimihety	Tsonga	Tswana
World Reserves %: Bauxite	0	3	0	0	0	0	0	0	0	0
Antimony	0	0	0	0	0	0	0	0	0	6
Barytes	0	0	0	0	0	0	0	0	0	0
Beryllium	0	0	0	0	0	4	0	0	0	4
Bismuth	0	0	0	0	0	0	0	0	1	0
Boron	0	0	0	0	0	0	0	0	0	0
Cadmium	0	0	0	0	0	0	0	0	0	7
Chromium	0	0	0	0	0	0	0	0	0	71
Cobalt	0	0	0	11	0	0	0	0.5	0	0.6
Copper	0	0	0	4	0	0	0	0	0	0.6
Fluorspar	0	0	0	0	0	0	0	0	0	13
Gold	0	0	0	0	0	0	0	0	0	47
Indium	0	0	0	0	0	0	0	0	0	0
Ind. diamond	0	0	0	0	0	0	0	0	0	0
Iron ore	0	0	0	0	0	0	0	0	0	4
Kaolin	0	0	0	0	0	0	0	0	0	2
Lead	0	0	0	2	0	0	0	0	0	3
Lithium	0	0	0	0	0	0	0	0	0	0
Magnesium	0	0	0	0	0	0	0	0	0	0.2
Manganese	0	0	0	0	0	0	0	0	0	45
Mercury	0	0	0	0	0	0	0	0	0	0
Molybdenum	0	0	0	0	0	0	0	0	0	0
Nickel	0	0	0	0	0	0	0	0.3	0	5
Niobium	0	0	2	0	0	0	0	0	0	0
Phosphate	0	0	0	0	0	0	0	0	0	20
Platinum group	0	0	0	0	0	0	0	0	0	89
Potash	0	0	0	0	0	0	0	0	0	0
Rare minerals	0	0	0	0	0	0	0	0	0	0
Rhenium	0	0	0	0	0	0	0	0	0	0
Selenium	0	0	0	0	0	0	0	0	0	0
Silver	0	0	0	0	0	0	0	0	0	0
Sulphur	0	0	0	0	0	0	0	0	0	0
Talc	0	0	0	0	0	0	0	0	0	0
Tantalum	0	0	0	0	0	0	0	0	0	0
Tellurium	0	0	0	0	0	0	0	0	0	0
Tin	0	0	12	0	0	0	0	0	1	0
Titanium A	0	0	0.3	0	0	0	0	0	0	0.5
Titanium B	0	0	0	0	0	0	0	0	0	18
Tungsten	0	0	0	0	0	0	0	0	0	4
Uranium	0	0	0	0	0	0	0	0	0	0
Vanadium	0	0	0	0	0	0	0	0	0	20
Vermiculite	0	0	0	0	0	0	0	0	0	40
Zinc	0	0	0	9	0	0	0	0	0	2
Zirconium	0	0	0	0	0	0	0	0	0	28
Total minerals: % sum	0	3	14	27	0	4	0	0.8	2	428
Number of Minerals	0	1	3	4	0	1	0	2	2	23
Oil reserves (/cap bbl)	0	31900	168000	0	0	0	0	0.2	0	0

Characteristics	Tuareg	Tukolor	Tumbuka	Turkish	Turkmen	Tutsi	Tuvaluan	Twa	Uighur	Ukrainian
World Reserves %: Bauxite	0	0	0	0	0	0	0	0	0	0
Antimony	0	0	0	2	0.1	0	0	0	0	0
Barytes	0	0	0	2	0.1	0	0	2	0	0
Beryllium	0	0	0	0	0	0	0	0	0	0
Bismuth	0	0	0	0	0	0	0	0	0	0
Boron	0	0	0	29	1	0	0	0	0	0
Cadmium	0	0	0	0.6	0	0	0	0	0	0.1
Chromium	0	0	0	0	0	0	0	0	0	0
Cobalt	0	0	11	0	0	0	0	0	0	0.1
Copper	0	0	4	0	0	0	0	0	0	0
Fluorspar	0	0	0	0.1	0	0	0	0	0	0.1
Gold	0	0	0	0	0.1	0	0	0	0	0
Indium	0	0	0	0	0	0	0	0	0	0.1
Ind. diamond	0	0	0	0	0	0	0	0	0	0
Iron ore	0	0	0	0	0.1	0	0	0	0	0.1
Kaolin	0	0	0	0	0	0	0	0	0	0.1
Lead	0	0	0	0.1	0	1	0	0	0	0
Lithium	0	0	0	0	0	0	0	0	0	0
Magnesium	0	0	0	2	0.1	0	0	0	0	0.1
Manganese	0	0	4	0	0.1	0	0	0	0	0.1
Mercury	0	0	0	3	0.2	0	0	0	0	0.2
Molybdenum	0	0	0	0	0	0	0	0	0	0
Nickel	0	0	0	0	0	0	0	0	0	0
Niobium	0	0	0	0	0	0	0	0	0	0
Phosphate	0	0	0	0	0	0	0	0	0	0.1
Platinium group	0	0	9	0	0	0	0	0	0	0
Potash	0	0	0	0.2	0	0	0	0	0	0.3
Rare minerals	0	0	0	0	0	0	0	0	0	0
Rhenium	0	0	0	0	0	0	0	0	0	0
Selenium	0	0	0	0	0	0	0	0	0	0.1
Silver	0	0	0	0	0.5	0	0	0	0	0.1
Sulphur	0	0	0	0	0	0	0	0	0	0
Talc	0	0	0	0	0.2	0	0	0	0	0.2
Tantalum	0	0	0	0	0	0	0	0	0	0
Tellurium	0	0	0	0	0	0	0	0	0	0
Tin	0	0	0	0	0	0	0	0	0	0
Titanium A	0	0	0	0	0.1	0	0	0	0	0.1
Titanium B	0	0	0	0	0	0	0	0	0	0
Tungsten	0	0	9	3	0	0	0	0	0	0
Uranium	0	0	0	0	0	0	0	0	0	0
Vanadium	0	0	0	0	0	0	0	0	0	0
Vermiculite	0	0	0	0	0	0	0	0	0	0
Zinc	1	0	0	0	0.3	1	0	2	0	0.1
Zirconium	0	0	0	0.1	0	0	0	0	0	0.2
Total minerals: % sum	0.2	0	27	42	0.9	0.5	0	0.6	0	0.3
Number of Minerals	0	0	4	7	3	0	0	0	0	2
Oil reserves (/cap bbl)	0	0	0	7800	283000	0	0	0	0	22400

Characteristics	Urdu	Uzbek	Vanuatuan	Vietnamese	Wallon	White	Wolof	Xhosa	Yalunka	Yao
World Reserves %: Bauxite	0	0	0	0	0	2	0	0	0.6	0.4
· Antimony	0	0	0	0.1	0	13	0	6	0	27
· Barytes	0	0	0	0	0	7	0	0	0	12
· Beryllium	0	0	0	0.3	0	26	0	4	0	0.2
· Bismuth	0	0	0	0.1	0	10	0	0	0	10
· Boron	0	0	0	0	0	0	0	0	0	4
· Cadmium	0	0	0	0	0	0.9	0	7	0	1
· Chromium	0	0	0	0.1	0	12	0	71	0	0
· Cobalt	0	0	0	0	0	1	0	0.6	0	0
· Copper	0	0	0	0.1	0	9	0	0.6	0	0
· Fluorspar	0	0	0	0.1	0	10	0	13	0	0
· Gold	0	0	0	0	0	0	0	47	0	6
· Indium	0	0	0	0.1	0	0	0	0	0	0
· Ind. diamond	0	0	0	0.3	0	5	0	4	0	0.5
· Iron ore	0	0	0	0.1	0	25	0	2	0	0
· Kaolin	0	0	0	0	0	12	0	0	0	0.3
· Lead	0	0	0	0	0	0.8	0	3	0	0.5
· Lithium	0	0	0	0	0	2	0	0	0	4
· Magnesium	0	0	0	0.4	0	33	0	0.2	0	0
· Manganese	0	0	0	0	0	6	0	45	0	16
· Mercury	0	0	0	0	0	7	0	0	0	0.9
· Molybdenum	0	0	0	0.1	0	0.6	0	0	0	4
· Nickel	0	0	0	0	0	11	0	5	0	5
· Niobium	0	0	0	0	0	11	0	0	0	0.8
· Phosphate	0	0	0	0.1	0	9	0	20	0	0
· Platinium group	0	0	0	0.1	0	0	0	89	0	0.8
· Potash	0	0	0	0.1	0	24	0	0	0	0
· Rare minerals	0	0	0	0.3	0	1	0	0	0	2
· Rhenium	0	0	0	0.1	0	0	0	0	0	27
· Selenium	0	0	0	0	0	12	0	0	0	0
· Silver	0	0.2	0	0	0	4	0	0	0	0
· Sulphur	0	0	0	0	0	7	0	0	0	4
· Talc	0	0	0	0.1	0	5	0	0	0	0
· Tantalum	0	0	0	0	0	0	0	0	0	0
· Tellurium	0	0	0	0	0	0.5	0	0	0	0
· Tin	0	0	0	0.4	0	0	0	0.5	0.5	13
· Titanium A	0	0	0	0.1	0	36	0	18	0.2	8
· Titanium B	0	0	0	0.1	0	10	0	4	0	8
· Tungsten	0	0	0	0	0	8	0	0	0	23
· Uranium	0	0	0	0.4	0	0	0	20	0	0.9
· Vanadium	0	0	0	0.3	0	0	0	40	0	7
· Vermiculite	0	0	0	0	0	0	0	2	0	0
· Zinc	0	0	0	0	0	0	0	0	0	0
· Zirconium	0	0	0	0	0	0	0	28	0	0.5
Total minerals: % sum	0	0.2	0	4	0	373	0	428	1	195
Number of Minerals	0	0.1	0	0.3	0	31	0	23	5	15
Oil reserves (/cap bbl)	3220	0	0	8190	0	150000	0	0	4	10300

Characteristics	Yi-Miao	Yoruba	Yugoslav	Zambo	Zulu
World Reserves %: Bauxite	0.7	0	0	0	0
Antimony	52	0	0.8	0	5
Barytes	24	0	0	0	0
Beryllium	0	0	0	0	3
Bismuth	19	0	0	0	0
Boron	8	0	0	0	0
Cadmium	3	0	0	0	6
Chromium	0	0	0	0	62
Cobalt	0	0	0	0	0.5
Copper	0	0	0	0	0.5
Fluorspar	11	0	0	0	11
Gold	0	0	0	0	41
Indium	9	0	2	0	0
Ind. diamond	1	0	0	0	0
Iron ore	5	0	0	0	3
Kaolin	1	0	0	0	2
Lead	9	0	0	0	2
Lithium	0	0	0.1	0	0
Magnesium	30	0	0	0	0.2
Manganese	2	0	0	0	4
Mercury	8	0	0	0	0
Molybdenum	9	0	0	0	0
Nickel	2	1	0	0	5
Niobium	0	0	0	0	0
Phosphate	2	0	0	0	18
Platinium group	0	0	4	0	77
Potash	3	0	0	0	0
Rare minerals	51	0	0	0	0
Rhenium	0	0	0	0	0
Selenium	0	0	0	0	0
Silver	7	0	0.9	0	0
Sulphur	0	0	0	0	0
Talc	7	12	0	0	0
Tantalum	0	0.3	0	0	0
Tellurium	0	0	0	0	0
Tin	25	0	0	0	0.4
Titanium A	15	0	0	0	15
Titanium B	15	0	0	0	4
Tungsten	45	0	0.1	0	0
Uranium	2	0	0	0	0.7
Vanadium	14	0	0	0	18
Vermiculite	0	0	0	0	35
Zinc	3	0	0	0	2
Zirconium	1	0	0	0	25
Total minerals: % sum	375	14	8	0	375
Number of Minerals	29	3	3	0	20
Oil reserves (/cap bbl)	19800	163000	8420	0	0

7

LAND RESOURCES ACROSS ETHNIC CULTURES

Many teachings on ethnic cultures are directly related to local terrain. This chapter provides comparative statistics for a variety of variables characterizing each ethnic group's land-based resources (excluding minerals, covered in Chapter 6). For a full discussion of the methodology used to generate these estimates, please refer to Chapter 1 which gives important caveats. This chapter first gives summary statistics of the variables reported: the number of countries/cultures for which each variable was available, the number of ethnic cultures covered, weighted averages (by population) and simple averages; these averages can be used as benchmarks. Then a lengthy comparative table is presented which provides raw statistics across the ethnic groups defined in Chapter 1.

Most of the variables are self explanatory, though some merit commentary. All of the statistics should be considered as estimates which have undergone rounding and certain adjustments. Land-related estimates cover the amount of land available, its current use, the degree to which it is protected by law, and the extent to which it may be exposed to earthquakes, volcanism, soil degradation, overgrazing, and deforestation. Elevation and time zone location are also given; these statistics are estimated for inhabited regions. Then, each group is characterized as being located in or exposed to the earth's tectonic plates, vegetation zones (Biomes), and zoological zones.

Summary Statistics:
Land Resources

Characteristics	Number of Countries Covered	Number of Ethnic Groups Covered	Weighted Average by Pop 1994	Simple Average	Simple Standard Deviation
Land: Total Area (km sq)	234	426	4142445.82	1182579.22	2379052.89
: Density (pop/km sq)	234	426	161.92	137.45	785.53
: # of boundaries	233	425	6.62	4.17	2.87
: Total boundary (km)	234	426	10542.05	4175.85	4521.99
: Terrain (3=mountains)	234	426	2.17	1.95	1.00
Land Usage: Arable %	232	424	22.67	12.57	12.10
: Permanent crops %	232	424	1.46	2.36	5.42
: Meadows & pastures %	232	424	18.71	21.15	18.44
: Forest & woodland %	232	424	24.33	28.00	21.27
: Other %	232	424	29.92	31.36	22.25
: Irrigated %	221	418	5.55	2.28	7.43
: % Protected	191	409	3.43	4.14	4.45
: % Partially Protected	192	410	3.05	2.32	4.11
Risks: Earthquake (1=high)	234	426	0.43	0.17	0.36
: Volcanism	234	426	0.12	0.08	0.25
: Soil degradation	234	426	0.55	0.30	0.44
: Desertification	234	426	0.63	0.39	0.47
: Overgrazing	234	426	0.22	0.15	0.33
: Deforestation	234	426	0.61	0.44	0.47
Elevation: average (m)	234	426	209.70	382.24	535.26
: Highest point (m)	193	414	5801.48	3438.32	2175.77
: Lowest point (m)	193	414	-35.59	51.23	167.94
Timezone (GMT)	233	426	3.96	2.38	3.53
Tectonic plate: African	234	426	0.18	0.53	0.49
: Eurasian	234	426	0.72	0.35	0.47
: Indo-Australian	234	426	0.27	0.13	0.32
: Pacific	234	426	0.07	0.06	0.22
: American	234	426	0.12	0.05	0.19
: Nasca	234	426	0.00	0.01	0.08
: Caribbean	234	426	0.02	0.01	0.12
Biome: Desert (1=yes)	234	426	0.27	0.25	0.41
: Monsoon	234	426	0.46	0.10	0.28
: Tropical rain forest	234	426	0.35	0.39	0.47
: Savanna	234	426	0.35	0.46	0.49
: Mediterranean	234	426	0.10	0.10	0.28
: Temperate grassland	234	426	0.43	0.17	0.36
: Temperate forest	234	426	0.44	0.18	0.37
: Mountain	234	426	0.40	0.17	0.36
: Taiga	234	426	0.03	0.03	0.17
: Tundra	234	426	0.03	0.01	0.10
: Polar	234	426	0.03	0.02	0.13
Zoology: Neotropical	234	426	0.08	0.05	0.21
: Nearctic	234	426	0.07	0.03	0.15
: Ethiopian	234	426	0.14	0.49	0.49
: Oriental	234	426	0.52	0.16	0.36
: Palearctic	234	426	0.66	0.32	0.46
: Australian	234	426	0.03	0.06	0.23

Characteristics	Abadkis	Abkhaz	Acholi	Afar	Afro-European	Akan	Albanian	Ambo	Amerind	Amerind-Mestizo
Land: Total Area (km sq)	141000	69700	236000	922000	11000	239000	50500	1250000	2140000	2770000
:Density (pop/km sq)	150	79	82	40	228	69	109	8	52	12
:# of boundaries	2	4	5	3	0	3	2	4	3	5
:Total boundary (km)	2930	1460	2700	3900	0	2090	1190	5200	4450	9670
:Terrain (3=mountains)	4	3	3	2	3	2	3	0	3	3
Land Usage: Arable %	17	.	23	0.7	19	5	22	2	12	9
:Permanent crops %	0	.	.	.	6	6	4	.	1	4
:Meadows & pastures %	13	.	25	30	18	15	17	23	33	52
:Forest & woodland %	33	.	30	18	28	37	33	43	28	22
:Other %	37	3	13	16	29	36	23	32	25	13
:Irrigated %	2	.	.	2	3	.	0.5	2	2	1
:% Protected	8	.	8	0.7	.	5	0.6	.	6	3
:Partially Protected	1	3	4	0.7	.	.	.	1	4	2
Risks: Earthquake (1=high)	0	0	0	0.2	0	0	0	0	.	1
:Volcanism	0	0	0	0.7	0	0	0	0	.	.
:Soil degradation	1	0	1	0.7	0	1	0	1	0.3	1
:Desertification	0	0	0	0.7	0	0	0	0	0.9	0
:Overgrazing	0	0	1	0.7	0	1	0	1	0.8	.
:Deforestation	1	0	1	0.7	0	1	0	1	0.9	1
Elevation: average (m)	1340	490	1190	1590	32	65	.	43	1200	25
:Highest point (m)	8850	5070	5100	4200	2260	885	2760	2620	5370	6960
:Lowest point (m)	60	3	610	-130	-5	0	0	.	-11	-42
Timezone (GMT)	6	3	3	3	1	0	1	1	-7	-3
Tectonic plate: African	0	0	1	1	1	1	0	1	0	0
:Eurasian	1	1	0	0	0	0	1	0	0	0
:Indo-Australian	0	0	0	0	0	0	0	0	0	0
:Pacific	0	0	0	0	0	0	0	0	0.7	1
:American	0	0	0	0	0	0	0	0	0.8	1
:Nasca	0	0	0	0	0	0	0	0	0	1
:Caribbean	0	0	0	0	0	0	0	0	0	1
Biome: Desert (1=yes)	1	0	0	0.9	0	0	0	1	0.2	1
:Monsoon	0	0	0	0	0	0	0	0	0	0
:Tropical rain forest	0	0	1	0	0	1	0	0	0	1
:Savanna	0	0	1	0.7	0	1	0	1	0.7	1
:Mediterranean	0	0	0	0	1	0	0.9	0	0	0
:Temperate grassland	0	0	0	0	0	0	0	0	0	0
:Temperate forest	1	1	0	0	0	0	0.4	0	0	1
:Mountain	1	1	1	0	0	0	0.1	0	0.8	1
:Taiga	0	0	0	0	0	0	0	0	0	0
:Tundra	0	0	0	0	0	0	0	0	0	0
:Polar	0	0	0	0	0	0	0	0	0	0
Zoology: Neotropical	0	0	0	0	0	0	0	0	0.8	1
:Nearctic	0	0	0	0	0	0	0	0	0.1	0
:Ethiopian	0	0	1	0.9	0	1	0	1	0	0
:Oriental	0	0	0	0	0	0	0	0	0	0
:Palearctic	1	1	0	0	1	0	0.9	0	0	0
:Australian	0	0	0	0	0	0	0	0	0	0

Characteristics	Amhara	Ana-Ife	Andorran	Angolares	Anouis	Antandroy	Arab, other	Arab Berber	Arab Emirian	Arab Lebanese
Land: Total Area (km sq)	1220000	56800	450	63800	322000	587000	829000	1690000	83600	10400
.. Density (pop/km sq)	43	69	118	115	45	23	58	3	22	277
.. # of boundaries	4	3	2	0.7	4	2	5	6	3	2
.. Total boundary (km)	5140	1650	125	838	3110	0	3090	4280	1020	454
.. Terrain (3=mountains)	3	2	3	3	2	2	2	1	1	2
Land Usage: Arable %	12	25	2	2	9	4	14	3	0	21
.. Permanent crops %	1	1	0	15	4	0	2	0	0	9
.. Meadows & pastures %	41	4	56	4	9	58	22	8	2	1
.. Forest & woodland %	24	28	22	28	26	26	6	0	0	8
.. Other %	22	42	20	30	52	11	56	91	98	61
.. Irrigated %	0	0	0	5	6	1	2	0	0	7
.. % Protected	3	1	0	0	0.3	2	0.5	0.1	5	0.3
.. % Partially Protected	0	1	0	4	0	1	0.4	0	0	0
Risks: Earthquake (1=high)	1	0	0	0.7	0	0	0.5	0	0	0
.. Volcanism	1	0	0	0.3	0	0	0	0	0	0
.. Soil degradation	1	0	0	0	0	1	0.3	0	0	0
.. Desertification	1	0	0	0	0	1	0.3	0	0	0
.. Overgrazing	1	1	1	0.3	0	1	0.3	0	0	0
.. Deforestation	1	1	1	0	1	1	0	0	0	0
Elevation: average (m)	2140	20	1080	71	7	1380	134	23	5	17
.. Highest point (m)	4620	986	2950	2250	1750	2880	3200	2200	1930	3080
.. Lowest point (m)	-125	0	840	0	0	3	-66	-45	0	0
Timezone (GMT)	3	0	1	0	0	3	2	1	4	2
Tectonic plate: African	1	1	0	1	1	1	0.8	1	0	0
.. Eurasian	0	0	1	0	0	0	0.5	0	1	1
.. Indo-Australian	0	0	0	0	0	0	0.1	0	0	0
.. Pacific	0	0	0	0	0	0	0	0	0	0
.. American	0	0	0	0	0	0	0	0	0	0
.. Nasca	0	0	0	0	0	0	0	0	0	0
.. Caribbean	0	0	0	0	0	0	0	0	0	0
Biome: Desert (1=yes)	1	0	0	0	0	1	0.6	1	1	0
.. Monsoon	0	0	0	0	0	0	0	0	0	0
.. Tropical rain forest	0	1	0	1	1	0	0	0	0	0
.. Savanna	1	1	0	0	1	1	0	0	0	0
.. Mediterranean	0	0	0	0	0	0	0.4	0	0	1
.. Temperate grassland	0	0	0	0	0	0	0	0	0	0
.. Temperate forest	0	0	0	0	0	0	0	0	0	0
.. Mountain	1	0	1	0	0	0	0	0	0	1
.. Taiga	0	0	0	0	0	0	0	0	0	0
.. Tundra	0	0	0	0	0	0	0	0	0	0
.. Polar	0	0	0	0	0	0	0	0	0	0
Zoology: Neotropical	0	0	0	0	0	0	0	0	0	0
.. Nearctic	0	0	0	0	0	0	0	0	0	0
.. Ethiopian	1	1	0	1	1	1	0.6	1	0	0
.. Oriental	0	0	0	0	0	0	0	0	0	0
.. Palearctic	0	0	1	0	0	0	0.9	1	1	1
.. Australian	0	0	0	0	0	0	0	0	0	0

Characteristics	Arab Omani	Arab Palestin.	Arab Quatar	Arab Saudi	Arab Sudanic	Arab Total	Arauca-nian	Armenian	Assamese	Assyrian
Land: Total Area (km sq)	212000	6720	11000	2150000	2380000	11300000	757000	184000	47000	435000
::Density (pop/km sq)	8	247	44	8	10	51	18	111	35	46
::# of boundaries	4	2	2	9	8	5	3	5	2	7
::Total boundary (km)	1370	413	60	4410	7520	3630	6170	1650	1080	3450
::Terrain (3=mountains)	2	3	0	1	2	2	4	3	3	3
Land Usage: Arable %	0	26	0	1	5	1	7	11	2	12
::Permanent crops %	5	2	0	0	0	1	0	0.3	2	1
::Meadows & pastures %	5	26	5	39	25	23	16	0.5	5	9
::Forest & woodland %	0	2	0	1	19	6	21	1	70	3
::Other %	95	44	95	59	51	58	56	12	23	75
::Irrigated %	0.2	1	0	0	0.9	1	2	17	0	4
::% Protected	0	0.3	0	9	0.4	0.3	18	6	19	0
::% Partially Protected	0	0	0	0	0.3	0.4	1	0.2	18	0
Risks: Earthquake (1=high)	0	0	0	0	0	0.3	1	0	0	1
::Volcanism	0	0.2	0	0	0	0.4	0	0.1	0	0
::Soil degradation	0	0.2	0	1	1	0.2	1	0.1	0	1
::Desertification	0	0	0	0	0	0.2	0	0.1	0	0
::Overgrazing	1	0	0	0	0	0.2	0	0	0	0
::Deforestation	0	0	0	0	1	0.9	0	0	0	0
Elevation: average (m)	6	474	10	298	241	159	268	896	2420	34
::Highest point (m)	3030	3080	105	3210	3210	3150	6890	4270	7550	3610
::Lowest point (m)	0	0	3	3	17	-47	-4	271	97	3
::Timezone (GMT)	4	2	3	3	2	2	-4	3	6	3
Tectonic plate: African	0	0	0	0	1	0	0	0	0	0
::Eurasian	1	1	1	1	0	1	0	1	0	1
::Indo-Australian	0	0	0	0	0	0	0	0	1	0
::Pacific	0	0	0	0	0	0	0	0	0	0
::American	0	0	0	0	0	0	1	0	0	0
::Nasca	0	0	0	0	0	0	0	0	0	0
::Caribbean	0	0	0	0	0	0	0	0	0	0
Biome: Desert (1=yes)	1	1	1	1	1	1	0	0	0	0
::Monsoon	0	0	0	0	0	0	0	0	1	0
::Tropical rain forest	0	0	0	0	0	0	0	0	0	0
::Savanna	0	0	0	0	0	0	0	0	0	0
::Mediterranean	0	1	0	0	0	0.5	1	1	0	0
::Temperate grassland	0	0	0	0	0	0	1	0	0	0
::Temperate forest	0	0	0	0	0	0	1	0	0	0
::Mountain	0	0	0	0	0	0	1	1	1	1
Zoology: Neotropical	0	0	0	0	0	0	1	0	0	0
::Nearctic	0	0	0	0	0	0	0	0	0	0
::Ethiopian	1	0	0	1	1	0.7	0	0	0	0
::Oriental	0	0	0	0	0	0	0	0	1	0
::Paleartic	1	1	1	1	0	0.7	0	1	0	1
::Australian	0	0	0	0	0	0.8	0	0	0	0

Characteristics	Austrian	Avar	Aymara	Azande	Azerbaijani	Bagirmi-Sara	Bahraini	Bai	Bakhtiari	Bakongo
Land: Total Area (km sq)	83800	86600	1190000	2220000	1060000	1280000	620	960000	1650000	1250000
..Density (pop/km sq)	93	85	12	15	56	5	857	126	38	8
..# of boundaries	7						0		6	4
..Total boundary (km)	2640	2010	6840	7930	4180	5970		23200	5490	5200
..Terrain (3=mountains)	4	3	3	2	3	2		3	3	2
Land Usage: Arable %	17	18	2	3	12		2	10	8	0
..Permanent crops %	1	0	0	0	0		2	0	0	2
..Meadows & pastures %	24	25	23	8	26	36	6	31	27	23
..Forest & woodland %	39	57	53	65	55	11		14	11	43
..Other %	19	70	20	24	26	51	90	45	54	32
..Irrigated %	0	2	0.5	0.2	2		0	0	2	0
..% Protected	0	0	6	4	0		0	3	5	2
..% Partially Protected	25	0			0	0.3	0	1		1
Risks: Earthquake (1=high)	0	0	0.3	0.4	0	0	0	0	0	0
..Volcanism	0	0	0.5	0	0	0	0	1	0	0
..Soil degradation	0	0	1	0	0.6	0	0	0	0	0
..Desertification	0	0	0.5	0	0.6	1	0	1	1	1
..Overgrazing	0	0		0.3	0	0	0	0	0	0
..Deforestation	0	0	0.5	0	0	0	0	0	0	0
Elevation: average (m)	202	990	1320	287	933	300	0.9	28	913	43
..Highest point (m)	3800	4470	6530	4380	5190	3410	134	8850	5600	2620
..Lowest point (m)	115	-28	36	30	-26	160	-154	-154	-28	
Timezone (GMT)	1	3	-4	1	3	1	3	8	4	1
Tectonic plate: African	0	0	0	1	0	1	0	0	0	1
..Eurasian	1	1	0	0	1	0	1	1	1	0
..Indo-Australian	0	0	0	0	0	0	0	0	0	0
..Pacific	0	0	0	0	0	0	0	0	0	0
..American	0	0	1	0	0	0	0	0	0	0
..Nasca	0	0	1	0	0	0	0	0	0	0
..Caribbean	0	0	0	0	0	0	0	0	0	0
Biome: Desert (1=yes)	0	0	0	0	0	0	1	0	1	0
..Monsoon	0	0	0	0	0	0	0	0	0	0
..Tropical rain forest	0	0	0	0.2	0	0	0	0	0	1
..Savanna	0	0	0	0.8	0	1	0	0	0	0
..Mediterranean	0	0	0	0	0	0	0	0	0	0
..Temperate grassland	0	0	0	0	0	0	0	0	0	0
..Temperate forest	1	0	0	0	0	0	0	1	0	0
..Mountain	0	1	1	0	1	0	0	0	1	0
..Taiga	0	0	0	0	0	0	0	0	0	0
..Tundra	0	0	0	0	0	0	0	0	0	0
..Polar	0	0	0	0	0	0	0	0	0	0
Zoology: Neotropical	0	0	1	0	0	0	0	0	0	0
..Nearctic	0	0	0	0	0	0	0	0	0	0
..Ethiopian	0	0	0	1	0	1	0	0	0	1
..Oriental	0	0	0	0	0	0	0	1	0	0
..Palearctic	1	1	0	0	1	0	1	1	1	0
..Australian	0	0	0	0	0	0	0	0	0	0

Characteristics	Balante	Baluchi	Bambara	Bamileke-Bamum	Banda	Bangi-Ngale	Bantu	Baoule	Bari	Bariba
Land: Total Area (km sq)	36100	1050000	1240000	475000	1150000	2350000	398000	322000	2510000	113000
:Density (pop/km sq)	28	118	8	26	9	18	28	42	11	45
:# of boundaries	2	4	7	6	6	7	4	5	8	4
:Total boundary (km)	724	6340	7240	4590	6160	8340	3040	3110	7700	1990
:Terrain (3=mountains)	0	3	1	1	3	2	2	2	2	2
Land Usage: Arable %	9	20	20	3	3	3	7	9	5	12
:Permanent crops %	1	0	2	2	0	0	0	4	5	4
:Meadows & pastures %	46	14	25	18	5	4	13	9	24	4
:Forest & woodland %	38	6	7	54	68	78	61	26	20	35
:Other %	6	59	66	13	24	15	20	52	51	45
:Irrigated %	0	13	0	0	7	0	0.1	0	0	0
:% Protected	0	0.3	3	4	0	4	8	6	4	7
:% Partially Protected	0	0.7	0	2	3	0	1	0.3	0.3	0
Risks: Earthquake (1=high)	0	0.7	0	0	0	0	0	0	0	0
:Volcanism	0	0.1	0	1	0	0	0	0	0	0
:Soil degradation	0	0.3	0	0	0.7	0	1	0	0	0
:Desertification	0	0.3	0	1	0.7	0	0	0	0	0
:Overgrazing	0	0	0	1	0	0	0	0	1	0
:Deforestation	1	1	1	0	0	0	1	1	0	1
Elevation: average (m)	20	528	316	387	353	290	1370		235	17
:Highest point (m)	4250	7650	1150	4100	2540	511	2590	1750	3190	681
:Lowest point (m)	0	0	22	0	233	0	157	0	0	0
Timezone (GMT)	-1	5	0	1	1	2	2	0	2	1
Tectonic plate: African	1	0	1	1	1	1	1	1	1	1
:Eurasian	0	1	0	0	0	0	0	0	0	0
:Indo-Australian	0	0	0	0	0	0	0	0	0	0
:Pacific	0	0	0	0	0	0	0	0	0	0
:American	0	0	0	0	0	0	0	0	0	0
:Nasca	0	0	0	0	0	0	0	0	0	0
:Caribbean	0	0	0	0	0	0	0	0	0	0
Biome: Desert (1=yes)	0	1	0	0	0	0	0	0	0	0
:Monsoon	0	0	0	0	0	0	0	0	0	0
:Tropical rain forest	1	0	0	1	0	1	1	1	0	0
:Savanna	0	0	1	0	1	0	0	0	1	1
:Mediterranean	0	0	0	0	0	0	0	0	0	0
:Temperate grassland	0	0	0	0	0	0	0	0	0	0
:Temperate forest	0	0	0	0	0	0	0	0	0	0
:Mountain	0	0	0	0	0	0	0	0	0	0
:Taiga	0	0	0	0	0	0	0	0	0	0
:Tundra	0	0	0	0	0	0	0	0	0	0
:Polar	0	0	0	0	0	0	0	0	0	0
Zoology: Neotropical	0	0	0	0	0	0	0	0	0	0
:Nearctic	0	0	0	0	0	0	0	0	0	0
:Ethiopian	1	0	1	1	1	1	1	1	1	1
:Oriental	0	0	0	0	0	0	0	0	0	0
:Palearctic	0	1	0	0	0	0	0	0	0	0
:Australian	0	0	0	0	0	0	0	0	0	0

Characteristics	Barotze	Baskhir	Basque	Bassa	Batswana	Bayad	Beja	Belgian	Belorus-sian	Bemba
Land: Total Area (km sq)	753000	17100000	503000	111000	600000	1570000	2510000	29600	2280000	753000
..Density (pop/km sq)	12	9	77	26	2	1	11	342	45	12
..# of boundaries	2	15	4	3	3	2	8	4	6	2
..Total boundary (km)	5660	20100	1900	1590	4010	8110	7700	1350	5310	5660
..Terrain (3=mountains)	2	2	3	1	0	3	0	0	1	2
Land Usage: Arable %	7	0	31	3	2	1	5	24	26	7
..Permanent crops %	0	0	10	2	0	0	0	1	0.1	0
..Meadows & pastures %	47	0	21	39	75	79	24	20	14	47
..Forest & woodland %	27	0	31	55	21	10	20	21	0.7	27
..Other %	19	0	7	0	0	10	51	34	47	19
..Irrigated %	0	0	6	0	0	0	4	0	0.8	0
..% Protected	8	1	0	1	17	4	0.3	0	0.1	8
..% Partially Protected	0	0	7	0	2	0	0	2	0	0
Risks: Earthquake (1=high)	0	0	0	0	0	0	0	0	0	0
..Volcanism	0	0	0	0	0	0	0	0	0	0
..Soil degradation	1	0	1	0	1	0	1	0	0	1
..Desertification	0	0	0	0	1	0	0	0	0	0
..Overgrazing	1	0	1	0	1	0	0	0	0	1
..Deforestation	0	0	0	1	0	0	0	0	0	0
Elevation: average (m)	1280	156	445	23	1010	1310	235	83	153	1280
..Highest point (m)	2160	5640	3400	1380	1510	4360	3190	689	1170	2160
..Lowest point (m)	329	-28	0	0	513	553	0	4	62	329
Timezone (GMT)	2	8	1	1	2	8	2	1	2	2
Tectonic plate: African	1	0	0	1	1	0	1	0	0	1
..Eurasian	0	1	1	0	0	1	0	1	1	0
..Indo-Australian	0	0	0	0	0	0	0	0	0	0
..Pacific	0	0	0	0	0	0	0	0	0	0
..American	0	0	0	0	0	0	0	0	0	0
..Nasca	0	0	0	0	0	0	0	0	0	0
..Caribbean	0	0	0	0	0	0	0	0	0	0
Biome: Desert (1=yes)	0	0	0	0	1	1	1	0	0.2	0
..Monsoon	0	0	0	0	0	0	0	0	0	0
..Tropical rain forest	0	0	0	1	0	0	0	0	0	0
..Savanna	1	0	0	0	1	0	0	0	0	1
..Mediterranean	0	0	1	0	0	0	0	0	0	0
..Temperate grassland	0	1	0	0	0	1	0	0	0	0
..Temperate forest	0	1	1	0	0	0	0	1	1	0
..Mountain	0	0	1	0	0	1	0	0	0	0
..Tundra	0	0	0	0	0	0	0	0	0	0
..Taiga	0	1	0	0	0	0	0	0	0	0
..Polar	0	0	0	0	0	0	0	0	0	0
Zoology: Neotropical	0	0	0	0	0	0	0	0	0.09	0
..Nearctic	0	0	0	0	0	0	0	0	0.01	0
..Ethiopian	1	0	0	1	1	0	1	0	0.1	1
..Oriental	0	0	0	0	0	0	0	0	0.1	0
..Palearctic	0	1	1	0	0	1	0	1	0.1	0
..Australian	0	0	0	0	0	0	0	0	0	0

Characteristics	Bengali	Berber	Bete	Betsileo	Betsimi-Saraka	Bhutia	Bihari	Black	Black Amerind	Boa
Land: Total Area (km sq)	144000	1140000	322000	587000	587000	47000	142000	6300000	1140000	2350000
: Density (pop/km sq)	849	43	42	23	23	35	351	65	30	18
: # of boundaries	2	4	5	0	0	2	2	4	5	7
: Total boundary (km)	4240	3560	3110	0	0	1080	3300	8500	7410	8340
: Terrain (3=mountains)	1	3	9	4	4	3	3	3	3	3
Land Usage: Arable %	67	13	9	58	58	2	31	15	4	3
: Permanent crops %	2	0.7	4	26	26		0.6	2	2	0
: Meadows & pastures %	4	23	9	11	11	5	10	26	29	4
: Forest & woodland %	16	8	26			70	28	34	49	78
: Other %	11	56	52	11	11	23	30	22	16	15
: Irrigated %	14	0.6	0.6	2	2	1		8	0	0
: % Protected	0.7	0.5	0.3	2	2	9	0.9	4	8	4
: % Partially Protected						18		0.5		0
Risks: Earthquake (1=high)	0	1	0	1	1	0	0	0.5	0	0
: Volcanism	0	0	0	0	0	0	0	0.4	0	0
: Soil degradation	0	0	0	1	1	0	0	0.4	1	0
: Desertification	1	1	0	0	0	0	1	0.4	0	0
: Overgrazing	0	0	0	0	0	0	0		0	0
: Deforestation	1	0	1	1	1	0	1	0.4	1	0
Elevation: average (m)	8	58		1380	1380	2420	956	317	1560	290
: Highest point (m)	958	3690	1750	2880	2880	7550	6580	4420	5800	5110
: Lowest point (m)	0	-49	0			97	43	-38	-5	0
Timezone (GMT)	6	0.4	0	3	3	6	6	0.1	-5	2
Tectonic plate: African	0	1	1	1	1	0	0	0.8	0	1
: Eurasian	1	0	0	0	0	1	1	0	0	0
: Indo-Australian	1	0	0	0	0	0	1	0	0	0
: Pacific	0	0	0	0	0	0	0	0	0	0
: American	0	0	0	0	0	0	0	0	1	0
: Nasca	0	0	0	0	0	0	0	0	0	0
: Caribbean	0	0	0	0	0	0	0	0	0	0
Biome: Desert (1=yes)	0	1	0	0	0	0	0.3	0.8	0	0
: Monsoon	1	0	0	0	0	1	1	0.4	0	0
: Tropical rain forest	1	0	1	1	1	0	1	0.3	1	1
: Savanna	0	0	1	0	0	0	0	0.4	0	0
: Mediterranean	0	1	0	0	0	0	0	0.1	0	0
: Temperate grassland	0	0	0	0	0	0	0	0.8	0	0
: Temperate forest	0	0	0	0	0	0	0	0.7	0	0
: Mountain	0	0	0	0	0	1	0	0.5	0	0
Zoology: Neotropical	0	0	0	0	0	0	0	0	1	0
: Nearctic	0	0	0	0	0	0	0	0	0	0
: Ethiopian	0	0	1	1	1	0	0	0.4	0	1
: Oriental	1	0	0	0	0	1	1	0.6	0	0
: Palearctic	0	1	0	0	0	1	0.7	0.1	0	0
: Australian	0	0	0	0	0	0	0	0	0	0

Characteristics	Bobo	Bounty Mutineers	Brazilian	Breton	Bubi	Bulgarian	Bullom	Bura	Burman	Bush Negro
Land: Total Area (km sq)	533000	42	8512000	544000	28100	126000	71700	924000	677000	154000
:Density (pop/km sq)	28	48	69	104	14	81	63	115	66	3
:# of boundaries	6	0		8	2	4	2	4	5	3
:Total boundary (km)	4280	0	1200	2880	539	1960	958	4050	5880	1640
:Terrain (3=mountains)	1	3	2	3		3	2	2	3	1
Land Usage: Arable %	8	0	20	32	5	35	23	31	15	0
:Permanent crops %	0	18	4	2	4	3		3	1	0
:Meadows & pastures %	34	0	55	23	4	18	31	23	49	0
:Forest & woodland %	21	54	17	27	61	33	29	15	34	95
:Other %	37	0		16	26	11	15	28		5
:Irrigated %	0			1	0	11	0	0	0	0
:% Protected	7	0	6	10	0	2	1	3	0.3	4
:% Partially Protected	7	0	0.6	9	0	1	0	1	0	0
Risks: Earthquake (1=high)	0	0	0	0	0	0	0	0	0	0
:Volcanism	0	0	0	0	0	0	0	1	0	0
:Soil degradation	0.3	0	0	0	0	0	1	1	1	0
:Desertification	0.7	0	0	0	0	0	0	0	0	0
:Overgrazing	0.7	0	0	0	0	1	0	1	0	0
:Deforestation	7	7	0.4	0	0	0	1	0	1	0
Elevation: average (m)	307		64	60	20	547	26	3	6	
:Highest point (m)	856	5	1800	4810	3010	2870	1940	2420	5880	1180
:Lowest point (m)	105	0	-0.6	-3	0	0	0	0	0	4
Timezone (GMT)	0	5	0.6	1	1	2	0	1	7	-4
Tectonic plate: African	1	0	0.6	0	1	0	1	1	0	0
:Eurasian	0	0	0	1	0	1	0	0	1	0
:Indo-Australian	0	0	0	0	0	0	0	0	0	0
:Pacific	0	0.4	0	0	0	0	0	0	0	0
:American	0	0	0.4	0	0	0	0	0	0	1
:Nasca	0	0	0	0	0	0	0	0	0	0
:Caribbean	0	0	0	0	0	0	0	0	0	0
Biome: Desert (1=yes)	0	0	0	0	0	0	0	0.3	0	0
:Monsoon	0	0	0	0	0	0	0	0	1	0
:Tropical rain forest	0	1	1	0	1	0	1	0	1	1
:Savanna	1	0	0	0	0	0	0	1	0	0
:Mediterranean	0	0	0	0	0	0	0	0	0	0
:Temperate grassland	0	0	0	0	0	0	0	0	0	0
:Temperate forest	0	0	0	1	0	1	0	0	0	0
:Mountain	0	0	0	0	0	0	0	0	0	0
:Taiga	0	0	0	0	0	0	0	0	0	0
:Tundra	0	0	0	0	0	0	0	0	0	0
:Polar	0	0	0	0	0	0	0	0	0	0
Zoology: Neotropical	0	0.3	1	0	0	0	0	0	0	1
:Nearctic	0	0	0	0	0	0	0	0	0	0
:Ethiopian	1	0	0	0	1	0	1	1	0	0
:Oriental	0	0	0	0	0	0	0	0	1	0
:Palearctic	0	0	0	1	0	1	0	0	0	0
:Australian	0	0.7	0	0	0	0	0	0	0	0

Characteristics	Bushman	Capver-dien	Caroli-nians	Catalan	Chahar Aimak	Chamba	Chamorro	Chiga	Chin	Chinese
Land: Total Area (km sq)	600000	92100	477	505000	648000	475000	524	236000	677000	985000
Density (pop/km sq)	2	107	100	78	30	26	223	82	66	2160
# of boundaries	3	1	0	4	4	6	0	5	5	
Total boundary (km)	4010	1210	0	1900	5830	4590	0	2700	5880	2890
Terrain (3=mountains)	3	3	3	3	4	2	3	3	3	2
Land Usage: Arable %	2	32	1	31	12	13	8	23	15	16
Permanent crops %	0	6	0	10	0	2	0	9	1	5
Meadows & pastures %	75	40	19	21	46	18	16	25	49	33
Forest & woodland %	6	16	0	31	3	54	13	30	34	44
Other %	21	7	0	7	3	13	30	13		5
Irrigated %	1	0		6		0		0		1
% Protected	7	6	0	7	0.3	4	0.3	8	0.3	0.1
% Partially Protected	2	1	1	0	0.2	2		4	1	0.1
Risks: Earthquake (1=high)	0			0	0	0		0		
Volcanism	0	0	0	0	1	1	0.3	1	1	0.1
Soil degradation	1	0	0	1	1			1		
Desertification	1	0	0	0			0			
Overgrazing	0	0	0	1	1		0	1	0	0
Deforestation	0	0	0	0	1			1	0	
Elevation: average (m)	1010	95	206	446	1820	387	112	1190		23
Highest point (m)	1510	2350		3400	7480	4100		5100	5880	2640
Lowest point (m)	513	1		0	259	0		610	0	-6
Timezone (GMT)	2	1	9	1	5	1	10	3	7	6
Tectonic plate: African	1	1	0	0	0	1	0	1	0	0
Eurasian	0	0	0	1	1	0	0	0	1	1
Indo-Australian	0	0	0	0	0	0	0	0	0	0
Pacific	0	0	1	0	0	0	1	0	0	0
American	0	0	0	0	0	0	0	0	0	0
Nasca	0	0	0	0	0	0	0	0	0	0
Caribbean	0	0	0	0	0	0	0	0	0	0
Biome: Desert (1=yes)	1	1	0	0	1	0	0	0	0	0
Monsoon	0	0	0	0	0	0	0	0	0	
Tropical rain forest	0	0	1	0	0	1	1	0	1	
Savanna	1	0	0	0	0	1	0	1	0	
Mediterranean	0	0	0	1	0	0	0	0	0	
Temperate grassland	0	0	0	0	0	0	0	0	0	
Temperate forest	0	0	0	0	0	0	0	0	0	
Mountain	0	0	0	0	1	0	0	0	0	
Taiga	0	0	0	0	0	0	0	0	0	
Tundra	0	0	0	0	0	0	0	0	0	
Polar	0	0	0	0	0	0	0	0	0	
Zoology: Neotropical	0	0	0	0	0	0	0	0	0	0
Nearctic	0	0	0	0	0	0	0	0	0	0
Ethiopian	1	1	0	0	0	1	0	1	0	0.1
Oriental	0	0	1	0	1	0	1	0	1	0.9
Paleartic	0	0	0	1	1	0	0	0	0	
Australian	0	0	1	0	0	0	1	0	0	0

Characteristics	Chinese Mainland	Chokwe	Chuang	Chuvash	Circassian	Coloured	Comorian	Creole	Croatian	Czech
Land: Total Area (km sq)	9600000	1940000	9600000	17100000	704000	1220000	38700	24500	55300	299000
··Density (pop/km sq)	578	14	126	9	73	32	267	392	86	129
··# of boundaries	0	6	13	15	6	6	0	0	5	0
··Total boundary (km)	0	7180	23200	20100	2590	4970	0	261	1760	200
··Terrain (3=mountains)	2	3	3	2	3	2	3	3	3	3
Land Usage: Arable %	24	0	10	0	27	10	33	34	30	0.1
··Permanent crops %	1	11	0	0	4	1	8	3	17	0
··Meadows & pastures %	55	65	31	0	11	65	10	35	19	0.1
··Forest & woodland %	15	21	14	0	23	3	17	25	19	0.8
··Other %	14	0	45	0	35	21	33	8	10	98
··Irrigated %	8	3	0	0	0.4	6	0.1	1	5	0
··% Protected	3	0.4	3	1	0.2	4	0.1	0	5	6
··% Partially Protected	1	0	0	0	0.9	0	0	0	0	0
Risks: Earthquake (1=high)	0	0	1	0	0.1	0	0	0	1	0
··Volcanism	0	0.4	0	0	0.1	0	0.1	0	0	1
··Soil degradation	0	0	1	0	0.1	0	0	0	0	0
··Desertification	0	0.4	1	0	0.1	0	0	0	0	0
··Overgrazing	0	0	0	0	0	0	0	0	0	0
··Deforestation	8	0	1	0	0.1	0	0.1	0	0.8	0
Elevation: average (m)	8	199	28	156	492	12	142	37	131	100
··Highest point (m)	4000	4190	8850	5640	4750	3450	2390	919	1920	5780
··Lowest point (m)	0	1	-154	-28	-45	2	3	1	0.2	0
Timezone (GMT)	8	1	8	8	3	2	3	0.7	2	0.8
Tectonic plate: African	0	1	0	0	1	1	1	1	0	0
··Eurasian	1	0	1	1	0.9	0	0	0	1	1
··Indo-Australian	0	0	0	0	0	0	0	0	0	0
··Pacific	0	0	0	0	0	0	0	0	0	0
··American	0	0	0	0	0	0	0	0	0	0
··Nasca	0	0	0	0	0	0	0	0	0	0
··Caribbean	0	0	0	0	0	0	0	0	0	0
Biome: Desert (1=yes)	0	0	0	0	0	1	0	0	0	0
··Monsoon	1	0.4	1	0	0	0	0	0	0	0
··Tropical rain forest	0	0.6	1	0	0	0	1	0.9	0	0
··Savanna	0	1	0	0	0	1	0	0.1	0	0
··Mediterranean	0	0	0	0	0.9	1	0	0	0	0
··Temperate grassland	0	0	0	1	0	0	0	0	0.8	0
··Temperate forest	1	0	1	1	1	0	0	0	1	1
··Mountain	0	0	0	1	0	1	0	0	0.2	0
··Taiga	0	0	0	1	0	0	0	0	0	0
··Tundra	0	0	0	1	0	0	0	0	0	0
··Polar	0	0	0	1	0	0	0	0	0	0
Zoology: Neotropical	0	0	0	0	0	0	0	0.3	0	0
··Nearctic	0	0	0	0	0	0	0	0.1	0	0
··Ethiopian	0	1	0	0	0	1	1	0.7	0	0
··Oriental	1	0	1	0	0	0	0	0	0	0
··Palearctic	1	0	1	1	1	0	0	0	1	1
··Australian	0	0	0	0	0	0	0	0	0	0

Characteristics	Dagestani	Dai	Damara	Dan	Danish	Dinka	Dogon	Dong	Dravidian	Duala
Land: Total Area (km sq)	14800000	9600000	824000	283000	44100	2510000	1240000	9600000	3290000	28100
: Density (pop/km sq)	19	126	2	39	120	11	8	126	273	14
: # of boundaries	14	13	4	5	1	8	7	13	6	2
: Total boundary (km)	17700	23200	3940	2830	77	7700	7240	23200	14100	539
: Terrain (3=mountains)	2	3	2			2	1	3	3	
Land Usage: Arable %	2	10	0	8	61	5		10	55	5
: Permanent crops %			0	4	0				4	4
: Meadows & pastures %	3	31	64	8	6	24	25	31	4	4
: Forest & woodland %	0	14	22	28	12	20	7	14	23	61
: Other %	8	45	13	53	21	51	66	45	17	26
: Irrigated %	10	5	0	0.2	9	1			13	0
: % Protected	1	0	13		9	0.3	3	3	4	0
: % Partially Protected	0	3	0		0		0	1	3	0
Risks: Earthquake (1=high)	0	1	0	0	0	0	0	1	1	0
: Volcanism	0	0	1	0	0	0	0	0	1	0
: Soil degradation	0	1	0	0	0	1	0	1	1	0
: Desertification	0	0	1	0	0	1	0	0	0	0
: Overgrazing	0	1	0	0	0	1	1	1	1	0
: Deforestation	0	0	0	0.8	0	0	0	0	1	0
Elevation: average (m)	270		1650	10		235	316		114	20
: Highest point (m)	5480	8850	2580	1680	182	3190	1150	8850	8600	301
: Lowest point (m)	-28	-154	-2		-7		22	-154		
Timezone (GMT)	4	8	1	0	1	2	0	8	6	1
Tectonic plate: African	0	0	1	1	0	1	1	0	0	1
: Eurasian	1	1	0	0	1	0	0	1	0	0
: Indo-Australian	0	0	0	0	0	0	0	0	1	0
: Pacific	0	0	0	0	0	0	0	0	0	0
: American	0	0	0	0	0	0	0	0	0	0
: Nasca	0	0	0	0	0	0	0	0	0	0
: Caribbean	0	0	0	0	0	0	0	0	0	0
Biome: Desert (1=yes)	0.9	1	1	0	0	1	1	1	0	0
: Monsoon	0	0	0	0	0	0	0	0	1	0
: Tropical rain forest	0	1	0	0.8	0	0	0	1	1	1
: Savanna	0	0	1	1	0	1	1	0	0	1
: Mediterranean	0	0	0	0	0	0	0	0	0	0
: Temperate grassland	0.9	1	0	0	0	0	0	1	0	0
: Temperate forest	0.9	1	0	0	1	0	0	1	0	0
: Mountain	0.9	1	0	0	0	0	0	1	1	0
: Taiga	0.9	0	0	0	0	0	0	0	0	0
: Tundra	0	0	0	0	0	0	0	0	0	0
: Polar	0	0	0	0	0	0	0	0	0	0
Zoology: Neotropical	0	0	0	0	0	0	0	0	0	0
: Nearctic	0	0	0	0	0	0	0	0	0	0
: Ethiopian	0	0	1	1	0	1	1	0	0	1
: Oriental	0	1	0	0	0	0	0	1	1	0
: Palearctic	1	1	0	0	1	0	0	1	1	0
: Australian	0	0	0	0	0	0	0	0	0	0

Characteristics	Duala-Landa-B.	Dujia	Dutch	Dyola	Edo	Egyptian	English	Estonian	Euro-nesian	European
Land: Total Area (km sq)	475000	9600000	758000	938000	924000	1000000	245000	45100	2860	3350000
Density (pop/km sq)	26	126	77	26	115	56	240	35	77	16
# of boundaries	6	13	2	6	4	4	1	2		4
Total boundary (km)	4590	23200	7090	5650	4050	2690	360	557		8080
Terrain (3=mountains)	2	3	2	1	2	3	2	0	3	
Land Usage: Arable %	13	10	9	5	31	2	29	22	19	8
Permanent crops %	2		0.2	0	3	0	0		24	3
Meadows & pastures %	18	31	33	21	23	0	48	11		44
Forest & woodland %	54	14	51	10	15	0	9	31	47	26
Other %	13	45	4	63	28	95	14	21	10	19
Irrigated %	0	0	2	0.7	0	0.8	1	0	0	0.9
% Protected	4	0	0	0.5	3	0.7	0	8	0	0.5
% Partially Protected	2	3	0	0.2	1	0	19	0	0	2
Risks: Earthquake (1=high)	0	1	0	0	0	0	0	0	0	0.1
Volcanism	1	0	0	0	0	0	0	0	1	0.1
Soil degradation	0	1	0	0	1	1	0	0	0	0.8
Desertification	1	0	0	0.8	1	1	0	0	0	0.7
Overgrazing	1	1	0	0	0	1	0	0	0	0.1
Deforestation	1	0	0	0.2	3	0	0	0	0	0.1
Elevation: average (m)	387	28	82	239	3	24	45	46	0	125
Highest point (m)	4100	8850	4690	884	2420	2640	1340	318	1860	6280
Lowest point (m)	0	-154	-4	17	0	-133	-3	0	0	-29
Timezone (GMT)	1	8	0	0	1	2	0	2	-11	-2
Tectonic plate: African	1	0	0.2	0	1	1	0	0	0	
Eurasian	0	1	0	1	1	0	1	1	0	0.1
Indo-Australian	0	0	0	0	0	0	0	0	1	0.1
Pacific	0	0	0	0	0	0	0	0	0	0.8
American	0	0	0	0	0	0	0	0	0	0
Nasca	0	0	0	0	0	0	0	0	0	0
Caribbean	0	0	0	0	0	0	0	0	0	0
Biome: Desert (1=yes)	0	1	0.8	0.8	0	1	0	0	0	0.7
Monsoon	0	1	0	0	1	0	0	0	0	0
Tropical rain forest	1	0	0	0	1	0	0	0	1	0.1
Savanna	1	0	0	1	1	0	0	0	0	0.7
Mediterranean	0	0	0	0	0	1	0	0	0	0
Temperate grassland	0	0	1	0	0	0	1	0	0	0.8
Temperate forest	0	1	0.8	0	0	0	1	1	0	0.9
Mountain	0	1	0.1	0	0	0	0	0	0	0.1
Taiga	0	0	0.8	0	0	0	0	0	0	0.0
Tundra	0	0	0	0	0	0	0	0	0	0
Polar	0	0	0	0	0	0	0	0	0	0.8
Zoology: Neotropical	0	0	0	0	0	0	0	0	0	0.1
Nearctic	0	0	0	0	0	0	0	0	0	0.1
Ethiopian	1	0	0	1	1	1	0	0	0	0
Oriental	1	1	0	0	0	0	0	0	0	0
Palearctic	0	1	0.8	0	0	1	1	1	0	0.8
Australian	0	0	0.2	0	0	0	0	0	1	0.1

Characteristics	Ewa-Adja	Ewe	Fang	Fijian	Finnish	Fleming	Fon	Forros	French	Fulani
Land: Total Area (km sq)	56800	239000	404000	18300	412000	30500	113000	960	1620000	746000
::Density (pop/km sq)	69	69	22	40	15	328	45	132	99	77
::# of boundaries	3	3	5	0	3	4	4	0	7	5
::Total boundary (km)	1650	2090	3920	0	2600	1390	1990	0	3550	4050
::Terrain (3=mountains)	2	2	1	3	1	1	2	3	2	2
Land Usage: Arable %	25	5	11	8	8	24	12	1	28	22
::Permanent crops %	1	1	2	5	0.2	1	4	36	2	2
::Meadows & pastures %	4	15	17	3	0	20	4	0	21	22
::Forest & woodland %	28	37	58	65	75	21	35	62	28	21
::Other %	42	36	13	19	17	34	45	0	21	32
::Irrigated %	1	0	0	0.3	2	0	0	0	2	0.1
::% Protected	1	5	3	0	0	2	7	0	9	4
::% Partially Protected	0	0	0	0	0	0	0	0	8	2
Risks: Earthquake (1=high)	0	0	0	0	0	0	0	0	0	0.1
::Volcanism	0	1	0	0	0	0	0	0	0	0.7
::Soil degradation	1	0	0.8	0	0	0	1	1	0	0.8
::Desertification	0	1	0	0	0	0	0	0	0	0.2
::Overgrazing	1	1	0.8	0	0	0	1	0	0	0.3
::Deforestation	1	1	0.9	0	0	0	1	1	0	0.3
Elevation: average (m)	20	65	298		14	76	17	17	73	74
::Highest point (m)	986	885	3570	1320	1400	694	681	2020	4920	2120
::Lowest point (m)	0	0	0	0	0	0	0	0	0.2	15
Timezone (GMT)	1	0	1	11	2	1	1	0	0.9	0.7
Tectonic plate: African	1	1	1	0	0	0	1	1	0	1
::Eurasian	0	0	0	0	1	1	0	0	1	0
::Indo-Australian	0	0	0	0	0	0	0	0	0	0
::Pacific	0	0	0	1	0	0	0	0	0	0
::American	0	0	0	0	0	0	0	0	0	0
::Nasca	0	0	0	0	0	0	0	0	0	0
::Caribbean	0	0	0	0	0	0	0	0	0	0
Biome: Desert (1=yes)	0	0	0	0	0	0	0	0	0	0.1
::Monsoon	0	0	0	0	0	0	0	0	0	0
::Tropical rain forest	0	0	0.9	1	0	0	0	1	0	0
::Savanna	1	1	0	0	0	0	1	0	0	0.8
::Mediterranean	0	0	0	0	0	0	0	0	0.1	0
::Temperate grassland	0	0	0	0	0	0	0	0	0	0
::Temperate forest	0	0	0	0	0.1	1	0	0	0.9	0
::Mountain	0	0	0	0	0	0	0	0	0.1	0
::Taiga	0	0	0	0	1	0	0	0	0	0
::Tundra	0	0	0	0	0	0	0	0	0	0
::Polar	0	0	0	0	0	0	0	0	0	0
Zoology: Neotropical	0	0	0	0	0	0	0	0	0	0
::Nearctic	0	0	0	0	0	0	0	0	0	0
::Ethiopian	1	1	1	0	0	0	1	1	0	1
::Oriental	0	0	0	0	0	0	0	0	0	0
::Paleartic	0	0	0	0	1	1	0	0	1	0
::Australian	0	0	0	1	0	1	0	0	0	0

Characteristics	Fur	Ga-Adangme	Gagauz	Galician	Ganda	Garifuna	Gbaya	Georgian	German	Gibral-tarian
Land: Total Area (km sq)	2510000	239000	361000	505000	236000	23000	623000	91100	863000	7
: Density (pop/km sq)	11	69	106	78	82	9	5	79	206	4810
: # of boundaries	8	3	4	4	5	2	5	4	9	1
: Total boundary (km)	7700	2090	1970	1900	2700	516	5200	1500	4760	1
: Terrain (3=mountains)	2	2	4	3	3	1	1	3	1	1
Land Usage: Arable %	5	5	41	31	23	2	3	30	27	
: Permanent crops %	0	7	2	10	9	0	0	4		
: Meadows & pastures %	24	15	10	21	25	44	64	12	20	
: Forest & woodland %	20	37	11	31	30	52	28	26	31	
: Other %	51	36	35	7	13	0	0	28	20	100
: Irrigated %		0	0.2	6	0	0	9	3		
: % Protected	4	5	0	0	8	0	4	3	0.4	
: % Partially Protected	0.3	0	0.4	7	4	5	0	3	15	
Risks: Earthquake (1=high)	0	0	0.6	0	0	0	0	0	0	0
: Volcanism	0	0	0.4	0	0	0	0	0	0	0
: Soil degradation	1	1	0	0	1	0	0	0	0	0
: Desertification	0	0	0	1	0	0	1	0	0	0
: Overgrazing	5	1	0	0	1	5	0	0	0	3
: Deforestation	0	1	0	1	0	0	1	0	0	
Elevation: average (m)	235	65	305	446	1190		381	489	123	
: Highest point (m)	3190	885	2480	3400	5100	1120	1410	5070	3130	
: Lowest point (m)	0	0	0.5	0	610		335	0	0.8	
Timezone (GMT)	2	0	2	1	3	-6	1	3	0.9	3
Tectonic plate: African	1	1	0	0	1	0	1	0	0	
: Eurasian	0	0	1	1	0	0	0	1	0.9	1
: Indo-Australian	0	0	0	0	0	0	0	0	0	0
: Pacific	0	0	0	0	0	0	0	0	0	0
: American	0	0	0	0	0	0	0	0	0	0
: Nasca	0	0	0	0	0	0	0	0	0	0
: Caribbean	0	0	0	0	0	1	0	0	0	0
Biome: Desert (1=yes)	1	0	0	0	0	0	0	0	0.1	0
: Monsoon	0	0	0	0	0	0	0	0	0	0
: Tropical rain forest	0	1	0	0	1	1	1	0	0	0
: Savanna	1	1	0	0	1	0	1	0	0	0
: Mediterranean	0	0	0	1	0	0	0	0	0.1	1
: Temperate grassland	0	0	0.4	0	0	0	0	0	0.1	0
: Temperate forest	0	0	0.4	1	0	0	0	1	0.1	0
: Mountain	0	0	0.6	0	0	0	0	1	0.1	0
: Taiga	0	0	0	0	0	0	0	0	0	0
: Tundra	0	0	0	0	0	0	0	0	0	0
: Polar	0	0	0	0	0	0	0	0	0	0
Zoology: Neotropical	0	0	0	0	0	1	0	0	0	0
: Nearctic	0	0	0	0	0	0	0	0	0	0
: Ethiopian	1	1	0	0	1	0	1	0	0	0
: Oriental	0	0	0	0	0	0	0	0	0.1	0
: Palearctic	0	0	1	1	0	0	0	1	0.9	1
: Australian	0	0	0	0	0	0	0	0	0.0	0

Characteristics	Gilaki	Gilber-tese	Gio	Gisu	Gola	Grebo	Greek	Green-landic	Grosi	Guiana Chinese
Land: Total Area (km sq)	1650000	717	111000	236000	111000	111000	253000	2180000	274000	91000
:Density (pop/km sq)	38	105	26	82	26	26	81	0	36	1
:# of boundaries	5	0	3	5	3	3	4	0	6	2
:Total boundary (km)	5490	0	1590	2700	1590	1590	1350	0	3190	1180
:Terrain (3=mountains)	3		1	3	1	1	3	1	1	1
Land Usage: Arable %	8	51	3	23	3	3	24	0	10	0
··Permanent crops %			2	9			8			0
··Meadows & pastures %	27	3	39	25	39	39	37	1	37	0
··Forest & woodland %	11	46	55	30	55	55	20		26	82
··Other %	54		1	13	1	1	11	99	27	18
··Irrigated %	2						7			0
··% Protected	5	39	1	8	1	1	0.8		10	0
··% Partially Protected	3			4			0.7		8	
Risks: Earthquake (1=high)	0	0	0	0	0	0	0.9	0	0	0
:Volcanism	0	0	0	0	0	0	0	0	0	0
:Soil degradation	1	0	0	0	0	0	0	0	0	0
:Desertification	0	0	0	0	0	0	0	0	0	0
:Overgrazing	1	0	0	1	0	0	0	0	1	0
:Deforestation	1	0	1	1	1	1	0	0	1	0
Elevation: average (m)	913	2	23	1190	23	23	20	25	304	9
:Highest point (m)	5600	75	1380	5100	1380	1380	2930	3700	747	830
:Lowest point (m)	-28			610			-0.1	-3	135	0
Timezone (GMT)	4	-12	1	3	1	1	0.9	-3	0	-4
Tectonic plate: African	0	0	1	1	1	1	0	0	1	0
··Eurasian	1	0	0	0	0	0	1	0	0	0
··Indo-Australian	0	0	0	0	0	0	0	0	0	0
··Pacific	0	1	0	0	0	0	0	0	0	0
··American	0	0	0	0	0	0	0	1	0	1
··Nasca	0	0	0	0	0	0	0	0	0	0
··Caribbean	0	0	0	0	0	0	0	0	0	0
Biome: Desert (1=yes)	0	0	0	0	0	0	0	0	0	0
··Monsoon	0	0	0	1	0	0	0	0	0	0
··Tropical rain forest	0	1	1	0	1	1	0	0	0	1
··Savanna	0	0	0	0	0	0	0	0	1	0
··Mediterranean	0	0	0	0	0	0	1	0	0	0
··Temperate grassland	0	0	0	0	0	0	0	0	0	0
··Temperate forest	0	0	0	0	0	0	0	0	0	0
··Mountain	1	0	0	0	0	0	0	0	0	0
··Taiga	0	0	0	0	0	0	0	0	0	0
··Tundra	0	0	0	0	0	0	0	0	0	0
··Polar	0	0	0	0	0	0	0	1	0	0
Zoology: Neotropical	0	0	0	0	0	0	0	0	0	1
··Nearctic	0	0	0	0	0	0	0	1	0	0
··Ethiopian	0	0	1	1	1	1	0	0	1	0
··Oriental	0	0	0	0	0	0	0	0	0	0
··Palearctic	1	0	0	0	0	0	1	0	0	0
··Australian	0	1	0	0	0	0	0	0	0	0

Characteristics	Guianese Creole	Gurage	Gurma	Gurung	Gypsy	Han Chinese	Hani	Hausa	Haya	Hazara-Dari
Land: Total Area (km sq)	91000	1220000	179000	47000	145000	9600000	9600000	979000	945000	648000
..Density (pop/km sq)	1	43	59	35	100	126	126	97	30	30
..# of boundaries	2	4	4	3	3	13	13	5	7	4
..Total boundary (km)	1180	5140	2240	1080	2020	23200	23200	4330	3400	5830
..Terrain (3=mountains)	1	3	2	3	3	3	3	2	3	4
Land Usage: Arable %	0	12	14	0	37	10	10	26	5	12
..Permanent crops %	0	1	3	5	2	0	0	2	1	0
..Meadows & pastures %		41	17	70	15	31	31	20	40	46
..Forest & woodland %	82	24	30	23	23	14	14	13	47	3
..Other %	18	22	36		15	45	45	38	7	3
..Irrigated %	0	0	0	19	9	5	5	5	0	
..% Protected		3	9	18	4	0	0	0	14	0.3
..% Partially Protected	0	0	2			3	3	4	10	0.2
Risks: Earthquake (1=high)	0	1	0	0	0.7	1	1	2	0	1
..Volcanism	0	1	0.3	0	0.2	0	0	0	0	0
..Soil degradation	0	1	0.6	0	0.0	1	1	0.2	0	1
..Desertification	0	1	0.1	0	0.3	0	0		0	1
..Overgrazing	0	1		0	233	1	1	42	4	1
..Deforestation	9	1	116	2420	2280	28	28	2370	14	1
Elevation: average (m)	830	2140	884	7550	2	8850	8850	33	5890	1820
..Highest point (m)		4620	39	97		-154	-154	1	0	7480
..Lowest point (m)	-4	-125		6		8	8		3	259
Timezone (GMT)	0	3	0	1	0.9	1	1	1	1	5
Tectonic plate: African	0	1	1	0	0	0	0	1	1	0
..Eurasian	0	0	0	0	0	1	1	0	0	1
..Indo-Australian	0	0	0	1	0	0	0	0	0	0
..Pacific	0	0	0	0	0	0	0	0	0	0
..American	1	0	0	0	0	0	0	0	0	0
..Nasca	0	0	0	0	0	0	0	0	0	0
..Caribbean	0	0	0	0	0	0	0	0	0	0
Biome: Desert (1=yes)	0	1	0	0	0	1	1	0.2	0	1
..Monsoon	0	0	0	1	0	0	0	0.8	0	0
..Tropical rain forest	1	0	0	0	0	0	0	0.1	1	0
..Savanna	0	1	1	0	0	0	0	1	0	0
..Mediterranean	0	0	0	0	0.3	0	0	0	0	0
..Temperate grassland	0	0	0	0	0.9	1	1	0	0	0
..Temperate forest	0	0	0	0	0	0	0	0	0	0
..Mountain	1	1	0	1	0	1	1	0	0	1
..Taiga	0	0	0	0	0	0	0	0	0	0
..Tundra	0	0	0	0	0	0	0	0	0	0
..Polar	0	0	0	0	0	0	0	0	0	0
Zoology: Neotropical	1	0	0	0	0	0	0	0	0	0
..Nearctic	0	0	0	0	0	0	0	0	0	0
..Ethiopian	0	1	1	0	0	0	0	1	1	0
..Oriental	0	0	0	1	0	1	1	0	0	1
..Palearctic	0	0	0	0	0.9	1	1	0	0	1
..Australian	0	0	0	0	0	0	0	0	0	0

Characteristics	Hehet-Bena	Herero	Hottentot	Hui-Vighur	Humbe-Nyaneka	Hungarian	Hutu	Ibibio	Icelander	Igbo
Land: Total Area (km sq)	945000	824000	600000	9600000	1250000	93000	27000	923000	103000	924000
:Density (pop/km sq)	30	2	2	126	8	109	262	115	3	115
:# of boundaries	7	3	3	13	4	5	4	4	0	4
:Total boundary (km)	3400	3940	4010	23200	5200	2310	927	4040	0	4050
:Terrain (3=mountains)	3	2	2	3	2	1	2	2	1	2
Land Usage: Arable %	5	1	0	10	2	49	35	31	0	31
:Permanent crops %	1	0	0	0	0	3	10	3	0	3
:Meadows & pastures %	40	64	75	31	23	14	25	23	23	23
:Forest & woodland %	47	22	2	14	43	19	7	15	1	15
:Other %	7	13	21	45	32	11	24	28	76	28
:Irrigated %	0	0	0	0	0	3	0	0	0	0
:% Protected	14	13	17	3	2	6	7	3	9	3
:% Partially Protected	10	2	2	1	1	4	1	1	7	1
Risks: Earthquake (1=high)	0	0	0	1	0	0.2	0	0	1	0
:Volcanism	0	0	0	0	0	0	0	0	1	0
:Soil degradation	0	1	1	1	1	0	1	1	0	1
:Desertification	0	1	1	1	0	0	0	0	0	0
:Overgrazing	0	1	1	1	0	0	0.6	0	0	0
:Deforestation	0	0	0	0	1	0	1	1	0	1
Elevation: average (m)		1650	1010			106	1230			
:Highest point (m)	5890	2580	1510	8850	2620	1290	3740	2420	2120	2420
:Lowest point (m)	0	0	0	-154	0	65	876	0	0	0
Timezone (GMT)	3	2	2	8	1	1	2	1	0	1
Tectonic plate: African	1	1	1	0	1	0	1	1	0	1
:Eurasian	0	0	0	1	0	0.9	0	0	1	0
:Indo-Australian	0	0	0	0	0	0	0	0	0	0
:Pacific	0	0	0	0	0	0	0	0	0	0
:American	0	0	0	0	0	0	0	0	1	0
:Nasca	0	0	0	0	0	0	0	0	0	0
:Caribbean	0	0	0	0	0	0	0	0	0	0
Biome: Desert (1=yes)	0	1	1	1	0	0	0	0	0	0
:Monsoon	0	0	0	0	0	0	0	0	0	0
:Tropical rain forest	0	0	0	0	0	0	0	1	0	1
:Savanna	1	0	0	0	1	0	1	0	0	1
:Mediterranean	0	0	0	0	0	0	0	0	0	0
:Temperate grassland	0	0	0	0	0	0.9	0	0	0	0
:Temperate forest	0	0	0	0	0	0	0	0	0	0
:Mountain	0	0	0	1	0	0	1	0	0	0
:Taiga	0	0	0	0	0	0	0	0	0	0
:Tundra	0	0	0	0	0	0	0	0	1	0
:Polar	0	0	0	0	0	0	0	0	0	0
Zoology: Neotropical	0	0	0	0	0	0	0	0	0	0
:Nearctic	0	0	0	0	0	0	0	0	0	0
:Ethiopian	1	1	1	0	1	0	1	1	0	1
:Oriental	0	0	0	1	0	0	0	0	0	0
:Palearctic	0	0	0	1	0	0.9	0	0	1	0
:Australian	0	0	0	0	0	0	0	0	0	0

Characteristics	Ijaw	Indian	Indo-Aryan	Indo-nesian	Iranian	Irish	Issa	Italian	Japanese	Javanese
Land: Total Area (km sq)	924000	792000	3290000	1910000	797000	122000	22000	2220000	510000	1920000
:Density (pop/km sq)	115	288	273	90	161	105	23	153	330	101
:# of boundaries	4	2	6	0	4	1	2	7	0	2
:Total boundary (km)	4050	1770	14100	0	6710	359	517	4850	207	2670
:Terrain (3=mountains)	2	2	1	1	3	1	1	3	3	1
Land Usage: Arable %	31	14	55	1	26	18	0	26	11	8
:Permanent crops %	3	1	4	14	6	0	0	8	2	3
:Meadows & pastures %	23	5	23	51	4	64	0	18	68	7
:Forest & woodland %	15	11	17	35	64	6	0	32	17	67
:Other %	28	42	13	35	15	11	0	16	17	15
:Irrigated %		26			3	0.3		7	9	9
:% Protected	3	3	4			6		6	6	6
:% Partially Protected	1		3		1		0.4	5		3
Risks: Earthquake (1=high)	0	0.1		0	1	0	0	0.7	0	0
:Volcanism	0	0.1	0	0	0	0	0	0.7	0	0
:Soil degradation	1		1	0	1	0	0	0	0	0
:Desertification	1	0.1	1	0	1	0	0	0	0	0
:Overgrazing	0			0	0	0	0	0	0	0
:Deforestation	3	0	1	3	0	0	0	0.2	0	0
Elevation: average (m)		26	114		275	25		244		
:Highest point (m)	2420	2680	8600	1630	8530	1130	2060	4370	3780	5030
:Lowest point (m)		-6		11		-0.8	-153	-0.1	-4	
Timezone (GMT)	1	3	6	1	5	0	3	1	9	8
Tectonic plate: African	1						1	0.2		
:Eurasian	0	0.5	1	1	1	1	0	0.8	1	0
:Indo-Australian	0	0.2	1	1	0	0	0	0	0	1
:Pacific	0		0	1	0	0	0	0	1	0
:American	0		0	0	0	0	0	0	0	0
:Nasca	0		0	0	0	0	0	0	0	0
:Caribbean	0		0	0	0	0	0	0	0	0
Biome: Desert (1=yes)	0	0.2	0	0	1	0	1	0	0	0
:Monsoon	0	0.7	1	0	0	0	0	0	0	0
:Tropical rain forest	1	0.1	1	1	0	0	0	0	0	1
:Savanna	1		0	0	0	0	0	0	0	0
:Mediterranean	0	0.1	0	0	0	0	0	0.7	0	0
:Temperate grassland	0	0.2	0	0	0	0	0	0	0	0
:Temperate forest	0	0.1	0	0	0	1	0	0.2	1	0
:Mountain	0		0	0	1	0	0	0.3	0	0
:Taiga	0		0	0	0	0	0	0	0	0
:Tundra	0		0	0	0	0	0	0	0	0
:Polar	0		0	0	0	0	0	0	0	0
Zoology: Neotropical	0		0	0	0	0	0	0	0	0
:Nearctic	0	0.2	0	0	0	0	0	0	0	0
:Ethiopian	1	0.1	0	0	0	0	1	0	0	0
:Oriental	0	0.3	1	0	0	0	0	0	0	1
:Palearctic	0	0.2	0	0	1	1	0	0.8	1	0
:Australian	0	0.1	0	1	0	0	0	0	0	1

Characteristics	Jewish	Jola	Kalenjin	Kamba	Kanuri	Kara-kalpak	Kare	Karen	Kavango	Kazakh
Land: Total Area (km sq)	156000	196000	583000	583000	982000	447000	623000	677000	824000	3330000
·Density (pop/km sq)	228	40	45	45	97	48	5	66	2	25
·# of boundaries	6	5	5	5	4	5	5	5	4	6
·Total boundary (km)	1560	2640	3480	3480	4330	6220	5200	5880	3940	12700
·Terrain (3=mountains)	1	1	3	3	2	1	1	3	1	2
Land Usage: Arable %	22	27	3	3	26	10	3	15	1	14
·Permanent crops %	4	0	1	1	2	0	0	1	0	0
·Meadows & pastures %	35	30	7	7	21	47	5	0	64	53
·Forest & woodland %	5	31	4	4	13	0	64	49	22	5
·Other %	33	12	85	85	37	43	28	34	13	28
·Irrigated %	9	1	6	6	0	.	0	2	0	4
·% Protected	0.2	1	0	0	4	0	9	0.3	13	0.1
·% Partially Protected	0.8	1	0	0	2	0	9	0	0	0.4
Risks: Earthquake (1=high)	0	0	1	1	0	0	4	1	0	0.1
·Volcanism	0	0	1	1	0	0	0	0	0	
·Soil degradation	0	1	1	1	1	0	0	0	1	0.1
·Desertification	0	0	0	0	0.1	0	0	0	0	0.1
·Overgrazing	0.9	1	1	1	0	0	1	1	1	
·Deforestation	0	1	1	1	1	0	0	1	0	0.1
Elevation: average (m)	369	24	887	887	42	21	381	6	1650	76
·Highest point (m)	1380	581	5200	5200	2390	4640	1410	5880	2580	6940
·Lowest point (m)	-315	0			32	-12	335			-110
·Timezone (GMT)	2	0	3	3	1	5	1	7	-2	5
Tectonic plate: African	0.2	1	1	1	1	0	1	0	1	0
·Eurasian	0.8	0	0	0	0	1	0	1	0	1
·Indo-Australian	0	0	0	0	0	0	0	1	0	0
·Pacific	0	0	0	0	0	0	0	0	0	0
·American	0	0	0	0	0	0	0	0	0	0
·Nasca	0	0	0	0	0	0	0	0	0	0
·Caribbean	0	0	0	0	0	0	0	0	0	0
Biome: Desert (1=yes)	0.9	0	0	0	0.1	1	0	0	1	0.1
·Monsoon	0	0	0	0	0	0	0	1	0	0
·Tropical rain forest	0	0	0	0	0	0	1	1	0	0
·Savanna	0	1	1	1	0.8	0	1	0	1	0
·Mediterranean	0.8	0	0	0	0	0	0	0	0	0
·Temperate grassland	0	0	0	0	0	0	0	0	0	0.8
·Temperate forest	0.1	0	0	0	0	0	0	0	0	0.1
·Mountain	0	0	1	1	0	0	0	0	0	0.1
·Taiga	0	0	0	0	0	0	0	0	0	0
·Tundra	0	0	0	0	0	0	0	0	0	0
·Polar	0	0	0	0	0	0	0	0	0	0
Zoology: Neotropical	0	0	0	0	0	0	0	0	0	0
·Nearctic	0	0	0	0	0	0	0	0	0	0
·Ethiopian	0	1	1	1	1	0	1	0	1	0
·Oriental	0	0	0	0	0	0	0	1	0	0.1
·Paleartic	1	0	0	0	0	1	0	0	0	0.1
·Australian	0	0	0	0	0	0	0	0	0	0

Characteristics	Kebu-Akposo	Khmer	Kikuyu	Kimbundu	Kisii	Kissi	Klao	Kongo	Kono	Konzo
Land: Total Area (km sq)	56800	243000	583000	1250000	583000	211000	111000	2030000	71700	2350000
:Density (pop/km sq)	69	72	45	8	45	33	26	16	63	18
:# of boundaries	3	3	3	4	5	5	3	7	7	7
:Total boundary (km)	1650	3010	3480	5200	3480	2910	1590	7890	958	8340
:Terrain (3=mountains)	2	2	3	2	3	2	1	2	2	2
Land Usage: Arable %	25	19	7	2	7	9	3	3	23	3
:Permanent crops %	1	3	1	2	1	0.4	2		3	
:Meadows & pastures %	4	3	7	23	7	16	39	8	31	4
:Forest & woodland %	28	66	4	43	4	39	39	75		78
:Other %	42	11	85	32	85	35	55	14	29	15
:Irrigated %	1									
:% Protected	11	0.9	6	2	6	0.6	1	0.3		4
:% Partially Protected	1			1		0.2		0.6	1	
Risks: Earthquake (1=high)										
:Volcanism	0	0	0	0	0	0	0	0	0	0
:Soil degradation	0	0	0	0	0	0	0	0	0	0
:Desertification	0	0	0	0	0	0.2	0	0	0	0
:Overgrazing	0	0	0	0	0	0.2	0	0	0	0
:Deforestation	1	1	1	1	1	1	1	0.2	1	0
Elevation: average (m)	20	11	887	43	887	42	23	325	26	290
:Highest point (m)	986	2040	5200	2620	5200	1790	1380	4450	1940	5110
:Lowest point (m)	0	0	0	0	0	0	0	0	0	0
Timezone (GMT)	0	7	3	1	3	0	0	1	0	2
Tectonic plate: African	1		1	1	1	1	1	1	1	1
:Eurasian	0	1	0	0	0	0	0	0	0	0
:Indo-Australian	0	0	0	0	0	0	0	0	0	0
:Pacific	0	0	0	0	0	0	0	0	0	0
:American	0	0	0	0	0	0	0	0	0	0
:Nasca	0	0	0	0	0	0	0	0	0	0
:Caribbean	0	0	0	0	0	0	0	0	0	0
Biome: Desert (1=yes)	0	0	0	0	0	0	0	0	0	0
:Monsoon	0	1	0	0	0	0	0	0	0	0
:Tropical rain forest	0	0	0	0	0	1	1	1	1	1
:Savanna	1	0	1	1	1	0.8	0	0	0	0
:Mediterranean	0	0	0	0	0	0	0	0	0	0
:Temperate grassland	0	0	0	0	0	0	0	0	0	0
:Temperate forest	0	0	0	0	0	0	0	0	0	0
:Mountain	0	0	1	0	1	0	0	0	0	1
:Taiga	0	0	0	0	0	0	0	0	0	0
:Tundra	0	0	0	0	0	0	0	0	0	0
:Polar	0	0	0	0	0	0	0	0	0	0
Zoology: Neotropical	0	0	0	0	0	0	0	0	0	0
:Nearctic	0	0	0	0	0	0	0	0	0	0
:Ethiopian	1	0	1	1	1	1	1	1	1	1
:Oriental	0	1	0	0	0	0	0	0	0	0
:Palearctic	0	0	0	0	0	0	0	0	0	0
:Australian	0	0	0	0	0	0	0	0	0	0

Characteristics	Koranko	Korean	Kotoko	Kpelle	Kru	Kurd	Kuwaiti	Kyrgyz	Ladino	Lango
Land: Total Area (km sq)	71700	491000	1280000	159000	111000	965000	17800	218000	109000	236000
: Density (pop/km sq)	63	351	5	26	26	57	106	25	92	82
: # of boundaries	2	2	6	4	3	6	2	4	4	5
: Total boundary (km)	958	1520	5970	2220	1590	3800	462	4060	1690	2700
: Terrain (3=mountains)	2	3	2	1	1	3	0	3	3	4
Land Usage: Arable %	23	20	2	3	3	18	0	9	12	23
: Permanent crops %	2	1	2	2	1	0	0	0	4	9
: Meadows & pastures %	31	2	36	6	2	18	8	42	12	25
: Forest & woodland %	29	67	11	40	39	14	0	0	40	30
: Other %	15	10	51	50	55	47	92	49	32	13
: Irrigated %	0	11	0.3	0.9	0	3	0		1	0
: % Protected	1	5			1	0.1	1		8	8
: % Partially Protected	0								0.5	4
Risks: Earthquake (1=high)	1					0.4			1	
: Volcanism		1				0.3			1	
: Soil degradation	1		1			0.3	1		1	1
: Desertification						0.4				
: Overgrazing	1						1			1
: Deforestation	1		1	1	1				1	1
Elevation: average (m)	26	64	300	31	23	520	5	707	1500	1190
: Highest point (m)	1940	2470	3410	1510	1380	4820	281	6940	4220	5100
: Lowest point (m)	0	-9	160	0	0	-19	3	499	0	610
Timezone (GMT)	0	9	1	0	0	0.4	3	5	-6	3
Tectonic plate: African	1	0	1	1	1	0	0	0	0	1
: Eurasian	0	1	0	0	0	1	1	1	0	0
: Indo-Australian	0	0	0	0	0	0	0	0	0	0
: Pacific	0	0	0	0	0	0	0	0	0	0
: American	0	0	0	0	0	0	0	0	0	0
: Nasca	0	0	0	0	0	0	0	0	0	0
: Caribbean	0	0	0	0	0	0	0	0	1	0
Biome: Desert (1=yes)	0	0	0	0	0	0.6	1	0.1	0	0
: Monsoon	0	0	0	0	0	0	0	0	0	0
: Tropical rain forest	0	0	0	0.4	1	0	0	0	1	0
: Savanna	1	0	1	0	0	0	0	0	0	1
: Mediterranean	0	0	0	0	0	0.4	0	0	0	0
: Temperate grassland	0	0	0	0	0	0	0	0	0	0
: Temperate forest	0	1	0	0	0	0	0	0	0	0
: Mountain	0	0	0	0	0	0.3	0	1	0	0
: Taiga	0	0	0	0	0	0	0	0	0	0
: Tundra	0	0	0	0	0	0	0	0	0	0
: Polar	0	0	0	0	0	0	0	0	0	0
Zoology: Neotropical	0	0	0	0	0	0	0	0	1	0
: Nearctic	0	0	0	0	0	0	0	0	0	0
: Ethiopian	1	0	1	1	1	0	0	0	0	1
: Oriental	0	0	0	0	0	0	0	0	0	0
: Palearctic	0	1	0	0	0	1	1	1	0	0
: Australian	0	0	0	0	0	0	0	0	0	0

Characteristics	Lao	Latvian	Lezgin	Li	Liechten-steiner	Limba	Lithua-nian	Lobi	Loma	Lomwe
Land: Total Area (km sq)	468000	64100	86600	9600000	160	71700	65200	299000	111000	118000
Density (pop/km sq)	95	42	85	126	178	63	58	39	26	90
# of boundaries	4	4	7	13	2	2	4	5	3	3
Total boundary (km)	4900	1080	2010	23320	78	958	1270	3150	1590	2880
Terrain (3=mountains)	2	0	3	3	3	2	0		1	2
Land Usage: Arable %	29	27	18	10	25	23	49	9	1	25
Permanent crops %	3			0		3		2	3	
Meadows & pastures %	1	13	25	31	38	31	22	23	2	20
Forest & woodland %	35	39	57	14	19	29	17	26	39	50
Other %	32	21	70	45	18	15	12	40	55	5
Irrigated %	6			5	0	0		8		1
% Protected	9	3		0		0	2	4	1	1
% Partially Protected	4	0	0	3	38	1				4
Risks: Earthquake (1=high)	0	0	0	1	0	0	2	0	0	0
Volcanism	0.2	0	0	0	0	0	0	0	0	0
Soil degradation	0	0	0	1	0	0	0	0.5	0	0
Desertification	0	0	0	0	0	0	0	0	0	0
Overgrazing	0.2	0	0	1	0	0	1		0	0
Deforestation	0.2	0	0	1	5	1	0	0.5	0	1
Elevation: average (m)	2640	46	990	28	465	26	46	150	23	1010
Highest point (m)	12	311	4470	8850	2600	1940	292	1270	1380	3000
Lowest point (m)	7		-28	-154	430	0		65	0	37
Timezone (GMT)	7	2	3	8	1	0	2	0	0	2
Tectonic plate: African	0	0	0	0	0	1	0	1	1	1
Eurasian	1	1	1	1	1	0	1	0	0	0
Indo-Australian	0	0	0	0	0	0	0	0	0	0
Pacific	0	0	0	0	0	0	0	0	0	0
American	0	0	0	0	0	0	0	0	0	0
Nasca	0	0	0	0	0	0	0	0	0	0
Caribbean	0	0	0	0	0	0	0	0	0	0
Biome: Desert (1=yes)	0	0	0	1	0	0	0	0	0	0
Monsoon	1	0	0	0	0	0	0	0	0	0
Tropical rain forest	1	0	0	0	0	1	0	0	1	1
Savanna	0	0	0	0	0	0	0	1	0	0
Mediterranean	0	0	0	0	0	0	0	0	0	0
Temperate grassland	0	0	0	0	0	0	0	0	0	0
Temperate forest	0	1	1	0	0	0	1	0	0	0
Mountain	0	0	0	0	1	0	0	0	0	0
Taiga	0	0	0	0	0	0	0	0	0	0
Tundra	0	0	0	0	0	0	0	0	0	0
Polar	0	0	0	0	0	0	0	0	0	0
Zoology: Neotropical	0	0	0	0	0	0	0	0	0	0
Nearctic	0	0	0	0	0	0	0	0	0	0
Ethiopian	0	0	0	0	0	1	0	1	1	1
Oriental	1	0	0	1	0	0	0	0	0	0
Palearctic	0	1	1	1	1	0	1	0	0	0
Australian	0	0	0	0	0	0	0	0	0	0

Characteristics	Lotuko	Luba	Luchasi	Luena	Lugbara	Luhya	Lumbe	Lunda	Luo	Luri
Land: Total Area (km sq)	2510000	2350000	1250000	1250000	2350000	583000	1250000	1250000	583000	1650000
: Density (pop/km sq)	11	18	8	8	18	45	8	8	45	38
: # of boundaries	8	7	4	4	7	5	4	4	5	5
: Total boundary (km)	7700	8340	5200	5200	8340	3480	5200	5200	3480	5490
: Terrain (3=mountains)	2	2	2	2	2	3	2	2	3	3
Land Usage: Arable %	5	3	2	2	3	3	2	2	3	8
: Permanent crops %	0	0	0	0	0	1	0	0	1	0
: Meadows & pastures %	24	4	23	23	4	7	23	23	7	27
: Forest & woodland %	20	78	43	43	78	4	43	43	4	11
: Other %	51	15	32	32	15	85	32	32	85	54
: Irrigated %	1	0	0	0	0	0	0	0	0	2
: % Protected	4	4	2	2	4	6	2	2	6	5
: % Partially Protected	0.3	0	1	1	0	0	1	1	0	3
Risks: Earthquake (1=high)	0	0	0	0	0	0	0	0	0	1
: Volcanism	0	0	0	0	0	1	0	0	1	0
: Soil degradation	1	0	1	1	0	0	1	1	0	1
: Desertification	0	0	0	0	0	0	0	0	0	0
: Overgrazing	1	0	0	0	0	0	0	0	0	1
: Deforestation	0	0	1	1	0	1	1	1	1	1
Elevation: average (m)	235	290	1112	1112	290	887	1112	1112	887	913
: Highest point (m)	3190	5110	2620	2620	5110	5200	2620	2620	5200	5600
: Lowest point (m)	0	0	0	0	0	0	0	0	0	-28
Timezone (GMT)	2	2	1	1	2	3	1	1	3	4
Tectonic plate: African	1	1	1	1	1	1	1	1	1	0
: Eurasian	0	0	0	0	0	0	0	0	0	1
: Indo-Australian	0	0	0	0	0	0	0	0	0	0
: Pacific	0	0	0	0	0	0	0	0	0	0
: American	0	0	0	0	0	0	0	0	0	0
: Nasca	0	0	0	0	0	0	0	0	0	0
: Caribbean	0	0	0	0	0	0	0	0	0	0
Biome: Desert (1=yes)	1	0	0	0	0	0	0	0	0	1
: Monsoon	0	0	0	0	0	0	0	0	0	0
: Tropical rain forest	0	1	0	0	1	0	0	0	0	0
: Savanna	1	1	1	1	1	1	1	1	1	0
: Mediterranean	0	0	0	0	0	0	0	0	0	1
: Temperate grassland	0	0	0	0	0	0	0	0	0	0
: Temperate forest	0	0	0	0	0	0	0	0	0	0
: Mountain	0	0	0	0	0	0	0	0	0	1
: Taiga	0	0	0	0	0	0	0	0	0	0
: Tundra	0	0	0	0	0	0	0	0	0	0
: Polar	0	0	0	0	0	0	0	0	0	0
Zoology: Neotropical	0	0	0	0	0	0	0	0	0	0
: Nearctic	0	0	0	0	0	0	0	0	0	0
: Ethiopian	1	1	1	1	1	1	1	1	1	0
: Oriental	0	0	0	0	0	0	0	0	0	0
: Palearctic	0	0	0	0	0	0	0	0	0	1
: Australian	0	0	0	0	0	0	0	0	0	0

Characteristics	Luxem-burger	Macedo-nian	Madurese	Magars	Maka	Makonde	Makua	Malagasy	Malawi	Malay
Land: Total Area (km sq)	2590	48500	1920000	141000	464000	945000	800000	587000	802000	342000
: Density (pop/km sq)	151	79	101	150	25	30	20	23	20	211
: # of boundaries	3	5	2	2	6	3	2	0	6	4
: Total boundary (km)	359	947	2670	2930	4630	3400	4560	0	4570	2890
: Terrain (3=mountains)	1	1	1	3	2	3	2	2	2	2
Land Usage: Arable %	24	5	8	17	12	5	4	4	4	8
: Permanent crops %	1	2	3	0	2	1	0	0	0	9
: Meadows & pastures %	20	22	7	13	19	40	56	58	56	0.2
: Forest & woodland %	21	29	67	33	55	47	20	26	20	57
: Other %	34	33	15	37	13	7	20	11	20	27
: Irrigated %	0	9	13	2	0	0	0	0	0	5
: % Protected	0	5	8	8	4	14	0	2	0	5
: % Partially Protected	0	1	1	1	2	1	0	1	0	3
Risks: Earthquake (1=high)	0	1	1	1	0	1	0	0	0	0
: Volcanism	0	0	1	0	0.9	0	0	0	0	0
: Soil degradation	0	0	0	0	0.9	0	0	0	0	0
: Desertification	0	0	0	0	0.9	0	0	0	0	0
: Overgrazing	0	0	0	0	0	0	0	0	0	0
: Deforestation	1	0	1	1	1	1	1	1	1	1
Elevation: average (m)	300	174		1340	393	14	35	1380	35	19
: Highest point (m)	559	2920	5030	8850	3890	5890	2440	2870	2440	3740
: Lowest point (m)	130			60		0				0
Timezone (GMT)	1	1	8	6	1	3	2	3	2	8
Tectonic plate: African	0	0	0	0	1	1	1	1	1	0
: Eurasian	1	1	1	1	0	0	0	0	0	1
: Indo-Australian	0	0	1	0	0	0	0	0	0	0
: Pacific	0	0	0	0	0	0	0	0	0	0
: American	0	0	0	0	0	0	0	0	0	0
: Nasca	0	0	0	0	0	0	0	0	0	0
: Caribbean	0	0	0	0	0	0	0	0	0	0
Biome: Desert (1=yes)	0	0	0	0	0	0	0	0	0	0
: Monsoon	0	0	0	0	0	0	0	0	0	0
: Tropical rain forest	0	0	1	0	1	0	0	0	0	1
: Savanna	0	0	0	0	0	1	1	1	1	0
: Mediterranean	0	1	0	0	0	0	0	0	0	0
: Temperate grassland	0	0	0	0	0	0	0	0	0	0
: Temperate forest	1	0	0	0	0	0	0	0	0	0
: Mountain	0	0	0	1	0	0	0	0	0	0
: Taiga	0	0	0	0	0	0	0	0	0	0
: Tundra	0	0	0	0	0	0	0	0	0	0
: Polar	0	0	0	0	0	0	0	0	0	0
Zoology: Neotropical	0	0	0	0	0	0	0	0	0	0
: Nearctic	0	0	0	0	0	0	0	0	0	0
: Ethiopian	0	0	0	0	1	1	1	1	1	0
: Oriental	0	0	1	1	0	0	0	0	0	1
: Paleartic	1	1	0	0	0	0	0	0	0	0
: Australian	0	0	1	0	0	0	0	0	0	0

Characteristics	Malay Christian	Malay Coastal	Malay Muslim	Malinke	Maltese	Mambwe	Manchu-Tibetian	Mandara	Mande	Mandingo
Land: Total Area (km sq)	300000	1920000	300000	414000	320	753000	9600000	475000	274000	196000
:Density (pop/km sq)	222	101	222	32	1130	12	126	26	36	40
:# of boundaries	0	0	0	5	0	7	13	6	6	5
:Total boundary (km)	3	2670	3	3670	0	5660	23200	4590	3190	2640
:Terrain (3=mountains)	1	2	1	2	0	2	3	2	1	0
Land Usage: Arable %	26	8	26	7	38	0	10	13	10	27
:Permanent crops %	11	3	11	1	3	7	0	2	0	0
:Meadows & pastures %	4	7	4	15	0	47	31	18	37	30
:Forest & woodland %	40	67	40	29	0	27	14	54	26	31
:Other %	19	15	19	48	59	19	45	13	27	12
:Irrigated %	5	1	5	0.3	0		5			1
:% Protected	2	3	2	0.6	3	8	3	4	1	
:% Partially Protected	1	1	1				1	2		1
Risks: Earthquake (1=high)	1	1	1	0	0	0	1	1	0	1
:Volcanism	0	1	0	0.2	0	0	0	0	0	0
:Soil degradation	0	0	0	0	0	1	1	0	0	0
:Desertification	0	0	0	0.8	0	0	1	1	0	1
:Overgrazing	1	1	1		0	1		1	0	1
:Deforestation	1	1	1		0	1	1	1	0	1
Elevation: average (m)	16	7	16	81	71	1280	28	387	304	24
:Highest point (m)	2950	5030	2950	1550	253	2160	8850	4100	747	581
:Lowest point (m)	0	8	8	4	0	329	-154		135	0
Timezone (GMT)	8	8	8	0	2	2	8	1	0	0
Tectonic plate: African	0	0	0	1	0	1	0	1	1	1
:Eurasian	1	1	1	0	1	0	1	0	0	0
:Indo-Australian	0	1	0	0	0	0	1	0	0	0
:Pacific	0	0	0	0	0	0	0	0	0	0
:American	0	0	0	0	0	0	0	0	0	0
:Nasca	0	0	0	0	0	0	0	0	0	0
:Caribbean	0	0	0	0	0	0	0	0	0	0
Biome: Desert (1=yes)	0	0	0	0	0	0	0	0	0	0
:Monsoon	1	1	1	0	0	0	1	0	0	0
:Tropical rain forest	1	1	1	0.2	0	0	0	0	0	1
:Savanna	0	0	0	0.7	0	1	0	1	1	0
:Mediterranean	0	0	0	0	1	0	0	0	0	0
:Temperate grassland	0	0	0	0	0	0	1	0	0	0
:Temperate forest	0	0	0	0	0	0	1	0	0	0
:Mountain	0	0	0	0	0	0	1	0	0	0
:Taiga	0	0	0	0	0	0	0	0	0	0
:Tundra	0	0	0	0	0	0	0	0	0	0
:Polar	0	0	0	0	0	0	0	0	0	0
Zoology: Neotropical	0	0	0	0	0	0	0	0	0	0
:Nearctic	0	0	0	0	0	0	0	0	0	0
:Ethiopian	0	0	0	1	0	1	0	1	1	1
:Oriental	1	1	1	0	0	0	1	0	0	0
:Palearctic	0	0	0	0	1	0	1	0	0	0
:Australian	0	0	0	0	0	0	0	0	0	0

Characteristics	Mandyako	Mano	Manx (Norse-C.)	Manzan-Darani	Maori	Maravi	Masa	Masalit Maba	Maya	Mbaka
Land: Total Area (km sq)	36100	111000	588	1650000	269000	245000	1280000	1280000	23000	623000
.: Density (pop/km sq)	28	26	119	38	13	75	5	5	9	5
.: # of boundaries	2	3	0	3	0	4	6	6	2	5
.: Total boundary (km)	724	1590	0	5490	0	3440	5970	5970	516	5200
.: Terrain (3=mountains)	9	1	1	3	2	2	2	2	1	1
Land Usage: Arable %	1	3		8	2	21	0	0	2	3
.: Permanent crops %										
.: Meadows & pastures %	46	39		27	53	25	36	36	44	5
.: Forest & woodland %	38	55		11	38	45	11	11	52	64
.: Other %	6			54	7	8	51	51		28
.: Irrigated %	0	0		2		0	0.3	0.3	0	
.: % Protected	0	1		5	11	10			5	9
.: % Partially Protected	0			3	1	3				4
Risks: Earthquake (1=high)	0	0	0	1	1	0	0	0	0	0
.: Volcanism	0	0	0	1	1	0	0	0	0	0
.: Soil degradation	0	0	0	0	0	0.2	0	0	0	0
.: Desertification	0	0	0	0	0	0.2	1	1	0	0
.: Overgrazing	0	0	0	0	0	0	0	0	0	0
.: Deforestation	0	0	0	0	0	0	0	0	0	1
Elevation: average (m)	20	23	87	913	66	1070	300	300		381
.: Highest point (m)	4250	1380		5600	3760	2830	3410	3410	1120	1410
.: Lowest point (m)	0	0		-28	0	95	160	160	-6	335
Timezone (GMT)	0	0	0	4	12	2	1	1	-6	1
Tectonic plate: African	1	1	0	0	0	1	1	1	0	1
.: Eurasian	0	0	1	1	0	0	0	0	0	0
.: Indo-Australian	0	0	0	0	1	0	0	0	0	0
.: Pacific	0	0	0	0	1	0	0	0	0	0
.: American	0	0	0	0	0	0	0	0	1	0
.: Nasca	0	0	0	0	0	0	0	0	0	0
.: Caribbean	0	0	0	0	0	0	0	0	0	0
Biome: Desert (1=yes)	0	0	0	0	0	0	1	1	0	0
.: Monsoon	0	0	0	0	0	0	0	0	0	0
.: Tropical rain forest	0	1	0	0	0	0	0	0	1	1
.: Savanna	1	0	0	0	0	1	0	0	0	0
.: Mediterranean	0	0	0	0	0	0	0	0	0	0
.: Temperate grassland	0	0	0	0	0	0	0	0	0	0
.: Temperate forest	0	0	1	0	1	0	0	0	0	0
.: Mountain	0	0	0	1	0	0	0	0	0	0
.: Taiga	0	0	0	0	0	0	0	0	0	0
.: Tundra	0	0	0	0	0	0	0	0	0	0
.: Polar	0	0	0	0	0	0	0	0	0	0
Zoology: Neotropical	0	0	0	0	0	0	0	0	1	0
.: Nearctic	0	0	0	0	0	0	0	0	1	0
.: Ethiopian	1	1	0	0	0	1	1	1	0	1
.: Oriental	0	0	0	0	0	0	0	0	0	0
.: Palearctic	0	0	1	1	0	0	0	0	0	0
.: Australian	0	0	0	0	1	0	0	0	0	0

Characteristics	Mbete	Mbochi	Mbum	Mbunda	Melanesian	Mende	Merina	Meru	Mestizo	Miao Man
Land: Total Area (km sq)	298000	342000	968000	1250000	295000	71700	587000	583000	2170000	237000
..Density (pop/km sq)	6	7	10	8	10	63	23	45	40	19
..# of boundaries	4	5	6	4		2	0	4	4	5
..Total boundary (km)	3750	5500	5500	5200	505	958		3480	6120	5080
..Terrain (3=mountains)	0.6	2	2	2	0.3	2	2	3	3	3
Land Usage: Arable %		0	0.5	2	0.9	23	4	3	9	4
..Permanent crops %	0.6		26		1		1	1	1	3
..Meadows & pastures %	22	29	31	23	76	31	58	1	29	58
..Forest & woodland %	71	62	38	43	21	29	26	4	37	35
..Other %	4	7		32		15	11	85	23	
..Irrigated %	0		3				2		2	1
..% Protected	0	0		2	0	1	2	6	8	
..% Partially Protected	4	4	0.2							0
Risks: Earthquake (1=high)				0	0.9	0	0	0		1
..Volcanism	0	0	0.1		0.6		1	1	0.6	
..Soil degradation	0		0.2	1		1			0.3	
..Desertification	0		0.2		0		1	1	0.5	1
..Overgrazing		0		1		1			0.1	
..Deforestation	1								0.8	5
Elevation: average (m)	211	513	336		27	26	1380	887	1030	
..Highest point (m)	1010	981	3190	2620	3660	1940	2880	5200	5010	2820
..Lowest point (m)		1	156	43					-0.2	70
..Timezone (GMT)	1	1	1	1	10	0	3	3	-5	7
Tectonic plate: African	1	1	1	1		1	1	1		
..Eurasian										1
..Indo-Australian					1					
..Pacific					0.9				0.3	
..American									0.9	
..Nasca										
..Caribbean									0.1	
Biome: Desert (1=yes)									0.6	
..Monsoon									0.2	1
..Tropical rain forest	1	1		1	1	1	1		0.8	
..Savanna			0.4	1				1	0.1	
..Mediterranean									0.6	
..Temperate grassland									0.1	
..Temperate forest									0.8	1
..Mountain										
..Taiga										
..Tundra										
..Polar										
Zoology: Neotropical									0.4	
..Nearctic										
..Ethiopian	1	1	1	1		1	1	1		
..Oriental										1
..Palearctic										
..Australian					1					

Characteristics	Micronesian	Mixed	Moldovan	Mon	Mon-Khmer	Monegasque	Mongo	Mongol-Buryat	Mongol-Dariganga	Mongol-Dorbed
Land: Total Area (km sq)	1290	3590	4410000	677000	237000	2	2350000	1570000	1570000	1570000
Density (pop/km sq)	208	216	96	66	19	15300	18	1	1	1
# of boundaries	0	0	6	5	5	4		2	2	2
Total boundary (km)	0	0	6400	5880	5080	4	8340	8110	8110	8110
Terrain (3=mountains)	2	3		3	3	1	2	3	3	3
Land Usage: Arable %	19	15	38	15	4		3			
Permanent crops %	4	5	0.2	1	0		0			
Meadows & pastures %	7	4	30	1	3		4	79	79	79
Forest & woodland %	23	24	0.7	49	58		78	10	10	10
Other %		52	0.3	34	35	100	15	10	10	10
Irrigated %	0	0.8		0.3	1			0	0	0
% Protected	0	0.1	0.7				4	4	4	4
% Partially Protected	0						0	0	0	0
Risks: Earthquake (1=high)	0	0.3	0	1	1	0	0	0	0	0
Volcanism	0		0.7	0	0	0	0	0	0	0
Soil degradation	0	0.3		0	1	0	0	0	0	0
Desertification	0	0.3	0	0	0	0	0	0	0	0
Overgrazing	0	0.3	0.1	0	0	0	0	0	0	0
Deforestation	0	0.3		0	0	0	0	0	0	0
Elevation: average (m)	28	20	173	6	5	55	290	1310	1310	1310
Highest point (m)	2370	2320	1880	5880	2820	140	5110	4360	4360	4360
Lowest point (m)	0	0.1	-7	0	70	0	0	553	553	553
Timezone (GMT)	11	0.7	4	7	7	1	2	8	8	8
Tectonic plate: African	0	0	0	0	0	0	1	0	0	0
Eurasian	0	0.1	1	1	1	1	0	1	1	1
Indo-Australian	0	0.7	0	1	0	0	0	0	0	0
Pacific	0.8	0	0	0	0	0	0	0	0	0
American	0	0.2	0	0	0	0	0	0	0	0
Nasca	0.2	0	0	0	0	0	0	0	0	0
Caribbean	0	0	0	0	0	0	0	0	0	0
Biome: Desert (1=yes)	0.3	0.1	0.3	0	0	0	0	0	0	0
Monsoon	0	0.6	0	1	1	0	0	0	0	0
Tropical rain forest	0.3	0.5	0	0	0	0	1	0	0	0
Savanna	0	0	0	0	0	0	0	0	0	0
Mediterranean	0	0	0	0	0	1	0	0	0	0
Temperate grassland	0.7	0	0.9	0	0	0	0	1	1	1
Temperate forest	0	0	0.3	0	0	0	0	0	0	0
Mountain	0	0	0.3	0	0	0	0	0	0	0
Taiga	0	0	0.3	0	0	0	0	0	0	0
Tundra	0	0	0	0	0	0	0	0	0	0
Polar	0	0	0	0	0	0	0	0	0	0
Zoology: Neotropical	0	0.3	0	0	0	0	0	0	0	0
Nearctic	0.7	0.1	0	0	0	0	0	0	0	0
Ethiopian	0	0.7	0	0	0	0	1	0	0	0
Oriental	0.2	0	0	1	1	0	0	0	0	0
Palearctic	0	0	1	0	0	1	0	1	1	1
Australian	0.3	0	0	0	0	0	0	0	0	0

Characteristics	Mongol-Khalka	Mongoloid	Montene-grin	Moor	Morvians	Mossi	Mpongwe	Mubi	Mulatto	Muong
Land: Total Area (km sq)	1570000	4290000	102000	629000	49500	261000	268000	1280000	6080000	330000
Density (pop/km sq)	1	249	103	115	108	48	5	5	45	213
# of boundaries	2	7	2			5	3	6	8	3
Total boundary (km)	8110	15600	2230	2960		2800	2550	5970	11100	3820
Terrain (3=mountains)	3	1	2	0.4		1	1	2	2	2
Land Usage: Arable %		48	30	7		8		0	9	2
Permanent crops %	0	0.8	2	7			18		2	2
Meadows & pastures %	79	8	5	25		29	78	36	23	1
Forest & woodland %	0	22	25	24		30	2	11	56	40
Other %	10	21	20	37		30	0	51	10	35
Irrigated %	10	12	3	3		0	0	0	1	3
% Protected	4	3		6		8	4		6	2
% Partially Protected	0	0.2		2		5		0.3	2	0
Risks: Earthquake (1=high)	0	0.2	0	0.4	1	0.4	0	0	0.1	0
Volcanism	0	0.2	0	0.6		1		0	0	0
Soil degradation	1	1	0	0.4		1		1		0
Desertification	0	0.8	0	0.6		1		0	0.8	0
Overgrazing			0	0.4		1		0	0.8	0
Deforestation	1	1	0	6				0	0.8	0
Elevation: average (m)	1310	101	132	1590		219		300	850	13
Highest point (m)	4360	8640				796	1020	3410	3260	3140
Lowest point (m)	553	-24		-2		87		160	-5	
Timezone (GMT)	8	-6	1	0.6		1	3	1	-4	7
Tectonic plate: African	0	0	0	0.4		0.4	1	1	0.9	0
Eurasian	1	0.8	1	0	1	0	0	0	0	1
Indo-Australian	0	0	0	0	0	0	0	0	0	0
Pacific	0	0	0	0	0	0	0	0	0	0
American	0	0	0	0	0	0	0	0	0.9	0
Nasca	0	0	0	0	0	0	0	0	0	0
Caribbean	0	0	0	0	0	0	0	0	0	0
Biome: Desert (1=yes)	1	0.1	0	0.6	0	1	0	0	0.7	0
Monsoon	0	0.8	0	0.4	0	0	0	0	0.9	1
Tropical rain forest	0	0.8	0	0	0	0	1	0	0.8	0
Savanna	0	0	0	0	0	1	0	1	0	0
Mediterranean	0	0	1	0	0	0	0	0	0	0
Temperate grassland	1	0.2	0	0	0	0	0	0	0.7	0
Temperate forest	0	0.2	1	0	0	0	0	0	0.7	0
Mountain	0	0.2	0	0	0	0	0	0	0.1	0
Taiga	1	0	0	0	0	0	0	0	0	0
Tundra	0	0	0	0	0	0	0	0	0	0
Polar	0	0	0	0	0	0	0	0	0	0
Zoology: Neotropical	0	0	0	0	0	0	0	0	0.8	0
Nearctic	0	0	0	0	0	0	0	0	0.1	0
Ethiopian	0	0	0	0.6	0	1	1	1	0	0
Oriental	1	1	0	0	0	0	0	0	0	1
Paleartic	0	1	1	0.4	1	0	0	0	0	0
Australian	0	0	0	0	0	0	0	0	0	0

Characteristics	Nama	Nauruan	Ndebele	Nepalese	Nether-lander	Newar	Ngbandi	Ngoni	Nkole	Norman-French D.
Land: Total Area (km sq)	824000	20	393000	141000	37300	141000	623000	118000	236000	150
··Density (pop/km sq)	2	485	28	150	410	150	5	90	82	558
··# of boundaries	4	0	4	4	2	2	5	3	5	0
··Total boundary (km)	3940	0	3080	2930	1030	2930	5200	2880	2700	0
··Terrain (3=mountains)	2	0	2	4	0	4	1	2	3	1
Land Usage: Arable %	0	0	7	17	25	17	3	25	23	0
··Permanent crops %		0	0	13	34	13	5	0	3	0
··Meadows & pastures %	64	0	13	33	9	33	64	20	25	0
··Forest & woodland %	22	0	61	37	31	37	28	50	30	0
··Other %	13	100	19	2	15	2	0	5	13	0
··Irrigated %	0		0	8	9	8	9	11		0
··% Protected	13		8	1	3	1	4	4	8	0
··% Partially Protected	2								4	0
Risks: Earthquake (1=high)	0	0	0	1	0	1	0	0	0	0
··Volcanism	0	0	0	0	0	0	0	0	0	0
··Soil degradation	1	0	1	1	0	1	0	0	1	0
··Desertification	0	0	0	0	0	0	0	0	0	0
··Overgrazing		0	1	0	0	0	0	1	1	0
··Deforestation	0	0	1	1	3	1	1	1	1	5
Elevation: average (m)	1650	27	1410	1340		1340	381	1010	1190	
··Highest point (m)	2580	64	2580	8850	321	8850	1410	3000	5100	
··Lowest point (m)	-2	0	165	60	-7	60	335	37	610	
··Timezone (GMT)	1	12	2	6	1	6	1	2	3	0
Tectonic plate: African	1	0	1	0	0	0	1	1	1	0
··Eurasian	0	0	0	1	1	1	0	0	0	1
··Indo-Australian	0	0	0	0	0	0	0	0	0	0
··Pacific	0	1	0	0	0	0	0	0	0	0
··American	0	0	0	0	0	0	0	0	0	0
··Nasca	0	0	0	0	0	0	0	0	0	0
··Caribbean	0	0	0	0	0	0	0	0	0	0
Biome: Desert (1=yes)	1	0	0	0	0	0	0	0	0	0
··Monsoon	0	0	0	1	0	1	0	0	0	0
··Tropical rain forest	0	1	0	0	0	0	1	0	0	0
··Savanna	0	0	1	0	0	0	0	1	1	0
··Mediterranean	0	0	0	0	0	0	0	0	0	0
··Temperate grassland	0	0	0	0	0	0	0	0	0	0
··Temperate forest	0	0	0	0	1	0	0	0	0	1
··Mountain	0	0	0	1	0	1	0	0	0	0
··Taiga	0	0	0	0	0	0	0	0	0	0
··Tundra	0	0	0	0	0	0	0	0	0	0
··Polar	0	0	0	0	0	0	0	0	0	0
Zoology: Neotropical	0	0	0	0	0	0	0	0	0	0
··Nearctic	0	0	0	0	0	0	0	0	0	0
··Ethiopian	1	0	1	0	0	0	1	1	1	0
··Oriental	0	0	0	1	0	1	0	0	0	0
··Palearctic	0	0	0	0	1	0	0	0	0	1
··Australian	0	1	0	0	0	0	0	0	0	0

Characteristics	North-Western	Norwegian	Nuba	Nuer	Nung Sukuma	Nupe	Nyamwezi (Galla)	Nyoros	Ometo	Oromo
Land: Total Area (km sq)	753000	324000	2510000	2510000	330000	924000	945000	236000	1220000	1220000
Density (pop/km sq)	12	13	11	11	213	115	30	82	43	43
# of boundaries	8	3	8	8	3	4	7	5	4	4
Total boundary (km)	5660	2580	7700	7700	3820	4050	3400	2700	5140	5140
Terrain (3=mountains)	2	3	5	5	2	2	3	3	3	3
Land Usage: Arable %	7	3	0	0	22	31	5	23	12	12
Permanent crops %	0	0	0	0	1	3	1	9	1	1
Meadows & pastures %	47	0	24	24	40	23	40	25	41	41
Forest & woodland %	27	27	20	20	35	15	47	30	24	24
Other %	19	70	51	51	2	28	7	13	22	22
Irrigated %	0	0	1	1	0	0	0	0	0	0
% Protected	8	13	4	4	3	3	14	8	3	3
% Partially Protected	0	1	0.3	0.3	0	1	10	4	0	0
Risks: Earthquake (1=high)	0	0	0	0	0	0	0	0	1	1
Volcanism	0	0	0	0	0	1	0	1	1	1
Soil degradation	1	0	1	1	1	1	1	1	1	1
Desertification	0	0	1	1	0	1	0	0	1	1
Overgrazing	0	0	1	1	0	1	0	0	1	1
Deforestation	1	0	0	0	1	1	1	1	1	1
Elevation: average (m)	1280	96	235	235			14	1190	2140	2140
Highest point (m)	2160	2470	3190	3190	3140	2420	5890	5100	4620	4620
Lowest point (m)	329	0						610	-125	-125
Timezone (GMT)	2	1	2	2	7	1	3	3	3	3
Tectonic plate: African	1	0	1	1	0	1	1	1	1	1
Eurasian	0	1	0	0	1	0	0	0	0	0
Indo-Australian	0	0	0	0	0	0	0	0	0	0
Pacific	0	0	0	0	0	0	0	0	0	0
American	0	0	0	0	0	0	0	0	0	0
Nasca	0	0	0	0	0	0	0	0	0	0
Caribbean	0	0	0	0	0	0	0	0	0	0
Biome: Desert (1=yes)	0	0	1	1	0	0	0	0	1	1
Monsoon	0	0	0	0	1	0	0	0	0	0
Tropical rain forest	0	0	0	0	1	1	0	1	0	0
Savanna	1	0	1	1	0	1	1	1	1	1
Mediterranean	0	0	0	0	0	0	0	0	0	0
Temperate grassland	0	0	0	0	0	0	0	0	0	0
Temperate forest	0	1	0	0	0	0	0	0	0	0
Mountain	0	1	0	0	0	0	0	0	1	1
Taiga	0	1	0	0	0	0	0	0	0	0
Tundra	0	1	0	0	0	0	0	0	0	0
Polar	0	0	0	0	0	0	0	0	0	0
Zoology: Neotropical	0	0	0	0	0	0	0	0	0	0
Nearctic	0	0	0	0	0	0	0	0	0	0
Ethiopian	1	0	1	1	0	1	1	1	1	1
Oriental	0	0	0	0	1	0	0	0	0	0
Palearctic	0	1	0	0	0	0	0	0	0	0
Australian	0	0	0	0	0	0	0	0	0	0

Characteristics	Osete	Ovambo	Ovim-bundu	Pacific Islander	Pakistani	Palauans	Palaung-Wa	Papuan New Guin.	Pashtun	Pepel
Land: Total Area (km sq)	69700	824000	1250000	20	197000	458	237000	462000	648000	36100
..Density (pop/km sq)	79	4	4	485	146	35	19	9	30	28
..# of boundaries	4	2					5	1	4	2
..Total boundary (km)	1460	3940	5200		616		5080	820	5830	724
..Terrain (3=mountains)	3				2	2	3	3	4	0
Land Usage: Arable %		1	2		17		4	0	12	9
..Permanent crops %		0	0		1		0	1	0	1
..Meadows & pastures %		64	23		0		3	0	46	
..Forest & woodland %		22	43		31		58	71	3	46
..Other %		13	32	100	15		35	28	3	38
..Irrigated %		0	0		27		1	0		6
..% Protected	3	13	2		11		0	0.1	0.3	
..% Partially Protected	0	2	1		0.2		0	0	0.2	
Risks: Earthquake (1=high)	0	0	0	0	1	0	0	1	1	0
..Volcanism	0	0	0	0	0	0	1	1	0	0
..Soil degradation	0	0	0	0	0	0	0	0	0	0
..Desertification	0	1	1	0	0.1	0	0	0	0	0
..Overgrazing	0	0	0	0	0	0	1	0	1	0
..Deforestation	0	0	0	0	0	3	5	0	1	0
Elevation: average (m)	490	1650	43	27	63		2820	17	1820	20
..Highest point (m)	5070	2580	2620	64	1420	9	70	4510	7480	4250
..Lowest point (m)	3	-2	1	12	-1		7	0	259	0
Timezone (GMT)	3	1	1	0	0.8	9		10	5	0
Tectonic plate: African	1	1	1	0	0	0	0	0	0	1
..Eurasian	1	0	0	0	0.2	0	1	0	1	0
..Indo-Australian	0	0	0	0	0.7	0	0	1	0	0
..Pacific	0	0	0	1	0	1	0	1	0	0
..American	0	0	0	0	0	0	0	0	0	0
..Nasca	0	0	0	0	0	0	0	0	0	0
..Caribbean	0	0	0	0	0	0	0	0	0	0
Biome: Desert (1=yes)	0	0	0	0	0.3	0	0	0	1	0
..Monsoon	0	0	0	0	0.1	0	1	0	0	0
..Tropical rain forest	0	0	0	1	0	1	0	1	0	1
..Savanna	1	1	1	0	0	0	0	0	0	0
..Mediterranean	1	0	0	0	0.6	0	0	0	0	0
..Temperate grassland	0	0	0	0	0	0	0	0	0	0
..Temperate forest	1	0	0	0	0	0	0	0	0	0
..Mountain	0	0	0	0	0.1	0	0	0	1	0
..Taiga	0	0	0	0	0	0	0	0	0	0
..Tundra	0	0	0	0	0	0	0	0	0	0
..Polar	0	0	0	0	0	0	0	0	0	0
Zoology: Neotropical	0	0	0	0	0	0	0	0	0	0
..Nearctic	0	0	0	0	0	0	0	0	0	0
..Ethiopian	0	1	1	0	0	0	0	0	0	1
..Oriental	1	0	0	0	0.1	0	1	0	1	0
..Paleartic	0	0	0	0	0.9	0	0	0	1	0
..Australian	0	0	0	1	0	0	0	1	0	0

Characteristics	Persian	Polinisian	Polinesian Chinese	Polinesian European	Polish	Portuguese	Punjabi	Punu	Puyi	Pygmy
Land: Total Area (km sq)	1640000	90800	3940	3710	346000	5930000	810000	293000	9600000	342000
:Density (pop/km sq)	38	46	54	56	122	105	159	6	126	7
:# of boundaries	5	0	0	0	3	7	4	4	13	5
:Total boundary (km)	5480	0	0	0	3000	1050	6780	3550	23200	5500
:Terrain (3=mountains)	3	2	2	2	2	1	3	0.7	3	0
Land Usage: Arable %	8	10	1	1	47	15	26	0	10	2
::Permanent crops %	0	20	19	19	1	2	0	0.7	0	0
::Meadows & pastures %	27	31	5	5	13	15	6	22	31	29
::Forest & woodland %	11	28	31	29	28	58	4	73	14	62
::Other %	54		44	46	10	10	64	4	45	7
::Irrigated %	2	0.3	0	0	0.7		19	0	5	0
:% Protected	5	0.8	.	.		2	5	0	3	0
:% Partially Protected	3	0.7	0	0		0.3	3	4	1	4
Risks: Earthquake (1=high)	0	0.4	0	0	0		1	0	0	0
::Volcanism	0	0	0	0	0	0	0	0	1	0
::Soil degradation	1	0	0	0	0	0	1	0	0	0
::Desertification	1	0	0	0	0	0	1	0	1	0
::Overgrazing	1	0	0	0	0	0.7	1	0	0	0
::Deforestation		0	0	0	0	0	0	0	0	0
Elevation: average (m)	907	26	2	2	106	709	277	175	28	513
::Highest point (m)	5590	2830	2240	2240	2470	2860	8610	1010	8850	981
::Lowest point (m)	-28		-6	-5	-1	-0.2	0	1	-154	1
Timezone (GMT)	3	3			1	0.3	5	1	8	1
Tectonic plate: African	0	0	0	0	0	0.3	0	1	0	1
::Eurasian	1	0	0	0	1		1	0	1	0
::Indo-Australian	0	0.4	1	1	0	0	1	0	0	0
::Pacific	0	1	0	0	0	0	0	0	0	0
::American	0	0	0	0	0	0.7	0	0	0	0
::Nasca	0	0.5	0	0	0	0	0	0	0	0
::Caribbean	1	0	0	0	0	0	0	0	0	0
Biome: Desert (1=yes)	0	0	0	0	0	0.7	0	0	1	0
::Monsoon	0	0	1	1	0	0	1	1	0	0
::Tropical rain forest	0	0.6	0	0	0	0.7	0	1	0	1
::Savanna	1	0	0	0	0	0.7	1	1	1	1
::Mediterranean	0	0	0	0	0	0.3	0	0	0	0
::Temperate grassland	1	0	0	0	0	0.7	0	0	0	0
::Temperate forest	0	0.4	0	0	1		0	0	0	0
::Mountain	1	0	0	0	0	0	1	0	1	0
Zoology: Neotropical	0	0.1	0	0.1	0	0.7	0	0	0	0
::Nearctic	0	0	0	0	0	0	0	0	0	0
::Ethiopian	0	0	0	0	0	0	0	1	0	1
::Oriental	0	0	0	0	0	0	1	0	1	0
::Palearctic	1	0	0	0	1	0.7	1	0	1	0
::Australian	0	0.9	1	0.9	0	0.3	0	0	0	0

Characteristics	Quechua	Rakhine	Romanian	Romansch	Rundi	Russian	Ruthenian	Rwanda	Saho	Sakalava
Land: Total Area (km sq)	958000	677000	237000	41300	2200000	14300000	49500	1910000	93700	587000
..Density (pop/km sq)	23	66	98	166	30	17	108	31	37	23
..# of boundaries	4	5	4	5		13	0	7	0	0
..Total boundary (km)	5410	5880	2900	1850	7870	17770	0	7160	0	0
..Terrain (3=mountains)	3	3	2	4	2	2	0	2	0	2
Land Usage: Arable %	4	15	43	10	6	6	0	7	0	4
..Permanent crops %	0.9	1	2	1	0.5	0.2	0	8	0	
..Meadows & pastures %	20	1	19	40	73	0.6	0	68	0	58
..Forest & woodland %	53	49	28	26	15	0.5	0	15	0	26
..Other %	22	34	7	23			0		0	11
..Irrigated %		2	11							2
..% Protected	4	0.3	5	0	4	1	1	0.5		1
..% Partially Protected	0.6		4	18	0.2			0.8		
Risks: Earthquake (1=high)	0.9	1	1					0		0
..Volcanism	0.9				0.1			0.2		0
..Soil degradation								0		1
..Desertification								0.2		0
..Overgrazing	0.7							0.2		1
..Deforestation	0.9	1	0	0	0.1	0.1				0
Elevation: average (m)	784		82	521	322	159		478		1380
..Highest point (m)	6570	5880	2540	4630	4950	5290		5110		2880
..Lowest point (m)	7	0		193	50	-24		127		0
Timezone (GMT)	-5	7	2	1	2	7		2	3	3
Tectonic plate: African					1			1		1
..Eurasian			1	1		1	1			
..Indo-Australian		1								
..Pacific										
..American	1									
..Nasca										
..Caribbean										
Biome: Desert (1=yes)	0.6									
..Monsoon		1								
..Tropical rain forest	0.6	1								
..Savanna	0.3									
..Mediterranean										
..Temperate grassland						0.9				
..Temperate forest			1			0.9	1			
..Mountain	1			1						
..Taiga						0.8				
..Tundra						0.8				
..Polar						0.8				
Zoology: Neotropical	1									
..Nearctic										
..Ethiopian					1			1		1
..Oriental		1								
..Paleartic			1	1		1	1			
..Australian	0	0	0	0	0	0	0	0	0	0

Characteristics	Samoan	Sanga	Sanmarinese	Sara	Scandinavian	Senufo	Serbian	Serer	Servicais Tongas	Shan
Land: Total Area (km sq)	1650000	342000	60	623000	16400	617000	199000	196000	960	677000
:Density (pop/km sq)	0.5	7	375	5	65	30	98	40	132	66
:# of boundaries	0.5	5	1	5	0.4	6	4	5	0	5
:Total boundary (km)	1720	5500	39	5200	24	4480	2130	2640	0	5880
:Terrain (3=mountains)	3	2	1	1	0.6	2	2	2	3	15
Land Usage: Arable %	18	2	17	3	23	7	28	27	3	1
:Permanent crops %	18	0	0	0	2	2	5	0	36	0
:Meadows & pastures %	5	29	0	5	4	18	20	30	1	49
:Forest & woodland %	48	62	83	64	70	20	26	31	0	34
:Other %	13	0	0	28	3	53	19	12	62	0.2
:Irrigated %	0.4	0	0	0	9	5	4	1	0	0.3
:% Protected	2	4	0	9	3	2	3	1	0	0
:% Partially Protected	0.2	0	0	4	19	0	0	16	0	1
Risks: Earthquake (1=high)	0.8	0	0	0	0	0	1	1	1	0
:Volcanism	0.8	0	0	0	0	0	0	1	0	0
:Soil degradation	0.2	0	0	0	0	0	0	0	0	0
:Desertification	0	1	0	1	0	0	0	0	0	0
:Overgrazing	0	0	0	0	0	0	0	0	0	1
:Deforestation	4	0	0	0	0	0.3	0.1	0.1	1	6
Elevation: average (m)	2770	513	17	381	17	150	130	24	17	5880
:Highest point (m)	-18	981	739	1410	173	1420	2510	581	2020	0
:Lowest point (m)	-10	0	50	335	-7	26	0	0	0	7
Timezone (GMT)	0	1	1	1	0.4	0	1	0	1	0
Tectonic plate: African	0.7	1	0	1	0	1	0	1	1	1
:Eurasian	0.8	0	1	0	1	0	1	0	0	1
:Indo-Australian	0	0	0	0	0	0	0	0	0	0
:Pacific	0	0	0	0	0	0	0	0	0	0
:American	0	0	0	0	0	0	0	0	0	0
:Nasca	0.2	0	0	0	0	0	0	0	0	0
:Caribbean	0.8	0	0	0	0	0	0	0	0	0
Biome: Desert (1=yes)	0	0	0	0	0	0.3	0.8	0	0	0
:Monsoon	0	0	0	0	0	0.5	0.1	0	0	0
:Tropical rain forest	0.2	1	0	1	0	1	0	1	1	1
:Savanna	0.2	0	0	1	0	0	0	1	0	0
:Mediterranean	0	0	1	0	0	0	0.2	0	0	0
:Temperate grassland	0	0	0	0	0	0	0	0	0	0
:Temperate forest	0	0	0	0	0	0	0	0	0	0
:Mountain	0.2	0	0	0	0	0	0	0	0	0
:Taiga	0.2	0	0	0	0.4	0	0	0	0	0
:Tundra	0	0	0	0	0.6	0	0	0	0	0
:Polar	0	0	0	0	0.6	0	0	0	0	0
Zoology: Neotropical	0	0	0	0	0	0	0	0	0	0
:Nearctic	0.2	0	0	0	0.4	0	0	0	0	0
:Ethiopian	0	1	0	1	0	1	0	1	1	0
:Oriental	0	0	0	0	0	0	0	0	0	1
:Palearctic	0	0	1	0	0.6	0	1	0	0	0
:Australian	0.8	0	0	0	0.4	0	0	0	0	0

Characteristics	Shilluk	Shona	Siamese	Sidamo	Sindhi	Sinhalese	Slavic Muslims	Slovak	Slovene	Soga
Land: Total Area (km sq)	2510000	471000	514000	1220000	804000	65200	51400	97000	22000	236000
: Density (pop/km sq)	11	26	111	43	159	276	85	109	97	82
: # of boundaries	8	4	4	3	4	0	5	4	4	5
: Total boundary (km)	7700	3360	4860	5140	6770	0	1380		1030	2700
: Terrain (3=mountains)	2	2	2		3		3		3	3
Land Usage: Arable %	5	6	34	12	26	16	20		11	23
: Permanent crops %			4			17		0.2	2	9
: Meadows & pastures %	24	21		41	6		25		20	25
: Forest & woodland %	20	53	30	24	4	37	35		44	30
: Other %	51	19	31	22	64	23	17		23	13
: Irrigated %			7		9	8		0.1		
: % Protected	4		11	3	5	12	0.5	0.27	4	8
: % Partially Protected	0.3	0.7	5		3	4	0.1	0.1	0.1	4
Risks: Earthquake (1=high)	0				1		1	1	1	0
: Volcanism	0			1						0
: Soil degradation	1			1						1
: Desertification				1	1					
: Overgrazing	0			1						
: Deforestation	1		1	1				1		1
Elevation: average (m)	235	1150		2140					132	1190
: Highest point (m)	3190	2540	2600	4620	8610	2510	1910	4380	2820	5100
: Lowest point (m)	0	138	0	-125	0	0	0	25	0	610
Timezone (GMT)	2	2	7	3	5	6	1	1	1	3
Tectonic plate: African	1	1	0	1	0	0	0	0	0	1
: Eurasian	0	0	1	0	1	0	1	1	1	0
: Indo-Australian	0	0	0	0	0	1	0	0	0	0
: Pacific	0	0	0	0	0	0	0	0	0	0
: American	0	0	0	0	0	0	0	0	0	0
: Nasca	0	0	0	0	0	0	0	0	0	0
: Caribbean	0	0	0	0	0	0	0	0	0	0
Biome: Desert (1=yes)	0	0	0	0	1	0	0	0	0	0
: Monsoon	0	0	1	0	0	0	0	0	0	0
: Tropical rain forest	0	0	1	0	0	1	0	0	0	0
: Savanna	1	1	0	1	0	0	0	0	0	1
: Mediterranean	0	0	0	0	0	0	0	0	0	0
: Temperate grassland	0	0	0	0	0	0	0	0	0	0
: Temperate forest	0	0	0	0	0	0	1	1	1	0
: Mountain	0	0	0	0	0	0	0	0	0	0
: Taiga	0	0	0	0	0	0	0	0	0	0
: Tundra	0	0	0	0	0	0	0	0	0	0
: Polar	0	0	0	0	0	0	0	0	0	0
Zoology: Neotropical	0	0	0	0	0	0	0	0	0	0
: Nearctic	0	0	0	0	0	0	0	0	0	0
: Ethiopian	1	1	0	1	0	0	0	0	0	1
: Oriental	0	0	1	0	1	1	0	0	0	0
: Paleartic	0	0	0	0	0	0	1	1	1	0
: Australian	0	0	0	0	0	0	0	0	0	0

Characteristics	Somali	Somba	Songhai	Soninke	Sotho	Sotho North	Spanish	Sundanese	Suriname	Susu
Land: Total Area (km sq)	687000	113000	1250000	1010000	743000	1220000	3250000	1920000	960	246000
Density (pop/km sq)	18	45	7	17	44	32	58	101	188	26
# of boundaries	3	4	7	6	4	6	6	2	2	6
Total boundary (km)	2570	1990	6490	6100	3340	4970	6300	2670	0	3400
Terrain (3=mountains)	1	2	1	0.8	2	2	3	2	2	2
Land Usage: Arable %	0.3	12	2	6	10	10	22	8	8	6
Permanent crops %	0.1	4	0	0	0.6	1	2	3	0	12
Meadows & pastures %	45	4	16	25	65	65	20			42
Forest & woodland %	15	35	5	11	2	3	44	67	67	40
Other %	37	45	77	57	22	21	4	15	15	0
Irrigated %	0.2	0	0.4	0.3	0.6	1	1	13	13	0.7
% Protected	0.3	7	5		4	6	5	10	10	0
% Partially Protected	0.1	0	0	3	2	4	0	3		0
Risks: Earthquake (1=high)	0.1	0	0	0	0	0	0	1	0	0
Volcanism	1	0	0	0	0	0	0	1	0	0
Soil degradation	1	1	0.5	0.1	0.4	0	0.6	0	0	0
Desertification	1	0	1	0.9	0.4	0	0	0	0	0
Overgrazing	1	1	0.5	0.1	0.4	0	1	0	0	1
Deforestation	1	0	0.5	0.2	0	0	0	0	0	0
Elevation: average (m)	195	17	271	241	638	12	649		23	46
Highest point (m)	2610	681	1570	995	3460	3450	3340	5030		1750
Lowest point (m)	-11	1	107	16	612	2	-0.7	8	-4	0
Timezone (GMT)	3	1	0.5	0.1	1	1	0.6	8		0
Tectonic plate: African	1	1	1	1	1	1	0.4	0	0	1
Eurasian	0	0	0	0	0	0	0.6	1	0	0
Indo-Australian	0	0	0	0	0	0	0	1	0	0
Pacific	0	0	0	0	0	0	0	0	0	0
American	0	0	0	0	0	0	0	0	1	0
Nasca	0	0	0	0	0	0	0	0	0	0
Caribbean	0	0	0	0	0	0	0	0	0	0
Biome: Desert (1=yes)	1	0	1	0.8	0	0	0.3	0	0	0
Monsoon	0	0	0	0	0	0	0	1	0	0
Tropical rain forest	0	1	0	0	0	0	0	1	1	1
Savanna	0	1	1	1	0.6	1	0	0	0	1
Mediterranean	0	0	0	0	0	0	0.4	0	0	0
Temperate grassland	0	0	0	0	0.6	0	0.4	0	0	0
Temperate forest	0	0	0	0	0	0	0.6	0	0	0
Mountain	0	0	0	0	0.1	0	0.3	0	0	0
Taiga	0	0	0	0	0	0	0	0	0	0
Tundra	0	0	0	0	0	0	0	0	0	0
Polar	0	0	0	0	0	0	0	0	0	0
Zoology: Neotropical	0	0	0	0	0	0	0.4	0	1	0
Nearctic	0	0	0	0	0	0	0	0	0	0
Ethiopian	1	1	1	1	1	1	0	0	0	1
Oriental	0	0	0	0	0	0	0	1	0	0
Paleartic	0	0	0	0	0	0	0.6	0	0	0
Australian	0	0	0	0	0	0	0	0	0	0

Characteristics	Swahili	Swazi	Swedish	Swiss	Tahitian	Tai	Taiwanese (Dari)	Tajik	Tama	Tamang
Land: Total Area (km sq)	914000	17400	445000	159	19100	306000	36000	407000	1280000	141000
..Density (pop/km sq)	37	47	19	186	9	164	578	36	5	150
..# of boundaries	7	2	2	2	0	4		4	6	2
..Total boundary (km)	3290	535	2210	78		4140		4940	5970	2930
..Terrain (3=mountains)	3	3	2	3	1	2	2	3	2	4
Land Usage: Arable %	5	8	7	25		17	24	9		17
..Permanent crops %	1	0	0						2	0
..Meadows & pastures %	39	67	2	38	14	2	5	36	36	13
..Forest & woodland %	45	6	64	19	51	45	55	1	11	33
..Other %	7	19	27	18	35	35	15	37	51	37
..Irrigated %	0	2	0	0	0	4	14			0
..% Protected	14	0	6			2	8	0.6	0.3	2
..% Partially Protected	10	3	5	38		1	3	0.1	0.3	8
Risks: Earthquake (1=high)						0	1	0.5	0	1
..Volcanism						0	0	0.5	0	0
..Soil degradation						0.3	0	0.5	0	0
..Desertification							0	0.5	0	1
..Overgrazing							0	0.5		0
..Deforestation	4					0.3	8		0	0
Elevation: average (m)		1160		463				1030	300	1340
..Highest point (m)	5890	1860	2080	2600	1630	3060	4000	7150	3410	8850
..Lowest point (m)	0	21	0	430	0	18		245	160	60
Timezone (GMT)	3	2	1	1	11	7	8	5	1	6
Tectonic plate: African	1	1							1	
..Eurasian			1	1		1	1	0.5		1
..Indo-Australian										
..Pacific					1					
..American										
..Nasca										
..Caribbean										
Biome: Desert (1=yes)								0.1	1	
..Monsoon										
..Tropical rain forest					1					
..Savanna	1	1								
..Mediterranean										
..Temperate grassland										
..Temperate forest			1							
..Mountain				1				0.5		1
..Taiga			1							
..Tundra										
..Polar										
Zoology: Neotropical										
..Nearctic										
..Ethiopian	1	1							1	
..Oriental						1	1	0.5		1
..Palearctic			1	1				0.5		
..Australian					1					

Characteristics	Tamil (Tubu)	Tatar	Teda	Teke	Tem-Kabre	Temne	Teso	Thai	Tharu	Tigre
Land: Total Area (km sq)	65600	1460000	1280000	1790000	56800	71700	236000	330000	141000	567000
·Density (pop/km sq)	273	12	5	15	69	63	82	213	150	40
·# of boundaries	0	13	6	6	3	2	5	3	2	2
·Total boundary (km)		18200	5970	7560	1650	958	2700	3820	2930	2160
·Terrain (3=mountains)	1	2	2	3	2	2	2	2	4	1
Land Usage: Arable %	16		2	1	25	23	23	22	17	5
·Permanent crops %	17	7		1			9		1	0.4
·Meadows & pastures %	37		36	74	4	31	25	40	13	17
·Forest & woodland %	23	0.2	11	13	28	29	30	35	33	10
·Other %		5	51		42	15	13	35	37	9
·Irrigated %	8	0				0	0		2	0
·% Protected	12		0.3	3	1	1	8	5	8	1
·% Partially Protected	4	0		1	1	0	4	3	1	0.4
Risks: Earthquake (1=high)	0	1	0	0	0	0	0	2	0	0.4
·Volcanism	0	0	0	0	0	0	0	0	0	0.4
·Soil degradation	1	0	1	0	0	1	1	0	1	0.4
·Desertification	0	0	0	0.3	0	0	0	0	0	0.4
·Overgrazing	0	0	0	0	0	0	0	0	0	0.4
·Deforestation	1	0	0	0	0	1	0	1	0	898
Elevation: average (m)	7	148	300	352	20	26	1190	13	1340	4620
·Highest point (m)	2520	5620	3410	3970	986	1940	5100	3140	8850	-125
·Lowest point (m)	0	-25	160				610		60	
Timezone (GMT)	6	8	1	1	1	0	3	7	6	3
Tectonic plate: African	0	0	1	1	1	1	1	0	0	0.4
·Eurasian	0	1	0	0	0	0	0	1	1	0
·Indo-Australian	1	0	0	0	0	0	0	0	0	0
·Pacific	0	0	0	0	0	0	0	0	0	0
·American	0	0	0	0	0	0	0	0	0	0
·Nasca	0	0	0	0	0	0	0	0	0	0
·Caribbean	0	0	0	0	0	0	0	0	0	0
Biome: Desert (1=yes)	0	0.9	1	0	0	0	0	0	0	0.4
·Monsoon	1	0	0	1	0	1	1	1	1	0
·Tropical rain forest	0	0	0	0	1	1	0	0	0	0
·Savanna	0	0	0	0	1	0	1	0	0	0
·Mediterranean	0	0.1	0	0	0	0	0	0	0	0
·Temperate grassland	0	0.8	0	0	0	0	0	0	0	0
·Temperate forest	0	0.8	0	0	0	0	0	0	0	0
·Mountain	0	0.8	0	0	0	0	0	0	0	0.4
·Taiga	0	0.8	0	0	0	0	0	0	0	0
·Tundra	0	0	0	0	0	0	0	0	0	0
·Polar	0	0	0	0	0	0	0	0	0	0
Zoology: Neotropical	0	0	0	0	0	0	0	0	0	0
·Nearctic	0	0	0	0	0	0	0	0	0	0
·Ethiopian	0	0	1	1	1	1	1	0	0	0.4
·Oriental	1	0	0	0	0	0	0	1	1	0
·Palearctic	0	1	0	0	0	0	0	0	0	0
·Australian	0	0	0	0	0	0	0	0	0	0

Characteristics	Tigrinya	Tikar	Tiv	Tonga	Tongan	Toros	Tribal	Tsimihety	Tsonga	Tswana
Land: Total Area (km sq)	910000	475000	924000	753000	694	236000	144000	587000	797000	1220000
: Density (pop/km sq)	42	26	115	12	139	82	849	23	20	32
: # of boundaries	3	6	4	7		5			6	6
: Total boundary (km)	3720	4590	4050	5660		2700	4250		4550	4970
: Terrain (3=mountains)	2	2	2		2	3	1	2		1
Land Usage: Arable %	9	13	31	7	25	23	67	4	4	1
: Permanent crops %	0.7	2	3	7	54	9	2	1	0	0
: Meadows & pastures %	30	18	23	47	13	25	4	58	56	65
: Forest & woodland %	17	54	25	27	2	30	16	26	20	3
: Other %	16	13	28	19		13	11	11	20	21
: Irrigated %	0	0	0	0	0	0	1	1	0	1
: % Protected	2	4	3	8		8	4	2		6
: % Partially Protected	0.7	2	1	0		4	0.7	1		4
Risks: Earthquake (1=high)	0.7	0	0	0	0	0	0	0	0	0
: Volcanism	0.7	1	0	1	0	1	0	1	0	0
: Soil degradation	0.7	0	1	0	0	0	0	0	1	0
: Desertification	0.7	1	1	1	1	1	1	1	0	0
: Overgrazing	0.7	1	1	0	0	0	0	0	0	0
: Deforestation	0.7	1	0	1	0	1	1	1	1	0
Elevation: average (m)	1550	387	3	1280		1190		1380	41	12
: Highest point (m)	4620	4100	2420	2160	1050	5100	957	2880	2430	3450
: Lowest point (m)	-125	0	0	329	13	610	0	3	0.1	2
Timezone (GMT)	3	1	1	2	13	3	6	3	2	1
Tectonic plate: African	0.7	1	1	1	0	1	1	1	1	1
: Eurasian	0	0	0	0	0	0	0	0	0	0
: Indo-Australian	0	0	0	0	0	0	1	0	0	0
: Pacific	0	0	0	0	1	0	0	0	0	0
: American	0	0	0	0	0	0	0	0	0	0
: Nasca	0	0	0	0	0	0	0	0	0	0
: Caribbean	0.7	0	0	0	0	0	0	0	0	0
Biome: Desert (1=yes)	0.0	0	0	0	0	0	0	0	0	1
: Monsoon	0	0	0	0	0	0	0	0	0	0
: Tropical rain forest	0.7	1	0	0	1	1	1	1	0	0
: Savanna	0	1	1	1	0	1	1	1	1	1
: Mediterranean	0.0	0	0	0	0	0	0	0	0	0
: Temperate grassland	0	0	0	0	0	0	0	0	0	0
: Temperate forest	0.7	0	0	0	0	0	0	0	0	0
: Mountain	0	0	0	0	0	0	0	0	0	0
: Taiga	0	0	0	0	0	0	0	0	0	0
: Tundra	0	0	0	0	0	0	0	0	0	0
: Polar	0	0	0	0	0	0	0	0	0	0
Zoology: Neotropical	0	0	0	0	0	0	0	0	0	0
: Nearctic	0.0	0	0	0	0	0	0	0	0	0
: Ethiopian	0.0	1	1	1	0	1	0	1	1	1
: Oriental	0	0	0	0	0	0	1	0	0	0
: Paleartic	0.7	0	0	0	0	0	0	0	0	0
: Australian	0	0	0	0	1	0	0	0	0	0

Characteristics	Tuareg	Tukolor	Tumbuka	Turkish	Turkmen	Tutsi	Tuvaluan	Twa	Uighur	Ukrainian
Land: Total Area (km sq)	1010000	313000	753000	748000	789000	27200	51	27000	2230000	2300000
..Density (pop/km sq)	15	35	12	83	22	252	414	260	10	77
..# of boundaries	7	7	6	6	4	3	0	4	5	8
..Total boundary (km)	5950	2980	5660	2730	4270	937	0	928	10400	6170
..Terrain (3=mountains)	1	1	2	3	2	2	0	2	2	2
Land Usage: Arable %	4	23	7	30	6	37	0	35	15	49
..Permanent crops %	0	0	0	4	0.2	9	2	10	0	2
..Meadows & pastures %	24	31	47	12	52	27	0	25	57	12
..Forest & woodland %	11	29	27	26	3	6	0	7	4	0.7
..Other %	61	17	19	28	35	21	98	23	24	27
..Irrigated %	0	0.9	0	0.3	2	0	0	1	0.2	3
..% Protected	4	10	8	0.5	0.3	5	0	7	0	0.8
..% Partially Protected	5	5	0	0.7	0.1	0	0	1	0	0.1
Risks: Earthquake (1=high)	0	0	0	1	1	1	1	0	0	0
..Volcanism	0	0	0	0	0	0.5	0	1	0	0
..Soil degradation	0.2	0.9	1	0.9	0.7	0	0	0	0	0
..Desertification	0.8	0.1	0	0	0.4	0	0	0	0	0
..Overgrazing	0.4	0.9	1	0.9	0.3	1	0	0	0	0
..Deforestation	0.2	0.9	0	0	0	0	0	0.6	0	0
Elevation: average (m)	295	21	1280	450	393	1130	2	1210	202	174
..Highest point (m)	1220	628	2160	4980	4170	3510	7	3710	7020	2520
..Lowest point (m)	84	-0.4	329	0.2	-34	853	0	873	0.9	-3
Timezone (GMT)	0	0	2	2	4	2	12	2	6	2
Tectonic plate: African	1	1	1	0	0	1	0	1	0	0
..Eurasian	0	0	0	1	1	0	0	0	1	1
..Indo-Australian	0	0	0	0	0	0	0	0	0	0
..Pacific	0	0	0	0	0	0	1	0	0	0
..American	0	0	0	0	0	0	0	0	0	0
..Nasca	0	0	0	0	0	0	0	0	0	0
..Caribbean	0	0	0	0	0	0	0	0	0	0
Biome: Desert (1=yes)	0.8	0.1	0	0	0.9	0	0	0	0.8	0
..Monsoon	0	0	0	0	0	0	0	0	0	0
..Tropical rain forest	0	0	0	0	0	0	1	1	0	0
..Savanna	1	1	1	0	0	1	0	0	0	0
..Mediterranean	0	0	0	0.9	0	0	0	0	0	0
..Temperate grassland	0	0	0	0.1	0.1	0	0	0	0	0.9
..Temperate forest	0	0	0	0	0	0	0	0	0	0
..Mountain	0	0	0	0	0	0	0	0	0	0
..Taiga	0	0	0	0	0	0	0	0	0	0
..Tundra	0	0	0	0	0	0	0	0	0	0
..Polar	0	0	0	0	0	0	0	0	0	0
Zoology: Neotropical	0	0	0	0	0	0	0	0	0	0
..Nearctic	0	0	0	0	0	0	0	0	0	0
..Ethiopian	1	1	1	0	0	1	0	1	0	0
..Oriental	0	0	0	0	0	0	0	0	0	0
..Palearctic	0	0	0	1	1	0	0	0	1	1
..Australian	0	0	0	0	0	0	1	0	0	0

Characteristics	Urdu	Uzbek	Vanuatuan	Vietnamese	Wallon	White	Wolof	Xhosa	Yalunka	Yao
Land: Total Area (km sq)	804000	477000	14800	408000	30500	7720000	228000	1220000	71700	5140000
::Density (pop/km sq)	159	44	11	210	328	33	40	32	63	99
::# of boundaries	4	5	0	3	4	3	5	6	2	9
::Total boundary (km)	6770	5990	0	3860	1390	8540	2670	4970	958	13700
::Terrain (3=mountains)	3	1	3	2	2	3	0	2	2	3
Land Usage: Arable %	26	10	1	22	24	0.5	25	10	23	14
::Permanent crops %	0	0	5	1	1	0.5	0	1	1	1
::Meadows & pastures %	6	46	2	1	20	29	29	65	31	31
::Forest & woodland %	4	0.3	91	40	21	31	30	3	29	27
::Other %	64	41	1	35	34	23	16	21	15	28
::Irrigated %	19	0.8	0	3	0	1	1	6	0	3
::% Protected	5	0.1	0	3	2	0.5	0	4	0	4
::% Partially Protected	3	0.1	1	2	0	0.7	1	0	1	
Risks: Earthquake (1=high)	1	0.1	1	0	0	0.1	0	0	0	0.5
::Volcanism	0	0.1	1	0	0	0.09	0	0	0	0.5
::Soil degradation	1	0.1	0	0	0	0.7	0.9	0	0	0.7
::Desertification	1	0.1	0	0	0	0.1	0.1	0	0	
::Overgrazing	0	0.1	0	0	0	0.8	0.9	0	0	
::Deforestation	0	0.1	0	0	0	0.2	1	0	1	0.9
Elevation: average (m)	277	228	20		76	222	22	12	26	361
::Highest point (m)	8610	5180	1880	3160	694	5370	574	3450	1940	5950
::Lowest point (m)	0	47	1	-0.7	0	-60	-0.1	2	0	-68
Timezone (GMT)	5	5	11	7	1	-5	0	2	0	5
Tectonic plate: African	0	0	0	0	0	0.1	1	1	1	
::Eurasian	1	0.9	0	1	1	0.9	0	0	0	0.5
::Indo-Australian	1	0	1	0	0	0	0	0	0	0.5
::Pacific	0	0	1	0	0	0	0	0	0	0
::American	0	0	0	0	0	0.9	0	0	0	0
::Nasca	0	0	0	0	0	0	0	0	0	0
::Caribbean	0	0	0	0	0	0	0	0	0	0
Biome: Desert (1=yes)	1	0.8	0	0	0	0.09	0	1	0	0
::Monsoon	0	0	0	1	0	0	0	0	0	0
::Tropical rain forest	0	0	1	1	0	0	0	0	1	0
::Savanna	1	0	0	0	0	0	1	1	1	0.5
::Mediterranean	0	0.1	0	0	0	0.2	0	0	0	0
::Temperate grassland	0	0.9	0	0	0	0.3	0	1	0	0.5
::Temperate forest	0	0.1	0	0	1	0.1	0	1	0	0.5
::Mountain	1	0	0	0	0	0.8	0	1	0	0.5
::Taiga	0	0	0	0	0	0.8	0	0	0	0
::Tundra	0	0	0	0	0	0.2	0	0	0	0
::Polar	0	0	0	0	0	0	0	0	0	0
Zoology: Neotropical	0	0	0	0	0	0.2	0	0	0	0
::Nearctic	0	0	0	0	0	0.7	0	0	0	0
::Ethiopian	0	0	0	0	0	0	1	1	1	0
::Oriental	1	0	0	1	0	0	0	0	0	0.5
::Paleartic	1	0.1	0	0	1	0.1	0	0	0	0.5
::Australian	0	0	1	0	0	0.1	0	0	0	0

Characteristics	Yi-Miao	Yoruba	Yugoslav	Zambo	Zulu
Land: Total Area (km sq)	9600000	902000	294000	129000	1220000
:Density (pop/km sq)	126	114	196	32	29
:# of boundaries	13	4	8	2	6
:Total boundary (km)	23200	3990	3830	1230	5030
:Terrain (3=mountains)	3	2	2	2	2
Land Usage: Arable %	10	30	27	9	0.9
:Permanent crops %	3	3	1	1	
:Meadows & pastures %	31	23	20	43	58
:Forest & woodland %	14	16	32	35	3
:Other %	45	28	20	12	29
:Irrigated %	5		0.9		6
:% Protected	3	3	0.2	0.3	4
:% Partially Protected	0	1	17	1	0
Risks: Earthquake (1=high)	1	0	0	1	0
:Volcanism	1	1	0	1	0.1
:Soil degradation	1	1	0	1	0.1
:Desertification	1	0	0	0	0.1
:Overgrazing	0	1	0	1	0
:Deforestation	1	4	0		
Elevation: average (m)	28		79	56	46
:Highest point (m)	8850	2370	3090	2110	3270
:Lowest point (m)	-154	0	21		24
Timezone (GMT)	8	1	1	-6	2
Tectonic plate: African	0	1	0	0	1
:Eurasian	1	0	1	0	0
:Indo-Australian	0	0	0	0	0
:Pacific	0	0	0	0	0
:American	0	0	0	0	0
:Nasca	0	0	0	0	0
:Caribbean	0	0	0	0	0
Biome: Desert (1=yes)	1	0	0	0	0
:Monsoon	0	0	0	1	0
:Tropical rain forest	1	1	0	1	0
:Savanna	0	1	0	0	0
:Mediterranean	0	0	0	0	0
:Temperate grassland	1	0	0.2	0	0.9
:Temperate forest	1	0	0.8	0	0.9
:Mountain	1	0	0	0	0.9
:Taiga	1	0	0	0	0
:Tundra	0	0	0	0	0
:Polar	0	0	0	0	0
Zoology: Neotropical	0	0	0	1	0
:Nearctic	0	0	0	0	0
:Ethiopian	0	1	0	0	1
:Oriental	1	0	0	1	0
:Paleartic	1	0	1	0	0
:Australian	0	0	0	0	0

8

MARINE RESOURCES ACROSS ETHNIC CULTURES

Many discussions of ethnic cultures focus on the role of the seas, oceans and marine environments (see Chapter 2). This chapter provides comparative statistics for a variety of variables characterizing each ethnic group's marine-based resources. For a full discussion of the methodology used to generate these estimates, please refer to Chapter 1 which gives important caveats. This chapter first gives summary statistics of the variables reported: the number of countries/cultures for which each variable was available, the number of ethnic cultures covered, weighted averages (by population) and simple averages; these averages can be used as benchmarks. Then a lengthy comparative table is presented which provides raw statistics across the ethnic groups defined in Chapter 1.

Most of the variables are self explanatory, though some merit commentary. All of the statistics should be considered as estimates which have undergone rounding and certain adjustments. Some are in their aggregate form; "Coastline", for example, measures the average length of coastline, in kilometers, per group. Others are given on a per capita basis; "Coastline/cap" measures the average length of coastline per capita for each group. Depending on the variable, "capita" may signify per person, per 1000 persons, or per million persons. The aggregate measure reflects the total accessible resource to the population, whereas the per capita measure indicates the quantity available if the resource was uniquely divisible. The extent to which each group can be characterized by its marine biologic zone, and prevailing winds is also given. Some groups can be exposed to multiple marine biologic and prevailing wind conditions (generated form ocean currents and topology).

Summary Statistics:
Marine Resources

Characteristics	Number of Countries Covered	Number of Ethnic Groups Covered	Weighted Average by Pop 1994	Simple Average	Simple Standard Deviation
Coastline: length (km)	226	423	9823.49	4133.03	10785.37
: length km/cap	226	423	141.95	3368.11	39954.38
Zones: Sea territory	233	425	21.62	27.38	50.50
: Continental shelf (m)	229	421	98.39	69.49	89.43
: Exclusive fishing (nm)	228	421	19.14	31.42	67.41
: Extend. econ. zone (nm)	229	423	98.00	66.77	89.05
: 200-Mi EEZ, area	204	417	1202766.01	402961.02	876964.83
: Contiguous zone (nm)	226	420	7.09	2.83	6.86
Inland waterways (km)	231	422	35735.69	7401.42	22095.58
Inland waterways/cap	231	422	0.11	0.20	0.68
Water area: (km sq)	231	425	199102.17	514853.58	4882343.70
: area/cap	231	425	4.96	156.68	1940.24
Access: Number of ports	204	375	10.17	4.89	6.05
: Natural Harbour (1=yes)	214	420	0.00	0.01	0.07
: Number of outlets	204	417	0.06	0.35	0.73
: Island (1=yes)	234	426	0.09	0.14	0.34
: Landlocked (1=yes)	232	426	0.04	0.21	0.39
Ships: Number/cap	190	410	6.13	28.26	144.79
: tonnage (dwt)/cap	190	410	111.20	1018.57	5425.35
Offshore Reserves: oil/cap	204	417	0.06	0.12	0.55
: gas/cap	204	417	0.19	1.44	22.54
Fish supply kgrm/year/cap	204	417	0.37	14.42	88.89
Marine Biology: Arctic	232	426	0.07	0.02	0.12
: NW American Boreal	232	426	0.04	0.01	0.06
: N Pacific, American	232	426	0.04	0.00	0.04
: Tropical East Pacific	232	426	0.06	0.08	0.26
: South Pacific	232	426	0.01	0.01	0.08
: Antiboreal	232	426	0.00	0.00	0.00
: Atlantic Boreal	232	426	0.10	0.05	0.19
: Atlantic Warm Temp	232	426	0.19	0.19	0.73
: Tropical Indo-West-Pacif	232	426	0.55	0.25	0.42
: East Asia Boreal	232	426	0.05	0.01	0.11
: North Pacific, East Asia	232	426	0.26	0.03	0.18
: Indo-Australian	232	426	0.04	0.02	0.13
: Tropical Atlantic	232	426	0.15	0.27	0.43
Coral reef (1=yes)	233	426	0.31	0.20	0.38
Salinities	234	426	32.95	27.19	13.92
Ocean circulation	232	426	0.32	0.57	0.97
Prevailing Wind: Polar	232	426	0.00	0.01	0.07
: Westerlies Zone	232	426	0.12	0.08	0.25
: Subtropical	232	426	0.10	0.08	0.26
: Monsoon Zone	232	426	0.32	0.09	0.28
: Trades Zone	232	426	0.60	0.68	0.45
: Intertropical	232	426	0.08	0.13	0.31
: Transition	232	426	0.00	0.00	0.05
No oceans (1=yes)	232	426	0.08	0.09	0.26
Fresh water (cub/kil)	122	356	204.06	34.33	97.86

Characteristics	Abadkis	Abkhaz	Acholi	Afar	Afro-European	Akan	Albanian	Ambo	Amerind	Amerind-Mestizo
Coastline: length (km)	0	310	0	13000	1020	539	570	1600	8400	4990
: length km/cap	0	57	0	3600	407	33	133	156	118	149
Zones: Sea territory	0	0	0	1	12	200	13	20	18	200
: Continental shelf (m)	0	.	0	1	0	100	13	200	26	200
: Excl. fish (nm)	0	.	0	.	0	0	0	0	2	0
: Extend. econ. zone (nm)	0	0	0	30	0	0	0	0	190	0
: 200-Mi EEZ, area	0	0	0	1020	298000	218000	20000	506000	2620000	1160000
: Contiguous zone (nm)	0	.	0	4	0	155	28	0	0	0
Inland waterways (km)	0	0	0	0	0	155	28	0	5400	11000
: Inland waterways/cap	0	0	0	0	0	0.5	0.3	0	0.1	0.3
Water area: (km sq)	4000	0	36300	9030000	160	8520	1350	0	53700	30200
: area/cap	0.2	0	2	227	0.1	0.5	0.3	0	0.6	0.9
Access: Number of ports	0	2	0	2	1	0	0	4	11	6
: Natural Harbour (1=yes)	1	0	0	0	0	0	0	0	0	0
: Number of outlets	0	0	1	0	1	0	0	0	0	0
: Island (1=yes)	1	0	0	0	0	0	0	0	0	0
: Landlocked (1=yes)	1	0	0	0	0	0	0	0	0	0
Ships: Number/cap	0	9	0.1	0	2	0.7	6	3	10	2
: tonnage (dwt)/cap	0	184	0.3	0.9	6	5	101	11	183	30
Offshore Reserves: oil/cap	0	0	0	0.2	0	2	0	0.3	0.3	0
: gas/cap	0	0	0	0	0	0	0	0.2	0.4	0
Fish supply kgrm/year/cap	0	0	0	0	0	0	0	0	0.1	0
Marine Biology: Arctic	0	0	0	0	0	0	0	0	0.1	0
: NW American Boreal	0	0	0	0	0	0	0	0	0.1	0
: N Pacific, American	0	0	0	0	0	0	0	0	0.9	0
: Tropical East Pacific	0	0	0	0	0	0	0	0	0	1
: South Pacific	0	0	0	0	0	0	0	0	0	0
: Antiboreal	0	0	0	0	0	0	0	0	0	0
: Atlantic Boreal	0	0	0	0	0	0	0	0	0.1	0
: Atlantic Warm Temp.	0	0	0	0	1	0	0	0	0.1	0
: Tropical Indo-West-Pacif	0	0	0	0	0	0	0	0	0	0
: East Asia Boreal	0	0	0	0	0	0	0	0	0	0
: North Pacific, East Asia	0	0	0	0	0	0	0	0	0	0
: Indo-Australian	0	0	0	0	0	0	0	0	0	0
: Tropical Atlantic	0	1	0	0	1	1	1	1	1	1
Coral reef (1=yes)	0	0	0	0.9	1	0	0	0	0.9	0
Salinities	2	40	2	34	36	35	35	34	34	34
Ocean circulation	0	1	0	0.9	1	1	1	1	0.2	-1
Prevailing Wind: Polar	0	0	0	0	0	0	0	0	0	0
: Westerlies Zone	0	0	0	0	1	0	1	0	0.1	1
: Subtropical	0	0	0	0	0	0	0	0	0.1	0
: Monsoon Zone	0	0	0	0.1	0	0	0	0	0.1	0
: Trades Zone	0	1	0	0.7	0	1	0	1	0.1	1
: Intertropical	1	0	0	0	0	0	0	0	0.9	0
: Transition	0	0	0	0	0	0	0	0	0	0
No oceans (1=yes)	0	1	1	0	0	0	0	0	0	0
Fresh water (cub/kil)	3	.	0.2	2	0.3	0.3	0.3	0.5	71	28

Characteristics	Amhara	Ana-Ife	Andorran	Angolares	Anouis	Antandroy	Arab, other	Arab Berber	Arab Emirian	Arab Lebanese
Coastline: length (km)	1090	56	0	1300	515	4830	1000	1740	1450	225
:length km/cap	14	14	0	614	38	364	58	568	794	78
Zones: Sea territory	12	30	0	12	12	50	14	11	3	12
:Continental shelf (m)	0	0	0	138	200	150	88	0	0	0
:Excl. fish (nm)	0	0	0	0	0	150	1	0	0	0
:Extend. econ. zone (nm)	0	200	0	200	200	0	0	0	200	0
:200-Mi EEZ, area	0	1030	0	1260000	105000	1290000	113000	324000	59300	22600
:Contiguous zone (nm)	0	25	0	0	0	0	7	0	0	0
Inland waterways (km)	0	0	0	566	980	566	291	0	0	0
Inland waterways/cap	0	0	0	0.1	0.1	0	0	0	0	0
Water area: (km sq)	121000	2400	0	304	4460	5500	1580	0	0	0
:area/cap	0	0.6	.	0	0.3	0.4	0.1	0	0	0
Access: Number of ports	2	2	0	5	0	4	8	6	7	170
:Natural Harbour (1=yes)	0	0	0	0	0	0	0	0	0	0.1
:Number of outlets	0	0	2	0	0	1	0	0	0	0.7
:Island (1=yes)	0	0	0	0.3	0.2	1	0	0	0	0
:Landlocked (1=yes)	0	0	1	0	0	0	0	0	0	0
Ships: Number/cap	0.4	5	0	10	0	1	44	8	50	48
:tonnage (dwt)/cap	2	5	0	66	0	3	0.1	239	691	149
Offshore Reserves: oil/cap	0	0	0	0	0	0	0.3	0.2	4	0
:gas/cap	0	0	0	0	0	0	0	0.4	12	0
Fish supply kgrm/year/cap	0	0	0	105	0.6	0	0	0	16	0
Marine Biology: Arctic	0	0	0	0	0	0	0	0	0	0
:NW American Boreal	0	0	0	0	0	0	0	0	0	0
:N Pacific, American	0	0	0	0	0	0	0	0	0	0
:Tropical East Pacific	0	0	0	0	0	0	0	0	0	0
:South Pacific	0	0	0	0	0	0	0	0	0	0
:Antiboreal	0	0	0	0	0	0	0	0	0	0
:Atlantic Boreal	0	0	0	0	0	0	0	0	0	0
:Atlantic Warm Temp	0	0	0	0.7	0	0	0.7	1	0	0
:Tropical Indo-West-Pacif	0	0	0	0	0	0	0.2	0	1	0
:East Asia Boreal	0	0	0	0	0	0	0	0	0	0
:North Pacific, East Asia	0	0	0	0	0	0	0	0	0	0
:Indo-Australian	0	0	0	0	0	1	0	0	0	0
:Tropical Atlantic	0	0	0	0.3	0.7	0	0	0	0	0
Coral reef (1=yes)	0	0	0	0	0	1	0.1	0	1	0
Salinities	38	35	2	34	35	35	33	38	38	39
Ocean circulation	1	-1	0	-0.7	1	1	0.1	0.9	1	1
Prevailing Wind: Polar	0	0	0	0	0	0	0	0	0	0
:Westerlies Zone	0	0	1	0	0	0	0.2	1	0	0
:Subtropical	0	0	0	0.7	0	0	0.9	0	1	1
:Monsoon Zone	0	0	0	0	0	0	0	0	0	0
:Trades Zone	1	1	0	0.3	1	1	0.4	0	0	0
:Intertropical	0	0	0	0	0	0	0	0	0	0
:Transition	0	0	0	0	0	0	0	0	0	0
No oceans (1=yes)	1	1	1	0	1	1	0	0	0	1
Fresh water (cub/kil)	2	0.1	.	11	0.7	16	11	3	0.9	0.8

Characteristics	Arab Omani	Arab Palestin.	Arab Quatar	Arab Saudi	Arab Sudanic	Arab Total	Arauca-nian	Armenian	Assamese	Assyrian
Coastline: length (km)	2090	43	563	2510	764	1150	6440	455	0	58
: length km/cap	1250	15	1150	152	28	96	466	28	0	3
Zones: Sea territory	12	2	3	12	11	13	12	12	0	12
: Continental shelf (m)	200	0	0	0	179	83	200	0.8	0	0
: Excl. fish (nm)						0.7	200	0.4		
: Extend. econ. zone (nm)	200	0	0	0	0	34		1	0	0
: 200-Mi EEZ, area	562000	22600	24000	1870000	82100	307000	2290000	27700	0	686
: Contiguous zone (nm)	0	0	0	18	16	9	24	0	0	0
Inland waterways (km)	0	0	0	0	3850	614	725	47		573
Inland waterways/cap	0	0	0	0	0.2	0.1	0.1	0	0	0
Water area: (km sq)	0	211	0	0	119000	13700	8150	4500		950
: area/cap	0	0.1	0	0	5	0.7	0.6	0.6	0	0
Access: Number of ports	2		3	7		0.7	8	1	1	3
: Natural Harbour (1=yes)					0.2			0	0	
: Number of outlets	0	0	0	0			0		1	0
: Island (1=yes)	0	0	0	0	0.1		0	0.7	0	0
: Landlocked (1=yes)	0	0	0	0	0.2		4	0.3	0	2
Ships: Number/cap	2	48	47	7		5	53	24	0	7
: tonnage (dwt)/cap	5	149	1210	76	0.3	55	0.2		0	
Offshore Reserves: oil/cap	1	0	6	5		0.6			0	
: gas/cap	25	0	457	4		0.1	2		0	
Fish supply kgrm/year/cap	0	0	0	0		0.5	0	0	0	0
Marine Biology: Arctic	0	0	0	0	0	0	0	0	0	0
: NW American Boreal	0	0	0	0	0	0	0	0	0	0
: N Pacific, American	0	0	0	0	0	0	0	0	0	0
: Tropical East Pacific	0	0	0	0	0	0	0	0	0	0
: South Pacific	0	0	0	0	0	0	0	0	0	0
: Antiboreal	0	0	0	0	0	0	0	0	0	0
: Atlantic Boreal	0	0	0	0	0	0	0	0	0	0
: Atlantic Warm Temp	0	0	0	0	0	0.6	0	0.2	0	0
: Tropical Indo-West-Pacif	1	1	1	1	0.9	0.3	1	0.1	0	1
: East Asia Boreal	0	0	0	0	0	0	0	0	0	0
: North Pacific, East Asia	0	0	0	0	0	0	0	0	0	0
: Indo-Australian	0	0	0	0	0	0	0	0	0	0
: Tropical Atlantic	0	0	0	0	0	0	0	0	0	0
Coral reef (1=yes)	0	0	0	0	0.9	0.2	0	0	0	0
Salinities	37	39	38	41	36	35	35	12	30	38
Ocean circulation	1	1	1	1	1	0.4	-1	2	2	0
Prevailing Wind: Polar	0	0	0	0	0	0	0	0	0	0
: Westerlies Zone	0	0	0	0	0	0.1	1	1	0	0
: Subtropical	0	0	0	0	0	0.9	1	1	1	1
: Monsoon Zone	0	0	0	0	0.9	0.1	0	0	0	0
: Trades Zone	0	0	0	0	0.9		0	0	0	0
: Intertropical	1	1	1	1	0		0	0	0	1
: Transition	0	0	0	0	0.7	0.3	0	0.2	0	0
No oceans (1=yes)	0	0	0	0			0	0	0	0
Fresh water (cub/kil)	0.4	0.8	.	4	17	10	17	31	0	43

Characteristics	Austrian	Avar	Aymara	Azande	Azerbai-jani	Bagirmi-Sara	Bahraini	Bai	Bakhtiari	Bakongo
Coastline: length (km)	0	0	1170	203	2000	0	161	14500	3180	1600
:length km/cap	0	0	51	11	33	0	303	8	50	156
Zones: Sea territory	0	0	97	41	8	0	3	12	12	20
:Continental shelf (m)	0	0	97	141	32	0	0	0	0	0
:Excl. fish (nm)	0	0	0	0	0	0	0	0	0	0
:Extend. econ. zone (nm)	0	0	0	0	0	0	0	0	50	200
:200-Mi EEZ, area	0	0	380000	19700	97600	2000	5150	110000	156000	506000
:Contiguous zone (nm)	0	0	4	4	324	0.3	0	0.1	0	0
Inland waterways (km)	446	0	11400	11500	7700	0	0	0	517	0
Inland waterways/cap	0.1	0	0.8	0.3	0.5	0	0	0.1	0.1	0
Water area: (km sq)	1120	500	9860	81600	0	24800	0	271000	12000	0
:area/cap	0.1	0.1	0.7	2	0	4	0	0.2	0.2	0
Access: Number of ports	2	0	1	3	2	0	4	12	0.7	4
:Natural Harbour (1=yes)	3	0	0.5	0	0	0	0	0	0	0
:Number of outlets	1	0	0.8	0.1	0	2	0	0	0	0
:Island (1=yes)	3	0	12	0.1	0	0	1	0	0	0
:Landlocked (1=yes)	0	1	0	1	0	1	0	0	0	0
Ships: Number/cap	0	0	0.4	0	0.3	3	28	17	3	3
:tonnage (dwt)/cap	27	0	0	0	0	0	299	0	13	0
Offshore Reserves: oil/cap	0	0	0	0	0	0	3	0	0.6	11
:gas/cap	0	0	0	0	0	0	48	0	0.5	0.3
Fish supply kgrm/year/cap	0	0	0.4	0.7	0	0	48	0	0	0.2
Marine Biology: Arctic	0	0	0	0	0	0	0	0	0	0
:NW American Boreal	0	0	0	0	0	0	0	0	0	0
:N Pacific, American	0	0	0	0	0	0	0	0	0	0
:Tropical East Pacific	0	0	0	0	0	0	0	0	0	0
:South Pacific	0	0	0	0	0	0	0	0	0	0
:Antiboreal	0	0	0	0	0	0	0	0	0	0
:Atlantic Boreal	0	0	0	0	0	0	0	0	0	0
:Atlantic Warm Temp	0	0	0	0	0	0	0	0	0	0
:Tropical Indo-West-Pacif	0	0	0	0	0	0	0	0	0	0
:East Asia Boreal	0	0	0	0	0	0	0	0	0	0
:North Pacific, East Asia	0	0	0	0	0	0	0	0	0	0
:Indo-Australian	0	0	0	0	0	0	0	0	0	0
:Tropical Atlantic	0	0	0	0	0	0	0	0	0	1
Coral reef (1=yes)	0	0	0	0	0	0	1	0	0	0
Salinities	2	40	17	31	39	2	38	34	38	34
Ocean circulation	0	1	0.6	0.4	0.4	0	1	0	0	-1
Prevailing Wind: Polar	0	0	0	0	0	0	0	0	0	0
:Westerlies Zone	0	0	0	0	0	0	0	0	0	0
:Subtropical	0	0	0.5	0	0	0	0	0	0	0
:Monsoon Zone	0	0	0	0	0	0	0	0	0	0
:Trades Zone	0	0	0	0	0	0	0	0	0	0
:Intertropical	1	0	0	0.9	1	0	1	1	1	1
:Transition	0	0	0	0.2	0	0	0	0	0	0
No oceans (1=yes)	1	1	0	1	0	1	0	1	0	1
Fresh water (cub/kil)	3	1	4	4	45	0.2	0	460	45	0.5

Characteristics	Balante	Baluchi	Bambara	Bamileke-Bamum	Banda	Bangi-Ngale	Bantu	Baoule	Bari	Bariba
Coastline: length (km)	274	1640	0	402	11	37	93	515	853	121
: length km/cap	292	23		32	0.3	0.9	10	38	31	24
Zones: Sea territory	12	11		50	4	12	6	12	12	200
: Continental shelf (m)		132		0			0		200	0
: Excl. fish (nm)		15			61					
: Extend. econ. zone (nm)	200	132			314	200		200		
: 200-Mi EEZ, area	151000	257000		15400		1030	24100	105000	91600	1720
: Contiguous zone (nm)		16							18	
Inland waterways (km)	0	202	1820	2090	5170	15100	4110	980	4070	2000
: Inland waterways/cap			0.2	0.2	0.3	0.4	0.4	0.1	0.1	0.4
Water area: (km sq)	8120	20200	20000	6000	23800	77800		4460	130000	
: area/cap	8	0.2	2	0.5	2	2	0.4	0.3	5	1
Access: Number of ports	1	4		1	3	3	4	2	2	
: Natural Harbour (1=yes)		0	0	0	0.7	0	2	0	0	0.2
: Number of outlets			2		0.7		0			
: Island (1=yes)		1	0		0.1		1			
: Landlocked (1=yes)			1							
Ships: Number/cap		9		0.2				0.6	0.3	
: tonnage (dwt)/cap		0.2		0.3		0.4		0.7		
Offshore Reserves: oil/cap		0.2		0.4						
: gas/cap				0.1						
Fish supply kgrm/year/cap										
Marine Biology: Arctic										
: NW American Boreal										
: N Pacific, American										
: Tropical East Pacific										
: South Pacific										
: Antiboreal										
: Atlantic Boreal										
: Atlantic Warm Temp										
: Tropical Indo-West-Pacif		1								
: East Asia Boreal										
: North Pacific, East Asia										
: Indo-Australian										
: Tropical Atlantic	1			1		1	1	1	1	1
Coral reef (1=yes)										
Salinities	36	36	2	33	10	33	1	35	40	33
Ocean circulation	-1	0.7	0	1	1	1	2	1	1	1
Prevailing Wind: Polar										
: Westerlies Zone										
: Subtropical										
: Monsoon Zone		0.7								
: Trades Zone										
: Intertropical	1		1	1		1	1	1	1	1
: Transition										
No oceans (1=yes)	0	0	1	0	0	0	0	0	1	0
Fresh water (cub/kil)	.	116	1	0.4	0.3	0.7	1	0.7	19	0.1

Characteristics	Barotze	Baskhir	Basque	Bassa	Batswana	Bayad	Beja	Belgian	Belorussian	Bemba
Coastline: length (km)	0	37700	4950	579	0	0	853	62	4610	0
: length km/cap	0	253	193	202	0	0	31	6	37	0
Zones: Sea territory	0	12	12	200	0	0	12	12	2	0
: Continental shelf (m)	0	200	0.7	200	0	0	200	193	25	0
: Excl. fish (nm)	0	0	0	0	0	0	0	0	0	0
: Extend. econ. zone (nm)	0	200	200	0	0	0	0	0	28	0
: 200-Mi EEZ, area	0	0	1220000	230000	0	0	91600	2650	0	0
: Contiguous zone (nm)	0	0	0	0	0	0	18	0	0	0
Inland waterways (km)	2250	124000	1040	15100	0	199	4070	1730	14900	2250
Inland waterways/cap	0.3	0.8	0	0	0	0.1	0.2	0.2	0.5	0.3
Water area: (km sq)	11900	79400	5330	0	15000	0	130000	271	10400	11900
: area/cap	1	0.5	0.1	0	1	0	0.1	0	0.4	1
Access: Number of ports	0	24	23	5	1	0	5	5	0	0
: Natural Harbour (1=yes)	2	0	0	4	0	0	2	0	3	2
: Number of outlets	0	0	0	0	3	2	0	0	0	0
: Island (1=yes)	1	0	0	0	0	0	0	0	0	1
: Landlocked (1=yes)	0	1	0	0	1	1	0	0	0	0
Ships: Number/cap	0	11	8	539	0	0	0	7	0.8	0
: tonnage (dwt)/cap	0	94	102	33400	0	0	0	215	0.2	0
Offshore Reserves: oil/cap	0	0	0	0	0	0	0	0	0	0
: gas/cap	0	0	0	0	0	0	0	0	0	0
Fish supply kgrm/year/cap	0	0	0	0	0	0	0.3	2	0.0	0
Marine Biology: Arctic	0	0	0	0	0	0	0	0	0	0
: NW American Boreal	0	0	0	0	0	0	0	0	0	0
: N Pacific, American	0	0	0	0	0	0	0	0	0	0
: Tropical East Pacific	0	0	0	0	0	0	0	0	0	0
: South Pacific	0	0	0	0	0	0	0	0	0	0
: Antiboreal	0	0	0	0	0	0	0	0	0	0
: Atlantic Boreal	0	0	0	0	0	0	0	0	0	0
: Atlantic Warm Temp	0	0	1	0	0	0	0	0	0	0
: Tropical Indo-West-Pacif	0	0	0	0	0	0	1	0	0	0
: East Asia Boreal	0	0	0	0	0	0	0	0	0	0
: North Pacific, East Asia	0	0	0	0	0	0	0	0	0	0
: Indo-Australian	0	0	0	0	0	0	0	0	0	0
: Tropical Atlantic	0	0	0	1	0	0	0	0	0	0
Coral reef (1=yes)	0	0	0	1	0	0	1	0	0	0
Salinities	2	32	35	35	2	0	40	33	0.7	2
Ocean circulation	0	-1	-1	-1	0	0	-1	-1	-0.1	0
Prevailing Wind: Polar	0	0	0	0	0	0	0	0	0.9	0
: Westerlies Zone	0	1	1	0	0	1	0	1	0.1	0
: Subtropical	1	1	0	0	0	0	1	0	0.1	1
: Monsoon Zone	0	0	0	0	0	0	0	0	0	0
: Trades Zone	0	0	0	0	0	0	0	0	0	0
: Intertropical	0	0	0	1	0	0	0	0	0	0
: Transition	0	0	0	0	0	0	0	0	0	0
No oceans (1=yes)	1	0	0	0	1	1	0	0	0	1
Fresh water (cub/kil)	0.4	.	45	0.1	0.1	0.6	19	9	0.1	0.4

Characteristics	Bengali	Berber	Bete	Betsileo	Betsimi-Saraka	Bhutia	Bihari	Black	Black Amerind	Boa
Coastline: length (km)	581	1590	515	4830	4830	0	167	11200	2410	37
: length km/cap	5	59	38	364	364	0	1	170	79	0.9
Zones: Sea territory	12	12	12	50	50	0	3	55	12	12
: Continental shelf (m)	0.1	126	200	150	150	0	0	171	200	
: Excl. fish (nm)				150	150	0	0	16		
: Extend. econ. zone (nm)	200	126	200	150	150	0	57	129	200	200
: 200-Mi EEZ, area	77000	226000	105000	1290000	1290000	0	22100	4250000	603000	1030
: Contiguous zone (nm)	18	15				0	5	8	8	
Inland waterways (km)	8240	0	980	566	566	0	2370	30500	14300	15100
Inland waterways/cap	0.1	0	0.1			0	0.2	0.2	0.4	0.4
Water area: (km sq)	10100	224	4460	5500	5500	0	5750	107000	100000	77800
: area/cap	0.1	0	0.3	0.4	0.4	0	0.1	16	3	2
Access: Number of ports	2	10	2	4	4	0	2		7	3
: Natural Harbour (1=yes)	0	0	0	0	0	0	0.7	0	0	0
: Number of outlets	0	0	0	1	1	0	0.7	0.2		0
: Island (1=yes)	1	0	0	0	0	0	0.4			0
: Landlocked (1=yes)		0	0	1	1	1	1	30		0
Ships: Number/cap	4	3	0.6	3	3	0	0	661	1	0
: tonnage (dwt)/cap	0	26	0.7	0	0	0	0	0.2	11	0.4
Offshore Reserves: oil/cap	0	0	0	0	0	0	0	2	0	0
: gas/cap	0	0	0	0	0	0	0	0.4	0	0
Fish supply kgrm/year/cap	0	0	0	0	0	0	0	0.4	0	0
Marine Biology: Arctic	0	0	0	0	0	0	0	0	0	0
: NW American Boreal	0	0	0	0	0	0	0	0.4	0	0
: N Pacific American	0	0	0	0	0	0	0	0.4	0	0
: Tropical East Pacific	0	0	0	0	0	0	0	0	0	0
: South Pacific	0	0	0	0	0	0	0	0.4	0	0
: Antiboreal	0	0	0	0	0	0	0	0.4	0	0
: Atlantic Boreal	0	0	0	0	0	0	0	0.1	0	0
: Atlantic Warm Temp	0	1	0	0	0	0	0	0	0	0
: Tropical Indo-West-Pacif	1	0	0	1	1	0	0.3	0	0	0
: East Asia Boreal	0	0	0	0	0	0	0	0.3	0	0
: North Pacific, East Asia	0	0	0	0	0	0	0	0.9	0	0
: Indo-Australian	0	0	0	0	0	0	0	0.4	0	0
: Tropical Atlantic	0	0	1	0	0	0	0	0	1	1
Coral reef (1=yes)	1	0	0	1	1	0	0	0.3	0	0
Salinities	30	36	35	35	35	32	0	36	30	33
Ocean circulation	1	-0.6	1	1	1	0	0	0.2	1	0
Prevailing Wind: Polar	0	0	0	0	0	0	0	0.4	0	0
: Westerlies Zone	0	0.6	0	0	0	0	0	0.7	0	0
: Subtropical	0	1	0	0	0	0	0	0.9	0	0
: Monsoon Zone	1	0	0	1	1	0	0.9	0.1	0	0
: Trades Zone	0	0	1	0	0	0	0	0	1	0
: Intertropical	0	0	0	0	0	0	0	0	0	1
: Transition	0	0	0	0	0	0	0	0	0	0
No oceans (1=yes)	0	0	0	1	1	1	0.7	0.9	0	0
Fresh water (cub/kil)	22	8	0.7	16	16	0	8	225	5	0.7

Characteristics	Bobo	Bounty Mutineers	Brazilian	Breton	Bubi	Bulgarian	Bullom	Bura	Burman	Bush Negro
Coastline: length (km)	0	37	1280	3410	296	430	402	853	3060	385
: length km/cap	0	284000	1220	163	750	40	89	8	46	1170
Zones: Sea territory	0	2	12	12	12	11	200	30	12	12
Continental shelf (m)	0	144	200	200	0	0		200	200	27
Excl. fish (nm)	0	200	0	0	0	198	0	0	0	0
Extend. econ. zone (nm)	0	0	200	200	0	0	0	200	200	200
200-Mi EEZ, area	0		1190000	341000	283000	31500	156000	211000		109000
Contiguous zone (nm)	0	9	0	12	0	0	0	0	24	0
Inland waterways (km)	486	0	606	8450	0	594	700	8580	3100	4390
Inland waterways/cap	0	0	0.1	0.1	0	0.1	0.2	0.1	0.1	0.1
Water area: (km sq)	5650	0	951	1390	0	344	120	13000	18800	1810
: area/cap	0.6	0.3	0.1	0.1	0	0	0	0.1	0.1	0.5
Access: Number of ports	0		0.5	54	2	6	3	0	0.3	2
Natural Harbour (1=yes)	0	1	0	0	0	0	0	0	0	0
Number of outlets	2	0	0	0	0	0	0	0	0	0
Island (1=yes)	0	1	0	0	0	0	0	0	0	0
Landlocked (1=yes)	1	0	0	0	0	0	1	0	0	0
Ships: Number/cap	0		7	4	5	14	1	0.5	0	16
: tonnage (dwt)/cap	0	0	91	97	17	204	1	0.7	30	33
Offshore Reserves: oil/cap	0	0	0	0	0	0	0	0	0	0
: gas/cap	0	0	130	0.5	0	0	0	0.1	0.1	0
Fish supply kgrm/year/cap	0		0	0	0	0	0	0	0	48
Marine Biology: Arctic	0	0	0	0	0	0	0	0	0	0
NW American Boreal	0	0	0	0	0	0	0	0	0	0
N Pacific, American	0	0	0	0	0	0	0	0	0	0
Tropical East Pacific	0	0	0	0	0	0	0	0	0	0
South Pacific	0	0	0	0	0	0	0	0	0	0
Antiboreal	0	0	0	0	0	0	0	0	0	0
Atlantic Boreal	0	0	0	0	0	0	0	0	0	0
Atlantic Warm Temp	0	0	0.6	0	0	0	0	0	0	0
Tropical Indo-West-Pacif	0	0	0	0	0	0	0	0	0	0
East Asia Boreal	0	0	0	0	0	0	0	0	0	0
North Pacific, East Asia	0	0	0	0	0	0	0	0	0	0
Indo-Australian	0	0	0	0	0	0	0	0	0	0
Tropical Atlantic	0	0	0.4	0	0	0	0	0	0	0
Coral reef (1=yes)	0	0.3	0	0	0	0	0	0	0	0
Salinities	2	35	35	34	32	39	35	33	30	35
Ocean circulation	0	1	-0.3	-1	1	1	-1	1	1	1
Prevailing Wind: Polar	0		0	0	0	0	0	0	0	0
Westerlies Zone	0	0.7	0	1	0	0	0	0	0	0
Subtropical	0	0.1	0.6	0	0	0	0	0	0	0
Monsoon Zone	0		0	0	0	0	0	0	0	0
Trades Zone	0	0.3	0.4	0	0	0	0	0	0	0
Intertropical	1	0	0	0	1	0	1	1	1	1
Transition	0		0	0	0	1	0	0	0	0
No oceans (1=yes)	0	0	0	0	0	0	0	0	0	0
Fresh water (cub/kil)	0.5		11	40		14	0.4	4	4	

Characteristics	Bushman	Capver-dien	Caroli-nians	Catalan	Chahar Aimak	Chamba	Chamorro	Chiga	Chin	Chinese
Coastline: length (km)	0	1790	.	4960	0	402	126	0	3060	5110
: length km/cap	0	150	.	127	0	32	.	0	46	173
Zones: Sea territory	0	12	3	12	0	50	3	0	12	12
: Continental shelf (m)	0	200	200	0	0	0	200	0	200	172
: Excl. fish (nm)	0	0	0	0	0	0	0	0	0	49
: Extend. econ. zone (nm)	0	200	200	200	0	0	200	0	200	133
: 200-Mi EEZ, area	0	1770000	.	1220000	0	1540	.	0	.	879000
: Contiguous zone (nm)	0	.	12	.	0	0	12	0	24	2
Inland waterways (km)	0	820	0	1050	1200	2090	0	0	3100	5700
Inland waterways/cap	0	0.1	0	.	0.1	0.2	0	0	0.1	0.1
Water area: (km sq)	15000	440	0	5350	0	6000	0	36300	18800	22700
: area/cap	11			0.1		0.5		2	0.4	0.5
Access: Number of ports	0	7	3	23	2	1	2	1	3	0.6
: Natural Harbour (1=yes)	0	0	1	0	1	0	1	0	1	0.2
: Number of outlets	3	0	0	8	0	0	0	1	0	0.4
: Island (1=yes)	0	1	1	0	0	0	1	0	0	0.4
: Landlocked (1=yes)	1	0	0	0	1	0	0	1	0	
Ships: Number/cap	0	7		102	0	0.2		0.1	2	.34
: tonnage (dwt)/cap	0	91			0	0.3		0.3	30	970
Offshore Reserves: oil/cap	0	0	0	0	0	0.4	0	0	0.1	0.8
: gas/cap	0	0	0	0	0	0.1	0	0	0	0.5
Fish supply kgrm/year/cap	0	0	0	0	0	0	0	0	0	0.1
Marine Biology: Arctic	0	0	0	0	0	0	0	0	0	0.1
: NW American Boreal	0	0	0	0	0	0	0	0	0	0.1
: N Pacific, American	0	0	0	0	0	0	0	0	0	
: Tropical East Pacific	0	0	0	0	0	0	0	0	0	
: South Pacific	0	0	0	0	0	0	0	0	0	
: Antiboreal	0	0	0	0	0	0	0	0	0	
: Atlantic Boreal	0	0	0	0	0	0	0	0	0	0.0
: Atlantic Warm Temp	0	0	0	0	0	0	0	0	0	0.1
: Tropical Indo-West-Pacif	0	0	0	0	0	0	0	0	0	0.8
: East Asia Boreal	0	0	0	0	0	0	0	0	0	0.0
: North Pacific, East Asia	0	0	0	0	0	0	0	0	0	0.0
: Indo-Australian	0	0	0	0	0	0	0	0	0	0.0
: Tropical Atlantic	0	1	1	1	0	1	1	0	1	0.1
Coral reef (1=yes)	0	0	0	0	0	0	0	0	0	0.8
Salinities	2	35	35	35	2	33	35	2	30	33
Ocean circulation	0	-1	-1	-1	0	1	0	0	1	-0.4
Prevailing Wind: Polar	0	0	0	0	0	0	0	0	0	0.1
: Westerlies Zone	0	0	0	0	0	0	0	0	0	0.4
: Subtropical	0	1	1	1	1	1	1	1	1	0.7
: Monsoon Zone	0	0	0	0	0	0	0	0	0	0.2
: Trades Zone	0	0	0	0	0	0	0	0	0	0.0
: Intertropical	0	0	0	0	1	0	0	0	0	
: Transition	0	0	0	0	0	0	0	0	0	
No oceans (1=yes)	0	0	0	0	0	0	0	0	0	
Fresh water (cub/kil)	0.1	11	.	45	26	0.4	.	0.2	4	59

Characteristics	Chinese Mainland	Chokwe	Chuang	Chuvash	Circassian	Coloured	Comorian	Creole	Croatian	Czech
Coastline: length (km)	1450	612	14500	37700	6410	2880	621	265	1750	54200
length km/cap	46	58	8	253	108	73	541	1060	361	5290
Zones: Sea territory	12	15	12	12	6	12	14	11	12	0.3
Continental shelf (m)			0	200		200		131	200	0.5
Excl. fish (nm)		200	0		0	200	9	0	12	
Extend. econ. zone (nm)	200	0	0	200	178	0	197	157	12	4
200-Mi EEZ, area	0	187000	110000	0	211000	1020000	80800	748000	0	
Contiguous zone (nm)	0	0	0.1	0	1070	0	0	0	0	4510000
Inland waterways (km)	0	9540	271000	124000	0	0	35	723	327	0
Inland waterways/cap		0.3	0.2	0.8	8770	0	0	0.9	0.1	363
Water area: (km sq)	3720	49200	12	79400	0.2	0	344	255	128	0
area/cap	0.2	2		0.5	4	7	0.2	0.3	0	98500
Access: Number of ports	0	3	12	24			0	2	7	7
Natural Harbour (1=yes)		0	0	0		0	0	0	0	0
Number of outlets	1	0	0	0	0	0	0	0.8	0	0
Island (1=yes)	0	1	1	0	1	0.2	1	0	0	0
Landlocked (1=yes)		1				0			0	0
Ships: Number/cap	11	4	17	11	11	5	5	18	14	2
tonnage (dwt)/cap	429	0.1		94	105	4	4	128	31	42
Offshore Reserves: oil/cap	0.1	0.1	0	0	0	0	0	0	0	0.1
gas/cap	0	0	0	0	0	0	0	55	0	0.4
Fish supply kgrm/year/cap	0	0	0	0	0	0	0	0	0	0.8
Marine Biology: Arctic	0	0	0	0	0	0	0	0	0	0
NW American Boreal	0	0	0	0	0	0	0	0	0	0
N Pacific. American	0	0	0	0	0	0	0	0	0	0
Tropical East Pacific	0	0	0	0	0	0	0	0	0	0
South Pacific	0	0	0	0	0	0	0	0	0	0
Antiboreal	0	0	0	0	0	0	0	0	0	0
Atlantic Boreal	0	0	0	0	0	0	0	0	0	0
Atlantic Warm Temp	0	0	0	0	0	0	0	0	0	0
Tropical Indo-West-Pacif	1	1	1	1	1	1	1	0.7	1	0
East Asia Boreal	0	0	0	0	0	0	0	0	0	0
North Pacific, East Asia	1	0	0	0	0	0	0	0	0	0
Indo-Australian	0	0	0	0	0	0	0	0	0	0
Tropical Atlantic	0	0	0	0	0	0	0	0.9	0	0
Coral reef (1=yes)	0	0	0	0	0.1	0	1	0.9	0	0
Salinities	34	33	34	32	39	35	35	35	33	0.8
Ocean circulation	0	-0.4	0	-1	1	1	1	0.4	1	0
Prevailing Wind: Polar	0	0	0	0	0	0	0	0	0	0
Westerlies Zone	0	0	0	0	0	0	0	0	0	0
Subtropical	1	1	1	1	1	1	1	0.9	1	0
Monsoon Zone	0	0	0	1	0	0	0	0.2	0	0
Trades Zone	0	0	0	0	0	0	0	0	0	0
Intertropical	0	0	0	0	0	0	0	0	0	0
Transition										
No oceans (1=yes)	0	0	0	0	0	0	0	0	1	0
Fresh water (cub/kil)		0.6	460		14	9	16	0.4	5	42

Characteristics	Dagestani	Dai	Damara	Dan	Danish	Dinka	Dogon	Dong	Dravidian	Duala
Coastline: length (km)	32500	14500	1490	527	3440	853	0	14500	7000	296
: length km/cap	218	8	950	69	674	31	0	8	9	750
Zones: Sea territory	10	12	6	47	3	12	0	12	12	12
: Continental shelf (m)	173	0	0	200	200	200	0	0	200	0
: Excl. fish (nm)	0	0	12	0	199	0	0	0	0	0
: Extend. econ. zone (nm)	173	0	0	163	0.8	0	0	0	200	0
: 200-Mi EEZ, area	0	0	500000	128000	75700	91600	0	0	2020000	283000
: Contiguous zone (nm)	0	0	0	0	4	18	0	0	24	0
Inland waterways (km)	107000	110000	0	797	421	4070	1820	110000	19100	0
Inland waterways/cap	0.8	0.1	0	0.1	0.1	0.1	0.2	0.1	0.1	0
Water area: (km sq)	68700	271000	1000	6440	755	130000	20000	271000	314000	0
: area/cap	0.5	0.2	0.6	0.6	0.1	5	2	0.2	0.4	0
Access: Number of ports	21	12	1	2	5	2	0	12	7	2
: Natural Harbour (1=yes)	0	0	0	0	0	0	0	0	0	0
: Number of outlets	0	0	0	0	0	0	2	0	0	0
: Island (1=yes)	0	0	0	0	0	0	0	0	0	0
: Landlocked (1=yes)	0	0	0	0	0	0	1	0	0	0
Ships: Number/cap	10	1	0	101	97	0.3	0	1	0.4	5
: tonnage (dwt)/cap	81	17	0	624	1320	2	0	17	1	17
Offshore Reserves: oil/cap	0	0	0	0	0.7	0	0	0	0	0
: gas/cap	0	0	0	0	0.7	0	0	0	0.1	0
Fish supply kgrm/year/cap	0.9	0	16	16	4	0	0	0	0	0
Marine Biology: Arctic	0	0	0	0	0	0	0	0	0	0
: NW American Boreal	0	0	0	0	0	0	0	0	0	0
: N Pacific, American	0	0	0	0	0	0	0	0	0	0
: Tropical East Pacific	0	0	0	0	0	0	0	0	0	0
: South Pacific	0	0	0	0	0	0	0	0	0	0
: Antiboreal	0	0	0	0	0	0	0	0	0	0
: Atlantic Boreal	0.9	0	0	0	1	0	0	0	0	0
: Atlantic Warm Temp	0.1	1	1	1	0	1	1	1	0	0
: Tropical Indo-West-Pacif	0.9	0	0	0	0	0	0	0	1	0
: East Asia Boreal	0	1	0	0	0	0	0	1	0	0
: North Pacific, East Asia	0	0	0	0	0	0	0	0	0	0
: Indo-Australian	0	0	0	0	0	0	0	0	0	0
: Tropical Atlantic	0	0	1	1	0	1	0	0	0	1
Coral reef (1=yes)	0	1	0	0	0	0	0	1	1	0
Salinities	0.33	34	35	35	34	40	2	34	34	32
Ocean circulation	-0.7	0	-1	0.6	1	1	0	0	1	1
Prevailing Wind: Polar	0	0	0	0	0	0	0	0	0	0
: Westerlies Zone	0.9	0	1	0	1	0	0	0	0	0
: Subtropical	0.1	0	0	0	0	0	0	0	0	0
: Monsoon Zone	0	1	0	0	0	0	0	1	1	0
: Trades Zone	0.1	0	0	0	0	0	0	0	0	0
: Intertropical	0	0	0	1	0	1	1	0	0	1
: Transition	0	0	0	0	0	0	0	0	0	0
No oceans (1=yes)	.	0	0	0	0	1	1	0	0	0
Fresh water (cub/kil)	0.1	460	0.1	0.6	1	19	1	460	380	.

Characteristics	Duala-Landa-B.	Dujia	Dutch	Dyola	Edo	Egyptian	English	Estonian	Euro-nesian	European
Coastline: length (km)	402	14500	44700	20	853	2450	12400	1390	403	12800
: length km/cap	32	8	3550	21	8	44	215	878	1830	1130
Zones: Sea territory	50	12	12	49	30	12	3		12	143
: Continental shelf (m)			152		200	200	200			197
: Excl. fish (nm)			197		200	200	200			29
: Extend. econ. zone (nm)			3						200	30
200-Mi EEZ, area	15400		3570000	4800	211000	174000	942000		96000	1850000
: Contiguous zone (nm)						18				0.1
Inland waterways (km)	2090	110000	2750	1470	8580	173	2740	250		8270
Inland waterways/cap	0.2	0.1	0.1	0.2	0.1			0.2		0.3
Water area: (km sq)	6000	271000	574000	15400	13000	6000	3230	1900		126000
: area/cap	0.5	0.2	24	2	0.1	0.5	0.1			4
Access: Number of ports	1	12	6	1	6		0.7	3	1	6
: Natural Harbour (1=yes)										
: Number of outlets				2					1	0.1
: Island (1=yes)				0.8			1			
: Landlocked (1=yes)										3
Ships: Number/cap	0.2		5		0.5	4	8	64	14	31
: tonnage (dwt)/cap	0.3	17	15		0.7	28	114	370	26	0.2
Offshore Reserves: oil/cap	0.4		0.1		0.1	0.1	0.2			0.5
: gas/cap	0.1		0.3				0.7			0.1
Fish supply kgrm/year/cap			0.8	5			0.4		266	0.1
Marine Biology: Arctic			0.8							0.7
: NW American Boreal										
: N Pacific, American										0.1
: Tropical East Pacific										
: South Pacific										
: Antiboreal			0.8							
: Atlantic Boreal			0.2							
: Atlantic Warm Temp										
: Tropical Indo-West-Pacif				0.2						
: East Asia Boreal				0.9						
: North Pacific, East Asia										
: Indo-Australian										
: Tropical Atlantic										
Coral reef (1=yes)	1	1	1	1	1	1	1	1	1	0.1
Salinities	33	34	32		33	39	35	34	35	0.1
Ocean circulation	1		0.2	1		1	-1	-1	1	33
Prevailing Wind: Polar			0.1							-0.6
: Westerlies Zone										0.1
: Subtropical		1					1	1	1	0.9
: Monsoon Zone	1			1	1	1				
: Trades Zone				0.2						0.1
: Intertropical			0.2							
: Transition						1				
No oceans (1=yes)										
Fresh water (cub/kil)	0.4	460	35	1	4	56	28	0	0	25

Characteristics	Ewa-Adja	Ewe	Fang	Fijian	Finnish	Fleming	Fon	Forros	French	Fulani
Coastline: length (km)	56	539	459	1130	1660	64	121	209	9690	597
:length km/cap	14	33	194	1550	267	6	24	1650	586	23
Zones: Sea territory	30	200	53	12	4	12	200	12	12	28
:Continental shelf (m)	0	100	21	200	199	200	0	0	195	128
:Excl. fish (nm)	0	0	0	200	23	0	0	0	23	140
:Extend. econ. zone (nm)	200	0	0	200	0	0	0	200	172	140
:200-Mi EEZ, area	1030	218000	68700	1130000	134000	2740	1720	128000	833000	147000
:Contiguous zone (nm)	0	0	0	0	6	0	0	0	10	2
Inland waterways (km)	25	155	1820	163	6120	1790	0	0	7680	5380
Inland waterways/cap	0	0	0.2	0.2	1	0.2	0	0	0.1	0.1
Water area: (km sq)	2400	8520	5980	0	37100	280	2000	0	87800	9550
:area/cap	0.6	0.5	0.6	0	7	0.6	0.4	0	2	0.1
Access: Number of ports	0	0.2	0.1	4	11	5	0.1	2	47	0.5
:Natural Harbour (1=yes)	0	0	0	0	0	0	0	1	0.1	0.3
:Number of outlets	0	0	0	0	0	0	0	0	0	0
:Island (1=yes)	0	0	0	1	0	0	0	0	0	0.1
:Landlocked (1=yes)	0	0	0	0	0	0	0	0	0	0
Ships: Number/cap	5	0.7	1	34	25	3	0	16	4	0.3
:tonnage (dwt)/cap	5	0.5	0.7	86	212	5	0.2	10	89	0.4
Offshore Reserves: oil/cap	0	0	0.1	0	0	0	0	0	0	0.1
:gas/cap	0	0	0.3	0	0	0	0	0	0.6	0.6
Fish supply kgrm/year/cap	0	2	0	60	7	2	0	339	0.6	0.2
Marine Biology: Arctic	0	0	0	0	0	0	0	0	0.1	0
:NW American Boreal	0	0	0	0	0	0	0	0	0	0
:N Pacific American	0	0	0	0	0	0	0	0	0	0
:Tropical East Pacific	0	0	0	0	0	0	0	0	0	0
:South Pacific	0	0	0	1	0	0	0	0	0	0
:Antiboreal	0	0	0	0	0	0	0	0	0	0
:Atlantic Boreal	0	0	0	0	1	8	0	0	0.1	0
:Atlantic Warm Temp	0	0	0	0	0	0	0	0	0.9	0.9
:Tropical Indo-West-Pacif	0	0	0	0	0	0	0	0	0	0
:East Asia Boreal	0	0	0	0	0	0	0	0	0	0
:North Pacific, East Asia	0	0	0	0	0	0	0	0	0	0
:Indo-Australian	0	0	0	0	0	0	0	0	0	0
:Tropical Atlantic	1	1	1	0	0	0	1	1	0	0
Coral reef (1=yes)	0	0	0	1	0	0	0	0	0	0
Salinities	35	35	33	35	34	34	33	33	33	29
Ocean circulation	-1	1	1	1	-1	1	1	1	0.9	0.1
Prevailing Wind: Polar	0	0	0	0	1	0	0	0	0.1	0
:Westerlies Zone	0	0	0	0	1	1	0	0	0	0
:Subtropical	0	0	0	0	0	0	0	0	0	0
:Monsoon Zone	1	1	1	1	0	0	1	1	0	0
:Trades Zone	0	0	0	0	0	0	0	0	0	0.8
:Intertropical	0	0	0	0	0	0	0	0	0	0.2
:Transition	0	0	0	0	0	1	0	0	0	0
No oceans (1=yes)	0	0	0	0	0	9	0	0	0	0
Fresh water (cub/kil)	0.1	0.3	0.4	.	4	9	0.1	.	39	2

Characteristics	Fur	Ga-Adangme	Gagauz	Galician	Ganda	Garifuna	Gbaya	Georgian	German	Gibraltarian
Coastline: length (km)	853	539	3150	4960	0	386	0	517	2120	12
: length km/cap	31	333	53	127	0	1930	0	58	51	384
Zones: Sea territory	12	200	3	12	0	3	0	0.2	14	3
: Continental shelf (m)	200	100	0	0	0	0	0	0	187	200
: Excl. fish (nm)	0	0	0	0	0	0	0	0	173	0
: Extend. econ. zone (nm)	0	0	0	200	0	0	0	200	3	0
: 200-Mi EEZ, area	91600	218000	104000	1220000	0	30900	0	7120	393000	0
: Contiguous zone (nm)	18	0	0	0	0	0	0	36	0.2	0
Inland waterways (km)	4070	155	525	1050	0	825	800	0.1	8640	0
Inland waterways/cap	0.1	0	0	0	0	0	0.2	0	0.1	0
Water area: (km sq)	130000	8520	4300	5350	36300	160	0	295	13100	0
: area/cap	5	0.5	0.2	0.1	2	0.8	0	2	0.2	0
Access: Number of ports	2	2	12	23	0	4	0	2	39	1
: Natural Harbour (1=yes)	0	0	0	2	1	0	1	0	0	0
: Number of outlets	0	0	0	8	0	0	1	0	0.2	0
: Island (1=yes)	0	0	1	0	0	0	0	0	0	0
: Landlocked (1=yes)	0	0	0	0	1	0	1	0	0.1	0
Ships: Number/cap	0.3	0.7	0.4	0	0.1	135	0	9	0.8	0
: tonnage (dwt)/cap	2	5	0	102	0.3	242	0	182	77	0
Offshore Reserves: oil/cap	0	0	0	0	0	0	0	0	0	0
: gas/cap	0	0	0	0	0	0	0	0	0.9	0
Fish supply kgrm/year/cap	0	0	0	0	0	0	0	0	0.9	0
Marine Biology: Arctic	0	0	0	0	0	0	0	0	0.0	0
: NW American Boreal	0	0	0	0	0	0	0	0	0	0
: N Pacific, American	0	0	0	0	0	0	0	0	0	0
: Tropical East Pacific	0	0	0	0	0	0	0	0	0	0
: South Pacific	0	0	0	0	0	0	0	0	0	0
: Antiboreal	0	0	0	0	0	0	0	0	0	0
: Atlantic Boreal	0	0	0	1	0	0	0	0	0.1	1
: Atlantic Warm Temp	0	0	0	0	0	0	0	0	0.1	0
: Tropical Indo-West-Pacif	0	0	0	0	0	0	0	0	0.1	0
: East Asia Boreal	0	0	0	0	0	0	0	0	0	0
: North Pacific, East Asia	0	0	0	0	0	0	0	0	0	0
: Indo-Australian	0	0	0	0	0	0	0	0	0	0
: Tropical Atlantic	0	1	0	0	0	1	0	0	0	0
Coral reef (1=yes)	0	0	0	0	0	1	0	0	0	0
Salinities	40	35	17	35	0	35	2	40	33	36
Ocean circulation	1	1	2	1	2	1	0	1	-0.7	1
Prevailing Wind: Polar	0	0	0	0	0	0	0	0	0.9	0
: Westerlies Zone	0	0	0	1	0	0	0	1	0.1	1
: Subtropical	0	0	0	0	0	0	0	0	0.1	0
: Monsoon Zone	1	0	0	0	0	0	0	0	0	0
: Trades Zone	1	1	0	0	0	1	0	0	0	0
: Intertropical	0	1	0	0	1	0	1	0	0	0
: Transition	0	0	0.4	0	0	0	0	0	0.0	0
No oceans (1=yes)	0	0	0	0	0	0	0	1	0	1
Fresh water (cub/kil)	19	0.3	16	45	0.2	.	0.1	16	39	.

Characteristics	Gilaki	Gilber-tese	Gio	Gisu	Gola	Grebo	Greek	Green-landic	Grosi	Guiana Chinese
Coastline: length (km)	3180	1140	579	0	579	579	13000	44100	0	378
length km/cap	50	15200	202	0	202	202	1300	770000	0	3090
Zones: Sea territory	12	12	200	0	200	200	6	3	0	12
Continental shelf (m)	10	10	200	0	200	200	199	200	0	200
Excl. fish (nm)	50	200	0	0	0	0	8	200	0	0
Extend. econ. zone (nm)	200	0	230000	0	230000	230000	0	0	0	200
200-Mi EEZ, area	156000	0	0	0	0	0	520000	4	0	160000
Contiguous zone (nm)	0	5	0	0	0	0	0	0	0	0
Inland waterways (km)	517	0	0	0	0	0	307	0	0	230
Inland waterways/cap	0	0.1	0	0	0	0	0	0	0	0
Water area: (km sq)	12000	0	15100	36300	15100	15100	10500	1830000	0	1850
area/cap	0.2	0	5	2	5	5	0.3	32000	0	15
Access: Number of ports	7	2	4	0	4	4	0.1	7	0	1
Natural Harbour (1=yes)	0	0	0	0	0	0	0	0	0	0
Number of outlets	0	0	0	1	0	0	0.1	0	2	0
Island (1=yes)	0	1	0	0	0	0	0	1	0	0
Landlocked (1=yes)	0	0	0	1	0	0	0	1	1	0
Ships: Number/cap	3	67	539	0.1	539	539	222	0	0	0
tonnage (dwt)/cap	13	36	3340	0.3	3340	3340	6600	0	0	0
Offshore Reserves: oil/cap	0.6	0	0	0	0	0	0.1	0	0	0
gas/cap	0.5	0	0	0	0	0	0	0	0	0
Fish supply kgrml/year/cap	0	0	0	0	0	0	2	1550	0	359
Marine Biology: Arctic	0	0	0	0	0	0	0	1	0	0
NW American Boreal	0	0	0	0	0	0	0	0	0	0
N Pacific. American	0	0	0	0	0	0	0	0	0	0
Tropical East Pacific	0	0	0	0	0	0	0	0	0	0
South Pacific	0	0	0	0	0	0	0	0	0	0
Antiboreal	0	0	0	0	0	0	0	0	0	0
Atlantic Boreal	0	0	0	0	0	0	0	0	0	0
Atlantic Warm Temp	0	0	0	0	0	0	1	0	0	0
Tropical Indo-West-Pacif	0	1	0	0	0	0	0	0	0	0
East Asia Boreal	0	0	0	0	0	0	0	0	0	0
North Pacific, East Asia	0	0	0	0	0	0	0	0	0	0
Indo-Australian	0	0	0	0	0	0	0	0	0	0
Tropical Atlantic	0	0	1	0	1	1	0	0	0	1
Coral reef (1=yes)	0	1	0	0	0	0	0	0	0	1
Salinities	38	35	35	2	35	35	4	34	2	35
Ocean circulation	0	-1	-1	0	-1	-1	0.9	-1	0	-1
Prevailing Wind: Polar	0	0	0	0	0	0	0	1	0	0
Westerlies Zone	1	0	0	0	0	0	0	0	0	0
Subtropical	0	0	0	0	0	0	1	0	0	0
Monsoon Zone	0	0	0	0	0	0	0	0	0	0
Trades Zone	0	1	0	0	0	0	0	0	0	1
Intertropical	0	0	1	1	1	1	0	0	1	0
Transition	0	0	0	0	0	0	0	0	0	0
No oceans (1=yes)	1	0	0	1	0	0	0	0	1	0
Fresh water (cub/kil)	45	.	0.1	0.2	0.1	0.1	9	.	0.2	.

Characteristics	Guianese Creole	Gurage	Gurma	Gurung	Gypsy	Han Chinese	Hani	Hausa	Haya	Hazara-Dari
Coastline: length (km)	378	1090	200	0	3890	14500	14500	707	1420	0
: length km/cap	3090	14	16	0	708	8	8	25	49	0
Zones: Sea territory	12	12	78	0	9	12	12	165	50	0
: Continental shelf (m)	200	0	33	0	83	0	0	0	0	0
: Excl. fish (nm)	0	0	0	0	0	0	0	0	0	0
: Extend. econ. zone (nm)	200	0	76	0	143	0	0	165	0	0
: 200-Mi EEZ, area	16000	0	72800	0	26000	0	0	174000	223000	0
: Contiguous zone (nm)	0	0	0	0	0	0	0	0	0	0
Inland waterways (km)	230	0	61	0	911	110000	110000	7160	0	1200
Inland waterways/cap	2	0		0	0.1	0.1	0.1	0.1		0.1
Water area: (km sq)	1850	121000	3860	0	1110000	271000	271000	10900	59100	0
: area/cap	15	2	0.4	0	79	0.2	0.2	0.1	6	0
Access: Number of ports	1	2	0.1	0	5	12	12	0.6	0	2
: Natural Harbour (1=yes)	0	0	0.6	1	0	0	0	0.3	0	0
: Number of outlets	0	0	0.3	0	0	0	0	0.2	0	1
: Island (1=yes)	0	0	0.2	1	0	0	0	0.4	0	0
: Landlocked (1=yes)	0	0	4	0	0	0	0	0.5	0	1
Ships: Number/cap		0.4		0	11			0.1	0.5	0
: tonnage (dwt)/cap	0	2	0.5	0	163	1	1	0.9	2	1
Offshore Reserves: oil/cap	0.9	0		0	0	0	0		0	0
: gas/cap	0	0	0	0	0	1	1	0.1	0.1	0
Fish supply kgrm/year/cap	359	0	0	0	0.7	17	17	0.9	0	0
Marine Biology: Arctic	0	0	0	0	0	0	0	0	0	0
: NW American Boreal	0	0	0	0	0	0	0	0	0	0
: N Pacific, American	0	0	0	0	0	0	0	0	0	0
: Tropical East Pacific	0	0	0	0	0	0	0	0	0	0
: South Pacific	0	0	0	0	0	0	0	0	0	0
: Antiboreal	0	0	0	0	0	0	0	0	0	0
: Atlantic Boreal	0	0	0	0	0	0	0	0	0	0
: Atlantic Warm Temp	0	0	0	0	0	0	0	0	0	0
: Tropical Indo-West-Pacif	0	0	0	0	0	0	0	0	0	0
: East Asia Boreal	0	0	0	0	0	1	1	0	0	0
: North Pacific, East Asia	0	0	0	0	0	0	0	0	0	0
: Indo-Australian	0	0	0	0	0	1	1	0	0	0
: Tropical Atlantic	0	0	0	0	0	0	0	0	0	0
Coral reef (1=yes)	1	1	0.7	3	0	34	34	0.8	35	2
Salinities	35	38	25	2	28	34	34	27	35	
Ocean circulation	1	1	0.5	0	1	1	1	0.3	1	0
Prevailing Wind: Polar	0	0	0	0	0	0	0	0	0	0
: Westerlies Zone	0	0	0	0	0	0	0	0	0	0
: Subtropical	0	0	0	0	0	0	0	0	0	0
: Monsoon Zone	0	0	0	0	0	1	1	0	0	1
: Trades Zone	1	1	1	1	0	0	0	1	1	0
: Intertropical	0	0	0	0	0	0	0	0	0	0
: Transition	0	0	0	0	0	0	0	0	0	0
No oceans (1=yes)	0	1	1	0	1	0	0	0.1	0	1
Fresh water (cub/kil)		2	0.2	0	20	460	460	3	0.5	26

Characteristics	Hehet-Bena	Herero	Hottentot	Hui-Vighur	Humbe-Nyaneka	Hungarian	Hutu	Ibibio	Icelander	Igbo
Coastline: length (km)	1420	1490	0	14500	1600	2540	0	853	4990	853
: length km/cap	49	950	0	8	156	420	0	9	17600	8
Zones: Sea territory	50	6	0	12	20	2	0	30	12	30
: Continental shelf (m)	0	12	0	0	200	30	0	200	200	200
: Excl. fish (nm)	0	0	0	0	0	1	0	0	0	0
: Extend. econ. zone (nm)	0	0	0	0	200	28	0	200	200	200
: 200-Mi EEZ, area	223000	500000	0	0	506000	40500	0	211000	867000	211000
: Contiguous zone (nm)	0	0	0	0	0	0	0	0	0	0
Inland waterways (km)	.	0	0	110000	0	1580	1720	8570	0	8580
Inland waterways/cap	.	0	0	0.1	0	0.1	0.2	0.1	0	0.1
Water area: (km sq)	59100	1000	15000	271000	0	638000	0	13000	2750	13000
: area/cap	2	0.6	11	12	0	51	0.2	0.1	10	0.1
Access: Number of ports	6	1	3	12	4	3	0	6	7	6
: Natural Harbour (1=yes)	0	0	0	0	0	0	0	0	0	0
: Number of outlets	0	0	3	0	0	2	2	0	1	0
: Island (1=yes)	0	0	0	0	0	0	0	0	1	0
: Landlocked (1=yes)	0	0	1	0	0	1	1	0	0	0
Ships: Number/cap	0.5	0	0	0	0	0.8	0	0.5	64	0.5
: tonnage (dwt)/cap	2	0	0	0	0	0.3	0	0.7	195	0.7
Offshore Reserves: oil/cap	0.1	0	0	0	0	0	0	0.1	0	0.1
: gas/cap	0	0	0	0	0	0	0	0	0	0
Fish supply kgrm/year/cap	0	16	0	17	11	39	0	0	354	0
Marine Biology: Arctic	0	0	0	0	0	0	0	0	0	0
: NW American Boreal	0	0	0	0	0	0	0	0	0	0
: N Pacific, American	0	0	0	0	0	0	0	0	0	0
: Tropical East Pacific	0	0	0	0	0	0	0	0	0	0
: South Pacific	0	0	0	0	0	0	0	0	0	0
: Antiboreal	0	0	0	0	0	0	0	0	0	0
: Atlantic Boreal	0	0	0	0	0	0	0	0	1	0
: Atlantic Warm Temp	0	0	0	0	0	0	0	0	0	0
: Tropical Indo-West-Pacif	1	0	0	0	0	0	0	0	0	0
: East Asia Boreal	0	0	0	0	0	0	0	0	0	0
: North Pacific, East Asia	0	0	0	1	0	0	0	0	0	0
: Indo-Australian	0	0	0	0	0	0	0	0	0	0
: Tropical Atlantic	0	1	0	0	1	0	0	1	0	1
Coral reef (1=yes)	1	0	0	0	1	0	0	0	0	0
Salinities	35	35	0	34	34	0	0	33	35	33
Ocean circulation	-1	-1	0	0	-1	0.2	0.2	0	-1	0
Prevailing Wind: Polar	0	0	0	0	0	0	0	0	0	0
: Westerlies Zone	0	0	1	1	0	1	0	0	1	0
: Subtropical	0	1	0	0	0	0	0	0	0	0
: Monsoon Zone	1	0	0	0	0	0	0	0	0	0
: Trades Zone	0	0	0	0	1	0	0	0	0	0
: Intertropical	0	0	0	0	0	0	1	1	0	1
: Transition	0	0	0	0	0	0	0	0	0	0
No oceans (1=yes)	0	0	0	1	0	1	1	0	0	0
Fresh water (cub/kil)	0.5	0.1	0.1	460	0.5	0.9	0.2	4	.	4

Characteristics	Ijaw	Indian	Indo-Aryan	Indo-nesian	Iranian	Irish	Issa	Italian	Japanese	Javanese
Coastline: length (km)	853	4590	7000	2250	1040	4710	314	5870	13700	54700
: length km/cap	8	420	8	12700	16	357	631	111	110	282
Zones: Sea territory	30	14	12	12	12	3	12	54	14	12
: Continental shelf (m)	200	176	200	200	198	60	0	197	3	0
: Excl. fish (nm)	200	115	200	200	198	200			197	
: Extend. econ. zone (nm)		136					200	0.6	1	200
: 200-Mi EEZ, area	211000	972000	2020000	1310000	316000	548000	6170	1160000	3880000	541000
: Contiguous zone (nm)	0	1	24	0	24		24		0.1	
Inland waterways (km)	8580	4480	19100		0	1120	0	13100	2490	21600
Inland waterways/cap	0.1	0.1	0.4	300		0.1		0.2	0.2	0.1
Water area: (km sq)	13000	15700	314000	2	25000	1930	20	23700	3190	92900
: area/cap	0.1	0.6	0.7		0.2	0.1		0.1	0.3	0.5
Access: Number of ports	0.6	0.5		1	0.3	0.5	1	10	18	0.8
: Natural Harbour (1=yes)	0	0	0	0	0	0	0	0	0	0
: Number of outlets	0	0	4		0	0	0	0	1	0
: Island (1=yes)	0	0.4	0.7	0	0	1	0	0	0	1
: Landlocked (1=yes)	0	0	0	0	0	0	0	0	0	0
Ships: Number/cap	0.5	55	0.4		0.6	15	4	11	30	4
: tonnage (dwt)/cap	0.7	1010	1	0.5	12	72	5	146	288	15
Offshore Reserves: oil/cap	0.1	0.3			0.3	0.5		0.1	0.6	0.2
: gas/cap	0	0.9		0	0.1	0.1		0.2		0
Fish supply kgrm/year/cap	0	1	0	125	0	0	0	0	0	0
Marine Biology: Arctic	0	1	0	0	0	0	0	0	0	0
: NW American Boreal	0	0.1	0	0	0	0	0	0	0	0
: N Pacific, American	0	0.1	0	1	0	0	0	0	0	0
: Tropical East Pacific	0	0.1	0	0	0	0	0	0	0	0
: South Pacific	0	0	0	0	0	0	0	0	0	0
: Antiboreal	0	0.1	0	0	0	0	0	0	0	0
: Atlantic Boreal	0	0.2	0	0	0	1	0	0	0	0
: Atlantic Warm Temp	0	0.5	0	0	0	0	0	0.8	0	0
: Tropical Indo-West-Pacif	0	0	1	1	1	0	1	0	0	0
: East Asia Boreal	0	0.3	0	0	0	0	0	0	1	0
: North Pacific, East Asia	0	0.6	0	0	0	0	0	0	1	0
: Indo-Australian	0	0	0	0	0	0	0	0	0	1
: Tropical Atlantic	1	0	0	0	0	0	0	0	0	0
Coral reef (1=yes)	0	0.2	1	1	1	0.4	1	0.2	0	1
Salinities	33	34	34	35	37	35	38	37	33	35
Ocean circulation	0	0.2	0	0	0	0.7	0	0.8	0	0
Prevailing Wind: Polar	0	0.1	0	0	0	0.1	0	0	0	0
: Westerlies Zone	0	0.7	0	0	0	1	0	0.2	1	0
: Subtropical	1	0.2	0	1	1		1	0.2	0	1
: Monsoon Zone	0		1	0	0	0	0	0	0	0
: Trades Zone	0	0	0	0	0	0	0	0	0	0
: Intertropical	0	0	0	0	0	0	0	0	0	0
: Transition	0	0	0	0	0	0	0	0	0	0
No oceans (1=yes)	0	0.7	0	0	1	0	0	0.7	0	0
Fresh water (cub/kil)	4	47	380		153	9		50	109	82

Characteristics	Jewish	Jola	Kalenjiin	Kamba	Kanuri	Kara-kalpak	Kare	Karen	Kavango	Kazakh
Coastline: length (km)	887	531	536	536	709	0	0	3060	1490	1840
: length km/cap	74	67	21	21	7	0	0	46	950	1
Zones: Sea territory	7	12	12	12	25	0	0	12	6	2
: Continental shelf (m)	3	200	0	0	166	0	0	200	0	0
: Excl. fish (nm)	1	200	0	0	0	0	0	0	12	0
: Extend. econ. zone (nm)	0	0	200	200	166	0	0	200	0	0
: 200-Mi EEZ, area	29300	206000	118000	118000	175000	0	0	0	500000	0
: Contiguous zone (nm)	0	24	0	0	0	0	0	24	0	0
Inland waterways (km)	547	899	0	0	7220	1100	800	3100	0	14000
Inland waterways/cap	0	0.1	0	0	0.1	0.1	0.2	0.1	1000	0.1
Water area: (km sq)	4780	4190	13400	13400	11400	22000	0	18800	1000	72100
: area/cap	0.4	0.5	0.5	0.5	0.6	1	0	0.4	0.6	0.4
Access: Number of ports	0.3	0.4	0.2	0.2	0.3	0	0	0.3	0.1	2
: Natural Harbour (1=yes)	0	0	0	0	0	0	0	0	0	0
: Number of outlets	0	0	0	0	0	0	1	0	0	0
: Island (1=yes)	0	0	0	0	0	0	0	0	0	0
: Landlocked (1=yes)	0	0	0	0	0	1	1	0	0	0
Ships: Number/cap	.5	0.8	0.2	0.2	0.2	0	0	2	0	0.7
: tonnage (dwt)/cap	123	.2	0.4	0.4	0.4	0	0	30	0	.9
Offshore Reserves: oil/cap	0	0	0	0	0.5	0	0	0	0	0
: gas/cap	0	0	0	0	0.9	0	0	0.1	0	0
Fish supply kgrm/year/cap	0	0	0	0	0.1	0	0	0	16	0
Marine Biology: Arctic	0	0	0	0	0	0	0	0	0	0
: NW American Boreal	0	0	0	0	0	0	0	0	0	0
: N Pacific. American	0	0	0	0	0	0	0	0	0	0
: Tropical East Pacific	0	0	0	0	0	0	0	0	0	0
: South Pacific	0	0	0	0	0	0	0	0	0	0
: Antiboreal	0	0	0	0	0	0	0	0	0	0
: Atlantic Boreal	0	0	0	0	0	0	0	0	0	0.9
: Atlantic Warm Temp	0.9	0	0	0	0	0	0	0	0.9	0.1
: Tropical Indo-West-Pacif	0	0	0	0	0	0	0	0	0.1	0
: East Asia Boreal	0	0	0	0	0	0	0	0	0	0
: North Pacific. East Asia	0	0	0	0	0	0	0	0	0	0.1
: Indo-Australian	0	0	0	0	0	0	0	0	0	0
: Tropical Atlantic	0	1	0	0	0.8	0	0	0	0	0
Coral reef (1=yes)	0	0	0	0	0	0	0	0	0	0
Salinities	37	36	35	35	27	40	2	30	35	38
Ocean circulation	1	-1	-1	-1	0.3	1	0	-1	-1	0.9
Prevailing Wind: Polar	-1	0	0	0	0	0	0	0	0	0
: Westerlies Zone	0	0	0	0	0	0	0	0	0	0
: Subtropical	0.2	0	0	0	0	0	0	0	0	0.1
: Monsoon Zone	0	0	0	0	0	0	0	0	0	0
: Trades Zone	0	0	0	0	0.1	0	0	0	0	0.9
: Intertropical	1	1	1	1	0	1	0	0	1	0
: Transition	0	0	0	0	0	0	0	0	0	0
No oceans (1=yes)	0.9	0	0	0	0	0	0	0	0	0.9
Fresh water (cub/kil)	2	1	1	1	3	1	0.1	4	0.1	413

Characteristics	Kebu-Akposo	Khmer	Kikuyu	Kimbundu	Kisii	Kissi	Klao	Kongo	Kono	Konzo
Coastline: length (km)	56	1100	536	1600	536	357	579	58	402	37
: length km/cap	14	50	21	156	21	61	202	12	89	0.9
Zones: Sea territory	30	12	12	20	12	50	200	42	200	12
: Continental shelf (m)	0	200	0	200	0	0	200	0	0	0
: Excl. fish (nm)	0	0	0	0	0	0	200	0	0	0
: Extend. econ. zone (nm)	200	200	200	0	200	160	0	168	0	200
: 200-Mi EEZ, area	1030	150000	118000	506000	118000	88100	230000	4780	156000	1030
: Contiguous zone (nm)	0	20	0	0	0	0	0	0	0	0
Inland waterways (km)	25	4860	13400	0	13400	1170	0	13400	700	15100
Inland waterways/cap	0	0.2	0.5	0	0.5	0.2	0	0.4	0.2	0.4
Water area: (km sq)	2400	4150	0	0	0	24	15100	65500	120	77800
A: area/cap	0.6	0.2	0.2	4	0.2	2	5	3	3	3
Access: Number of ports	0.2	0.3	0	0	0	0	4	0	0	0
: Natural Harbour (1=yes)	0	0	0	0	0	0	0	0	0	0
: Number of outlets	0	1	0	3	0	0	0	0	0	0
: Island (1=yes)	0	0	0	0	0	0	0	0	0	0
: Landlocked (1=yes)	0	0	0	0	0	0	0	0	0	0
Ships: Number/cap	5	4	0	0	0	0	0	0	1	0
: tonnage (dwt)/cap	5	0	0	0	0	0	539	0.3	0	0.4
Offshore Reserves: oil/cap	0	0.1	0.2	11	0.2	0.4	3340	0.3	0	0
: gas/cap	0	0	0.4	0.3	0.4	0.2	0	0.2	0	0
Fish supply kgrm/year/cap	0	0.1	0	0.2	0	0	0	3	0	0
Marine Biology: Arctic	0	0	0	0	0	0	0	0	0	0
: NW American Boreal	0	0	0	0	0	0	0	0	0	0
: N Pacific, American	0	0.1	0	0	0	0	0	0	0	0
: Tropical East Pacific	0	0	0	0	0	0	0	0	0	0
: South Pacific	0	0	0	0	0	0	0	0	0	0
: Antiboreal	0	0	0	0	0	0	0	0	0	0
: Atlantic Boreal	0	0	0	0	0	0	0	0	0	0
: Atlantic Warm Temp	0	0.9	0	0	0	0	0	0	0	0
: Tropical Indo-West-Pacif	0	0	0	0	0	0	0	0	0	0
: East Asia Boreal	0	0	0	0	0	0	0	0	0	0
: North Pacific, East Asia	0	0	0	0	0	0	0	0	0	0
: Indo-Australian	0	0	0	0	0	0	0	0	0	0
: Tropical Atlantic	0	0	0	0	0	0	0	0	0	0
Coral reef (1=yes)	1	1	1	1	1	1	1	1	1	1
Salinities	35	0.31	35	34	35	35	35	33	35	33
Ocean circulation	-1	-0.9	-1	-1	-1	-1	-1	0.2	-1	0
Prevailing Wind: Polar	0	0	0	0	0	0	0	0	0	0
: Westerlies Zone	0	0	0	0	0	0	0	0	0	0
: Subtropical	0	0.2	0	0	0	0.2	0	0	0	0
: Monsoon Zone	0	0.9	0	0	0	0.8	0	0	0	0
: Trades Zone	0	0	0	0	0	0	0	0	0	0
: Intertropical	1	0	1	1	1	0	1	1	1	1
: Transition	0	0	0	0	0	0	0	0	0	0
No oceans (1=yes)	0	6	0	0	0	0	0	0	0	0
Fresh water (cub/kil)	0.1	6	1	0.5	1	0.6	0.1	0.6	0.4	0.7

Characteristics	Koranko	Korean	Kotoko	Kpelle	Kru	Kurd	Kuwaiti	Kyrgyz	Ladino	Lango
Coastline: length (km)	402	2980	0	497	579	3820	499	0	400	0
: length km/cap	89	72	0	150	202	64	263	0	40	0
Zones: Sea territory	200	12	0	134	200	11	12	0	12	0
: Continental shelf (m)	0	2	0	130	200	10	0	0	0	0
: Excl. fish (nm)	0	8	0	70	0	17	0	0	0	0
: Extend. econ. zone (nm)	0	67	0	0	0	75	0	0	200	0
: 200-Mi EEZ, area	156000	346000	0	174000	230000	143000	12000	0	99100	0
: Contiguous zone (nm)	0	0.1	0	0	0	0	0	0	0	0
Inland waterways (km)	700	5400	2000	456	0	791	0	632	625	0
Inland waterways/cap	0.2	0.1	0.3	0.1	0	0	0	0.1	0.1	0
Water area: (km sq)	120	10700	24800	9750	15100	8070	0	8260	460	36300
: area/cap	0.1	0.1	4	2	5	0.2	0	0	3	2
Access: Number of ports	3	0	0	3	4	0.5	3	0	3	0
: Natural Harbour (1=yes)	0	0	2	0	0	0	0	0	0	0
: Number of outlets	0	0	0	0	0	0	0	0	0	1
: Island (1=yes)	0	0	1	0	0	0	0	0	0	0
: Landlocked (1=yes)	1	1	1	0	0	0	1	0	1	1
Ships: Number/cap	1	34	0	0	0	0	0	0	0	0
: tonnage (dwt)/cap	0	0	0	0	0	0	0	0	0	0
Offshore Reserves: oil/cap	0	0	3	0	0	6	33	0.9	0	0.1
: gas/cap	0	0	0	0	0	51	2000	0	0	0.3
Fish supply kgrm/year/cap	0	0	0	350	539	0.2	0	0	0	0
Marine Biology: Arctic	0	0	0	21700	33400	0.2	0	0	0	0
: NW American Boreal	0	0	0	0	0	0	0	0	0	0
: N Pacific American	0	0	0	0	0	0	0	0	0	0
: Tropical East Pacific	0	0	0	0	0	0	0	0	0	0
: South Pacific	0	0	0	0	0	0	0	0	0	0
: Antiboreal	0	0	0	0	0	0	0	0	0	0
: Atlantic Boreal	0	0	0	0	0	0	0	0	0	0
: Atlantic Warm Temp	0	0	0	0	0	0	0	0	0	0
: Tropical Indo-West-Pacif	0	0	0	0	0	0	0	0	0	0
: East Asia Boreal	0	0	0	0	0	0	0	0	0	0
: North Pacific, East Asia	0	0	0	0	0	0.4	0	0.1	0	0
: Indo-Australian	0	0	0	0	0	0.6	0	0	0	0
: Tropical Atlantic	1	1	0	1	1	0	1	0	1	2
Coral reef (1=yes)	0	0	0	0	0	0	0	0	0	0
Salinities	35	32	2	35	35	38	38	3	33	0
Ocean circulation	-1	-0.9	0	-1	-1	0.4	-1	2	1	0
Prevailing Wind: Polar	0	0	0	0	0	0	0	0	0	0
: Westerlies Zone	0	0	0	0	0	0	0	0	0	0
: Subtropical	0	1	0	0	0	1	0	1	0	1
: Monsoon Zone	1	0	0	0	0	0	0	0	1	0
: Trades Zone	0	0	0	0	0	0	1	0	1	0
: Intertropical	0	0	0	1	1	0	0	0	0	0
: Transition	0	0	0	0	0	0	0	0	0	1
No oceans (1=yes)	1	0	0	0	0	1	0	0	1	0
Fresh water (cub/kil)	0.4	38	0.2	0.3	0.1	31	0.5	0.1	0.7	0.2

Characteristics	Lao	Latvian	Lezgin	Li	Liechten-steiner	Limba	Lithua-nian	Lobi	Loma	Lomwe
Coastline: length (km)	2690	531	0	14500	0	402	113	266	579	0
: length km/cap	47	198	0	8	0	89	30	20	202	0
Zones: Sea territory	10	12	0	12	0	200	12	6	200	0
: Continental shelf (m)	167	.	0	0	0	0	.	103	200	0
: Excl. fish (nm)	0	200	0	0	0	0	200	0	0	0
: Extend. econ. zone (nm)	167	0	0	0	0	0	0	103	0	0
: 200-Mi EEZ, area	271000	0	0	110000	0	156000	0	54100	230000	0
: Contiguous zone (nm)	0	0	0	0.1	0	0	0	0	0	0
Inland waterways (km)	3970	300	500	271000	0	700	597	507	0	144
Inland waterways/cap	0.1	0.1	0.1	0.1	0	0.2	0.2	0.2	0	0
Water area: (km sq)	2850	0	0	271000	0	120	0	2500	15100	2440
: area/cap	0.1	0	0	0.2	0	3	0	0.2	5	2
Access: Number of ports	0	4	0	12	0	0	2	0	4	4
: Natural Harbour (1=yes)	4	0	0	0	0	0	0	1	0	0
: Number of outlets	0	0	0	0	0	0	0	0	0	0
: Island (1=yes)	0.5	0	0	1	0	0	0	0.5	0	0
: Landlocked (1=yes)	0	0	1	0	1	0	0	0.3	0	1
Ships: Number/cap	0.2	49	0	17	0	0	19	4	539	0
: tonnage (dwt/cap)	4	500	0	0	0	0	128	0	33400	0
Offshore Reserves: oil/cap	19	0	0	0	0	0	0	0	0	0
: gas/cap	0.1	0	0	0	0	0	0	0	0	2
Fish supply kgrm/year/cap	0.3	0	0	0	0	0	0	0	0	0
Marine Biology: Arctic	0	0	0	0	0	0	0	0	0	0
: NW American Boreal	0	0	0	0	0	0	0	0	0	0
: N Pacific American	0	0	0	0	0	0	0	0	0	0
: Tropical East Pacific	0	0	0	0	0	0	0	0	0	0
: South Pacific	0	0	0	0	0	0	0	0	0	0
: Antiboreal	0	0	0	0	0	0	0	0	0	0
: Atlantic Boreal	0	1	1	0	0	0	1	0	0	0
: Atlantic Warm Temp	0	0	0	0	0	0	0	0	0	0
: Tropical Indo-West-Pacif	0	0	0	1	0	0	0	0	0	0
: East Asia Boreal	0	0	0	0	0	0	0	0	0	0
: North Pacific, East Asia	0.8	0	0	0	0	0	0	0	0	0
: Indo-Australian	0	0	0	0	0	0	0	0	0	0
: Tropical Atlantic	0	0	0	0	0	1	0	1	1	1
Coral reef (1=yes)	0	0	0	1	0	0	0	0.5	0	0
Salinities	26	34	40	34	0	35	34	18	35	2
Ocean circulation	0.3	-1	-1	0	-1	-1	-1	1	-1	0
Prevailing Wind: Polar	0	0	0	0	0	0	0	0	0	0
: Westerlies Zone	0	1	1	0	1	0	1	0	0	0
: Subtropical	0	0	0	1	0	0	0	0	0	0
: Monsoon Zone	0.8	0	0	0	0	0	0	0	0	0
: Trades Zone	0	0	0	0	0	1	0	1	1	2
: Intertropical	0	0	0	0	0	0	0	0	0	0
: Transition	0	0	0	0	0	0	0	0	0	0
No oceans (1=yes)	0	0	1	1	1	0	0	0	0	0
Fresh water (cub/kil)	27	.	.	460	.	0.4	.	0.5	0.1	0.2

Characteristics	Lotuko	Luba	Luchasi	Luena	Lugbara	Luhya	Lumbe	Lunda	Luo	Luri
Coastline: length (km)	853	37	1600	1600	37	536	1600	1600	536	3180
: length km/cap	31	0.9	156	156	0.9	21	156	156	21	50
Zones: Sea territory	12	12	20	20	12	12	20	20	12	120
: Continental shelf (m)	200	200			200	0			0	50
: Excl. fish (nm)	0		200	200		200	200	200	200	
: Extend. econ. zone (nm)										
200-Mi EEZ, area	91600	1030	506000	506000	1030	118000	506000	506000	118000	156000
: Contiguous zone (nm)	18									0
Inland waterways (km)	4070	15100			15100					517
Inland waterways/cap	0.1	0.4			0.4					
Water area: (km sq)	130000	77800			77800	13400			13400	12000
: area/cap						0.5			0.5	0.2
Access: Number of ports	5	2	4	4	2		4	4		
: Natural Harbour (1=yes)										
: Number of outlets		3			3					
: Island (1=yes)										
: Landlocked (1=yes)	0.3					0.2			0.2	
Ships: Number/cap	0.2	0.4	3	3	0.4		3	3		3
: tonnage (dwt)/cap			1	1		0.24	1	1		13
Offshore Reserves: oil/cap			1	1		0.4	1	1	0.2	0.6
: gas/cap			0.3	0.3			0.3	0.3	0.4	0.5
Fish supply kgrm/year/cap			0.2	0.2			0.2	0.2		
Marine Biology: Arctic										
: NW American Boreal										
: N Pacific American										
: Tropical East Pacific										
: South Pacific										
: Antiboreal										
: Atlantic Boreal										
: Atlantic Warm Temp										
: Tropical Indo-West-Pacif						1			1	
: East Asia Boreal										
: North Pacific, East Asia										
: Indo-Australian										
: Tropical Atlantic	1	1	1	1	1		1	1		1
Coral reef (1=yes)										
Salinities	40	33	34	34	33	35	34	34	35	38
Ocean circulation	1		-1	-1			-1	-1		
Prevailing Wind: Polar										
: Westerlies Zone										
: Subtropical										
: Monsoon Zone										
: Trades Zone	1	1	1	1	1	1	1	1	1	1
: Intertropical										
: Transition										
No oceans (1=yes)	1									
Fresh water (cub/kil)	19	0.7	0.5	0.5	0.7	1	0.5	0.5	1	45

Characteristics	Luxem-burger	Macedo-nian	Madurese	Magars	Maka	Makonde	Makua	Malagasy	Malawi	Malay
Coastline: length (km)	0	6660	54700	0	386	1420	2470	4830	2470	4270
: length km/cap	0	655	281	0	39	49	156	368	155	216
Zones: Sea territory	0	2	12	0	60	50	12	50	12	12
: Continental shelf (m)	0	23	0	0	0	0	0	150	0	191
: Excl. fish (nm)	0	25	0	0	0	0	0	150	0	165
: Extend. econ. zone (nm)	0		200	0	0	0	200	150	200	191
: 200-Mi EEZ, area	0	256000	5410000	0	17600	223000	561000	1290000	562000	434000
: Contiguous zone (nm)	0	0	0	0	0		0	0	0	0
Inland waterways (km)	37	69	21600	4000	2230	0	3740	566	3750	3170
Inland waterways/cap	0.1	0	0.1	0.2	0.2	0	0.2	0	0.2	0.1
Water area: (km sq)	0	737	93000	0	5600	59100	17500	5500	17500	1310
: area/cap	0	0.2	0.5	0	0.5	2	0.2	0.4	0	0.7
Access: Number of ports	1	4	8	0	0	6	3	0	3	0
: Natural Harbour (1=yes)	0	0	0	0	1	0	0	0	0	0
: Number of outlets	1	0	0	1	0	0	0	0	0	0
: Island (1=yes)	0	0	1	1	0	0	0	1	0	0
: Landlocked (1=yes)	1	0	0	1	0	0	0	0	0	0
Ships: Number/cap	133	18	4	0	0.2	0.5	0	0	0	20
: tonnage (dwt)/cap	6670	552	15	0	0.5	0.2	0	0	0	302
Offshore Reserves: oil/cap	0	0	0	0	0.2	0.1	0	0	0	0.2
: gas/cap	0	0	0.2	0	0	0	0	0	0	0.3
Fish supply kgrm/year/cap	0	0.9	0	0	1	0	0.9	3	0.9	4
Marine Biology: Arctic	0	0	0	0	0	0	0	0	0	0
: NW American Boreal	0	0	0	0	0	0	0	0	0	0
: N Pacific American	0	0	0	0	0	0	0	0	0	0
: Tropical East Pacific	0	0	0	0	0	0	0	0	0	0
: South Pacific	0	0	0	0	0	0	0	0	0	0
: Antiboreal	0	0	0	0	0	0	0	0	0	0
: Atlantic Boreal	0	0	0	0	0	0	0	0	0	0
: Atlantic Warm Temp	0	0	0	0	0	0	0	0	0	0
: Tropical Indo-West-Pacif	0	0	1	0	0	1	1	1	0	1
: East Asia Boreal	0	0	0	0	0	0	0	0	0	0
: North Pacific, East Asia	0	0	0	0	0	0	0	0	0	0
: Indo-Australian	0	0	0	0	0	0	0	0	0	0
: Tropical Atlantic	0	0	0	0	1	0	0	0	0	0
Coral reef (1=yes)	0	0	1	0	0	0	0	1	0	1
Salinities	2	5	35	2	33	35	35	35	35	34
Ocean circulation	0	1	1	0	1	1	1	1	1	1
Prevailing Wind: Polar	0	0	0	0	0	0	0	0	0	0
: Westerlies Zone	1	1	0	0	0	0	0	0	0	0
: Subtropical	0	0	0	0	0	0	0	0	0	0
: Monsoon Zone	0	0	1	1	0	0	0	0	0	1
: Trades Zone	0	0	0	0	1	1	1	1	1	0
: Intertropical	0	0	0	0	0	0	0	0	0	0
: Transition	0	0	0	0	0	0	0	0	0	0
No oceans (1=yes)	1	0	0	1	0	0	0	0	1	0
Fresh water (cub/kil)	.	11	82	3	0.4	0.5	0.8	16	0.8	12

Characteristics	Malay Christian	Malay Coastal	Malay Muslim	Malinke	Maltese	Mambwe	Manchu-Tibetian	Mandara	Mande	Mandingo
Coastline: length (km)	22500	54700	22500	293	140	0	14500	402	0	531
: length km/cap	408	281	408	52	389	0	8	32	0	67
Zones: Sea territory	100	12	100	29	12	0	12	50	0	12
: Continental shelf (m)	0	0	0	48	200	0	0	0	0	200
: Excl. fish (nm)	0	0	0	0	25	0	0	0	0	200
: Extend. econ. zone (nm)	200	200	200	143	0	0	0	0	0	0
200-Mi EEZ, area	1890000	5410000	1890000	63500	66200	0	0	15400	0	206000
: Contiguous zone (nm)	0	0	0	0	24	0	0	0	0	24
Inland waterways (km)	3220	21600	3220	1180	0	2250	110000	2090	0	899
Inland waterways/cap	0	0.1	0	0	0	0.3	0.1	0.2	0	0.1
Water area: (km sq)	1830	93000	1830	5120	0	11900	271000	6000	400	4190
: area/cap	0	0.5	0	0.6	0	0.2	0.2	0.5	0	0.5
Access: Number of ports	8	0	8	0	2	0	12	1	0	4
: Natural Harbour (1=yes)	0	0	0	0.4	0	0	0	0	0	0
: Number of outlets	1	1	1	0	1	1	1	1	2	0
: Island (1=yes)	0	0	0	0.2	1	0	0	0	0	0
: Landlocked (1=yes)	0	0	0	0.2	0	1	0	0	1	0
Ships: Number/cap	13	4	13	0	2330	0	17	0.2	0	0
: tonnage (dwt)/cap	205	15	205	0	49800	0	17	0.3	0	0
Offshore Reserves: oil/cap	0	0	0	0	0	0	0	0.4	0	0
: gas/cap	0.6	0.2	0.6	0	0	0	0	0.1	0	0.8
Fish supply kgrm/year/cap	0	0	0	0.8	0	0	0	0	0	0.2
Marine Biology: Arctic	0	0	0	0	0	0	0	0	0	0
: NW American Boreal	0	0	0	0	0	0	0	0	0	0
: N Pacific American	0	0	0	0	0	0	0	0	0	0
: Tropical East Pacific	0	0	0	0	0	0	0	0	0	0
: South Pacific	0	0	0	0	0	0	0	0	0	0
: Antiboreal	0	0	0	0	0	0	0	0	0	0
: Atlantic Boreal	0	0	0	0	0	0	0	0	0	0
: Atlantic Warm Temp	0	0	0	0	1	0	0	0	0	0
: Tropical Indo-West-Pacif	1	1	1	0	0	0	0	0	0	0
: East Asia Boreal	0	0	0	0	0	0	0	0	0	0
: North Pacific, East Asia	0	0	0	0	0	0	1	0	0	0
: Indo-Australian	0	0	0	0	0	0	0	0	0	0
: Tropical Atlantic	0	0	0	1	0	1	0	1	1	1
Coral reef (1=yes)	1	1	1	0	1	0	1	1	0	1
Salinities	34	35	34	29	38	2	34	33	2	36
Ocean circulation	0	0	0	0	0	0	0	0	0	-1
Prevailing Wind: Polar	0	0	0	0	0	0	0	0	0	0
: Westerlies Zone	0	0	0	0.5	0	0	0	0	0	0
: Subtropical	0	1	0	0.6	1	0	1	0	0	0
: Monsoon Zone	1	0	1	0	0	0	0	0	0	0
: Trades Zone	0	0	0	0	0	0	0	1	1	1
: Intertropical	0	0	0	0	0	0	0	0	0	0
: Transition	0	0	0	0	0	0	0	0	0	0
No oceans (1=yes)	0	0	0	0	1	1	0	1	1	0
Fresh water (cub/kil)	30	82	30	0.8	.	0.4	460	0.4	0.2	1

Characteristics	Mandyako	Mano	Manx (Norse-C.)	Manzan-Darani	Maori	Maravi	Masa	Masalit Maba	Maya	Mbaka
Coastline: length (km)	274	579	113	3180	15100	0	0	0	386	0
: length km/cap	292	202	1610	50	4310	0	0	0	1930	0
Zones: Sea territory	12	200	3	12	12	0	0	0	3	0
: Continental shelf (m)	0	200	200	50	200	0	0	0		0
: Excl. fish (nm)	200	0	200	0	0	0	0	0	0	0
: Extend. econ. zone (nm)	0	0	0	0	200	0	0	0	0	0
: 200-Mi EEZ, area	151000	230000	0	156000	4830000	0	0	0	30900	0
: Contiguous zone (nm)	0	0	0	0	0	0	0	0	0	0
Inland waterways (km)	0	0	0	517	1610	565	2000	2000	825	800
Inland waterways/cap	0	0	0	0	0.5	0.1	0.3	0.3	4	0.2
Water area: (km sq)	8120	15100	0	12000	10	21900	24800	24800	160	0
: area/cap	8	5	3	0.2	0	2	4	4	0.8	0
Access: Number of ports	1	4	3	0.7	5	3			0.4	0
: Natural Harbour (1=yes)	0	0		0	0				0	1
: Number of outlets	0	0	1	0	0	2	2	2	4	0
: Island (1=yes)	0	0	0	0	1	0	0	0	0	1
: Landlocked (1=yes)	0	0	0	0	0	1	1	1	0	0
Ships: Number/cap	0	539		3	7	0	0	0	135	0
: tonnage (dwt)/cap	0	33400		13	74	0	0	0	242	0
Offshore Reserves: oil/cap	0	0		0.6	0	0	0	0	0	0
: gas/cap	0	0		0.5	2	0	0	0	0	0
Fish supply kgrm/year/cap	0	0	0	0	0	3	3	3	0	2
Marine Biology: Arctic	0	0	0	0	0	0	0	0	0	0
: NW American Boreal	0	0	0	0	0	0	0	0	0	0
: N Pacific, American	0	0	0	0	0	0	0	0	0	0
: Tropical East Pacific	0	0	0	0	0	0	0	0	0	0
: South Pacific	0	0	0	0	0	0	0	0	0	0
: Antiboreal	0	0	0	0	0	0	0	0	0	0
: Atlantic Boreal	0	0	0	0	0	0	0	0	0	0
: Atlantic Warm Temp	0	0	0	0	0	0	0	0	0	0
: Tropical Indo-West-Pacif	0	0	0	0	0	0	0	0	0	0
: East Asia Boreal	0	0	0	0	0	0	0	0	0	0
: North Pacific, East Asia	0	0	0	0	0	0	0	0	0	0
: Indo-Australian	0	0	0	0	0	0	0	0	0	0
: Tropical Atlantic	1	1	1	1	0	0	0	0	0	0
Coral reef (1=yes)	0	0	0	0	1	0	0	0	1	0
Salinities	36	35	35	38	34	2	2	2	35	2
Ocean circulation	-1	-1	-1	0	1	0	0	0	0	0
Prevailing Wind: Polar	0	0	1	0	0	0	0	0	0	0
: Westerlies Zone	0	0	1	0	1	0	0	0	0	0
: Subtropical	0	0	0	0	0	0	0	0	0	0
: Monsoon Zone	0	0	0	0	0	0	0	0	0	0
: Trades Zone	1	1	0	1	0	0	0	0	1	0
: Intertropical	0	0	0	0	0	0	0	0	0	0
: Transition	0	0	0	0	0	0	0	0	0	0
No oceans (1=yes)	0	0	0	0	0	1	1	1	0	1
Fresh water (cub/kil)	0.1	0.1		45	1	0.2	0.2	0.2	0	0.1

Characteristics	Mbete	Mbochi	Mbum	Mbunda	Melane-sian	Mende	Merina	Meru	Mestizo	Miao Man
Coastline: length (km)	593	169	94	1600	4980	402	4830	536	5470	0
: length km/cap	444	69	7	156	6620	89	364	21	131	0
Zones: Sea territory	141	200	12	20	12	200	50	12	62	0
: Continental shelf (m)	0	0	0	0	139	0	150	0	115	0
: Excl. fish (nm)	89	0	0	200	0	0	150	200	15	0
: Extend. econ. zone (nm)	0	0	0	0	200	0	150	0	122	0
: 200-Mi EEZ, area	137000	24700	3600	506000	2030000	156000	1290000	118000	1750000	0
: Contiguous zone (nm)	0	0	0	0	0	0	0	0	4	0
Inland waterways (km)	2730	4390	1790	0	6740	700	566	0	11300	4590
Inland waterways/cap	2	0	0.3	0	3	0.2	0	0	0.2	1
Water area: (km sq)	6130	500	15600	0	6450	120	5500	13400	42200	6000
: area/cap	4	0.2	2	0	2	0	0.4	0.5	0.7	1
Access: Number of ports	3	2	1	4	4	3	4	0	8	0
: Natural Harbour (1=yes)	0	0	0	0	0	0	0	0	0	0
: Number of outlets	0	0	1	0	1	0	1	0	0.1	3
: Island (1=yes)	0	0	0	0	0	0	0	1	0	0
: Landlocked (1=yes)	0	0	1	0	1	1	1	0	0	1
Ships: Number/cap	13	0	0.8	3	9	1	3	0.2	13	0
: tonnage (dwt)/cap	2	2	0.6	1.1	21	1	0	0.4	197	0.2
Offshore Reserves: oil/cap	0.4	19	0.1	0.3	0	0	0	0	0.2	0.3
: gas/cap	22	0	2	0.2	74	0	0	0	0.4	0
Fish supply kgrm/year/cap	0	0	0	0	0	0	0	0	0.2	0
Marine Biology: Arctic	0	0	0	0	0	0	0	0	0	0
: NW American Boreal	0	0	0	0	0	0	0	0	0	0
: N Pacific, American	0	0	0	0	0	0	0	0	0	0
: Tropical East Pacific	0	0	0	0	0	0	0	0	0.7	0
: South Pacific	0	0	0	0	1	0	0	0	0	0
: Antiboreal	0	0	0	0	0	0	0	0	0	0
: Atlantic Boreal	0	0	0	0	0	0	0	0	0	0
: Atlantic Warm Temp	0	0	0	0	0	0	0	0	0.1	0
: Tropical Indo-West-Pacif	0	0	0	0	1	0	1	1	0	0
: East Asia Boreal	0	0	0	0	0	0	0	0	0	0
: North Pacific, East Asia	0	0	0	0	0	0	0	0	0	0
: Indo-Australian	0	0	0	0	0	0	0	0	0	0
: Tropical Atlantic	0	0	0	0	0	0	0	0	0	0
Coral reef (1=yes)	1	0	0	1	1	1	1	1	0.1	2
Salinities	0	32	8	34	35	35	35	35	0.8	0
Ocean circulation	32	1	2	-1	0.4	-1	1	1	0.5	0
Prevailing Wind: Polar	1	0	0	0	0.4	0	0	0	3.3	0
: Westerlies Zone	0	0	0	0	0.1	0	0	0	0.3	0
: Subtropical	0	0	0	0	0	0	0	0	0.1	0
: Monsoon Zone	0	0	0	0	0.9	0	0	0	0.2	1
: Trades Zone	0	0	0	0	0.5	0	0	0	0.9	0
: Intertropical	1	1	0.2	1	0	1	1	1	0.5	0
: Transition	0	0	0	0	0	0	0	0	0	0
No oceans (1=yes)	0	0	0	0	0	0	0	0	0	1
Fresh water (cub/kil)	0.1	0	0.2	0.5	0.1	0.4	16	1	26	1

Characteristics	Micronesian	Mixed	Moldovan	Mon	Mon-Khmer	Monegasque	Mongo	Mongol-Buryat	Mongol-Dariganga	Mongol-Dorbed
Coastline: length (km)	4020	542	9780	3060	0	4	37	0	0	0
: length km/cap	38000	1370	68	46	0	140	0.9	0	0	0
Zones: Sea territory	10	12	3	12	0	12	12	0	0	0
: Continental shelf (m)	195	124	55	200	0	0	0	0	0	0
: Excl. fish (nm)	0	48	0	0	0	0	200	0	0	0
: Extend. econ. zone (nm)	200	181	55	200	0	0	0	0	0	0
: 200-Mi EEZ, area	59400	261000	0	0	0	0	1030	0	0	0
: Contiguous zone (nm)	12	0.1	0	24	0	0	0	0	0	0
Inland waterways (km)	0	0	31800	3100	4590	0	15100	199	199	199
Inland waterways/cap	0	0	0.7	0.1	1	0	0.4	0.1	0.1	0.1
Water area: (km sq)	23	131	20200	18800	6000	0	77800	0	0	0
: area/cap	0.2	0.2	0.5	0.4	0	0	3	0	0	0
Access: Number of ports	2	0	7	0.3	0	0	0	0	0	0
: Natural Harbour (1=yes)	0	0	0	0	3	0	0	0	0	2
: Number of outlets	0	1	0	0	0	0	0	2	2	0
: Island (1=yes)	1	0	0	0	1	0	0	1	1	1
: Landlocked (1=yes)	0	0	0	0	0.2	1	0	0	0	0
Ships: Number/cap	4	214	0	2	0.3	0	0	0	0	0
: tonnage (dwt)/cap	97	6770	9	30	0	0	0.4	0	0	0
Offshore Reserves: oil/cap	0	0.1	72	0.1	0	0	0	0	0	0
: gas/cap	0	0	0	0	0	0	0	0	0	0
Fish supply kgrm/year/cap	8	33	0	0	0	0	0	0	0	0
Marine Biology: Arctic	0	0	0.3	0	0	0	0	0	0	0
: NW American Boreal	0	0	0	0	0	0	0	0	0	0
: N Pacific, American	0	0	0	0	0	0	0	0	0	0
: Tropical East Pacific	0	0	0	0	0	0	0	0	0	0
: South Pacific	0.8	0	0	0	0	0	0	0	0	0
: Antiboreal	0	0	0	0	0	0	0	0	0	0
: Atlantic Boreal	0	0	0.3	0	0	0	0	0	0	0
: Atlantic Warm Temp	0	0	0.1	0	0	1	0	0	0	0
: Tropical Indo-West-Pacif	0.2	0.4	0	0	0	0	0	0	0	0
: East Asia Boreal	0	0	0.3	0	2	0	0	0	0	0
: North Pacific, East Asia	0	0	0	0	0	0	0	0	0	0
: Indo-Australian	0	0	0	0	0	0	0	0	0	0
: Tropical Atlantic	0	0	0	0	0	0	0	0	0	0
Coral reef (1=yes)	0.7	0.6	0	1	1	0	1	0	0	1
Salinities	35	0.5	1	30	0	37	33	0	0	1
Ocean circulation	0.7	35	1	1	0	1	0	0	0	0
Prevailing Wind: Polar	0	0.6	0	0	0	0	0	0	0	0
: Westerlies Zone	0	0	0.1	0	0	0	0	0	0	0
: Subtropical	0	0	0	0	0	0	0	0	0	0
: Monsoon Zone	0.7	0	0.3	0	0	0	0	0	0	0
: Trades Zone	0.3	0.7	0	0	0	0	0	0	0	0
: Intertropical	0	0.6	0	0	1	1	1	1	1	1
: Transition	0	0	1	1	0	0	0	1	1	1
No oceans (1=yes)	0	0	0	0	0	0	0	0	0	0
Fresh water (cub/kil)	.	0.2	0.1	4	1	.	0.7	0.6	0.6	0.6

Characteristics	Mongol-Khalka	Mongoloid	Montene-grin	Moor	Morvians	Mossi	Mpongwe	Mubi	Mulatto	Muong
Coastline: length (km)	0	8190	.	998	45400	192	885	0	5860	3440
: length km/cap	0	8	.	232	8520	12	702	0	108	49
Zones: Sea territory	0	12	.	46	0	71	100	0	146	12
: Continental shelf (m)	0	168	.	200	0	36	150	0	195	200
: Excl. fish (nm)	0	0	.	0	0	0		0	0.4	0
: Extend. econ. zone (nm)	0	168	.	200	0			0	56	200
: 200-Mi EEZ, area	0	1690000	.	306000	0	77900	214000	0	2340000	723000
: Contiguous zone (nm)		20	0	10	172	55	1600	2000	3	24
Inland waterways (km)	199	3360	0	215	0		1	0.3	0.7	17700
Inland waterways/cap	0.1	0		0	14100000	3300	10000	24800	36400	0.3
Water area: (km sq)	0	307000		537	2640	0.3	8	4	0.3	4200
: area/cap	0	0.3	2	0.1		0.7	3		48700	0.1
Access: Number of ports	0	0.8		0	0	1		0	0.4	3
: Natural Harbour (1=yes)	2	0		0				2	10	0
: Number of outlets	0	0	0	0				0	0	0
: Island (1=yes)	1	0.5	4	0.4		0.6	6	1	0.2	3
: Landlocked (1=yes)	0	4	142	1		0.2	22		28	9
Ships: Number/cap	0	0		11			3		563	
: tonnage (dwt)/cap	0	0		0		0			0	0
Offshore Reserves: oil/cap	0	0	0	0	0	0.5	24	3	2	1
: gas/cap	0	0	0	0	0	0	0	0	0	0
Fish supply kgrm/year/cap	0	0	0	0	0	0	0	0	0	0
Marine Biology: Arctic	0	0	0	0	0	0	0	0	0	0
: NW American Boreal	0	0	0	0	0	0	0	0	0	0
: N Pacific, American	0	0	0	0	0	0	0	0	0	0
: Tropical East Pacific	0	0	0	0	0	0	0	0	0	0
: South Pacific	0	0	0	0	0	0	0	0	0	0
: Antiboreal	0	0	1	0	0	0	0	0	0	0
: Atlantic Boreal	0	0	0	0	0	0	0	0	1	1
: Atlantic Warm Temp	0	1	0	0.4	0	0	0	0	0	0
: Tropical Indo-West-Pacif	0	0	0	0	0	0	0	0	0	0
: East Asia Boreal	0	0	0	0	0	0	0	0	0	0
: North Pacific, East Asia	0	0.2	0	0	0	0	0	0	0	0
: Indo-Australian	0	0	0	0.6	0	0.4	1	0	0.7	0
: Tropical Atlantic	0	0.8	39	0.4	0	12	32	2	0.1	33
Coral reef (1=yes)	0	34		35		2	1		0.9	-1
Salinities	0	0.8	0	-0.2	0	0	1	0	36	0
Ocean circulation	0	0	0	0	0	0	0	0	0.3	0
Prevailing Wind: Polar	0	0	0	0	0	0	0	0	0	0
: Westerlies Zone	1	0.2	1	1	0	1	1	1	0.7	1
: Subtropical	0	0.8	0	0	0	0	0	0	0.1	0
: Monsoon Zone	0	0	1	0	0	0	0	0	0.1	0
: Trades Zone	0	0	0	0	0	0	0	0	0	0
: Intertropical	0	0	1	0	0	0	0	0	0	0
: Transition	1	0		0		0	0		0	33
No oceans (1=yes)	0	0	1	3	.	0.2	0.1	0.2	27	-1
Fresh water (cub/kil)	0.6	393	.	3	.	0.2	0.1	0.2	27	5

Characteristics	Nama	Nauruan	Ndebele	Nepalese	Nether-lander	Newar	Ngbandi	Ngoni	Nkole	Norman-French D.
Coastline: length (km)	1490	30	0	0	451	0	0	0	0	62
: length km/cap	950	2680	0	0	29	0	0	0	0	808
Zones: Sea territory	6	12	0	0	12	0	0	0	0	3
: Continental shelf (m)					0					200
: Excl. fish (nm)	12	200	0	0	200	0	0	0	0	200
: Extend. econ. zone (nm)	0	0	0	0		0	0	0	0	0
: 200-Mi EEZ, area	500000	431000	0	0	84700	0	0	0	0	0
: Contiguous zone (nm)	0	0	0	0	12	0	0	0	0	0
Inland waterways (km)	0	0	0	0	4610	0	0	144	0	0
Inland waterways/cap	0	0	0	0	0.3	0	0	0	0	0
Water area: (km sq)	1000	0	4020	4000	3370	4000	800	24400	36300	0
: area/cap	0.6	0	0.4	0.2	0.2	0.2	0.2	2	2	0
Access: Number of ports	1	1	0	0	39	0	0	4	0	3
: Natural Harbour (1=yes)	0	0	2	1		1	1	2	0	1
: Number of outlets	0	1	0	0		0	0	0	1	1
: Island (1=yes)	0	1								
: Landlocked (1=yes)	0	0	1	1		1	1	1	1	0
Ships: Number/cap	0	103	0	0	34	0	0	0	0	0
: tonnage (dwt)/cap	0	598	0	0	295	0	0	0	0	0
Offshore Reserves: oil/cap	0	0	0	0	0.1	0	0	0	0.1	0
: gas/cap	0	0	0	0	0.7	0	0	0	0.3	0
Fish supply kgrm/year/cap	16	0	0	0	0	0	0	0	0	0
Marine Biology: Arctic	0	0	0	0	0	0	0	0	0	0
: NW American Boreal	0	0	0	0	0	0	0	0	0	0
: N Pacific, American	0	0	0	0	0	0	0	0	0	0
: Tropical East Pacific	0	0	0	0	0	0	0	0	0	0
: South Pacific	0	0	0	0	0	0	0	0	0	0
: Antiboreal	0	0	0	0	0	0	0	0	0	0
: Atlantic Boreal	0	0	0	0	1	0	0	0	0	1
: Atlantic Warm Temp	0	0	0	0	1	0	0	0	0	0
: Tropical Indo-West-Pacif	0	0	0	0	0	0	0	0	0	0
: East Asia Boreal	0	0	0	0	0	0	0	0	0	0
: North Pacific, East Asia	0	0	0	0	0	0	0	0	0	0
: Indo-Australian	0	0	0	0	0	0	0	0	0	0
: Tropical Atlantic	0	0	0	0	0	0	0	0	0	0
Coral reef (1=yes)	1	1	0	0		0	0	0	0	0
Salinities	35	35	2	2	34	2	2	2	2	34
Ocean circulation	-1	-1	0	0	-1	0	0	0	0	-1
Prevailing Wind: Polar	0	0	0	0	0	0	0	0	0	0
: Westerlies Zone	0	0	0	0	1	0	0	0	0	1
Subtropical	1	1	1	1	0	1	0	0	0	0
: Monsoon Zone	0	0	0	0	0	0	0	0	0	0
: Trades Zone	1	1	0	0	0	0	1	1	1	0
: Intertropical	0	0	0	0	0	0	0	0	0	0
: Transition	0	0	0	0	0	0	0	0	0	0
No oceans (1=yes)	0	0	1	1	0	1	1	1	1	0
Fresh water (cub/kil)	0.1		1	3	15	3	0.1	0.2	0.2	

Characteristics	North-Western	Norwegian	Nuba	Nuer	Nung Sukuma	Nupe	Nyamwezi (Galla)	Nyoros	Ometo	Oromo
Coastline: length (km)	0	21900	853	853	3440	853	1420	0	1090	1090
: length km/cap	0	4630	31	31	49	8	49	0	14	14
Zones: Sea territory	0	4	12	12	12	30	50	0	12	12
: Continental shelf (m)	0	200	200	200	200	200	0	0	0	0
: Excl. fish (nm)	0	0	0	0	0	0	0	0	0	0
: Extend. econ. zone (nm)	0	200	0	0	200	200	0	0	0	0
: 200-Mi EEZ, area	0	2030000	91600	91600	723000	211000	223000	0	0	0
: Contiguous zone (nm)	0	10	18	18	24	0	0	0	0	0
Inland waterways (km)	2250	1580	4070	4070	17700	8580	0	0	0	0
Inland waterways/cap	0.3	0.4	0.1	0.1	0.3	0.1	0	0	0	0
Water area: (km sq)	11900	16400	130000	130000	4200	13000	59100	36300	121000	121000
: area/cap		4	5	5	0.1	0.1	2	2	2	2
Access: Number of ports	1	6	2	2	3	6	6	2	0	0
: Natural Harbour (1=yes)	0	0	0	0	0	0	0	1	0	0
: Number of outlets	2	0	0	0	0	0	0	0	0	0
: Island (1=yes)	1	0	0	0	0	0	0	0	0	0
: Landlocked (1=yes)	0	0	0	0	0	0	0	0	0	0
Ships: Number/cap	0	277	0.3	0.3	0	0.5	0.5	0.1	0.4	0.4
: tonnage (dwt)/cap	0	8460	0.2	0.2	0	0.7	0.2	0.3	0.2	0.2
Offshore Reserves: oil/cap	0	3	0	0	3	0.1	0.1	0	0	0
: gas/cap	0	24	0	0	9	0	0	0	0	0
Fish supply kgrm/year/cap	0	10	0	0	9	0	0	0	0	0
Marine Biology: Arctic	0	0	0	0	0	0	0	0	0	0
: NW American Boreal	0	0	0	0	0	0	0	0	0	0
: N Pacific American	0	0	0	0	0	0	0	0	0	0
: Tropical East Pacific	0	0	0	0	0	0	0	0	0	0
: South Pacific	0	0	0	0	0	0	0	0	0	0
: Antiboreal	0	0	0	0	0	0	0	0	0	0
: Atlantic Boreal	0	1	0	0	0	0	0	0	0	0
: Atlantic Warm Temp	0	0	0	0	0	0	0	0	0	0
: Tropical Indo-West-Pacif	0	0	0	0	0	0	0	0	0	0
: East Asia Boreal	0	0	0	0	0	0	0	0	0	0
: North Pacific; East Asia	0	0	0	0	0	0	0	0	0	0
: Indo-Australian	0	0	0	0	0	0	0	0	0	0
: Tropical Atlantic	0	0	1	1	1	1	1	0	1	1
Coral reef (1=yes)	0	0	0	0	0	0	0	0	0	0
Salinities	2	34	40	40	33	33	35	0	38	38
Ocean circulation	0	-1	1	1	-1	1	1	0	1	1
Prevailing Wind: Polar	0	0	0	0	0	0	0	0	0	0
: Westerlies Zone	0	1	0	0	0	0	0	0	0	0
: Subtropical	0	0	0	0	0	0	0	0	0	0
: Monsoon Zone	0	0	0	0	0	0	0	0	0	0
: Trades Zone	0	0	0	0	0	0	0	0	0	0
: Intertropical	1	0	1	1	1	1	1	1	1	1
: Transition	0	0	0	0	0	0	0	0	0	0
No oceans (1=yes)	1	0	0	0	0	0	0	0	0	0
Fresh water (cub/kil)	0.4	2	19	19	5	4	0.5	0.2	2	2

Characteristics	Ossete	Ovambo	Ovim-bundu	Pacific Islander	Pakistani	Palauans	Palaung-Wa	Papuan New Guin.	Pashtun	Pepel
Coastline: length (km)	310	1490	1600	30	7960	·	0	5150	0	274
: length km/cap	57	950	156	2680	566	·	0	1230	0	292
Zones: Sea territory	0	12	20	12	12	3	0	12	0	12
: Continental shelf (m)	·				136	200		200		
: Excl. fish (nm)	0				119	200				
: Extend. econ. zone (nm)	0		200	200	59			200		200
: 200-Mi EEZ, area	0	500000	506000	431000	652000	12	0	2350000		151000
: Contiguous zone (nm)	0	0	0	0	0.1	0	0	0	0	0
Inland waterways (km)	0				2100		4590	10900	1200	
Inland waterways/cap	0				0.1		1	3	0.1	
Water area: (km sq)	0	1000			2320		6000	9980		8120
: area/cap	0	0.6			0.1		0	2	0	8
Access: Number of ports	2	0	4	1	0	1	0	5	0	1
: Natural Harbour (1=yes)	0	0	0	0	0	·	0	0	0	0
: Number of outlets	0	0	0	0	0.6	·	3	0	2	0
: Island (1=yes)	0	0	0	1	0	1	0	1	0	0
: Landlocked (1=yes)	0	0	0	0	0	0	0	0	1	0
Ships: Number/cap	9	0	3	103	20	·	0.2	9	0	0
: tonnage (dwt)/cap	184	0	11	598	368	·	0.3	11	0	0
Offshore Reserves: oil/cap	0	0	0.3	0	53	·	0	0	0	0
: gas/cap	0	0	0.2	0	4	·	0	0	0	0
Fish supply kgrm/year/cap	0	16	0	0	0	·	0	5	0	0
Marine Biology: Arctic	0	0	0	0	0	0	0	0	0	0
: NW American Boreal	0	0	0	0	0	0	0	0	0	0
: N Pacific American	0	0	0	0	0	0	0	0	0	0
: Tropical East Pacific	0	0	0	0	0	0	0	0	0	0
: South Pacific	0	0	0	1	0	1	0	1	0	0
: Antiboreal	0	0	0	0	0	0	0	0	0	0
: Atlantic Boreal	0	0	0	0	0	0	0	0	0	0
: Atlantic Warm Temp	0	1	0	0	0	0	0	0	0	0
: Tropical Indo-West-Pacif	0	0	0	0	1	0	0	0	0	0
: East Asia Boreal	0	0	0	0	0	0	0	0	0	0
: North Pacific, East Asia	0	0	0	0	0	0	0	0	0	0
: Indo-Australian	0	0	0	0	0	0	0	0	0	0
: Tropical Atlantic	0	0	1	0	0	0	0	0	0	1
Coral reef (1=yes)	0	0	0	1	0	1	0	0	0	0
Salinities	40	35	34	35	35	34	2	35	2	36
Ocean circulation	0	·	·	·	-0.2	·	0	0	0	·
Prevailing Wind: Polar	0	0	0	0	0.6	0	0	0	0	0
: Westerlies Zone	1	0	0	0	0.3	0	0	0	0	0
: Subtropical	0	1	1	0	0	0	1	1	0	1
: Monsoon Zone	0	0	0	0	0.2	0	0	0	0	0
: Trades Zone	0	0	0	1	0.2	1	0	0	0	0
: Intertropical	0	0	0	0	0	0	0	0	0	0
: Transition	0	0	0	0	0	0	0	0	0	0
No oceans (1=yes)	1	0	1	1	0	0	1	1	1	1
Fresh water (cub/kil)	·	0.1	0.5	0	22	·	1	0.1	26	0

Characteristics	Persian	Polinisian	Polinesian Chinese	Polinesian European	Polish	Portu-guese	Punjabi	Punu	Puyi	Pygmy
Coastline: length (km)	3160	6990	2630	2470	720	6030	1090	644	14500	169
: length km/cap	51	13100	12000	11600	31	102	11	488	8	69
Zones: Sea territory	12	12	12	12	12	141	12	134	12	200
:: Continental shelf (m)		190	200	200		199	200	99		
:: Excl. fish (nm)	50				197	61	0.1			
:: Extend. econ. zone (nm)	0.2	200	200	200	0.3	0.3	200			
:: 200-Mi EEZ, area	155000	1790000			45900	2720000	322000	150000	110000	24700
:: Contiguous zone (nm)			12	11		0.2	2		0.1	
Inland waterways (km)	517	525	0	0	3940	34700		2540		4390
Inland waterways/cap	0	0.4			0.1	0.3		2		2
Water area: (km sq)	11900	176	281	263	12400	42300	25700	6800	271000	500
: area/cap	0.2	0.1		1	0.3	0.4	0.3	4	0.2	0.2
Access: Number of ports	7	0	2	2	7	11	3	3	12	0.2
:: Natural Harbour (1=yes)	0	0	0	0	0	1	0	0	0	2
:: Number of outlets		1	0	0						
:: Island (1=yes)	0	0	1	1	0	0	0	0	0	0
:: Landlocked (1=yes)	0	0	0	0	0	0	0	0	0	0
Ships: Number/cap	3	10	.	.	7	3	0.2	4	1	1
:: tonnage (dwt)/cap	14	156			104	72	4	15	17	19
Offshore Reserves: oil/cap	0.6	0.5	0	0	0.5	0		0.3	0	
:: gas/cap	0.6	98	170	170		0.1		22		
Fish supply kgrm/year/cap	0	0	0	0	0	0	0	0	0	1
Marine Biology: Arctic	0	0	0	0	0	0	0	0	0	0
:: NW American Boreal	0	0	0	0	0	0	0	0	0	0
:: N Pacific American	0	0	0	0	0	0	0	0	0	0
:: Tropical East Pacific	0	0	0	0	0	0	0	0	0	0
:: South Pacific	0	0.7	1	1	0	0	0	0	0	0
:: Antiboreal	0	0	0	0	0	0	0	0	0	0
:: Atlantic Boreal	0	0	0	0	1	0.3	0	0	0	0
:: Atlantic Warm Temp	0	0	0	0	0	0.3	0	0	0	0
:: Tropical Indo-West-Pacif	1	0	1	1	0	0	1	0	0	0
:: East Asia Boreal	0	0	0	0	0	0	0	0	1	0
:: North Pacific, East Asia	0	0	0	0	0	0	0	0	0	0
:: Indo-Australian	0	0	0	0	0	0	0	0	0	0
:: Tropical Atlantic	0	0	0	0	0	0	0	1	0	1
Coral reef (1=yes)	0	0.3	0	0	0	0.7	0	0	0	1
Salinities	38	35	35	35	34	36	37	32	34	32
Prevailing Wind: Polar	0	0	0	0	-1	-0.3	0	0	0	1
:: Westerlies Zone	0	0	0	0	1	1	0	0	1	
:: Subtropical	0	0.3	1	1	1	0.7	0	0	1	
:: Monsoon Zone	1	0	0	0	0	0	1	0	0	
:: Trades Zone	0	0.5	0	0	0	0	0	0	0	
:: Intertropical	0	0.2	0	0	0	0	0	1	0	1
:: Transition	0	0	0	0	0	1	0	0	0	
No oceans (1=yes)	0	0	0	0	0	0	0	0	0	0
Fresh water (cub/kil)	45	1	.	.	17	28	153	0.1	460	0

Characteristics	Quechua	Rakhine	Romanian	Romansch	Rundi	Russian	Ruthenian	Rwanda	Saho	Sakalava
Coastline: length (km)	2100	3060	225	0	35	31400	45400	29	112000	4830
: length km/cap	122	46	10	0	0.8	219	8520	0.7	32100	364
Zones: Sea territory	178	12	12	0	11	10		0		50
: Continental shelf (m)	178	200	199	0	187	181	0	158	0	150
: Excl. fish (nm)	0	200	0	0	0	0.1	0	0	0	150
: Extend. econ. zone (nm)	0	0	199	0	0	181	0	0	0	150
: 200-Mi EEZ, area	816000	24	31900	0	963	1090	0	815	0	1290000
: Contiguous zone (nm)	0	0	0	0	0	0		0		
Inland waterways (km)	7010	3100	1720	1210	14100	103000	172	12000	0	566
Inland waterways/cap	0.4	0.1	0.1	0.2	0.4	0.8		0.3		
Water area: (km sq)	6650	18800	7160	1520	72900	68300	14100000	69200	82200000	5500
: area/cap	0.4	0.4	0.3	0.2	2	0.5	2640	2	23600	0.4
Access: Number of ports	4	0.3	0	0	3	2		3		4
: Natural Harbour (1=yes)	0.2	0	1	4	0.1	0		0.2		0
: Number of outlets	0.1	0	176	0	0.1	0		0.1		0
: Island (1=yes)	0.2	0	1	4	0.4	0	0	0.4	0	1
: Landlocked (1=yes)	0	2	0	1	0	10	0	0	0	0
Ships: Number/cap	26	30	1	88	0	87	0	0	0	1
: tonnage (dwt)/cap	0	0.1	176	0	0	0	0	0	0	3
Offshore Reserves: oil/cap	0.5	0	0	0	0	0	0	0	0	0
: gas/cap	0	0	0	0	0	0.8	0	0	0	0
Fish supply kgrm/year/cap	0.9	0	0	0	0.9	0	0	0.8	0	0
Marine Biology: Arctic	0.6	0	0	0	0	0	0	0	0	0
: NW American Boreal	0	0	0	0	0	0	0	0	0	0
: N Pacific, American	0	0	0	0	0	0	0	0	0	0
: Tropical East Pacific	0	0	0	0	0	0	0	0	0	0
: South Pacific	0	0	0	0	0	0	0	0	0	0
: Antiboreal	0	0	0	0	0	0	0	0	0	0
: Atlantic Boreal	0	0	0	0	0	0	0	0	0	0
: Atlantic Warm Temp	0	0	0	0	0	0	0	0	0	0
: Tropical Indo-West-Pacif	0	0	0	0	0	0	0	0	0	1
: East Asia Boreal	0	0	0	0	0	0	0	0	0	0
: North Pacific, East Asia	0	0	0	0	0	0	0	0	0	0
: Indo-Australian	0	0	0	0	0	0	0	0	0	0
: Tropical Atlantic	0	0	0	0	0	0	0	0	0	0
Coral reef (1=yes)	0	1	1	0	0	0	0	0	0	1
Salinities	31	30	39	2	31	32	0	26	0	35
Ocean circulation	-0.4	1	1	0	0.1	-0.7	0	0.4	0	1
Prevailing Wind: Polar	0	0	0	0	0	0.1	0	0	0	0
: Westerlies Zone	0	0	1	1	0	0.8	0	0	0	0
: Subtropical	0.9	0	0	0	0	0	0	0	0	0
: Monsoon Zone	0	1	0	0	1	0	0	1	0	1
: Trades Zone	0	0	0	0	0	0	0	0	0	1
: Intertropical	0	0	0	0	0	0	0	0	0	0
: Transition	0	0	0	0	0	0.1	0	0	0	0
No oceans (1=yes)	0	0	0	1	0	0.1	0	1	0	0
Fresh water (cub/kil)	5	4	25	3	0.7	33		0.6		16

Characteristics	Samoan	Sanga	Sanmari-nese	Sara	Scandina-vian	Senufo	Serbian	Serer	Servicais Tongas	Shan
Coastline: length (km)	3790	169		0	1710	274	9250	531	209	3060
length km/cap	1460	69		0	10500	20	916	67	1650	46
Zones: Sea territory	9	200		0	3	6	196	12	12	12
Continental shelf (m)	68	0		0	200		20	200	0	200
Excl. fish (nm)	0			0	200	106	11	200		0
Extend. econ. zone (nm)	200			0					200	200
200-Mi EEZ, area	1400000	24700		0	68600	55600	625000	206000	128000	0
Contiguous zone (nm)	4	4		0	4			24		24
Inland waterways (km)	7210	4390		800	150	1120	59	899		3100
Inland waterways/cap	0.2	2		0.2	0.1	0.1		0.1		0.1
Water area: (km sq)	36200	500		0	252	8990	100000	4190		18800
area/cap	0.8	0.2		0	0.1	0.8	11	0.5		0.4
Access: Number of ports	0.6		0.2			0.2	2	4	2	0.3
Natural Harbour (1=yes)	0.2	2	0	0	0.3					0
Number of outlets		0	1	1	0	0.9	0	0	1	0
Island (1=yes)	0.8	0	0	0	0.6	0.0	0	0		0
Landlocked (1=yes)		0	1	1	0	0.5	0	0		0
Ships: Number/cap	11	0	0	0	96	0.3	4	0.8	16	2
tonnage (dwt)/cap	39	2	0	0	1300	0.4	11	0.2	10	30
Offshore Reserves: oil/cap	0		0	0	0.1	0	0.1	0	0	0
gas/cap		0	0	0	0.7	0	0.1	0	0	0.1
Fish supply kgrm/year/cap	176	19	0	0	4	0	0	0	339	0
Marine Biology: Arctic	0.2	0	0	0	0	0	0	0	0	0
NW American Boreal	0.2	0	0	0	0	0	0	0	0	0
N Pacific, American	0.7	0	0	0	0	0	0	0	0	0
Tropical East Pacific		0	0	0	0	0	0	0	0	0
South Pacific	0.2	0	0	0	1	0	0	0	0	0
Antiboreal	0.2	0	0	0	0	0	0	0	0	0
Atlantic Boreal	0.2	0	0	0	0	0	0	0	0	0
Atlantic Warm Temp		0	0	0	0	0	0	0	0	0
Tropical Indo-West-Pacif		0	0	0	0	0	0	0	0	0
East Asia Boreal		0	0	0	0	0	0	0	0	0
North Pacific, East Asia		0	0	0	0	0	0	0	0	0
Indo-Australian		0	0	0	0	0	0	0	0	0
Tropical Atlantic		0	0	0	0	0	0	1	0	0
Coral reef (1=yes)	0.2	1	1	0	1	0.5	1	1	1	1
Salinities	0.8	0	0	2		19		0	0	0
Ocean Circulation	35	32	39		35		33	36	33	30
Prevailing Wind: Polar	0.8	1	1	2	-0.3	1	1	-1	1	1
Westerlies Zone		0	0	0	1	0	0	0	0	0
Subtropical	0.2	0	0	0	0	0	0	0	0	0
Monsoon Zone		0	0	0	0	0	0	0	0	0
Trades Zone	0.1	0	0	0	0	0	0	0	0	0
Intertropical	1	1	1	1	1	1	1	1	1	1
Transition	0	0	0	0	0	0	0	1	0	0
No oceans (1=yes)	0	0	1	0	1	0	1	0	0	0
Fresh water (cub/kil)	467	0		0.1		0.9	42	1		4

Characteristics	Shilluk	Shona	Siamese	Sidamo	Sindhi	Sinhalese	Slavic Muslims	Slovak	Slovene	Soga
Coastline: length (km)	853	460	3220	1090	1050	1340	1780	45400	55	0
:length km/cap	31	29	57	14	8	94	367	8480	21	0
Zones: Sea territory	12	2	12	12	12	12	12	0.1	12	0
::Continental shelf (m)	200		200		200	199	200	0.9	197	0
::Excl. fish (nm)						07	12	0.9	5	0
::Extend. econ. zone (nm)		37	200		200	201	120		5	0
::200-Mi EEZ, area	91600	105000	325000		319000	521000		3210000	0	0
::Contiguous zone (nm)	18	0	3850	0	24	24	1	0	34	0
Inland waterways (km)	4070	698	0.1	0	0	214	0	196	0	3630
Inland waterways/cap	0.1	0.1	2230	121000	25200	0	128	0	14	2
Water area: (km sq)	130000	6630			0.2	864	0	13100000	0	
::area/cap		0.6		2	0.3	2	7	2270	1	
Access: Number of ports	5	3	5	2	0	0		5	0	0
::Natural Harbour (1=yes)	2	2	0		0	1	0	0.6	0	0
::Number of outlets	0	0	0	0	0	0	0	0	0	0
::Island (1=yes)	0	0.8	5	0.4	0	03	0.4	0	0	0.1
::Landlocked (1=yes)	0	0.2	23	0.2	0.2	3	0.9	0.1	0.8	0.3
Ships: Number/cap	0.3	0.3	0.1		4	27		03		
::tonnage (dwt)/cap	2		0.4			0		0.6		
Offshore Reserves: oil/cap		0	0	0	0	2	0	0	0	0
::gas/cap	0	0	0	0	0	0	0	0	0	0
Fish supply kgrm/year/cap	0	0	0	0	0	0	0	0	0	0
Marine Biology: Arctic	0	0	0	0	0	0	0	0	0	0
::NW American Boreal	0	0	0	0	0	0	0	0	0	0
::N Pacific, American	0	0	0	0	0	0	0	0	0	0
::Tropical East Pacific	0	0	0	0	0	0	0	0	0	0
::South Pacific	0	0	0	0	0	0	0	0	0	0
::Antiboreal	0	0	0	0	0	0	0	0	0	0
::Atlantic Boreal	0	0	0	0	0	0	0	0	0	0
::Atlantic Warm Temp	0	0	0	0	0	0	0	0	0	0
::Tropical Indo-West-Pacif	1	0	1	1	1	1	1	0	1	0
::East Asia Boreal	0	0	0	0	0	0	0	0	0	0
::North Pacific, East Asia	0	0	0	0	0	0	0	0	0	0
::Indo-Australian	0	0	0	0	0	0	0	0	0	0
::Tropical Atlantic	0	0.2	0	0	0	0	0	0	0	0
Coral reef (1=yes)	1	0.7	1	1	1	1	1	1	1	1
Salinites	40	2	31	38	37	33		0.1	38	2
Ocean circulation	1	0	0	0	1	1	1	0	1	0
Prevailing Wind: Polar	0	0	0	0	0	0	0	0	0	0
::Westerlies Zone	0	0	0	0	0	0	0	0	0	0
::Subtropical	0	0	0	0	0	0	0	0	0	0
::Monsoon Zone	1	1	1	1	1	1	1	0	1	1
::Trades Zone	1	1	1	1	1	1	1	0	1	0
::Intertropical	0	0	0	0	0	0	0	0	0	0
::Transition	0	0	0	0	0	0	0	0	0	0
No oceans (1=yes)	0	0	0	0	0	0	0	0	1	2
Fresh water (cub/kil)	19	1	32	2	153	6	.	31	5	0.2

Characteristics	Somali	Somba	Songhai	Soninke	Sotho	Sotho North	Spanish	Sundanese	Suriname	Susu
Coastline: length (km)	2830	121	0	115	1720	2880	5820	54700	364	346
: length km/cap	288	24	0	32	44	73	108	281	2020	54
Zones: Sea territory	181	200	0	18	7	12	80	12	12	12
: Continental shelf (m)	2	0	0	37	120	200	75	0	0	0
: Excl. fish (nm)	0	0	0	27	120	200	1	0	0	0
: Extend. econ. zone (nm)	0	0	0	0	0	0	126	200	0	200
: 200-Mi EEZ, area	705000	1720	0	36700	609000	1020000	1880000	5410000	0	71000
: Contiguous zone (nm)	0.2	0	0	3	0	0	0.1	0	0	0
Inland waterways (km)	0	0	1080	1590	0	0	17800	21600	0	1300
Inland waterways/cap	0	0	0.1	0.2	0	0	0.2	0.1	0	0.2
Water area: (km sq)	19800	2000	10300	15700	0	0	23700	93000	0	0
: area/cap	1	0.4	1	0	0	0	0.3	0.5	0	0
Access: Number of ports	4	1	0	2	0	0	19	0	3	2
: Natural Harbour (1=yes)	0	0	0	0	7	7	0	8	0	0
: Number of outlets	0	0	2	0	0	0	0	0	0	0
: Island (1=yes)	0	0	1	0	0	0	0	1	1	0
: Landlocked (1=yes)	0.5	0	0	0.8	0.4	0.2	6	4	0	0
Ships: Number/cap	0	0	0	0.1	0.4	0.5	84	15	.	0
: tonnage (dwt)/cap	1	0.2	0	0.4	0.1	0	0	0.2	0	2
Offshore Reserves: oil/cap	0	0	0	0	3	0	0	0	0	0
: gas/cap	0	0	0	0	0	0	0	0	0	0.2
Fish supply kgrm/year/cap	0	0	0	0	0	0	0	0	102	0
Marine Biology: Arctic	0	0	0	0	0	0	0	0	0	0
: NW American Boreal	0	0	0	0	0	0	0	0	0	0
: N Pacific, American	0	0	0	0	0	0	0	0	0	0
: Tropical East Pacific	0	0	0	0	0	0	0	0	0	0
: South Pacific	0	0	0	0	0	0	0	0	0	0
: Antiboreal	0	0	0	0	0	0	0	0	0	0
: Atlantic Boreal	0	0	0	0	0	0	0	0	0	0
: Atlantic Warm Temp	0	0	0	0	0	0	0	0	0	0
: Tropical Indo-West-Pacif	0	0	0	0	0	0	0	0	0	0
: East Asia Boreal	0	0	0	0	0	0	0	0	0	0
: North Pacific, East Asia	0	0	0	0	0	0	0	0	0	0
: Indo-Australian	0	0	0	0	0	0	0	0	0	0
: Tropical Atlantic	0	0	0	0	0	0	0	0	0	0
Coral reef (1=yes)	0.1	1	1	1	1	1	0.6	1	1	1
Salinities	38	33	2	9	21	35	36	1	1	35
Ocean circulation	1	1	0	1	0.8	0	-0.6	35	36	-1
Prevailing Wind: Polar	0	0	0	0	0	0	0	0	0	0
: Westerlies Zone	0	0	0	0	0	0	1	0	0	0
: Monsoon Zone	0.9	0	0	0	0	0	0.4	0	0	0
: Subtropical	0.1	1	0.1	0.9	1	1	0	1	1	1
: Trades Zone	0	0	0.5	0.2	0	0	0	0	0	35
: Intertropical	0	0	0	0	0	0	0	0	0	-1
: Transition	0	0	0	0	0	0	0	0	0	0
No oceans (1=yes)	0	0	0	0	0	0	0	0	0	0
Fresh water (cub/kil)	0.9	0.1	0.9	1	6	9	41	82	.	0.7

Characteristics	Swahili	Swazi	Swedish	Swiss	Tahitian	Tai	Taiwanese (Dari)	Tajik	Tama	Tamang
Coastline: length (km)	1380	0	3160	0	2250	2580	1450	0	0	0
:length km/cap	109	0	374	0	12700	37	46	0	0	0
Zones: Sea territory	49	0	12	0	200	9	12	0	0	0
::Continental shelf (m)	7	0	200	0	200	150	0	0	0	0
::Excl. fish (nm)	0	0	193	0	0	0	200	0	0	0
::Extend. econ. zone (nm)	7	0	0.2	0	200	150	0	0	0	0
::200-Mi EEZ, area	223000	0	155000	0	1310000	541000	0	0	0	0
::Contiguous zone (nm)	0	0	0.2	0	0	18	0	0	0	0
Inland waterways (km)	0	0	2220	0	0	14400	0	758	2000	0
Inland waterways/cap	0	0	0.3	0	0	0.3	0	0.1	0.3	0
Water area: (km sq)	57100	160	38100	0	300	4650	3720	2770	24800	4000
:: area/cap	2	0.2	4	0	2	0.1	0.2	0.2	4	0.2
Access: Number of ports	6	0	7	0	4	2	0.5	2	0	0
::Natural Harbour (1=yes)	0	0	0	0	0	0	0	0.5	0	1
::Number of outlets	0	1	0	2	0	0.8	0	0.9	2	0
::Island (1=yes)	0	0	0	0	1	0.3	1	0	0	1
::Landlocked (1=yes)	0	1	0	1	0	0	0	1	1	1
Ships: Number/cap	0.5	0	31	0	0	0	11	0	0	0
::tonnage (dwt)/cap	0.2	0	388	0	0	0	429	0	0	0
Offshore Reserves: oil/cap	0.1	0	0	0	0	0.7	0.1	0.1	0	0
::gas/cap	0	0	0.3	0	0	0	0	0	0	0
Fish supply kgrm/year/cap	0	0	3	0	125	6	3	0	3	0
Marine Biology: Arctic	0	0	0	0	0	0	0	0	0	0
::NW American Boreal	0	0	0	0	0	0	0	0	0	0
::N Pacific, American	0	0	0	0	0	0	0	0	0	0
::Tropical East Pacific	0	0	0	0	0	0	0	0	0	0
::South Pacific	0	0	0	0	1	0	0	0	0	0
::Antiboreal	0	0	0	0	0	0	0	0	0	0
::Atlantic Boreal	0	0	1	0	0	0	0	0	0	0
::Atlantic Warm Temp	0	0	0	0	0	0	0	0	0	0
::Tropical Indo-West-Pacif	1	0	0	0	0	1	0	0	0	0
::East Asia Boreal	0	0	0	0	0	0	0	0	0	0
::North Pacific, East Asia	0	0	0	0	0	0	1	0	0	0
::Indo-Australian	0	0	0	0	0	0	0	0	0	0
::Tropical Atlantic	0	0	0	0	0	0	0	0	0	0
Coral reef (1=yes)	1	0	0	0	1	0	0	0	0	0
Salinities	35		35		35	25	34	5		
Ocean circulation	1		-1		1	-0.2	0	2		
Prevailing Wind: Polar	0	0	0	0	0	0	0	0	0	0
::Westerlies Zone	0	0	1	1	0	0	0	1	0	0
::Subtropical	0	0	0	0	0	0	0	0	0	0
::Monsoon Zone	1	0	0	0	0	1	1	0	2	1
::Trades Zone	0	0	0	0	1	0	0	0	0	0
::Intertropical	0	0	0	0	0	0	0	0	0	0
::Transition	0	0	0	0	0	0	0	0.5	0	0
No oceans (1=yes)	0	1	0	1	0	0	0	0.5	0	1
Fresh water (cub/kil)	0.5		4	0.2		4	0.1	26	0.2	3

Characteristics	Tamil (Tubu)	Tatar	Teda	Teke	Tem-Kabre	Temne	Teso	Thai	Tharu	Tigre
Coastline: length (km)	1340	31800	0	74	56	402	0	3440	0	65400
: length km/cap	75	214	0	20	14	89	0	49	0	1870
Zones: Sea territory	12	10	0	64	30	200	0	12	0	5
: Continental shelf (m)	200	169	0	145	0	0	0	200	0	0
: Excl. fish (nm)	0	0	0	0	0	0	0	0	0	0
: Extend. econ. zone (nm)	200	169	0	7570	200	0	0	200	0	0
: 200-Mi EEZ, area	518000	0	0	0	1030	156000	0	723000	0	0
: Contiguous zone (nm)	24	0	0	0	0	0	0	24	0	0
Inland waterways (km)	215	105000	2000	12100	25	700	36300	17700	4000	0
Inland waterways/cap	0	0.8	0.3	0.4	0	0.2	2	0.3	0.2	0
Water area: (km sq)	870	71400	24800	56400	2400	120		4200		47800000
: area/cap	0	0.6	4	0.2	0.6		0	0.1		197
Access: Number of ports	2	20	0	3	0	3	0	3	0	2
: Natural Harbour (1=yes)	0	0	0	0	2	0	1	3	1	0
: Number of outlets	0	0	2	0	0	0	0	9	0	0
: Island (1=yes)	1	0	1	0	0	1	0	0	0	0
: Landlocked (1=yes)	0	0	0	0	0	1	1	0	1	0
Ships: Number/cap	2	10	0	0	5	1	0.1	1	0	0
: tonnage (dwt)/cap	24	84	0	0	5	1	0.3	0	0	0
Offshore Reserves: oil/cap	0	0	0	0.3	0	0	0	0	0	0.2
: gas/cap	0	0	0	0.5	0	0	0	0	0	0.7
Fish supply kgrm/year/cap	0	0.8	3	0.3	0	0	0	0	0	0
Marine Biology: Arctic	0	0	0	0	0	0	0	0	0	0
: NW American Boreal	0	0	0	0	0	0	0	0	0	0
: N Pacific, American	0	0	0	0	0	0	0	0	0	0
: Tropical East Pacific	0	0	0	0	0	0	0	0	0	0
: South Pacific	0	0	0	0	0	0	0	0	0	0
: Antiboreal	0	0	0	0	0	0	0	0	0	0
: Atlantic Boreal	0	0.8	0	0	0	0	0	0	0	0
: Atlantic Warm Temp	0	0.1	0	0	0	0	0	0	0	0
: Tropical Indo-West-Pacif	0	0	0	0	0	0	0	0	0	0
: East Asia Boreal	0	0	0	0	0	0	0	0	0	0
: North Pacific, East Asia	0	0	0	0	0	0	0	0	0	0
: Indo-Australian	0	0	0	0	0	0	0	0	0	0
: Tropical Atlantic	0	0.8	0	0	0	0	0	0	0	0
Coral reef (1=yes)	0	0	0	0	0	0	0	0	0	0.4
Salinities	33	33	2	33	35	35	2	33	2	0.4
Ocean circulation	-1	-0.7	0	0.3	-1	-1	0	-1	0	16
Prevailing Wind: Polar	0	0	0	0	0	0	0	0	0	0.4
: Westerlies Zone	0	0.8	0	0	0	0	0	0	0	0
: Subtropical	0	0.1	0	0	0	0	0	0	0	0
: Monsoon Zone	0	0	0	0	0	0	0	1	1	0
: Trades Zone	1	0	1	1	0	0	0	0	0	0.4
: Intertropical	0	0	0	0	1	1	1	0	0	0
: Transition	0	0	0	0	0	0	0	0	0	0
No oceans (1=yes)	0	0	1	1	1	1	1	0	1	0.4
Fresh water (cub/kil)	6	.	0.2	0.5	0.1	0.4	0.2	5	3	2

Characteristics	Tigrinya	Tikar	Tiv	Tonga	Tongan	Toros	Tribal	Tsimihety	Tsonga	Tswana
Coastline: length (km)	31700	402	853	0	416	0	580	4830	2460	2880
: length km/cap	8900	32	8	0	4330	0	5	364	154	73
Zones: Sea territory	9	50	30	0	12	0	12	50	12	12
: Continental shelf (m)	0	0	200	0	200	0	0	150	0	200
: Excl. fish (nm)	0	0	0	0	200	0	0	150	0	200
: Extend. econ. zone (nm)	0	0	200	0	0	0	0	150	199	0
: 200-Mi EEZ, area	0	15440	211000	0	0	0	200	1290000	559000	1020000
: Contiguous zone (nm)	0	0	0	0	0.1	0	76800	0	0	0
Inland waterways (km)	0	2090	8580	2250	0	0	18	566	3730	0
Inland waterways/cap	0	0.2	0.1	0.3	0	0	0.1	0	0.2	0
Water area: (km sq)	22800000	6000	13000	11900	30	36300	10100	5500	17400	0
: area/cap	582	0.5	0.6	1	0.3	2	0.1	0.4	0.2	0
Access: Number of ports	2	0	0	1	1	1	1	1	3	7
: Natural Harbour (1=yes)	0	0	0	0	0	0	0	0	0	0
: Number of outlets	0	0	0	2	0	0	0	0	0	0
: Island (1=yes)	0	0	0	1	1	1	0	1	0	0
: Landlocked (1=yes)	0	0	0	0	0	0	4	0	0	0
Ships: Number/cap	0	0.2	0.5	0	83	0	0	0	0	0
: tonnage (dwt)/cap	0	0.3	0.7	0	138	0	0	0	0	0
Offshore Reserves: oil/cap	0.3	0.4	0.1	0	0	0.1	0	0	0.9	0.2
: gas/cap	1	0.1	1	0	0	0.3	0	0	0.2	0.5
Fish supply kgrm/year/cap	0	0	0	0	232	0	0	0	0	0
Marine Biology: Arctic	0	0	0	0	0	0	0	0	0	0
: NW American Boreal	0	0	0	0	0	0	0	0	0	0
: N Pacific. American	0	0	0	0	0	0	0	0	0	0
: Tropical East Pacific	0	0	0	0	0	0	0	0	0	0
: South Pacific	0	0	0	0	0	0	0	0	0	0
: Antiboreal	0	0	0	0	0	0	0	0	0	0
: Atlantic Boreal	0	0	0	0	0	0	0	0	0	0
: Atlantic Warm Temp	0	0	0	0	0	0	0	0	0	0
: Tropical Indo-West-Pacif	0	0	0	0	0	0	0	0	0	0
: East Asia Boreal	0	0	0	0	0	0	0	0	0	0
: North Pacific, East Asia	0	0	0	0	0	0	0	0	0	0
: Indo-Australian	0	0	0	0	0	0	0	0	0	0
: Tropical Atlantic	0	0	0	0	0	2	0	0	0	0
Coral reef (1=yes)	0	1	1	1	1	0	1	1	1	1
Salinities	0	0	0	0	0	0	0	0	0	0
Ocean circulation	0.7	0	0	0	0	0	0	0	0	0
Prevailing Wind: Polar	27	33	33	2	35	2	30	35	35	35
: Westerlies Zone	0.7	1	0	0	1	0	1	1	1	0
: Subtropical	0	0	0	0	0	0	0	0	0	0
: Monsoon Zone	0	0	0	0	0	0	0	0	0	0
: Trades Zone	0	0	0	0	0	0	0	0	0	1
: Intertropical	0.7	1	1	1	1	1	1	1	1	0
: Transition	0	0	0	0	0	0	0	0	0	1
No oceans (1=yes)	0	0	0	0	0	0	0	0	0	0
Fresh water (cub/kil)	2	0.4	4	0.4	.	0.2	23	16	0.8	9

Characteristics	Tuareg	Tukolor	Tumbuka	Turkish	Turkmen	Tutsi	Tuvaluan	Twa	Uighur	Ukrainian
Coastline: length (km)	0	562	0	6860	1030	0	64	0	0	6450
: length km/cap	0	106	0	119	17	0	2640	0	0	107
Zones: Sea territory	0	20	0	6	6	0	12	0	0	1
: Continental shelf (m)	0	200	0	7	4	0	7	0	0	134
: Excl. fish (nm)	0	172	0	7	12	0	7	0	0	20
: Extend. econ. zone (nm)	0	28	0	191	0	0	193	0	0	126
: 200-Mi EEZ, area	0	199000	0	232000	46300	0	699000	0	0	33500
: Contiguous zone (nm)	0	21	0	0	0	0	0.2	0	0	0
Inland waterways (km)	1080	899	2250	1370	294	0	0	0	117	15800
Inland waterways/cap	0.1	0.1	0.3	0	0	0	0	0	0	0.3
Water area: (km sq)	11300	3650	11900	9420	3310	1820	0	1730	39600	19000
: area/cap	1	0.5	1	0.2	0.1	0.3	0	0.2	3	0.3
Access: Number of ports	0	4	0	5	0	0	2	0	3	10
: Natural Harbour (1=yes)	0	0	0	1	0.1	1	0	1	0	1
: Number of outlets	2	0	2	0	0	0	0	2	0	0
: Island (1=yes)	0	0	0	0	0.1	1	1	0	0	0
: Landlocked (1=yes)	1	0	1	0	1	1	0	1	1	0
Ships: Number/cap	0	0.8	0	17	0	0	439	0	0	0
: tonnage (dwt)/cap	0	0.2	0	243	0	0	1380	0	0	0
Offshore Reserves: oil/cap	0	0	0	0	0.6	0	0	0	0	0
: gas/cap	0	0	0	0	0.3	0	0	0	0	0
Fish supply kgrm/year/cap	0	0	0	0	0	0	1	0	0	13
Marine Biology: Arctic	0	0	0	0	0	0	0	0	0	0
: NW American Boreal	0	0	0	0	0	0	0	0	0	0
: N Pacific, American	0	0	0	0	0	0	0	0	0	0
: Tropical East Pacific	0	0	0	0	0	0	0	0	0	0
: South Pacific	0	0	0	0	0	0	1	0	0	0
: Antiboreal	0	0	0	0	0	0	0	0	0	0
: Atlantic Boreal	0	0	0	0	0	0	0	0	0	0
: Atlantic Warm Temp	0	0	0	1	0	0	0	0	0	1
: Tropical Indo-West-Pacif	0	0	0	0	0	0	0	0	0	0
: East Asia Boreal	0	0	0	0	0	0	0	0	0	0
: North Pacific, East Asia	0	0	0	0	0	0	0	0	0	0
: Indo-Australian	0	0	0	0	0	0	0	0	0	0
: Tropical Atlantic	0	1	0	0	0	0	0	0	0	0
Coral reef (1=yes)	0	0	0	0	0	0	1	0	0	0
Salinities	2	36	2	39	36	2	35	2	32	38
Ocean circulation	0	-1	0	0.9	0.8	0	0	0	0	0.8
Prevailing Wind: Polar	0	0	0	0	0	0	0	0	0	0.9
: Westerlies Zone	0	0.1	0	0.1	0.1	0	0	0	0	0
: Subtropical	0	0.9	0	0.9	0.1	0	0	0	0	0.1
: Monsoon Zone	0	0	0	0	0	0	0	0	0	0
: Trades Zone	0.2	0	0	0.1	0.6	0	0	0	0	0
: Intertropical	0	0	0	0	0	0	0	0	0	0
: Transition	0	0	0	0	0	0	0	0	0	0
No oceans (1=yes)	1	0	1	0	1	1	0	1	1	0
Fresh water (cub/kil)	0.9	1	0.4	16	39	0.1	.	0.2	0.8	28

Characteristics	Urdu	Uzbek	Vanuatuan	Vietnamese	Wallon	White	Wolof	Xhosa	Yalunka	Yao
Coastline: length (km)	1050	0	2530	3590	64	16500	522	2880	402	7880
: length km/cap	8	0	15400	53	6	173	81	73	89	26
Zones: Sea territory	12	0	12	12	12	23	23	12		8
: Continental shelf (m)	200	0	200	200	200	189	191	200	200	0
: Excl. fish (nm)	0	0	0.1	0.1	0	18	182		0	0
: Extend. econ. zone (nm)	200	0	200	200	200	162	9	200		29
: 200-Mi EEZ, area	319000	0	617000	777000	2740	6080000	195000	1020000	156000	81200
: Contiguous zone (nm)	24	0	24	24	0	9	22	0	0	0
Inland waterways (km)	0	989	0	17800	1790	33200	876	0	700	57600
Inland waterways/cap	0	0.1	0	0.2	0.2	0.2	0.1	0.7	0.2	0.1
Water area: (km sq)	25200	18200	0	6240	280	154000	3880	0	120	151000
: area/cap	0.2	0.2	0	0.1	0.3	22	0.4	0.2	3	0.2
Access: Number of ports	0.3	0.9	4	0	5	0	0	0.5	0	0.8
: Natural Harbour (1=yes)	0	0	0	0	0	0.1	0	0	0	0
: Number of outlets	0	0.1	0	0.3	0	0	0.7	0	0	0.7
: Island (1=yes)	0	0	1	0	0	4	0.2	0	1	0
: Landlocked (1=yes)	0	0.2	0	0	0	125	0	0	1	0.3
Ships: Number/cap	0.2	0	726	3	3	0.1	0.9	0	0	0.8
: tonnage (dwt)/cap	4	0	18000	10	5	0.4	0	0	0	0
Offshore Reserves: oil/cap	0	0	0	0	0	0.2	0	0	0	0
: gas/cap	0	0	190	0	0	0.7	0	0	0	0
Fish supply kgrm/year/cap	0	0	0	0	2	0.7	0	0	0	0
Marine Biology: Arctic	0	0	0	0	0	0.1	0	0	0	0
: NW American Boreal	0	0	0	0	0	0	0	0	0	0
: N Pacific, American	0	0	0	0	0	0	0	0	0	0
: Tropical East Pacific	0	0	0	0	0	0	0	0	0	0
: South Pacific	0	0	1	0	0	0	0	0	0	0
: Antiboreal	0	0	0	0	0	0	0	0	0	0
: Atlantic Boreal	0	0	0	0	1	0.7	0	0	0	0
: Atlantic Warm Temp	0	0	0	0	8	0.7	0	0	0	0
: Tropical Indo-West-Pacif	1	0	1	1	0	0.1	0	1	0	0.7
: East Asia Boreal	0	0	0	0	0	0	0	0	0	0
: North Pacific, East Asia	0	0	0	0	0	0	0	0	0	0.5
: Indo-Australian	0	0	0	0	0	0.2	0	0	0	0
: Tropical Atlantic	0	0	0	0	0	0.9	1	1	0	0
Coral reef (1=yes)	0	0	1	1	0	0	0	0	0	0.1
Salinities	37	33	35	33	34	35	36	35	35	23
Ocean circulation	-1	-1	-1	-1	-1	0.1	-1	0	-1	0.8
Prevailing Wind: Polar	0	0	0	0	0	0.7	0	0	0	0
: Westerlies Zone	0	0.9	0	0	1	0.8	0	0	0	0
: Subtropical	0	0.1	0	0	0	0.1	0.1	1	0	0
: Monsoon Zone	1	0	0	1	0	0	0	0	1	0.5
: Trades Zone	1	0	1	0	0	0	0	0	0	0.5
: Intertropical	0	0	0	0	0	0	0	0	0	0
: Transition	0	0.8	0	0	0	0	0	0	0	0
No oceans (1=yes)	0	0	0	0	-1	0	0	0	0	0
Fresh water (cub/kil)	153	26	.	9	9	337	1	9	0.4	239

Characteristics	Yi-Miao	Yoruba	Yugoslav	Zambo	Zulu
Coastline: length (km)	14500	836	1210	910	2520
: length km/cap	8	9	23	220	64
Zones: Sea territory	12	35	157	200	10
: Continental shelf (m)	0	195	157	200	175
: Excl. fish (nm)	0				175
: Extend. econ. zone (nm)	0	194			0
: 200-Mi EEZ, area	0	207000	173000	160000	889000
: Contiguous zone (nm)	0	0	0	0	0
Inland waterways (km)	110000	8330	5280	2220	35
Inland waterways/cap	0.1	0.1	0.1	0.5	0
Water area: (km sq)	271000	12700	3620	9240	1
: area/cap	0.2	0.1	0.1	5	0
Access: Number of ports	12	6	35		7
: Natural Harbour (1=yes)	10	0	0.6		0.2
: Number of outlets	0	0	0	0	0
: Island (1=yes)	0	0	0.2	0.2	0.1
: Landlocked (1=yes)	0	0	9	0.3	0.1
Ships: Number/cap	1	0.4	81	0	4
: tonnage (dwt)/cap	17	6			0
Offshore Reserves: oil/cap	0	0.1	0.1	0	0
: gas/cap	0	0	0	0	0
Fish supply kgrm/year/cap	0	0	0	0	0
Marine Biology: Arctic	0	0	0	0	0
: NW American Boreal	0	0	0	0	0
: N Pacific, American	0	0	0	0	0
: Tropical East Pacific	0	0	0	0	0
: South Pacific	0	0	0	0	0
: Antiboreal	0	0	0	0	0
: Atlantic Boreal	0	0	0	0	0
: Atlantic Warm Temp	0	0	0.8	0	0.9
: Tropical Indo-West-Pacif	0	0	0.8	0	0
: East Asia Boreal	1	0	0	0	0
: North Pacific, East Asia	1	0	0	0	0
: Indo-Australian	0	0	0	1	0
: Tropical Atlantic	0	1	0	0	0.9
Coral reef (1=yes)	0	0	0	1	0
Salinities	34	33	28	33	31
Ocean circulation	0	0	-0.4	1	0.2
Prevailing Wind: Polar	0	0	0.8	0	0
: Westerlies Zone	0	0	0	0	0
: Subtropical	1	0	0.2	0	0.9
: Monsoon Zone	0	0	0	0	0
: Trades Zone	0	1	0	1	0
: Intertropical	1	0	0	0	0.1
: Transition	0	0	0	0	0.1
No oceans (1=yes)	0	0	0	0	0
Fresh water (cub/kil)	460	4	33	0.9	8

9

CLIMATIC RESOURCES ACROSS ETHNIC CULTURES

Many of the authors cited in Chapter 1 have noted the effects of climate on various ethnic cultures. This chapter provides comparative statistics for a variety of climatic variables across ethnic cultures. For a full discussion of the methodology used to generate these estimates, please refer to Chapter 1 which gives important caveats. This chapter first gives summary statistics of the variables reported: the number of countries/cultures for which each variable was available, the number of ethnic cultures covered, weighted averages (by population) and simple averages; these averages can be used as benchmarks. Then a lengthy comparative table is presented which provides raw statistics across the ethnic groups defined in Chapter 1.

Most of the variables are self explanatory, though some merit commentary. All of the statistics should be considered as estimates which have undergone rounding and certain adjustments. Meteorological estimates are averages recorded over a 30-year or similar period. For example, "Temp monthly high (min C)" records the lowest level of monthly high temperatures, in Celsius; "Temp monthly high (max C)" measures the highest recorded level of monthly high temperatures. Some of the variables represent interactions. For example, the variable "High temp @ max humidity" is the estimate for the highest temperature during the month when average afternoon humidity is at its highest (a proxy for physiological heat/humidity stress). Similarly, the variable "High humid @ max temp" estimates the maximum humidity level during the month having the highest temperature. Other variables measure the extent to which certain climatic events (e.g. snowfall) are likely to occur where an ethnic group resides. "Flooding risk (10=high)" and other risk variables estimate whether these are a common occurrence. Finally, climatic types are given across groups based on Trewartha's modification of Koppen's classification scheme. A given group can be exposed to more than one climatic type, or (as a group's population may be geographically dispersed) be exposed only partially to a climatic type.

Summary Statistics:
Climatic Resources

Characteristics	Number of Countries Covered	Number of Ethnic Groups Covered	Weighted Average by Pop 1994	Simple Average	Simple Standard Deviation
Latitude (absolute degrees)	234	426	28.80	21.60	16.05
Temperature: degrees (C)	234	426	17.53	20.35	7.63
: monthly high (min C)	234	426	22.08	25.98	8.96
: monthly high (max C)	234	426	41.04	38.37	4.49
: monthly low (min C)	234	426	-8.11	0.81	15.65
: monthly low (max C)	234	426	15.57	15.49	5.76
Humidity: morning min (%)	234	426	56.94	67.29	18.20
: morning max (%)	234	426	81.77	86.13	7.99
: afternoon min (%)	234	426	42.00	49.89	17.45
: afternoon max (%)	234	426	70.28	73.74	9.93
High temp @ max humidity	234	426	23.73	22.33	11.09
High humidity @ max temp	234	426	51.55	56.16	18.09
Rain: monthly min (mm)	234	426	15.93	18.74	24.21
: monthly max (mm)	234	426	198.17	243.24	205.71
: days/month min	234	426	3.18	3.36	3.81
: days/month max	234	426	13.24	15.65	6.05
Snow: persistent (1=yes)	234	426	0.44	0.22	0.40
: intermittent (1=yes)	234	426	0.50	0.30	0.44
Frost present (1=yes)	234	426	0.62	0.54	0.48
Evaporation (1=low)	234	426	0.31	-0.03	0.85
Barometric pressure: July	234	426	1008.07	1011.67	5.07
: January	234	426	1018.43	1014.74	4.61
Risks: Typhoon (10=high)	234	426	2.57	0.79	2.61
: Flooding (10=high)	234	426	5.48	1.69	3.63
: Tropical storm (10=high)	234	426	0.09	260.17	1.20
: Windstorm (10=high)	234	426	2.18	1.39	3.35
: Drought (10=high)	234	426	2.91	1.81	3.66
Climate Type: Tropical wet	234	426	0.07	0.16	0.36
: Tropical monsoon	234	426	0.21	0.10	0.28
: Tropical wet & dry	234	426	0.37	0.37	0.47
: Steppe, low latitude	234	426	0.35	0.26	0.42
: Desert, low latitude	234	426	0.18	0.20	0.38
: Steppe, middle latitude	234	426	0.30	0.08	0.26
: Desert, middle latitude	234	426	0.25	0.05	0.21
: Subtropical, humid	234	426	0.51	0.12	0.32
: Mediterranean	234	426	0.06	0.07	0.24
: Marine, west coast	234	426	0.10	0.09	0.27
: Cont humid hot summer	234	426	0.33	0.07	0.24
: Cont humid cool summer	234	426	0.34	0.08	0.27
: Subarctic	234	426	0.03	0.02	0.13
: Tundra	234	426	0.03	0.02	0.12
: Ice cap	234	426	0.00	0.00	0.05
: Dry steppe wasteland	234	426	0.03	0.10	0.29
: Temperate highland	234	426	0.04	0.02	0.12
: Temp desert dry summer	234	426	0.00	0.01	0.08
: Temp desert dry winter	234	426	0.01	0.02	0.12
: Highland	234	426	0.37	0.20	0.39

Characteristics	Abadkis	Abkhaz	Acholi	Afar	Afro-European	Akan	Albanian	Ambo	Amerind	Amerind-Mestizo
Latitude (abs degrees)	27	41	0.2	12	18	7	42	8	23	39
Temperature: degrees (C)	17	13	24	21	26	27	13	26	16	17
: monthly high (min C)	24	20	29	29	33	32	19	28	24	25
: monthly high (max C)	36	40	36	37	36	38	41	37	33	40
: monthly low (min C)	-2	-15	15	4	14	15	-14	14	-3	-6
: monthly low (max C)	18	14	15	11	20	21	10	21	10	6
Humidity: morning min (%)	68	57	78	56	77	95	71	77	69	81
: morning max (%)	90	80	89	85	88	97	86	84	87	92
: afternoon min (%)	53	40	54	36	61	61	42	74	33	60
: afternoon max (%)	84	65	72	73	73	77	68	78	58	79
High temp @ max humid	28	9	25	24	31	27	13	28	22	14
High humid @ max temp	61	45	56	44	70	68	43	70	37	61
Rain: monthly min (mm)	3	40	46	4	15	15	36	0	10	56
: monthly max (mm)	373	75	175	229	180	178	165	117	181	109
: days/month min	0.2	12	9	2	2	1	1	4	4	6
: days/month max	21		19	22	9	10	15	8	24	9
Snow: persistent (1=yes)	1	1	0	0	0	0	0	0	0.1	0
: intermittent (1=yes)	1	1	0	0	0	0	1	0	0.1	1
Frost present (1=yes)	1	1	0	0	0	0	1	0	0.1	1
Evaporation (1=low)			1	0.7	-1	-1	-1	-1	-0.1	
Barometric pressure: July	1000	1010	1010	1010	1010	1010	1010	1020	1010	1010
: January	1020	1020	1010	1020	1020	1010	1020	1010	1020	1000
Risks: Typhoon (10=high)	0	0	0	0	0	0	0	0	0	0
: Flooding (10=high)	0	0	0	0	0	0	0	0	0.2	0
: Tropical storm (10=high)	0	0	0	0	0	0	0	0	0	0
: Windstorm (10=high)	0	0	0	0	0	0	0	0	0	0
: Drought (10=high)	0	0	0	0.1	0	0	0	0	0.1	0
Climate Type: Tropical wet	0	0	0	0	0	1	0	0	0	0
: Tropical monsoon	0	0	0	0	0	0	0	0	0	0
: Tropical wet & dry	0	0	1	0	1	0	0	0	0	1
: Steppe, low latitude	0	0	0	0	0	0	0	1	0	0
: Desert, low latitude	0	0	0	0.1	0	0	0	0	0.9	0
: Steppe, middle latitude	0	0	0	0	0	0	0	0	0.1	0
: Desert, middle latitude	0	0	0	0	0	0	0	0	0.8	0
: Subtropical, humid	1	1	0	0	0	0	0	0	0.1	0
: Mediterranean	0	0	0	0	0	0	1	0	0.1	0
: Marine, west coast	0	0	0	0	0	0	0	0	0	0
: Cont humid hot sum	0	0	0	0	0	0	0	0	0	0
: Cont humid cool sum	0	0	0	0	0	0	0	0	0	0
: Subarctic	0	0	0	0	0	0	0	0	0	0
: Tundra	0	0	0	0	0	0	0	0	0	0
: Ice cap	0	0	0	0	0	0	0	0	0	0
: Dry steppe wasteland	0	0	0	0	0	0	0	0	0	0
: Temperate highland	0	0	0	0	0	0	0	0	0	0
: Temp desert dry sum	0	0	0	0	0	0	0	0	0	0
: Temp desert dry win	0	0	0	0	0	0	0	0	0	0
: Highland	1	1	1	0.9	0	0	0	0	0.9	0

Characteristics	Amhara	Ana-Ife	Andorran	Angolares	Anouis	Antandroy	Arab, other	Arab Berber	Arab Emirian	Arab Lebanese
Latitude (abs degrees)	12	6	42	27	6	19	32	32	25	34
Temperature: degrees (C)	17	27	9	21	26	18	25	24	25	21
: monthly high (min C)	27	32	13	24	31	27	25	28	29	25
: monthly high (max C)	34	35	36	38	36	35	45	46	48	42
: monthly low (min C)	0	15	-18	3	15	12	-0.7	0.8	3	-1
: monthly low (max C)	7	21	5	15	20	15	12	17	23	18
Humidity: morning min (%)	56	95	78	65	93	85	60	55	61	64
: morning max (%)	86	97	87	84	96	94	82	73	82	72
: afternoon min (%)	33	61	55	55	71	49	41	52	59	57
: afternoon max (%)	73	77	79	74	82	71	64	72	65	70
High temp @ max humid	21	27	11	19	29	26	17	29	36	17
High humid @ max temp	44	68	48	57	72	64	44	68	64	57
Rain: monthly min (mm)	5	15	34	13	41	8	0.9	0.1	0	0
: monthly max (mm)	300	178	105	123	495	300	72	91	36	191
: days/month min	2	1	4	1	3	0	0.5	0.2	0	0
: days/month max	28	10	15	13	18	7	8	11	2	15
Snow: persistent (1=yes)	0	0	0	0	0	0	0	0	0	0
: intermittent (1=yes)	0	0	0	0	0	0	0.4	0	0	0
Frost present (1=yes)	0	0	1	0	0	0	0.9	1	0	0
Evaporation (1=low)	-1	-1	-1	0.7	-1	-1	-0.7	-1	-1	-1
Barometric pressure: July	1010	1010	1020	1020	1010	1020	1010	1010	999	1010
: January	1020	1010	1020	1020	1010	1010	1020	1020	1020	1020
Risks: Typhoon (10=high)	0	0	0	0	0	0	0	0	0	0
: Flooding (10=high)	0	0	0	0	0	0	0	0	0	0
: Tropical storm (10=high)	0	0	0	0	0	0	0	0	0	0
: Windstorm (10=high)	0	0	0	0	0	0	0	0	0	0
: Drought (10=high)	0	1	0	0.3	1	1	1	1	1	0
Climate Type: Tropical wet	0	0	0	1	1	0	0	0	0	0
: Tropical monsoon	0	0	0	0	0	0	0	0	0	0
: Tropical wet & dry	0	1	0	0	0	1	0	0	0	0
: Steppe, low latitude	0	0	0	0	0	1	0.4	0	0	0
: Desert, low latitude	0	0	0	0	0	0	0.4	0	1	0
: Steppe, middle latitude	0	0	0	0	0	0	0	0	0	0
: Desert, middle latitude	0	0	0	0	0	0	0	0	0	0
: Subtropical, humid	0	0	0	0	0	0	0	0	0	0
: Mediterranean	0	0	0	0	0	0	0.5	1	0	1
: Marine, west coast	0	0	0	0	0	0	0	0	0	0
: Cont humid hot sum	0	0	0	0	0	0	0	0	0	0
: Cont humid cool sum	0	0	0	0	0	0	0	0	0	0
: Subarctic	0	0	0	0	0	0	0	0	0	0
: Tundra	0	0	0	0	0	0	0	0	0	0
: Ice cap	0	0	0	0	0	0	0	0	0	0
: Dry steppe wasteland	0	0	0	0	0	0	0	0	0	0
: Temperate highland	0	0	0	0	0	0	0	0	0	0
: Temp desert dry sum	0	0	0	0	0	0	0	0	0	0
: Temp desert dry win	0	0	0	0	0	0	0	0	0	0
: Highland	1	0	1	0	0	0	0	0	0	0

Characteristics	Arab Omani	Arab Palestin.	Arab Quatar	Arab Saudi	Arab Sudanic	Arab Total	Arauca- nian	Armenian	Assamese	Assyrian
Latitude (abs degrees)	23	32	25	24	12	29	36	40	27	33
Temperature: degrees (C)	29	20	26	23	29	23	17	10	17	21
: monthly high (min C)	31	25	29	30	40	27	27	14	24	25
: monthly high (max C)	47	42	48	45	48	45	37	40	36	49
: monthly low (min C)	11	-3	3	-7	5	-0.6	-4	-25	-2	-8
: monthly low (max C)	26	12	23	19	19	14	6	11	-1	-2
Humidity: morning min (%)	58	50	61	33	19	53	70	61	18	18
: morning max (%)	82	76	82	65	70	79	93	88	68	32
: afternoon min (%)	60	67	59	19	10	37	38	37	90	84
: afternoon max (%)	80	14	65	44	44	60	64	74	53	12
High temp @ max humid	33	40	36	21	36	20	14	4	84	52
High humid @ max temp	72		64	31	13	41	40	37	28	18
Rain: monthly min (mm)		0	0	0		0.6		8	61	13
: monthly max (mm)	28	143	36	25	97	73	84	59	3	0
: days/month min		0	0	0	0	0.4	0	2	373	28
: days/month max	2	12	2	4	8	8	84	11	0.2	0
Snow: persistent (1=yes)	0	0	0	0	0	0.3	0	1	21	5
: intermittent (1=yes)	2	1		1	1	0.3	0	1	1	0
Frost present (1=yes)	0		0		1	0.9	1	1	1	
Evaporation (1=low)	-1	1	-1	-1		-0.7		0.7		-1
Barometric pressure: July	1000	1010	999	1010	1010	1010	1010	1010	1000	1010
: January	1020	1020	1020	1020	1010	1020	1010	1020	1020	1020
Risks: Typhoon (10=high)	0	0	0	0	0	0	0	0	0	0
: Flooding (10=high)	0	0	0	0	10	0	0	0	0	0
: Tropical storm (10=high)	1	0	1	0	1	0.3	0	0	10	0
: Windstorm (10=high)	0	0	0	0	0	0.1	0	0	0	0
: Drought (10=high)	0	0	0	1	0	0	1	0	0	0
Climate Type: Tropical wet	0	0	0	0	0	0	1	0	0	0
: Tropical monsoon	0	0	0	0	0	0	1	0	0	0
: Tropical wet & dry	0	0	0	0	0	0.3	0	0	0	0
: Steppe, low latitude	0	0	0	0	0	0.6	0	0	0	0
: Desert, low latitude	1	0	1	1	1	0	1	0	0	0
: Steppe, middle latitude	0	0	0	0	0	0	0	0	0	1
: Desert, middle latitude	0	0	0	0	0	0.3	0	0.1	0	0
: Subtropical, humid	0	0	0	0	0	0	0	0.1	1	0
: Mediterranean	0	1	0	0	0	0	1	0.9	0	0
: Marine, west coast	0	0	0	0	0	0	0	0	0	0
: Cont humid hot sum	0	0	0	0	0	0	0	0	0	0
: Cont humid cool sum	0	0	0	0	0	0	0	0	0	0
: Subarctic	0	0	0	0	0	0	0	0	0	0
: Tundra	0	0	0	0	0	0	0	0	0	0
: Ice cap	0	0	0	0	0	0	0	0	0	0
: Dry steppe wasteland	0	0	0	0	0.9	0.1	0	0	0	0
: Temperate highland	0	0	0	0	0	0	0	0	0	0
: Temp desert dry sum	1	0	1	0	0	0	0	0	0	0
: Temp desert dry win	0	0	0	0	0	0	0	0	0	0
: Highland	0	0	0	0	0	0	0	0.9	0	0

Characteristics	Austrian	Avar	Aymara	Azande	Azerbai-jani	Bagirmi Sara	Bahraini	Bai	Bakhtiari	Bakongo
Latitude (abs degrees)	47	40	14	8	36	12	26	35	33	8
Temperature: degrees (C)	8	14	17	26	14	28	25	11	15	26
: monthly high (min C)	13	12	23	34	16	36	29	13	18	28
: monthly high (max C)	38	40	30	39	42	46	45	43	43	37
: monthly low (min C)	-23	-27	3	12	-23	8	5	-23	-21	14
: monthly low (max C)	9	10	9	19	13	19	24	15	15	21
Humidity: morning min (%)	72	62	84	74	53	32	69	46	47	77
: morning max (%)	86	91	94	89	82	93	85	74	77	84
: afternoon min (%)	49	36	56	49	38	10	63	46	39	74
: afternoon max (%)	76	75	77	66	75	72	22	74	75	78
High temp @ max humid	3	3	25	32	8	31	65	30	11	28
High humid @ max temp	54	36	65	57	39	13		72	41	77
Rain: monthly min (mm)	39	8	4	3	35		0	2	3	0
: monthly max (mm)	84	53	63	191	49	320	18	243	46	117
: days/month min	10	2	1	0.2	7	0	0	3	0.2	0
: days/month max	15	11	12	14	1	22	2	13	4	8
Snow: persistent (1=yes)	1	1	1	0	1	0	0	1	1	0
: intermittent (1=yes)	1	1	1	0	1	0	0	1	1	0
Frost present (1=yes)	1	1	1	0.2	1	0	0	1	1	0
Evaporation (1=low)	1	1	-0.5	0.8	-0.6	0	0	1	-1	-1
Barometric pressure: July	1010	1010	1020	1010	1000	1010	999	1010	999	1020
: January	1020	1020	1010	1010	1020	1010	1020	1030	1020	1010
Risks: Typhoon (10=high)	0	0	0	0	0	0	0	0	0	0
: Flooding (10=high)	0	0	0	3	0	0	0	1	0	1
: Tropical storm (10=high)	0	0	0	0.7	0	0	0	0	0	0
: Windstorm (10=high)	0	0	0	0.7	0	0	0	0	0	0
: Drought (10=high)	0	0	0	0.2	0	1	0	0	0	0
Climate Type: Tropical wet	0	0	0	0	0	0	0	0	0	0
: Tropical monsoon	0	0	0	0	0	0	0	0	0	0
: Tropical wet & dry	0	0	0	0	0	1	0	0	0	1
: Steppe, low latitude	0	0	0	0	0	0	0	0	0	0
: Desert, low latitude	0	0	0	0	0	0	1	0	0	0
: Steppe, middle latitude	0	0	0	0	0.6	0	0	0	0	0
: Desert, middle latitude	0	0	0	0	0.6	0	0	0	0	0
: Subtropical, humid	0	0	0	0	0.4	0	0	0	0	0
: Mediterranean	0	0	0	0	0	0	0	0	0	0
: Marine, west coast	0	0	0	0	0	0	0	0	0	0
: Cont humid hot sum	0	0	0	0	0	0	0	0	0	0
: Cont humid cool sum	1	0	0	0	0	0	0	0	0	0
: Subarctic	0	0	0	0	0	0	0	0	0	0
: Tundra	0	0	0	0	0	0	0	0	0	0
: Ice cap	0	0	0	0	0	0	0	0	0	0
: Dry steppe wasteland	0	0	0	0.2	0	1	0	0	0	0
: Temperate highland	0	0	0.5	0	0	0	0	0	0	0
: Temp desert dry sum	0	0	0	0	0	0	0	0	0	0
: Temp desert dry win	0	0	0	0	0	0	0	1	1	0
: Highland	0	1	1	0.7	0.4	0	0	1	1	0

Characteristics	Balante	Baluchi	Bambara	Bamileke-Bamum	Banda	Bangi-Ngale	Bantu	Baoule	Bari	Bariba
Latitude (abs degrees)	12	30	14	4	5	7	18	6	12	6
Temperature: degrees (C)	28	19	29	25	26	25	18	26	29	27
: monthly high (min C)	35	22	36	31	33	32	26	31	40	31
: monthly high (max C)	43	46	47	36	37	36	35	36	48	35
: monthly low (min C)	13	-10	8	14	14	14	0.5	15	5	18
: monthly low (max C)	21	-16	19	17	18	19	9	20	9	22
Humidity: morning min (%)	70	29	33	97	89	88	44	93	18	83
: morning max (%)	87	62	94	98	96	95	77	96	67	91
: afternoon min (%)	45	25	18	62	53	61	28	71	10	68
: afternoon max (%)	74	61	73	75	72	73	58	82	41	78
High temp @ max humid	31	26	31	27	30	31	26	29	37	26
High humid @ max temp	72	29	40	67	56	71	28	72	13	74
Rain: monthly min (mm)	0	0	0	23	4	2	0	41	0	13
: monthly max (mm)	254	188	348	295	225	222	193	495	71	366
: days/month min	13	0.7	1	3	1	0.1	0.6	1	6	1
: days/month max		10	17	24	18	16	18	18		13
Snow: persistent (1=yes)	0	0	0	0	0	0	0	0	0	0
: intermittent (1=yes)	0	1	0	0	0	0	0	0	0	0
Frost present (1=yes)	0	1	0	0	0	0	-1	0	-1	0
Evaporation (1=low)	-1	-1	-1	0	-1	-1	-1	0	0	0
Barometric pressure: July	1010	999	1010	1010	1010	1010	1020	1010	1010	1010
: January	1010	1020	1010	1010	1010	1010	1010	1010	1010	1010
Risks: Typhoon (10=high)	0	0	0	0	0	0	0	0	0	0
: Flooding (10=high)	0	7	0	0	7	0	0	0	0	0
: Tropical storm (10=high)	0	0	0	0	0	0	0	0	0	0
: Windstorm (10=high)	1	0	1	1	0.3	1	1	1	1	1
: Drought (10=high)	0	0	0	0	0.3	0	0.3	0	0	0
Climate Type: Tropical wet	0	0	0	1	0	1	1	0	0	0
: Tropical monsoon	1	0	0	0	0	0	0	0	0	0
: Tropical wet & dry	0	0	1	0	1	0	0	1	1	1
: Steppe, low latitude	0	0	0	0	0	0	0	0	0	0
: Desert, low latitude	0	0	0	0	0	0	0	0	0	0
: Steppe, middle latitude	0	0	0	0	0	0	0	0	0	0
: Desert, middle latitude	0	0	0	0	0	0	0	0	0	0
: Subtropical, humid	0	0	0	0	0	0	0	0	0	0
: Mediterranean	0	0	0	0	0	0	0	0	0	0
: Marine, west coast	0	0	0	0	0	0	0	0	0	0
: Cont humid hot sum	0	0	0	0	0	0	0	0	0	0
: Cont humid cool sum	0	0	0	0	0	0	0	0	0	0
: Subarctic	0	0	0	0	0	0	0	0	0	0
: Tundra	0	0	0	0	0	0	0	0	0	0
: Ice cap	0	0	0	0	0	0	0	0	0	0
: Dry steppe wasteland	0	1	0	0	0	0	0	0	0	0
: Temperate highland	0	0	0	0	0	0	0	0	0	0
: Temp desert dry sum	0	0	0	0	0	0	0	0	0	0
: Temp desert dry win	0	0	0	0	0	0	0	0	0	0
: Highland	0	0	0	0	0.3	0	0	0	0	0

Characteristics	Barotze	Baskhir	Basque	Bassa	Batswana	Bayad	Beja	Belgian	Belorus-sian	Bemba
Latitude (abs degrees)	20	55	40	6	24	48	12	51	53	20
Temperature: degrees (C)										
: monthly high (min C)	21	3	14	25	20	-4	29	10	4	21
: monthly high (max C)	28	32	16	29	31	-6	40	13	32	28
: monthly low (min C)	38	-32	39	34	42	36	48	37	-32	38
: monthly low (max C)	4	5	-10	13	-4	-44	4	-17	5	4
Humidity: morning min (%)	14	58	8	20	-10	1	5	6	59	14
: morning max (%)	39	87	58	87	55	64	19	87	87	39
: afternoon min (%)	85	43	86	95	74	88	18	94	43	85
: afternoon max (%)	19	83	33	76	55	40	67	65	83	19
High temp @ max humid	71	-5	71	86	74	75	01	86	-5	71
High humid @ max temp	26	54	9	27	29	-16	41	6	54	26
Rain: monthly min (mm)	23	36	33	80	63	54	37	68	35	23
: monthly max (mm)	231	88	11	31	0	0	13	53	86	231
: days/month min	0	12	53	996	107	76	0	95	12	0
: days/month max	21	23	2	5	0.1	0	71	13	22	21
Snow: persistent (1=yes)	0	0	10	26	8	1	0	21		0
: intermittent (1=yes)	0	1	1	0	0	0	6	1	0.1	0
Frost present (1=yes)	0	0	1	-1	0	1	0	1	0.1	0
Evaporation (1=low)	0		-1		-1	0	1	1	0.9	0
Barometric pressure: July	1020	1010	1020	1010	1020	1010	1010	1020	1010	1020
: January	1010	1020	1020	1010	1010	1030	1010	1010	1020	1010
Risks: Typhoon (10=high)	0	0	0	0	0	0	0	0	0	0
: Flooding (10=high)	0	0	0	0	0	0	0	0	0	0
: Tropical storm (10=high)	0	0	0	1	1	0	1	0	0	0
: Windstorm (10=high)	0	0	0	1	0	0	0	0	0	0
: Drought (10=high)	1	0	0	0	0	0	0	0	0	1
Climate Type: Tropical wet	1	0	0	1	0	0	0	0	0	1
: Tropical monsoon	0	0	0	1	0	0	0	0	0	0
: Tropical wet & dry	0	0	0	0	0	0	0	0	0	0
: Steppe, low latitude	0	0	0	0	1	0	0	0	0	0
: Desert, low latitude	0	0	0	0	0	0	1	0	0	0
: Steppe, middle latitude	0	1	0	0	0	1	0	0	0	0
: Desert, middle latitude	0	0	0	0	0	0	0	0	0	0
: Subtropical, humid	0	0	0	0	0	0	0	0	0	0
: Mediterranean	0	0	1	0	0	0	0	0	0	0
: Marine, west coast	0	0	0	0	0	0	0	1	0	0
: Cont humid hot sum	0	0	0	0	0	0	0	0	0.1	0
: Cont humid cool sum	0	1	0	0	0	0	0	0	0	0
: Subarctic	0	0	0	0	0	0	0	0	0.1	0
: Tundra	0	1	0	0	0	0	0	0	0	0
: Ice cap	0	0	0	0	0	0	0	0	0.1	0
: Dry steppe wasteland	0	1	0	0	0	0	0	0	0	0
: Temperate highland	0	0	0	0	0	0	0	0	0.1	0
: Temp desert dry sum	0	0	0	0	0	0	0	0	0	0
: Temp desert dry win	0	1	0	0	0	0	0	0	0.1	0
: Highland	0	1	0	0	0	0	0	0		0

Characteristics	Bengali	Berber	Bete	Betsileo	Betsimi-Saraka	Bhutia	Bihari	Black	Black Amerind	Boa
Latitude (abs degrees)	23	35	6	19	19	27	26	29	6	7
Temperature: degrees (C)										
: monthly high (min C)	25	23	26	18	18	17	19	18	14	25
: monthly high (max C)	29	26	31	27	27	24	25	28	22	32
: monthly low (min C)	42	46	36	35	35	36	38	39	24	36
: monthly low (max C)	24	8	15	1	1	-2	0.6	-6	4	14
Humidity: morning min (%)	37	80	20	12	12	18	20	14	7	19
: morning max (%)	74	86	93	85	85	68	59	73	82	88
: afternoon min (%)	37	58	96	94	94	90	85	84	88	95
: afternoon max (%)	74	70	71	49	49	53	48	53	51	61
High temp @ max humid	31	58	82	71	71	84	81	63	64	73
High humid @ max temp	42	16	29	26	26	28	29	18	19	31
Rain: monthly min (mm)	4	61	72	64	64	61	56	59	53	71
: monthly max (mm)	437	104	41	300	300	373	391	48	51	3
: days/month min	0	0.3	495	8	8	0.2	0.1	139	160	222
: days/month max	16	11	3	7	7	21	20	6	6	0.1
Snow: persistent (1=yes)	0	1	18	21	21	0	0.7	13	20	16
: intermittent (1=yes)	0		0	0	0	1	0.7	0.5	1	0
Frost present (1=yes)	1	-1	0	0	0	1	0.1	0.5	-1	0
Evaporation (1=low)	-1		0	-1	-1		1	0.1		1
Barometric pressure: July	1000	1010	1010	1020	1020	1000	1000	1020	1010	1010
: January	1020	1020	1010	1010	1010	1020	1020	1020	1010	1010
Risks: Typhoon (10=high)	0	0	0	0	0	0	0	4	0	0
: Flooding (10=high)	10	0	0	1	1	10	3	2	0	0
: Tropical storm (10=high)	0	0	0	0	0	0	0	0.1	0	0
: Windstorm (10=high)	0	0	0	0	1	0	0	0.4	0	0
: Drought (10=high)	1	0	1	1	1	1	3	2	1	10
Climate Type: Tropical wet	0	0	1	1	1	0	0	0.4	0	1
: Tropical monsoon	0	0	0	0	0	0	0	0.1	1	0
: Tropical wet & dry	1	0	0	0	0	0	1	0.3	1	1
: Steppe, low latitude	0	0	0	0	0	0	0	0.8	0	0
: Desert, low latitude	0	0.6	0	0	0	0	0	0.5	1	1
: Steppe, middle latitude	0	0.4	0	0	0	0	0	0.4	1	0
: Desert, middle latitude	0	0	0	0	0	0	0	0.7	0	0
: Subtropical, humid	0	0	0	0	0	0	0	0.1	0	0
: Mediterranean	0	0	0	0	0	0	0	0.3	0	0
: Marine, west coast	0	1	0	0	0	0	0	0.4	0	0
: Cont humid hot sum	0	0	0	0	0	0	0	0.4	0	0
: Cont humid cool sum	0	0	0	0	0	0	0	0	0	0
: Subarctic	0	0	0	0	0	0	0	0	0	0
: Tundra	0	0	0	0	0	0	0	0	0	0
: Ice cap	0	0	0	0	0	0	0	0	0	0
: Dry steppe wasteland	0	0	0	0	0	0	0	0	0	0
: Temperate highland	0	0	0	0	0	0	0	0.1	0	0
: Temp desert dry sum	0	0.7	0	0	0	0	0.7	0.4	0	0
: Temp desert dry win	0	1	0	0	0	0	0		0	0
: Highland	0	0	0	0	0	1	0		0	1

Characteristics	Bobo	Bounty Mutineers	Brazilian	Breton	Bubi	Bulgarian	Bullom	Bura	Burman	Bush Negro
Latitude (abs degrees)	12	28	27	46	3	43	8	9	19	5
Temperature: degrees (C)	29	24	22	12	26	9	27	28	28	27
: monthly high (min C)	37	30	25	15	29	16	31	34	34	33
: monthly high (max C)	48	36	39	40	32	37	35	40	41	37
: monthly low (min C)	9	13	6	-15	17	-21	19	16	13	17
: monthly low (max C)	19	19	16	9	19	8	21	21	22	19
Humidity: morning min (%)	37	70	66	82	85	71	80	81	71	85
: morning max (%)	84	78	85	91	95	90	91	87	89	91
: afternoon min (%)	19	68	56	54	85	46	67	65	52	66
: afternoon max (%)	69	75	76	82	95	78	82	80	88	80
High temp @ max humid	31	29	20	57	30	2	28	29	29	30
High humid @ max temp	25	73	56	35	89	46	71	72	64	67
Rain: monthly min (mm)	0	59	13	12	5	28	3	25	3	70
: monthly max (mm)	296	232	270	64	302	87	902	460	582	342
: days/month min	1	6	3	17	3	7	0.7	2	0.3	8
: days/month max	15	18	19		24	13	28	20	26	23
Snow: persistent (1=yes)	0	0	0	0	0	0	0	0	0	0
: intermittent (1=yes)	0	0	0	1	0	1	0	0	0	0
Frost present (1=yes)	0	1	0	1	0	1	0	0	0	0
Evaporation (1=low)	-0.3	-0.7	0.6	0	-1	0	-1	0	0	-0.1
Barometric pressure: July	1010	1020	1020	1010	1010	1010	1010	1010	1010	1010
: January	1010	1010	1020	1020	1020	1020	1020	1010	1020	1010
Risks: Typhoon (10=high)	0	0	0	0	0	0	0	0	0	0
: Flooding (10=high)	0	0	0	0	1	0	0	0	1	0
: Tropical storm (10=high)	0	0	0.4	0	0	0	0	0	0	0
: Windstorm (10=high)	0	0	0	1	0	0	0	0	0	0
: Drought (10=high)	1	0	0	0	0	0	0	1	0	0
Climate Type: Tropical wet	0	0	0.6	0	1	0	0	0	0	0
: Tropical monsoon	0	0	0	0	0	0	1	0	1	0.9
: Tropical wet & dry	0.7	0	0.4	0	0	0	0	1	0	0
: Steppe, low latitude	0.3	0	0	0	0	0	0	0	0	0
: Desert, low latitude	0	0	0	0	0	0	0	0	0	0
: Steppe, middle latitude	0	0	0	0	0	0	0	0	0	0
: Desert, middle latitude	0	0	0	0	0	0	0	0	0	0
: Subtropical, humid	0	0.3	0	0	0	0	0	0	0	0
: Mediterranean	0	0	0	0	0	0	0	0	0	0
: Marine, west coast	0	0.7	0	1	0	0	0	0	0	0
: Cont humid hot sum	0	0	0	0	0	0	0	0	0	0
: Cont humid cool sum	0	0	0	0	0	1	0	0	0	0
: Subarctic	0	0	0	0	0	0	0	0	0	0
: Tundra	0	0	0	0	0	0	0	0	0	0
: Ice cap	0	0	0	0	0	0	0	0	0	0
: Dry steppe wasteland	0.3	0	0	0	0	0	0	0	0	0
: Temperate highland	0	0	0	0	0	0	0	0	0	0
: Temp desert dry sum	0	0	0	0	0	0	0	0	0	0
: Temp desert dry win	0	0	0	0	0	0	0	0	0	0
: Highland	0	0	0	0	0	0	0	0	0	0

Characteristics	Bushman	Capver-dien	Caroli-nians	Catalan	Chahar Aimak	Chamba	Chamorro	Chiga	Chin	Chinese
Latitude (abs degrees)	24	39	17	40	33	4	14	0.2	19	15
Temperature: degrees (C)	20	20	26	15	10	25	27	24	28	25
: monthly high (min C)	31	21	29	16	14	31	29	29	34	32
: monthly high (max C)	42	40	32	39	40	36	32	36	41	38
: monthly low (min C)	-4	-1	19	-10	-21	14	19	12	13	7
: monthly low (max C)	10	13	22	8	-11	17	22	15	22	21
Humidity: morning min (%)	55	62	85	58	51	97	85	78	71	83
: morning max (%)	74	85	91	86	80	98	91	89	89	90
: afternoon min (%)	55	48	69	33	22	62	69	54	52	58
: afternoon max (%)	74	72	79	71	70	75	79	72	88	72
High temp @ max humid	29	15	28	9	2	27	28	25	29	28
High humid @ max temp	63	49	77	33	23	67	77	56	64	66
Rain: monthly min (mm)	0	3	69	11	0	23	69	46	3	52
: monthly max (mm)	107	111	338	53	102	295	338	175	582	308
: days/month min	0.1	2	11	2	0.1	3	11	9	0.3	6
: days/month max	8	15	23	10	7	24	23	19	26	17
Snow: persistent (1=yes)	0	0	0	0	1	0	0	0	0	0.1
: intermittent (1=yes)	0	0	0	0	1	0	0	0	0	0.1
Frost present (1=yes)	1	0	0	1	1	0	0	0	0	0
Evaporation (1=low)	-1	-1	1	-1	-1	1	0	1	1	1
Barometric pressure: July	1020	1020	1010	1020	999	1010	1010	1010	1010	1010
: January	1010	1020	1010	1020	1020	1010	1010	1010	1020	1020
Risks: Typhoon (10=high)	0	0	10	0	0	0	0	0	0	3
: Flooding (10=high)	0	0	0	0	0	0	0	0	10	0
: Tropical storm (10=high)	0	0	0	0	0	0	0	0	0	3
: Windstorm (10=high)	0	0	0	0	0	0	0	0	0	0
: Drought (10=high)	1	0	0	0	0	0	0	0	0	0
Climate Type: Tropical wet	0	0	1	0	0	0	1	0	0	0
: Tropical monsoon	0	0	0	0	0	0	0	0	1	0
: Tropical wet & dry	0	0	0	0	0	1	0	1	0	0
: Steppe, low latitude	1	1	0	0	0	0	0	0	0	0
: Desert, low latitude	0	0	0	0	0	0	0	0	0	0
: Steppe, middle latitude	0	0	0	0	1	0	0	0	0	0
: Desert, middle latitude	0	0	0	0	0	0	0	0	0	0
: Subtropical, humid	0	0	0	0	0	0	0	0	0	0.4
: Mediterranean	0	0	0	1	0	0	0	0	0	0.1
: Marine, west coast	0	0	0	0	0	0	0	0	0	0
: Cont humid hot sum	0	0	0	0	0	0	0	0	0	0.6
: Cont humid cool sum	0	0	0	0	0	0	0	0	0	0.1
: Subarctic	0	0	0	0	0	0	0	0	0	0.1
: Tundra	0	0	0	0	0	0	0	0	0	0
: Ice cap	0	0	0	0	0	0	0	0	0	0
: Dry steppe wasteland	0	0	0	0	0	0	0	0	0	0
: Temperate highland	0	0	0	0	0	0	0	0	0	0.4
: Temp desert dry sum	0	0	0	0	0	0	0	0	0	0
: Temp desert dry win	0	0	0	0	0	0	0	0	0	0.1
: Highland	0	0	0	0	0	0	0	1	1	0.3

Characteristics	Chinese Mainland	Chokwe	Chuang	Chuvash	Circassian	Coloured	Comorian	Creole	Croatian	Czech
Latitude (abs degrees)	24	7	35	55	38	30	12	16	45	50
Temperature: degrees (C)	21	25	11	3	10	19	25	25	11	5
..monthly high (min C)	30	31	13	2	16	29	30	29	20	13
..monthly high (max C)	38	36	43	32	39	39	33	35	42	38
..monthly low (min C)	0	14	-23	-32	-23	-2	18	12	-25	-28
..monthly low (max C)	19	20	15	5	8	7	21	19	8	6
Humidity: morning min (%)	90	84	46	58	52	71	75	81	71	74
..morning max (%)	93	91	74	87	85	91	80	88	86	87
..afternoon min (%)	62	66	46	43	25	54	72	62	45	45
..afternoon max (%)	75	75	74	83	69	67	78	76	76	78
High temp @ max humid	18	30	30	-5	7	17	28	25	5	0.9
High humid @ max temp	64	73	72	54	26	54	73	65	46	49
Rain: monthly min (mm)	66	2	3	36	9	8	65	21	44	19
..monthly max (mm)	305	183	243	88	51	89	381	113	94	69
..days/month min	7	0.1	2	12	0.9	2	1	1	8	10
..days/month max	14	13	13	23		10	15	12	14	13
Snow: persistent (1=yes)	0	0	1	1	0.9		0	0	0	1
..intermittent (1=yes)	0	0				1				
Frost present (1=yes)	1	0	1	1	0.9				1	1
Evaporation (1=low)	0		1		0.9					1
Barometric pressure: July	1010	1020	1010	1010	-0.1	-1	0.1	0.6	-1	-1
..January	1020	1010	1030	1020	1010	1010	-1	-0.7	1010	1010
Risks: Typhoon (10=high)	10		10	0	1020	1010	1020	1020	1020	1020
..Flooding (10=high)	0	4	0	0	0	0	0	1010	0	0
..Tropical storm (10=high)	0	0	0	0	0	0	0	0	0.1	0
..Windstorm (10=high)	0	6	0	0	0	0	0	0.7	0	0
..Drought (10=high)	0	0.6	0	0	0	1	0	0.2	0	0
Climate Type: Tropical wet	0	0.1	0	0	0	0	0.1	0.6	0	0
..Tropical monsoon	0	0.4	0	0	0	0	0	0.7	0	0
..Tropical wet & dry	0	0.4	0	0	0	0	0.1	0.3	0	0
..Steppe, low latitude	0	0	0	0	0	0	0	0.2	0	0
..Desert, low latitude	0	0	0	0	0	1	0	0	0	0
..Steppe, middle latitude	0	0	0	0	1	0	0	0	0	0
..Desert, middle latitude	0	0	0	0	0	0	0	0	0	0
..Subtropical, humid	0	0	1	0	0	0	0	0	0	0
..Mediterranean	0	0	0	0	0	1	0	0	0	0
..Marine, west coast	0	0	0	0	0	0	0	0	0	0
..Cont humid hot sum	1	0	1	1	0	0	0	0	1	0
..Cont humid cool sum	0	0	0	1	0	0	0	0	0	1
..Subarctic	0	0	0	0	0	0	0	0	0	0
..Tundra	0	0	0	0	0	0	0	0	0	0
..Ice cap	0	0	0	0	0	0	0	0	0	0
..Dry steppe wasteland	0	0	0	0	0.9	0	0	0	0	0
..Temperate highland	0	0	0	0	0	1	0	0	0	0
..Temp desert dry sum	0	0	0	0	0	0	0	0	0	0
..Temp desert dry win	0	0	0	0	0	1	0	0	0	0
..Highland	0	0.6	1	1	0	0	0	0	0	0

Characteristics	Dagestani	Dai	Damara	Dan	Danish	Dinka	Dogon	Dong	Dravidian	Duala
Latitude (abs degrees)	53	35	24	6	56	12	14	35	21	3
Temperature: degrees (C)	4	11	18	26	8	29	29	11	24	26
: monthly high (min C)	3	13	25	31	10	40	36	13	28	29
: monthly high (max C)	33	43	36	36	33	48	47	43	46	32
: monthly low (min C)	-31	-23	-4	15	-24	19	8	-23	-1	17
: monthly low (max C)	6	6	9	20	8	19	19	46	22	19
Humidity: morning min (%)	59	15	27	92	70	18	33	46	35	85
: morning max (%)	88	46	62	96	89	67	94	74	80	95
: afternoon min (%)	42	74	11	72	59	10	18	46	19	85
: afternoon max (%)	82	46	35	83	87	41	73	74	64	95
High temp @ max humid	-4	74	28	29	4	37	31	30	34	30
High humid @ max temp	52	30	23	73	62	13	40	72	20	89
Rain: monthly min (mm)	32			39	32	71			3	5
: monthly max (mm)	83	243	79	589	71		348	243	180	302
: days/month min	11	2	0.1	3		0	0	2	0.2	
: days/month max	21	13		19	17	6	17	13		24
Snow: persistent (1=yes)	0.1									0
: intermittent (1=yes)		1						1		
Frost present (1=yes)	1	1		0	1	0	0	1	0	
Evaporation (1=low)	0	1	-1	-0.2		-1	-1			-1
Barometric pressure: July	1010	1010	1020	1010	1010	1010	1010	1010	1000	1010
: January	1020	1030	1010	1010	1010	1010	1010	1030	1020	1020
Risks: Typhoon (10=high)	0	0	0	0	0	0	0	0	0	0
: Flooding (10=high)										
: Tropical storm (10=high)		1						1	1	
: Windstorm (10=high)										
: Drought (10=high)	0	0		0	0	1	0	0	0	0
Climate Type: Tropical wet				1						1
: Tropical monsoon				1		1	1			1
: Tropical wet & dry			1						1	
: Steppe, low latitude										
: Desert, low latitude	0		1							
: Steppe, middle latitude										
: Desert, middle latitude	1									
: Subtropical, humid		1						1	1	
: Mediterranean					1					
: Marine, west coast	0.9				1					
: Cont humid hot sum										
: Cont humid cool sum	0.9									
: Subarctic	0.9									
: Tundra	0.9									
: Ice cap	0.9									
: Dry steppe wasteland										
: Temperate highland	0.9									
: Temp desert dry sum	0									
: Temp desert dry win	0									
: Highland	1	1						1	1	

Characteristics	Duala-Landa-B.	Dujia	Dutch	Dyola	Edo	Egyptian	English	Estonian	Euro-nesian	European
Latitude (abs degrees)	4	35	51	14	9	28	53	59	14	38
Temperature: degrees (C)	25	11	6	28	28	24	12	5	26	15
: monthly high (min C)	31	13	13	35	34	31	14	7	32	23
: monthly high (max C)	36	43	39	46	40	47	34	33	34	39
: monthly low (min C)	14	-23	-32	8	16	1	-10	-33	17	-9
: monthly low (max C)	17	15	4	19	21	17	4	5	21	-6
Humidity: morning min (%)	97	46	79	41	81	50	70	70	75	79
: morning max (%)	98	74	91	94	87	70	87	91	82	91
: afternoon min (%)	62	46	46	20	65	18	56	58	73	57
: afternoon max (%)	75	74	78	74	80	41	81	89	79	78
High temp @ max humid	27	30	-3	31	29	20	7	-1	30	12
High humid @ max temp	67	72	57	37	72	24	59	63	79	61
Rain: monthly min (mm)	23	243	56	0	25	5	37	36	81	53
: monthly max (mm)	295	3	93	385	460	0	64	73	455	123
: days/month min	3	2	11	0	2	1	11	12	7	6
: days/month max	24	13	16	17	20	0	15	20	22	12
Snow: persistent (1=yes)	0	1	0.8	0	0	0	1	1	0	0.2
: intermittent (1=yes)	0	1	0.2	0	0	1	1	0	0	0.8
Frost present (1=yes)	0	1	1	1	0	1	1	1	1	0.9
Evaporation (1=low)	0	1	1	0	0	1	1	0	0	0
Barometric pressure: July	1010	1010	1010	1010	1010	1010	1010	1010	1010	1010
: January	1010	1030	1020	1010	1010	1020	1010	1020	1010	1010
Risks: Typhoon (10=high)	0	10	0	0	0	0	0	0	0	0.8
: Flooding (10=high)	0	0	0	0	0	0	0	0	0	0.7
: Tropical storm (10=high)	0	0	0	8	0	0	0	0	0	0.1
: Windstorm (10=high)	0	0	0	0	1	1	0	0	0	0.1
: Drought (10=high)	1	0	0	0	0	0	0	0	0	0
Climate Type: Tropical wet	0	0	0	1	1	0	0	0	1	0.7
: Tropical monsoon	1	0	0	0	1	1	0	1	0	0.1
: Tropical wet & dry	0	1	0	0.8	0	0	1	0	0	0.7
: Steppe, low latitude	0	0	0	0	0	0	0	0	0	0
: Desert, low latitude	0	0	0	0	0	0	0	0	0	0
: Steppe, middle latitude	0	0	0	0	0	0	0	0	0	0
: Desert, middle latitude	0	0	0	0	0	0	0	0	0	0.2
: Subtropical, humid	0	0	0	0	0	0	0	0	0	0
: Mediterranean	0	0	0	0	0	0	0	0	0	0.1
: Marine, west coast	0	1	0.8	0	1	1	1	0	0	0.1
: Cont humid hot sum	0	0	0	0	0	0	0	0	0	0
: Cont humid cool sum	0	1	0.2	0	0	0	0	0	0	0
: Subarctic	0	0	0.8	0	0	0	0	0	0	0.2
: Tundra	0	0	0.8	0	0	0	0	0	0	0
: Ice cap	0	0	0.8	0.8	0	0	0	0	0	0.1
: Dry steppe wasteland	0	0	0	0	0	0	0	0	0	0.1
: Temperate highland	0	1	0	0	1	0	0	1	0	0.1
: Temp desert dry sum	0	0	0	0	0	0	0	0	0	0
: Temp desert dry win	0	0	0	0	0	0	0	0	0	0
: Highland	0	1	0.8	0	0	0	0	0	0	0.1

Characteristics	Ewa-Adja	Ewe	Fang	Fijian	Finnish	Fleming	Fon	Forros	French	Fulani
Latitude (abs degrees)	6	7	3	18	62	51	6	0.2	47	10
Temperature: degrees (C)	27	27	25	25	5	10	27	25	11	28
: monthly high (min C)	32	32	31	32	13	13	31	31	15	34
: monthly high (max C)	38	38	36	37	33	37	35	33	40	40
: monthly low (min C)	15	15	15	13	-33	-17	18	13	-18	15
: monthly low (max C)	21	21	17	19	-5	6	22	20	5	20
Humidity: morning min (%)	95	95	94	76	70	87	83	73	81	74
: morning max (%)	97	97	97	82	91	94	91	83	91	89
: afternoon min (%)	61	61	65	73	58	65	68	70	52	56
: afternoon max (%)	77	77	77	79	89	86	78	79	81	79
High temp @ max humid	27	27	28	28	-0.9	6	26	29	5	29
High humid @ max temp	68	68	70	77	63	68	74	76	56	65
Rain: monthly min (mm)	15	15	18	125	36	53	13	0	38	16
: monthly max (mm)	178	178	307	368	73	95	366	150	69	510
: days/month min	1	1	3	13	12	13	1	0	12	1
: days/month max	10	10	23	21	20	21	13	10	17	20
Snow: persistent (1=yes)	0	0	0	0	0	0	0	0	0	0
: intermittent (1=yes)	0	0	0	0	0.1	1	0	0	0.1	0
Frost present (1=yes)	0	0	0	0	1	1	0	0	0.9	0
Evaporation (1=low)	1	0	-0.2	0	1	1	0	-1	1	-0.3
Barometric pressure: July	1010	1010	1010	1010	1010	1020	1010	1020	1010	1010
: January	1010	1010	1010	1010	1010	1010	1010	1010	1020	1010
Risks: Typhoon (10=high)	0	0	0	0	0	0	0	0	0	0
: Flooding (10=high)	0	0	0	0	0	0	0	0	0	0
: Tropical storm (10=high)	0	0	0	1	0	0	0	0	0	0
: Windstorm (10=high)	1	1	1	0	0	0	1	0	9	0.7
: Drought (10=high)	0	0	0	0	0	0	1	0	0	0
Climate Type: Tropical wet	0	0	1	1	0	0	0	1	0	0.1
: Tropical monsoon	1	1	0	0	0	0	1	0	0	0
: Tropical wet & dry	1	1	0.9	0	0	0	1	0	0	0.7
: Steppe, low latitude	0	1	0	1	0	0	0	0	0	0
: Desert, low latitude	0	0	0	0	0	0	0	0	0	0.1
: Steppe, middle latitude	0	0	0	0	0	0	0	0	0	0
: Desert, middle latitude	0	0	0	0	0	0	0	0	0.1	0.1
: Subtropical, humid	0	0	0	0	0	0	0	0	0	0
: Mediterranean	0	0	0	0	0	0	0	0	0	0.6
: Marine, west coast	0	0	0	0	0.1	1	0	0	0	0
: Cont humid hot sum	0	0	0	0	0	0	0	0	0.1	0.2
: Cont humid cool sum	0	0	0	0	0	0	3	0	0.1	0
: Subarctic	0	0	0	0	1	0	0	0	0.1	0
: Tundra	0	0	0	0	1	0	0	0	0	0
: Ice cap	0	0	0	0	0	0	0	0	0	0
: Dry steppe wasteland	0	0	0	0	0	0	0	0	0	0.7
: Temperate highland	1	0	0	0	0	0	0	0	0	0
: Temp desert dry sum	0	0	0	0	0	0	0	0	0	0
: Temp desert dry win	0	0	0	0	0	0	0	0	0	0
: Highland	0	0	0	0	0	0	0	0	0.1	0

Characteristics	Fur	Ga-Adangme	Gagauz	Galician	Ganda	Garifuna	Gbaya	Georgian	German	Gibraltarian
Latitude (abs degrees)	12	7	43	40	0.2	17	4	41	49	36
Temperature: degrees (C)	29	27	11	15	24	26	27	13	9	26
: monthly high (min C)	40	32	11	16	29	32	34	20	15	23
: monthly high (max C)	48	38	36	39	36	36	38	40	38	38
: monthly low (min C)	5	15	-25	-10	12	9	14	-15	-22	
: monthly low (max C)	19	21	8	8	15	18	18	14	8	14
Humidity: morning min (%)	18	95	62	58	78	90	90	57	78	72
: morning max (%)	67	97	89	86	89	94	96	80	91	81
: afternoon min (%)	10	61	39	33	54	86	49	40	51	60
: afternoon max (%)	41	77	78	71	72	91	72	65	80	72
High temp @ max humid	37	27	2	9	25	28	29	9	5	19
High humid @ max temp	13	68	42	33	56	87	49	40	54	60
Rain: monthly min (mm)	0	15	21	11	46	56	5	15	39	1
: monthly max (mm)	71	178	72	53	175	305	226	74	82	152
: days/month min	0	1	5	10	9	4	2	7	17	0
: days/month max	6	10	11		19	16	19	12	12	10
Snow: persistent (1=yes)	0	0	0.4	0	0	0	0	1	0.1	0
: intermittent (1=yes)	0	0	1	1	0	0	0	1	0.9	0
Frost present (1=yes)	0	0	1	1	0	0	0	1	0.9	0
Evaporation (1=low)	1	0	0.6	1	1	1	1	1		1
Barometric pressure: July	1010	1010	1010	1020	1010	1010	1010	1010	1010	1020
: January	1010	1010	1020	1020	1010	1020	1010	1020	1010	1020
Risks: Typhoon (10=high)	0	0	0	0	0	0	0	0	0	0
: Flooding (10=high)	0	1	0.4	0	1	1	0	0	0.6	0
: Tropical storm (10=high)	0	0	0	0	0	0	0	0	0	0
: Windstorm (10=high)	0	0	0	0	0	0	0	0	0	0
: Drought (10=high)	1	1	0.6	0	1	0	0	0	0.2	0
Climate Type: Tropical wet	0	0	0	0	0	1	0	0	0	0
: Tropical monsoon	0	0	0	0	0	0	0	0	0	0
: Tropical wet & dry	0	1	0	0	1	0	1	0	0	0
: Steppe, low latitude	1	0	0	0	0	0	0	0	0	0
: Desert, low latitude	0	0	0	0	0	0	0	0	0	0
: Steppe, middle latitude	0	0	0	0	0	0	0	0	0	0
: Desert, middle latitude	0	0	0	0	0	0	0	0	0	0
: Subtropical, humid	0	0	0	0	0	0	0	1	0	0
: Mediterranean	0	0	0	0	0	0	0	0	0	1
: Marine, west coast	0	0	0	1	0	0	0	0	0.5	0
: Cont humid hot sum	0	0	0.4	0	0	0	0	0	0.2	0
: Cont humid cool sum	0	0	0	0	0	0	0	0	0.1	0
: Subarctic	0	0	0	0	0	0	0	0	0	0
: Tundra	0	0	0	0	0	0	0	0	0	0
: Ice cap	0	0	0	0	0	0	0	0	0	0
: Dry steppe wasteland	1	0	0	0	0	0	0	0	0	0
: Temperate highland	0	0	0	0	0	0	0	0	0.1	0
: Temp desert dry sum	0	0	0	0	0	0	0	0	0	0
: Temp desert dry win	0	0	0	0	0	0	0	0	0	0
: Highland	0	0	0	0	1	0	0	1	0.1	0

Characteristics	Gilaki	Gilber-tese	Gio	Gisu	Gola	Grebo	Greek	Green-landic	Grosi	Guiana Chinese
Latitude (abs degrees)	33	1	6	0.2	6	6	38	64	12	5
Temperature: degrees (C)	15	28	25	24	25	25	18	-2	29	27
: monthly high (min C)	18	34	29	29	29	29	21	-11	38	33
: monthly high (max C)	43	35	34	36	34	34	43	-24	48	36
: monthly low (min C)	-21	19	13	12	13	13	-7	-29	9	18
: monthly low (max C)	15	21	20	15	20	20	16	-2	19	21
Humidity: morning min (%)	47	68	87	78	87	87	49	83	38	73
: morning max (%)	77	75	95	89	95	95	79	92	81	86
: afternoon min (%)	39	68	76	54	76	76	35	83	19	69
: afternoon max (%)	75	74	86	72	86	86	64	92	67	83
High temp @ max humid	11	31	27	25	27	27	14	8	31	29
High humid @ max temp	41	73	80	56	80	80	35	86	20	69
Rain: monthly min (mm)	46	94	31	46	31	31	8	31		31
: monthly max (mm)		315	996	175	996	996	72	84	277	551
: days/month min	0.2	15	5	9	5	5	2	10	0	4
: days/month max	4	15	26	19	26	26	16	13	14	26
Snow: persistent (1=yes)	1	0						1		
: intermittent (1=yes)	1	0						1		
Frost present (1=yes)	1	0	0	0	0	0	0	1	0	0
Evaporation (1=low)	-1	-1	-1	-1	-1	-1	0.9	-1	-1	-1
Barometric pressure: July	999	1010	1010	1010	1010	1010	1010	1010	1010	1010
: January	1020	1010	1010	1010	1010	1010	1020	996	1010	1010
Risks: Typhoon (10=high)	0	0	0	0	0	0	0	0	0	0
: Flooding (10=high)	0	1	1	1	1	1	0	0	0	0
: Tropical storm (10=high)	0	0	0	0	0	0	0	0	0	0
: Windstorm (10=high)	0	0	0	0	0	0	0	0	0	0
: Drought (10=high)	0	0	0	0	0	0	0	0	0	0
Climate Type: Tropical wet	0	1	1	0	1	1	0	0	0	1
: Tropical monsoon	0	0	0	0	0	0	0	0	0	0
: Tropical wet & dry	0	0	0	0	0	0	0	0	1	0
: Steppe, low latitude	0	0	0	0	0	0	0	0	0	0
: Desert, low latitude	0	0	0	0	0	0	0	0	0	0
: Steppe, middle latitude	0	0	0	0	0	0	0	0	0	0
: Desert, middle latitude	0	0	0	0	0	0	0	0	0	0
: Subtropical, humid	1	0	0	0	0	0	0	0	0	0
: Mediterranean	0	0	0	0	0	0	1	0	0	0
: Marine, west coast	0	0	0	0	0	0	0	0	0	0
: Cont humid hot sum	0	0	0	0	0	0	0	0	0	0
: Cont humid cool sum	0	0	0	0	0	0	0	0	0	0
: Subarctic	0	0	0	0	0	0	0	0	0	0
: Tundra	0	0	0	0	0	0	0	1	0	0
: Ice cap	0	0	0	0	0	0	0	1	0	0
: Dry steppe wasteland	0	0	0	0	0	0	0	0	0	0
: Temperate highland	0	0	0	0	0	0	0	0	0	0
: Temp desert dry sum	0	0	0	0	0	0	0	0	0	0
: Temp desert dry win	0	0	0	0	0	0	0	0	0	0
: Highland	0	0	0	1	0	0	0	0	0	0

Characteristics	Guianese Creole	Gurage	Gurma	Gurung	Gypsy	Han Chinese	Hani	Hausa	Haya	Hazara-Dari
Latitude (abs degrees)	5	12	8	27	45	35	35	9	4	33
Temperature: degrees (C)	27	17	27	17	8	11	11	28	22	10
: monthly high (min C)	33	27	34	24	14	13	13	35	31	14
: monthly high (max C)	36	34	41	36	39	43	43	41	36	40
: monthly low (min C)	18	0	13	-2	-27	-23	-23	15	8	-21
: monthly low (max C)	21	7	20	18	8	15	15	21	16	-11
Humidity: morning min (%)	73	56	79	68	66	46	46	72	70	51
: morning max (%)	86	86	92	90	90	74	74	88	84	80
: afternoon min (%)	69	33	49	53	52	46	46	56	36	22
: afternoon max (%)	83	73	74	84	84	74	74	78	56	70
High temp @ max humid	29	21	28	28	3	30	30	29	28	2
High humid @ max temp	69	44	54	61	53	72	72	63	48	23
Rain: monthly min (mm)	31	5	3	3	27	3	3	21	0	0
: monthly max (mm)	551	300	206	373	101	243	243	414	152	102
: days/month min	4	2	0.7	0.2	13	2	2	2	0	0.7
: days/month max	26	28	11	21	0.5	13	13	19	12	7
Snow: persistent (1=yes)	0	0	0	0	1	1	1	0	0	1
: intermittent (1=yes)	0	0	0	0	1	1	1	0	0	1
Frost present (1=yes)	0	0	0	1	1	1	1	0	0	1
Evaporation (1=low)	-1	-1	0.4	-1	1	1	1	-0.2	1	-1
Barometric pressure: July	1010	1010	1010	1000	1010	1010	1010	1010	1020	999
: January	1010	1020	1010	1020	1020	1030	1030	1010	1010	1020
Risks: Typhoon (10=high)	0	0	0	0	0	10	10	0	0	0
: Flooding (10=high)	0	0	0	0	0	0	0	0.1	0	0
: Tropical storm (10=high)	0	0	0	0	0	0	0	0	0	0
: Windstorm (10=high)	0	0	7	0	0	0	0	0.8	0	0
: Drought (10=high)	1	0	10	1	0	0	0	0.8	1	0
Climate Type: Tropical wet	1	0	0	0	0	0	0	0	1	0
: Tropical monsoon	0	0	0	0	0	0	0	0	0	0
: Tropical wet & dry	0	0	1	0	0	0	0	0.8	1	0
: Steppe, low latitude	0	0	0	0	0	0	0	0.2	0	0
: Desert, low latitude	0	0	0	0	0	0	0	0	0	0
: Steppe, middle latitude	0	0	0	0	0	0	0	0	0	0
: Desert, middle latitude	0	0	0	0	0	0	0	0	0	0
: Subtropical, humid	0	0	0	0	0.7	1	1	0	0	0
: Mediterranean	0	0	0	0	0.3	0	0	0	0	0
: Marine, west coast	0	0	0	0	0	0	0	0	0	0
: Cont humid hot sum	0	0	0	0	0	1	1	0	0	0.8
: Cont humid cool sum	0	0	0	0	0	0	0	0	0	0.2
: Subarctic	0	0	0	0	0	0	0	0	0	0
: Tundra	0	0	0	0	0	0	0	0	0	0
: Ice cap	0	0	0	0	0	0	0	0	0	0
: Dry steppe wasteland	0	0	0	0	0	0	0	0	0	0
: Temperate highland	0	1	0	0	0	0	0	0	0	1
: Temp desert dry sum	0	0	0	0	0	0	0	0	0	0
: Temp desert dry win	0	0	0	0	0	0	0	0.8	0	0
: Highland	0	1	0	1	0	1	1	0	1	0

Characteristics	Hehet-Bena	Herero	Hottentot	Hui-Vighur	Humbe-Nyaneka	Hungarian	Hutu	Ibibio	Icelander	Igbo
Latitude (abs degrees)	4	24	24	35	8	47	7	9	64	9
Temperature: degrees (C)	22	18	20	11	26	9	22	28	5	28
monthly high (min C)	31	25	31	13	28	14	26	34	10	34
monthly high (max C)	36	36	42	43	37	39	29	40	23	40
monthly low (min C)	8	-4	-4	-23	14	-25	14	16	-17	16
monthly low (max C)	16	9	10	15	21	8	16	21	1	21
Humidity: morning min (%)	70	27	55	46	77	69	57	81	75	81
morning max (%)	84	62	74	74	84	88	83	87	83	87
afternoon min (%)	36	11	55	46	74	49	57	65	67	65
afternoon max (%)	56	35	74	74	78	82	83	80	80	80
High temp @ max humid	28	28	30	30	28	4	26	29	4	29
High humid @ max temp	48	23	63	72	77	49	60	72	72	72
Rain: monthly min (mm)	0	0	0	2	0	32	6	25	42	25
monthly max (mm)	152	79	107	243	117	80	159	460	94	460
days/month min	12	0.1	0.1	13	8	7	2	2	15	2
days/month max	0	8	8	1	0	14	21	20	21	20
Snow: persistent (1=yes)	0	0	0	1	0	0	0	0	1	0
intermittent (1=yes)	0	0	0	1	0	1	0	0	0	0
Frost present (1=yes)	0	1	1	1	0	1	0	0	1	0
Evaporation (1=low)	1	-1	-1	-1	-1	0.9	1	0	0	0
Barometric pressure: July	1020	1020	1020	1010	1020	1010	1010	1010	1010	1010
January	1010	1010	1010	1030	1010	1020	1010	1010	999	1010
Risks: Typhoon (10=high)	0	0	0	0	0	0	0	0	0	0
Flooding (10=high)	0	0	0	0	0	0	0.4	0	0	0
Tropical storm (10=high)	0	0	0	0	0	0	0	0	0	0
Windstorm (10=high)	1	1	1	1	1	0	0	0	0	0
Drought (10=high)	0	0	0	0	0	0	0.6	0	0	0
Climate Type: Tropical wet	0	0	0	0	0	0	0	0	0	0
Tropical monsoon	0	0	0	0	0	0	0	1	0	1
Tropical wet & dry	1	0	0	0	1	0	0	0	0	0
Steppe, low latitude	0	0	1	0	0	0	0	0	0	0
Desert, low latitude	0	1	0	0	0	0	0	0	0	0
Steppe, middle latitude	0	0	0	0	0	0	0	0	0	0
Desert, middle latitude	0	0	0	1	0	0	0	0	0	0
Subtropical, humid	0	0	0	0	0	0	0	0	0	0
Mediterranean	0	0	0	0	0	0	0	0	0	0
Marine, west coast	0	0	0	0	0	0.1	0	0	1	0
Cont humid hot sum	0	0	0	0	0	1	0	0	0	0
Cont humid cool sum	0	0	0	0	0	0	0	0	0	0
Subarctic	0	0	0	0	0	0	0	0	1	0
Tundra	0	0	0	0	0	0	0	0	0	0
Ice cap	0	0	0	0	0	0	0	0	0	0
Dry steppe wasteland	0	1	0	0	0	0	0	0	0	0
Temperate highland	0	0	0	0	0	0	0	0	0	0
Temp desert dry sum	0	0	0	0	0	0	0	0	0	0
Temp desert dry win	0	0	0	1	0	0	0	0	0	0
Highland	1	0	0	1	0	0	0.6	0	0	0

Characteristics	Ijaw	Indian	Indo-Aryan	Indo-nesian	Iranian	Irish	Issa	Italian	Japanese	Javanese
Latitude (abs degrees)	9	18	21	22	29	53	11	36	37	5
Temperature: degrees (C)	28	24	24	24	22	10	32	18	15	28
: monthly high (min C)	34	30	28	29	24	14	34	22	22	33
: monthly high (max C)	40	37	46	37	48	31	47	40	38	37
: monthly low (min C)	16	9	-1	11	-4	-11	17	-3	-8	19
: monthly low (max C)	21	18	22	18	17	4	23	13	16	21
Humidity: morning min (%)	81	80	35	68	19	74	57	73	71	90
: morning max (%)	87	89	80	76	54	88	84	87	92	95
: afternoon min (%)	65	60	19	66	19	69	43	48	48	61
: afternoon max (%)	80	73	64	74	54	86	74	71	69	75
High temp @ max humid	29	26	34	28	34	9	32	16	28	29
High humid @ max temp	72	66	20	70	23	72	43	50	66	71
Rain: monthly min (mm)	25	61	3	51	12	43	2	22	48	43
: monthly max (mm)	460	192	180	145	256	71	5	130	232	300
: days/month min	2	8	0.2	6	13	10	0.3	3	5	4
: days/month max	20	16	8	16	13	14	0.3	12	12	18
Snow: persistent (1=yes)	0	0.1	0	0	1	1	0	0.8	1	0
: intermittent (1=yes)	0	0.1	0	0	1	1	0	0.8	1	0
Frost present (1=yes)	0	0.3	0	0	1	1	0	-0.7	1	0
Evaporation (1=low)	0	0.1	0	-1	-1	0.3	-1			
Barometric pressure: July	1010	1010	1000	1020	999	1010	1010	1020	1010	1010
: January	1010	1010	1020	1010	1020	1010	1010	1020	1020	1010
Risks: Typhoon (10=high)	0	0	1	0	0	0	0	0	0	0
: Flooding (10=high)	0	4	0	0	0	0	0	0	0.1	1
: Tropical storm (10=high)	0	2	0	0	0	0	0	0	0	0
: Windstorm (10=high)	0	0	0	0	0	0	0	0	0.1	0
: Drought (10=high)	1		1	1	1		1			1
Climate Type: Tropical wet		0.5		1						1
: Tropical monsoon		0.2								
: Tropical wet & dry	1	0.3	1							
: Steppe, low latitude		0.1								
: Desert, low latitude		0.1					1			
: Steppe, middle latitude					1					
: Desert, middle latitude					1					
: Subtropical, humid		0.1							1	
: Mediterranean		0.1						1		
: Marine, west coast		0.1				1				
: Cont humid hot sum										
: Cont humid cool sum										
: Subarctic										
: Tundra										
: Ice cap										
: Dry steppe wasteland		0								
: Temperate highland		0.1								
: Temp desert dry sum										
: Temp desert dry win		0								
: Highland		0.3								1

Characteristics	Jewish	Jola	Kalenjin	Kamba	Kanuri	Kara-kalpak	Kare	Karen	Kavango	Kazakh
Latitude (abs degrees)	35	14	2	2	9	41	4	19	24	42
Temperature: degrees (C)	17	28	18	18	28	13	27	28	18	7
: monthly high (min C)	22	35	26	26	35	16	34	34	25	7
: monthly high (max C)	41	43	31	31	41	42	38	41	36	42
: monthly low (min C)	-7	12	5	5	15	-17	14	13	-4	-30
: monthly low (max C)	10	21	11	11	21	5	18	22	9	-11
Humidity: morning min (%)	51	70	74	74	72	52	90	71	27	56
: morning max (%)	80	88	89	89	88	77	96	89	62	87
: afternoon min (%)	35	45	40	40	56	41	49	52	11	36
: afternoon max (%)	69	74	62	62	78	69	72	88	35	78
High temp @ max humid	10	31	22	22	29	3	29	29	28	0.9
High humid @ max temp	39	72	40	40	63	42	49	64	23	42
Rain: monthly min (mm)	6	6	15	15	21	5	5	3	0	5
: monthly max (mm)	124	254	211	211	418	23	226	582	79	46
: days/month min	2	0	5	5	2	5	2	0.3	0.1	2
: days/month max	12	13	17	17	19	11	19	26	8	11
Snow: persistent (1=yes)	0.2									1
: intermittent (1=yes)	0.1									1
Frost present (1=yes)						1				1
Evaporation (1=low)	-0.6				-0.1					0
Barometric pressure: July	1010	1010	1010	1010	1010	1010	1010	1010	1020	1010
: January	1020	1010	1010	1010	1010	1020	1010	1020	1010	1030
Risks: Typhoon (10=high)										
: Flooding (10=high)	0.1	0.1					1	1		
: Tropical storm (10=high)										
: Windstorm (10=high)	0.1	0.1								
: Drought (10=high)	0.1				0.3	1				
Climate Type: Tropical wet	0	0	0	0	0	0	0	0	0	0
: Tropical monsoon	0	0	0	0	0	0	0	0	0	0
: Tropical wet & dry	0	1	1	1	0	0	1	1	1	0
: Steppe, low latitude	0	0	0	0	0.8	0	0	0	0	0
: Desert, low latitude	0	0	0	0	0.2	0	0	0	0	0
: Steppe, middle latitude	0	0	0	0	0	0	0	0	0	0.9
: Desert, middle latitude	0	0	0	0	0	1	0	0	0	0.1
: Subtropical, humid	0	0	0	0	0	0	0	0	0	0
: Mediterranean	0.8	0	0	0	0	0	0	0	0	0
: Marine, west coast	0	0	0	0	0	0	0	0	0	0
: Cont humid hot sum	0	0	0	0	0	0	0	0	0	0
: Cont humid cool sum	0	0	0	0	0	0	0	0	0	0
: Subarctic	0	0	0	0	0	0	0	0	0	0
: Tundra	0	0	0	0	0	0	0	0	0	0
: Ice cap	0	0	0	0	0	0	0	0	0	0
: Dry steppe wasteland	0	0	0	0	0.8	0	0	0	1	0.1
: Temperate highland	0	0	0	0	0	0	0	0	0	0.1
: Temp desert dry sum	0.2	0	0	0	0	0	0	0	0	0
: Temp desert dry win	0	0	0	0	0	1	0	0	0	0
: Highland	0	0	1	1	0	0	0	1	0	0.1

Characteristics	Kebu-Akposo	Khmer	Kikuyu	Kimbundu	Kisii	Kissi	Klao	Kongo	Kono	Konzo
Latitude (abs degrees)	6	12	2	8	2	9	6	6	8	7
Temperature: degrees (C)	27	27	18	26	18	27	25	25	27	25
: monthly high (min C)	32	34	26	28	26	31	29	32	31	32
: monthly high (max C)	38	41	31	37	31	36	34	36	35	36
: monthly low (min C)	15	13	5	14	5	17	13	14	19	14
: monthly low (max C)	21	22	11	21	11	21	20	19	21	19
Humidity: morning min (%)	95	74	74	77	74	82	87	86	80	88
: morning max (%)	97	86	89	84	89	93	95	94	91	95
: afternoon min (%)	61	68	40	74	40	64	76	60	67	61
: afternoon max (%)	77	82	62	78	62	86	86	73	82	73
High temp @ max humid	27	30	22	28	22	28	27	31	28	31
High humid @ max temp	68	71	40	77	40	70	80	70	71	71
Rain: monthly min (mm)	15	8	15	1	15	3	31	3	3	3
: monthly max (mm)	178	271	211	117	211	1220	996	233	902	222
: days/month min	1	1	5	0	5	0.2	5	0.1	0.7	0.1
: days/month max	10	18	17	8	17	29	26	15	28	16
Snow: persistent (1=yes)	0	0	0	0	0	0	0	0	0	0
: intermittent (1=yes)	0	0	0	0	0	0	0	0	0	0
Frost present (1=yes)	0	0	0	0	0	0	0	0	0	0
Evaporation (1=low)	0	0.1	0	-1	0	-1	-1	0.8	-1	-1
Barometric pressure: July	1010	1010	1010	1020	1010	1010	1010	1010	1010	1010
: January	1010	1010	1010	1010	1010	1010	1010	1010	1010	1010
Risks: Typhoon (10=high)	0	0	0	0	0	0	0	0	0	0
: Flooding (10=high)	0	0.8	0	1	0	0.8	0	8	0	0
: Tropical storm (10=high)	0	0.8	0	0	0	0	0	0	0	0
: Windstorm (10=high)	1	0	1	1	1	0	0	0	1	1
: Drought (10=high)	0	0	0	1	0	0	0	0	0	0
Climate Type: Tropical wet	0	0	0	0	0	0	0	0	0	0
: Tropical monsoon	0	0	0	0	0	0	1	0	1	0
: Tropical wet & dry	1	1	0	1	0	1	0	1	0	0
: Steppe, low latitude	0	0	0	0	0	0	0	0	0	0
: Desert, low latitude	0	0	0	0	0	0	0	0	0	0
: Steppe, middle latitude	0	0	0	0	0	0	0	0	0	0
: Desert, middle latitude	0	0	0	0	0	0	0	0	0	0
: Subtropical, humid	0	0	0	0	0	0	0	0	0	0
: Mediterranean	0	0	0	0	0	0	0	0	0	0
: Marine, west coast	0	0	0	0	0	0	0	0	0	0
: Cont humid hot sum	0	0	0	0	0	0	0	0	0	0
: Cont humid cool sum	0	0	0	0	0	0	0	0	0	0
: Subarctic	0	0	0	0	0	0	0	0	0	0
: Tundra	0	0	0	0	0	0	0	0	0	0
: Ice cap	0	0	0	0	0	0	0	0	0	0
: Dry steppe wasteland	0	0	0	0	0	0	0	0	0	0
: Temperate highland	0	0	0	0	0	0	0	0	0	0
: Temp desert dry sum	0	0	0	0	0	0	0	0	0	0
: Temp desert dry win	0	0	0	0	0	0	0	0	0	0
: Highland	0	0	1	0	1	0.8	0	0.8	0	1

Characteristics	Koranko	Korean	Kotoko	Kpelle	Kru	Kurd	Kuwaiti	Kyrgyz	Ladino	Lango
Latitude (abs degrees)	8	37	12	7	6	35	29	42	14	0.2
Temperature: degrees (C)	27	10	28	26	25	14	25	3	19	24
: monthly high (min C)	7	7	36	30	26	19	28	12	28	29
: monthly high (max C)	35	35	46	35	34	43	48	38	32	36
: monthly low (min C)	19	-20	8	14	13	-19	1	-32	5	12
: monthly low (max C)	21	16	19	20	20	-13	26	8	12	15
Humidity: morning min (%)	80	71	32	86	87	46	45	64	81	78
: morning max (%)	91	87	93	95	95	82	77	86	92	89
: afternoon min (%)	67	51	70	71	76	27	41	39	51	54
: afternoon max (%)	82	71	72	86	86	67	65	72	72	72
High temp @ max humid	28	29	31	27	27	11	18	-1	26	25
High humid @ max temp	71	68	13	76	80	28	46	47	55	56
Rain: monthly min (mm)	3	17		21	31		3	21	3	46
: monthly max (mm)	902	322	320	1100	996	43	28	95	274	175
: days/month min	0.7	5		3	5	0.5		5	2	9
: days/month max	28	15	22	27	26	0.6	3	11	23	19
Snow: persistent (1=yes)	0	0.4		0	0	0.7	0	0.1	0	0
: intermittent (1=yes)	0	0.7		0	0	-0.1	0	0	0	0
Frost present (1=yes)	0	0.4		0	0	-0.6		0.1	0	0
Evaporation (1=low)	-1	-1	-1	-1	-1		-1	-1	-1	-1
Barometric pressure: July	1010	1010	1010	1010	1010	1000	999	1000	1010	1010
: January	1010	1020	1010	1010	1010	1020	1020	1020	1020	1010
Risks: Typhoon (10=high)	0	7	0	0	0	0	0	0	0	0
: Flooding (10=high)	0	0	0	0	0	0	0	0	0	0
: Tropical storm (f0=high)	0	0	0	0	0	0	0	0	10	0
: Windstorm (10=high)	0	3	0	0	0	0	0	0	10	0
: Drought (10=high)	0	0	10	0	0	0	0	0	0	0
Climate Type: Tropical wet	0	0	0	0	0	0	0	0	0	0
: Tropical monsoon	0	0	0	1	1	0	0	0	0	0
: Tropical wet & dry	1	0	1	0	0	0	0	0	0	1
: Steppe, low latitude	0	0	0	0	0	0	0	0	0	0
: Desert, low latitude	0	0	0	0	0	0	1	0	0	0
: Steppe, middle latitude	0	0	0	0	0	0.6	0	0.9	0	0
: Desert, middle latitude	0	0	0	0	0	0	0	0	0	0
: Subtropical, humid	0	0	0	0	0	0	0	0	0	0
: Mediterranean	0	0	0	0	0	0.8	0	0	1	0
: Marine, west coast	0	0	0	0	0	0	0	0	0	0
: Cont humid hot sum	0	0	0	0	0	0	0	0	0	0
: Cont humid cool sum	0	1	0	0	0	0	0	0	0	0
: Subarctic	0	0	0	0	0	0	0	0	0	0
: Tundra	0	0	0	0	0	0	0	0	0	0
: Ice cap	0	0	0	0	0	0	0	0	0	0
: Dry steppe wasteland	0	0	0	0	0	0	0	0.1	0	0
: Temperate highland	0	0	0	0	0	0	0	0	0	0
: Temp desert dry sum	0	0	0	0	0	0.4	0	0	0	0
: Temp desert dry win	0	0	0	0	0	0	0	0	0	0
: Highland	0	0	0	0	0	0	0	0	0	1

Characteristics	Lao	Latvian	Lezgin	Li	Liechten-steiner	Limba	Lithua-nian	Lobi	Loma	Lomwe
Latitude (abs degrees)	14	57	40	35	47	8	54	9	6	15
Temperature: degrees (C)	27	4	14	11	8	27	5	27	25	19
: monthly high (min C)	36	7	12	13	15	31	7	34	29	28
: monthly high (max C)	41	33	40	43	38	35	33	42	34	34
: monthly low (min C)	10	-33	-27	-23	-23	19	-33	12	13	-1
: monthly low (max C)	22	5	10	15		21	5	20	20	13
Humidity: morning min (%)	87	70	62	46	80	80	70	66	87	50
: morning max (%)	93	91	91	74	92	91	91	89	95	89
: afternoon min (%)	56	58	36	46	51	67	58	46	76	28
: afternoon max (%)	73	89	75	74	76	82	89	75	86	66
High temp @ max humid	32	-1	3	30	3	28	-1	30	27	27
High humid @ max temp	61	63	36	72	52	71	63	47	80	28
Rain: monthly min (mm)		36	8	3	64	3	36	21	31	0
: monthly max (mm)	305	73	53	243	136	902	73	390	996	218
: days/month min	5	12	2	2	12	0.7	12	2	5	0.1
: days/month max	15	20	11	13	15	28	20	16	26	19
Snow: persistent (1=yes)	0	1	1	1	1	0	1	0	0	0
: intermittent (1=yes)	0	0	1	1	0	0	0	0	0	0
Frost present (1=yes)	0	1	1	1	1	0	1	0	0	0
Evaporation (1=low)	0.2									
Barometric pressure: July	1010	1010	1010	1010	1010	1010	1010	1010	1010	1020
: January	1010	1020	1020	1030	1010	1010	1020	1010	1010	1010
Risks: Typhoon (10=high)				10						
: Flooding (10=high)	2							0.5		
: Tropical storm (10=high)										
: Windstorm (10=high)								0.5		
: Drought (10=high)										
Climate Type: Tropical wet	0	0	0	0	0	0	0	0	0	0
: Tropical monsoon	0	0	0	0	0	1	0	0	1	0
: Tropical wet & dry	1	0	0	0	0	0	0	1	0	1
: Steppe, low latitude	0	0	0	0	0	0	0	0	0	0
: Desert, low latitude	0	0	0	0	0	0	0	0	0	0
: Steppe, middle latitude	0	0	0	0	0	0	0	0	0	0
: Desert, middle latitude	0	0	0	0	0	0	0	0	0	0
: Subtropical, humid	0	0	0	1	0	0	0	0	0	0
: Mediterranean	0	0	0	0	0	0	0	0	0	0
: Marine, west coast	0	0	0	0	0	0	0	0	0	0
: Cont humid hot sum	0	0	0	0	0	0	0	0	0	0
: Cont humid cool sum	0	1	0	0	0	0	1	0	0	0
: Subarctic	0	0	0	0	0	0	0	0	0	0
: Tundra	0	0	0	0	0	0	0	0	0	0
: Ice cap	0	0	0	0	0	0	0	0	0	0
: Dry steppe wasteland	0	0	0	0	0	0	0	0	0	0
: Temperate highland	0	0	0	0	0	0	0	0	0	0
: Temp desert dry sum	0	0	0	0	0	0	0	0	0	0
: Temp desert dry win	0	0	0	0	0	0	0	0	0	0
: Highland	0	0	1	1	1	0	0	0	0	0

Characteristics	Lotuko	Luba	Luchasi	Luena	Lugbara	Luhya	Lumbe	Lunda	Luo	Luri
Latitude (abs degrees)	12	7	8	8	7	2	8	8	2	33
Temperature: degrees (C)	29	25	26	26	25	18	26	26	18	15
monthly high (min C)	40	32	28	28	32	26	28	28	26	18
monthly high (max C)	48	36	37	37	36	31	37	37	31	43
monthly low (min C)	5	14	14	14	14	5	14	14	5	-21
monthly low (max C)	19	19	21	21	19	11	21	21	11	15
Humidity: morning min (%)	18	88	77	77	88	74	77	77	74	47
morning max (%)	67	95	84	84	95	89	84	84	89	77
afternoon min (%)	10	61	74	74	61	40	74	74	40	39
afternoon max (%)	41	73	78	78	73	62	78	78	62	75
High temp @ max humid	37	31	28	28	31	22	28	28	22	11
High humid @ max temp	13	71	77	77	71	40	77	77	40	41
Rain: monthly min (mm)	0	3	0	0	3	15	0	0	15	3
monthly max (mm)	71	222	117	117	222	211	117	117	211	46
days/month min	0	0.1	0	0	0.1	5	0	0	5	0.2
days/month max	6	16	8	8	16	17	8	8	17	4
Snow: persistent (1=yes)	0	0	0	0	0	0	0	0	0	1
intermittent (1=yes)	0	0	0	0	0	0	0	0	0	1
Frost present (1=yes)	0	0	0	0	0	0	0	0	0	1
Evaporation (1=low)	-1	1	-1	-1	1	0	-1	-1	0	-1
Barometric pressure: July	1010	1010	1020	1020	1010	1010	1020	1020	1010	999
January	1010	1010	1010	1010	1010	1010	1010	1010	1010	1020
Risks: Typhoon (10=high)	0	0	0	0	0	0	0	0	0	0
Flooding (10=high)	0	1	0	0	1	1	0	0	1	0
Tropical storm (10=high)	0	0	0	0	0	0	0	0	0	0
Windstorm (10=high)	0	0	0	0	0	0	0	0	0	0
Drought (10=high)	1	0	0	0	0	0	0	0	0	0
Climate Type: Tropical wet	0	1	0	0	1	0	0	0	0	0
Tropical monsoon	0	0	0	0	0	0	0	0	0	0
Tropical wet & dry	1	0	1	1	0	1	1	1	1	0
Steppe, low latitude	0	0	0	0	0	0	0	0	0	0
Desert, low latitude	0	0	0	0	0	0	0	0	0	0
Steppe, middle latitude	0	0	0	0	0	0	0	0	0	0
Desert, middle latitude	0	0	0	0	0	0	0	0	0	0
Subtropical, humid	0	0	0	0	0	0	0	0	0	0
Mediterranean	0	0	0	0	0	0	0	0	0	0
Marine, west coast	0	0	0	0	0	0	0	0	0	0
Cont humid hot sum	0	0	0	0	0	0	0	0	0	0
Cont humid cool sum	0	0	0	0	0	0	0	0	0	0
Subarctic	0	0	0	0	0	0	0	0	0	0
Tundra	0	0	0	0	0	0	0	0	0	0
Ice cap	0	0	0	0	0	0	0	0	0	0
Dry steppe wasteland	0	0	0	0	0	0	0	0	0	0
Temperate highland	0	0	0	0	0	0	0	0	0	1
Temp desert dry sum	0	0	0	0	0	0	0	0	0	0
Temp desert dry win	0	0	0	0	0	0	0	0	0	0
Highland	0	0	0	0	0	0	0	0	0	0

Characteristics	Luxem- burger	Macedo- nian	Madurese	Magars	Maka	Makonde	Makua	Malagasy	Malawi	Malay
Latitude (abs degrees)	49	44	5	27	4	4	23	19	23	5
Temperature: degrees (C)	9	10	28	17	25	22	26	18	27	28
: monthly high (min C)	11	20	33	24	31	31	34	27	34	35
: monthly high (max C)	37	41	37	36	36	36	46	35	46	37
: monthly low (min C)	-20	-20	19	-2	14	8	7	1	7	17
: monthly low (max C)	5	8	21	18	17	16	17	12	17	21
Humidity: morning min (%)	85	67	90	68	96	70	65	85	65	94
: morning max (%)	95	92	95	90	97	84	75	94	75	96
: afternoon min (%)	58	45	61	53	62	36	57	49	57	58
: afternoon max (%)	91	75	75	84	75	56	67	71	67	67
High temp @ max humid	4	4	29	28	27	28	29	26	29	33
High humid @ max temp	61	42	71	61	67	48	65	64	65	65
Rain: monthly min (mm)	42	28	43	3	21	0	13	8	13	88
: monthly max (mm)	84	66	300	373	295	152	130	300	130	292
: days/month min	13	4	4	0.2	3	0	2	7	2	10
: days/month max	20	13	18	21	23	12	9	21	9	19
Snow: persistent (1=yes)	0	0	0	1	0	0	0	0	0	0
: intermittent (1=yes)	1	1	0	1	0	0	0	0	0	0
Frost present (1=yes)	1	-1	0	1	0	-1	-1	-1	-1	1
Evaporation (1=low)	1	1	1	1	1	1	1	1	1	1
Barometric pressure: July	1010	1010	1010	1000	1010	1020	1020	1020	1020	1010
: January	1020	1020	1010	1020	1010	1010	1010	1010	1010	1010
Risks: Typhoon (10=high)	0	0	0	0	0	0	0	0	0	0
: Flooding (10=high)	0	0	1	0	0	1	1	1	1	8
: Tropical storm (10=high)	0	0	0	0	0	0	0	0	0	0
: Windstorm (10=high)	0	0	0	0	0	0	0	0	0	0
: Drought (10=high)	0	0	1	0	0.1	0	0	0	0	0.9
Climate Type: Tropical wet	0	0	0	1	1	0	0	0	0	0
: Tropical monsoon	0	0	1	0	0	0	0	1	0	1
: Tropical wet & dry	0	0	0	0	0	1	1	0	1	0
: Steppe, low latitude	0	0	0	0	0	0	0	0	0	0
: Desert, low latitude	0	0	0	0	0	0	0	0	0	0
: Steppe, middle latitude	0	0	0	0	0	0	0	0	0	0
: Desert, middle latitude	0	0	0	0	0	0	0	0	0	0
: Subtropical, humid	0	0	0	0	0	0	0	0	0	0
: Mediterranean	0	0.9	0	0	0	0	0	0	0	0
: Marine, west coast	1	0.1	0	0	0	0	0	0	0	0
: Cont humid hot sum	0	0	0	0	0	0	0	0	0	0
: Cont humid cool sum	0	0	0	0	0	0	0	0	0	0
: Subarctic	0	0	0	0	0	0	0	0	0	0
: Tundra	0	0	0	0	0	0	0	0	0	0
: Ice cap	0	0	0	0	0	0	0	0	0	0
: Dry steppe wasteland	0	0	0	0	0	0	0	0	0	0
: Temperate highland	0	0	0	0	0	0	0	0	0	0
: Temp desert dry sum	0	0	0	0	0	0	0	0	0	0
: Temp desert dry win	0	0	0	0	0	1	0	0	0	0
: Highland	0	0	1	1	0	1	0	0	0	0.8

Characteristics	Malay Christian	Malay Coastal	Malay Muslim	Malinke	Maltese	Mambwe	Manchu-Tibetian	Mandara	Mande	Mandingo
Latitude (abs degrees)	11	5	11	10	36	20	35	4	12	14
Temperature: degrees(C)	27	28	27	27	23	21	11	25	29	28
: monthly high (min C)	34	33	34	32	22	22	13	31	38	35
: monthly high (max C)	38	37	38	39	40	38	43	36	48	43
: monthly low (min C)	14	19	14	14	5	4	-23	14	9	12
: monthly low (max C)	22	21	22	20	18	14	15	17	19	21
Humidity: morning min (%)	85	90	85	74	71	39	46	97	38	70
: morning max (%)	93	95	93	94	78	85	74	98	81	88
: afternoon min (%)	55	61	55	52	59	19	46	62	19	45
: afternoon max (%)	74	75	74	82	68	71	74	75	67	74
High temp @ max humid	31	29	31	29	16	26	30	27	31	31
High humid @ max temp	61	71	61	61	62	23	72	67	20	72
Rain: monthly min (mm)	13	43	13					23		
: monthly max (mm)	432	300	432	817	110	231	243	295	277	254
: days/month min	3	4	3	0.8	0	0	2	3	0	0
: days/month max	24	18	24	23	13	21	13	24	14	13
Snow: persistent (1=yes)	0	0	0	0	0	0	1	0	0	0
: intermittent (1=yes)	0	0	0	0	0	0	1	0	0	0
Frost present (1=yes)	0	0	0	0	0	0	1	0	0	0
Evaporation (1=low)	1	1	1	-0.8	-1	0	1	0	0	-1
Barometric pressure: July	1010	1010	1010	1010	1010	1020	1010	1010	1010	1010
: January	1020	1010	1020	1010	1020	1010	1030	1010	1010	1010
Risks: Typhoon (10=high)	10	10	10	0	0	0	10	0	0	0
: Flooding (10=high)	0	0	0	0.7	0	0	0	0	0	0
: Tropical storm (10=high)	0	0	0	0.1	0	0	0	0	0	0
: Windstorm (10=high)	0	0	0	0	0	0	0	0	0	0
: Drought (10=high)	0	0	0	0.2	0	0	0	0	0	0
Climate Type: Tropical wet	1	1	1	0	0	0	0	0	0	0
: Tropical monsoon	0	0	0	0	0	0	0	0	0	0
: Tropical wet & dry	0	0	0	1	0	1	0	1	1	1
: Steppe, low latitude	0	0	0	0	0	0	0	0	0	0
: Desert, low latitude	0	0	0	0	0	0	0	0	0	0
: Steppe, middle latitude	0	0	0	0	0	0	0	0	0	0
: Desert, middle latitude	0	0	0	0	0	0	0	0	0	0
: Subtropical, humid	0	0	0	0	0	0	1	0	0	0
: Mediterranean	0	0	0	0	1	0	0	0	0	0
: Marine, west coast	0	0	0	0	0	0	0	0	0	0
: Cont humid hot sum	0	0	0	0	0	0	0	0	0	0
: Cont humid cool sum	0	0	0	0	0	0	0	0	0	0
: Subarctic	0	0	0	0	0	0	0	0	0	0
: Tundra	0	0	0	0	0	0	0	0	0	0
: Ice cap	0	0	0	0	0	0	0	0	0	0
: Dry steppe wasteland	0	0	0	0.2	0	0	0	0	0	0
: Temperate highland	0	0	0	0	0	0	1	0	0	0
: Temp desert dry sum	0	0	0	0	0	0	0	0	0	0
: Temp desert dry win	0	0	0	0	0	0	0	0	0	0
: Highland	0	1	0	0	0	0	1	0	0	0

Characteristics	Mandyako	Mano	Manx (Norse-C.)	Manzan-Darani	Maori	Maravi	Masa	Masalit Maba	Maya	Mbaka
Latitude (abs degrees)	12	6	54	33	41	16	12	12	17	4
Temperature: degrees (C)	28	25	12	15	15	20	28	28	26	27
...monthly high (min C)	35	29	14	18	19	28	36	36	32	34
...monthly high (max C)	43	34	34	43	31	35	46	46	36	38
...monthly low (min C)	13	13	-10	-21	-2	13	8	8	9	14
...monthly low (max C)	21	20	7	-15	5		19	19	18	18
Humidity: morning min (%)	70	87	70	47	73	48	32	32	90	90
...morning max (%)	87	95	87	77	81	88	93	93	94	96
...afternoon min (%)	45	76	56	39	67	26	10	10	86	49
...afternoon max (%)	74	86	81	75	78	67	72	72	91	72
High temp @ max humid	31	27	7	11	13	27	31	31	28	29
High humid @ max temp	72	80	59	41	71	27	13	13	87	49
Rain: monthly min (mm)	0	31	37	3	81	0	0	0	56	5
...monthly max (mm)	254	996	64	46	137	221	320	320	305	226
...days/month min	0	5	11	0.2	9	0.1	0	0	4	2
...days/month max	13	26	15	4	18	19	22	22	16	19
Snow: persistent (1=yes)	0	0	0	1	1	0	0	0	0	0
...intermittent (1=yes)	0	0	1	1	1	0	0	0	0	0
Frost present (1=yes)	0	0	0	0	0	0	0	0	0	0
Evaporation (1=low)	-1	-1	-1	-1	-1	0	-1	-1	-1	-1
Barometric pressure: July	1010	1010	1010	999	1010	1020	1010	1010	1010	1010
...January	1010	1010	1010	1020	1010	1010	1010	1010	1020	1010
Risks: Typhoon (10=high)	0	0	0	0	0	0	0	0	0	0
...Flooding (10=high)	0	0	0	0	0	0	0	0	0	0
...Tropical storm (10=high)	0	0	0	0	0	0	0	0	0	0
...Windstorm (10=high)	0	0	0	0	0	0	0	0	0	0
...Drought (10=high)	0	0	0	0	0	0.2	0	0	0	0
Climate Type: Tropical wet	0	0	0	0	0	0	0	0	0	1
...Tropical monsoon	0	0	0	0	0	0	0	0	0	0
...Tropical wet & dry	1	1	0	0	0	1	1	1	1	0
...Steppe, low latitude	0	0	0	0	0	0	0	0	0	0
...Desert, low latitude	0	0	0	0	0	0	0	0	0	0
...Steppe, middle latitude	0	0	0	0	0	0	0	0	0	0
...Desert, middle latitude	0	0	0	0	0	0	0	0	0	0
...Subtropical, humid	0	0	0	0	0	0	0	0	0	0
...Mediterranean	0	0	0	0	0	0	0	0	0	0
...Marine, west coast	0	0	1	0	1	0	0	0	0	0
...Cont humid hot sum	0	0	0	1	0	0	0	0	0	0
...Cont humid cool sum	0	0	0	0	0	0	0	0	0	0
...Subarctic	0	0	0	0	0	0	0	0	0	0
...Tundra	0	0	0	0	0	0	0	0	0	0
...Ice cap	0	0	0	0	0	0	0	0	0	0
...Dry steppe wasteland	0	0	0	0	0	0	0	0	0	0
...Temperate highland	0	0	0	0	0	0	0	0	0	0
...Temp desert dry sum	0	0	0	0	0	0	0	0	0	0
...Temp desert dry win	0	0	0	0	0	0	0	0	0	0
...Highland	0	0	0	0	0	0	0	0	0	0

Characteristics	Mbete	Mbochi	Mbum	Mbunda	Melanesian	Mende	Merina	Meru	Mestizo	Miao Man
Latitude (abs degrees)	2	4	9	8	9	8	19	2	17	18
Temperature: degrees (C)	26	25	27	26	27	27	18	18	18	26
: monthly high (min C)	33	32	34	28	32	31	27	26	26	33
: monthly high (max C)	37	37	42	37	37	35	35	31	33	40
: monthly low (min C)	15	12	11	14	17	19	1	5	3	4
: monthly low (max C)	19	19	18	21	21	21	12	11	11	21
Humidity: morning min (%)	82	77	58	77	73	80	85	74	75	71
: morning max (%)	93	89	95	84	79	91	94	89	88	87
: afternoon min (%)	63	54	30	74	71	67	49	40	44	71
: afternoon max (%)	76	71	73	78	79	82	71	62	63	87
High temp @ max humid	30	31	30	28	29	28	26	22	24	31
High humid @ max temp	71	65	33	77	72	71	64	40	48	74
Rain: monthly min (mm)	2	0	6	0	77	3	8	15	17	3
: monthly max (mm)	340	292	296	117	221	902	300	211	152	302
: days/month min	0.4	0	1	0	5	0.7	7	5	4	1
: days/month max	15	9	22	8	11	28	21	17	19	18
Snow: persistent (1=yes)	0	0	0	0	0	0	0	0	0.2	0
: intermittent (1=yes)	0	0	0	0	0	0	0	0	0.3	0
Frost present (1=yes)	0	0	0	0	0.6	0	1	0	0.3	1
Evaporation (1=low)	-0.6	0	0.6	0.1	0.1	-1	-1	0	-0.4	0
Barometric pressure: July	1020	1020	1010	1020	1010	1010	1020	1010	1020	1010
: January	1010	1010	1010	1010	1010	1010	1010	1010	1010	1010
Risks: Typhoon (10=high)	0	0	0	0	4	0	0	0	3	1
: Flooding (10=high)	0	0	0	0	0	0	0	0	0.4	0
: Tropical storm (10=high)	0	0	8	0	0	0	0	0	0.1	0
: Windstorm (10=high)	0	0	0.2	0	0	0	0	0	0.3	0
: Drought (10=high)	1	1	6	1	0	1	1	0	0.6	0
Climate Type: Tropical wet	0	0	0.2	0	1	0	0	0	0	1
: Tropical monsoon	1	1	0.6	1	0	0	1	0	0.1	0
: Tropical wet & dry	0	0	0	1	0	1	1	1	0.2	0
: Steppe, low latitude	1	1	0	1	0	0	0	1	0	0
: Desert, low latitude	0	0	0	0	0	0	0	0	0	0
: Steppe, middle latitude	0	0	0	0	0	0	0	0	0	0
: Desert, middle latitude	0	0	0	0	0	0	0	0	0	0
: Subtropical, humid	0	0	0	0	0	0	0	0	0	0
: Mediterranean	0	0	0	0	0	0	0	0	0	0
: Marine, west coast	0	0	0	0	0	0	0	0	0	0
: Cont humid hot sum	0	0	0	0	0	0	0	0	0	0
: Cont humid cool sum	0	0	0	0	0	0	0	0	0	0
: Subarctic	0	0	0	0	0	0	0	0	0	0
: Tundra	0	0	0	0	0	0	0	0	0	0
: Ice cap	0	0	0	0	0	0	0	0	0	0
: Dry steppe wasteland	0	0	0	0	0	0	0	0	0	0
: Temperate highland	0	0	0	0	0	0	0	0	0	0
: Temp desert dry sum	0	0	0	0	0	0	0	0	0	0
: Temp desert dry win	0	0	0	0	0	0	0	0	0	0
: Highland	0	0	0	0	0	0	0	1	0.4	0

Characteristics	Micronesian	Mixed	Moldovan	Mon	Mon-Khmer	Monegasque	Mongo	Mongol-Buryat	Mongol-Dariganga	Mongol-Dorbed
Latitude (abs degrees)	9	16	49	19	18	43	7	48	48	48
Temperature: degrees (C)	28	25	8	28	26	17	25	-4	-4	-4
: monthly high (min C)	31	30	6	34	33	19	32	-6	-6	-6
: monthly high (max C)	34	35	34	41	40	34	36	36	36	36
: monthly low (min C)	21	11	-27	13	4	-1	14	-44	-44	-44
: monthly low (max C)	23	19	8	22	21	14	19	1	1	1
Humidity: morning min (%)	82	74	66	71	71	67	88	64	64	64
: morning max (%)	88	84	91	89	87	79	95	88	88	88
: afternoon min (%)	74	58	48	52	71	67	61	40	40	40
: afternoon max (%)	80	74	84	88	87	75	73	75	75	75
High temp @ max humid	30	27	-2	29	31	23	31	-16	-16	-16
High humid @ max temp	79	68	55	64	74	72	71	54	54	54
Rain: monthly min (mm)	56	13	32	3	3	21	3	0	0	0
: monthly max (mm)	284	113	90	582	302	123	222	76	76	76
: days/month min	12	3	9	0.3	1	1	0.1	1	1	1
: days/month max	24	12	16	26	18	7	16	10	10	10
Snow: persistent (1=yes)	0	0	0.3	0	0	0	0	1	1	1
: intermittent (1=yes)	0	0	0.7	0	0	0	0	1	1	1
Frost present (1=yes)	0	0	0	0	0	0	0	1	1	1
Evaporation (1=low)	0.4		0.7							
Barometric pressure: July	1010	1020	1010	1010	1010	1010	1010	1010	1010	1010
: January	1010	1010	1020	1020	1010	1020	1010	1030	1030	1030
Risks: Typhoon (10=high)	10	0	0	0	0	0	0	0	0	0
: Flooding (10=high)	0	0	0	10	10	0	1	0	0	0
: Tropical storm (10=high)	0	0	0	0	0	0	0	0	0	0
: Windstorm (10=high)	0	3	0	1	1	1	0	0	0	0
: Drought (10=high)	0	5	0	1	0	1	0	0	0	0
Climate Type: Tropical wet	1	0	0	0	0	0	1	0	0	0
: Tropical monsoon	0	0	0	1	1	0	0	0	0	0
: Tropical wet & dry	0	0	0	0	0	0	0	0	0	0
: Steppe, low latitude	0	0	0	0	0	0	0	0	0	0
: Desert, low latitude	0	0	0	0	0	0	0	0	0	0
: Steppe, middle latitude	0	0	0	0	0	0	0	0	0	0
: Desert, middle latitude	0	0	0	0	0	0	0	0	0	0
: Subtropical, humid	0	0.7	0	0	0	0	0	0	0	0
: Mediterranean	0	0.3	0	0	0	1	0	0	0	0
: Marine, west coast	0	0	0.3	0	0	0	0	0	0	0
: Cont humid hot sum	0	0	0.3	0	0	0	0	0	0	0
: Cont humid cool sum	0	0	0.3	0	0	0	0	1	1	1
: Subarctic	0	0	0.3	0	0	0	0	0	0	0
: Tundra	0	0	0	0	0	0	0	0	0	0
: Ice cap	0	0	0	0	0	0	0	0	0	0
: Dry steppe wasteland	0	0	0	0	0	0	0	0	0	0
: Temperate highland	0	0	0.3	0	0	0	0	0	0	0
: Temp desert dry sum	0	0	0	0	0	0	0	0	0	0
: Temp desert dry win	0	0	0	0	0	0	0	0	0	0
: Highland	0	0	0.3	0	0	0	1	0	0	0

Characteristics	Mongol-Khalka	Mongoloid	Montene-grin	Moor	Morvians	Mossi	Mpongwe	Mubi	Mulatto	Muong
Latitude (abs degrees)	48	23	44	14	48	10	0.2	12	15	15
Temperature: degrees (C)	-4	22	9	27	6	28	27	28	24	25
: monthly high (min C)	-6	26	20	34	10	36	33	36	31	33
: monthly high (max C)	36	46	42	42	39	44	37	46	37	43
: monthly low (min C)	-44	-4	-25	10	-27	11	17	8	10	6
: monthly low (max C)	1	21	8	22	4	20	19	19	17	22
Humidity: morning min (%)	64	37	71	59	74	58	85	32	83	74
: morning max (%)	88	79	85	85	90	87	95	93	88	83
: afternoon min (%)	40	23	46	45	51	34	69	10	65	67
: afternoon max (%)	75	66	76	73	82	71	79	72	72	76
High temp @ max humid	-16	33	5	31	3	30	30	31	28	23
High humid @ max temp	-54	28	47	66	53	37	75	13	69	72
Rain: monthly min (mm)	0	3	46	29	26	5	3	0	42	18
: monthly max (mm)	76	190	96	215	84	242	373	320	152	343
: days/month min	1	0.5	8	3	9	0.4	0.7	0	7	7
: days/month max	10	0.9	14	10	15	13	19	22	14	16
Snow: persistent (1=yes)	1	0.2	0	0	1	0	0	0	0.1	0
: intermittent (1=yes)	0	0.2	1	0	1	0	0	0	0.1	0
Frost present (1=yes)	1	0.2	1	0.6	1	0	0	1	-0.3	0
Evaporation (1=low)	1	0.2	-1	-1	-1	0	-1	-0		-1
Barometric pressure: July	1010	1000	1010	1010	1010	1010	1010	1010	1020	1010
: January	1030	1020	1020	1020	1020	1010	1020	-1010	1010	1010
Risks: Typhoon (10=high)	0	2	0	0	0	0	0	0	0	0
: Flooding (10=high)	0	0	0	0	0	0	0	0	0	0
: Tropical storm (10=high)	0	0	0	0	0	4	0	0	0	0
: Windstorm (10=high)	0	0	0	0	0	1	0	0	0	0
: Drought (10=high)	0	0	0	1	0	0	0	1	0	1
Climate Type: Tropical wet	0	0	0	0	0	0	0	0	0	0
: Tropical monsoon	0	0	0	0	0	0	1	0	0	0
: Tropical wet & dry	0	0	0	0	0	1	0	1	0	1
: Steppe, low latitude	1	0	0	0	0	0	0	0	0	0
: Desert, low latitude	0	0	0	0.4	0	0.4	0	0	0.1	0
: Steppe, middle latitude	0	0.8	0	0	0	1	0	0	0.8	0
: Desert, middle latitude	0	0.8	0	0.6	0	0	0	0	0.7	0
: Subtropical, humid	0	0	0	0	0	0	0	0	0	0
: Mediterranean	0	0.2	1	0	0	1	1	1	0	1
: Marine, west coast	1	0.2	0	0	1	0	0	0	0.7	0
: Cont humid hot sum	0	0	0	0	0	0	0	0	0.7	0
: Cont humid cool sum	0	0	0	0	1	0	0	0	0	0
: Subarctic	0	0	0	0	0	0	0	0	0	0
: Tundra	0	0	0	0	0	0	0	0	0	0
: Ice cap	0	0	0	0	0	0	0	0	0	0
: Dry steppe wasteland	0	0	0	0	0	0	0	0	0	0
: Temperate highland	0	0	0	0	0	0	0	0	0	0
: Temp desert dry sum	0	0	0	0	0	0	0	0	0	0
: Temp desert dry win	0	0.2	0	0	0	0	0	0	0	0
: Highland	0	0.2	0	0	0	0	0	0	0	0

Characteristics	Nama	Nauruan	Ndebele	Nepalese	Newar	Nether-lander	Ngbandi	Ngoni	Nkole	Norman-French D.
Latitude (abs degrees)	24	0.3	19	27	27	52	4	15	0.2	49
Temperature: degrees (C)	18	28	18	17	17	9	27	19	24	12
: monthly high (min C)	25	34	26	24	24	15	34	28	29	14
: monthly high (max C)	36	35	35	36	36	34	38	34	36	34
: monthly low (min C)	-4	19	0	-2	-2	-20	14	-1	12	-10
: monthly low (max C)	9	21	9	18	18	6	18	13	15	7
Humidity: morning min (%)	27	68	43	68	68	78	90	50	78	70
: morning max (%)	62	75	77	90	90	89	96	89	89	87
: afternoon min (%)	11	68	26	53	53	65	49	28	54	56
: afternoon max (%)	35	74	57	84	84	85	72	66	72	81
High temp @ max humid	28	31	26	28	28	6	29	27	25	7
High humid @ max temp	23	73	26	61	61	68	49	28	56	59
Rain: monthly min (mm)	79	94	195	3	3	40	226	218	46	37
: monthly max (mm)	0.1	315	0.6	373	373	71	2	0.1	175	64
: days/month min	0	5	0	0.2	0.2	12	0	0	9	11
: days/month max	8	15	18	21	21	20	19	19	19	15
Snow: persistent (1=yes)	0	0	0	0	0	0	0	0	0	0
: intermittent (1=yes)	0	0	0	1	1	1	0	0	1	1
Frost present (1=yes)	1	0	-1	1	1	1	0	0	0	1
Evaporation (1=low)	-1	1	1	1	1	1	1	0	1	1
Barometric pressure: July	1020	1010	1020	1000	1000	1010	1010	1020	1010	1010
: January	1010	1010	1010	1020	1020	1020	1010	1010	1010	1020
Risks: Typhoon (10=high)	0	0	0	0	0	0	0	0	0	0
: Flooding (10=high)	0	0	0	0	0	0	0	0	0	0
: Tropical storm (10=high)	0	0	0	0	0	0	0	0	0	0
: Windstorm (10=high)	0	0	0	0	0	0	0	0	0	0
: Drought (10=high)	0	1	1	0	0	0	1	0	0	0
Climate Type: Tropical wet	0	1	0	0	0	0	1	0	0	0
: Tropical monsoon	0	0	0	0	0	0	0	0	0	0
: Tropical wet & dry	0	0	1	0	0	0	0	1	0	0
: Steppe, low latitude	1	0	0	0	0	0	0	0	0	0
: Desert, low latitude	0	0	0	0	0	0	0	0	0	0
: Steppe, middle latitude	0	0	0	0	0	0	0	0	0	0
: Desert, middle latitude	0	0	0	0	0	0	0	0	0	0
: Subtropical, humid	0	0	0	0	0	0	0	0	0	0
: Mediterranean	0	0	0	0	0	0	0	0	0	0
: Marine, west coast	0	0	0	0	0	1	0	0	0	1
: Cont humid hot sum	0	0	0	0	0	0	0	0	0	0
: Cont humid cool sum	0	0	0	0	0	0	0	0	0	0
: Subarctic	0	0	0	0	0	0	0	0	0	0
: Tundra	0	0	0	0	0	0	0	0	0	0
: Ice cap	0	0	0	0	0	0	0	0	0	0
: Dry steppe wasteland	0	0	0	0	0	0	0	0	1	0
: Temperate highland	0	0	0	0	0	0	0	0	0	0
: Temp desert dry sum	0	0	0	0	0	0	0	0	0	0
: Temp desert dry win	0	0	0	0	0	0	0	0	0	0
: Highland	0	0	0	1	1	0	0	0	0	0

Characteristics	North-Western	Norwegian	Nuba	Nuer	Nung Sukuma	Nupe	Nyamwezi (Galla)	Nyoros	Ometo	Oromo
Latitude (abs degrees)	20	64	12	12	15	9	4	0.2	12	12
Temperature: degrees (C)	21	5	29	29	25	28	22	24	17	17
: monthly high (min C)	28	11	40	40	33	34	31	29	27	27
: monthly high (max C)	38	34	48	48	43	40	36	36	34	34
: monthly low (min C)	4	-26	5	5	6	16	8	16	0	0
: monthly low (max C)	14	4	19	19	22	21	16	15	7	7
Humidity: morning min (%)	39	68	18	18	74	81	70	78	56	56
: morning max (%)	85	88	67	67	83	87	84	89	86	86
: afternoon min (%)	19	52	10	10	67	65	36	54	33	33
: afternoon max (%)	71	85	41	41	76	80	56	72	73	73
High temp @ max humid	26	0	37	37	23	29	28	25	21	21
High humid @ max temp	23	59	13	13	72	72	48	56	44	44
Rain: monthly min (mm)	0	26	0	0	18	25	0	46	0	0
: monthly max (mm)	231	95	71	71	343	460	152	175	300	300
: days/month min	0	0	0	0	7	20	0	9	2	2
: days/month max	21	14	6	6	16	0	12	19	28	28
Snow: persistent (1=yes)	0	1	0	0	0	0	0	0	0	0
: intermittent (1=yes)	0	1	0	0	0	0	0	1	0	-1
Frost present (1=yes)	0	1	1	1	1	1	1	1	-1	-1
Evaporation (1=low)	0	1	0	0	0	0	0	1	0	0
Barometric pressure: July	1020	1010	1010	1010	1010	101	1020	1010	1010	1010
January	101	1010	101	1010	1010	101	1010	1010	1020	1020
Risks: Typhoon (10=high)	0	0	0	0	0	0	0	0	0	0
: Flooding (10=high)	0	0	0	0	0	0	0	0	0	0
: Tropical storm (10=high)	0	0	0	0	0	0	0	0	0	0
: Windstorm (10=high)	0	0	0	0	0	0	0	0	0	0
: Drought (10=high)	0	0	1	1	1	1	1	0	0	0
Climate Type: Tropical wet	0	0	0	0	0	0	0	1	0	0
: Tropical monsoon	0	0	0	0	0	0	0	0	0	0
: Tropical wet & dry	0	0	1	1	1	1	1	0	0	0
: Steppe, low latitude	1	0	0	0	0	0	0	0	0	0
: Desert, low latitude	0	0	0	0	0	0	0	0	0	0
: Steppe, middle latitude	0	0	0	0	0	0	0	0	0	0
: Desert, middle latitude	0	0	0	0	0	0	0	0	0	0
: Subtropical, humid	0	0	0	0	0	0	0	0	0	0
: Mediterranean	0	0	0	0	0	0	0	0	0	0
: Marine, west coast	1	1	0	0	0	0	0	0	0	0
: Cont humid not sum	0	0	0	0	0	0	0	0	0	0
: Cont humid cool sum	0	0	0	0	0	0	0	0	0	0
: Subarctic	0	1	0	0	0	0	0	0	0	0
: Tundra	0	0	0	0	0	0	0	0	0	0
: Ice cap	0	0	0	0	0	0	0	0	0	0
: Dry steppe wasteland	0	0	0	0	0	0	0	1	0	0
: Temperate highland	0	0	0	0	0	0	0	0	0	0
: Temp desert dry sum	0	0	0	0	0	0	0	0	0	0
: Temp desert dry win	0	0	0	0	0	0	0	0	0	0
: Highland	0	0	0	1	0	0	1	1	1	1

Characteristics	Ossete	Ovambo	Ovim-bundu	Pacific Islander	Pakistani	Palauans	Palaung-Wa	Papuan New Guin.	Pashtun	Pepel
Latitude (abs degrees)	41	24	8	0.3	40	15	18	7	33	12
Temperature: degrees (C)	13	18	26	28	18	29	26	28	10	28
: monthly high (min C)	20	25	28	34	21	32	33	32	14	35
: monthly high (max C)	40	36	37	35	38	35	40	37	40	43
: monthly low (min C)	-15	-4	14	19	-3	22	4	18	-21	13
: monthly low (max C)	14	9	21	21	13	23	21	21	-11	21
Humidity: morning min (%)	57	27	77	68	69	81	71	72	51	70
: morning max (%)	80	62	84	75	86	87	87	78	80	87
: afternoon min (%)	40	11	74	68	58	76	71	69	22	45
: afternoon max (%)	65	35	78	74	77	80	87	78	70	74
High temp @ max humid	9	28	28	31	18	31	31	28	2	31
High humid @ max temp	40	23	77	73	62	80	74	69	23	72
Rain: monthly min (mm)	15	0	0	94	29	46	3	18	0	0
: monthly max (mm)	75	79	117	315	84	264	302	193	102	254
: days/month min	7	0.1	0	5	7	12	1	2	0.1	0
: days/month max	12	.8	8	15	12	24	8	8	.7	13
Snow: persistent (1=yes)	1	0	0	0	0	0	0	0	1	0
: intermittent (1=yes)	1	0	0	0	0.6	0	0	-1	1	0
Frost present (1=yes)	1	-1	-1	-1	0.6	-1	-1	0	-1	-1
Evaporation (1=low)	1				0.3		1	-1		
Barometric pressure: July	1010	1020	1020	1010	1010	1010	1010	1010	999	1010
: January	1020	1010	1010	1010	1010	1010	1010	1010	1020	1010
Risks: Typhoon (10=high)	0	0	0	0	0	0	0	0	0	0
: Flooding (10=high)	0	0	0	0	0	0	0	0	0	0
: Tropical storm (10=high)	0	0	1	0	0	0	0	0	0	0
: Windstorm (10=high)	0	0	1	0	3	0	0	0	0	0
: Drought (10=high)	0	1	1	1	0	1	1	1	1	1
Climate Type: Tropical wet	0	0	0	1	0	1	1	1	0	0
: Tropical monsoon	0	0	0	0	0	0	0	0	0	0
: Tropical wet & dry	0	1	1	0	0	0	0	0	0	1
: Steppe, low latitude	0	0	0	0	0.1	0	0	0	0	0
: Desert, low latitude	0	0	0	0	0.2	0	0	0	0	0
: Steppe, middle latitude	0	0	0	0	0	0	0	0	1	0
: Desert, middle latitude	0	0	0	0	0	0	0	0	1	0
: Subtropical, humid	0	0	0	0	0	0	0	0	0	0
: Mediterranean	0	0	0	0	0.6	0	0	0	0	0
: Marine, west coast	0	0	0	0	0	0	0	0	0	0
: Cont humid hot sum	0	0	0	0	0	0	0	0	0	0
: Cont humid cool sum	1	0	0	0	0	0	0	0	0	0
: Subarctic	0	0	0	0	0	0	0	0	0	0
: Tundra	0	0	0	0	0	0	0	0	0	0
: Ice cap	0	0	0	0	0	0	0	0	0	0
: Dry steppe wasteland	0	0	0	0	0	0	0	0	0	0
: Temperate highland	0	0	0	0	0	0	0	0	0	0
: Temp desert dry sum	0	0	0	0	0.3	0	0	0	0	0
: Temp desert dry win	0	0	0	0	0	0	0	0	0	0
: Highland	1	0	0	0	0	0	0	0	0	0

Characteristics	Persian	Polinisian	Polinesian Chinese	Polinesian European	Polish	Portu- guese	Punjabi	Punu	Puyi	Pygmy
Latitude (abs degrees)	33	24	17	17	52	24	29	2	35	4
Temperature: degrees (C)	15	23	26	26	7	23	22	26	11	25
: monthly high (min C)	18	28	32	32	11	28	24	33	13	32
: monthly high (max C)	43	33	34	34	35	39	48	37	43	37
: monthly low (min C)	-21	11	17	17	-29	6	-4	15	-23	12
: monthly low (max C)	15	16	21	21	7	16	17	19	15	19
Humidity: morning min (%)	47	75	75	75	80	76	19	82	46	77
: morning max (%)	77	82	82	82	93	87	54	93	74	89
: afternoon min (%)	39	71	73	73	56	62	19	64	46	54
: afternoon max (%)	75	79	79	79	87	74	54	76	74	71
High temp @ max humid	11	25	30	30	2	24	34	30	30	31
High humid @ max temp	41	77	79	79	63	64	34	72	72	65
Rain: monthly min (mm)	3	84	81	81	31	30	22	2	2	2
: monthly max (mm)	46	327	455	455	95	128	258	346	243	292
: days/month min	0.2	8	27	27	11	6	13	0.5	2	9
: days/month max	4	21	22	22	16	14	13	16	13	9
Snow: persistent (1=yes)	1	0.3	0	0	1	0	1	0	1	0
: intermittent (1=yes)	1	0.3	0	0	0	0.3	1	0	1	0
Frost present (1=yes)	1	0.4	0	0.1	1	-0.3	1	-0.7	1	0
Evaporation (1=low)	-1	-0.2	0	0	1		-1		-1	0
Barometric pressure: July	999	1010	1020	1020	1010	1020	999	1020	1010	1020
: January	1020	1010	1010	1010	1020	1010	1020	1010	1030	1010
Risks: Typhoon (10=high)	0	2	0	0	0	0	0	0	0	0
: Flooding (10=high)	0	0	0	0	0	7	0	0	10	0
: Tropical storm (10=high)	0	0	1	0.6	0	0	0	0	0	0
: Windstorm (10=high)	0	0	0	0	0	0.2	0	0	0	0
: Drought (10=high)	0	0	0	0	0	0	0	0	0	0
Climate Type: Tropical wet	0	0.7	1	1	0	0	0	0	0	1
: Tropical monsoon	0	0	0	0	0	0	0	0	0	0
: Tropical wet & dry	0	0.3	0	0	0	0	0	1	0	0
: Steppe, low latitude	1	0	0	0	0	0	1	0	0	0
: Desert, low latitude	1	0	0	0	0	0	0	0	0	0
: Steppe, middle latitude	0	0	0	0	0	0	0	0	0	0
: Desert, middle latitude	0	0	0	0	0	0	0	0	0	0
: Subtropical, humid	0	0	0	0	0	0.7	0	0	1	0
: Mediterranean	0	0	0	0	0	0.7	0	0	0	0
: Marine, west coast	0	0	0	0	0	0.3	0	0	0	0
: Cont humid hot sum	0	0	0	0	0	0	0	0	0	0
: Cont humid cool sum	0	0	0	0	1	0	0	0	0	0
: Subarctic	0	0	0	0	0	0	0	0	0	0
: Tundra	0	0	0	0	0	0	0	0	0	0
: Ice cap	0	0	0	0	0	0	0	0	0	0
: Dry steppe wasteland	0	0	0	0	0	0	0	0	0	0
: Temperate highland	0	0	0	0	0	0	0	0	0	0
: Temp desert dry sum	0	0	0	0	0	0	0	0	0	0
: Temp desert dry win	0	0	0	0	0	0	0	0	0	0
: Highland	0	0	0	0	0	0	0	0	0	0

Characteristics	Quechua	Rakhine	Romanian	Romansch	Rundi	Russian	Ruthenian	Rwanda	Saho	Sakalava
Latitude (abs degrees)	8	19	45	47	7	54	48	5	15	19
Temperature: degrees (C)	18	28	8	9	25	4	6	25	31	18
: monthly high (min C)	25	34	16	15	32	3	10	31	33	27
: monthly high (max C)	32	41	41	38	36	33	39	36	44	35
: monthly low (min C)	5	13	-32	-23	14	-31	-27	14	17	1
: monthly low (max C)	11	22	8	7	19	6	4	18	23	12
Humidity: morning min (%)	87	71	58	80	86	59	74	86	56	85
: morning max (%)	94	89	89	92	94	87	90	94	83	94
: afternoon min (%)	55	52	58	51	61	43	51	60	44	49
: afternoon max (%)	73	88	89	76	74	83	82	73	74	71
High temp @ max humid	21	29	4	3	31	-4	-4	30	31	26
High humid @ max temp	60	64	59	52	70	53	53	68	43	64
Rain: monthly min (mm)	7	3	26	64	3	33	26	12	0	8
: monthly max (mm)	71	582	121	136	216	84	84	212	23	300
: days/month min	2	0.3	5	12	0.2	11	9	2	0.1	7
: days/month max	10	26	13	15	16	21	15	17	3	21
Snow: persistent (1=yes)	0.3	0	1	1	0	0.1	1	0	0	0
: intermittent (1=yes)	0	0	1	1	0	0.1	1	0	0	0
Frost present (1=yes)	-0.7	0	1	1	0.1	1	1	0.2	0	0
Evaporation (1=low)	-0.9	-1	-1	-1	-1	0.1	-1	-1	-1	-1
Barometric pressure: July	1020	1010	1010	1010	1010	1010	1010	1010	1010	1020
: January	1010	1020	1020	1020	1010	1020	1020	1010	1020	1010
Risks: Typhoon (10=high)	0	0	0	0	0	0	0	0	0	0
: Flooding (10=high)	0	0	0	0	0	0	0	0	0	0
: Tropical storm (10=high)	0	1	0	0	0	0	0	0	0	0
: Windstorm (10=high)	1	0	0	0	9	0	0	9	0	0
: Drought (10=high)	0.1	0	1	0	0.9	0	1	0.9	0	0
Climate Type: Tropical wet	0	0	0	0	0	0	0	0	0	0
: Tropical monsoon	0	1	0	0	0	0	0	0	0	0
: Tropical wet & dry	0	0	0	0	0	0	0	0	0	1
: Steppe, low latitude	0.6	0	0	0	0	0	0	0	0	0
: Desert, low latitude	0.3	0	0	0	0	0	0	0	1	0
: Steppe, middle latitude	0.1	0	0	0	0	0	0	0	0	0
: Desert, middle latitude	0	0	0	0	0	0	0	0	0	0
: Subtropical, humid	0	0	0	0	0	0.9	0	0	0	0
: Mediterranean	0	0	0	0	0	0	0	0	0	0
: Marine, west coast	0	0	0	0	0	0	0	0	0	0
: Cont humid hot sum	0	0	1	0	0	0.9	1	0	0	0
: Cont humid cool sum	0	0	0	0	0	0.8	0	0	0	0
: Subarctic	0	0	0	0	0	0	0	0	0	0
: Tundra	0	0	0	0	0	0	0	0	0	0
: Ice cap	0	0	0	0	0	0	0	0	0	0
: Dry steppe wasteland	0	0	0	0	0	0.8	0	0.2	0	0
: Temperate highland	0	0	0	0	0	0	0	0	0	0
: Temp desert dry sum	0	0	0	0	0	0	0	0	0.2	0
: Temp desert dry win	0	0	0	0	0	0	0	0	0	0
: Highland	0.7	0	0	0	0.9	0.8	0	1	1	0

Characteristics	Samoan	Sanga	Sanmari- nese	Sara	Scandina- vian	Senufo	Serbian	Serer	Servicais Tongas	Shan
Latitude (abs degrees)	19	4	44	8	60	10	44	14	0.2	19
Temperature: degrees (C)	24	25	17	27	7	27	9	28	25	28
: monthly high (min C)	30	32	19	34	11	34	20	35	31	34
: monthly high (max C)	35	37	40	38	26	41	42	43	33	41
: monthly low (min C)	9	12	-6	14	-15	12	-25	12	13	13
: monthly low (max C)	19	19	12	18	5	20	8	21	20	22
Humidity: morning min (%)	74	77	70	90	77	66	71	70	73	71
: morning max (%)	82	89	87	96	88	93	86	88	83	89
: afternoon min (%)	68	54	42	49	72	46	45	45	70	52
: afternoon max (%)	75	71	70	72	85	77	76	74	79	88
High temp @ max humid	26	31	13	29	10	30	5	31	29	29
High humid @ max temp	74	65	43	49	76	54	46	72	76	64
Rain: monthly min (mm)	78	0	15	5	54	22	44	0	0	3
: monthly max (mm)	395	292	129	226	132	416	94	254	150	582
: days/month min	7	0	9	2	14	2	8	0		0.3
: days/month max	20	9	11	19	23	17	14	13	10	26
Snow: persistent (1=yes)	0.2	0	1	0	0.6	0	0	0	0	0
: intermittent (1=yes)	0.2	0	1	0	0.4	0	1	0	0	0
Frost present (1=yes)	0.2	0	1	0	1	1	1	0	0	0
Evaporation (1=low)	1	0	-1	1		-0.3	-1	-1	-1	1
Barometric pressure: January	1010	1020	1010	1010	1010	1010	1010	1010	1020	1010
: July	1010	1010	1020	1010	1010	1010	1020	1010	1010	1020
Risks: Typhoon (10=high)	8	0	0	0	0	0	0	0	0	0
: Flooding (10=high)	0	10	0	10	0	5	0	10	0	10
: Tropical storm (10=high)	0	0	0	0	0	0	0	0	0	0
: Windstorm (10=high)	0	0	0	0	0	0	0	0	0	0
: Drought (10=high)	0.8	0	0	0	0	0.5	0	0	0	0
Climate Type: Tropical wet	0	0	0	0	0	0	0	0	1	0
: Tropical monsoon	0.2	0	0	0	0	0	0	0	0	0
: Tropical wet & dry	0.2	1	0	1	0	0.5	0	1	0	1
: Steppe, low latitude	0.2	1	0	0	0	0.1	0	1	0	0
: Desert, low latitude	0.2	0	0	0	0	0.3	0	0	0	0
: Steppe, middle latitude	0	0	0	0	0	0	0	0	0	0
: Desert, middle latitude	0.2	0	0	0	0	0	0	0	0	0
: Subtropical, humid	0	0	0	0	0	0	0	0	0	0
: Mediterranean	0.2	0	1	0	0	0	0	0	0	0
: Marine, west coast	0	0	1	0	1	0	0	0	0	0
: Cont humid hot sum	0	0	0	0	0	0	1	0	0	0
: Cont humid cool sum	0	0	0	0	0	0	0	0	0	0
: Subarctic	0	0	0	0	1	0	0	0	0	0
: Tundra	0	0	0	0	0	0	0	0	0	0
: Ice cap	0	0	0	0	0	0	0	0	0	0
: Dry steppe wasteland	0.2	0	0	0	0	0	0	0	0	0
: Temperate highland	0	0	0	0	0	0	0	0	0	0
: Temp desert dry sum	0	0	0	0	0	0	0	0	0	0
: Temp desert dry win	0	0	0	0	0	0	0	0	0	0
: Highland	0.2	0	0	0	0	0.3	0	0	0	0

Characteristics	Soga	Slovene	Slovak	Slavic Muslims	Sinhalese	Sindhi	Sidamo	Siamese	Shona	Shilluk
Latitude (abs degrees)	0.2	46	48	45	8	29	12	13	20	12
Temperature: degrees (C)	24	9	6	10	27	22	17	28	19	29
: monthly high (min C)	29	20	10	20	31	24	27	37	28	40
: monthly high (max C)	36	42	39	41	36	48	34	41	37	48
: monthly low (min C)	12	-25	-27	-22	15	-4	0	11	1	5
: monthly low (max C)	15	8	4	7	22	17	7	22	11	19
Humidity: morning min (%)	78	71	74	70	71	19	56	90	47	18
: morning max (%)	89	85	90	93	80	54	86	94	77	67
: afternoon min (%)	54	46	51	40	66	19	33	53	32	10
: afternoon max (%)	72	76	82	77	78	54	73	70	59	41
High temp @ max humid	25	5	3	3	29	34	21	32	27	37
High humid @ max temp	56	47	53	42	76	23	44	58	34	13
Rain: monthly min (mm)	46	46	26	33	69	12	5	5	2	7
: monthly max (mm)	175	96	83	87	370	258	300	305	182	71
: days/month min	9	8	8	8	6	1	2	1	0.9	0
: days/month max	19	14	15	14	19	13	28	15	16	6
Snow: persistent (1=yes)	0	0		0	0		0	0	0	0
: intermittent (1=yes)			1						0.8	
Frost present (1=yes)			1	1		1		0	0	1
Evaporation (1=low)	1	-1	1	1	-1	-1	-1	0	-1	0
Barometric pressure: July	1010	1010	1010	1010	1010	999	1010	1010	1020	1010
: January	1010	1020	1020	1020	1010	1020	1020	1010	1010	1010
Risks: Typhoon (10=high)	0	0	0	0	0	0	0	0	0	0
: Flooding (10=high)	0	0	0	0	1	0	0	0	1	1
: Tropical storm (10=high)	0	0	0	0	0	0	0	0	0	0
: Windstorm (10=high)	0	0	0	0	0	0	0	0	1	0
: Drought (10=high)	0	0	0	0	0	1	1	0	0.8	0
Climate Type: Tropical wet	0	0	0	0	0	0	0	0	0	0
: Tropical monsoon	0	0	0	0	1	0	0	0	0	0
: Tropical wet & dry	1	0	0	0	0	0	0	1	1	1
: Steppe, low latitude	0	0	0	0	0	0	0	0	0	0
: Desert, low latitude	0	0	0	0	0	1	0	0	0	0
: Steppe, middle latitude	0	0	0	0	0	0	0	0	0	0
: Desert, middle latitude	0	0	0	0	0	0	0	0	0	0
: Subtropical, humid	0	0	0	0	0	0	0	0	0	0
: Mediterranean	0	0	0	0	0	0	0	0	0	0
: Marine, west coast	0	1	0	0	0	0	0	0	0	0
: Cont humid hot sum	0	0	1	1	0	0	0	0	0	0
: Cont humid cool sum	0	0	0	0	0	0	0	0	0	0
: Subarctic	0	0	0	0	0	0	0	0	0	0
: Tundra	0	0	0	0	0	0	0	0	0	0
: Ice cap	0	0	0	0	0	0	0	0	0	0
: Dry steppe wasteland	0	0	0	0	0	0	0	0	0	0
: Temperate highland	0	0	0	0	0	0	0	0	0	0
: Temp desert dry sum	0	0	0	0	0	0	0	0	0	0
: Temp desert dry win	0	0	0	0	0	0	0	0	0	0
: Highland	1	0	0	0	0	0	1	0	0	0

Characteristics	Somali	Somba	Songhai	Soninke	Sotho	Sotho North	Spanish	Sundanese	Suriname	Susu
Latitude (abs degrees)	6	6	14	14	29	30	31	5	12	10
Temperature: degrees (C)										
: monthly high (min C)	27	27	29	28	17	19	18	28	27	27
: monthly high (max C)	30	31	37	36	27	26	22	33	31	31
: monthly low (min C)	14	35	47	46	39	39	39	37	36	36
: monthly low (max C)	36	18	8	8	-5	-2	-3	19	17	17
Humidity: morning min (%)	20	22	19	20	7	7	11	21	22	21
: morning max (%)	76	83	30	41	63	71	67	90	76	83
: afternoon min (%)	85	91	93	93	85	91	87	95	79	94
: afternoon max (%)	71	68	15	23	42	54	45	61	66	63
High temp @ max humid	79	78	71	73	57	67	72	75	72	87
High humid @ max temp	28	26	31	31	21	17	16	29	30	28
Rain: monthly min (mm)	0.4	74	29	45	46	54	46	71	67	70
: monthly max (mm)	74	13			8	8	22	43	20	3
: days/month min	114	366	271	333	90	89	85	300	112	1300
: days/month max	0.4	13	15	16	2	2	4	4	4	0.1
Snow: persistent (1=yes)	20			0.1	10	10	12	18	16	29
: intermittent (1=yes)			0.5		1	1	0.6			
Frost present (1=yes)	0.1						0.7			
Evaporation (1=low)							-0.6			
Barometric pressure: July	-1		-1	-1	-1	-1	-0.6		-1	-1
: January	1010	1010	1010	1010	1010	1010	1020	1010	1010	1010
Risks: Typhoon (10=high)	1010	1010	1010	1010	1010	1010	1020	1010	1010	1010
: Flooding (10=high)				1			3			
: Tropical storm (10=high)										
: Windstorm (10=high)	9	10	10	0.5			0.1	1	10	
: Drought (10=high)	9			0.8			0.3	10		
Climate Type: Tropical wet										
: Tropical monsoon		1	1	1					1	1
: Tropical wet & dry		1				1		1		1
: Steppe, low latitude	0.9			0.9			0.3			
: Desert, low latitude	0.9			0.9	0.6		0.3			
: Steppe, middle latitude										
: Desert, middle latitude										
: Subtropical, humid										
: Mediterranean					0.6	1	0.3			
: Marine, west coast					0.6	1	0.6			
: Cont humid hot sum					0.6	1	0.4			
: Cont humid cool sum										
: Subarctic										
: Tundra										
: Ice cap										
: Dry steppe wasteland										
: Temperate highland										
: Temp desert dry sum								1		
: Temp desert dry win	0.1		0.5	0.9	0.6	0		1		
: Highland										

Characteristics	Swahili	Swazi	Swedish	Swiss	Tahitian	Tai	Taiwanese (Dari)	Tajik	Tama	Tamang
Latitude (abs degrees)	5	26	60	47	22	16	24	36	12	27
Temperature: degrees (C)										
: monthly high (min C)	22	17	6	8	24	25	21	11	28	17
: monthly high (max C)	31	27	10	15	29	33	30	16	36	24
: monthly low (min C)	36	27	35	38	37	42	38	41	46	36
: monthly low (max C)	8	-5	-28	-23	11	5	0	-24	8	-2
Humidity: morning min (%)	16	9	8	7	18	22	19	10	19	18
: morning max (%)	70	59	66	80	68	73	90	55	32	68
: afternoon min (%)	84	81	89	92	76	84	93	81	93	90
: afternoon max (%)	37	59	53	51	66	68	62	29	10	53
High temp @ max humid	57	81	86	76	74	79	75	67	72	84
High humid @ max temp	28	24	2	3	28	25	18	3	31	28
Rain: monthly min (mm)	49	79	59	52	70	73	64	30	13	61
: monthly max (mm)	2	20	25	64	51	14	66	2		
: days/month min	160	254	76	136	145	333	305	77	320	373
: days/month max	0.2	3	10	12	6	5	7	0.6	0	0.2
Snow: persistent (1=yes)	12	16	17	15	16	17	14	9	22	21
: intermittent (1=yes)	0	0	1	1	0	0	0	0	0	1
Frost present (1=yes)	0	0	1	0	0	0	0	0.6	0	
Evaporation (1=low)	0	-1	1	1		1	1	-1	1	
Barometric pressure: July	0.9				-1					-1
: January	1020	1020	1010	1010	1020	1010	1010	1000	1010	1000
Risks: Typhoon (10=high)	1010	1010	1010	1010	1010	1010	1020	1020	1010	1020
: Flooding (10=high)	0	0	0	0	0	7	0	0	0	0
: Tropical storm (10=high)	0	0	0	0	0	0	0	0	0	0
: Windstorm (10=high)	0	0	0	0	0	1	0	0	0	0
: Drought (10=high)	0	0	0	0	0		0	0.9	0	0
Climate Type: Tropical wet	1	0	0	0	1	0	0	0	0	0
: Tropical monsoon	0	0	0	0	0	0	0	0	0	0
: Tropical wet & dry	0	0	0	0	0	1	0	0	1	0
: Steppe, low latitude	0	0	0	0	0	0	0	0	0	0
: Desert, low latitude	0	0	0	0	0	0	0	0	0	0
: Steppe, middle latitude	0	0	0	0	0	0	0	0	0	0
: Desert, middle latitude	0	0	0	0	0	0	0	0	0	0
: Subtropical, humid	0	1	0	0	0	0	1	0	0	0
: Mediterranean	0	0	0	0	0	0.7	0	0.1	0	0
: Marine, west coast	0	0	0	0	0	0	0	0	0	0
: Cont humid hot sum	0	0	0	0	0	0	0	0	0	0
: Cont humid cool sum	0	0	1	0	0	0	0	0	0	0
: Subarctic	1	0	0	0	0	0	0	0	0	0
: Tundra	0	0	0	0	0	0	0	0	0	0
: Ice cap	0	0	0	0	0	0	0	0	0	0
: Dry steppe wasteland	0	0	0	0	0	0	0	0	0	0
: Temperate highland	0	0	0	0	0	0	0	0	0	0
: Temp desert dry sum	0	0	0	0	0	0	0	0	0	0
: Temp desert dry win	0	1	0	0	0	0	0	0	0	0
: Highland	1	0	0	0	0	0	0	0	0	1

Characteristics	Tamil (Tubu)	Tatar	Teda	Teke	Tem-Kabre	Temne	Teso	Thai	Tharu	Tigre
Latitude (abs degrees)	8	53	12	6	6	8	0.2	15	27	14
Temperature: degrees (C)	27	4	28	25	27	27	24	25	17	25
:monthly high (min C)	31		36	32	32	31	29	33	24	30
:monthly high (max C)	36	33	46	36	38	35	36	43	36	40
:monthly low (min C)	15	-31	8	13	15	19	12	6	-2	10
:monthly low (max C)	22	-6	19	19	21	21	15	22	18	16
Humidity: morning min (%)	71	58	32	85	85	80	78	74	68	56
:morning max (%)	80	86	93	93	97	91	89	83	90	84
:afternoon min (%)	66	42	10	59	61	67	54	67	53	39
:afternoon max (%)	78	81	72	72	77	82	72	76	84	74
High temp @ max humid	29	-4	31	31	27	28	25	23	28	27
High humid @ max temp	76	52	13	69	68	71	56	72	61	43
Rain: monthly min (mm)	69	31	0	2	15	3	46	18	3	2
:monthly max (mm)	371	79	320	241	178	902	175	343	373	139
:days/month min	6	10	0	0.1	1	0.7	9	7	0.2	0.9
:days/month max	19	20	22	14	10	28	19	16	21	13
Snow: persistent (1=yes)	0	0	0	0	0	0	0	0	0	0
:intermittent (1=yes)	0	0.1	0	0	0	0	0	0	0	0
Frost present (1=yes)	0	-0.1	0	0	0	0	0	0	0	0
Evaporation (1=low)	-1		-1	0.7	0	-1	1	1	1	0.4
Barometric pressure: July	1010	1010	1010	1010	1010	1010	1010	1010	1000	1010
January	1010	1020	1010	1010	1010	1010	1010	1010	1020	1020
Risks: Typhoon (10=high)	0	0	0	0	0	0	0	0	0	0
:Flooding (10=high)	0	0	0	0	0	0	0	0	0	0
:Tropical storm (10=high)	0	0	0	0	0	0	0	0	0	0
:Windstorm (10=high)	1	0	0	7	1	1	0	1	0	0
:Drought (10=high)	0	0	1	1	1	0	1	0	0	0
Climate Type: Tropical wet	0	0	0	1	0	1	1	1	0	0
:Tropical monsoon	0	0	0	0	0	0	0	0	0	0
:Tropical wet & dry	1	0	0	0	1	0	0	0	0	0
:Steppe, low latitude	0	0	0	0	0	0	0	0	0	0
:Desert, low latitude	0	0.1	1	0	0	0	0	0	0	0
:Steppe, middle latitude	0	0.9	0	0	0	0	0	0	0	0
:Desert, middle latitude	0	0.9	0	0	0	0	0	0	0	0
:Subtropical, humid	0	0	0	0	0	0	0	0	1	0
:Mediterranean	0	0	0	0	0	0	0	0	0	0
:Marine, west coast	0	0.8	0	0	0	0	0	0	0	0
:Cont humid hot sum	0	0.8	0	0	0	0	0	0	0	0
:Cont humid cool sum	0	0.8	0	0	0	0	1	0	0	0
:Subarctic	0	0	0	0	0	0	0	0	0	0
:Tundra	0	0.8	0	0	0	0	0	0	0	0
:Ice cap	0	0	0	0	0	0	0	0	0	0
:Dry steppe wasteland	0	0.8	0	0	0	0	0	0	0	0
:Temperate highland	0	0	0	0	1	0	0	0	0	0
:Temp desert dry sum	0	0.8	0	0	0	0	0	0	0	0
:Temp desert dry win	0		0	0.7	0	0	1	0	1	1
:Highland	0	0.8	0	0	0	0	1	0	1	1

Characteristics	Tigrinya	Tikar	Tiv	Tonga	Tongan	Toros	Tribal	Tsimihety	Tsonga	Tswana
Latitude (abs degrees)	13	4	9	20	21	0.2	23	19	23	30
Temperature: degrees (C)	21	25	28	21	27	24	25	18	26	19
: monthly high (min C)	29	31	34	28	32	29	29	27	34	29
: monthly high (max C)	37	36	40	38	34	36	42	35	46	39
: monthly low (min C)	5	14	16	4	17	12	7	1	7	-2
: monthly low (max C)	11	17	21	14	21	15	24	12	17	7
Humidity: morning min (%)	56	97	81	39	75	78	37	85	65	71
: morning max (%)	85	98	87	85	82	89	74	94	75	91
: afternoon min (%)	36	62	65	19	73	54	37	49	57	54
: afternoon max (%)	73	75	80	71	79	72	74	71	67	67
High temp @ max humid	24	27	29	26	30	25	31	26	29	17
High humid @ max temp	44	67	72	23	79	56	42	64	65	54
Rain: monthly min (mm)	4	23	25		81	46		8	13	8
: monthly max (mm)	223	295	460	231	455	175	437	300	131	89
: days/month min	3	3	2		3	3	0			2
: days/month max	21	24	20	21	22	9	16	21	9	10
Snow: persistent (1=yes)	0	0	0	0	0	0	0	0	0	0
: intermittent (1=yes)	0	0	0	0	0	0	0	0	0	0
Frost present (1=yes)	0	0	0	0	0	0	0	0	0	0
Evaporation (1=low)	-1	0	0	0	0	-1	-1	-1	-1	-1
Barometric pressure: July	1010	1010	1010	1020	1010	1010	1000	1020	1020	1010
: January	1020	1010	1010	1010	1010	1010	1020	1010	1010	1010
Risks: Typhoon (10=high)	0	0	0	0	0.1	0	0	0	0	0
: Flooding (10=high)	0	0	0	0	0	0	0	0	0	0
: Tropical storm (10=high)	0	0	0	0	0	0	0	0	0	0
: Windstorm (10=high)	0	0	0	0	0	0	0	0	0	0
: Drought (10=high)	0	1	1	1	1	1	1	1	0	1
Climate Type: Tropical wet	0	0	0	0	1	1	0	0	0	0
: Tropical monsoon	0	0	0	0	0	0	0	0	0	0
: Tropical wet & dry	0	1	1	1	0	0	1	1	0	0
: Steppe, low latitude	0	0	0	0	0	0	0	0	0	1
: Desert, low latitude	0	0	0	0	0	0	0	0	0	0
: Steppe, middle latitude	0	0	0	0	0	0	0	0	0	0
: Desert, middle latitude	0	0	0	0	0	0	0	0	0	0
: Subtropical, humid	0	0	0	0	0	0	0	0	1	0
: Mediterranean	0	0	0	0	0	0	0	0	0	0
: Marine, west coast	0	0	0	0	0	0	0	0	0	0
: Cont humid hot sum	0	0	0	0	0	0	0	0	0	0
: Cont humid cool sum	0	0	0	0	0	0	0	0	0	0
: Subarctic	0	0	0	0	0	0	0	0	0	0
: Tundra	0	0	0	0	0	0	0	0	0	0
: Ice cap	0	0	0	0	0	0	0	0	0	0
: Dry steppe wasteland	0	0	0	0	0	0	0	0	0	0
: Temperate highland	0	0	0	0	0	0	0	0	0	0
: Temp desert dry sum	0	0	0	0	0	0	0	0	0	0
: Temp desert dry win	0	0	0	0	0	0	0	0	0	0
: Highland	1	0	0	0	0	0	0	0	0	0

Characteristics	Tuareg	Tukolor	Tumbuka	Turkish	Turkmen	Tutsi	Tuvaluan	Twa	Uighur	Ukrainian
Latitude (abs degrees)	13	15	20	39	36	9	8	8	43	51
Temperature: degrees (C)	29	27	21	9	14	22	28	22	5	5
...monthly high (min C)	37	35	28	15	17	26	33	26	6	7
...monthly high (max C)	47	43	38	38	42	29	36	29	41	35
...monthly low (min C)	8	11	4	-25	-18	15	18	14	-33	-26
...monthly low (max C)	19	21	14	7	14	17	22	17	9	9
Humidity: morning min (%)	33	67	39	55	50	57	75	57	59	68
...morning max (%)	90	88	85	86	78	82	82	83	90	91
...afternoon min (%)	17	43	19	26	37	57	76	57	35	49
...afternoon max (%)	71	73	71	71	70	82	81	83	78	84
High temp @ max humid	31	31	26	6	6	27	30	26	-4	-1
High humid @ max temp	31	31	23	27	38	59	80	60	39	55
Rain: monthly min (mm)	0	0	0	11	4	6	199	6	9	30
...monthly max (mm)	299	233	231	50	36	151	298	158	32	89
...days/month min	0	0	0	2	0.7	1	12	2	3	8
...days/month max	15	12	21	0	0.5	20	15	21	7	14
Snow: persistent (1=yes)	0	0	0	0.9	0	0	0	0	1	1
...intermittent (1=yes)	0	0	0	0	0.4	0	0	0	0.8	0.9
Frost present (1=yes)	0	0.1	0	1	0.9	0	0	0	1	1
Evaporation (1=low)	-0.2	-1	0	0	-1	-1	-1	-1	-0.2	0.9
Barometric pressure: July	-0.8	1010	1020	1010	1000	1010	1010	1010	1010	1010
...January	1010	1010	1010	1020	1020	1010	1010	101	1030	1020
Risks: Typhoon (10=high)	1010	0	0	0	0	0	0.4	0	0	0
...Flooding (10=high)	0	9	0	0	0	0	0	0	0	0
...Tropical storm (10=high)	0	0	0	0	0	0	0	0	0	0
...Windstorm (10=high)	0	1	1	0	0	0	0	0	0	0
...Drought (10=high)	1	0	1	0	0	0	1	0	0	0
Climate Type: Tropical wet	0	0	0	0	0	0.5	0	0.4	0	0
...Tropical monsoon	0	0	0	0	0	0.5	0.6	0.6	0	0
...Tropical wet & dry	0.8	0.9	0	0	0	0.5	0	0	0	0
...Steppe, low latitude	0.2	0.1	0	0	0	0	0	0	0.2	0
...Desert, low latitude	0.8	0	0	0	0.4	0	0	0	0	0
...Steppe, middle latitude	0	0	0	0	0	0	0	0	0.8	0
...Desert, middle latitude	0	0.9	0	0.9	0	0	0	0	0.8	0
...Subtropical, humid	0	0	0	0	0	0	0	0	0	0
...Mediterranean	0	0	0	0	0	0	0	0	0	0.1
...Marine, west coast	0	0	0	0	0	0	0	0	0	0.1
...Cont humid hot sum	0	0	0	0	0	0	0	0	0	0
...Cont humid cool sum	0	0	0	0	0	0	0	0	0	0
...Subarctic	0	0	0	0	0	0	0	0	0	0.1
...Tundra	0.6	0.9	0	0.9	0.4	0	0	0	0	0.1
...Ice cap	0	0	0	0	0	0	0	0	0	0.1
...Dry steppe wasteland	0	0	0	0	0	0	0	0	0	0
...Temperate highland	0	0	0	0	0	0.5	0	0.6	0	0.1
...Temp desert dry sum										
...Temp desert dry win										
...Highland										

Characteristics	Urdu	Uzbek	Vanuatuan	Vietnamese	Wallon	White	Wolof	Xhosa	Yalunka	Yao
Latitude (abs degrees)	29	40	17	16	51	37	15	30	8	26
Temperature: degrees (C)	22	12	25	24	10	14	27	19	27	16
: monthly high (min C)	24	16	32	33	13	24	35	29	31	21
: monthly high (max C)	48	42	37	43	37	40	43	3	35	40
: monthly low (min C)	-4	-19	13	6	-1	-1	12	-2	19	-11
: monthly low (max C)	17	13	19	22	6	-1	21	7	19	-15
Humidity: morning min (%)	19	53	76	74	87	70	69	71	21	50
: morning max (%)	54	78	82	83	94	83	88	91	80	79
: afternoon min (%)	19	39	73	67	65	47	43	54	91	42
: afternoon max (%)	54	69	79	76	86	59	74	67	67	70
High temp @ max humid	34	3	28	23	66	11	31	17	82	29
High humid @ max temp	23	40	77	72	68	53	70	54	28	56
Rain: monthly min (mm)	12	5	125	18	53	55	258	8	71	3
: monthly max (mm)	258	35	368	340	95	116	13	89	3	218
: days/month min	1	1	13	7	13	13	0	2	902	1
: days/month max	13	6	21	16	21	0.8	0	10	0.7	14
Snow: persistent (1=yes)	1		0	0	1	0.8	-1	0	28	0.5
: intermittent (1=yes)	1	0.9	0	0		0.6		0	0	0.5
Frost present (1=yes)	1		0	0	1	1010	1010	-1	0	0.4
Evaporation (1=low)	-1	-1		-1		1020	1010	1010	-1	1010
Barometric pressure: July	999	1000	1020	1010	1020	0	9	1010	1010	1020
: January	1020	1020	1010	1010	1010	0.2	0.5	1010	1010	5
Risks: Typhoon (10=high)	0	0	0	10	0	0.3	0	0	0	7
: Flooding (10=high)	10	0	0	0	0	0.1	0	0	0	0
: Tropical storm (10=high)	0	0	1	0	0	0.2	0	0	0	0
: Windstorm (10=high)	0	0	0	0	0	0.9	0	0	0	0
: Drought (10=high)	0	0	0	1	0	0.8	1	1	1	1
Climate Type: Tropical wet	0	0	0	0	0	0.7	0	0	0	0
: Tropical monsoon	0	0	0	0	0	0	0	0	0	0.3
: Tropical wet & dry	0	0	0	0	0	0.9	0	0	0	0.1
: Steppe, low latitude	1	0	0	0	0	0.1	0	0	0	0
: Desert, low latitude	1	0.2	0	1	0	0.1	0	0	0	0
: Steppe, middle latitude	0	0.9	0	0	0	0.7	0	1	0	0.5
: Desert, middle latitude	0	0	0	0	0	0.7	0	0	0	0.5
: Subtropical, humid	0	0	0	0	0		0	0	0	0.5
: Mediterranean	0	0	0	0	0		0	0	0	0
: Marine, west coast	0	0	0	0	0		0	1	0	0
: Cont humid hot sum	0	0	0	1	1		0.9	1	0	0.5
: Cont humid cool sum	0	0	0	0	0		0	0	0	0.5
: Subarctic	0	0	0	0	0		0	0	0	0
: Tundra	0	0	0	0	0		0	0	0	0
: Ice cap	0	0	0	0	0	0	0	0	0	0
: Dry steppe wasteland	0	0	0	0	0	0	0	0	0	0
: Temperate highland	0	0	0	0	0	0	0	0	0	0
: Temp desert dry sum	0	0	0	0	0	0	0	0	0	0
: Temp desert dry win	0	0	0	0	0	0	0	-1	0	0
: Highland	0	0	0	0	0	0.7	0	0	0	0.5

Characteristics	Yi-Miao	Yoruba	Yugoslav	Zambo	Zulu
Latitude (abs degrees)	35	9	50	12	28
Temperature: degrees (C)	11	28	8	27	20
:monthly high (min C)	13	34	14	31	30
:monthly high (max C)	43	40	38	34	40
:monthly low (min C)	-23	16	-24	20	-0.8
:monthly low (max C)	15	21	8	23	8
Humidity: morning min (%)	46	81	77	80	66
:morning max (%)	74	87	90	92	91
:afternoon min (%)	46	65	50	44	49
:afternoon max (%)	74	80	80	70	67
High temp @ max humid	30	29	4	27	19
High humid @ max temp	72	72	53	73	50
Rain: monthly min (mm)	3	25	38		7
:monthly max (mm)	243	456	77	296	102
:days/month min	2	2	11	1	2
:days/month max	13	20	17	21	10
Snow: persistent (1=yes)	1	0	0.2	0	0
:intermittent (1=yes)	1	0	1	0	0
Frost present (1=yes)	1	0	1	0	0.9
Evaporation (1=low)	1	-1	1	-1	-1
Barometric pressure: July	1010	1010	1010	1010	1010
:January	1030	1010	1020	1010	1010
Risks: Typhoon (10=high)	10	0	0	0	0
:Flooding (10=high)	10	1	0	0	0
:Tropical storm (10=high)	0	0	0	0	0
:Windstorm (10=high)	1	0.3	0	0	1
:Drought (10=high)	1	1	0	0	0
Climate Type: Tropical wet	0	0	0	1	0
:Tropical monsoon	0	1	0	0	0
:Tropical wet & dry	0	1	0	0	0
:Steppe, low latitude	0	0	0	0	0
:Desert, low latitude	0	0	0	0	0
:Steppe, middle latitude	1	0	0	0	0.9
:Desert, middle latitude	1	0	0	0	0.1
:Subtropical, humid	0	0	0	0	0
:Mediterranean	0	0	0.8	0	0.9
:Marine, west coast	0	0	0.2	0	0.9
:Cont humid hot sum	1	0	0	0	0.9
:Cont humid cool sum	0	0	0	0	0
:Subarctic	0	0	0	0	0
:Tundra	0	0	0	0	0
:Ice cap	0	0	0	0	0
:Dry steppe wasteland	0	0	0	0	0
:Temperate highland	0	0	0	0	0.9
:Temp desert dry sum	0	0	0	0	0
:Temp desert dry win	0	1	0	0	0
:Highland	1	0	0	0	0.0

10

SELECT BIBLIOGRAPHY

PHYSIOECONOMIC EFFECTS ON ETHNIC CULTURE

This bibliography cites research works focusing on the relationship between ethnic groups and physioeconomic factors, especially climate.

Abel, E. L. et al. "Seasonal, monthly, and day of week trends in homicide as affected by alcohol and race." *Alcoholism Clinical and Experimental Research* 9, no. 3 (May 1985): 281-283. Topics discussed include: consumption, victims, ethnic differences, drinking patterns.

Abelson, A. et al. "Altitude, migration, and fertility in the Andes." *Soc Biol* 21, no. 1 (March 1974): 12-27. Topics discussed include: Caucasoid race, ethnic groups, Indians, South America, transients, migrants.

Bangham, C. et al. "Fertility of Nepalese Sherpas at moderate altitudes: comparison with high altitude data." *Ann Hum Biol* 7, no. 4 (July 1980): 323-330. Topics discussed include: China ethnology, marriage, menarche, Nepal, sex ratio.

Beals, K. L. "Brain size, cranial morphology, climate, and time machines." *Current Anthropology* 25, no. 3 (June 1984): 301-330. Topics discussed include: head measures, ethnic groups, environment, morphology, evolution.

Bradbury, T. N. "Racial factors and season of birth in schizophrenia: A reinterpretation of Gallagher, McFalls, and Jones." *Journal of Abnormal Psychology* 95, no. 2 (May 1986): 187-188. Topics discussed include: methodology, ethnic differences.

Cabezas, G. M. et al. "The nutritional status of the Kung population (the Kalahari Desert)." *Rev Enferm* 16, no. 175 (March 1993): 81-84. Topics discussed include: Angola, Botswana, diet, food supply, Namibia, water supply, desert climates, ethnic groups, nutrition.

Cervinka, R. "Psychosocial aspects of fitness for employment in the tropics." *Offentl Gesundheitswes* 45, no. 4 (April 1983): 180-182. Topics discussed include: Germany, ethnology, Nigeria, timing, personality, personnel management, personnel selection.

Chance, N. "Implications of environmental stress. Strategies of developmental change in the North." *Arch Environ Health* 17, no. 4 (October 1968): 571-577. Topics discussed include: acclimation, acculturation, arctic regions, cold climates, crowding, Indians, North America, religion, psychology, social behavior, social welfare.

Cohen, P. "The influence on survival of season of onset of childhood acute lymphoblastic leukemia." *Chronobiol Int* 4, no. 2 (1987): 291-297. Topics discussed include: ethnic groups, Israel, epidemiology, mortality, cycles.

Erhardt, C. L. et al. "Seasonal patterns of conception in New York City." *Am J Public Health* 61, no. 11 (November 1971): 2246-2258. Topics discussed include: birth, death, ethnic groups, illegitimacy, income, maternal age, menstruation, pregnancy, Puerto Rico, gender effects, timing, fertilization.

Feldman, D. A. "The history of the relationship between environment and culture in ethnological thought: An overview." *J of the Hist of the Behavioral Sci* 11, no. 1 (1975): 67-81. Topics discussed include: ethnology, cultural ecology.

Fox, R. et al. "A study of temperature regulation in New Guinea people." *Philos Trans R Soc Lond Biol* 268, no. 893 (1 August 1974): 375-391. Topics discussed include: acclimation, body constitution, chlorides analysis, blood supply, effects on heart beat, tropical climates, thermoregulation, ethnic groups.

Frazen, E. "Medical aspects of work in tropical countries." *Z Arztl Fortbild Jena* 72, no. 19 (1 October 1978): 950-955. Topics discussed include: aerospace medicine, development, Europe, ethnology, malaria, tropical climates, work-related medicine.

Gribbin, J. R. *Climate and mankind*. 56 pages. World Climate Conference (Geneva, Switzerland). London: Earthscan, 1979. Topics discussed include: climatic changes.

Grivetti, L. E. "Geographical location, climate and weather, and magic: Aspects of agricultural success in the Eastern Kalahari, Botswana." *Social Science Information* 20, no. 3 (1981): 509-536. Topics discussed include: magic ritual, success, Botswana, Africa, ethnic groups, environment effects, geography, rites, workers.

Hayes, J. "Emphysema in a non industrialized tropical island." *Thorax* 24, no. 5 (September 1969): 623-625. Topics discussed include: age effects, air pollution, ethnic groups, Jamaica, lung pathology, pulmonary emphysema, pathology, epidemiology, gender effects.

Hunter, J. "The summer disease. Some field evidence on seasonality in childhood lead poisoning." *Soc Sci Med* 12, no. 2D (June 1978): 85-94. Topics discussed include: preschool children, ethnic groups, blood, mass screening, maternal fetal exchange, Michigan, pregnancy, risk, skin pigmentation, epidemiology.

Jaremin, B. "Acute non inflammatory chemical diarrhoeas among employees of Polish building enterprise in a tropical country." *Bull Inst Marit Trop Med Gdynia* 37, no. 3-4 (1986): 229-237. Topics discussed include: acute disease, epidemiology, diarrhea treatment, Iraq, ethnology, seasonality, water supply.

---. "Limited, intragroup epidemics of acute infectious diseases of the upper respiratory tracts and throat among workers of a Polish construction site in a tropical country." *Bull Inst Marit Trop Med Gdynia* 38, no. 1-2 (1987): 42-49. Topics discussed include: Iraq, work-related drug treatment, ethnology, respiratory tract infections, seasonality, tropical climates, propagation.

Korochkin, I. "Adaptation and morbidity among Soviet engineers in tropical countries." *Sov Med* no. 8 (1990): 56-59. Topics discussed include: Nigeria, work-related diseases, etiology, seasonality, USSR, ethnology, acclimation, physiology, epidemiology, transients, migrants.

Krylov, V. et al. "Metabolic indicators in children depending on their national ethnic background and climatic geographical zones of residence." *Lab Delo* no. 1 (1978): 25-28. Topics discussed include: arctic regions, Siberia, amino acids, blood, glucose analysis, cold climates, electrolytes, lipids.

Macdonald, E. "Demographic variation in cancer in relation to industrial and environmental influence." *Environ Health Perspect* 17 (October 1976): 153-166. Topics discussed include: age effects, air analysis, pollution, climatic effects, ethnic groups, neoplasms mortality, gender effects, Texas, exposure, industry.

Mann, I. C. *Culture, race, climate, and eye disease; an introduction to the study of geographical ophthalmology.* 580 pages. Springfield, IL: C. C. Thomas, 1966. Topics discussed include: geography, ethnology, culture.

Marshall, R. "An analysis of the seasonal variation of coronary heart disease and respiratory disease mortality in New Zealand." *Int J Epidemiol* 17, no. 2 (June 1988): 325-331. Topics discussed include: age effects, ethnology, etiology, epidemiology, New Zealand, gender effects.

Mason, E. et al. "Variations in basal metabolic rate responses to changes between tropical and temperate climates." *Hum Biol* 44, no. 1 (February 1972): 141-172. Topics discussed include: age effects, calorimetry, ethnic groups, India, oxygen consumption, residential mobility, timing, acclimation.

Massey, D. et al. "A demonstration of the effect of seasonal migration on fertility." *Demography* 21, no. 4 (November 1984): 501-517. Topics discussed include: preschool, marriage, Mexico, rural areas, population, socioeconomics, timing, ethnology, transients, migrants.

Mavlanov, K. et al. "Seasonal dynamics of the indices of humoral immunity in children aged 3 months to 1 year in relation to nutrition in an arid zone." *Vopr Pitan 1992* no. 4 (July 1992): 26-29. Topics discussed include: Caucasoid race, Mongoloid race, Turkmenistan ethnology, desert climates.

Montesquieu, C. d. S. d. *The Spirit of Laws.* Anne M. Cohler, Basia Carolyn Miller and Harold Samuel Stone, translators, Cambridge; New York: Cambridge University Press, 1989; original 1748. Topics discussed include: climate, culture, civilization, mortality, fertility, alcohol, labor, laws, economics.

Mueller, W. et al. "A multinational Andean genetic and health program. VIII. Lung function changes with migration between altitudes." *Am J Phys Anthropol* 51, no. 2 (August 1979): 183-195. Topics discussed include: adaptation, Chile, ethnic groups, Indians, South America, development, occupations, gender effects, Spain, ethnology, histology, travel.

Nelson, E. et al. "Climatic and social associations with postneonatal mortality rates within New Zealand." *N Z Med J* 101, no. 849 (13 July 1988): 443-446. Topics discussed include: ethnic groups, New Zealand, socioeconomics, temperature, sudden infant death.

Nonaka, K. et al. "Effects of maternal birth season on birth seasonality in the Canadian population during the seventeenth and eighteenth centuries." *Hum Biol* 62, no. 5 (October 1990): 701-717. Topics discussed include: Canada, fertility, France, ethnology, history, medicine, marriage, childbearing age.

Odinaev, F. "The characteristics of the development and course of pneumoconiosis under the conditions of a mountain climate." *Gig Tr Prof Zabol* no. 7 (1992): 13-14. Topics discussed include: mining, epidemiology, silicosis, ethnology, etiology, Tajikistan epidemiology, altitude, pneumoconiosis.

Parker, P.M. *Climatic Effects on Individual, Social and Economic Behavior: A Physioeconomic Review of Research Across Disciplines,* Bibliographies and Indexes in Geography, Number 2, Westport, Connecticut; London: Greenwood Press, 1995 (ISBN: 0-313-29400-3).

Paulozzi, L. "The seasonality of mortality in Alaska." *Soc Sci Med D* 15, no. 3 (August 1981): 335-339. Topics discussed include: Alaska, demography, Eskimos, ethnic groups, infants, sociology, medicine.

Planalp, J. M. *Heat stress and culture in North India.* 557 pages. United States. Army Medical Research and Development Command. United States Army Medical Research and Development Commmand Special technical report, Washington: U.S. Army Medical Research and Development Command, 1971. Topics discussed include: India, ethnology, physiology.

Ricketts, T. et al. "An evaluation of subsidized rural primary care programs: II. The environmental contexts." *Am J Public Health* 73, no. 4 (April 1983): 406-413. Topics discussed include: health, services, economics, ethnic groups, labor, supply, distribution, rural areas.

Scaglion, R. "Seasonal births in a Western Abelam village, Papua New Guinea." *Hum Biol* 50, no. 3 (September 1978): 313-323. Topics discussed include: agriculture, ethnic groups, New Guinea, birth rate.

Shapiro, A. "Heat, ethnic differences, and creativity in the Negev desert." *J Educ Psychol* 67, no. 2 (April 1975): 183-187. Topics discussed include: cross-cultural analysis, Europe, heart rate, intelligence, Israel, Morocco ethnology, creativity, desert climates, ethnic groups.

Sharma, V. M. et al. "Ethnic variations in psychological performance under altitude stress." *Aviation, Space, and Environmental Medicine* 47 (March 1976): 248-251. Topics discussed include: stress, ethnic groups, variations, depression, anxiety, concentration, eye coordination, India.

Vallery, M. J. et al. "Can a protracted stay in the tropics permanently lower basal metabolic rates of European expatriates?" *Ann Hum Biol* 7, no. 3 (May 1980): 267-271. Topics discussed include: Africa, Asia, Caucasoid race, France, ethnology, timing, adaptation, basal metabolism, tropical climate.

Velcek, F. et al. "Traumatic death in urban children." *J Pediatr Surg* 12, no. 3 (June 1977): 375-384. Topics discussed include: accidents, traffic, ethnic groups, fires, New York City, seasonality, gender effects, socioeconomics, population, wounds, injuries, mortality.

Visscher, B. et al. "Latitude, migration, and the prevalence of multiple sclerosis." *Am J Epidemiol* 106, no. 6 (December 1977): 470-475. Topics discussed include: California, China, ethnology, Europe, genetics, medicine, Israel, Japan, diagnosis, South Africa, Washington, demography, epidemiology, transients, migrants.

Witkowski, S. R. et al. "Climate, clothing, and body-part nomenclature." *Ethnology* 24 (July 1985): 197-214. Topics discussed include: anatomy, terminology, language, culture, anatomy, dress.

Wong, M. "Sudden unexplained death syndrome. A review and update." *Trop Geogr Med* 44, no. 4 (October 1992): S1-19. Topics discussed include: Asia, autopsy, causality, culture, pathology, ethnic groups, risk, seasonality, gender effects, Singapore, socioeconomics.

Zunnunov, Z. "Physical work capacity as a criterion of human resistance under the hot climatic conditions of an arid zone." *Fiziol Zh SSSR* 78, no. 6 (June 1992): 18-24. Topics discussed include: acclimatization physiology, ethnic groups, exercise test, Uzbekistan, desert climate, exercise physiology, physical endurance physiology, tropical climates.

11

INDEXES

INDEX OF ETHNIC GROUPS

INDEX OF SUBJECTS

About the Author

PHILIP M. PARKER is an Associate Professor at the European Institute of Business Administration (INSEAD) in Fontainebleau, France, where he teaches graduate courses in multivariate statistics, research methodology, and international marketing. He holds undergraduate degrees in biology and economics, and graduate degrees in finance and managerial economics. He received his Ph.D. in Business Economics from the Wharton School of the University of Pennsylvania in 1988. His research interests include evaluating cross-national effects of physical environment on human behavior and the resulting implications for business and economic policy. Dr. Parker has consulted on various projects with international development agencies and has conducted field research and training with private concerns in Europe, Africa, the Middle East, Asia, Latin America and North America. He has recently published articles in academic and industry journals on various economic and business topics, including the diffusion of innovations, marketing and industrial organization.

ISBN 0-313-29767-3

90000>

EAN

9 780313 297670

HARDCOVER BAR CODE